Wolfgang Lindner
Can Türker   Yannis Tzitzikas
Athena Vakali (Eds.)

Current Trends in Database Technology – EDBT 2004 Workshops

EDBT 2004 Workshops PhD, DataX, PIM, P2P&DB, and ClustWeb
Heraklion, Crete, Greece, March 14-18, 2004
Revised Selected Papers

 Springer

Volume Editors

Wolfgang Lindner
Massachusetts Institute of Technology, CSAIL
32 Vassar Street, Cambridge, MA 02139, USA
E-mail: wolfgang@csail.mit.edu

Marco Mesiti
University of Milan, DICo
Via Comelico 39/41, 20135 Milan, Italy
E-mail: mesiti@dico.unimi.it

Can Türker
Swiss Federal Institute of Technology Zurich
8092 Zurich, Switzerland
E-mail: tuerker@inf.ethz.ch

Yannis Tzitzikas
University of Namur, Institute of Informatics
Rue Grandgagnage 21, 5000 Namur, Belgium
E-mail: ytz@info.fundp.ac.be

Athena Vakali
Aristotle University, Department of Informatics
54124 Thessaloniki, Greece
E-mail: avakali@csd.auth.gr

Library of Congress Control Number: 2004115768

CR Subject Classification (1998): H.2, H.3, H.4, H.5.1, C.2.4, K.4.4

ISSN 0302-9743
ISBN 3-540-23305-9 Springer Berlin Heidelberg New York

Springer is a part of Springer Science+Business Media

springeronline.com

© Springer-Verlag Berlin Heidelberg 2004
Printed in Germany

Typesetting: Camera-ready by author, data conversion by Scientific Publishing Services, Chennai, India
Printed on acid-free paper   SPIN: 11328957   06/3142   5 4 3 2 1 0

Preface

This volume comprises papers from the following five workshops that were part of the complete program for the International Conference on Extending Database Technology (EDBT) held in Heraklion, Greece, March 2004:

- ICDE/EDBT Joint Ph.D. Workshop (PhD)
- Database Technologies for Handling XML-information on the Web (DataX)
- Pervasive Information Management (PIM)
- Peer-to-Peer Computing and Databases (P2P&DB)
- Clustering Information Over the Web (ClustWeb)

Together, the five workshops featured 61 high-quality papers selected from approximately 180 submissions. It was, therefore, difficult to decide on the papers that were to be accepted for presentation. We believe that the accepted papers substantially contribute to their particular fields of research. The workshops were an excellent basis for intense and highly fruitful discussions. The quality and quantity of papers show that the areas of interest for the workshops are highly active. A large number of excellent researchers are working on the aforementioned fields producing research output that is not only of interest for other researchers but also for industry. The organizers and participants of the workshops were highly satisfied with the output. The high quality of the presenters and workshop participants contributed to the success of each workshop. The amazing environment of Heraklion and the location of the EDBT conference also contributed to the overall success. Last, but not least, our sincere thanks to the conference organizers – the organizing team was always willing to help and if there were things that did not work, assistance was quickly available.

On the basis of the reviews and discussions during the workshops, 55 authors were asked to submit revised versions of their workshop papers for these LNCS postproceedings. When revising their papers, authors were asked to consider not only the comments of the reviewers but also the comments of other workshop participants. The revised papers underwent a second reviewing process before they were accepted for these postproceedings.

ICDE/EDBT Ph.D. Workshop (PhD)

Continuing in its tradition, the Ph.D. Workshop brought together Ph.D. students in the field of database technology outside of the ICDE/EDBT conference series. It offers Ph.D. students the opportunity to present, discuss, and receive feedback on their research in a constructive and international environment.

For the first time the Ph.D. Workshop was actually a real distributed event. The first session was held in conjunction with the 9th International Conference on Extending Database Technology (EDBT) on March 18, 2004, in Heraklion (Greece). The second session was held in conjunction with the 20th International Conference on Data Engineering (ICDE) on March 29, 2004, in Boston (USA).

As for the statistics: we received 86 submissions (from 21 countries). After a careful review process (each paper was evaluated by three committee members followed by an online discussion), 21 papers were selected for presentation at the workshop, out of which 18 contributors were invited to submit revised and extended versions of their papers for these proceedings.

Workshop Chair

Wolfgang Lindner   Massachusetts Institute of Technology (USA)

Program Committee

Karl Aberer	EPFL Lausanne (Switzerland)
Anastassia Ailamaki	Carnegie Mellon University (USA)
Walid G. Aref	Purdue University (USA)
Phil Bernstein	Microsoft (USA)
Elisa Bertino	Purdue University (USA)
Michael Böhlen	Free University of Bolzano-Bozen (Italy)
Stefano Ceri	University of Milan (Italy)
Klaus Dittrich	University of Zurich (Switzerland)
Georgios Evangelidis	University of Macedonia (Greece)
Michael Franklin	UC Berkeley (USA)
Dina Goldin	University of Connecticut (USA)
Christian S. Jensen	Aalborg University (Denmark)
Björn Þór Jónsson	Reykjavik University (Iceland)
Martin Kersten	CWI (Netherlands)
Tan Kian Lee	NUS (Singapore)
Peter Lockemann	University of Karlsruhe (Germany)
Bertram Ludaescher	UC San Diego (USA)
Samuel Madden	MIT (USA)
David Maier	Oregon Health and Science University (USA)
Ioana Manolescu	INRIA (France)
Holger Meyer	University of Rostock (Germany)
Klaus Meyer-Wegener	University of Erlangen-Nuremberg (Germany)
Felix Naumann	Humboldt University Berlin (Germany)
Erich Neuhold	IPSI Fraunhofer (Germany)
Dimitris Papadias	Hong Kong University (China)
Jan Paredaens	University of Antwerp (Belgium)
Neoklis Polyzotis	UC Santa Cruz (USA)
Ken Salem	University of Waterloo (Canada)
Timos Sellis	National Technical University of Athens (Greece)
Heiko Schuldt	UMIT (Austria)
Peter Triantafillou	University of Patras (Greece)
David Toman	University of Waterloo (Canada)

Database Technologies for Handling XML-Information on the Web (DataX)

Since XML was proposed by the W3C in 1998, the database community has been working on ways to manage semistructured information by extending traditional database systems and by proposing new native XML-based systems in order to store, maintain, exchange, and securely access XML documents. DataX brought together experts from several fields of information technology to discuss new interesting results and applications of XML data management. An invited paper reports the current assessment of the area and outlines the promising challenges for the next few years. Moreover, the technical program addresses important topics concerning querying and indexing of XML sources along with the evolution of XML schema and applications. Finally, a panel deals with important questions in XML data management.

Workshop Chairs

Barbara Catania	University of Genoa (Italy)
Akmal B. Chaudhri	IBM developerWorks (UK)
Giovanna Guerrini	University of Pisa (Italy)
Marco Mesiti	University of Milan (Italy)

Program Committee

Ricardo Baeza-Yates	University of Chile (Chile)
Zohra Bellahsene	LIRMM (France)
Stéphane Bressan	NUS (Singapore)
Barbara Catania	University of Genoa (Italy)
Akmal B. Chaudhri	IBM developerWorks (UK)
Klaus R. Dittrich	University of Zurich (Switzerland)
Elena Ferrari	University of Insubria (Italy)
Mary F. Fernandez	AT&T Research (USA)
Giorgio Ghelli	University of Pisa (Italy)
Sergio Greco	University of Calabria (Italy)
Giovanna Guerrini	University of Pisa (Italy)
Hosagrahar V. Jagadish	University of Michigan (USA)
Zoé Lacroix	Arizona State University (USA)
Anna Maddalena	University of Genoa (Italy)
Gianni Mecca	University of Basilicata (Italy)
Marco Mesiti	University of Milan (Italy)
M. Tamer Özsu	University of Alberta (Canada)
Rajeev Rastogi	Bell Labs (USA)
Ralf Schenkel	Max-Planck Institute (Germany)
Divesh Srivastava	AT&T Research (USA)
Rainer Unland	University of Essen (Germany)
Athena Vakali	Aristotle University of Thessaloniki (Greece)

External Reviewers

Bernd Amann	Elio Masciari	Cristina Sirangelo
Giovanni Conforti	Pietro Mazzoleni	Dominique Stein
Sergio Flesca	Andrea Perego	Andrea Tagarelli
Ela Hunt	Mark Roantree	Pierangelo Veltri
Anne Laurent	Awny Sayed	Alessandro Verri
Paolo Manghi	Carlo Sartiani	Ning Zhang

Pervasive Information Management (PIM)

Wireless connectivity, along with increasingly small and powerful mobile devices and sensors, enables a wide range of new applications that will radically change the way information is managed and processed today. Information becomes ubiquitous, highly distributed and at the same time accessible from everywhere at any time. Information access takes place in highly dynamic and unstable networks. Nevertheless, users and application developers will expect information processing to continue under similar guarantees as those offered by today's stationary and more or less centralized systems, even if some nodes of the pervasive information network are (temporarily) disconnected and/or are in motion. Examples of these guarantees are those given by database management systems, e.g., consistency and durability of data. Additional challenges stem from the fact that mobile devices, in particular embedded devices and sensors, are less powerful than their stationary counterparts; they are smaller (resulting, for example, in smaller in- and output devices and less available storage), have restricted energy supplies, and communicate via expensive and unreliable wireless communication media.

The papers accepted for this postconference proceedings address a broad range of issues in pervasive information systems. New and existing concepts and techniques are developed in the light of the rapidly increasing mobility of users and the great advances in system infrastructures, mobile devices, and sensor technologies.

Workshop Chairs

Can Türker	ETH Zurich (Switzerland)
Birgitta König-Ries	TU München (Germany)

Program Committee

Karl Aberer	EPFL Lausanne (Switzerland)
Michel E. Adiba	University of Grenoble (France)
Christoph Gollmick	University of Jena (Germany)
Hagen Höpfner	University of Magdeburg (Germany)
Valérie Issarny	INRIA Rocquencourt (France)

Christian S. Jensen	Aalborg University (Denmark)
Birgitta König-Ries	TU München (Germany)
Sanjay Kumar Madria	University of Missouri-Rolla (USA)
Rainer Malaka	EML Heidelberg (Germany)
Kia Makki	Florida International University (USA)
Eduardo Mena	University of Zaragoza (Spain)
Evaggelia Pitoura	University of Ioannina (Greece)
Kurt Rothermel	University of Stuttgart (Germany)
George Samaras	University of Cyprus (Cyprus)
Kai-Uwe Sattler	University of Ilmenau (Germany)
Heiko Schuldt	UMIT Innsbruck (Austria)
Can Türker	ETH Zurich (Switzerland)
Özgür Ulusoy	Bilkent University (Turkey)
Jari Veijalainen	University of Jyväskylä (Finland)
Ouri Wolfson	University of Illinois (USA)

External Reviewers

Hidir Aras	Klaus Haller	Gregor Schiele
Martin Bauer	Martin Heusse	Roman Schmidt
Hu Cao	Sergio Ilarri	Chara Skouteli
Christos Christophi	Juhong Liu	Jie Wu
Tobias Drosdol	Philipp Obreiter	Bo Xu
Dimosthenis Georgiadis	Christoforos Panayiotou	Huabei Yin
Tirthankar Ghosh	Robert Porzel	

Peer-to-Peer Computing and Databases (P2P&DB)

The P2P paradigm holds many promises: it couples naturally with the Internet, the universal knowledge and service exchange medium; it favors scalability, by allowing the seamless plugging of data, services and computational resources into the global system; it increases system resilience, by avoiding unique points of failures; and it can speed up global access by distributing the indexing and query processing tasks to multiple computing nodes. This is all in contrast to the centralized architecture of current systems offering global access, such as search engines, Web directories, or mediators. The potential for progress is very encouraging, and there are already several systems that subscribe to the P2P computing paradigm, to some degree. On a theoretical level, researchers have started looking into models and algorithms to tackle basic problems in the P2P framework, as witnessed by the increasing number of papers in international workshops and conferences. This workshop, co-located with EDBT 2004 and focused on peer-to-peer systems and database computing, was no exception. It attracted quality papers, most of which provoked lively discussions amongst the participants.

Workshop Chairs

Carlo Meghini	ISTI-CNR (Italy)
Nicolas Spyratos	University of Paris-Sud (France)
Yannis Tzitzikas	University of Namur (Belgium)

Program Committee

Karl Aberer	EPFL Lausanne (Switzerland)
Anastasia Analyti	ICS-FORTH (Greece)
Paolo Atzeni	University of Rome 3 (Italy)
Diego Calvanese	Free University of Bozen-Bolzano (Italy)
Vassilis Christophides	ICS-FORTH (Greece)
Norbert Fuhr	University of Duisburg (Germany)
Mohand-Said Hacid	University Claude Bernard Lyon 1 (France)
Hatem Haddad	VTT (Finland)
Klaus P. Jantke	DFKI GmbH (Germany)
Ross King	Austrian Research Centers (Austria)
Matthias Klusch	DFKI GmbH (Germany)
Manolis Koubarakis	Technical University of Crete (Greece)
Heikki Mannila	Helsinki University of Technology (Finland)
John Mylopoulos	University of Toronto (Canada)
Wolfgang Nejdl	University of Hannover (Germany)
Evaggelia Pitoura	University of Ioannina (Greece)
Philippe Rigaux	University of Paris-Sud (France)
Thomas Risse	IPSI Fraunhofer (Germany)
Marie-Christine Rousset	University of Paris-Sud (France)
Luciano Serafini	Cultural Institute of Trentino (Italy)
Vagan Terziyan	University of Jyväskylä (Finland)

External Reviewers

Josenildo Costa da Silva	Predrag Knežević	Henrik Nottelmann
Philippe Cudré-Mauroux	Georgia Koloniari	Loris Penserini
Sarunas Girdzijauskas	Jafar Movahedi	Christos Tryfonopoulos

Clustering Information over the Web (ClustWeb)

Web data management has become a critical emerging research area, due to the exponential increase in the information circulation and dissemination over the Web. Web data mining is an evolving field of high interest to a wide academic and technical community.

The ClustWeb workshop focused on the topic of clustering information over the Web, as an emerging topic in current Web data mining efforts. The papers presented and the panel presentation contributed to understanding the role of clustering mechanisms and methodologies in accessing Web information (such as documents, link paths, and users on the Web). The topics of the workshop are summarized in:

- clustering structured Web sources,
- similarity ranking on the Web graph,
- clustering query logs (in search engines), towards dissemination of information,
- protecting Web data in the framework of clustering

The ClustWeb workshop addressed the issues involved in the effect of Web data clustering on increasing Web information accessibility, decreasing lengths in Web navigation pathways, improving Web user request servicing, integrating various data representation standards, and extending current Web information organization practices.

Workshop Chairs

Jaroslav Pokorný   Charles University of Prague (Czech Republic)
Athena Vakali   Aristotle University of Thessaloniki (Greece)

Program Committee

Eleftherios Angelis   Aristotle University of Thessaloniki (Greece)
Boualem Benatallah   University of New South Wales in Sydney (Australia)
Salima Benbernou   University of Lyon 1 (France)
Igor Cadez   University of California, Irvine (USA)
Barbara Catania   University of Genoa (Italy)
Siobhán Clarke   Trinity College, Dublin (Ireland)
Elena Ferrari   University of Insubria (Italy)
Mohand-Said Hacid   University of Lyon 1 (France)
Carlos Hurtado   University of Chile (Chile)
Nick Koudas   AT&T Labs (USA)
Fang Li   Shanghai Jiao Tong University (China)
András Lukács   Hungarian Academy of Sciences (Hungary)
Marco Mesiti   University of Milan (Italy)
Apostolos Papadopoulos   Aristotle University of Thessaloniki (Greece)
Jaroslav Pokorný   Charles University (Czech Republic)
Yücel Saygin   Sabancı University (Turkey)
Václav Snášel   Technical University of Ostrava (Czech Republic)
Athena Vakali   Aristotle University of Thessaloniki (Greece)

Acknowledgments

We would sincerely like to thank all program committee members, as well as all external referees for their excellent work in evaluating the submitted papers. Also, we would like to thank all authors for submitting a paper to one of our workshops. Special thanks go to Andrea Perego from the University of Milan (Italy) who did an outstanding job in compiling these proceedings, as well as to Alfred Hofmann from Springer for his cooperation and advice in putting this volume together.

Cambridge, USA   Wolfgang Lindner (Program Chair PhD)
July 2004   Marco Mesiti (Program Co-chair DataX)
                                                       Can Türker (Program Chair PIM)
                                            Yannis Tzitzikas (Program Co-chair P2P&DB)
                                             Athena Vakali (Program Co-chair ClustWeb)

Table of Contents

Advanced Query Processing and Optimization

Data Models and Database Design

Information Retrieval and Interoperability

Database Technologies for Handling XML-Information on the Web (DataX)

Invited Paper

Indexing XML Documents

Querying XML Documents and Schema Evolution

XML Application

Panel

Pervasive Information Management (PIM)

Peer-to-Peer Computing and Databases (P2P&DB)

Routing

Query Evaluation

Data Structures

Clustering Information Over the Web (ClustWeb)

Invited Paper

Web Content Clustering

Web Logs and Selective Clustering

Panel

Querying Sliding Windows
Over On-line Data Streams*

Lukasz Golab

School of Computer Science,
University of Waterloo, Ontario, Canada
lgolab@uwaterloo.ca

Abstract. A data stream is a real-time, continuous, ordered sequence of items generated by sources such as sensor networks, Internet traffic flow, credit card transaction logs, and on-line financial tickers. Processing continuous queries over data streams introduces a number of research problems, one of which concerns evaluating queries over sliding windows defined on the inputs. In this paper, we describe our research on sliding window query processing, with an emphasis on query models and algebras, physical and logical optimization, efficient processing of multiple windowed queries, and generating approximate answers. We outline previous work in streaming query processing and sliding window algorithms, summarize our contributions to date, and identify directions for future work.

1   Introduction

Traditional databases have been used in applications that require persistent data storage and complex querying. Usually, a database consists of a set of unordered objects that are relatively static, with insertions, updates, and deletions occurring less frequently than queries. Queries are executed when posed and the answer reflects the current state of the database. However, a growing list of applications receive and process data as a sequence (stream) of items. This change was instigated by the following trends:

– the increasing ubiquity of wireless computing devices, envisioned to form sensor nets and collectively transmit a vast amount of information [1, 26],
– the increasing volume, popularity, and volatility of the World Wide Web, particularly on-line data feeds such as news, sports, and financial tickers [11, 35],
– the overwhelming volume of transaction logs (e.g. telephone call records, credit card transactions, or Web usage logs) that, even when processed off-line, may be so large as to restrict processing to one sequential scan of the data [13],
– the recent interest in the Internet measurement community to use a data management system for on-line analysis of network traffic [14, 31].

A data stream is a real-time, continuous, ordered sequence of items. Processing queries over data streams, which are expected to run continuously and return new answers

---

* This research is partially supported by the Natural Sciences and Engineering Research Council of Canada.

W. Lindner et al. (Eds.): EDBT 2004 Workshops, LNCS 3268, pp. 1–11, 2004.

as new data arrive, introduces novel challenges such as adapting query plans in response to changing stream arrival rates, sharing resources among similar queries, and generating approximate answers in limited space. Additionally, some continuous queries are not computable in bounded memory (e.g. Cartesian product of two infinite streams), some relational operators are blocking because they must consume the entire input before any results are produced (e.g. join or group-by), and some users may be interested only in the most recent data. These three problems may be solved by restricting the range of continuous queries to a sliding window of manageable size. In *count-based* sliding windows, only the last N tuples are of interest, whereas *time-based* sliding windows contain tuples which have arrived in the last T time units.

Sliding windows solve some of the difficulties caused by processing on-line data streams, but implementing windowed operators also raises additional issues. The fundamental problem is that as the window slides forward, old results must be removed in addition to appending new results generated by newly arrived tuples. For example, computing the maximum value in an infinite stream is trivial, but doing so in a sliding window of size N requires $\Omega(N)$ space—consider a sequence of non-increasing values, in which the oldest item in any given window is the maximum and must be replaced whenever the window moves forward. In general, the result set of a windowed operator can change in four ways. The arrival of a new tuple may add new tuples to the answer (e.g. join) or remove tuples from the answer (e.g. set difference). Moreover, an expired tuple may cause the removal of tuples in the result set (e.g. aggregates) or the addition of new tuples to the result set (e.g. set difference) [23].

The goal of this research is to examine the problems and trade-offs involved in sliding window query processing, and evaluate possible solutions. The particular research questions which we aim to answer are as follows.

- How should a data stream be modeled, which operators should be included in a windowed algebra, and which useful rewritings could a windowed algebra allow in logical query optimization?
- How should relational operators be modified to function effectively over sliding windows?
- What opportunities exist for shared evaluation of multiple windowed queries?
- What is the best load shedding strategy (e.g. dropping tuples or approximating the answer) for multiple windowed queries if the stream arrival rates are too high and the system is unable to keep up?

The remainder of this paper discusses previous work in sliding window query processing in Sect. 2, our contributions to date in Sect. 3, and directions for future work in Sect. 4. More details on this topic and on other issues in data stream management may be found in our recent survey [20].

2   Related Work

2.1   Query Languages and Semantics

All proposed data stream systems recognize the importance of sliding windows. The STREAM system includes CQL, which is an SQL-based query language for continuous queries [2]. CQL includes three types of operators: relation-to-relation, stream-to-relation, and relation-to-stream. Standard SQL is used to express relation-to-relation operators, and the SQL-99 windowing constructs serve as stream-to-relation operators by reducing an infinite stream to a finite table containing the most recent window of items. The relation-to-stream operators—Istream, Dstream, and Rstream—are used to convert static relations and sliding windows to an output stream. The Istream operator returns a stream of all those tuples which exist in the given relation at the current time, but did not exist at the current time minus one. Similarly, Dstream returns a stream of tuples that existed in the given relation in the previous time unit, but not at the current time. The Rstream operator streams the contents of the entire relation at the current time. Furthermore, time-based and count-based windows are supported, as are partitioned windows defined by splitting a window into groups and defining a separate count-based window on each group. Since stream algebras rely on time and ordering, synchronizing and comparing timestamps of tuples generated by remote sources is also discussed within the STREAM project—this problem is referred to as *query heartbeat generation* [29].

TelegraphCQ uses another SQL-like query language (called StreaQuel), augmented with a for-loop construct that specifies the window length and frequency of query re-execution as the window moves forward (or backward, or as one endpoint moves forward and the other moves backward) [9]. Moreover, GSQL is a streaming query language employed by AT&T Gigascope, which is a stream database for network applications [14]. GSQL is a subset of SQL that restricts all inputs and outputs to be streaming, requires an ordering attribute for each stream, allows binary windowed joins, and includes an order-preserving stream union.

An interesting alternative to declarative streaming query languages is the "boxes and arrows" interface of the Aurora stream processing system [1]. An Aurora query plan consists of boxes corresponding to query operators, and arrows connecting the operators and specifying data flow. The Aurora algebra, called SQuAl, includes seven operators, four of which are order-sensitive. The three order-insensitive operators are projection, union, and map, the last applying an arbitrary function to each of the tuples in the stream or a window thereof. The other four operators require an order specification, which includes the ordered field and a slack parameter. The latter defines the maximum disorder in the stream, e.g. a slack of two means that each tuple in the stream is either in sorted order, or at most two positions or two time units away from being in sorted order. The four order-sensitive operators are buffered sort (which takes an almost-sorted stream and the slack parameter, and outputs the stream in sorted order), windowed aggregates (in which the user can specify how often to advance the window and re-evaluate the aggregate), binary band join (which joins tuples whose timestamps are at most t units apart), and resample (which generates missing stream values by interpolation, e.g. given tuples with timestamps 1 and 3, a new tuple with timestamp 2 can be generated with an attribute value that is an average[1] of the other two tuples' values).

---

[1] Other resampling functions are also possible, e.g. the maximum, minimum, or weighted average of the two neighbouring data values.

2.2   Windowed Query Processing and Optimization

The *basic window model* was introduced in [35] to compute simple aggregates and was recently extended to windowed burst detection [36]. In this approach, the sliding window is partitioned into buckets (called basic windows), and only a summary and a timestamp are stored in each basic window. When the timestamp of the oldest basic window expires, a new basic window is inserted in its place, and the aggregate is updated using the new set of summaries. For instance, the windowed average may be incrementally maintained by storing partial sums and counts in each basic window.

A variation of the basic window model is presented in [8], with basic windows of various sizes arranged in a wavelet-like tree. For example, if the window size is sixteen tuples, the root stores summary information about all sixteen tuples, the left child summarizes tuples one through eight, the right child summarizes tuples nine through sixteen, and so on down to the leaves. If detailed information is required only for the newest tuples in the window, those subtrees (or leaves) which would normally summarize older tuples may be omitted from the tree.

Rather than waiting until the newest basic window fills up to refresh query results, [16] shows that restricting the sizes of the basic windows to powers of two and imposing a limit on the number of basic windows of each size yields an algorithm that approximates simple aggregates using logarithmic space. This algorithm has been used to approximately compute the windowed sum [16], windowed histogram [27], aggregates over time-based windows [12], as well as variance and k-medians clustering inside a window [6].

Recent work on sliding window joins includes binary windowed join algorithms [25], which extend the pipelined symmetric hash join [33], windowed join algorithms for tracking moving objects in sensor networks [22], and shared evaluation of windowed joins with various window sizes [24].

Previous work on sliding window query optimization consists of indexing techniques for sliding windows stored on disk [28], load shedding strategies for conjunctive queries [4], windowed joins [15, 30], and windowed aggregates [5], on-the-fly reordering of multi-way join plans [7, 34], as well as shared query processing by indexing query predicates [10] and by pre-computing aggregates shared by multiple queries [3]. Moreover, *punctuations*[2] [32] may be used instead of sliding windows to bound the memory requirements of some queries, or in conjunction with windows to avoid storing and later having to expire tuples that will not contribute to the query result and may be dropped immediately.

3   Results to Date

This section summarizes our existing research results. Thus far, we have focused on windowed join processing, indexing sliding windows stored in main memory, and incremental evaluation of complex windowed aggregates.

---

[2] A punctuation is a constraint that is encoded as a data item within a stream. Punctuations may be used to specify conditions that will be obeyed by all future tuples, e.g. no more tuples with attribute value greater than ten will appear in the remainder of the stream.

3.1 Windowed Joins

In [21], we developed a general framework and presented specific algorithms for evaluating joins over multiple sliding windows, given the constraint that all windows and hash tables must fit in main memory. Various window-specific issues that arise during join execution were considered, such as immediate or periodic generation of new results, immediate or periodic expiration of stale tuples out of the windows and hash tables, nested-loops or hash-based execution, and expiration techniques for time-based and count-based windows. Fundamentally, our algorithms extend the binary pipelined symmetric hash join [33] to multiple inputs and to deal with the aforementioned windowing issues during join processing.

We also developed a join ordering heuristic that considers stream arrival rates, window sizes, distinct value counts, and the frequency of query re-evaluation and expiration to choose an efficient execution order within our multi-join operator. The heuristic is based on ordering the most selective join first, but we have shown that other parameters must also be considered in some situations, such as those where one or more streams arrive much faster than others. Experiments with stand-alone prototypes of our multi-join algorithms validated our cost model and ordering heuristic, and showed that building large hash tables on the input windows is beneficial only if periodic expiration of stale tuples is performed.

3.2 Windowed Indices and Storage Structures

Since we have discovered in [21] that maintenance costs of windowed indices may be prohibitive if implemented without care, we investigated indexing further in [19]. As was the case with our join operators, we focused on main-memory query processing and returning exact answers. We used the basic window model [35], originally proposed for computing windowed aggregates, to define storage structures and query semantics for sliding windows. We proposed a circular array of pointers to basic windows as a default storage structure—as shown in Fig.1—and outlined several possibilities for storing the individual basic windows. The possibilities include storing individual tuples, distinct values and their multiplicities, or groups of distinct values and group multiplicities (range histograms) inside basic windows. We argued that the basic window model provides the only feasible index maintenance strategy (periodic insertion and deletion) as well as a natural approximation technique: if the system is unable to re-evaluate all queries after each basic window is appended, the basic window size can be increased, thereby decreasing system load but also increasing the delay in reporting answers generated by newly arrived tuples.

To motivate the need for two types of windowed indices, we classified streaming operators into four types based on the nature of the input and output: infinite versus windowed. Operators whose inputs and outputs are both infinite include on-the-fly selection. A windowed join is an example of a windowed-input, infinite-output operator as the inputs must be windowed to fit in finite memory, but output tuples may be streamed directly to the user. A windowed-output operator may have infinite or windowed input, and materializes the last window of results. Of those operators which require windowing the input, some are incrementally computable (e.g. simple aggregates), but others need to scan the entire window during re-evaluation. The latter may be further classified into

Location of pointer to oldest basic window

Circular array   Temporary buffer containing
the newest tuples

Basic windows

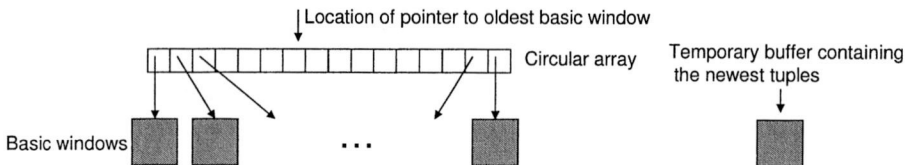

Fig. 1. Sliding window implemented as a circular array of pointers to basic windows. The newest basic window is temporarily buffered until it fills up, at which time it is inserted into the data structure by overwriting the pointer to the oldest basic window

set-valued operators (e.g. windowed intersection) that require access to distinct values in the window and their multiplicities, and attribute-valued operators (e.g. windowed join followed by a selection on another attribute) that need access to individual tuples during re-execution. Thus, some operators may benefit from set-valued indices, and others from attribute-valued indices. We proposed and evaluated solutions for both types of windowed indices in [19], including an approximation scheme for set-valued queries whereby we store range histograms in each basic window and, for example, return a windowed intersection in terms of intersecting ranges rather than intersecting distinct values.

3.3   Aggregates over Sliding Windows

When a sliding window is divided into basic windows, only distributive and algebraic aggregates may be computed incrementally. Complex aggregates, such as finding the k most frequent items or all items that occur with a frequency above a threshold τ, may need access to the entire window in the worst case. In [17], we gave an algorithm that uses the basic window model to find frequently occurring items in sliding windows, provided that the distribution of item types follows the power law (at least approximately). We tested our algorithm on IP traffic traces and obtained encouraging results.

In [18], we proposed three statistical models for the distribution of item types in data streams, and presented algorithms for finding frequent items in sliding windows with multinomially-distributed item frequencies. In what we call the *adversarial model*, items from various categories arrive at random, without conforming to any underlying distribution. This is the most general and difficult scenario, in which complex aggregates over sliding windows are typically maintained by periodically scanning the window and recomputing the answer. In the *stochastic model*, a stream is assumed to contain an arbitrary probability distribution, whose type and parameters remain fixed across the lifetime of the stream. In this model, maintaining statistics over sliding windows measures the variance of the distribution in the current window relative to the expected frequencies. Finally, in the *drifting model* the relative frequencies of the categories are assumed to vary over the lifetime of the stream, provided that they vary sufficiently slowly that for any given sliding window (of some fixed size) excerpted from the stream, with high probability the window could have been generated by a stochastic model. The drifting model is particularly suitable to sliding windows because the distribution is allowed to change, yet we may assume a stochastic model within a single sliding window without introducing significant error.

4   Directions for Future Research

We now outline our plans for future work in the area of sliding window query processing. We are interested in defining query semantics and an algebra over sliding windows, implementing sliding window operators, sharing resources during the execution of multiple windowed queries, and generating approximate answers with provable error guarantees.

4.1   Sliding Window Algebras and Query Semantics

In our previous work, the basic window model was used to specify query re-execution strategies. We intend to investigate whether this model may also be used to define a sliding window algebra, and in particular, whether incorporating the notion of (bulk) insertion and expiration into the algebra could be beneficial. This line of reasoning is closely related to StreaQuel, where the user may specify how often to advance the window and re-execute queries, to the SQuAl algebra, which includes explicit references to out-of-order tuple arrival, and to the notion of *negative tuples* [23], which may be used to implicitly expire old tuples out of their windows, i.e. rather than physically deleting a tuple, the presence of a negative tuple in the output stream would be understood to mean that the corresponding "real" tuple is no longer valid. Moreover, the notion of punctuations, or stream constraints in general, is also a candidate for direct inclusion into the algebra.

Another issue in streaming and windowed algebras concerns modeling various notions of time, order, and sequencing. Most of the proposed algebras and query languages are extensions of SQL and the relational model, augmented with windowing constructs. We are interested in applying insights from temporal, time series, sequence, array, and probabilistic[3] data models to the sliding window model, though fully-featured temporal logics are likely to be too powerful and impractical for on-line streams.

The basic window model is a possible solution for relaxing the notion of order in data streams: order across basic windows is preserved, but tuples inside a particular basic window can be considered as having arrived roughly at the same time. That is, rather than storing timestamps with each distinct tuple, only one timestamp is stored per basic window, meaning that each basic window is an unordered multiset. However, one problem with this model is that if the basic windows are defined in terms of time, then it is not possible to recover arbitrary count-based windows from the time-based partitions, and vice versa. For example, if the window is divided into basic windows that span one minute each, and the first two basic windows store one hundred tuples each, then it is impossible to select a count-based window of the last 150 tuples—this window should include the first fifty tuples in the second basic window, but there is no way to determine which tuples are the "first fifty" if order within the basic window is not preserved. Another consequence of the basic window model is that sharing a data stream among queries that are interested in windows with slightly different sizes is constrained in that the window sizes of interest must be multiples of the individual basic window size.

Lastly, we want to investigate the relative power and complexity of sliding window algebras derived from general stream algebras and vice versa. In what may be called *top-*

---

[3] Streaming measurements generated by primitive devices may be inaccurate.

down stream algebra design, one starts with a general streaming algebra, which is then restricted to form a sliding window algebra. In *bottom-up stream algebra design*, a sliding window algebra is developed first, followed by non-windowed streaming operators. It is unclear whether one method is easier (conceptually and computationally) than the other. For example, the Cartesian product is straightforward to evaluate over sliding windows, but intractable over infinite streams. Conversely, aggregates such as minimum and maximum may be evaluated on-the-fly in the infinite stream model, but require the storage of the entire window in the sliding window model.

4.2   Sliding Window Operators

We have already implemented some windowed operators (joins and simple aggregates) and indices that should be of use in any streaming system, regardless of the underlying algebra. We intend to continue this implementation and develop query rewritings involving physical operators (in addition to algebraic rewritings). Again, we want to exploit the basic window model to design efficient re-evaluation strategies for windowed operators. One issue in this context is that some operators, such as the sliding window join, may not benefit from periodic re-execution as prescribed by the basic window technique—the pipelined symmetric hash join [33] can in fact process a new tuple immediately upon arrival.

We also plan to extend our classification of windowed operators from [19] and better characterize groups of operators that can be efficiently executed over sliding windows. For example, some windowed-input operators may be implemented as infinite-input operators if one considers the input window to be an infinite stream of insertions and deletions (deletions may be implemented as negative tuples generated on the input stream [24]). This could be significant if there exists a general processing strategy for infinite-input operators that is more efficient than a processing strategy designed specifically for windowed-input operators.

Further research in implementing windowed operators may include storing some (or all) windows on disk as the access and update patterns of sliding windows should give rise to novel cache replacement and prefetching strategies. However, storing the windows on disk may be inappropriate for applications that deal with very high stream arrival rates (e.g. Internet traffic monitoring at a core router). Thus, it may be more practical to calculate approximate answers using the available main memory rather than computing exact answers using secondary storage.

4.3   Sliding Window Query Optimization

Possible optimization techniques include deriving functional dependencies over data streams, maintaining materialized views of continuous windowed queries, and ensuring scalability in the number of queries and stream arrival rates. In terms of scalable multi-query processing, an interesting open problem was proposed in [10]: sharing data structures for computing windowed aggregate queries with different select-project-join clauses. Coping with high arrival rates usually involves load shedding and providing approximate answers that are cheaper to compute. Our current, admittedly simple, load shedding solution was described above and consists of two steps: (a) enlarging the basic window size if the system is unable to re-execute continuous queries with the current frequency, and (b) summarizing distinct attribute values into groups when answering set-valued queries. Since sliding windows may be considered as approximations to infinite streams, we plan to study the effects of "approximating the approximation", e.g. shedding load by prematurely evicting tuples from their windows. The goal in this context is to present provable error guarantees on the results of windowed query plans consisting of multiple approximate operators.

5 Conclusions

This research is aimed at solving a challenging and practical problem in data stream management systems: sliding window query processing. Building on our initial work on sliding window operators and indices using the basic window model, we plan to extend our research to sliding window query algebras and semantics, logical and physical query optimization, generating approximate statistics over sliding windows with error guarantees, and shared evaluation of multiple windowed queries. We envision our current and expected contributions to be compatible with any data stream management system that requires support for sliding windows. Such systems are expected to gain considerable popularity as the data stream model finds widespread use in real-time Internet traffic measurement, next-generation sensor networks, and on-line transaction log processing.

References

1. D. Abadi, D. Carney, U. Cetintemel, M. Cherniack, C. Convey, S. Lee, M. Stonebraker, N. Tatbul, and S. Zdonik. Aurora: A new model and architecture for data stream management. *The VLDB Journal*, 12(2):120–139, Aug 2003.
2. A. Arasu, S. Babu, and J. Widom. The CQL continuous query language: Semantic foundations and query execution. Technical Report 2003-67, Stanford University, 2003.
3. A. Arasu and J. Widom. Resource sharing in continuous sliding-window aggregates. Technical Report 2004-15, Stanford University, 2004.
4. A. Ayad and J. Naughton. Static optimization of conjunctive queries with sliding windows over unbounded streaming information sources. In *Proc. ACM SIGMOD Int. Conf. on Management of Data*, 2004.
5. B. Babcock, M. Datar, and R. Motwani. Load shedding for aggregation queries over data streams. In *Proc. 20th Int. Conf. on Data Engineering*, pages 350–361, 2004.
6. B. Babcock, M. Datar, R. Motwani, and L. O'Callaghan. Maintaining variance and k-medians over data stream windows. In *Proc. 22nd ACM SIGACT-SIGMOD-SIGART Symp. Principles of Database Systems*, pages 234–243, 2003.
7. S. Babu, K. Munagala, J. Widom, and R. Motwani. Adaptive caching for continuous queries. Technical Report 2004-24, Stanford University, 2004.
8. A. Bulut and A. K. Singh. SWAT: Hierarchical stream summarization. In *Proc. 19th Int. Conf. on Data Engineering*, pages 303–314, 2003.
9. S. Chandrasekaran, O. Cooper, A. Deshpande, M. J. Franklin, J. M. Hellerstein, W. Hong, S. Krishnamurthy, S. Madden, V. Raman, F. Reiss, and M. Shah. TelegraphCQ: Continuous dataflow processing for an uncertain world. In *Proc. 1st Biennial Conf. on Innovative Data Syst. Res*, pages 269–280, 2003.
10. S. Chandrasekaran and M. J. Franklin. PSoup: a system for streaming queries over streaming data. *The VLDB Journal*, 12(2):140–156, Aug 2003.

11. J. Chen, D. DeWitt, F. Tian, and Y. Wang. NiagaraCQ: A scalable continuous query system for internet databases. In *Proc. ACM SIGMOD Int. Conf. on Management of Data*, pages 379–390, 2000.

12. E. Cohen and M. Strauss. Maintaining time-decaying stream aggregates. In *Proc. 22nd ACM SIGACT-SIGMOD-SIGART Symp. Principles of Database Systems*, pages 223–233, 2003.

13. C. Cortes, K. Fisher, D. Pregibon, A. Rogers, and F. Smith. Hancock: A language for extracting signatures from data streams. In *Proc. 6th ACM SIGKDD Int. Conf. on Knowledge Discovery and Data Mining*, pages 9–17, 2000.

14. C. Cranor, T. Johnson, O. Spatscheck, and V. Shkapenyuk. Gigascope: High performance network monitoring with an SQL interface. In *Proc. ACM SIGMOD Int. Conf. on Management of Data*, pages 647–651, 2003.

15. A. Das, J. Gehrke, and M. Riedewald. Approximate join processing over data streams. In *Proc. ACM SIGMOD Int. Conf. on Management of Data*, pages 40–51, 2003.

16. M. Datar, A. Gionis, P. Indyk, and R. Motwani. Maintaining stream statistics over sliding windows. In *Proc. 13th SIAM-ACM Symp. on Discrete Algorithms*, pages 635–644, 2002.

17. L. Golab, D. DeHaan, E. Demaine, A. Lopez-Ortiz, and J. I. Munro. Identifying frequent items in sliding windows over on-line packet streams. In *Proc. ACM SIGCOMM Internet Measurement Workshop*, pages 173–178, 2003.

18. L. Golab, D. DeHaan, A. Lopez-Ortiz, and E. Demaine. Finding frequent items in sliding windows with multinomially-distributed item frequencies. In *Proc. 16th Int. Conf. on Scientific and Statistical Database Management*, 2004.

19. L. Golab, S. Garg, and M. T. Özsu. On indexing sliding windows over on-line data streams. In *Advances in Database Technology — EDBT'04*, pages 712–729, 2004.

20. L. Golab and M. T. Özsu. Issues in data stream management. *ACM SIGMOD Record*, 32(2):5–14, 2003.

21. L. Golab and M. T. Özsu. Processing sliding window multi-joins in continuous queries over data streams. In *Proc. 29th Int. Conf. on Very Large Data Bases*, pages 500–511, 2003.

22. M. Hammad, W. Aref, and A. Elmagarmid. Stream window join: Tracking moving objects in sensor-network databases. In *Proc. 15th Int. Conf. on Scientific and Statistical Database Management*, pages 75–84, 2003.

23. M. Hammad, W. Aref, M. Franklin, M. Mokbel, and A. Elmagarmid. Efficient execution of sliding window queries over data streams. Technical Report CSD TR 03-035, Purdue University, 2003.

24. M. Hammad, M. J. Franklin, W. Aref, and A. Elmagarmid. Scheduling for shared window joins over data streams. In *Proc. 29th Int. Conf. on Very Large Data Bases*, pages 297–308, 2003.

25. J. Kang, J. Naughton, and S. Viglas. Evaluating window joins over unbounded streams. In *Proc. 19th Int. Conf. on Data Engineering*, pages 341–352, 2003.

26. S. Madden, M. J. Franklin, J. M. Hellerstein, and W. Hong. The design of an acquisitional query processor for sensor networks. In *Proc. ACM SIGMOD Int. Conf. on Management of Data*, pages 491–502, 2003.

27. L. Qiao, D. Agrawal, and A. El Abbadi. Supporting sliding window queries for continuous data streams. In *Proc. 15th Int. Conf. on Scientific and Statistical Database Management*, pages 85–94, 2003.

28. N. Shivakumar and H. García-Molina. Wave-indices: indexing evolving databases. In *Proc. ACM SIGMOD Int. Conf. on Management of Data*, pages 381–392, 1997.

29. U. Srivastava and J. Widom. Flexible time management in data stream systems. In *Proc. 23rd ACM SIGACT-SIGMOD-SIGART Symp. Principles of Database Systems*, 2004.

30. U. Srivastava and J. Widom. Memory-limited execution of windowed stream joins. Technical Report 2004-12, Stanford University, 2004.

31. M. Sullivan and A. Heybey. Tribeca: A system for managing large databases of network traffic. In *Proc. USENIX Annual Technical Conf.*, 1998.

32. P. Tucker, D. Maier, T. Sheard, and L. Faragas. Exploiting punctuation semantics in continuous data streams. *IEEE Trans. Knowledge and Data Eng.*, 15(3):555–568, 2003.

33. A. Wilschut and P. Apers. Dataflow query execution in a parallel main-memory environment. In *Proc. Int. Conf. on Parallel and Distributed Information Systems*, pages 68–77, 1991.

34. Y. Zhu, E. Rundensteiner, and G. Heineman. Dynamic plan migration for continuous queries over data streams. In *Proc. ACM SIGMOD Int. Conf. on Management of Data*, 2004.

35. Y. Zhu and D. Shasha. StatStream: Statistical monitoring of thousands of data streams in real time. In *Proc. 28th Int. Conf. on Very Large Data Bases*, pages 358–369, 2002.

36. Y. Zhu and D. Shasha. Efficient elastic burst detection in data streams. In *Proc. 9th ACM SIGKDD Int. Conf. on Knowledge Discovery and Data Mining*, pages 336–345, 2003.

MIRA: Multilingual Information Processing
on Relational Architecture

A. Kumaran

Department of Computer Science and Automation,
Indian Institute of Science, Bangalore, India
kumaran@csa.iisc.ernet.in

Abstract. In today's global village, it is critical that the key information tools, such as web search engines, *e-Commerce* portals and *e-Governance*, work across multiple natural languages, seamlessly. We propose a new flexible architecture – Multilingual Information processing on Relational Architecture (MIRA) – that supports the multilingual processing functionality of the primary storage mechanism for such deployments – the relational database systems, effectively and efficiently. We propose new linguistic matching operators that enhances the standard lexicographic matching of database systems into *phonetic* and *semantic* domains. We further show that the performance of the systems may be made *language-neutral*. Our proposed architecture is based on standards and hence amenable for easy implementation in any type of query processing and information retrieval systems. In this paper, we present our approach to implement the above architecture and outline the host of research issues that are opened up due to the inherently fuzzy nature of the alternative matching semantics.

1 Introduction

In an increasingly multilingual digital world[1], the key information and commerce applications, such as *e-Commerce* portals, digital libraries, search engines etc., must work across multiple natural languages, seamlessly. A critical requirement to achieve this goal is that the principal underlying data source – relational database management systems – should manage multilingual data effectively and efficiently. Our proposal, Multilingual Information processing on Relational Architecture (MIRA), attempts to enhance the relational database systems with multilingual features and to make the query performance nearly *language neutral*. Further, our proposed architecture is amenable for easy implementation in any type of query processing and information retrieval systems.

Specifically, we propose multilingual operators that extend and complement the standard lexicographic matching operator, to match text strings across languages based on enhanced matching semantics. We propose a *phonetic* matching operator that matches proper names, after transforming them to equivalent *phonemic* strings, and a *semantic* matching operator that matches attributes based on their *meanings*, transformed using

---

[1] Currently, two-thirds of Internet users are non-native English speakers [1] and it is predicted that the majority of web-data will be multilingual by 2010 [2].

W. Lindner et al. (Eds.): EDBT 2004 Workshops, LNCS 3268, pp. 12–23, 2004.

ontological hierarchies. In both cases, the performance of the operators is shown to be at a level acceptable for online user interaction. Further, to make the performance of queries on multilingual data comparable to monolingual processing, we propose a new compressed storage format that results in a near *language-neutral* performance when implemented on commercial database systems.

The alternative semantics for the matching operators and the inherently fuzzy nature of such matching opened up several interesting issues that may be possible extensions of our current research. We are also expanding the scope of our application domains, to test the viability of our multilingual architecture.

2   A Sample Multilingual Application

Consider a hypothetical e-Commerce application – *Books.com* that sells books across the globe, with a sample product catalog in multiple languages as shown in Figure 1. The product catalog shown may be considered as a logical view assembled from data from several databases (each aligned with the local language needs), but searchable in a unified manner for multilingual users.

Author	Author_FN	Title	Price	Category	Language
Durant	Will/Ariel	History of Civilization	$ 149.00	History	English
ஞேது	ஜ்வஹர்லால்	அிிய ேஜாிி	INR 250	சிிி்ிரம்	Tamil
Adams	Laurie S.	Arte Di Rinascita Italiana	€ 75.00	Arti Fini	Italian
Lebrun	François	L'Histoire De La France	€ 19.95	Histoire	French
بهنسي ك د	عفيفة	صبر التاريخ العمارة	SAR 95	معماري	Arabic
Gilderhus	Mark T.	History and Historians	£ 35.00	Historiography	English
नेहरू	जवाहरलाल	भारत एक खोज	INR 175	इतिहास	Hindi
Σαρρη	Κατερινα	Παιχνίδια στο Πιάνο	€ 12.00	Μουσική	Greek
Nehru	Jawaharlal	Letters to My Daughter	£ 15.00	Autobiography	English

Fig. 1. Hypothetical *Books.com* Catalog

2.1   Multilingual Name Searches

In this environment, suppose a user wants to search for the works of an author in all (or a specified set of) languages. The SQL:1999 compliant query requiring specification of the authors name in several languages is undesirable, due to requirement of lexical resources in each of the languages and high error levels in data input even when working on mono-lingual data[2]. We propose a simple query syntax, as shown in Figure 2, that takes input name in one language, namely `English`, but returns all *phonemically* equivalent names in the user-specified set of languages, namely, `English`, `Hindi`, `Arabic` and `Tamil`.

A sample phonetic query and the corresponding answer set, when issued on *Books.com*, are given in Figure 2. The returned tuples have in Author column the multi-lexical strings that are *phonemically close* to the query string in English, namely, `Nehru`.

---

[2] The error rate for name attributes in English is estimated to be approximately 3% [9].

The specification of ALL for the list of languages would have brought all records containing author names that are phonetically equivalent to Nehru, irrespective of the languages. The **Threshold** parameter specified in the query determines the quality of matches, as described later in the paper.

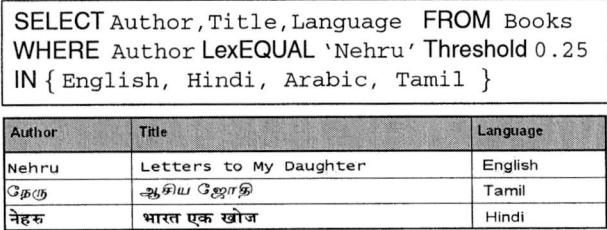

SELECT Author,Title,Language FROM Books
WHERE Author LexEQUAL 'Nehru' Threshold 0.25
IN { English, Hindi, Arabic, Tamil }

Author	Title	Language
Nehru	Letters to My Daughter	English
தேரு	ஆசிய ஜோதி	Tamil
नेहरु	भारत एक खोज	Hindi

Fig. 2. A Sample LexEQUAL Query and Result Set

We refer *matching on multilexical text strings, based on their phonemic equivalence* as **Multilexical Phonemic Matching**. Though restricted to proper names, such matching represent *a significant part of the user query strings in text databases and search engines, as proper and generic names constitute a fifth of normal corpora* [9].

2.2 Multilingual Concept Searches

Consider the query to retrieve all History books in *Books.com*, in a set of languages of users choice. The current SQL:1999 compliant query, having the selection condition as **Category** = "History" would return only those books that have *Category* as History, in English. A multilingual user may be served better if all the History books in all the languages (or in a set of languages specified by her) are returned. A simple SQL query, as given in Figure 3, and the corresponding result set may be desirable.

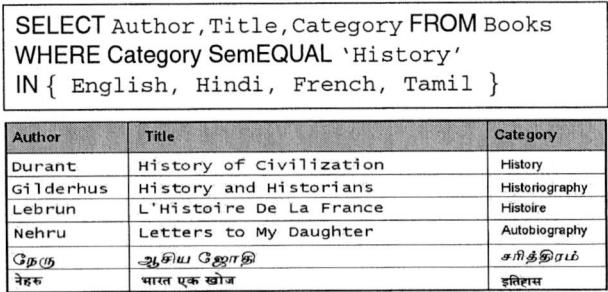

SELECT Author,Title,Category FROM Books
WHERE Category SemEQUAL 'History'
IN { English, Hindi, French, Tamil }

Author	Title	Category
Durant	History of Civilization	History
Gilderhus	History and Historians	Historiography
Lebrun	L'Histoire De La France	Histoire
Nehru	Letters to My Daughter	Autobiography
தேரு	ஆசிய ஜோதி	சரித்திரம்
नेहरु	भारत एक खोज	इतिहास

Fig. 3. A Sample SemEQUAL Query and Result Set

The output contains all books that have their category values that are semantically equivalent to History in English. Note that in addition to all books with *Category* having a value equivalent to History, the categories that are *subsumed* by History[3] are also retrieved. We refer *matching text strings based on their generalized meanings, irrespective of the languages*, as **Multilingual Semantic Matching**.

It should be specially noted here that though our solution methodology is designed for matching multilingual strings, it is equally applicable for extending the standard matching semantics of mono-lingual text strings. For example, the LexEQUAL operator may be used for matching the English name Catherine and all its variations, such as Kathrin and Katerina. Similarly, the SemEQUAL operator, may be used for matching Disk Drive with Computer Storage Devices.

3 MIRA Implementation Strategy

In this section, we outline our strategy for implementing the MIRA architecture. We explain the ontology of text data in relational systems and show how we define the semantics for the new operators for *phonemic* and *semantic* matching of multilingual text data.

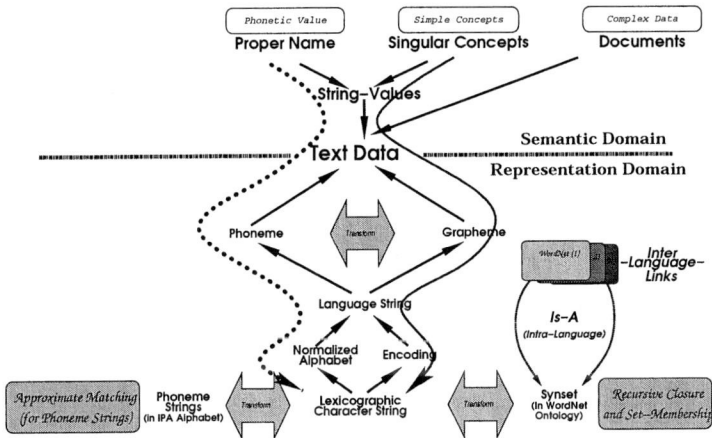

Fig. 4. Ontology for Text Data

Our view of storage and semantics of textual information in databases is shown in Figure 4. The semantics of *what* gets stored is sketched in the top part of the figure, and *how* the text data is stored is outlined by the lower half of the figure. Multilingual text strings are stored in a normalized alphabet (such as *English, Hindi, Arabic, Chinese*, etc.) and orthogonally in a specific encoding (such as *ASCII, Unicode*, etc.). Semantically, the text attributes may represent a wide variety of information, from simple strings to full documents; however, we consider only two specific type of attributes; first, those that store proper names, whose value is primarily in the vocalization of the name, tagged as

---

[3] Historiography (the study of of history writing and written histories) and Autobiography are considered as specialized branches of History itself.

Proper Names in the figure above. Second, those that lend themselves to be described using ontological hierarchies, tagged as *Singular Concepts* above. We broadly classify all other attributes as Documents which may require more sophisticated Natural Language Processing algorithms that process the documents on complex semantics.

3.1   Phonemic Matching Strategy

In this section we briefly sketch our phonetic matching approach that extends earlier works in monolingual world [16] to matching of multilingual names. We further enhance the performance of such matching by defining a phonemic index based on the classic *Soundex* algorithm [10] and by adopting *q-gram* techniques [7] that has been successfully used in approximate matching of monolingual names to multilingual world. Interested readers are referred to [13–15] for details of the matching algorithm and its performance.

LexEQUAL (S_l, S_r, e)
Input: Strings S_l, S_r, *Error Threshold, e*
                  Languages with TTP transformations, $\mathcal{S_L}$
1. $L_l \leftarrow$ Language of $S_l; L_r \leftarrow$ Language of S_r;
2.   **if** $L_l \in \mathcal{S_L}$ and $L_r \in \mathcal{S_L}$ **then**
3. $T_l \leftarrow$ transform(S_l, L_l); $T_r \leftarrow$ transform(S_r, L_r);
4. $Smaller \leftarrow (| \, T_l \, | \leq | \, T_r \, | \, ? \, |T_l| : |T_r|)$;
5.   **if** editdistance$(T_l, T_r) \leq (e * Smaller)$
6.   **then return** TRUE **else return** FALSE;
7.   **else return** NORESOURCE;

---

editdistance(S_L, S_R)
Input: String S_L, String S_R
Output: Edit-distance k
1. $L_l \leftarrow | \, S_L \, |; L_r \leftarrow | \, S_R \, |$;
2.   Create $DistMatrix[L_l, L_r]$ and initialize to $Zero$;
3.   **for** i **from** 0 **to** L_l **do** $DistMatrix[i, 0] \leftarrow i$;
4.   **for** j **from** 0 **to** L_r **do** $DistMatrix[0, j] \leftarrow j$;
5.   **for** i **from** 1 **to** L_l **do**
6.   **for** j **from** 1 **to** L_r **do**
7. $DistMatrix[i, j] \leftarrow$ Min $\left\{ \begin{array}{l} DistMatrix[i-1, j] + InsCost(S_{L_i}) \\ DistMatrix[i-1, j-1] + SubCost(S_{R_j}, S_{L_i}) \\ DistMatrix[i, j-1] + DelCost(S_{R_j}) \end{array} \right\}$
8.   **return** $DistMatrix[L_l, L_r]$;

Fig. 5. The LexEQUAL Algorithm

We propose a *phonemic* matching strategy (shown as dotted line in Figure 4) in LexEQUAL operator, as follows: First, the multilingual text strings are transformed to their equivalent *phonemic* representations in *International Phonetic Alphabet (IPA)*[4] [3], obtained using standard *text-to-phoneme (TTP)* converters. The phoneme strings are stored in the Unicode [4] encoding format, as specified by Unicode Consortium, using basic *Latin* and *IPA supplement* code charts. The resulting phoneme strings represent a normalized form of proper names across languages, thus providing a means of comparison. Further, when the text data is stored in multiple scripts, this may be the *only* means of comparing them. Since the phoneme sets of two languages are seldom identical, we employ approximate matching techniques to match the phoneme strings. Thus, the multilexical comparisons are *inherently fuzzy*, making it only possible to produce a likely, but not perfect, set of answers with respect to the user's intentions.

In the algorithm shown in Figure 5, the LexEQUAL operator accepts two *to-be-compared* multilingual text strings and a *User Match Threshold* parameter that determines the quality of match, as inputs. The strings are transformed to their equivalent phonemic strings in IPA [3] alphabet by the Transform function, implemented using standard *TTP* converters. The editdistance function computes the traditional *Levenshtein* edit distance or a modified distance metric, as appropriate. The value for the user match threshold parameter may be fixed by application administrators, depending on the domain and the application requirements.

LexEQUAL Match Quality. While the performance of above algorithm can be optimized, we emphasize that the ideal parameters will depend on the data set and the domain of interest. The *User Match Threshold* and *Cost Matrix* (*the replacement cost between a given pair of characters*) parameters may be tuned at user or application level, based on the characteristics of the domain. We detail our experiments and a methodology for tuning the parameters for optimal matching in [15].

LexEQUAL Operator Performance. Since the approximate matching implemented as UDF affects the query run-times adversely, we outline two different techniques for improving the performance of the query processing – the *Q-Gram Filters* and an *Approximate Phonetic Index*. Both these techniques cheaply return a set of candidate strings, which are further processed using the expensive UDF calls to weed out the *false-positives*. Our experimental results show that these techniques vastly improve the performance of phonetic matching.

3.2   Semantic Matching Strategy

Our strategy for matching multilingual data based on *semantics* in SemEQUAL operator is as shown in Figure 6. First, we convert the query string to a set of *concepts* using a standard linguistic resources, such as WordNet [5]. The WordNet is a *lexico-semantic* database that provides, the context for all noun word-forms in standard taxonomical hierarchies covering all concepts expressible in a language. We propose to leverage the rich semantic hierarchies available in WordNet and match two different word forms, based on the concept that they map on to in WordNet's taxonomic hierarchy. Further, the matching

---

[4] IPA provides a complete set of phonemes of all the world's languages, thus providing a common representation for the vocalization of the proper name.

may be on specializations of the *meaning* of the query string, using semantic closure[5] computed using WordNet. In addition to English WordNet, there are several initiatives such as *Euro-WordNet* and *Indo-WordNet* around the world [6], to interlink concepts of WordNets in different languages. Once the multilingual word forms are mapped onto semantic primitives using WordNet of the appropriate language, the resulting semantic primitives may be compared for equivalence, generalization or specialization based on the common concept hierarchy between the languages.

SemEQUAL ($String_{Data}$, $String_{Query}$, $\mathcal{T_L}$)
Input: Strings $String_{Data}$, $String_{Query}$
           Set of Target Languages $\mathcal{T_L}$
Output: TRUE or FALSE
           [*Optional*] Gloss of Matched Synset
1. $(L_D,L_Q) \leftarrow$ LangOf ($String_{Data}$, $String_{Query}$);
2. $(\mathcal{W}_D,\mathcal{W}_Q) \leftarrow$ WordNetOf (L_D,L_Q);
3. $S_D \leftarrow$ Synset of $String_{Data}$ in $\mathcal{W}_D$; $S_Q \leftarrow$ Synset of $String_{Query}$ in $\mathcal{W}_Q$;
4. $TC_Q \leftarrow$ TransitiveClosure($S_Q, \mathcal{T_L}$);
5.   **if** $TC_Q \cap S_D$ **is not empty then**
              return TRUE **else return** FALSE;
6.   [Opt.] **return** Gloss of the Matched Synset;

TransitiveClosure (S, $\mathcal{T_L}$)
Input: String S, Target Language Set $\mathcal{T_L}$
Output: The specializations of S
1. $L_S \leftarrow$ Language of String S;
2. $\mathcal{W_L} \leftarrow$ WordNet of Language L_S;
3. $S \leftarrow S_C \leftarrow$ Synsets of S in $\mathcal{W_L}$; $S_N \leftarrow \phi$;
4.   **repeat until no change in** S:
5.   **for every element** s **in** S_C
6. $S_N \leftarrow S_N \cup$ hypernyms of s
                  $\cup$ Synsets linked to s through
                  InterLangIndex to $L \in \mathcal{T_L}$
                  not yet traversed to;
7. $S \leftarrow S \cup S_N$; $S_C \leftarrow S_N$; $S_N \leftarrow \phi$;
8.   **return** S

Fig. 6. The SemEQUAL Algorithm

The SemEQUAL function takes as input, strings $String_{Data}$ and $String_{Query}$. The transitive closures are computed by the TransitiveClosure function, using Is-A relationships within a language and using Inter-Language-Index across languages. In the implementation, only the WordNets corresponding to the target languages specified in the query are traversed. Once the transitive closure is computed, set-processing

---

[5] The semantic closure of a concept in a taxonomic (or ontological) hierarchy, is the set of nodes reachable from a given node, by tracing the parent-child relationships.

routines are used for computing set-memberships. The output is TRUE if the specified matching condition is met. Since the query string, $String_{Query}$, may match on any one of the several synsets (which are possible semantics of the same word form), SemEQUAL may be made optionally to return the *Gloss* of the synset on which the $String_{Query}$ is matched.

The transitive closure function is implemented using the recursive SQL feature defined in SQL:1999 [8], which was found to be adequate *functionally* to implement the SemEQUAL operator. However, as expected, the cost of computing semantic closures was high. Since the linguistic ontological hierarchies are typically large (containing as much as 100,000 concepts), and since the domain-specific ontologies are typically much smaller than the WordNet ontology, our experiments with WordNet ontological hierarchies may provide a *worst-case* performance scenario for SemEQUAL matching.

SemEQUAL Operator Performance. We first analyzed the performance of SemEQUAL, expressed using standard SQL:1999 features, in relational database systems. A direct implementation on three commercial database systems indicates that supporting multilingual semantic processing is unacceptably slow. However, by tuning the schema and access structures to match the characteristics of WordNet, we are able to bring the response times down to *a few milliseconds*, which we expect to be sufficient for most applications. The details of our implementations and optimization techniques would be published in a forthcoming technical report.

3.3   General Multilingual Query Performance

While most commercial database systems support management of multilingual data, we found that the relative performance in handling multilingual data, compared with standard *Latin* based scripts was upto 300% slower. A comprehensive study of the differential performance of popular database management systems with respect to multilingual data is given in [12]. Worse, we found that the query optimizer's prediction accuracy differs substantially between them. We analyzed the parameters contributing to the slowdown and narrowed down the differential performance to primarily the storage size of the Unicode format and its effect on in-memory processing, and secondarily due to the Unicode-specific function call overheads.

To alleviate the primary problem, We propose Cuniform, a compressed format that is trivially convertible to Unicode, yet occupying equivalent storage space when the data is expressed in native ASCII-based scripts. Our initial experimental results with Cuniform indicate that it largely eliminates the performance degradation for multilingual scripts with small repertoires, and makes the performance of queries nearly *language-neutral*, for languages with small repertoire. Further, by partitioning the multilingual data in language specific tables, we may be able to achieve a higher performance than monolingual data, under certain assumptions on the distribution of data among different languages.

4   MIRA Implementation Architecture

Our proposed architecture for multilingual query processing is shown in Figure 7. The shaded boxes emphasize the new processing modules, and the iconized boxes represent resources (lexical or semantic) that are to be installed.

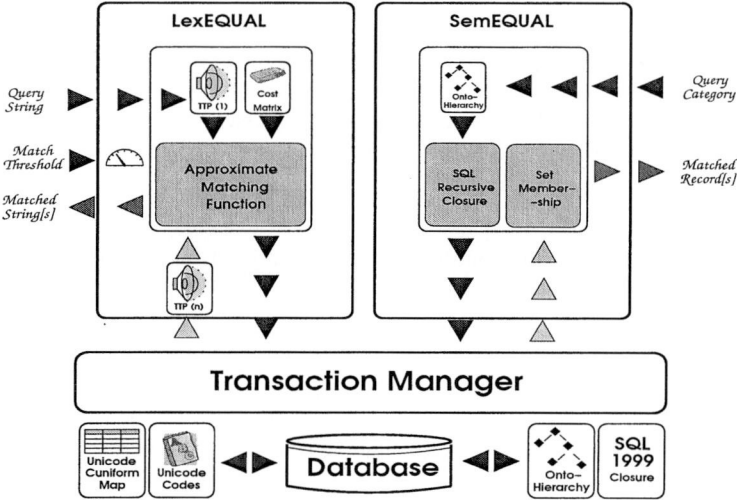

Fig. 7. MIRA Architecture

4.1   Design Goals for MIRA

We define the following design goals for the MIRA architecture, to implement the multilingual features and performance requirements in a usable, useful and scalable manner.

Relational Systems Oriented. Our focus is on relational database systems due to their popularity as data repositories for most operational data.

Attribute Data Oriented. Our architecture will focus on processing attribute-level data, for supporting multilingual keyword searches.

Standards Based. We rely on standard linguistic resources to promote uniformity and consistency across different information processing systems.

Light-Weight Processing Components. Our architecture will focus on OLTP environments, and hence light-weight components for handling text data.

Customizable Matching. The matching quality must be customizable by users, depending on the domain and application requirements.

Modular and Dynamic Architecture. The linguistic resources must be easily added, to make MIRA *language aware*, dynamically.

5   Conclusion and Future Research Issues

In our thesis, we propose an architecture for processing multilingual data transparently across languages, on the traditional information processing platforms, such as relational database management systems. A survey on the functionality and performance of the current systems indicate that the state-of-the-art falls short of these requirements on several counts, motivating our research on multi-lingual database systems.

From the efficiency perspective, we profiled in [12] the performance of standard relational operators (e.g. Select, Join) applied on multilingual data in commercial database systems. Our results showed that severe performance penalties may be incurred, upto about 300%, when compared against equivalent query processing on ASCII based data. We proposed efficient compressed storage format, Cuniform, to reduce these penalties and demonstrated that the query processing can be made nearly *language-neutral*.

From the functionality perspective, we introduced a new SQL multilingual operator called LexEQUAL [13–15], for *syntactic* matching of attribute data across languages. We confirmed the feasibility of our strategy by measuring the quality metrics, namely *Recall* and *Precision*, in matching a real, tagged multilingual data set. Further, we showed that the poor performance associated with the UDF implementation of approximate matching may be improved by orders of magnitude, by employing optimization techniques. We also proposed a new SQL operator – SemEQUAL, intended for matching multilingual text attribute data based on their meanings, leveraging the rich taxonomic hierarchies in cross-linked WordNets in different natural languages. Our experiments with Word-Net on three commercial database systems, confirmed the utility of the SemEQUAL operator, but underscored the inefficiencies in computing transitive closure, an essential component for semantic matching. By tuning the storage and access structures to match the characteristics of resources in the linguistic domain, we speeded up the closure computation by 2 to 3 orders of magnitude – to *a few milliseconds* – making the operator viable for supporting user online query processing.

In summary, in the performance area, we have profiled and optimized the multilingual performance of popular database systems. In the functional area, we have defined two operators – namely, LexEQUAL for *phonetic* matching and SemEQUAL for *semantic* matching of multilingual attributes, and shown that they may be efficiently implemented on existing relational database management systems. We expect that such operators may effectively and efficiently complement the standard lexicographic matching, thereby representing a first step towards the ultimate objective of achieving complete multilingual functionality in database systems.

5.1   Research Issues

The following open issues are being addressed as a part of our current research.

Real-Life Application and Multilingual Performance Suites. We need to identify a *real-life* application that can benefit from the multilingual processing and establish user work-flows using the multilingual operators. Such an application may provide a testbed for performance suites to calibrate and compare different database management systems on multilingual performance [11], along the lines of TPC benchmarks for OLTP applications.

Automatic Fine-tuning of Phonetic Match Quality. In LexEQUAL operator for phonetic matching, clearly the parameters for the best match quality depends on the phoneme set of the languages being considered and the requirements of the application domain. For example, a *Homeland Security* application may require tighter matches, where as a *Telephone Subscriber Search* application may be willing to tolerate much looser matches. We are currently automating the determination of optimal match parameters, based on user-defined training sets.

Approximate Indexes for Efficient Searches. Several approximate indexing methodologies offer search capability on pre-generated phonemic strings corresponding to names. We define the *Search Efficiency* of an index tree as the fraction of data elements in the database that were *examined*. The search efficiency indicates the effectiveness of the index structure in narrowing down the search. However, we find that all the approximate indexes are inefficient in searches, as shown in Figure 8. For example, about 75% of the strings in the database are retrieved as candidate matches for a user match threshold of 0.5, while less than 1% of the database are real matches.

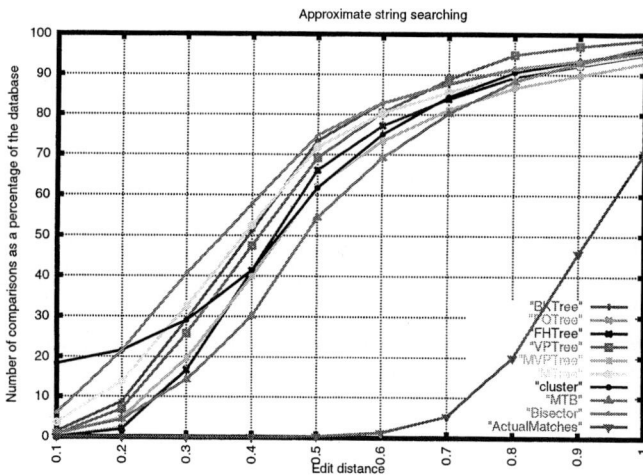

Fig. 8. Search Efficiency of Approximate Indexes

We are exploring the better partitioning and clustering techniques for building effective approximate indexes, to improve the search efficiency.

Domain-Specific Ontologies. While our performance experiments in semantic matching with WordNet taxonomic hierarchies had established performance characteristics of SemEQUAL, we expect the domain-specific ontologies to be more useful in semantic searching applications. Experiments (for performance and tightness) must be conducted using smaller and more precise domain specific ontologies, to ascertain the value of SemEQUAL operator.

References

1. The Computer Scope Limited. `http://www.NUA.ie/Surveys`.
2. The Web Fountain Project. `http://www.almaden.ibm.com/WebFountain`.
3. The International Phonetic Association. `http://www.arts.gla.ac.uk/IPA/`.
4. The Unicode Consortium. `http://www.unicode.org`.
5. The WordNet. `http://www.cogsci.princeton.edu/~wn`.
6. The Global WordNet Association. `http://www.globalwordnet.org`.
7. L. Gravano, P. Ipeirotis, H. Jagadish, N. Koudas, S. Muthukrishnan, and D. Srivastava. Approximate string joins in a database (almost) for free. In *Proc. of the 27th VLDB Conf., Rome, Italy*, 2001.
8. ISO/IEC. *Standard 9075-1-5:1999, Information Technology – Database Languages – SQL.* International Organization for Standardization, 1999.
9. D. Jurafskey and J. Martin. *Speech and Language Processing.* Pearson Education, 2000.
10. D. E. Knuth. *The Art of Computer Programming (Vol 3: Sorting and Searching).* Addison–Wesley, Reading, Massachusetts, United States, 2nd edition, 1993.
11. A. Kumaran and J. R. Haritsa. On database support for multilingual environments. In *Proc. of the 13th IEEE Research Issues in Data Engineering Workshop (held in conjunction with 19th IEEE Intl. Conf. on Data Engineering), Bangalore/Hyderabad, India*, 2003.
12. A. Kumaran and J. R. Haritsa. On the costs of multilingualism in database systems. In *Proc. of the 29th VLDB Conf., Berlin, Germany*, 2003.
13. A. Kumaran and J. R. Haritsa. LexEQUAL: Multilexical matching operator in SQL. In *Proc. of the 23rd ACM SIGMOD Intl. Conf. on Management of Data, Paris, France*, 2004.
14. A. Kumaran and J. R. Haritsa. Supporting multilexical queries in SQL. In *Proc. of the 20th IEEE Intl. Conf. on Data Engineering, Boston, United States*, 2004.
15. A. Kumaran and J. R. Haritsa. Supporting multiscript matching in database systems. In *Proc. of the 9th Extending Database Technology Conf., Heraklion-Crete, Greece*, 2004.
16. J. Zobel and P. Dart. Phonetic string matching: Lessons from information retrieval. In *Proc. of 19th ACM SIGIR Conf., Zurich, Switzerland*, 1996.

Index-Based Keyword Search
in Mediator Systems

Ingolf Geist

Department of Technical and Business Information Systems,
School of Computer Science,
University of Magdeburg, Germany
geist@iti.cs.uni-magdeburg.de

Abstract. Many users and applications require the integration of semi-structured data from autonomous, heterogeneous Web sources. Over the last years mediator systems have emerged that use domain knowledge to overcome the problem of structural heterogeneity. However, many users of these systems do not have a thorough knowledge of the complex global schemas and of the comprehensive query languages. Consequently, easy-to-use query interfaces like keyword search and browsing have to be supported. The aim of the proposed PhD project is the index-based realization of keyword searches in concept-based mediator systems. In order to avoid unnecessary source queries an index structure is maintained on the global level and used during query planning and processing.

1 Research Problem

Nowadays, many search requests require the usage of information from different, distributed, and autonomous (Web) sources. Applications can be found in scientific as well as e-commerce environments. Prominent examples are the integration of biological data sources, digital libraries, but also the search for stolen cultural assets is distributed over many sources[1], which drives this work. Many of these sources provide structured query interfaces, but cannot be indexed by Web search engines. Furthermore, most of them are not cooperative and provide semantically similar data in different structural representation. Consequently, there is still a need for systems, that integrate these semi-structured data sources into a global, integrated, not materialized view.

In the last years mediator systems have been proposed that use domain knowledge as an integration anchor to overcome the problems of structural heterogeneity (e.g [20]). These systems allow querying the sources with complex query languages and use complex integration models. During using the concept-based mediator prototype YACOB [23], which integrates several sources about stolen cultural assets, the experiences showed, normal users have difficulties to handle the concept schema, even if a graphical query interface based on browsing the global concept schema is provided. In fact, a simple *keyword search* was required, that comprises the meta data, here called concept level, as

---

[1] For instance, data about stolen cultural assets during World War II is distributed over at least 15 sites (http://www.lostart.de/links).

W. Lindner et al. (Eds.): EDBT 2004 Workshops, LNCS 3268, pp. 24–33, 2004.

well as the data, called instance level. This requirement led to the problem, how to map efficiently the keywords to structured source queries (in our case XPath). The proposed idea of this work is the usage of a global keyword index, which maps keywords to global query expressions that are decomposed by the mediator system to source queries, subsequently. Summarizing, the tasks of the PhD project are the identification of an effective keyword index structure, to provide an index-based query planning and processing, and to develop techniques to maintain the index structure in the context of autonomous, uncooperative Web sources.

2   State of the Art

The mediator architecture was introduced by Wiederhold [26] and has been utilized for integrating semi-structured data sources over the last years. Most prominent examples are TSIMMIS [13] and Information Manifold [19]. The MIX mediator system [6] represents a successor of TSIMMIS, which integrates XML data sources. All mentioned mediator systems integrate the local sources on structural level.

Integration systems using domain knowledge are e.g. KIND [20], SIMS [4], Context mediator [14] and the XML mediator STYX [3]. The systems uses different models to represent domain knowledge, e.g. subset of F-Logic, LOOM or ontologies. The integration approaches range from modeling local and global data in semantic concepts to mapping local XML fragments to global concepts. All systems support only simple "like"-queries on attribute level. Another direction in querying and using semantic data is the *Semantic Web*. Several languages are provided in this context (an overview is given in [21]).

Abiteboul requests for semi-structured query languages IR-style keyword query operators comprising schema data as well as instance data [1]. Several approaches follow this requirement [11, 25]. Furthermore, relevant to our research are keyword queries over structured databases, like relational systems [2, 8, 16, 22]. However, all systems deal only with centralized databases systems.

Data has to be obtained from the sources in order to build and maintain indexes on the global level. The standard crawling architecture [5] has to be refined for reducing costs and supporting sources, that cannot be crawled. Index update costs can be reduced by concentrating only on interesting parts of index and data. That leads to focused crawling [10, 24]. Some sources do not allow the complete crawling, but the provide limited query interfaces for accessing the data. They build the so called "Hidden Web" or "Deep Web" [7]. In order to index these sources special protocols were developed (e.g. [15]) or techniques like query-based sampling [9, 17] are used.

3   Proposed Approach

The PhD project is based on the YACOB mediator [23], a concept-based integration system. The system uses a two-level integration model: the *concept model* describes the domain knowledge using concept hierarchies and their associated properties. Special data values are expressed as category hierarchies.

Formally, the model is summarized as follows. A set of classes is defined as $\mathcal{T} = URI \times Name$ with URI the set of uniform resource identifier and $Name$ the set of valid names. The set of classes is distinguished into two disjoint subsets: concepts ($\mathcal{C} \subset \mathcal{T}$) describe kinds of instances, and categories ($\mathcal{V} \subset \mathcal{T}$ and $\mathcal{V} \cap \mathcal{C} = \emptyset$) describe sets of data values, so called synonyms.

Properties are assigned to categories. The set of properties is defined as $\mathcal{P} = Name \times \mathcal{C} \times (\mathcal{C} \cup \mathcal{V} \cup \{\mathcal{L}\})$ with one property consisting of a name, a concept it is assigned to, and either a concept, category, or the set of literals ($\mathcal{L}$) as instance domain. Moreover, concepts and categories are organized in disjoint specialization hierarchies. The *subClassOf* relationship is defined as **is_a** $\subseteq \mathcal{T} \times \mathcal{T}$ with: if t_2 **is_a** $t_1 : t_1 \in \mathcal{C} \wedge t_2 \in \mathcal{C} \vee t_1 \in \mathcal{V} \wedge t_2 \in \mathcal{V}$. Furthermore, properties are "inherited" by subconcepts, i.e. if c_2 **is_a** $c_1 \wedge c_1, c_2 \in \mathcal{C} : \forall (p, c_1, x) \in \mathcal{P} : \exists (p, c_2, x) \in \mathcal{P})$. A concept schema $CS = (\mathbf{C}, \mathbf{P}, \mathbf{V})$ consists of a set of concepts $\mathbf{C}$, a set of properties $\mathbf{P}$, and a set of categories $\mathbf{V}$.

As the local sources export their data in XML, the *instance model* follows the semi-structured model OEM [13]. The extension of a concept c is denoted as $\mathbf{ext}(c) = \{o = (id, elem, val) \mid c.name = elem \wedge \forall (p, c, x) \in \mathcal{P} : \exists i \in val : i.elem = p\}$. The local sources are integrated by specifying mappings, which describe how a local source supports a global concept. The mappings realize the GLaV approach [12] and are expressed in RDF, too. In detail, concept mappings, property, and category mappings define how one source supports the concept schema. Join mappings define intra-source relationships as joins over the global concept schema. Besides conventional join operations, similarity join operations can be specified, whose index support is discussed in the further work (Sec. 3.2).

The query language – CQuery – is concept-based and uses the known FLWR notation. CQuery comprises (*i*) selection of concepts using selection predicates, path expressions, and set operations between concept sets (**FOR** clause), (*ii*) obtaining and filtering instances (**LET** and **WHERE** clauses), and (*iii*) combining and projecting the results (**RETURN** clause). The following example returns information of all instances that are associated to the concept painting (or to one of the subconcepts) and contain "van Gogh" in the property artist.

```
FOR $c IN concept[name='painting']/*
LET $e := extension($c)
WHERE $e/artist = 'van Gogh'
RETURN
   <painting>$e</painting>
```

The complete description of the query planning/processing is not possible here because of given space limitation The interested reader is referred to [23]. The processing starts with translating the query into an algebraic expression. The necessary concepts are determined, and subsequently for each concept the instance expression (**WHERE** and **RETURN** clause) is evaluated and the results are combined. Using some heuristics the number of concepts is limited, and by applying the different mappings the global query is decomposed into source XPath queries. Finally, the results are combined using the outer union operation ($\uplus$).

3.1   Keyword Search

A keyword query consists of a set of keywords KW, and returns a set of global, integrated instances, that contain each of the keywords at least once in an associated meta data object (concept name, property name) or in a property value (category name or literal). Formally, the keyword search can be defined as: Given a set of keywords $KW = \{kw_1, \ldots, kw_n\}$ and a concept schema $CS = \{\mathbf{C}, \mathbf{P}, \mathbf{V}\}$, the result set O_{KW} of global instances is defined as:

$$O_{KW} = \{o = (id, elem, x) | \exists c \in \mathbf{C} : o \in \mathbf{ext}(c) \wedge$$
$$\bigwedge_{i=1}^{n} \big(contains(c.name, kw_i) \vee \exists c' \in \Phi_{is\_a}^{+}(c) : contains(c'.name, kw_i) \vee$$
$$\bigvee_{(p,c,v) \in \mathbf{P}} contains(p, kw_i) \vee$$
$$\exists v \in \mathbf{V} : v.name = x \wedge contains(v, kw_i) \vee \exists v' \in \Phi_{is\_a}^{+}(v) : contains(v', kw_i) \vee$$
$$ocontains(o, kw_i) \big) \} .$$

The predicate $contains(string, kw)$ evaluates to *true*, if the keyword kw is contained in $string$. The predicate $ocontains(object, kw)$ evaluates to *true*, if the keyword kw is contained in a value of the object or in the value of one of the subobjects, i.e. the keyword is contained as a value of a property. The expression $\Phi_{is\_a}^{+}$ returns all super-concepts or super-categories, i.e. it computes the transitive closure over the **is_a** relationship.

Consider the example keyword query $\{painting, gogh, flowers\}$. Possible matching objects are a painting object with artist "Gogh" and a title containing "flower", a book object with a title "Van Gogh's work" written by an author "Flowers", or another painting object with artist "Gogh" and the motif category "Flowers". The keyword search as defined here assumes no additional structural information are given, which rises the following problems addressed in the PhD project:

Extension of the Query Language. The query language as well as the corresponding algebra was extended by two constructs: the $\sim=$ operator and a refinement of the `extension` function. The $\sim=$ operator evaluates to *true*, if a keyword is contained in the compared object. It can be used for selecting concepts, properties and categories on the concept level as well as for filtering instance values. The `extension` function is used to return instances for a given list of concepts. The general keyword search is realized by passing keywords to the `extension` function, which returns instances that satisfy the above given keyword condition. The following example searches instances that contain the keywords "`painting flowers gogh`".

```
FOR $c IN concept/*        # select all concepts
LET $e := extension($c,'painting flowers gogh')
RETURN
   <painting>$e</painting>
```

This query is translated into the expression

$$\biguplus_{qe \in \mathbf{getQExpr}(\mathbf{C}, \{panting, flowers, gogh\})} \pi_{proj}(qe)$$

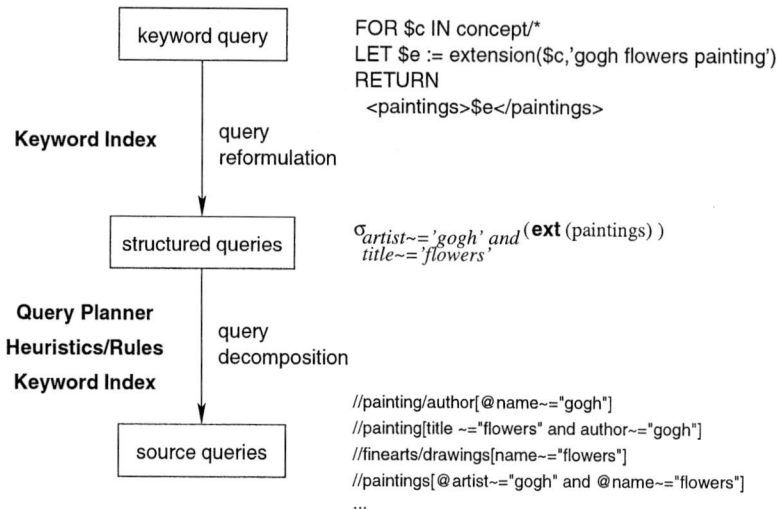

Fig. 1. Keyword query processing

with **C** all concepts existent in the schema and **getQExpr**(C, KW) a function returning a set of query expression of the form $\sigma_{cond}(\textbf{ext}(c))$, which are explained below. The operation $\uplus$ is the outer union operation.

Index-Based Keyword Query Processing. A general keyword query without structural information is processed in two steps:

(i) reformulating the unstructured keyword query in structured global algebra expression, and
(ii) decomposing these expressions into source queries, which are sent to the sources.

Step (i) is executed in the function **getQExpr**. The returned set comprises expressions of the form $\sigma_{cond}(\textbf{ext}(c))$. A predicate is defined as

$$pred_{ij} = \begin{cases} c/property = k & \text{if } k \in \textbf{V} \wedge k.name \sim= kw \\ c/property \sim= kw & \text{otherwise} \end{cases}$$

and the conjunctions as $conj_i = pred_{i1} \wedge \ldots \wedge pred_{ik}$. Then $cond$ is defined as $cond = conj_1 \vee \ldots \vee conj_m$. Using, the provided mappings the result query expressions are decomposed into XPath expressions in step (ii), which are executed by the sources. Fig. 1 illustrates the evaluation showing an example query.

The naive implementation of step (i) results in a combinatorial explosion. Therefore, we need information about the existence of the keywords and their different contexts. A context of a keyword is identified by the associated concept, a property as well as a category or an instance value and the type of the keyword. The kind of the string, where the keyword was extracted from, specifies the type of the keyword. In detail, the type is either a concept keyword, category keyword, a property keyword, or an instance value keyword. Fig. 2 shows extracted keywords from a small example. The keywords

keyword	role	concept	property
...	...	...	...
fine	r_c	finearts	–
paintings	r_c	paintings	–
title	r_p	paintings	title
vincent	r_v	paintings	artist
gogh	r_v	paintings	artist
flowers	r_v	paintings	artist
pantings	r_v	paintings	title
...	...	...	...

Keyword index

cultural asset | cultural asset

fine arts | fine arts

paintings | paintings   drawings | drawings

artist | artist   title | title   ...   ...

keywords from concept level

keywords from instance level

van	s1	215	Tarascon	s1	2
Gogh	s1	70	sun	s2	40
albrecht	s2	122	flowers	s2	90
dürer	s2	12	gras	s2	7
vincent	s1	87	vincent	s3	3
flowers	s3	7	paintings	s2	4
...			...		

concept — extracted keyword

property — associated

is_a — relationship

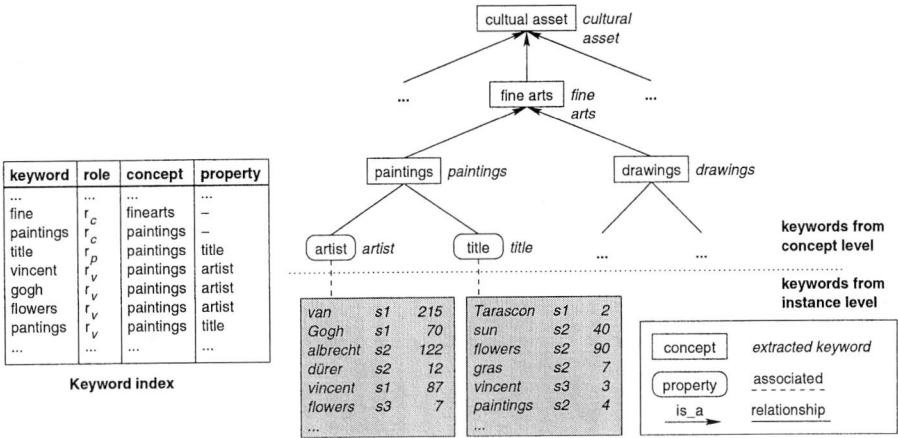

Fig. 2. Keyword index

are stored in an inverted index which comprises the keywords and their corresponding contexts. For instance, the keyword "flowers" occurs in an instance value and its context is specified by (concept: `paintings`, property: `title`). Based on this information a global query expression can be deduced to extract all instances supporting the keyword. For the given example, the query is $\sigma_{title\sim=flowers}(\textbf{ext}(paintings))$. That approach allows the easy implementation of the index within a relational database system.

The complete keyword query evaluation starts with the selection of the desired concepts. Then, the necessary query expressions are generated by function **getQExpr** for a set of keywords and the preselected concepts. For each query expression a possible further instance expression is added and the final expression is evaluated by the query processor of the mediator.

In detail, the function **getQExpr** works as illustrated in Fig. 3. Given are a set of concepts C and a set of keywords KW. Initially, all index entries ($\mathcal{E}_{cand}$) containing one of the keywords in KW are selected. Keywords found in meta objects (concept and category names) correspond also to sub-concepts and sub-categories, respectively. For example, the keyword "cultural" of the concept "cultural asset" applies to all direct and indirect subconcepts, e.g. "painting".

The next steps are executed separately for each found concept. If the current concept does not comprise entries for each keyword in KW it will be not processed, because no object can be found in the extension containing all keywords. Otherwise, we build all combinations of entries, i.e. of queries, that each given keyword occurs at least once. That is achieved by grouping the entries into sets E_{kw_i} for each keyword $kw_i \in KW$, $i = 1, \ldots, n$. Subsequently, the Cartesian product is computed. As each index entry corresponds to a predicate, one can interpret the result *Cond* as Disjunctive Normal Form. That means, each entry in *Cond* is a set of entries, which is translated to a conjunction of predicates, which are disjunctively connected in turn (function **translateToQExpr**). As parts of the global instances can originate from different sources, the index stores also the source of a instance value keyword supporting the creation of source queries.

Input:
    C – set of concepts
    $KW = \{kw_1, \ldots, kw_n\}$ – set of keywords
Output:
    QE – query expression of the form $\sigma_{cond}(\textbf{ext}(c))$
Given:
    $\mathcal{I}$ – set of index entries $e = \langle kw, role, concept, property, category \rangle$

function getQExpr(C,KW)
    $QE := \emptyset$
    /* including entries for sub-concepts and sub-categories */
    $\mathcal{E}_{cand} := \textbf{selectIndexEntries}(KW, \mathcal{I})$
    /* Assume $C_{\mathcal{E}_{cand}}$ the set of concepts occurring in $\mathcal{E}_{cand}$ */
    for each $c \in C_{\mathcal{E}_{cand}}$ **do**
        if $\mathcal{E}_{cand}$ comprises for concept c entries for each $kw_i \in KW$ **do**
            $Cond := \emptyset$
            /* build sets of entries for each keyword*/
            $E_{kw_i} := \{e : e \in \mathcal{E}_{cand}, e.kw = kw_i \wedge e.concept = c\}, i = 1, \ldots, n$
            /* compute Cartesian product of entries */
            $Cond := E_{kw_1} \times \ldots \times E_{kw_n}$
            /* build query expressions */
            $QE := QE \cup \textbf{translateToQExpr}(Cond)$
        od
    od

Fig. 3. getQExpr function evaluation

Evaluation. A first implementation within the YACOB prototype was used to evaluate the proposed approach. We evaluated the effectiveness of the index according to the reduction of source queries using real data sets. Using real[2] and generated query mixes showed a significant reduction of the number of source queries, e.g. the average number of source queries decreased from original 63 to 2.8 for queries comprising two keywords. That behavior is due to the distribution of the keywords over the different concepts. The distribution is normally not uniform but rather similar to a Zipf distribution [27], i.e. most keywords occur in one concept extension and only few occur in almost all concepts. As we cannot assume the index is complete in a real scenario, we tested partial indexes, which showed also a good performance according to the reduction of source queries as well as in order to provide a good recall.

3.2   Further Work

In the previous section we described the index-based keyword search. However, the present solution uses a static index, therefore the following issues are still in progress or planned for the future:

---

[2] Extracted from an access-log file of the Web database http://www.lostart.de.

Maintenance.   The local sources are assumed to be autonomous and uncooperative, i.e. neither do they allow a complete access to the data, nor do they provide the required information. Therefore, different maintenance methods are proposed: (*i*) a query-based sampling approach is used to (re-)build the indexes periodically. (*ii*) Extracting frequency information during query processing, that means, results of user queries are analyzed during runtime to improve the current index. The expected overhead can be reduced by using periodically the content of the semantic cache of the system [18] instead analyzing every query result. (*iii*) Using a focused crawling approach: that is, an overview about the frequency distribution of queries is maintained.

Based on this model, the index is periodically built and updated. All approaches showed in experiments advantages and disadvantages, therefore a hybrid approach is desired.

Ranked Queries.   The present approach supports boolean keyword search in combination of browsing the concept hierarchies. The combination allows a fast restriction of the result set sizes. Furthermore, the result set is subdivided into parts defined by the concept level.

However, there is still a need for ranking. The ranking should be based on the placement in the global concept hierarchy, i.e. an instance found in a sibling concept is less relevant, and the ranking of the instances returned by the sources. The approach requires the combination and the weighting of different ranks, but also offers new optimizations, like e.g. top-N operators.

Similarity Queries.   A second kind of text search includes *similarity queries*, i.e. to a given string all strings within a given distance are considered as similar. One popular measure is the edit or Levenshtein distance. Similarity queries can be used by the user directly or by integration operations which have to find duplicates. Unfortunately, most local sources do not support similarity queries directly, but substring or keyword queries. Hence, one has to map similarity queries to substring queries.

The filtering technique is one well-known approach to do this mapping. Assuming k errors are allowed between two strings, one can decompose the comparison string $k + 1$ substrings. The union of the results of these $k + 1$ substring queries contains all matching strings. To minimize the size of this preselection result, the most selective combination of substring queries has to be found. Therefore, one has to maintain frequency information on global level to make selectivity estimations.

Depending on the kind of substrings, possible structures are count-suffix trees, q-gram tables, or again keyword tables. In first tests, q-gram seemed to be most promising according to maintenance costs and query costs. Similar to the keyword search building and maintenance issues arise. Thus, the proposed methods of the keyword search can be generalized to this and possibly to other problems.

Further Evaluation.   The additional techniques and algorithms are to be evaluated using the prototype implementation. Especially, we want to test the adaptability to changing sources and workloads. Furthermore, the maintenance overhead has to be evaluated for different strategies.

4 Conclusion

The proposed work investigates the problem of index-supported keyword search over virtually integrated data. The integration system is an ontology-based mediator, as described before in the literature. A keyword search strategy has been developed. This integration allows a more efficient usage of the integrated data than browsing and structured queries alone. Furthermore, it does not require to materialize the data of the different sources into one site. Tests with a prototype in a static scenario showed promising results. Ideas for maintaining the global index based on techniques known from search engines have to be adopted to the proposed approach.

In order to complement the keyword search we pointed out the support of similarity queries. Here, global string similarity queries can be supported even if the source does not support them. Frequencies of occurrences of substrings have to maintained on the global site, which rises similar problems as for the keyword search. Hence, we can generalize our approach to more problems.

References

1. S. Abiteboul. Querying Semi-Structured Data. In *ICDT 1997*, volume 1186 of *LNCS*, pages 1–18. Springer, 1997.
2. S. Agrawal, S. Chaudhuri, and G. Das. DBXplorer: A System for Keyword-Based Search over Relational Databases. In *ICDE 2002*, pages 5–16, 2002.
3. B. Amann, C. Beeri, I. Fundulaki, and M. Scholl. Ontology-Based Integration of XML Web Resources. In *ISWC'2002*, volume 2342 of *LNCS*, pages 117–131. Springer, 2002.
4. Y. Arens, C.Y. Chee, C.-N. Hsu, and C.A. Knoblock. Retrieving and Integrating Data from Multiple Information Sources. *International Journal on Intelligent and Cooperative Information Systems*, 2(2):127–158, 1993.
5. R. Baeza-Yates and B. Ribeiro-Neto. *Modern Information Retrieval*. Addison-Wesley, 1999.
6. C.K. Baru, A. Gupta, B. Ludäscher, R. Marciano, Y. Papakonstantinou, P. Velikhov, and V. Chu. XML-Based Information Mediation with MIX. In *SIGMOD 1999*, pages 597–599, 1999.
7. M.K. Bergmann. The deep web: Surfacing hidden value, 2003. http://www.brightplanet.com/deepcontent/tutorials/DeepWeb/.
8. G. Bhalotia, A. Hulgeri, C. Nakhe, S. Chakrabarti, and S. Sudarshan. Keyword Searching and Browsing in Databases using Banks. In *ICDE 2002*, pages 431–440, 2002.
9. J.P. Callan and M.E. Connell. Query-based sampling of text databases. *Information Systems*, 19(2):97–130, 2001.
10. S. Chakrabarti, M. van den Berg, and B. Dom. Focused Crawling: a new approach to topic specfic Web resource discovery. *WWW8 / Computer Networks*, 31(11-16):1623–1640, 1999.
11. D. Florescu, D. Kossmann, and I. Manolescu. Integrating Keyword Search into XML Query Processing. *WWW9 / Computer Networks*, 33(1-6):119–135, 2000.
12. A. Friedmann, A. Levy, and T. Millstein. Navigational Plans for Data Integration. In *AAAI/IAAI 1999*, pages 67–73, 1999.
13. H. Garcia-Molina, Y. Papakonstantinou, D. Quass, A. Rajaraman, Y. Sagiv, J.D. Ullman, V. Vassalos, and J. Widom. The TSIMMIS Approach to Mediation: Data Models and Languages. *Journal of Intelligent Information Systems*, 8(2):117–132, 1997.
14. C.H. Goh, S. Bressan, S.E. Madnick, and M.D. Siegel. Context Interchange: New Features and Formalisms for the Intelligent Integration of Information. *ACM Transactions on Information Systems*, 17(3):270–293, 1999.

15. N. Green, P.G. Ipeirotis, and L. Gravano. SDLIP + STARTS = SDARTS a protocol and toolkit for metasearching. In *ACM/IEEE Joint Conference on Digital Libraries*, pages 207–214, 2001.
16. V. Hristidis and Y. Papakonstantinou. Discover: Keyword Search in Relational Databases. In *VLDB 2002*, pages 670–681, 2002.
17. P.G. Ipeirotis and L. Gravano. Distributed Search over the Hidden Web: Hirarchical Database Sampling and Selection. In *VLDB 2002*, 2002.
18. M. Karnstedt, K.-U. Sattler, I. Geist, and H. Höpfner. Semantic Caching in Ontology-based Mediator Systems. In *Berliner XML Tage 2003, 3rd Int. Workshop "Web und Datenbanken"*, pages 155–169, October 2003.
19. A.Y. Levy, A. Rajaraman, and J.J. Ordille. Querying Heterogeneous Information Sources Using Source Descriptions. In *VLDB 1996*, pages 251–262, 1996.
20. B. Ludäscher, A. Gupta, and M.E. Martone. Model-based Mediation with Domain Maps. In *ICDE 2001*, pages 82–90, 2001.
21. A. Magkanaraki, G. Karvounarakis, Ta Tuan Anh, V. Christophides, and D. Plexousakis. Ontology Storage and Querying. Technical Report 308, Foundation for Research and Technology Hellas, Institute of Computer Science, April 2002.
22. U. Masermann and G. Vossen. Design and Implementation of a Novel Approach to Keyword Searching in Relational Databases. In *ADBIS-DASFAA 2000*, pages 171–184, 2000.
23. K.-U. Sattler, I. Geist, and E. Schallehn. Concept-based Querying in Mediator Systems. *The VLDB Journal*, 2004. To appear.
24. S. Sizov, M. Theobald, S. Siersdorfer, G. Weikum, J. Graupmann, M. Biwer, and P. Zimmer. The BINGO! System for Information Portal Generation and Expert Web Search. In *CIDR 2003*, 2003.
25. A. Theobald and G. Weikum. The Index-Based XXL Search Engine for Querying XML Data with Relevance Ranking. In *EDBT 2002*, pages 477–495, 2002.
26. G. Wiederhold. Mediators in the Architecture of Future Information Systems. *IEEE Computer*, 25(3):38–49, 1992.
27. G. K. Zipf. *Human Behavior and the Principle of Least Effort*. Addison-Wesley, 1949.

Concept-Based Search on Semi-structured Data Exploiting Mined Semantic Relations

Jens Graupmann

Max-Planck Institut für Informatik, Saarbrücken, Germany
graupman@mpi-sb.mpg.de

Abstract. In this paper we show the current state of the ongoing research concerning our prototype for a search engine on semi-structured data incorporating rules mined on extracted structured data. We illuminate some ideas from the research field of data mining and how to apply them to the retrieval process. Additionally, we show technical aspects and features of our search engine.

1 Introduction

Today's web search engines are still following the paradigm of keyword based search. Although this is the best choice for large scale web search engines, in terms of throughput and scalability, it inherently limits their abilities to accomplish more meaningful query tasks. On the other hand, XML query engines (e.g., based on XQuery or XPath) have powerful query capabilities but at the same time their dedication to XML or even more powerful languages and data formats like RDF and OWL with a global schema is their weakness, due to the fact that most web information is still stored in diverse formats and does not conform to common schemas. These formats include static and also dynamically generated HTML documents that are only accessible through portal interfaces.

In this work we implement a new kind of search engine that works on semi-structured data and exploits rules mined in extracted structured information for query expansion. The search engine utilizes a light-weight but nevertheless expressive query language. First we briefly clarify some important aspects of the problem we try to solve:

- **Used Corpus and Its Internal Representation (Section 3):** We want to comprise as many data sources as possible, including HTML and XML. Thus we can not make strong assumptions about the data format and our internal representation can only include the least common denominator of these data formats. Furthermore we want to integrate information contained in autonomous sources like web portals.
- **Types of Queries That can (should) be Effectively Answered by Our System (Section 2):** Very often queries aim to find certain objects or more generally concepts having special properties, e.g. a book with the title 'Database systems' or a car with the make 'Audi'. We refer to this kind of query as a 'Concept-based query'.
- **Inclusion of Statistical Meta Data (Section 4):** Meta data plays a crucial role in our approach since statistical meta data collected during document indexing is used for query formulation and for query processing. We try to analyze this information and exploit contained regularities.

W. Lindner et al. (Eds.): EDBT 2004 Workshops, LNCS 3268, pp. 34–43, 2004.

- **Query Processing (Section 5):** We sketch our used query language and describe the evaluation process of a concept-based query. Furthermore we show how information obtained by analyzing the meta data is used to improve the query result.

The Main Research Question in the Context of This Work Is: How can we exploit structured (meta)data, that has been automatically extracted and transformed during indexing for semantically meaningful 'Concept-based' querying on semi-structured heterogeneous data without making great demands on the data sources. This research question involves techniques used in data mining in combination with emerging approaches in information retrieval.

In the following sections we show not only how to investigate this research question but also how a possible approach could be integrated in our search engine that is prototypically implemented and is still 'under construction'.

2 Concept-Based Search

Almost all web search engines support keyword based search, but this style of query is strongly limited in its expressiveness. The keywords in a query do not have any semantic interconnection other than boolean operators. Examples for desirable semantic connections are the following: one term is a synonym for another term or - like in our system - one term describes a concept or concept property while the other one is an instance value or a refinement of the first term. This fact also limits today's search engines in their ability to encompass Deep Web sources due to the fact that they are unable to assign keywords to matching form fields. Note that XML query languages, on the other hand, would easily support this feature, by interpreting some keywords as element names (i.e., XML tags), corresponding to concepts, and others as element contents, corresponding to instance values.

As an example, we consider the domain of car advertisements. Suppose we are looking for a brochure about the (car) Audi A4. For this information demand a typical query posed to a web search engine would be *brochure Audi A4*. This query could be ambiguous not only for a computer but also for a human user, because A4 is also a paper format. It is not clear whether we are looking for an A4 brochure about Audi or a brochure about an Audi A4.

If we can only use keywords to express this query, there is no way to specify this semantic relationship. With the query language of our system, however, a solution would be a more elaborated query like *car = 'Audi A4' AND brochure* or *Audi = 'A4' AND brochure* or an even more elaborated query like *car.make='AUDI' AND car.model='A4' AND brochure.format='A4'*.

3 Data Sources

As we want to include diverse data formats and autonomous data sources we have to transform them into a common format.

3.1 Restructuring Data

To include as many semi-structured data formats as possible we have to restrict ourselves to the least common denominator. This is the mean of nesting to express semantical relations. Of course XML has this feature, but almost every kind of semi-structured data format either has this property or other structural features can be exploited to generate such a nested structure that encodes latent relations between textual parts. HTML, for example, partly supports such nesting. A simple transformation of HTML to XML would not solve the problem resp. express the internal sematic stuture of the document since the main drawback of HTML - in its current version - is that it focusses on visual representation, not on structure. This well known shortcoming does not imply that HTML contains no structure information at all but it has to be interpreted, analyzed and transformed or annotated. Because of this the transformation of XML into HTML is mainly based on heuristics that mimic the cognition of a human while viewing a document. To check the applicability of these heuristics we apply additional techniques like classification of HTML tables (Section 4).

If XML were already ubiquitously used, the semantic relationships among query terms could be reflected by associating them with specific tags along the hierarchical structure of documents. However, there are many ways to encode the same information in an XML document, e.g. by using different tags or a different structure. Figure 1 gives an example for the diversity that one may face for the information *car.make='Audi' AND car.model='A4'*.

```
                                    |   <car>
                                    |     <make>Audi</make>
    <Audi model="A4" />             |     <model>A4</model>
                                    |   </car>
```

Fig. 1. Different ways of expressing information in XML

To cope with this structural and annotational diversity in non-schematic XML data, our system supports ontology-based similarity comparisons among different tag names and structures, and we answer queries by ranked result lists that reflect different similarity values. This feature was already present in our earlier work on ranked retrieval of XML data [9]; in this work we apply it to arbitrary web data, not just to XML repositories. To this end we transform HTML pages and other web formats into "semantically" annotated XML documents. Obviously, without solving an "AI-complete" problem, the resulting annotations are often not that insightful (e.g., when creating a tag "section" or "heading"), but in some cases relatively simple heuristics can lead to meaningful XML data with a more clear structure than the original HTML or Latex documents.

The following example (Figure 2) shows some of the heuristics that we use in our transformation component. Headers (for example the tag *h1*) are used in HTML in a way such that the text belonging to the header is a sibling node. Our system transforms the HTML code by including the text belonging to the header as a child node of a tag representing the original header. Another example for our heuristics, with richer semantics, is the transformation of the HTML code `<b>Make:</b>Audi` into the following structure: `<Make>Audi</Make>`. This is based on the heuristics that a bold term with a colon is the concept (descriptor) of the following string.

Fig. 2. Sample transformation from HTML to XML

We have implemented a framework with different modules to convert various data formats into XML. Currently these modules are HTML2XML (for XML) and PDF2XML (for PDF). Other modules are under development. These modules are mainly based on heuristic rules.

3.2 Web Services and the Deep Web

Many information sources are not accessible via crawling. Rather one needs to fill out a query form for retrieving documents that are dynamically generated from some underlying databases. The key difficulty in automatically generating meaningful queries against such web portals is to assign the appropriate values (which may be given merely as a set of keywords) to the available parameters of the form. For this task, our system first analyzes the interface (e.g., the HTML form) to determine the available parameters [6]. The result of the analysis is stored as meta information in a registry maintained by our search engine and used to generate wrappers that encapsulate the portal interface as a web service [8]. Thus, each HTML form that we can successfully analyze is represented by a WSDL interface in our system (see [4] for more details on generating web services). For example, a form with a field labeled "model" and a pull-down menu of possible values to be queried would be represented as an explicit web service parameter with an enumeration type. When our search engine receives a query for the keyword A4, it compares this term with the parameter names and values in enumeration types, and can successfully map A4 to the car model parameter.

4   Collecting Meta Information

In parallel to the indexing process we want to collect and analyze meta data to support the query formulation as well as the query processing step. We especially want to exploit statistical information about structured data that we extracted during the indexing process by using various techniques.

First we try to detect tables in our source data that could contain statistical - perhaps semanticlly meaningful - information. Since tables are mostly used for layout purposes this is a complicated problem. In our work we adopted the work presented in [10] to discover relevant table structures by classification. This classification is based on layout, content type and word group features like the average number of cells or the the average content length of cell values. Furthermore we apply an XPath-clustering algorithm (like proposed in [2]) to identify record structured information units within pages containing no tables. This is done by grouping XPath expressions with the same prefix[1]. Additionally we analyze HTML forms and extract the contained information[2]. The result of applying these techniques to a single page is a partially incomplete table schema (the extracted header information of the table if available) and the corresponding data records contained in the table. We insert our collected record structured data into a global table with open schema. This means that our global schema is extended if new rows are inserted that cannot be mapped onto an existing column.

During data extraction errors may occur when extracting the property descriptors (e.g. determining the table headers may fail or they might be missing at all) as well as during the extraction of instance data. For many subtasks algorithms and solutions are well known provided the correct abstraction. If we extract information consisting of some extracted property names (table header) with corresponding values (contained in the table body) and one 'column' without label but also with the corresponding values we can consider this value column as the probability distribution of a random variable. As a consequence we only have to compare this probability distribution with the distributions of possible candiate columns in our global schema. This can be done by computing the well known Kullbach-Leibler divergence of two value distributions p and q:

$$D(p||q) = \sum_{x \in X} p(x) log \frac{p(x)}{q(x)}$$

As a result we get a table with a schema comprising all attributes that we have found so far. This table is very sparse. For this reason it is possible to determine clusters that can be indentified by sharing many properties (not values) since instances of completely different concepts (e.g. cars or books) do not share any property (make & model vs. title & author) at all.

Because of the size of this global table (especially the number of attributes) extensive computations are costly and time-consuming. For this reason partitioning the table permits to pursuit a divide-and-conquer approach.

We try to partition our global table into partial tables with minimum overlapping of the specified attributes. Since every partial table only contains information about a special concept we refer to such a partial table as a concept cluster. Once we collected, preprocessed and splitted our meta information we want to use data mining techniques to

---

[1] This feature is also ongoing work but is beyond the scope of this paper.

[2] E.g., on a search form for cars we can extract the descriptors MAKE, MODEL, POWER with corresponding values if specified in the form (MAKE has possible values: Acura, Audi...).

discover relevant relationships among these attribute values. Because of the assignment of values to special properties we are looking for relationships between values assigned to different dimensions. This problem can be investigated by methods of the field of association analysis namley mining for multidimensional association rules as well as stochastical means.

Table 1. Extracted table content

(CAR)	MAKE	MODEL	POWER	YEAR
I_1	Audi	A6 TDI	103	1995
I_2	-	100 CC	85	1981
I_3	-	TDI	-	-
I_4	-	-	78	1993
I_5	Audi	100	103	1994
I_6	Audi	-	103	1995
I_7	Audi	100 CC	85	1982
I_8	VW	TDI	-	-

Consider the example values shown in Table 1 specifying eight extracted instances with their extracted schema (MAKE,MODEL,POWER,YEAR). I_1 and I_2 have almost no similarity by simply comparing the specified values. But if we analyzed our collected meta data we would find out that MODEL 100CC only occurs together with MAKE Audi. Because of this fact we simply could virtually add MAKE Audi to instance I_2. The same analysis for I_3 would show that occurence of TDI limits the possible values for MAKE to AUDI and VW. So we could bear in mind both completations. In contrast year 1993 would lead to multiple possible completions and therefore is useless to infer anything at all. We see that only some values for property p_i would determine a value for property p_j.

This means that dependencies between properties could exist in this table comparable to functional dependencies. Functional dependencies are very strong dependencies since they have to hold for all values. To discover more general dependencies we consider two properties as random variables. Similarly to the task of mining for functional dependencies the Chi-square dependence test only returns an overall measure for the dependency of random variables describing properties. To discover more general dependencies of two properties we construct their contingency table.

If we considered the values shown in table 2 as conditional probabilities, the probability $P(MAKE = AUDI|MODEL = A4)$ would be 0.97. But we also could consider every subset of properties, e.g.

$$P(MAKE = AUDI|MODEL = A4, YEAR = 1998).$$

In terms of data mining we could interpret the contingency table shown above as a two dimensional data cube. This would lead to the rule

$$MODEL = A4 \rightarrow MAKE = Audi$$

Table 2. Contingency table

Property	MAKE/MODEL		
(CAR)	A4	100	TDI
AUDI	97	61	38
VW	0	12	47
OPEL	0	0	2
...	0.3	0	13

with confidence 0.97 that is equivalent to the conditional probability shown above[3]. Currently we explore different approaches and techniques from data mining [1] and database technologies namely discovering functional dependencies [7].

5 Structured Querying of Unstructured Information

In this section we briefly sketch the query language used in our system and the query evaluation process using the mined relations.

5.1 Query Language

The internal query language of of our system resembles a highly simplified version of mainstream languages like SQL, XPath, or XQuery. Search conditions refer to concepts and values, which correspond to element names and contents in an XML setting and attribute names and values in an SQL setting. Unlike the established languages, however, we have added a similarity operator ~ that can be applied to concepts and values and was first introduced in the XXL query language [9]. This operator expands a term in the query with similar terms, supplied by an ontology. For example, a search for element names or content terms ~car would not only return *cars* but also *minivans* and other highly similar results. For efficiency, the system supports only conjunctions of search conditions, no negations and no disjunctions. We believe that this is sufficient to cover almost all queries that web or intranet users would pose. Pages or XML elements that satisfy one or more search conditions are bound to variables, and by using a variable as a prefix in other conditions we can specify when multiple conditions must be satisfied by the *same* page. To express that different pages should be connected (with a small distance), we use the variables in path expressions, as if all data were truly XML. In contrast to XPath or XQuery, a path expression can be satisfied across document boundaries; so we consider connectivity in a global data graph. Our query language includes the following types of conditions:

- **Keyword Conditions:** Simple keyword search is supported because of its benefit for querying data without global schema or even unknown strucuture (see also [3, 5] for keyword search in an XML context). An example for finding a page or XML element that contains the words "Audi A4" is: A[keyword]='Audi A4'.

---

[3] $support(A \rightarrow B) = P(A \cap B)$

- **Concept-Value Conditions:** This condition has the form *concept = value* and would be the preferred type of searching if all web or intranet data were richly annotated with concepts corresponding to XML tags and values appearing in element or attribute contents. The comparison operator could be generalized to include type-specific comparisons (e.g., on dates). An example for this condition type is `location=Cologne`.
- **Similarity Conditions:** It is possible to use the similarity operator ~ with every concept or value term, to include similar terms as approximate matches. The query `A.~car = BMW` not only searches cars, but may also return matches with element names like "automobile", "limousine", "motorbike", etc.
- **Path Conditions:** We support two kinds of path conditions. Reachability through a single link is expressed by a dot notation combining multiple variables, and reachability through a path of arbitrary length uses the wildcard symbol '#'. These conditions take into consideration hyperlinks, the parent-child relationship within XML documents, and also arbitrary XPointer or XLink references across document boundaries.

5.2   Query Processing and Ranked Retrieval

Internally the query processor transforms a query into an operator tree consisting of Java objects. A concept-value condition is evaluated by first looking up the occurrences of both the concept name and the value in the index and then comparing the relative positions of each occurrence pair. In a good match, the concept is found 'above' the value with regard to the document structure; that is, the value should occur in a child node or a descendant of the node that matches the concept name. The distance between the two matches is reflected in the scoring of a result.

Simple keyword conditions without ~ operator are fulfilled if the keyword occurs on a page. If the similarity operator is used and therefore this query condition is expanded with similiar terms a page is matched if one of these terms is found. The score for this condition depends on the similarity of the matched term compared to the original query term.

Path conditions (i.e., reachability through a single link or arbitrary path) refer to multiple pages bound to different variables. Whenever the query processor has determined candidate matches for local conditions and bound to variables, it tests the path condition using the materialized transitive closure, and discards candidates that are not connected or too far apart. The score of a path condition is based on the path length between the considered pages.

The order in which conditions are evaluated is determined by a coarse selectivity estimation using simple statistics about term frequencies. Portals are included if the concepts of one or more concept-value conditions can be matched with parameter descriptors of generated Web Services. In this case the corresponding values can be simply filled in or it is tried to match them with predefined values[4]. When portals are included into the search, the corresponding Web Services are invoked during query evaluation and their results are stored and indexed in a temporary table. The query processor treats the

---

[4] E.g., if the value in a HTML form is choosen by selecting a value of a selection box.

page with the query form and a result page returned by the portal as a single logical unit. This way, a result page is bound to the corresponding variable even if some conditions are actually satisfied by the query submission page (e.g., names of concepts appearing as labels in the form and values appearing in the result page).

An approach for expanding the query using our analyzed metadata data could be implemented as follows:

Once a user submitted a query we try to map the concepts of the query conditions onto columns (representing properties) in our global meta data table. This can lead to several candidates. Subsequently we try to map the specified value onto an instance value for this row. If this is not possible we cannot expand our query and evaluate our query as described in the second part of this section.

If we succeed we are able to determine the concept clusters that contain this attribute and select rules containing the corresponding property on their left side. We sort the rules by increasing confidence [5].

First the query is evaluated without expansion. If results are retrieved the result is presented together with possible query extensions to the user. The user can refine his query with additional query extensions. If no results are found by the initial query the query is automatically expanded by the rule with the highest confidence. This is iteratively done until results are found or no more rules for extension are available.

Additionally these rules are used to build consistent parameter assignments for portal interfaces, e.g. the meta data could be used to choose the value 'Audi' for the parameter 'Make' although the query simply is 'car=A4'. The overall ranking of a query match is computed on basis of the partial scores for all conditions, using a simple probabilistic model with independence assumptions.

6   Conclusion

The major contribution of this work is the application of data mining techniques to automatically extracted statistical information from structured elements of semi-structured data and the integration of these techniques into our prototype for a new kind of concept-based search engine. In addition we provide seamless integration of different data formats and autonomous data sources like deep web portals. Open issues are the selection of appropriate techniques for discovering useful dependencies within a large corpus of extracted data.

References

1. Sergej Brin, Rejeev Motwani, and Craig Silverstein. Beyond market baskets: Generalizing association rules to correlations. In *ACM Sigmod Conference*, 1997.
2. Hasan Davulcu, Srinivas Vadrevu, and Saravanakumar Nagarajan. OntoMiner: Bootstrapping and populating ontologies from domain specific Web sites. In *First Workshop on Semantic Web and Databases (SWDB)*, 2003.

---

[5] We know that this might lead to 'uninteresting' dependencies and that other measures like proposed in [1] could lead to better results.

3. Daniela Florescu, Donald Kossmann, and Ioana Manolescu. Integrating keyword search into XML query processing. In *9th WWW Conference*, 2000.
4. Jens Graupmann and Gerhard Weikum. The role of Web services in information search. *IEEE Data Engineering Bulletin*, 25(4), 2002.
5. Lin Guo, Feng Shao, Chavdar Botev, and Jayavel Shanmugasundaram. XRANK: Ranked keyword search over XML documents. In *ACM Sigmod Conference*, 2003.
6. Hai He, Weiyi Meng, Clement T. Yu, and Zonghuan Wu. WISE-Integrator: An automatic integrator of Web search interfaces for e-Commerce. In *28th Conference on Very Large Data Bases (VLDB)*, 2003.
7. Ykä Huhtala, Juha Kärkkäinen, Pasi Porkka, and Hannu Toivonen. TANE: An efficient algorithm for discovering functional and approximate dependencies. *The Computer Journal*, 42(2), 1999.
8. Sriram Raghavan and Hector Garcia-Molina. Crawling the hidden Web. In *26th Conference on Very Large Data Bases (VLDB)*, 2001.
9. A. Theobald and G. Weikum. The index-based XXL search engine for querying XML data with relevance ranking. In *7th Conference on Extending Database Technology (EDBT)*, 2002.
10. Yalin Wang and Jianying Hu. A machine learning approach for table detection on the Web. In *11th WWW Conference*, 2002.

Distributed and Scalable Similarity Searching in Metric Spaces

Michal Batko

Department of Information Technologies,
Masaryk University, Brno, Czech Republic
xbatko@fi.muni.cz

Abstract. In this paper, we address the problem of scalable distributed similarity searching. Our work is based on single-site metric space indexing algorithms. They provide efficient way to perform range and nearest neighbor queries on arbitrary data in general metric spaces. The metric spaces are excellent abstraction that allows comparison of very complex objects (such as audio files, DNA sequences, texts). We have exploited the SDDS (Scalable and Distributed Data Structures) paradigms and P2P (Peer to Peer) systems to form a metric space similarity searching structure in distributed environment. Our proposed method is fully scalable without any centralized part and it allows performing similarity queries on stored data.

1 Introduction

The problem of retrieving elements from a set of objects, which are close to a given query (using some similarity criterion), has a lot of applications – from pattern recognition to textual and multimedia information retrieval. The most general abstraction to implement such criterion is the *metric space*.

The advantage of the metric space approach to the data searching is its "extensibility", because in this way, we are able to perform both *exact match* and *similarity* queries on any collection of metric objects. Since any vector space is covered by a metric space with a proper distance function (for example the Euclidean distance), even the high-dimensional vector spaces are handled easily. Furthermore, there are also many metric functions able to quantify similarity between complex objects, such as free text or multimedia object features, that are very difficult to manage otherwise. For example, consider the *edit distance*, the *Hausdorff distance*, or the *Jacard coefficient*. The problem has recently attracted a lot of researchers to develop techniques to structure collections of metric objects in such a way so that the search requests are performed efficiently – see the recent surveys [1] and [4].

Though metric indexes are able to speedup retrieval considerably, the processing time is still an open problem. The evaluation metric distance functions can also take a considerable amount of computational time, and to search the partitioned space, we usually have to compute distances (using the metric function) between many objects. The time to compute a distance can also depend on the size of compared objects. For example, the *edit distance*, used to compare strings, has complexity $O(n \cdot m)$, where n and m represent the number of characters in the compared strings.

W. Lindner et al. (Eds.): EDBT 2004 Workshops, LNCS 3268, pp. 44–53, 2004.
© Springer-Verlag Berlin Heidelberg 2004

The distributed computer environment of present days is a suitable framework for parallel processing. With such infrastructure, parallel distance computations would enhance the search response time considerably. Modern computer networks have a large enough bandwidth, so it is becoming more expensive for an application to access a local disk than to access RAM of another computer on the network. In this paper, we try to apply current approaches to the distributed data processing – *Scalable and Distributed Data Structures*, SDDS, and *Peer to Peer*, P2P, communication – to the metric space indexing.

The rest of this paper is organized as follows. All necessary definitions for metric spaces and distributed data structures are presented in Sect. 2.1 and 2.2. Section 3 surveys the most significant papers for our research. The overview of goals, we want to accomplish, can be found in Sect. 4. The design of our scalable distributed structure for similarity searching in metric spaces is proposed in Sect. 5 and some preliminary experiments are shown in Sect. 6.

2 Preliminaries

2.1   Metric Space

Metric space is pair compound of a set of objects ($\mathcal{A}$) and a so-called metric function (d), which computes "distance" between any pair of objects from the set (i.e. the smaller distance, the closer or more similar are the objects). The distance is a positive real number and the function d has following properties:

$$\forall x \in \mathcal{A} : d(x, x) = 0 \qquad \qquad \textit{reflexivity}$$
$$\forall x, y \in \mathcal{A} : d(x, y) > 0 \qquad \qquad \textit{strict positiveness}$$
$$\forall x, y \in \mathcal{A} : d(x, y) = d(y, x) \qquad \qquad \textit{symmetry}$$
$$\forall x, y, z \in \mathcal{A} : d(x, y) \leq d(x, z) + d(z, y) \; \textit{triangle inequality}$$

There are two basic types for similarity search. The first is the *range* or *proximity* search. Its goal is to retrieve all objects which have distance from query object q at most the specified range r.

$$\{x \in \mathcal{A} \mid d(q, x) \leq r\}$$

We usually look for similar objects when searching in metric space, i.e. we look for the *nearest neighbor* object. We can extend this query to return n nearest neighbor objects to the query object q. The result is then a subset $\mathcal{K}$:

$$\mathcal{K} \subset \mathcal{A} : |\mathcal{K}| = n \wedge \forall u \in \mathcal{K}, v \in \mathcal{A} - \mathcal{K} : d(q, u) \leq d(q, v)$$

There are also other types of similarity queries (for example *similarity join* [3]). However, we use only the two previously mentioned queries in our research.

2.2   Scalable and Distributed Data Structures

The Scalable and Distributed Data Structures (SDDS) paradigm was first specified in [6]. In this article were also defined the most important properties that every SDDS should satisfy:

scalability   – data expand to new network nodes gracefully, and only when network nodes already used are efficiently loaded

no hot-spot   – there is no master site that must be accessed for resolving the address
of the searched objects, e.g., there is no centralized directory

independence – the file access and maintenance primitives, e.g., search, insertion,
split, etc., never require atomic updates to multiple nodes.

2.3   Peer to Peer Systems

We can define peer to peer (P2P) systems as distributed systems without any centralized
control or hierarchical organization, where the software running at each node is equivalent in functionality. Data in the system are distributed among the participating nodes.
Every node joined in P2P both hold data and perform queries.

P2P systems are popular because of the many benefits they offer: adaptation, self-
organization, load-balancing, fault-tolerance, availability through massive replication,
and the ability to pool together and harness large amounts of resources. For example,
file-sharing P2P systems distribute the main cost of sharing data, i.e. bandwidth and
storage, across all the peers in the network, thereby allowing them to scale without the
need for powerful and expensive servers.

3   Related Work

3.1   Scalable and Distributed Data Structures

The first SDDS proposed was the Distributed Linear Hashing (LH*) [6], which uses
linear hashing to split file among network sites. The hashing of primary key of the
file produces an identifier of the network site, which should hold the record. Every
site maintains two values needed for linear hashing function (local "view" of the site).
However, this information can be out of date. Therefore, there was proposed an updating
mechanism called Image Adjustment Message (IAM), which allows on use correcting
the values.

Another hash-based algorithm was the Distributed Dynamic Hashing (DDH) [2],
based on dynamic hashing. The advantage of DDH over LH* is that it can immediately
split any bucket (LH* according to LH can split only the bucket with token).

The last algorithm, we would like to mention in this section, is the Distributed Random Tree method (DRT) [5], which has introduced the approach to distribute a common
binary search tree. The structure maintains the linear order of keys (as opposed to LH*)
and it is thus able to perform range and nearest neighbor queries gracefully.

3.2   Peer to Peer Systems

As far as we know, no P2P system is currently using the metric space as the routing key.
However, a vector space based Content Addressable Network (CAN) [8] was proposed.
The CAN can route the query through the nodes using navigation, which stores all the
"in touch" neighbors at every site. The neighbor node, which is closer to the query
target, is chosen from the routing table and the query is forwarded (routed) there. We

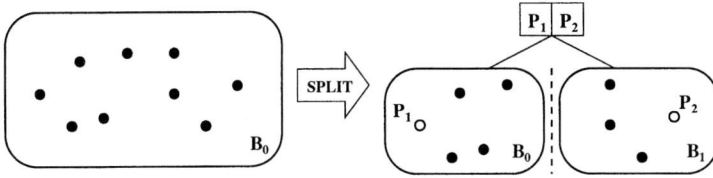

Fig. 1. Split of the bucket and modification of the tree

cannot describe all current P2P networks and all the research on this field due to space limitations of this paper, however we will at least cite a survey [7].

3.3 Metric Space Searching Methods

The idea of exploiting the metric spaces for similarity searching is quite old. Therefore, we will describe only the Generalized Hyperplane Tree (GHT) structure [9], because our proposed algorithms relay on this structure and we will refer to the description later. Other relevant methods can be found in the survey "Searching in Metric Spaces" [1].

GHT is a binary tree that allows storing metric space objects and quickly performing similarity search on them. The objects are kept in buckets of fixed capacity that are pointed from leaf nodes of the tree. Inner tree nodes contain pointers to a selected pair of objects (pivots). Elements closer to the first pivot go into left subtree and the objects nearest to the second one, into the right subtree.

We start by building a tree with only one root node pointing to a bucket B_0. When the bucket B_0 is full we must split it: we create a new empty bucket B_1 and move some objects (exactly one half if possible) into it to obtain space in B_0 (see Fig. 1). We can do that by choosing a pair of pivots P_1 and P_2 ($P_1 \neq P_2$) from B_0 and moving into bucket B_1 all objects O that satisfy the following condition.

$$d(P_1, O) > d(P_2, O) \tag{1}$$

Pivots P_1 and P_2 will be associated with a new root node and thus the tree will grow one level up. This split algorithm can be applied on any node and it is an autonomous operation (no other tree nodes need to be modified).

When we **Insert** a new object O we first traverse GHT to find the correct bucket. At each inner node, we test the condition (1): if it is true, we take the right branch; otherwise, the left branch is taken. This is done until a leaf node is found. Then we insert O into the pointed bucket and we split it, if necessary.

In order to perform a **Range Search** with query object Q and radius r, we recursively traverse GHT following the left child of each inner node if condition (2) is satisfied and right child if condition (3) is true.

$$d(P1, Q) - r \leq d(P2, Q) + r \tag{2}$$

$$d(P1, Q) + r > d(P2, Q) - r \tag{3}$$

Note that, since both the above conditions can be simultaneously satisfied (i.e., both the left and right subtree can be traversed) eventually more than one bucket can contain qualified objects.

The **Nearest Neighbor** is based on range searches with estimated radiuses. However, we will not describe the exact algorithm due to space limitations.

4   Objectives

Nearly all scalable and distributed structures proposed so far are aimed at primary key (attribute) search.However, there are many classes of objects that cannot be compared (for similarity) with just one attribute and the mapping to vector space has vast number of dimensions.

On the other side, the indexing techniques for metric spaces proposed so far use the centralized paradigm. Thus the scalability of such system is limited, because the number of computations necessary to satisfy a query grows with the file. Moreover, the centralized system has only a limited storage (either RAM or disks).

Therefore, the aim of our research is to combine the scalability of the distributed approach with the extensibility of the metric space indexing. The designed structure should scale gracefully through utilizing new nodes of the distributed environment. The search time should remain (nearly) constant for performed queries – the query could utilize more distributed nodes in order to retrieve results.

Moreover, the structure should be able to search in different types of objects. It should support primary key search with exact or range match, vector spaces with any dimension or even more complicated sets of objects, which only supports some similarity measurement. All those mentioned methods are easily transformed to a generic metric space with appropriate distance function.

5   Proposed Approach – GHT*

Our distributed similarity searching structure – GHT* – is based on GHT (the metric space part) and it exploits the techniques of DRT, DDH and CAN (the distributed part).

5.1   Architecture

The distributed environment is composed of network nodes (peers), which hold metric objects, execute similarity queries on stored data and communicate with other peers. Every peer is uniquely identified by its identificator *PID*.

Peers hold data in a set of buckets. Each bucket has a unique identifier within a peer, designated as *BID*. Each peer also maintains a GHT–like tree structure called the *address search tree (AST)*. It is used to route similarity range queries through the distributed network.

5.2   Address Search Tree

AST is a slightly modified GHT (defined in Sect. 3.3). Since buckets are distributed among the peers, peers have different bucket associations. In general, the tree leaf nodes

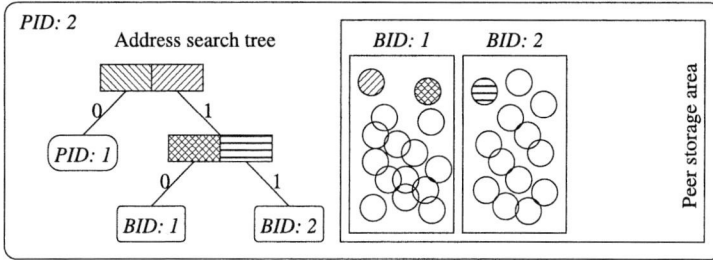

Fig. 2. Peer internal structure with address search tree and storage area with buckets full of objects

contain either a *PID*, if the bucket is on another peer, or a *BID*, if the bucket is held on the current peer. Figure 2 illustrates the peer internal structure.

Each peer has its own "view" of the distributed structure represented by its *AST*. The view may be out-of-date (in a way that some branches of the tree are missing), because any peer can split a bucket any time. This may cause sending insertion or search requests to incorrect peers, but this is not a problem. Whenever such misaddressing occurs, the request is forwarded to the correct peer and the caller is informed using update message (see Sect. 5.4).

When a peer wants to **insert** a new object, it first uses its local *AST*, and it finds a leaf node using the GHT pruning. If the leaf contains a *BID*, the inserting object is stored in the bucket *BID* located on the current peer – split is used if necessary. Otherwise (i.e. when *PID* pointer is found), the insert request is sent (forwarded) to a more appropriate peer *PID*. The same strategy is recursively used when an insert request is received through forwarding.

In order to perform a **range search** we again traverse the *AST* of the current peer. In general, we obtain a set of *PIDs* and a set of *BIDs*, because, as explained in Sect. 3.3, the execution of a range query may follow both the subtrees of an internal node in the *AST*. In this case, the query message is sent to all peers from the set of *PIDs*. All the buckets from the set of *BIDs* on current peer are tested for matching objects.

5.3 Bucket Splitting

Since the bucket capacity is limited, it must be split when an overflow occurs. Suppose a bucket in the peer with $PID = j$ overflows, the splitting is performed in the three following steps. First, we create a new bucket on either the peer j or another active peer (see Sect.). Second, for the created bucket, we choose a pair of pivots and we update the *AST*. This is performed using the dynamic pivot decision algorithm (not presented in this paper due to space limitations). Finally, we move some objects from current bucket to the new one according to the new pivots (the move is driven by condition (1) described in Sect. 3.3).

We do not address the reverse operation (joining the buckets after data removal) in this paper, because it is not properly solved yet. The problem is, that the *AST* of the other nodes may retain the old information about the two joined buckets. We are working on this issue now and the promising solution is the time–stamping of the nodes, so that the wrong path can be detected.

5.4   Update Message

The update message is sent to update the "view" of a peer, represented by its *AST*, whenever a misaddressing occurs. Such situation happens when the *PID* instead of the *BID* is found during the *AST* traversal and the request is forwarded. In this case, the receiving peer can have a more up to date view in its *AST*, so the sender's view must be updated.

The update message contains a subtree of the *AST* node representing the upgrade needed for the caller's "view". All necessary pivot objects are sent along with the update message.

5.5   Peer Joins

New peers may join the network any time and perform insert and query operations. In particular each joining peer J must know at least one other peer R already connected to the P2P network. Insert or range requests from J are sent to peer R (because peer J has an empty *AST* at the beginning), which either solves the request itself or uses the forwarding mechanism. The *AST* of node J is updated with the returned update messages during the operations and it becomes more accurate after a few inserts or range searches.

The peers that joined the network also offer their storage and computational capacity. This capacity is utilized by the structure during splits to scale gracefully over more peers. In Section 5.3 we have provided the split algorithm, which may require allocation of a bucket on a different peer. Such peer is chosen from the joined peers as follows.

Every peer with an unallocated storage capacity has to inform the other peers in the network. The peer adds a short description to every insert or range search request message it issues, so that the information spreads quickly among other peers in the network. The peers with some allocated buckets remember *PIDs* from the description and whenever they need to split a bucket onto another peer, they simply choose from the remembered ones. That information may become out-of-date, if the destination peer was contacted by another peer already. In that case the peer picks up next *PID* from the remembered ones and continues until the list is empty or a peer with available storage is found.

The peer leaving is not fully described here, because it is still in design phase. The peers, which did not use their available storage, can be removed safely. There are two problems with the peers that maintain some data. First, such a peer have to move the stored data to other peer with available storage capacity. This is not a big problem, since the peer has remembered peers with available capacity. Second, updates to the *AST* are needed. This is still an open problem, however, we are investigating the possibility of using the similar technique as for the bucket rejoining.

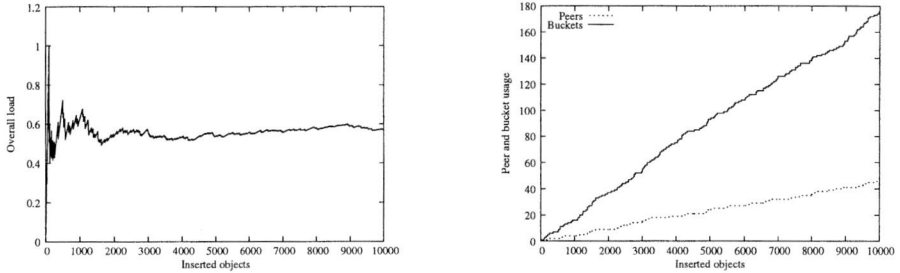

Fig. 3. Overall load of the structure during insertions (left) and number of peers and buckets responsible for holding the data (right)

6 Experimental Results

In this section we present a preliminary experimental evaluation based on a Java implementation of the proposed GHT* structure. For the preliminary evaluation and testing purposes, we have used a data–set of 10000 45–dimensional vectors and the L_2 distance function has been used. The vectors were synthetically generated with uniform distribution of distances. We are preparing more exhaustive experiments with larger data–sets and different metrics (for example edit distance for comparing texts or color histogram similarity function used to compare images). We also plan a comparative study with centralized metric space indexing techniques and distributed data structures (primary key and vector space).

We have chosen the available capacity at each peer to 5 buckets per peer at maximum with the maximal capacity of 100 objects per bucket. Objects were added using insert operation from different peers throughout the network, so that there were enough of peers with available capacity at any time.

We have measured the overall statistics of the structure first. The statistics was collected after every insertion. The left side of Fig. 3 is showing the overall load of the structure – i.e. the ratio between the number of inserted objects and the capacity of all active buckets. The second graph in Fig. 3 is displaying the evolution of the storage – number of peers that maintain a part of the structure and the overall number of buckets used.

We have achieved nearly 60% of overall structure load, which is a good result considering the distribution of the objects of the metric space used. However, in general these results strongly depend on the type of metric space used, on the actual distribution of the objects in the space, and on the pivot decision technique used. We can also see, that the evolution of the storage is linear with the number of inserted objects.

The main feature of GHT* is the ability to perform similarity searches. We have executed range searches on the entire data–set stored in GHT*. We have made two different sets of tests: one with a small radius, which returned about 10 object in average and another one with a bigger radius, which returned approximately 200 objects in average. We have executed both the types of query with 20 random generated query objects on a fresh peer (which has no knowledge of the structure, and hence has no AST at the start time).

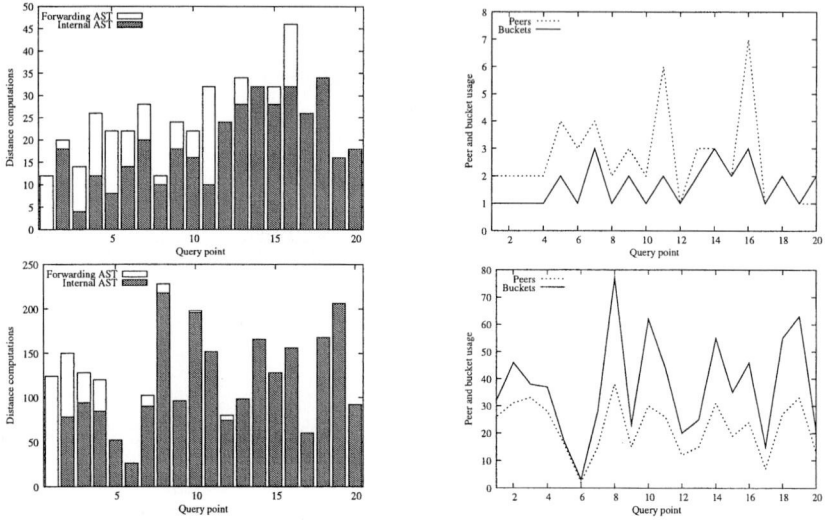

Fig. 4. Number of distance computations during a range query (left), number of peers and buckets accessed (right). The two graphs on the top represent the smaller evaluated radius, the two at the bottom are showing the bigger radius

The number of distance computations needed to address the correct buckets during the range search is shown on the left graphs in Fig. 4. The shaded bar represent the number of computations in the *AST* of the peer, which issued the query, the lighter part displays the computations in *AST* during forwarding. Those computations are performed on other peers to resolve the misaddressing. We do not mention the computations evaluated in every matching bucket (needed to get the exact objects that satisfy the query), since the number is highly dependent on the actual storage technique used in the bucket.

The right part of Fig. 4 is showing the number of peers and buckets accessed during the range query. We can see that the peer made addressing errors first and the queried peers have to perform some additional computations to correct the query. There is also the difference between small radius, which access only a few buckets and thus the peer is learning the "view" slowly, and the bigger radius, where the client has almost correct view after just a few queries.

7 Conclusion

As far as we know there has not been proposed metric space indexing structure, which uses distributed environment. Our structure is a first try to combine existing techniques for distributed searching and metric space indexing.

The GHT* structure allows storing data sets from any metric space and has many essential properties of the SDDS and P2P approaches. It is scalable – every peer can anytime perform an autonomous split gracefully distributing the structure over more peers. It has no hot spot – all peers use as precise addressing as possible and they all learn from misaddressing. Updates are performed locally and splitting never requires sending multiple messages to many peers. Finally, every peer can store data and perform similarity range queries at the same time.

We have implemented the first version of GHT* and performed some basic experiments. Even thought our experiments are still in the preliminary phase, we can conclude that the structure matches all the desired properties and thus it is able to perform metric space similarity search in the distributed environment. Future research concerns studies on the efficiency of the parallel processing, update operations, as well as some other forms of similarity search, such as the *nearest neighbor* queries.

References

1. Edgar Chávez, Gonzalo Navarro, Ricardo Baeza-Yates, and José Luis Marroquín. Searching in metric spaces. *ACM Computing Surveys*, 33(3):273–321, September 2001.
2. Robert Devine. Design and implementation of DDH: A distributed dynamic hashing algorithm. In *Proceedings of the 4th International Conference on Foundations of Data Organization and Algorithms (FODO)*, volume 730, pages 101–114, Chicago, 1993.
3. Vlastislav Dohnal, Claudio Gennaro, Pasquale Savino, and Pavel Zezula. Similarity join in metric spaces. In *Advances in Information Retrieval: 25th ECIR*, pages 452–467, 2003.
4. Gisli R. Hjaltason and Hanan Samet. Index-driven similarity search in metric spaces. *ACM Trans. Database Syst.*, 28(4):517–580, 2003.
5. Brigitte Kröll and Peter Widmayer. Distributing a search tree among a growing number of processors. In *Proceedings of the 1994 ACM SIGMOD International Conference on Management of Data / SIGMOD '94, Minneapolis, Minnesota*, pages 265–276, 1994.
6. Witold Litwin, Marie-Anne Neimat, and Donovan A. Schneider. LH* – A scalable, distributed data structure. *TODS*, 21(4):480–525, 1996.
7. Dejan S. Milojicic, Vana Kalogeraki, Rajan Lukose, Kiran Nagaraja, Jim Pruyne, Bruno Richard, Sami Rollins, and Zhichen Xu. Peer-to-peer computing. Technical Report HPL-2002-57, HP Laboratories, Palo Alto, March 2002.
8. Sylvia Ratnasamy, Paul Francis, Mark Handley, Richard Karp, and Scott Schenker. A scalable content-addressable network. In *Proc. of the 2001 conference on Applications, technologies, architectures, and protocols for computer communications*, pages 161–172, 2001.
9. Jeffrey K. Uhlmann. Satisfying general proximity/similarity queries with metric trees. *IPL: Information Processing Letters*, 40:175–179, 1991.

Pattern Based Management: Data Models and Architectural Aspects

Anna Maddalena

Dipartimento di Informatica e Scienze dell'Informazione,
Università degli Studi di Genova, Italy
`maddalena@disi.unige.it`

Abstract. Patterns are concise, but rich in semantic, representation of data (data mining results, multimedia features, Web structural information, etc.). Only few approaches exist to deal with heterogeneous patterns, even if this is an hot topic in most data-intensive and distributed applications. The aim of this thesis is to investigate the potentiality of pattern-based management. In particular, we plan to define sufficiently expressive pattern data models and languages to cope with different types of patterns. Besides, investigation of architectural issues concerning the usage of the proposed model and languages in centralized and advanced distributed environments will be exploited.

1 Introduction

The increasing opportunity of quickly collecting and cheaply storing large volumes of data, and the need for extracting concise information to be efficiently manipulated and intuitively analyzed, are posing new requirements for data management systems in both industrial and scientific applications. The determining property of such raw data is the vastness of their volume; moreover, a significant degree of heterogeneity may be present.

Clearly, data in such huge volumes do not constitute knowledge *per se*, i.e. little useful information can be deduced simply by their observation, so they hardly can be directly exploited by human beings. Thus, more elaborate techniques are required to extract the hidden knowledge and make these data valuable for end-users. A usual approach to deal with such huge quantity of data is to reduce the available data to knowledge artifacts (i.e., clusters, rules, frequent itemsets, etc.) through data processing methods (pattern recognition, data mining, knowledge extraction) that reduce data size while preserving as much as possible hidden/interesting information. These knowledge artifacts are also called *patterns*.

Several approaches have been proposed in the literature to cope with knowledge extraction and management problems. However, they usually consider a single type of knowledge artifact and mainly deal with the problem of defining languages for pattern extraction. Little emphasis has been posed in defining an overall environment to represent and efficiently manage different types of patterns.

As far as we know, the first general approach for pattern handling has been proposed in the context of the PANDA European project [25], which introduces the reference architecture and the logical foundations for pattern management. Results achieved in PANDA constitute the starting point of this work.

W. Lindner et al. (Eds.): EDBT 2004 Workshops, LNCS 3268, pp. 54–65, 2004.

Table 1. Examples of patterns

Application	Raw data	Type of pattern
market-basket analysis	sales transactions	item association rules
signal processing	complex signals	recurrent waveforms
mobile objects monitoring	measured trajectories	equations
information retrieval	documents	keyword frequencies
image recognition	image database	image features
market segmentation	user profiles	user clusters
music retrieval	music scores, audio files	rhythm, melody, harmony
system monitoring	system output stream	failure patterns
financial brokerage	trading records	stock trends
click-stream analysis	web-server logs	sequences of clicks
epidemiology	clinical records	symptom-diagnosis correlations
risk evaluation	customer records	decision trees

The aim of this PhD research work is to investigate the potentiality of pattern-based management systems. To this purpose, we plan to define sufficiently expressive pattern data models and languages to cope with different types of patterns. Architectural issues concerning storage and retrieval will also be investigated. In addition, since the capability to manage different types of patterns is much more important for data-intensive and distributed applications, we plan to exploit the usage of the proposed framework in distributed environments, considering the GRID as a special case.

This document is organized as follows. In Section 2, the pattern-based management problem is first introduced, then related work is discussed pointing out limitations of the current proposals. In Section 3, the goals of the thesis are presented in more details. Preliminary results already achieved are then presented in Section 4. Finally, Section 5 presents some concluding remarks.

2   Pattern Based Management: The Problem

Patterns can be thought as artifacts which effectively describe subsets of raw data (i.e. they are *compact*) by isolating and emphasizing some interesting properties (i.e. they are *rich in semantics*).

There are many different applicational contexts from which patterns can be generated and many different types of patterns. Some examples of patterns arising in different application domains are reported in Table 1.

Recently, pattern management issues are becoming much more important not only in centralized architectures but also in distributed ones. For example, the diffusion of the Web and the improvement of networking technologies speed up the requirement for distributed knowledge discovery and management systems. In such environments, it could be very useful to combine various types of knowledge under an homogeneous framework. As an example, a company, which produces food products and sells them through the Web, may be interested in combining knowledge concerning users which navigate its Web site, for example in the form of clusters, association rules, etc., generated by a clickstream analysis, with information concerning groups of products, generated, for instance, by a clustering technique. However, surprisely, the problem of directly storing and querying pattern-bases has received very limited attention so far in the commercial world and the database community.

In general, pattern management requires: (i) the definition of a model to represent patterns, (ii) specific languages to manipulate them, and (iii) the appropriate architectural support.

2.1   Pattern Model

A logical model for patterns must be general enough to represent in an homogeneous way different types of patterns extracted from different real-world application domains. As a minimum requirement, it must provide the representation of the pattern structure, some pattern measures, qualifying how well the pattern represents raw data, and raw data from which it has been generated.

Several approaches have been proposed to model (specific types of) patterns. Among them, we recall: (i) the Predictive Model Markup Language (PMML) [21], that uses XML to represent data mining models (i.e. the mining methodology used with mining parameters); (ii) the Java Data Mining API [18], that addresses the need for procedural support of all the existing and evolving data mining standards; (iii) the SQL/MM standard [17], by which mining models are represented as SQL types and made accessible through SQL syntax; (iv) Common Warehouse Model [10], whose main purpose is to enable easy interchange of warehouse and business intelligence metadata.

All the previous approaches seem not adequate to represent and handle different classes of patterns in a flexible, effective, and coherent way. Indeed, they consider a given list of predefined pattern types and they do not propose a general approach to pattern modeling.

Besides, the problem of mapping patterns against raw data is not considered, both from a modeling and a computational point of view. A specific mention is deserved by *inductive databases*, where data and rules inducted from data are uniformly represented and manipulated [22]. Under this approach, only association rules are considered. Furthermore, there is no clear separation between raw data and patterns.

The first attempt to introduce a *Pattern-Base Management System* (PBMS), capable of modeling, storing, and handling heterogeneous types of patterns, is related to the *PANDA (PAtterns for Next-generation DAtabase systems)* project. Indeed in PANDA, a pattern is modeled by: the *structure*, that qualifies the pattern by locating it within a pattern space; the *measure*, that quantifies the quality of the raw data representation achieved by the pattern itself; the *source*, describing the raw data the pattern relates to; the *formula*, describing the (approximate) mapping between the raw data space and the pattern space.

Although this approach represents an important step toward a unified pattern model, it still suffers of some limitations. First of all, relationships among raw data and patterns are not sufficiently formalized in the PANDA model. In particular, issues concerning the usage of different languages, leading to different expressive power and complexity results, for the formula representation have not been considered. Moreover, since raw data may change, synchronization between patterns and source data is an important issue not taken into account in PANDA. Another open issue is how advanced semantic information over raw data, such as ontologies, can be used in pattern representation. This issue has been considered only in the context of association rules [20] but no general approach has been proposed yet.

2.2 Pattern Languages

The difference in semantics between patterns and raw data discourages from adopting the same query language for both. Since raw data are managed by traditional DBMSs, they can be queried and retrieved using traditional query languages. On the other side, to retrieve patterns, a specific *pattern query language* has to be defined, capable of capitalizing on the peculiar semantics of patterns as defined in the model. Besides a pattern query language, there is also the need for a *pattern manipulation language*, by which patterns can be inserted, deleted, and updated.

Most of the limitations concerning existing pattern languages derive from the fact that few approaches exist to deal with heterogeneous patterns in a unified framework [12, 22]. Indeed, many of the proposed languages deal with specific types of patterns (in general, association rules) [6, 13–16, 20]. As far as we know, no pattern manipulation and query languages have been proposed yet to cope with heterogeneous patterns in a more general way.

2.3 Architectural Issues

From an architectural point of view, once a unified logical framework for pattern management has been defined, pattern storage and retrieval aspects have to be considered. In the PANDA project, three different storage schemes have been considered, based on relational, object-relational, and XML models. However, as far as we know, no specific physical model for patterns has been defined yet even if, due to pattern characteristics, ad-hoc storage and indexing techniques could greatly improve pattern query processing.

Besides the management of patterns in centralized architectures, pattern management is becoming an hot topic also for distributed environments. An important example is represented by the innovative paradigm of GRID computing [7], that complements Semantic Web with an infrastructure to handle large-scale distributed enterprise information systems. An important issue in this context is how heterogeneous resources of the GRID can be effectively managed. To this purpose, "GRID intelligence" [7] refers to an emerging research field that addresses how the data and information available on a GRID can be effectively acquired, preprocessed, represented, interchanged, integrated, and converted into useful knowledge. In this context, patterns play a fundamental role.

Since the concept of "Grid Intelligence" is a very recent one, only preliminary results have been obtained so far. The Knowledge Grid [7, 8] is a first proposal concerning how GRID services can be extended to deal with patterns management. However, problems concerning how such patterns should be modeled and efficiently retrieved have not been investigated yet.

3   The PhD Proposal

The PhD work started in March 2003, during my participation to the PANDA European project (2001-2004) [25]. It concerns three different aspects of pattern management, briefly discussed in the following.

3.1   Pattern Model

The first goal of the thesis is the development of a *pattern data model*, to represent pattern types and their instances. The model must be general enough to cope with different types of patterns. In defining such model, we start from the model proposed in PANDA [23] and we try to overcome some of the limitations identified in Section 2.1.

First of all, we plan to propose languages for formula specification (representing relationships between raw data and patterns) and to analyze their expressive power. To this purpose, we plan to consider constraint query languages [19].

Moreover, synchronization issues between pattern and raw data will be investigated. To this purpose, the pattern logical model will be enriched with temporal aspects to support the notions of transaction and validity time [24]. In the PBMS context, the pattern transaction time is the instant of time at which a pattern is generated and inserted in the PBMS. On the other hand, the concept of validity time has to be defined with respect to the validity time associated with the set of raw data the pattern represents.

Then, we plan to investigate how advanced semantic information over raw data, such as ontologies, can be used in pattern representation.

Finally, we plan to investigate the expressive power of the proposed model to understand which types of patterns can be represented. This of course depends on the language used to define pattern components.

3.2   Pattern Languages

We plan to define languages to manipulate and query patterns represented according to the proposed model. These issues have only been preliminarily investigated in PANDA [4], where the basic operations for pattern manipulation and retrieval have been identified. In the context of this thesis, we plan to formally define those languages, investigating expressive power and complexity issues.

In a pattern management system, traditional manipulation operations, such as insertion, deletion and update, have to be re-interpreted. In particular, the insertion operation corresponds to a pattern extraction process: new patterns are generated starting from raw data. Finally, pattern updates have to reflect modifications that occurred in the raw dataset associated with the pattern.

On the query language side, we plan to propose a calculus and an algebra for patterns, supporting both operations over patterns and operations binding patterns with raw data (so called *cross-over queries*). To this purpose, we plan to consider some existing calculus and algebra for complex objects, such as those presented in [1, 11] and extend them to cope with specific pattern components (see Section 4). Expressive power and equivalence of the proposed languages will also be investigated.

3.3   Architectural Goals

From an architectural point of view, we plan to propose a storage strategy for patterns and to investigate issues concerning the usage of such strategy during query processing.

Then, as a case study, we plan to investigate the potentiality of using the proposed pattern model and languages in the context of a distributed knowledge management environment, considering the GRID architecture as a special case. In particular, we plan to analyze how pattern management can be useful to represent GRID metadata, to handle GRID derived knowledge, and to support the mining process within the GRID environment.

4   Preliminary Results

In the following, we present in more details some preliminary results, obtained in the first period of my PhD work. The obtained results refer to the PBMS architecture defined in the context of the PANDA project [25].

A *Pattern-Base Management System* (PBMS) is a system for handling (i.e., storing, processing, and retrieving) patterns defined over raw data, to efficiently support pattern matching and pattern-related operations generating intensional information.

Figure 1 (taken from [23]) shows the reference architecture for a PBMS. On the bottom layer, a set of devices produce data, which are then organized and stored within databases or files. Knowledge discovery algorithms are applied over these data and generate patterns to be fed into the PBMS.

Within the PBMS, it is worth to distinguish three different layers. The *pattern layer* is populated with patterns. The *type layer* holds built-in and user-defined types for patterns. The *class layer* holds definitions of pattern classes, i.e., collections of semantically related patterns.

4.1   The Model

The model is based on the concepts of pattern types, patterns and pattern class [3, 4, 23]. A *pattern type* represents the intensional form of patterns, giving a formal description of their structure and relationship with source data. It is defined as a tuple composed of the following elements:

- the *structure schema s*, which defines the pattern space by describing the structure of the patterns instances of the pattern type;
- the *source schema d*, which defines the related source space by describing the dataset from which patterns, instances of the pattern type being defined, are constructed;
- the *measure schema m*, which describes the measures which quantify the quality of the source data representation achieved by the pattern; the role of this component is to enable the user to evaluate how accurate and significant for a given application each pattern is;
- the *formula f*, which describes the relationship between the source space and the pattern space, thus carrying the semantics of the pattern. Inside f, attributes are interpreted as free variables ranging over the components of either the source or the

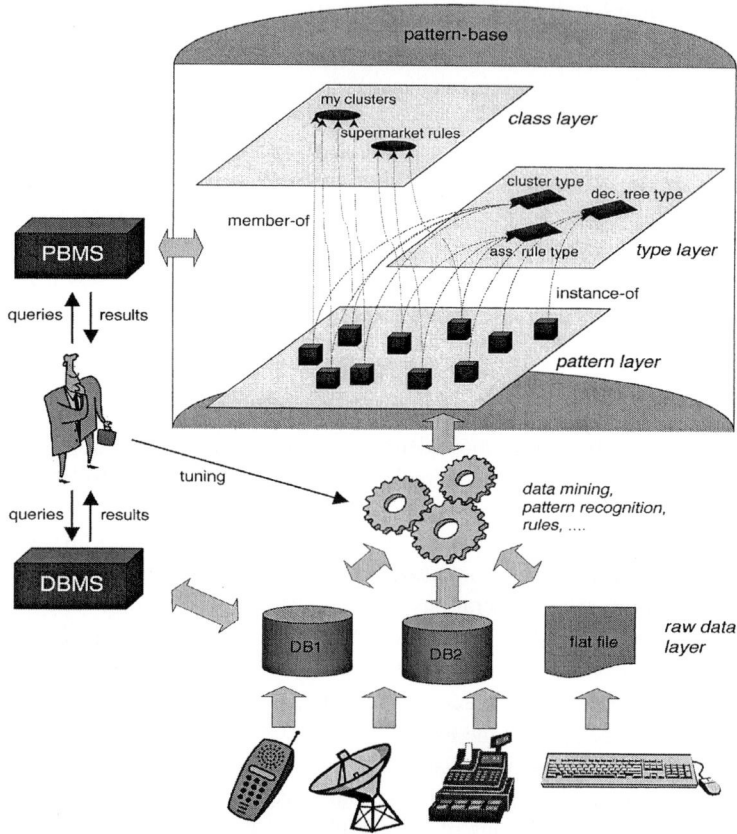

Fig. 1. The PBMS architecture

pattern space. Note that, though in some particular domains f may exactly express the inter-space relationship, in most cases it will describe it only approximatively.

Note that the proposed approach to pattern modeling is parametric on the language adopted for formulas, thus the achievable semantics for patterns strongly depends on the expressivity of the chosen language. In the following examples, we use a constraint calculus based on polynomial constraints which seems suitable for several types of patterns [19].

Patterns are instances of a specific pattern type. Thus, they are composed of the following elements:

- a pattern identifier (pid);
- a structure (s) that positions the pattern within the pattern space defined by its pattern type;
- a data source (d) that identifies the specific dataset from which the pattern has been generated;

- a measure (m) that estimates the quality of the raw data representation achieved by the pattern;
- a formula (f) which relates the pattern to the source data.

In particular, the formula is obtained by the formula f in the pattern type by: (i) instantiating each attribute appearing in ss with the corresponding value specified in s, and (ii) letting the attributes appearing in ds range over the source space.

Example 1. Given a domain D of values and a set of product sales transactions, a possible pattern type for modeling association rules over strings representing products is the following:

> n : AssociationRule
>
> s : TUPLE(head : SET(STRING), body : SET(STRING))
>
> d : BAG(transaction : SET(STRING))
>
> m : TUPLE(confidence : REAL, support : REAL)
>
> $f : \forall x(x \in$ head $\lor x \in$ body $\Rightarrow x \in$ transaction$)$

Assume that raw data include a relational table sales which stores sales transactions of a shop, having the following schema (transactionId, article, quantity). Using an extended SQL syntax to denote the dataset, an example of pattern instance for pattern type AssociationRule is the following:

> $pid : 512$
>
> s : (head $= \{'$Boots$'\}$, body $= \{'$Socks$', '$Hat$'\}$)
>
> d : 'SELECT SETOF(article) AS transaction
>
>   FROM sales
>
>   GROUP BY transactionId'
>
> m : (confidence $= 0.75$, support $- 0.55$)
>
> $f : \forall x(x \in \{'$Boots$', '$Socks$', '$Hat$'\} \Rightarrow x \in$ transaction$)$

In the pattern formula, transaction ranges over the data source space. On the other hand the values given to head and body within the structure are used to bind variables head and body in the formula of pattern type AssociationRule.   □

A *class* is a set of semantically related patterns and constitutes the key concept in defining a pattern query language. A class is defined for a given pattern type and contains only patterns of that type. It is important to note that a specific pattern may belong to any number of classes.

Example 2. Consider Example 1. The *Apriori* algorithm described in [2] could be used to generate relevant association rules from the dataset D intensionally described by the following SQL query:

> SELECT SETOF(article) AS transaction
>
> FROM sales
>
> GROUP BY transactionId.

Then, all the generated patterns could be inserted in a class called *SaleRules* for pattern type AssociationRule defined in Example 1. Note that the collection of patterns associated with the class can be later extended to include rules generated from a different dataset, let's say D', representing for instance the sales transaction recorded in a different store. □

To increase the expressivity of the logical model some interesting relationships between patterns have also been introduced (for formal details see [4]).

Among them, we recall: *specialization*, a sort of *IS-A* relationship (e.g. clusters of integer points can be seen as a specialization of generic clusters of points); *composition*, between a pattern and those used to define its structure; *refinement*, between a pattern and those belonging to its source component; in such case, the pattern data source is a collection of other patterns. Composition and refinement are key concepts in defining complex patterns.

Example 3. The following pattern type models clusters of association rules:

> n :ClusterOfRules
>
> ss :representative : AssociationRule
>
> ds :SET(rule : AssociationRule)
>
> ms :TUPLE(deviationOnConfidence : REAL, deviationOnSupport : REAL)
>
> f :rule.ss.head = representative.ss.head

Note that there is a refinement relationship between patterns of type ClusterOfRules and patterns of type AssociationRule, because the data source of a cluster of rules consists into a set of association rules.

In addition, since the representative of each cluster is an association rule, there exists a composition relationship between those two pattern types. □

4.2　Pattern Languages

As we have already discussed (see Section 3.2), languages for patterns have to deal with both pattern manipulation and querying issues. Several preliminary results concerning pattern languages have already been achieved [4, 5].

In particular, in [5] several operators useful to manipulate patterns have been identified and a preliminary proposal for an algebra for querying patterns has been presented. On the other side, in [9] the pattern model [3, 4, 23] and pattern manipulation operators proposed in [5] have been used to show how clustering results can be represented and managed under the proposed pattern framework.

In the following, the basic characteristics of the pattern query language and the pattern manipulation language are discussed (for additional technical details we refer the interested reader to [4, 5]).

The Pattern Query Language. The pattern query language supports the user in retrieving patterns from the Pattern Based Management System. Queries are executed against classes.

We defined some preliminary algebraic operators for pattern manipulation.

Besides typical relational operators (such as renaming, set-based operators), *projection* has been revisited to project out structure and measure components.

Selection allows one to select patterns belonging to a certain class satisfying a certain condition, involving any possible pattern component. Similarity predicates are also supported.

Operators providing a way to navigate hierarchies defined by the modeled relationships are also provided. Among them, we recall the *drill-down* and the *roll-up* operators, that, similarly to the ones defined for the data warehousing context, allow one to change the level of details of a certain pattern by navigating the refinement relationship. Concerning the composition relationship, we recall the *decomposition* operator, returning for each pattern a component pattern associated with a certain attribute of its structure.

Finally, *join* operators are proposed to combine patterns belonging to two different classes, thus generating new patterns instances of new pattern types. To perform a join operation the user has to specify a join predicate and a composition function. The join predicate expresses the condition over which the join is based, whereas the composition function defines the pattern type of the result.

The proposed language also supports operations binding patterns with raw data. Such operations are usually known as *cross-over queries* since for their execution two different systems - the PBMS and the system where raw data are stored - have to be used. Among them, we recall the *drill-through* operator which allows one to navigate from the pattern layer to the raw data layer, through pattern data sources and formulas, and the *covering* operator, which allows one to determine whether a fixed pattern represents a specified data source.

The Pattern Manipulation Language. A pattern manipulation language must provide the user primitives to generate patterns, by applying a mining process to raw data or from the scratch, and to insert them in the Pattern Based Management System. Besides that, it has to support pattern deletion and update. Moreover, since a pattern can be inserted in several classes, pattern generation and insertion into a class are defined as two distinct operators.

In defining the previous operators, traditional manipulation operators (insertion, deletion, and update) have been re-interpreted for the new context.

More precisely, pattern insertion is represented by an *extraction* operator, that allows one to extract a pattern from a raw dataset by applying a specific mining function. Patterns can also be generated by recomputing pattern measures against a new dataset or directly inserted in the Pattern Based Management System by the user, that in this case must be able to specify all pattern components.

The delete operation has the standard meaning, i.e., patterns satisfying specific conditions are selected and removed from the Pattern Based Management System. Since a pattern may belong to different classes, two versions of the delete operator are provided. The first one implements a restricted approach removing patterns from the PBMS only when they are inserted in no classes. The second one cascadely removes patterns from all classes they belong to and from the PBMS.

Finally, pattern updates have to reflect modifications occurred in the raw data dataset to patterns. Among update operators, we recall *synchronization*, which performs the recomputation of pattern measures to reflect modifications that occurred in its data source.

5   Concluding Remarks

The aim of this thesis is to investigate the potentiality of pattern-based management systems, developing pattern data and physical models and languages. The usage of the proposed model and languages in centralized and advanced distributed environments will also been exploited. Even if the importance of these issues has been recognized in the scientific literature, only few approaches have been proposed so far to deal with pattern management in an homogeneous way.

The PhD work started in March 2003, thus only preliminary results have been obtained up to now, some of which in the context of the PANDA European project [25]. In the next two years, we plan to further investigate model and architectural issues, as pointed out in Section 3.

References

1. S. Abiteboul and C. Beeri. The Power of Languages for the Manipulation of Complex Values. *VLDB Journal*, 4(4):727–794, 1995.
2. R. Agrawal and R. Srikant. Fast Algorithms for Mining Association Rules. In *Proc. 20th VLDB*, pages 487–499, 1994.
3. I. Bartolini, E. Bertino, B. Catania, P. Ciaccia, M. Golfarelli, M. Patella, and Stefano Rizzi. PAtterns for Next-generation DAtabase systems: Preliminary Results of the PANDA Project. In *Proc. of the 11th SEBD*, pages 293–300, 2003.
4. E. Bertino, B. Catania, M. Golfarelli, M. Halkidi, A. Maddalena, S. Skiadopoulos, S. Rizzi, M. Terrovitis, P. Vassiliadis, M. Vazirgiannis, and E. Vrachnos. The Logical Model for Patterns. PANDA Technical report TR-2003-02, 2003.
5. E. Bertino, B. Catania, and A. Maddalena. Towards a Language for Pattern Manipulation and Querying. In *Proc. of the 1st Int. Workshop on Pattern Representation and Management (PaRMa'04)*, 2004.
6. D. Braga, A. Campi, M. Klemettinen, and P.L. Lanzi. Mining Association Rules from XML Data. In *Proc. of the Int. Conf. on Data Warehousing and Knowledge Discovery (DaWak 2002)*, pages 21–30, 2002.
7. M. Cannataro. Knowledge Discovery and Ontology-based Services on the Grid. In *Proc. of Semantic Grid Workshop at GGF9*, 2003.
8. M. Cannataro and D. Talia. The Knowledge Grid. *Communication of the ACM*, 46(1):89–93, 2003.
9. B. Catania and A. Maddalena. A Framework for Cluster Management. In *Proc. of the Int. Workshop on Clustering Information over the Web (ClustWeb'04)*, 2004.
10. Common Warehouse Metamodel (CWM). http://www.omg.org/cwm, 2001.
11. L. Fegaras and D. Maier. Optimizing Object Queries Using an Effective Calculus. *ACM Transactions on Database Systems*, 25(4):457–516, 2000.
12. I. Geist. A Framework for Data Mining and KDD. In *Proc. of the 2002 ACM symposium on Applied computing*, pages 508–513. ACM Press, 2002.
13. I. Geist and K.U. Sattler. Towards Data Mining Operators in Database Systems: Algebra and Implementation. In *Proc. of the 2nd International Workshop on Databases, Documents, and Information Fusion (DBFusion 2002)*, 2002.
14. T. Imielinski and H. Mannila. A Database Perspective on Knowledge Discovery. *Communications of the ACM*, 39(11):58–64, 1996.

15. T. Imielinski and A. Virmani. MSQL: A query language for database mining. *Data Mining and Knowledge Discovery*, 2(4):373–408, 1999.
16. Information Discovery Data Mining Suite. `http://www.patternwarehouse.com/dmsuite.htm`, 2002.
17. ISO SQL/MM Part 6. `http://www.sql-99.org/SC32/WG4/Progression_Documents/FCD/fcd-datamining-2001-05.pdf`, 2001.
18. Java Data Mining API. `http://www.jcp.org/jsr/detail/73.prt`, 2003.
19. P. Kanellakis, G. Kuper, and P. Revesz. Constraint Query Languages. *Journal of Computer and System Sciences*, 51(1):25–52, 1995.
20. R. Meo, G. Psaila, and S. Ceri. An extension to SQL for mining association rules. *Data Mining and Knowledge Discovery*, 2(2):195–224, June 1998.
21. Predictive Model Markup Language (PMML). `http://www.dmg.org/pmmlspecs_v2/pmml_v2_0.html`, 2003.
22. L. De Raedt. A Perspective on Inductive Databases. *ACM SIGKDD Explorations Newsletter*, 4(2):69–77, 2002.
23. S. Rizzi, E. Bertino, B. Catania, M. Golfarelli, M. Halkidi, M. Terrovitis, P. Vassiliadis, M. Vazirgiannis, and E. Vrachnos. Toward a Logical Model for Patterns. In *Proc. of the 22nd Int. Conf. on Conceptual Modeling (ER 2003)*, pages 77–90, 2003.
24. R.T. Snodgrass. *The TSQL2 Temporal Query Language*. Kluwer, 1995.
25. The PANDA Project. `http://dke.cti.gr/panda/`, 2002.

Managing Dynamic Repositories
for Digital Content Components

André Santanchè and Claudia Bauzer Medeiros

Institute of Computing,
State University of Campinas – UNICAMP,
CP 6176, 13084-971 Campinas, SP, Brazil
{santanch,cmbm}@ic.unicamp.br

Abstract. The Semantic Web pursues interoperability at syntactic and semantic levels, to face the proliferation of data files with different purposes and representation formats. One challenge is how to represent such data, to allow users and applications to easily find, use and combine them. The paper proposes an infrastructure to meet those goals. The basis of the proposal is the notion of *digital content components* that extends the Software Engineering software component. The infrastructure offers tools to combine and extend these components, upon user request, managing them within dynamic repositories. The infrastructure adopt XML and RDF standards to foster interoperability, composition, adaptation and documentation of content data. This work was motivated by reuse needs observed in two specific application domains: education and agro-environmental planning.

1 Introduction

The reuse of digital content is an issue that is attracting increasing attention. In the context of this work, reuse can be defined as the practice of use an existing content object to build a new digital artifact using the object's content partial or totally [7, 13]. Reuse advantages include productivity improvement and cost reduction on development and maintenance. Furthermore, frequency of reuse may be a quality indicator, and content units designed for reuse can be quickly reconfigured.

On the other hand, there are several obstacles to supporting reuse; perhaps the most serious is the problem of proliferation of data, systems and users. Several directions are being followed towards solving these problems. One direction, which is investigated in this paper, is to exploit the advances in the area of software component reuse, from Software Engineering, combining them with database research on the Semantic Web and interoperability.

The Semantic Web [9] foresees a new generation of Web-based systems, where semantic descriptions of data and services will booster interoperability. In parallel, Software Engineering has reached a high level of maturity concerning reuse units, by developing the technology of software components. Our idea is to extend these principles, to comprise any digital content. From now on, this extended notion of component will be called *digital content component*; the term will be used in this paper to denote any kind of data e.g., pieces of software but also texts, audio, video, a result of a database query, and so forth.

W. Lindner et al. (Eds.): EDBT 2004 Workshops, LNCS 3268, pp. 66–77, 2004.

Software components are built by assembling code into a standard package that encapsulates implementation details. Well defined interfaces are associated with the package structure. These interfaces define how the component will be adopted and adapted into a new application, and how it will relate with other components and its execution environment.

By the same token, our proposal for a digital component structure involves the encapsulation of specific data representations into a package with a standard format, and public interfaces that support relationships among components.

Though the advantages of such generalization are evident, there remains the problem of putting it into practice. Thus, the paper is concerned with three main issues, having digital content reuse and interoperability in mind. The first issue concerns *establishing a model* to represent a digital content component, adopting interoperability standards preconized by the Semantic Web initiative. The second defines a *strategy to store and index* large volume of these components in a database. Finally it is necessary to *build a framework* to implement and manage content components. Our research has been motivated by reuse needs experienced by work developed at the State University of Campinas, Brazil (UNICAMP) in two application domains: education and agro-environmental planning.

The remainder of this text is organized as follows. Section 2 introduces related work. Section 3 presents the proposed digital content component model and discusses storage and implementation considerations. Finally, Section 4 presents concluding remarks and the present stage of this work.

2 Related Work

Related work involves research on software components and reusability in Software Engineering, and standards for digital content and interoperability in the Semantic Web. We discuss some attempts in these directions, starting from the software notion of component and evolving to the database concept of repository.

2.1 Packages

Content reuse can be enhanced via assembly into a standard package for distribution. In our work, *package* is defined as a structure that delimitates, organizes and describes one or more pieces of digital content suitable to reuse.

This packaging approach has already been adopted in the educational domains. The main example is the IMS Content Packaging Information Model [19], and based on that, the SCORM – Sharable Content Object Reference Model [5], a proposal to structure and distribute educational content in a package content form. Both aim at reusability, interoperability, location and adaptation facilities. They use XML to describe a hierarchical structure of each content package and their respective educational metadata. Metadata representation follows an IEEE standard for educational metadata, named LOM – Learning Object Metadata [8]. LOM has been coded in XML [23], with subsequent studies to represent LOM in RDF [10].

The adoption of open standards for component package structure and interface definition is a key approach to achieve interoperability. Within the Semantic Web context, XML and RDF are complementary standards, adequate to syntactic and semantic interoperability, respectively [4].

2.2   From Packages to Components

The package structure has limited capabilities. An evolution of this concept is achieved when packages are designed not only to transport content via a standard container, but to be connected with other packages and interact with them and their environment. This corresponds to the concept of *component*.

The component concept is often associated with the software component concept, which deals with software code. There is no agreement on the definition of the software component concept, though definitions are closely related [2].

Like a package, a component is designed to be a unit of independent deployment. There is a clear division between the content (encapsulated software implementation) and some external structure where this content is encapsulated.

However, components have higher specialized external structures, which publish component functionality by explicit contractual interfaces. To interact and work together, component structure and interface follow a model that specifies design constraints.

2.3   Component Repositories

Component reuse can only become effective with adoption of a structure to store and manage components in an efficient way. Many research initiatives concern component storage and retrieval, especially on techniques to index components. Indexation can be content-based or structure-based.

Prieto-Díaz [11] confronts two classification principles borrowed from library science, to apply in component indexation. First, the *enumerative* method uses a classification tree to organize components in categories and sub-categories. Second, the *faceted* method describes components by a set of attributes (named facets); each facet is specified by setting a pertinent term value (comparable to attribute value, but restricted on a list of possible values). Another option is using ontologies [20] to represent domain knowledge associated with components.

Still another indexation solution uses component structure. The basic method relies on component signature match [24], but it can be refined by a formal specification of component behavior, used as a basis to behavior match [25].

3   A Proposal for Digital Content Components

3.1   Components' Life Cycles

Any digital component infrastructure must support the entire cycle of component production, storage, retrieval and use – see Fig. 1. Production comprises the well known software component production process, which we propose to extend to any piece of data the user wants to share. Such components can be assembled automatically, or guided by the user, through a tool named *packager*. The figure shows packager modules that encapsulate distinct kinds of content components – spreadsheets, workflows, maps, etc. A packager takes the form of a plugin attached to a software, which deals with the content, or an independent module specialized to process some file formats. Components are stored in a dynamic repository, and managed by a repository manager, which is accessed by users to retrieve and combine them. Again in the figure, a developer uses an authoring tool to compose distinct components – workflow, maps and workflow runtime engine – into an executable unit to produce a map. This specific example reproduces a scenario we deal with in UNICAMP, but without support of content components. In this scenario, experts specify workflows to generate maps for environmental planning based on combining several kinds of data. These workflows can then be run to produce distinct kinds of environmental plans.

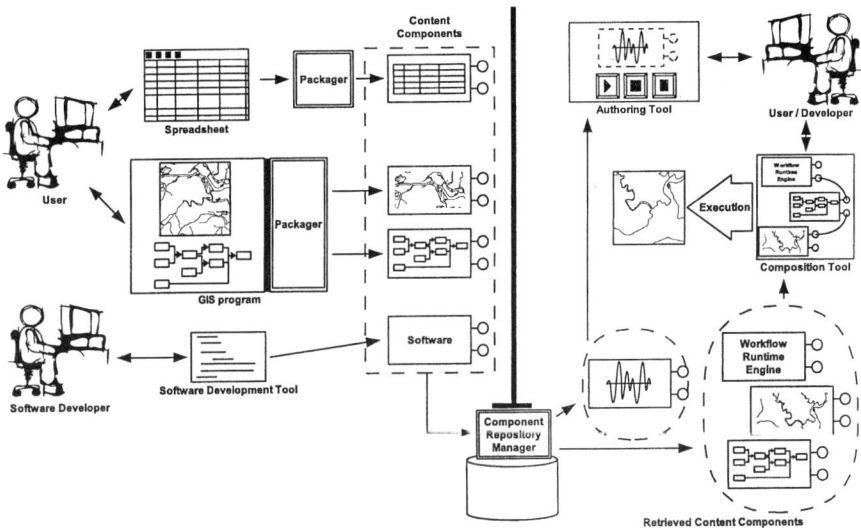

Fig. 1. Diagram of content component cycle for production/storage/use

The starting point for our work is the Anima project, an infrastructure for software components [14] developed by the first author. Anima is being used to create educational tools in several schools in the city of Salvador, Brazil. Anima comprises the complete cycle illustrated in Fig. 1, but restricted to software components and without database support. It provides support to building applications via component composition and uses RDF to represent component packages, including interface specification and component metadata. This allows applications to deal with software components implemented in different languages. An Anima application can be represented via a network of components whose configurations are stored in an XML file. This file can be dynamically converted into applications implemented in specific languages throughout XSLT sheets.

Moreover, Anima provides support to component execution and intercommunication via an XML based protocol.

With this background in mind, our research considers three aspects of content components: representation, storage/retrieval management and use.

3.2   Component Representation

Content Component Structure

A component's structure is defined to be a unit, composed of four distinct parts: (i) The content itself, in its original format; (ii) an XML specification of the internal structure used for component organization, based on SCORM [5], which allows a hierarchical description of components and sub-components; (iii) an RDF specification of component interfaces; (iv) RDF metadata to describe functionality, applicability, use restrictions, etc. Components can be recursively constructed from composition of other components, each of which in turn is structured by the same four parts. It is important to point out that XML has been proposed for aspect (ii), whereas all others are to be specified in RDF. These choices are based in the following criteria.

The internal organization structure follows a schema whose format and interpretation applies to all components. XML is a better choice in this case, where it acts as structuring element. Additionally, it allows inclusion of links to external pieces, allowing reuse by reference, as explained in [7]. External referenced entities include data generated by remote units, Web services, etc.

RDF is the choice to represent the interface and metadata, since descriptions and taxonomies are involved. RDF descriptions will promote straightforward indexation and component management support, and can be extended to represent ontologies with OWL [18]. RDF metadata with digital signature can ensure component provenance, and thus be used to control component quality based on the source.

Figure 2 shows a partial example of a component specification for encapsulating rainfall data. The content part stores a list of geographic positions for the rainfall stations coded in XML. The metadata part represents component's title and category. Specific terms employed – such as "XML Rainfall Station List" – are extracted from domain-dependent ontologies (e.g., see [12]).

The interface part shows three inputs and two outputs. All inputs are categorized as simple messages without parameters ("single"). Outputs describe in RDF how the contents are formatted (type arrow) for a given ontological context within a domain ontology (category arrow). This shows output should always contemplate not only syntactic information (i.e., XML schema), but also semantics (ontology terms).

This four-part structure for component representation, which extends the Software Engineering concept of software component to any kind of content, and promotes interoperability, is an important contribution of this work. Related work deals with some of these aspects in an isolated form, without an integration perspective.

Categories of Content Components

We differentiate between two kinds of component – process and passive components. A process component is a specific kind of digital content component. It encapsulates any kind of process description (sequences of instructions or plans) that can be executed by

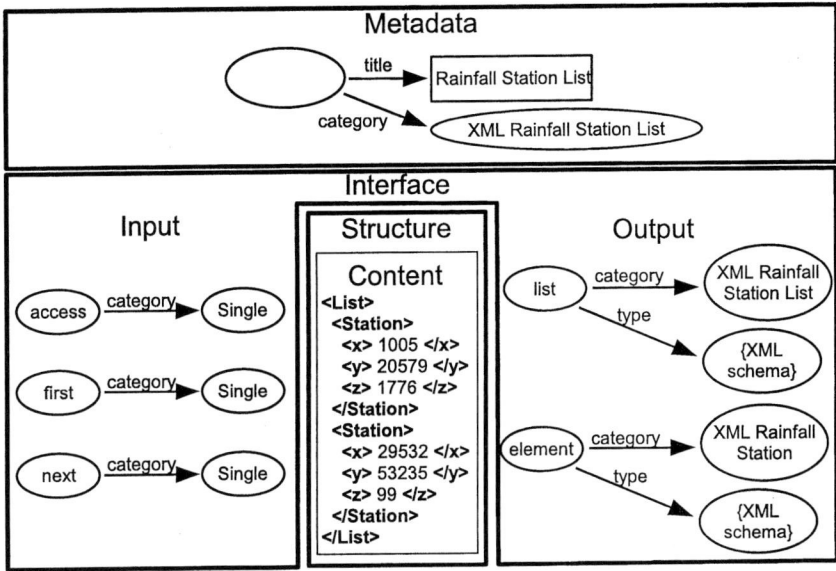

Fig. 2. Diagram of content component structure

a computer. Therefore, they usually define an input interface, and their results change according to different input values. The component of Fig. 2 is a non-process (passive) component, and contains data that can be used by a process component. A passive component's interface matches the input interfaces of process components enabled to use its contents.

In order to illustrate content component categories, we will borrow an example from scientific applications. In this context, scientists are interested not only in reusing results, but in sharing the whole process of experiment development. This originated the notion of scientific workflows (e.g. [1]), to specify and record experiments; this allows, among others, experiment reproducibility and therefore reuse. The WOODSS system [15], developed by us, follows this approach: it enables the capture of activities in agro-environmental planning to be stored as scientific workflows, which can be later edited, composed and re-executed.

WOODSS' users manage two main kinds of file: maps and workflows. The same workflow can be executed using different input maps. Workflows are an example of our process components, whereas maps are typically passive components. In our analogy, a "workflow component" can be linked to different passive "map components". Furthermore, one may envisage defining interfaces to workflows, in RDF, that will impose conditions on input files – e.g., indicating maps that can be acceptable as input.

Any digital content can potentially be packed in a component. The two requisites for packaging are: existence of an appropriate packager for its format and, for process components, existence of a runtime module enabled to run it. By the same token, two or more components can be attached and packed into a higher level component. For instance, consider a workflow component that receives two inputs: a map and a value v. It applies a sequence of filters to the map, based on value v – and generates another map as output. These components can be stored separately or composed into a more complex component that will deal with the specific map, and accept only input v.

Most process components cannot be executed directly, due to their need for interpreters or runtime modules, not embedded into their environment. In such cases, complementary attached components can perform this task. These complementary components are named *companion components*. Process components, moreover serve as companions to passive components, i.e., a passive component needs some sort of code to be processed.

The choice of the appropriate companion component to be associated to another (passive or process) component is determined by the application manager, and is influenced by the context. This allows dynamic component companion binding. Since this binding is defined by the application manager, it is transparent to end users. This allows a homogeneous treatment of passive and active components from the user's perspective.

Using the Components

Content components can be used in many ways. Three forms of expected use are: component insertion, content insertion and application construction.

In the first approach, components are inserted into documents or multimedia productions as content pieces. This use of components can be compared with the insertion of DDE/OLE objects into Windows documents, or insertion of embedded objects (such as Java applets) into Web pages. The components inserted are commonly passive components, or process components attached to passive components. For instance, a map component attached to a workflow component can be inserted in a scientific report.

The content insertion approach is similar to component insertion. However, the client unpacks component content and only this content is inserted into document or multimedia production, without component structure and metadata. In this approach, content components are used like content packages.

In the third usage form – application construction – components are used as basic blocks to construct applications. Here, just like in software component composition, an application is built from a network of interconnected components, following an architectural style [17].

This style guides digital content component usage and composition principles for construction of applications. A software architecture using components defines a configuration which involves components and connectors to bind components together. Our principles combine the Anima model for component composition with some aspects of the architectural style of C2 [22] – a message-based connection style for GUI software.

In our architecture each component is an independently executing peer, with its own state and thread of control. Components can only communicate asynchronously with other components via connectors – they can not use other forms of direct communication. Connectors transport messages; messages must offer support for at least XML, but can support another formats too (especially for performance purposes).

A message contains label, type and parameters represented in XML. The types' formats are defined by an XML schema and described by an associated RDF resource. The same schemes, taxonomies and descriptions are used in component interface description.

Figure 3 presents an example which combines process and passive components into an application intended to display informations about a set of rainfall stations. A modified version of the component illustrated in Fig. 2 will be used here, with some additional informations about the stations.

To compose components together the application adopts an architectural style named publish/subscribe [6]. Publish/subscribe style is based on messages produced by components and distributed by a message manager. Components subscribe to events they are interested in. Events are signalled by messages. In the example of Fig. 3, five components are subscribing to events (represented by a large arrow).

Publishers are components that raise events by publishing a message that is forwarded to every component that subscribes to that event. In the example, there are two visual software components (at the left side) that play a role of buttons and publish messages when the user clicks on them. The messages ("access" and "next") are dispatched to XML Rainfall Station List component, which subscribed to these events.

The "access" message induces the component to produce a "list" output message, which contains the list of all rainfall stations. Two components containing XSL stylesheets receive this message and convert it to a report and to a graphical representation of the rainfall station positions. The message "next" contains one rainfall station (the next of the sequence) and follows an equivalent path. This composition results in a browser of rainfall station lists.

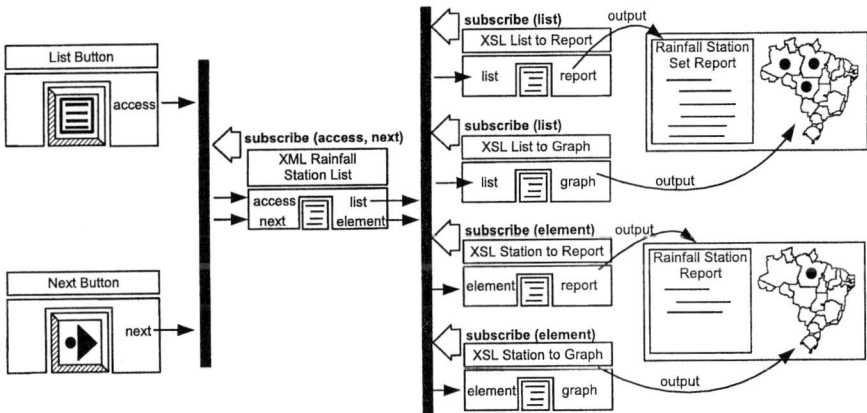

Fig. 3. Configuration that illustrates a content component composition

The configuration of components and connectors to form the application is stored in an XML document. This document contains the initial configuration of each component involved and the connectors configurations.

The representation of the connectors in the XML document depends on the architecture used to compose the components. In the publish/subscribe architecture, each connection is associated with a component subscription.

The framework of content components is designed to be flexible enough to adopt more than one architecture. Each kind of architecture is described and classified in a taxonomy by an RDF description. An XML schema determines the format used in the XML file that stores the configuration. Based on the RDF description the framework determines the role played by the components and connectors and how the configuration file will be interpreted.

3.3   Component Storage and Retrieval Management

A digital content component is a combination of raw data, XML data and RDF data. The solution requires devising a database capable to interpret and manage each format, since XML and RDF data will be used for indexation and internal structure exploration purposes.

There are many possible solutions to this problem. They involve, among others, considerations and tradeoffs between constructing a native XML DBMS versus a relational DBMS that maps XML (and RDF) data to their structure and vice-versa. The data can be dynamically mapped from XML and RDF to a relational database and vice-versa. Shanmugasundaram [16] proposes a process to map XML to a relational database, which unifies many partial solutions to this problem. RDF, on the other hand, is based in a strong connected network of interdependent description elements. Therefore, besides the mapping, it is necessary to devise a model to retrieve coherent fragments of RDF data [3], preventing the transfer of large data volumes for each query.

Other possible solutions are the use of a native XML database, alone or combined with a relational database. On the one hand XML data can be stored and indexed in a native way, on the other hand there are limitations to current XML database implementations, such as the need for consistency mechanisms, transaction support, etc. To store RDF data in an XML database will require a costly process to code and decode the descriptions from XML data.

One of the purposes of this project will be to identify the best storage solution, as well to combine it with a procedure to index and retrieve components. It will result in a dynamic component repository, in the sense that components may be dynamically combined. Indexation will be based on adapting and combining three techniques to the context of content component: use of ontologies [20], component signature match [24] and behavior match [25].

In many cases the connection of two components will need other intermediate components, responsible for adaptations and conversions. The component repository manager can find such components comparing input/output interfaces; however, this process can produce many options for the same connection. Metadata associated with components can then be used to help choose the adequate component configuration, e.g., for a given quality requirement.

Another direction is to use the notion of DBMS monitoring to track the rate of use of each repository component, and the rate of adopted combinations. This will help guide the search for adequate component combination, based on previous experience, and can indicate the quality of component, based on its use rate.

3.4   Reference Implementation Framework

The project includes a construction of a reference implementation framework to: provide an infrastructure for components execution and intercommunication; interact with a database to store/retrieve components; and provide support to component insertion, adaptation and reuse by applications. This framework will be based in the Anima infrastructure [14].

The Anima model is being extended to support any kind of content. This work includes the extension of Anima's software component model – presently based on modules coded in some program language – to deal with other types of process components, such as workflows and spreadsheets, which can act in many cases like software components. The construction of a workflow runtime component will be based in WOODSS. A spreadsheet runtime will explore a bridge to a spreadsheet system, such as the Universal Network Objects (UNO) [21], an interface-based component model of the OpenOffice system.

4 Concluding Remarks

This project combines work in Software Engineering with Semantic Web and database interoperability efforts. The main contribution is the formulation of an integrated view over these research areas, taking advantage from progress in the software components area to support development of applications in the Semantic Web. Another contribution is the four-part structure and the use of RDF to promote component specification interoperability, which will enhance component storage and indexation over different languages and standards.

The work proposed, under development, is based on previous experience in construction component-based applications for the educational domain [14], and on the use of scientific workflows, stored in databases, for reuse and interoperability of environmental applications [15].

Acknowledgments

This work was partially financed by UNIFACS, by grants from CNPq and FAPESP, and projects MCT-PRONEX SAI and CNPq WebMaps and AgroFlow.

References

1. Anastassia Ailamaki, Yannis E. Ioannidis, and Miron Livny. Scientific Workflow Management by Database Management. In *Proc. 10th IEEE International Conf. on Scientific and Statistical Database Management*, pages 190–201, 1998.
2. Felix Bachman et al. Volume II: Technical Concepts of Component-Based Software Engineering, 2nd Edition. Technical Report CMU/SEI-2000-TR-008, Carnegie Mellon University, July 2000.
3. Alex Barnell.   RDF Objects, November 2002.   http://www.hpl.hp.com/techreports/2002/HPL-2002-315.pdf, accessed on 10/2003.
4. Wolfram Conen and Reinhold Klapsing. A Logical Interpretation of RDF. *Linköping Electronic Articles in Computer and Information Science*, 5(13), 2000.   http://www.ep.liu.se/ea/cis/2000/013/.

5. Philip Dodds, editor. Sharable Content Object Reference Model (SCORM) – Version 1.2 – The SCORM Overview. Specification, Advanced Distributed Learning Initiative, October 2001. http://www.adlnet.org/screens/shares/dsp_displayfile.cfm? fileid=840, accessed on 10/2003.

6. Patrick Th. Eugster, Pascal A. Felber, Rachid Guerraoui, and Anne-Marie Kermarrec. The many faces of publish/subscribe. *ACM Comput. Surv.*, 35(2):114–131, 2003.

7. Franca Garzotto, Luca Mainetti, and Paolo Paolini. Information Reuse in Hypermedia Applications. In *Proc. of the the 7th ACM conf. on Hypertext*, pages 93–104. ACM Press, March 1996.

8. IEEE L.T.S.C. Draft Standard for Learning Object Metadata – IEEE 1484.12.1-2002, July 2002. http://ltsc.ieee.org/doc/wg12/LOM_1484_12_1_v1_Final_ Draft.pdf, accessed on 10/2003.

9. Robert Meersman and Amit P. Sheth. Special Section on Semantic Web and Data Management – Guest editor's introduction. *ACM SIGMOD Record*, 31(4):10–12, 2002.

10. Mikael Nilsson. IEEE Learning Object Metadata RDF binding, August 2002. http:// kmr.nada.kth.se/el/ims/md-lomrdf.html, accessed on 11/2003.

11. Rubén Prieto-Díaz. Classification of reusable modules. In Ted J. Biggerstaff and Alan J. Perlis, editors, *Software reusability: vol. 1, concepts and models*, pages 99–123. ACM Press, 1989.

12. Rob Raskin. Semantic Web for Earth and Environmental Terminology (SWEET). In *Proc. of NASA Earth Science Technology Conference 2003*, 2003.

13. Ann Rockley. *Fundamental Concepts of Content Reuse*, chapter 2, pages 23–42. New Riders, 2000.

14. André Santanchè and Cesar Augusto Camillo Teixeira. Anima: Promoting Component Integration in the Web. In *Proc. of 7th Brasilian Symp. on Multimedia and Hypermedia Systems*, pages 261–268, October 2001.

15. Laura A. Seffino, Claudia Bauzer Medeiros, Jansle V. Rocha, and Bei Yi. WOODSS – A spatial decision support system based on workflows. *Decision Support Systems*, 27(1-2):105–123, November 1999.

16. Jayavel Shanmugasundaram et al. A general technique for querying XML documents using a relational database system. *ACM SIGMOD Record*, 30(3), September 2001.

17. Mary Shaw and Paul C. Clements. A Field Guide to Boxology: Preliminary Classification of Architectural Styles for Software Systems. In *Proc. of the 21st International Computer Software and Applications Conference*, pages 6–13. IEEE Computer Society, 1997.

18. Michael K. Smith, Chris Welty, and Deborah L. McGuinness. OWL Web Ontology Language Guide – W3C Candidate Recommendation, August 2003. http://www.w3.org/ TR/2003/CR-owl-guide-20030818/, accessed on 11/2003.

19. Colin Smythe, editor. IMS Content Packaging Information Model. Specification, IMS Global Learning Consortium, Inc., June 2003. http://www.imsglobal.org/ content/packaging/, accessed on 11/2003.

20. Vijayan Sugumaran and Veda C. Storey. A Semantic-Based Approach to Component Retrieval. *SIGMIS Database*, 34(3):8–24, 2003.

21. Sun Microsystems. OpenOffice.org Developer's Guide, 2003. http://api. openoffice.org/docs/DevelopersGuide/DevelopersGuide.pdf, accessed on 01/2003.

22. Richard N. Taylor, Nenad Medvidovic, Kenneth M. Anderson, E. James Whitehead, Jr., Jason E. Robbins, Kari A. Nies, Peyman Oreizy, and Deborah L. Dubrow. A Component- and Message-Based Architectural Style for GUI Software. *IEEE Trans. Softw. Eng.*, 22(6):390–406, 1996.

23. Schawn Thropp and Mark McKell, editors. IMS Learning Resource Meta-Data XML Binding Specification, September 2001. `http://www.imsglobal.org/metadata/imsmdv1p2p1/`, accessed on 10/2003.
24. Amy Moormann Zaremski and Jeannette M. Wing. Signature Matching, a Tool for Using Software Libraries. *ACM Transactions on Software Engineering and Methodology*, April 1995.
25. Amy Moormann Zaremski and Jeannette M. Wing. Specification Matching of Software Components. In *Proc. of 3rd ACM SIGSOFT Symp. on the Foundations of Software Engineering*, October 1995.

Semantic Web Recommender Systems

Cai-Nicolas Ziegler

Institut für Informatik, Group DBIS,
Universität Freiburg, Germany
cziegler@informatik.uni-freiburg.de

Abstract. Research on recommender systems has primarily addressed centralized scenarios and largely ignored open, decentralized systems where remote information distribution prevails. The absence of superordinate authorities having full access and control introduces some serious issues requiring novel approaches and methods. Hence, our primary objective targets the successful deployment and integration of recommender system facilities for Semantic Web applications, making use of novel technologies and concepts and incorporating them into one coherent framework.

1 Introduction

Automated recommender systems intend to provide people with recommendations of products they might appreciate, taking into account their past product ratings profile and history of purchase or interest. Most successful systems apply so-called social filtering techniques [9], dubbed collaborative filtering [6]. These systems identify similar users and make recommendations based upon products people utterly fancy.

Unfortunately, common collaborative filtering methods fail when transplanted into decentralized scenarios. Analyzing the issues specific to these domains, we believe that two novel approaches may alleviate the prevailing problems, namely trust networks, along with trust propagation mechanisms, and taxonomy-driven profile generation and filtering. One aspect of our work hence addresses the conception of suitable components, specifically tailored to suit our decentralized setting, while another regards the seamless integration of these latter building bricks into one single, unified framework. Empirical analysis and performance evaluations are conducted at all stages.

2 Research Issues

Deploying recommender systems into the Semantic Web implies diverse, multi-faceted issues, some of them being inherent to decentralized systems in general, others being specific. Hereby, our devised Semantic Web recommender system performs all recommendation computations *locally* for one given user. Its principal difference from generic, centralized approaches refers to information storage, supposing all user and rating data *distributed* throughout the Semantic Web. Hence its decentralized nature. We thus come to identify several research issues:

W. Lindner et al. (Eds.): EDBT 2004 Workshops, LNCS 3268, pp. 78–89, 2004.
© Springer-Verlag Berlin Heidelberg 2004

- **Ontological Commitment.** Basically, the Semantic Web is made up of machine-readable content distributed all over the Web. In order to ensure that agents can understand and reason about the respective information, semantic interoperability via ontologies or common content models must be established. For instance, FOAF [5], an acronym for "Friend of a Friend", defines an ontology for establishing simple social networks and represents an open standard agents can rely upon.
- **Interaction Facilities.** Decentralized recommender systems have primarily been subject to multi-agent research projects. In suchlike settings, environment models are agent-centric, enabling agents to directly communicate with their peers and thus making synchronous message exchange feasible. The Semantic Web, being an aggregation of distributed metadata, constitutes an inherently data-centric environment model. Messages are exchanged by publishing or updating documents encoded in RDF, OWL, or similar formats. Hence, the communication becomes restricted to asynchronous message exchange only.
- **Security and Credibility.** Closed communities generally possess efficient means to control the users' identity and penalize malevolent behavior. Decentralized systems, among those peer-to-peer networks, open marketplaces and the Semantic Web, likewise, cannot prevent deception and insincerity. Spoofing and identity forging thus become facile to achieve [22]. Hence, some subjective means enabling each individual to decide which peers and content to rely upon are needed.
- **Computational Complexity and Scalability.** Centralized systems allow for estimating and limiting the community size and may thus tailor their filtering systems to ensure scalability. Note that user similarity assessment, which is an integral part of collaborative filtering [6], implies some computation-intensive processes. The Semantic Web will once contain millions of machine-readable homepages. Computing similarity measures for all these "individuals" thus becomes infeasible. Consequently, scalability can only be ensured when restricting these computations to sufficiently narrow neighborhoods. Intelligent filtering mechanisms are needed, still ensuring reasonable recall, i.e., not sacrificing too many relevant, like-minded agents.
- **Low Profile Overlap.** Interest profiles are generally represented by vectors indicating the user's opinion for every product. In order to reduce dimensionality and ensure profile overlap, some centralized systems like Ringo [20] require users to rate *small subsets* of the overall product space. These mandatory assessments, provisional tools for creating overlap-ensuring profiles, imply additional efforts for prospective users. Other recommenders, among those GroupLens and MovieLens [14], operate in domains where product sets are comparatively small. On the Semantic Web, virtually no restrictions can be imposed on agents regarding which items to rate. Hence, new approaches to ensure profile overlap are needed in order to make profile similarity measures meaningful.

3 Proposed Approach

Endeavors to ensure semantical interoperability through ontologies constitute the cornerstone of Semantic Web conception and have been subject to numerous research projects.

We do not concentrate our efforts on this aspect but suppose data compatibility from the outset. Our interest rather focuses on handling computational complexity, security, data-centric message passing, and profile vector overlap. Hereby, our approach builds upon two fundamental notions, namely taxonomy-driven interest profile assembly and trust networks. The exploitation of synergies of both intrinsically separate concepts helps us leverage recommender system facilities into the Semantic Web.

3.1   Information Model

The infrastructure of the Semantic Web defines interlinked XML-documents made up of machine-readable metadata. Our information model presented below well complies with its design goals and allows facile mapping into RDF, OWL, etc.:

- **Set of agents** $A = \{a_1, a_2, \ldots, a_n\}$. Set A contains all agents part of the community. Globally unique identifiers are assigned through URIs.
- **Set of products** $B = \{b_1, b_2, \ldots, b_m\}$. All products considered are comprised in set B. Hereby, unique identifiers may refer to product descriptions from an online shop agreed upon, such as Amazon.com, or globally accepted codes, like ISBNs in case of books.
- **Set of partial trust functions** $T = \{t_1, t_2, \ldots, t_n\}$. Every agent $a_i \in A$ has one partial trust function $t_i : A \rightarrow [-1, +1]^\perp$ that assigns continuous trust values to its peers. Functions $t_i \in A$ are partial since agents generally only rate small subsets of the overall community, hence rendering t_i sparse:

$$t_i(a_j) = \begin{cases} p, & \text{if trust}(a_i, a_j) = p \\ \perp, & \text{if no trust statement for } a_j \text{ from } a_i \end{cases} \tag{1}$$

We define high values for $t_i(a_j)$ to denote high trust from a_i in a_j, and negative values to express distrust, respectively. Values around zero indicate the absence of trust, not to be confused with explicit distrust [11].

- **Set of partial rating functions** $R = \{r_1, r_2, \ldots, r_n\}$. In addition to functions $t_i \in T$, every $a_i \in A$ has one partial function $r_i : B \rightarrow [-1, +1]^\perp$ that expresses his liking or dislike of product $b_k \in B$. No person can rate every available product, so functions $r_i \in B$ are necessarily partial.

$$r_i(b_k) = \begin{cases} p, & \text{if rates}(a_i, b_k) = p \\ \perp, & \text{if no rating for } b_k \text{ from } a_i \end{cases} \tag{2}$$

Intuitively, high positive values for $r_i(b_k)$ denote that a_i highly appreciates b_k, while negative values express dislike, respectively.

- **Taxonomy** C **over set** $D = \{d_1, d_2, \ldots, d_l\}$. Set D contains categories for product classification. Each category $d_e \in D$ represents one specific topic that products $b_k \in B$ may fall into. Topics express broad or narrow categories. The partial taxonomic order $C : D \rightarrow 2^D$ retrieves all immediate sub-categories $C(d_e) \subseteq D$ for topics $d_e \in D$. Hereby, we require that $C(d_e) \cap C(d_h) = \emptyset$ holds for all $d_e, d_h \in D, e \neq h$, hence imposing tree-like structuring, similar to single-inheritance class hierarchies known from object-oriented languages. Leaf topics d_e are topics with zero outdegree, formally $C(d_e) = \perp$, i.e., most specific categories. Furthermore, taxonomy C has

Similarity Computation. Taxonomy-driven interest profiles form the grounding for our novel filtering paradigm. Similarity computation between agents a_i, a_j, and between agents a_i and products b_k[1], respectively, requires some distance metric.

For our approach, we apply common nearest-neighbor techniques, namely Pearson correlation [6, 20] and cosine distance known from information retrieval. Hereby, profile vectors map *category* score vectors from C instead of plain product-rating vectors. High similarity evolves from interest in many identical or related branches, whereas negative correlation indicates diverging interests.

For instance, suppose a_i reads literature about Applied Mathematics only, and a_j about Algebra, then their computed similarity will be high, considering significant branch overlap from node Mathematics onward.

3.4   Recommendation Generation

We already indicated that two alternative designs are viable for post-filtering trust neighborhoods. We opt for product-user relevance, i.e., deferring supplementary neighborhood filtering into the recommendation process. We hence consider *all* peers part of the trust neighborhood, but weed out products not matching the active user a_i's profile.

The relevance of some product b_k one of a_i's trusted peers recommends then depends on various factors, the two most important aspects being the following ones:

- **Accorded trust** $t_i^c(a_j)$ **of peers** a_j **mentioning** b_k. Trust-based neighborhood formation substitutes finding nearest neighbors based upon interest similarity. Likewise, similarity ranks $c(a_i, a_j)$ become replaced by trust weights $t_i^c(a_j)$ for computing the predicted relevance of b_k for a_i.
- **Content-based relevance** $c_b(a_i, b_k)$ **of product** b_k **for user** a_i. Besides mere trustworthiness of peers a_j rating product b_k, the content-based relevance of b_k for the active user a_i is likewise important, e.g., one may consider the situation where even close friends recommend products not fitting our interest profile at all.

Since both functions, i.e., $t_i^c(a_j)$ and $c_b(a_i, b_k)$, operate on completely different scales, the conversion of these absolute weights into ranks seems appropriate. For instance, the trusted agent a_j with highest trust weight $t_i^c(a_j)$ obtains rank 1, and so forth. Likewise, the product b_k with highest similarity $c_b(a_i, b_k)$ to the active user a_i's interest profile becomes top-ranked.

Besides merging trustworthiness and content-based relevance ranks, other factors involved comprise product rating frequency and product description richness. Product rating frequency intends to reward products b_k recommended by numerous trusted peers, while description richness penalizes products bearing overly general taxonomic descriptions. The final ranks of products b_k eventually constitute the foundation for assembling top-N recommendation lists for the active user a_i.

---

[1] Supposing implicit product ratings only, the generation of taxonomy-driven profiles for products b_k equates profile generation for pseudo-user a_θ having implicitly rated b_k only.

3.5 Supplementary Fine-Tuning

Taxonomy-driven profile generation renders another mechanism, dubbed "topic diversification" [24], feasible. Hereby, our novel approach, optionally applicable on top of recommendation generation, allows rearrangement of the active user a_i's recommendation list in order to better reflect a_i's full range of interests, considering the impact of specific topics a_i implicitly declares interest in. For instance, suppose that novels classifying under Modern German Poetry have twice the share of Social Psychology in $a'i$'s reading list. Then post-processing of a_i's recommendation list by means of topic diversification procedures allows to fully account for that fact.

To our best knowledge, no similar approaches exist or have been documented in literature affiliated with recommender systems. Moreover, topic diversification becomes even more valuable when making recommendations *across* diverse domains of interest, e.g., books, DVDs, apparel, etc.

Other enhancements include considering *explicit* product ratings for recommendation generation whenever available. However, note that most scenarios only allow for collecting implicit ratings, e.g., purchase data, product mentions, etc., rather than explicit ones.

4 Real-World Deployment

Section 3.1 exposed our envisioned information infrastructure. We will show that such an architecture may actually come into life and become an integral part of the Semantic Web:

- **Social Networks.** FOAF defines machine-readable homepages based upon RDF and allows weaving acquaintance networks. Golbeck [5] proposed some modifications making FOAF support "real" trust relationships instead of mere acquaintance-ship.
- **Product Rating Information.** Moreover, FOAF networks seamlessly integrate with so-called "weblogs", which are steadily gaining momentum. These personalized "online diaries" are especially valuable with respect to product rating information. For instance, some crawlers extract certain hyperlinks from weblogs and analyze their makeup and content. Hereby, those referring to product pages from large catalogs like Amazon.com (*http://www.amazon.com*) count as implicit votes for these goods. Mappings between hyperlinks and some sort of unique identifier are required for diverse catalogs, though. Unique identifiers exist for *some* product groups like books, which are given "International Standard Book Numbers", i.e., ISBNs. Efforts to enhance weblogs with explicit, machine-readable rating information have also been proposed and are becoming increasingly popular. For instance, BLAM! (*http://www.pmbrowser.info/hublog/*) allows creating book ratings and helps embedding these into machine-readable weblogs.
- **Product Classification Taxonomies.** Besides user-centric information, i.e., agent a_i's trust relationships t_i and product ratings r_i, taxonomies for product classification play an important role within our approach. Luckily, these taxonomies exist for

certain domains. Amazon.com defines an extensive, fine-grained and deeply-nested taxonomy for books, containing thousands of topics. More important, Amazon.com provides books with subject descriptors referring to the latter taxonomy. Similar taxonomies exist for DVDs, CDs, and videos. Standardization efforts for product classification are channelled through the "United Nations Standard Products and Services Code" project (*http://www.unspsc.org/*). However, the UNSPSC's taxonomy provides much less information and nesting than, for instance, Amazon.com's taxonomy for books.

5   Experimental Setting

We created an experimental environment simulating the infrastructure proposed above. Hereby, by means of crawlers and screen scrapers, we gathered information from various trust-aware online communities like All Consuming (*http://www.allconsuming.net*), and Advogato (*http://www.advogato.org*), extracting information about approximately $10,000$ users a_i, their trust relationships t_i and implicit product ratings r_i. Ratings were obtained from All Consuming only.

Moreover, we captured Amazon.com's huge book taxonomy, made up of $13,525$ hierarchically arranged topics d_e, and categorization data about $11,031$ books b_k that All Consuming community members mentioned. Tailored crawlers search the Web for weblogs and ensure data freshness. All our experiments and empirical evaluations were based upon this "real-world" data.

6   Related Work

Recommender systems have begun attracting major research interest during the early nineties [6]. Nowadays, commercial and industrial systems are rife and wide-spread, detailed comparisons concerning features and approaches are given in [19]. Recommender systems differ from each other mainly through their filtering method. Hereby, distinctions between three types of filtering systems are made [6], namely collaborative, content-based and economic. Collaborative filtering systems [20] generate recommendations obtained from persons having similar interests. Content-based filtering only takes into account descriptions of products, based upon metadata and extracted features. Economic filtering has seen little practical application until now and exerts marginal impact only.

Modern recommender systems are hybrid, combining both content-based and collaborative filtering facilities in one single framework. Fab [2] counts among the first popular hybrid systems, more recent approaches have been depicted in [7] and [13]. Our filtering approach, comprising taxonomy-based profile generation and similarity computation, also exploits both content-based and collaborative filtering facilities. Trust networks add another supplementary level of filtering.

Initial attempts have been taken towards transplanting recommender systems into decentralized scenarios. Olsson [15] gives an extensive overview of existing approaches. Kautz et al. [9] extract implicit social network structures from the Web, using them as foundations for recommender system services operating on top of these networks. Jensen et al. [8] propose an approach called "explicit peer-based systems", which makes recommendations based upon friends' opinions.

7 Future Directions

Our past efforts have mainly focused on designing suitable trust metrics for computing trust neighborhoods [23], and conceiving metrics for making collaborative filtering applicable to decentralized architectures [22]. Moreover, we have shaped and synthesized an extensive infrastructure based upon "real-world" data from various communities and online stores.

Until now, our analysis has been largely confined to the book domain only. Future research will also include movies and other specific product groups and investigate the intrinsic differences between these groups. For instance, Amazon.com's taxonomy for DVD classification contains more topics than its book counterpart, though being less deep. We would like to better understand the impact that taxonomy structure may have upon profile generation and similarity computation.

Moreover, owing to the fact that our novel taxonomy-driven filtering approach yields excellent results compared to generic benchmark systems when dealing with information sparseness [24], we are planning to investigate our filtering paradigm's performance when applied to dense product rating datasets, likewise.

References

1. Alfarez Abdul-Rahman and Stephen Hailes. A distributed trust model. In *New Security Paradigms Workshop*, pages 48–60, Cumbria, UK, September 1997.
2. Marko Balabanović and Yoav Shoham. Fab – Content-based, collaborative recommendation. *Communications of the ACM*, 40(3):66–72, 1997.
3. Ellen Berscheid. Interpersonal attraction. In Daniel Gilbert, Susan Fiske, and Gardner Lindzey, editors, *The Handbook of Social Psychology*, volume II. McGraw-Hill, New York, NY, USA, 4th edition, 1998.
4. Thomas Beth, Malte Borcherding, and Birgit Klein. Valuation of trust in open networks. In *Proceedings of the 1994 European Symposium on Research in Computer Security*, pages 3–18, 1994.
5. Jennifer Golbeck, Bijan Parsia, and James Hendler. Trust networks on the Semantic Web. In *Proceedings of Cooperative Intelligent Agents*, Helsinki, Finland, August 2003.
6. David Goldberg, David Nichols, Brian Oki, and Douglas Terry. Using collaborative filtering to weave an information tapestry. *Communications of the ACM*, 35(12):61–70, 1992.
7. Zan Huang, Wingyan Chung, Thian-Huat Ong, and Hsinchun Chen. A graph-based recommender system for digital library. In *Proceedings of the Second ACM/IEEE-CS Joint Conference on Digital Libraries*, pages 65–73, Portland, OR, USA, 2002. ACM Press.
8. Carlos Jensen, John Davis, and Shelly Farnham. Finding others online: Reputation systems for social online spaces. In *Proceedings of the SIGCHI Conference on Human Factors in Computing Systems*, pages 447–454, Minneapolis, MN, USA, 2002. ACM Press.
9. Henry Kautz, Bart Selman, and Mehul Shah. Referral Web: Combining social networks and collaborative filtering. *Communications of the ACM*, 40(3):63–65, March 1997.

10. Raph Levien and Alexander Aiken. Attack-resistant trust metrics for public key certification. In *Proceedings of the 7th USENIX Security Symposium*, San Antonio, TX, USA, January 1998.

11. Stephen Marsh. *Formalising Trust as a Computational Concept*. PhD thesis, Department of Mathematics and Computer Science, University of Stirling, Stirling, UK, 1994.

12. Paolo Massa and Bobby Bhattacharjee. Using trust in recommender systems: an experimental analysis. In Christian Jensen, Stefan Poslad, and Theodosis Dimitrakos, editors, *Proceedings of the 2nd International Conference on Trust Management*, volume 2995 of *LNCS*, Oxford, UK, March 2004. Springer-Verlag.

13. Stuart Middleton, Harith Alani, Nigel Shadbolt, and David De Roure. Exploiting synergy between ontologies and recommender systems. In *Proceedings of the WWW2002 International Workshop on the Semantic Web*, volume 55 of *CEUR Workshop Proceedings*, Maui, HW, USA, May 2002.

14. Bradley Miller, Istvan Albert, Shyong Lam, Joseph Konstan, and John Riedl. MovieLens unplugged: Experiences with an occasionally connected recommender system. In *Proceedings of the ACM 2003 Conference on Intelligent User Interfaces (Accepted Poster)*, Chapel Hill, NC, USA, 2003. ACM.

15. Tomas Olsson. *Bootstrapping and Decentralizing Recommender Systems*. PhD thesis, Uppsala University, Uppsala, Sweden, 2003.

16. Michael O'Mahony, Neil Hurley, Nicolas Kushmerick, and Guénolé Silvestre. Collaborative recommendation: A robustness analysis. *ACM Transactions on Internet Technology*, 4(3), August 2004.

17. Lawrence Page, Sergey Brin, Rajeev Motwani, and Terry Winograd. The PageRank citation ranking: Bringing order to the Web. Technical report, Stanford Digital Library Technologies Project, 1998.

18. Ross Quillian. Semantic memory. In Marvin Minsky, editor, *Semantic Information Processing*, pages 227–270. MIT Press, Boston, MA, USA, 1968.

19. Ben Schafer, Joseph Konstan, and John Riedl. Recommender systems in e-commerce. In *Proceedings of the 1st ACM Conference on Electronic Commerce*, pages 158–166, Denver, CO, USA, 1999. ACM Press.

20. Upendra Shardanand and Patti Maes. Social information filtering: Algorithms for automating "word of mouth". In *Proceedings of the ACM CHI'95 Conference on Human Factors in Computing Systems*, volume 1, pages 210–217, 1995.

21. Rashmi Sinha and Kirsten Swearingen. Comparing recommendations made by online systems and friends. In *Proceedings of the DELOS-NSF Workshop on Personalization and Recommender Systems in Digital Libraries*, Dublin, Ireland, June 2001.

22. Cai-Nicolas Ziegler and Georg Lausen. Analyzing correlation between trust and user similarity in online communities. In Christian Jensen, Stefan Poslad, and Theodosis Dimitrakos, editors, *Proceedings of the 2nd International Conference on Trust Management*, volume 2995 of *LNCS*, pages 251–265, Oxford, UK, March 2004. Springer-Verlag.

23. Cai-Nicolas Ziegler and Georg Lausen. Spreading activation models for trust propagation. In *Proceedings of the IEEE International Conference on e-Technology, e-Commerce, and e-Service*, Taipei, Taiwan, March 2004. IEEE Computer Society Press.

24. Cai-Nicolas Ziegler, Georg Lausen, and Lars Schmidt-Thieme. Taxonomy-driven computation of product recommendations, 2004. Submitted for publication.

Trust Negotiation Systems

Anna Cinzia Squicciarini

Dipartimento di Informatica e Comunicazione,
Università degli Studi di Milano, Milano
squiccia@dico.unimi.it

Abstract. Trust negotiation is a promising approach for establishing trust in open systems like the Internet, where sensitive interactions may often occur between entities with no prior knowledge of each other. In this paper we present the work carried on so far in the area of trust negotiation as part of the Ph.D. activity. More precisely, we describe Trust-$\mathcal{X}$, the XML based framework for trust negotiations we have developed, and emphasize the open issues to be covered.

1   Introduction

The extensive use of the web for exchanging information and requiring or offering services require to deeply redesign the way access control is usually performed. In a conventional system, the identity of subjects is the main common access control mechanism used to make authorization decisions. Every entity that can access such systems has one or more identities in that domain. The underlying assumption is that entities in the system already know each other, and no trust issue arises. Therefore, the system relies on party identities to grant or deny authorizations. Even if in some contexts there is trust issue, like in traditional client-server systems, the trust establishment is often one-directional, in the sense that the server is a well-known service provider. Before requesting any service, the client must prove it is qualified for that service. In this case, trust establishment is often handled by uni-directional access control methods.

This paradigm is not suitable for open environments, where most of the interactions occur between strangers that do not know each other before the interaction takes place. The entities need not only to authenticate each other, but also to trust each other in order to exchange sensitive information and resources. Interactions are further complicated by the fact that usually the interacting entities belong to different security domains and/or do not have any pre existing relationships. In order to address such issues, *trust negotiation* [10] has been proposed as a new authorization model for open systems. The goal of a trust negotiation is to allow parties having no pre existing relationship to confidently perform sensitive interactions. In trust negotiation mutual trust is established through mutual exchange of properties of the parties, certified by digital credentials. Disclosure of credentials, in turn, is usually protected through the use of policies that specify which credentials must be received before the requested credential can be disclosed.

In this paper we present the work carried on in the area of trust negotiation as part of the Ph.D. activity. The remainder of this paper is organized as follows. In Section 2 we summarize the trust negotiation model, and discuss relevant open issues to be covered.

W. Lindner et al. (Eds.): EDBT 2004 Workshops, LNCS 3268, pp. 90–99, 2004.

In Section 3 we give an overview of Trust-$\mathcal{X}$, the core system for support of negotiations we have developed in the beginning of our Ph.D. activity. In Section 4 we focus on the new extensions we have recently added to the system, on the basis of the analysis performed over this preliminary version and an in-depth comparison of our system with the existing ones. Finally in Section 5 we point out the main issues we plan to investigate in future.

2 Open Issues in Trust Negotiations

Trust negotiation is an emerging and promising approach to establish trust between strangers in order to exchange sensitive resources. The notion of *resource* in trust negotiation comprises any sensitive object (e.g., health records, credit card numbers) whose disclosure needs to be protected. The approach of automated trust negotiation essentially differs from traditional identity based access control systems mainly in the following aspects:

- The involved parties are unknown to each other and usually belong to different security domains. Trust is dynamically established on the basis of parties properties, which are implemented using digital credentials. Digital credentials must be unforgeable and verifiable. To ensure such properties credentials are digitally signed using PKI [11]. Typically, a digital credential contains a set of attributes specified using name/value pairs. The document is signed using the issuer's private key and can be verified using the issuer's public key. The X.509 V3 standard [9] is the most used technique for encoding digital credentials.
- Every party can define ad hoc access control policies to control sensitive resource disclosure, known as *disclosure policies*. Disclosure policies inform a negotiation counterpart of the credentials to disclose to advance the negotiation. Essentially, disclosure policies state the conditions that the counterpart should satisfy, and are expressed as constraints against the credentials possessed and on associated attributes. Further, depending on their contents, credentials may be sensitive. For example, a credential may contain non-public attributes about an individual such as a credit card number.
- Parties establish trust directly without involving trusted third parties, other than credential issuers. The trust negotiation approach can employ a peer-to-peer architecture: all entities may possess sensitive resources to be protected and can act as clients as well as servers during different negotiations. Thus, they all must be equipped with a compliant negotiation system. Trust negotiation is triggered when a party acting as the client makes a request to the party acting as a server and controlling access to a sensitive resource according to an access control policy. Trust is thus incrementally built by iteratively disclosing digital credentials, in order to verify properties of the negotiating parties.
- The runtime system for trust negotiation includes a negotiation manager at each party to control all aspects of a negotiation. The manager may adopt a *strategy* to determine which credentials to disclose and when. The core of the system is a *compliance checker*, the module empowered to test whether disclosure policies are satisfied.

Although quite simple at first glance, a number of interesting theoretical and practical issues arise when dealing with trust negotiation systems, concerning aspects like policy language expressiveness and the associated infrastructures supporting trust negotiation processes. A first issue concerns the development of a solid and theoretical underpinning theory for trust languages and algorithms. A trust negotiation language should be powerful enough to express a wide range of protection requirements, including support for credential chains and authentication of the submitter. For what concern negotiation systems, the challenge is to devise solutions trading off among several requirements, often in conflict with each other. On one hand such systems should be flexible, scalable and portable, on the other hand they should support advanced functions, such as support for credential chains, authentication of multiple identities, complex compliance checker mode whose efficient implementation is often difficult. In particular, the compliance checker should be able to interpret a remote policy and check whether there exists a set of local credentials that satisfy the received policy, and the communication and computation costs should be not prohibitive. The system should also be strong enough to limit damages caused by intruders attacks or interception. Finally, completeness and termination are also desiderable properties: a negotiation should always succeed whenever possible, and efficiently terminate whenever a successful negotiation is not possible.

Trust negotiation for web-based applications has been recognized as an interesting and challenge research area to explore, and it has been the subject to intensive work in the recent years. As a result, a variety of systems and prototypes have been recently developed [6, 8, 12, 14]. However, all these proposals mainly focus on one of the aspects of trust negotiation, such as for instance policy and credential specification, or the selection of the negotiation strategy, but none of them provide a comprehensive solution to trust negotiation. Furthermore, most of the systems are based on some unrealistic assumptions that limit the applicability of the approach. For instance, TN systems usually assume that all the credentials associated with a party are at the user sites. However, in a large number of application environments credential storage is not centralized. None of the existing systems address how to obtain credentials, assuming that the entity disclosing credentials has full responsibility for obtaining and caching them locally. No real protection against attacks on negotiating parties is provided, such as credential theft or man identity theft [11]. The shortcomings we have identified in trust negotiation systems grew out of our analysis of existing trust negotiation systems [6, 8, 12, 14].

Such survey [3] led us devising Trust-$\mathcal{X}$, an XML-based framework supporting trust negotiation in a comprehensive and sound manner. In designing the framework we were first guided by the design criteria outlined in [10]: our goal was to address many of the trust negotiation requirements identified by the authors. In addition to the desiderata referred in [10], we have identified other dimensions in [3], such as the efficiency and the need of privacy protection mechanisms. We further elaborate on such issues and the solutions we have devised in next sections.

3   Core Trust-$\mathcal{X}$

Trust-$\mathcal{X}$ aims at providing a comprehensive infrastructure for trust negotiation, composed by a complete and expressive syntax formalized by the most used representation language (e.g. XML) and supported by an efficient and modular engine. The language, called $\mathcal{X}$-TNL, has been presented in [4] and has been developed to provide a powerful and complete language supporting negotiations. $\mathcal{X}$-TNL *certificates* are the means to convey information about the profile of the parties involved in the negotiation. A certificate can be either a *credential* or a *declaration*. The notion of certificate allows us to better support information exchange, and distinguish from certificates that need a digital signature of Authorities and those where digital signature is of the owner (owner and issuer are the same entity). A credential is a set of $\mathcal{X}$ properties of a party certified by a Certification Authority (CA) and digitally signed by the issuer, according to the standard defined by W3C for XML Signatures [1]. $\mathcal{X}$-TNL simplifies the task of credential specification because it provides a set of templates called *credential types*, for the specification of credentials with similar structure. A credential type is modeled as a DTD and a credential as a valid document with respect to the corresponding credential type.

Declarations, instead, are set of data without any certification, which use improves language flexibility and expressive power. Declarations, indeed, can encode data providing auxiliary information that are commonly required during negotiation process and that can not be modeled by credentials. (Examples of these information regard personal preferences and needs). All certificates associated with a party are collected into a unique XML document, called $\mathcal{X}$-$Profile$. Each $\mathcal{X}$-Profile is organized into $Data\ sets$, to optimize $\mathcal{X}$-profile organization. Each data set collects a class of credentials and declarations referring to a particular aspect of the life of their owner, and can thus facilitate certificate retrieval and exchange during negotiation.

A fundamental construct of $\mathcal{X}$-TNL is given by disclosure policies, that encode security requirements. Disclosure policies state the conditions under which a resource can be released during a negotiation. Conditions are expressed as constraints on the certificates possessed by the parties involved in the negotiation and on their attributes. Each party adopts its own Trust-$\mathcal{X}$ disclosure policies to regulate release of local information (that is, credentials or even policies through policy chains) and access to services. Similar to certificates, disclosure policies are encoded using XML. Additionally, Trust-$\mathcal{X}$ policies have been formalized as logical rules, to simplify the encoding of compliance checker and runtime systems algorithms. Expressing credentials and security policies using XML has several advantages. First, the protection of Web data and their security related information is uniform, in that credentials and policies are XML documents and thus can be protected using the same mechanisms developed for the protection of conventional XML documents. Furthermore, the use of an XML formalism for specifying credentials facilitates credential submission and distribution, as well as their verification by use of a query language such as XQuery [1]. Also, $\mathcal{X}$-TNL addresses the problem of vocabulary agreement, by using XML Namespaces. The use of namespaces combined with the certificate type system helps trust negotiation software to correctly interpret different credentials, even if they are issued by entities which do not share a common ontology.

Trust-$\mathcal{X}$ also comprises an architecture for negotiation management which is symmetric and peer-to-peer, as shown in Figure 1. A Trust-$\mathcal{X}$ negotiation consists of a set of phases, sequentially executed. The idea is to disclose policies at first, in order to limit

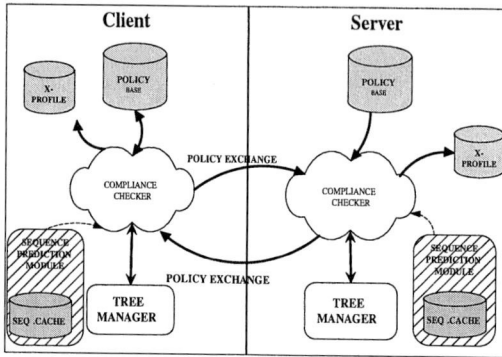

Fig. 1. Architecture for Trust-$\mathcal{X}$. Modules supported only by the Extended Trust-$\mathcal{X}$ are shadowed

credential release, and then disclose only those credentials that are necessary for the negotiation success. This distinction results in an effective protection of all the resources involved during negotiations: certificates and services are disclosed only after a complete counterpart policies evaluation, that is, only when the parties have found a sequence of certificate disclosure that make it possible to release the requested resource. The key phase of a Trust-$\mathcal{X}$ negotiation is thus the policy evaluation phase which consists of a bilateral and ordered policy exchange. The goal is to determine a sequence of credentials, called *trust sequence*, satisfying disclosure policies of both parties. During this phase, both client and server communicate disclosure policies adopted for the involved resources, until both client and server determine one or more set of policies that can be satisfied for all the resources and/or certificates involved. The policy evaluation phase is mostly executed by the *Compliance Checker*, whose goal is the evaluation of remote policies with respect to local policies and certificates,[1] and the selection of the strategy for carrying out the remainder of the negotiation.

More precisely, the flow of operations executed by the various Trust-$\mathcal{X}$ modules for processing a remote disclosure policy is sketched in Figure 2. To simplify the process a

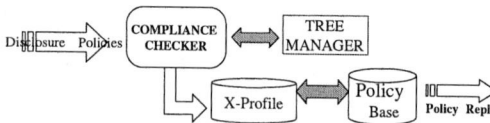

Fig. 2. Processing a disclosure policy

data structure is used, the *negotiation tree*, managed by the *tree manager*. A negotiation tree keeps track of the progress of the policy exchange, specifying a set of *negotiation*

---

[1] Certificates can be locally available in the $\mathcal{X}$-Profile or can be retrieved through certificate chains.

paths, where each path denotes a possible trust sequence. The path also keeps track of which certificates may contribute to the success of the negotiation, and of the correct order of certificate exchange. The policy evaluation phase ends when at least one trust sequence (corresponding to a path in the tree) is found, if there is compatibility between the policies of the parties. Once a trust sequence has been determined, the credential exchange phase is effectively executed. Functions required to carry out certificate disclosure include verification of certificate contents, checking for revocation, authentication of ownership (for credentials). The process ends with the disclosure of the requested resource or, if any unforeseen event happens, an interruption.

4   Extended Trust-$\mathcal{X}$

Although quite comprehensive and innovative, Trust-$\mathcal{X}$, as it was initially designed, had some missing features and weaknesses. For example, no mechanisms for efficiently carrying on negotiations was provided and a limited number of strategies were supported. No confidentiality of policies was actually achieved. Further, a deep analysis of our proposal let us understand that deferring the actual disclosure of certificates represented a potential privacy breach, since there are no guarantees about counterpart honesty until the end of the process. During policy exchange it was no possible to determine whether a party was lying or not until the actual credentials disclosure. Thus, the receiver might infer that the counterpart can satisfy the request, obtaining clues about the possession of sensitive credentials, even if it never actually obtains the credential. As a result, once a certificate offer appeared in a potential solution in the policy evaluation stage, the other party is practically free to invent policies and false promises to extract that certificate later during a failing certificate exchange phase. On the basis of such analysis the initial version of Trust-$\mathcal{X}$ has been enhanced in various ways, to both improve negotiation efficiency and flexibility as well as to support privacy and policies protection. We have then compared the resulting system with the other relevant negotiation frameworks. A summary of our analysis is reported in Table 1. As shown, all the presented languages have a well formed semantics, and all but TPL are monotonic. The specification of credential combination for expressing policies is also a requirement satisfied by all the proposed languages. The remaining requirements are all supported only by subsets of the analyzed systems. There is no system that address all requirements, however, thanks to the enhancements in the extended version, Trust-$\mathcal{X}$ results one of the best suited framework for trust negotiations.

Efficiency. Although the scenario we refer to is an open environment, we have identified a number of contexts in which the same type of negotiations will be likely executed several times between the same parties. In such contexts negotiations may be carried out following efficient and fast procedures, without jeopardizing negotiation security or resource protection. To support both trust and efficient negotiations, Trust-$\mathcal{X}$ has thus been extended to include the notion of *trust ticket* as well as the concept of *sequence caching*.

Trust tickets are a powerful means to reduce as much as possible the number of certificates and policies that need to be exchanged during negotiations. Trust tickets are

Table 1. Comparison of Trust-$\mathcal{X}$ with trust negotiation systems (Key: Y-Yes, N- No, P-Partial support)

Requirements	PSPL	TPL	Trust- X	KeyNote	Trust Builder
Well-defined semantics	Y	Y	**Y**	Y	Y
Monotonicity	Y	Y (DTPL)	**Y**	Y	Y
Credential combinations	Y	Y	**Y**	Y	Y
Constraints on attribute values	Y	Y	**Y**	N	Y
Inter-credential constraints	Y	Y	**Y**	N	Y
Credential chains	Y	Y	**P**	N	N
Authentication	Y	N	N	N	N
Who submits?	N	N	**N**	N	N
Sensitive Policies	Y	N	**Y**	N	Y
Compliance Checker Modes	Y	P	**Y**	N	P
Credential Validity	Y	Y	**Y**	Y	Y
Credential ownership	N	N	**P**	N	Y
Unified formalism	N	Y	**Y**	Y	N
Interoperable language	N	Y	**Y**	Y	N
Fast policy evaluation	N	N	**Y**	N	N

generated by each of the involved parties at the end of a successful negotiation and issued to the corresponding counterpart and locally stored by their owners into their $\mathcal{X}$- Profile, in a specific Data Set. A trust ticket certifies that parties have already successfully ended a negotiation for that resource, that is, they possess the necessary certificates to acquire the resource. The idea is that when a party asks for a resource, it can first be asked for a trust ticket for that resource. In this way parties can easily prove that they are trusted entities and thus they have all the requirements for successfully negotiating the requested resource. Note that the aim of trust tickets is completely different from that of tickets used by authentication services (e.g., Kerberos [11]). Trust tickets are used to certify that two parties have already successfully negotiated a resource and thus subsequent negotiations for the same resource can be simplified. By contrast, the ticket mechanism exploited by authentication services is not used to grant accesses to a resource. Rather, it is only used to denote that a client has been authenticated by the authentication server. Another mechanism we have introduced to efficiently carry on negotiations is based on the concept of *sequence caching*. By analyzing common trust negotiation applications, we have realized that in many scenarios there will be standard, off-the-shelf policies available for common, widely used resources (e.g., VISA cards, passports). In case of negotiations involving these common resources the sequences of certificates to be disclosed will be only regulated by such standard and predictable policies. In such cases it is possible to cache the sequences of certificates more often exchanged, instead of recalculating them for each negotiation. To better manage sequence reuse and storage each cached sequence is complemented by a set of additional information, to be used to determine the sequence usage. Under this approach during a negotiation, upon the end of introductory phase, a trust sequence previously cached is thus suggested by one of the parties. The applicability of a sequence is verified on the basis of the counterpart information collected during the first negotiation interactions. To support sequence caching, the basic architecture of Trust-$\mathcal{X}$, as shown in Figure 1, had to be consequently modified, by the addition of a module in charge of caching and suggesting the sequences. Such module, named *sequence prediction module*, consists of two main components: the cache memory and the prediction algorithm, which verifies whether this strategy can be applied to a specific negotiation. The cache memory collects all trust sequences recently executed that can be directly reused.

Policy Protection. Disclosure policies play a key role in trust negotiation. Unlike traditional decentralized systems, where policies are public or immediately available, disclosure policies may need to be disclosed gradually during negotiations, according to the level of trust reached so far by the parties. As pointed our by a number of researchers involved in the trust negotiation area [12–14], realistic disclosure policies tend indeed to contain sensitive information, because the details of a policy for disclosure certain set of credentials provide hints about credential content. Thus, to avoid unnecessary information leakage, in [2] we have introduced the concept of *policy prerequisites*. The idea of policy preconditions is to protect sensitive policies by introducing an order in policy disclosure. A disclosure policy is now specified by a possibly empty set of policy preconditions and a rule. The rule specifies which properties a party should possess either for obtaining access to a resource managed by the other party or for letting the other party to disclose the subsequent policy for the same resource. Policies belonging to a precondition set are related to the same resource of the policy with which they are associated. A further relevant use of precondition policies is that protection needs for a resource can be organized according to several policies logically linked (one policy is a precondition for the following and so on) and gradually disclosed during the policy evaluation phase of a negotiation. Modeling policy protection adds complexity to the algorithms and data structures proposed in the first version of Trust-$\mathcal{X}$. The *negotiation tree* indeed has now to keep track of the order in which the nodes should be considered, on the basis of the policies precondition satisfaction. Further, determining a solution is now more complex since it requires to find a portion of the tree, named *view*, denoting a sequence of certificates which corresponding *chain of policies* are all satisfied.[2]

Privacy Protection. Another issue we have recently investigated concerns privacy [5], since it is today one of the major concerns of users exchanging information through the Web. Indeed, one of the main weakness of trust negotiation systems is the lack of control or safeguard of personal information once it has been disclosed. Nothing is usually specified about the use of the information disclosed during a negotiation. Sensitive information obtained during the negotiation process may be distributed or sold to unauthorized parties later on. Another issue related with privacy arises because of sensitive attributes (e.g., age, credit rating and so on). A credential may contain several sensitive attributes, and very often just a subset of them is required to satisfy a counterpart policy. However, when a credential is exchanged, the receiver anyway gathers all the information contained in the credential. On the basis of such analysis, we have identified a number of innovative features that may be added to the Trust-$\mathcal{X}$ system, for preventing information leakage and limit privacy vulnerability. Such features include the support

---

[2] The formalization and a suite of algorithms supporting such approach can be found in [2].

different credential formats, each of which may provide a different degree of privacy protection, the notion of *context* associated with a policy, which allows one to both express privacy policies and to convey information which can be used to speed up the negotiation process. We also have begun to incorporate of our framework with the P3P [7] platform to support automated privacy protection.

5 Future Work

We plan to extend the work carried on so far in the area of trust negotiations along several directions. For what concern privacy, we wish to provide full support for P3P policies, to be exchanged at various steps of the negotiation. Our goal is, following the W3C guiding principle, to built the P3P system into a framework designed to facilitate data transfer. We are currently refining the suite of strategies supported by Trust-$\mathcal{X}$, to allow one to trade-off among efficiency, robustness, and privacy requirements. Other extensions include the development of mechanisms and modules to semi-automatically design privacy policies to be associated with disclosure policies, and techniques for recovery upon negotiation failures. Another interesting issue we will explore concerns the use of Trust-$\mathcal{X}$ in mobile environments. Although the problem of trust negotiations performed using desktop computers has been thoroughly explored, the issue of negotiations involving mobile devices is still an unexplored research area. This is anyway a promising and challenging research area, since it is expected that the number of wireless clients accessing Internet will rapidly increase in the next few years leading to an environment where the number of wireless clients accessing the Internet to perform mobile transactions will greatly exceed the number of clients accessing the Internet through networked computers. The development of a system supporting negotiations for mobile users presents significant challenges, mainly arising from the need of migrating trust negotiation concepts and their complex requirements into a mobile context. In this direction, we have identified a number of possible approaches to support mobile trust negotiations. Extending negotiation systems for the management of mobile users requires, for instance, to provide resource-compatibility with the resource constrained devices, that typically characterize these systems. We have already developed a prototype of core Trust-$\mathcal{X}$ on a platform based on Java and the Oracle DBMS. Future work also includes a full implementation of the system, to perform an extensive evaluation of the proposed strategies. Such prototype system will allow us to develop a systematic benchmark to asses the system performance under a variety of conditions.

Acknowledgments. I would like to thank my thesis advisors Professor Elisa Bertino of Purdue University, and Professor Elena Ferrari of University of Insubria, Como, and the TrustCom project for the financial support.

References

1. World Wide Web Consortium. http://www.w3.org/.
2. Elisa Bertino, Elena Ferrari, and Anna C. Squicciarini. Trust-$\mathcal{X}$ – A Peer to Peer Framework for Trust Establishment. To appear in TKDE, Transactions on Knowledge and Data Engineering, July 2004.

3. Elisa Bertino, Elena Ferrari, and Anna C. Squicciarini. Trust negotiations: Concepts, systems and languages. To appear in IEEE CISE, July 2004.
4. Elisa Bertino, Elena Ferrari, and Anna C. Squicciarini. $\mathcal{X}$-TNL – An XML based language for trust negotiations. In *Proc. 4th IEEE Int. Workshop on Policies for Distributed Systems and Networks (POLICY 2003)*, pages 81–84, 2003.
5. Elisa Bertino, Elena Ferrari, and Anna C. Squicciarini. Privacy preserving trust negotiation. In *4th Privacy Enhancing Technologies Workshop (Pet)*, May 2004.
6. Piero A. Bonatti and Pierangela Samarati. Regulating access services and information release on the Web. In *CCS 2000 Proc.*, pages 134–143, 2000.
7. Lorrie Cranor, Marc Langheinrich, Massimo Marchiori, Martin Presler-Marshall, and Joseph Reagle. The Platform for Privacy Preferences 1.0 (P3P1.0) Specification. W3C Recommendation, World Wide Web Consortium, April 2002. http://www.w3.org/TR/P3P.
8. Amir Herzberg, Yosi Mass, Joris Michaeli, Dalit Naor, and Yiftach Ravid. Access control meets public infrastructure, or: Assigning roles to strangers. In *S&P 2000 Proc.*, 2000.
9. Russell Housley, Tim Polk, Warwick Ford, and David Solo. Internet X.509 Public Key Infrastructure Certificate and certificate revocation list (CRL) profile. RFC 3280, Network Working Group, April 2002.
10. Kent E. Seamons, Marianne Winslett, Ting Yu, Bryan Smith, Evan Child, Jared Jacobson, Hyrum Mills, and Lina Yu. Requirements for policy languages for trust negotiation. In *POLICY 2002 Proc.*, pages 68–79, 2002.
11. William Stallings. *Cryptography and Network Security: Principles and Practice*. Prentice Hall, second edition, 1999.
12. William H. Winsborough and Ninghui Li. Protecting sensitive attributes in automated trust negotiation. In *WPES 2002 Proc.*, pages 41–51, 2002.
13. Ting Yu and Marianne Winslett. A unified Scheme for Resource protection in Automated Trust Negotiation. In *S&P 2003 Proc.*, pages 110–122, 2003.
14. Ting Yu, Marianne Winslett, and Kent E. Seamons. Supporting structured credentials and sensitive policies through interoperable strategies for automated trust negotiation. *ACM Transactions on Information and System Security*, 6(1):1–42, 2003.

Continuous Query Processing
in Spatio-Temporal Databases

Mohamed F. Mokbel

Dept. of Computer Sciences, Purdue University, West Lafayette IN, USA
mokbel@cs.purdue.edu

Abstract. In this paper, we aim to develop a framework for continuous query processing in spatio-temporal databases. The proposed framework distinguishes itself from other query processors by employing two main paradigms: (1) Scalability in terms of the number of concurrent continuous spatio-temporal queries. (2) Incremental evaluation of continuous spatio-temporal queries. Scalability is achieved thorough employing a *shared execution* paradigm. Incremental evaluation is achieved through computing only the updates to the previously reported answer. We distinguish between two types of updates; *positive* updates and *negative* updates. Positive or negative updates indicate that a certain object should be added to or removed from the previously reported answer, respectively. The proposed framework is applicable to a wide variety of continuous spatio-temporal queries where we do not have any constraints about the mutability of objects and queries (i.e., both objects and queries can be either stationary or moving) or the movement representation (i.e., movement can be represented either by sampling or trajectory).

1 Introduction

The rapid increase of spatio-temporal applications calls for new query processing techniques to deal with both the spatial and temporal domains. Examples of spatio-temporal applications include location-aware services, traffic monitoring, enhanced 911 service, and multimedia databases. Unlike traditional databases, spatio-temporal databases have the following distinguishing characteristics: (1) Most of spatio-temporal queries are continuous in nature. Unlike snapshot queries that are evaluated only once, continuous queries require continuous evaluation as the query result becomes invalid with the change of information [33]. (2) A large number of mobile and stationary objects, and consequently a large number of mobile and stationary concurrent continuous queries. (3) Any delay of the query response results in an obsolete answer. For example, consider a query that asks about the moving objects that lie in a certain region. If the query answer is delayed, the answer may be outdated where objects are continuously changing their locations.

Spatio-temporal databases need to support a wide variety of continuous spatio-temporal queries. For example, a continuous spatio-temporal range query may have various forms depending on the mutability of objects and queries. In addition, a range query may ask about the past, present, or the future. A naive way to process continuous

W. Lindner et al. (Eds.): EDBT 2004 Workshops, LNCS 3268, pp. 100–111, 2004.

spatio-temporal queries is to abstract the continuous queries into a series of snapshot spatio-temporal queries. Snapshot queries are issued to the server (e.g., a location-aware server) every T seconds. The naive approach incurs redundant processing where there may be only a slight change in the query answer between any two consecutive evaluations.

1.1 Motivation

The main objective in my PhD is to build a location-aware server [1, 18, 21] that has the ability to efficiently process a large number of stationary and moving objects and queries. In our attempt to build the location-aware server [1], we face the following challenges:

– Most of the existing query processing techniques focus on solving special cases of continuous spatio-temporal queries, e.g., [28, 30, 35, 36] are valid only for moving queries on stationary objects, [4, 8, 10, 23] are valid only for stationary range queries. Also, [15, 17, 23, 28] are valid only for sampling while [2, 25, 30, 31] require a trajectory representation. Trying to support a wide variety of spatio-temporal queries in a location-aware server results in implementing a variety of specific algorithms with different access structures. Maintaining different access structures and algorithms degrades the performance of the location-aware server.

– Most of the existing spatio-temporal algorithms focus on evaluating only one spatio-temporal query (e.g., [2, 14, 16, 28, 32, 30, 35, 36]). In a typical location-aware server [1, 18], there is a huge number of concurrently outstanding continuous spatio-temporal queries. Handling each query as an individual entity dramatically degrades the performance of the location-aware server.

– Most of the existing algorithms for continuous spatio-temporal queries model the continuous queries as a series of snapshot queries. Different approaches (e.g., *valid time* [36], *valid region* [35], *safe region* [23], *safe period* [8], *No-Action* region [34], and *trajectory model* [30]) are employed to allow for longer time intervals T between any two consecutive evaluations of spatio-temporal queries. Reissuing the spatio-temporal queries, even with longer time intervals, incurs redundant processing between each two consecutive executions, hence degrading the performance of a location-aware server.

– Most of the existing algorithms for continuous spatio-temporal queries require that the location-aware server sends a complete answer to the client with each reevaluation. In a typical location-aware server, query results are sent to clients via satellite servers [11]. Sending the whole answer each time consumes the network bandwidth and results in network congestion at the server side, thus degrading the ability of the server to process more queries.

Based on these challenges, we specify our goal as not to propose another spatio-temporal algorithm for very specific spatio-temporal queries. Instead, we aim to develop a general framework for spatio-temporal query processing that is scalable, incremental, and applicable to a wide variety of spatio-temporal queries.

1.2   The PhD Contribution

Although my PhD contributions are geared towards building scalable location-aware servers [1, 18], the main ideas and concepts can be utilized individually or together for any other spatio-temporal application. In general, the PhD contributions can be summarized as follows:

1. We go beyond the idea of reevaluating continuous spatio-temporal queries for every change of information. Instead, we employ an incremental evaluation paradigm that updates the query answer rather than evaluating it. By employing the incremental evaluation paradigm, we achieve two goals: (a) Reducing the required computations to evaluate continuous spatio-temporal queries. (b) Better utilization of the network bandwidth where we limit the data sent to queries to only the updates rather than the whole query answer.
2. We distinguish between two types of updates; *positive* updates and *negative* updates. Positive or negative updates indicate that a certain object should be added to or removed from the previously reported answer, respectively.
3. We support a wide variety of continuous spatio-temporal queries through a general framework. The proposed framework does not make any assumptions about the mutability of objects and queries or the movement representation.
4. We employ the *shared execution* paradigm as a means of achieving scalability in terms of the number of concurrently executed continuous queries.
5. We employ a recovery algorithm for *out-of-sync* clients; clients that are disconnected from the server for a short period of time. The recovery algorithm aims to keep out-of-sync clients updated with their results whenever they reconnect to the system.
6. We aim to realize our spatio-temporal query processor inside the Predator [27] database management system. In addition, we use a storage manager that is based on Shore [5] to store information and access structures for moving objects and moving queries.

1.3   Environment

This PhD work is part of the *Pervasive Location-Aware Computing Environments* project (PLACE, for short) [1], developed at Purdue University. The PLACE server receives information from moving objects and moving queries through GPS-like devices. In addition, the PLACE server keeps track of the locations of stationary objects (e.g., gas stations, hospitals, etc.). Once a moving object or query sends new information, the old information becomes persistent and is stored in a repository server.

The PLACE server [21] is implemented on top of the NILE query processor [13]; an extended version of the PREDATOR database management system [27] to handle continuously incoming data. For more details about the architecture and the query processor of the PLACE server, the reader is referred to [18, 20, 21].

2   Related Work

Most of the recent research in spatio-temporal query processing (e.g., [2, 16, 28, 30, 35, 36]) focus on continuously evaluating one spatio-temporal query at a time. Issues of scalability, incremental evaluation, mutability of both objects and queries, and client overhead are examples of challenges that either are overlooked wholly or partially by these approaches. Mainly, three different approaches are investigated: (1) The validity of the results. With each query answer, the server returns a valid time [36] or a valid region [35] of the answer. Once the valid time is expired or the client goes out of the valid region, the client resubmits the continuous query for reevaluation. The time T between each two consecutive evaluations relies on the accuracy of the valid time and the valid region. (2) Caching the results. The main idea is to cache the previous result either in the client side [28] or in the server side [16]. Previously cached results are used to prune the search for the new results of k-nearest-neighbor queries [28] and range queries [16]. (3) Precomputing the result. If the trajectory of the query movement is known apriori, then by using computational geometry for stationary objects [30] or velocity information for moving objects [16], we can identify which objects will be nearest-neighbors [2, 30] to or within a range [16, 25] from the query trajectory. If the trajectory information is changed, then the query needs to be reevaluated. The time T between each two consecutive evaluations relies on the accuracy of determining the future trajectory.

There is lot of research in optimizing the execution of multiple queries in traditional databases [26], continuous web queries [7], and continuous streaming queries [6, 12]. Optimization techniques for evaluating a set of continuous spatio-temporal queries are recently addressed for centralized [23] and distributed environments [4, 8]. Distributed environments assume that clients have computational and storage capabilities to share query processing with the server. The main idea of [4, 8] is to ship some part of the query processing down to the moving objects, while the server mainly acts as a mediator among moving objects. This assumption is not always realistic. In many cases, clients use cheap, low battery, and passive devices that do not have any computational or storage capabilities. For centralized environments, the Q-Index [23] does not assume any client overhead. The main idea of the Q-index is to build an R-tree-like [9] index structure on the queries instead of the objects. Then, at each time interval T, moving objects probe the Q-index to find the queries they belong to. The Q-index is limited in two aspects: (1) It performs reevaluation of all the queries every T time units. (2) It is applicable only for stationary queries.

In general, spatio-temporal queries can be evaluated using a spatio-temporal access method [19]. The TPR-tree [25] and its variants (e.g., the R^{EXP}-tree [24] and the TPR*-tree [31]) are used to index objects with future trajectories. However, there are no special mechanisms to support the continuous spatio-temporal queries in any of these access methods.

Our proposed framework distinguishes itself from other approaches, where we go beyond the idea of reevaluating continuous queries. Instead, we use incremental evaluation to compute only the updates of the previously reported result. In addition, unlike [4, 8], we do not assume any computational capabilities on the client side. Moreover, our framework is scalable to support a large number of concurrently outstanding continuous queries and can deal with many variations of continuous spatio-temporal queries.

3 Scalable Incremental Processing of Continuous Spatio-Temporal Queries

In this section, we present a scalable and incremental framework for continuously evaluating continuous spatio-temporal queries. The scalability is achieved by employing a *shared execution* paradigm for continuous spatio-temporal queries [18, 20]. With the shared execution, queries are indexed in the same way as data. Thus, evaluating a set of concurrent continuous spatio-temporal queries is reduced to a join between a set of moving objects and a set of moving queries [34]. Figure 1 gives an example of having a

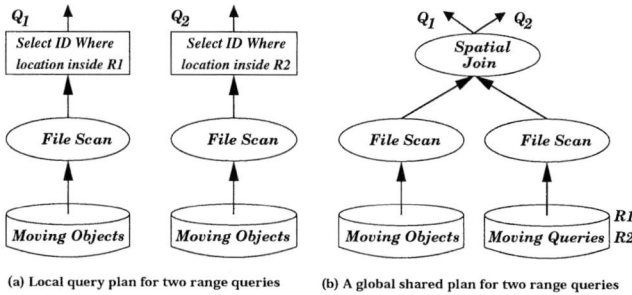

(a) Local query plan for two range queries   (b) A global shared plan for two range queries

Fig. 1. Shared execution of continuous queries

shared plan (Figure 1b) for two concurrent continuous queries (Figure 1a). Incremental evaluation is achieved through computing only the updates to the previously reported answer. We distinguish between two types of updates; *positive* updates and *negative* updates. A positive update of the form $(Q, +A)$ indicates that object A needs to be added to the answer set of query Q. Similarly, a negative update of the form $(Q, -A)$ indicates that object A is no longer part of the answer set of query Q. In general, we distinguish between three types of objects: *Stationary* objects, *moving* objects, and *predictive* objects. Moving objects can send only their current locations, while predictive objects have the ability to report their velocity vector. Thus, their future location can be predicted. Similarly, we have the same classification of queries, i.e., stationary, moving, and predictive queries.

3.1 Algorithms and Data Structures

The main idea of the continuous query processor is to treat both objects and queries similarly. Thus, we store both objects and queries in the same data structure. We use a simple grid structure that divides the space evenly into $N \times N$ equal sized grid cells. We utilize one grid structure that holds both objects and queries. Stationary and moving objects are mapped to specific grid cells using their locations. Predictive objects and all query types are clipped to multiple grid cells that overlap with the movement trajectory or query region, respectively.

An object entry O has the form $(OID, loc, t, QList)$, where OID is the object identifier, loc is the recent location of the object, t is the timestamp of the recently reported location loc, and $QList$ is the list of the queries that O is satisfying. A query Q is clipped to all grid cells that Q overlaps with. For any grid cell C, a query entry has the form $(QID, region, t, OList)$, where QID is the query identifier, $region$ is the recent rectangular region of Q that intersects with C, t is the timestamp of the recently reported region, and $OList$ is the list of objects in C that satisfy $Q.region$. k-nearest-neighbor queries are stored in the grid structure by considering the query region as the smallest circular region that contains the k nearest objects. Simple grid structures are commonly used to support different spatio-temporal queries (e.g., range queries [8], future queries [29], and aggregate queries [10]). In addition to the grid structure, we keep track of two auxiliary data structures; the object index and the query index. The object and query indexes are indexed on the OID and QID, respectively, and are used to provide the ability for searching the old locations of moving objects and queries given their identifiers. Using auxiliary data structures to keep track of the old locations is utilized in the LUR-tree [15] as a linked list and in the frequently updated R-tree [17] as a hash table.

Since a typical location-aware server receives a massive amount of updates from moving objects and queries, it becomes a huge overhead to handle each update individually. Thus, we buffer a set of updates from moving objects and queries for bulk processing. Basically the bulk processing is reduced to a spatial join between a set of objects (either stationary or moving) and a set of queries (either stationary or moving). Since, we are utilizing a grid structure, we use a spatial join algorithm similar to the one proposed in [22]. For each moving query Q, we keep track of the old (A_{old}) and new (A_{new}) query regions. A set of negative updates are produced for all objects that are in $Q.OList$ and lie in the area $A_{old} - A_{new}$. Then, we need only to evaluate the area $A_{new} - A_{old}$ to produce a set of *positive* updates. The area $A_{new} \cap A_{old}$ does not need to be reevaluated where the query result of this area is already reported to Q before. The efficiency of this incremental approach comes from the fact that the area $A_{new} \cap A_{old}$ is much larger than $A_{new} - A_{old}$. For any moving object O, we check the set of candidate queries that can intersect with the new location of O. Candidate queries are the queries that are stored in the same grid cell with O. The queries that are joined with O are compared with $O.QList$ to determine the set of positive and negative updates to be sent to the clients.

3.2   Examples

Example 1 (Spatio-Temporal Range-Queries). Figure 2a gives a snapshot of the database at time T_0 with nine moving objects, p_1 to p_9, and five continuous range queries, Q_1 to Q_5. At time T_1 (Figure 2b), only the objects p_1, p_2, p_3, and p_4 and the queries Q_1, Q_3, and Q_5 change their locations. The old query locations are plotted with dotted borders. Black objects are stationary, while white objects are moving. As a result of the change of database status from T_0 to T_1, the location-aware server reports the following updates: $(Q_1, -p_5), (Q_2, -p_1), (Q_3, +p_2), (Q_3, -p_7), (Q_3, -p_6), (Q_3, +p_8)$, and $(Q_4, -p_4)$.

Example 2 (Spatio-Temporal k-NN Queries). Figure 3a gives an example of two kNN queries where $k = 3$ issued at points Q_1 and Q_2. Assuming that both queries are issued at time T_0, we compute the first-time answer using any of the traditional algorithms of

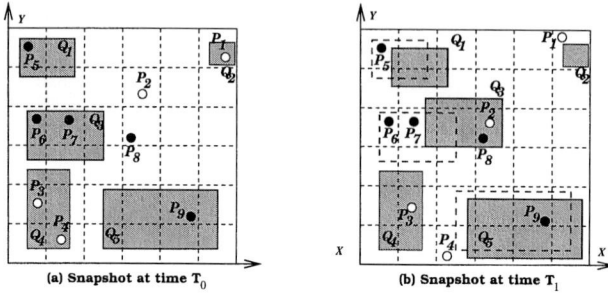

Fig. 2. Range queries

kNN queries. For Q_1, the answer would be $Q_1 = p_1, p_2, p_3$ while for Q_2, the answer would be $Q_2 = p_5, p_6, p_7$. In this case, we present Q_1 and Q_2 as circular range queries with radius equal to the distance of the kth neighbor. Later, at time T_1 (Figure 3b), objects

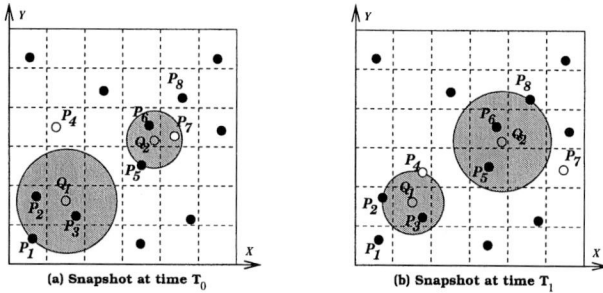

Fig. 3. k-NN queries

p_4 and p_7 are moved. For Q_1, object p_4 intersects with the query region. This results in invalidating the furthest neighbor of Q_1, which is p_1. Thus, two update tuples are reported $(Q_1, -p_1)$ and $(Q_1, +p_4)$. For Q_2, the object p_7 was part of the answer at time T_0. However, after p_7 moves, we find that p_8 becomes more near to Q_2 than p_7. Thus, two updates are reported, $(Q_2, -p_7)$ and $(Q_2, +p_8)$. Notice that unlike range queries, k-NN queries can change their location and size over time.

Example 3 (Predictive Spatio-Temporal Range-Queries). Figure 4a gives an example of querying the future. Five moving objects p_1 to p_5, have the ability to report their current locations at time T_0 and a velocity vector that is used to predict their future locations at times T_1 and T_2. The range query Q is interested in objects that will intersect with its region at time $T_2 > T_0$. At time T_0 the rectangular query region is joined with the lines representation of the moving objects. The returned answer set of Q is (p_1, p_3). At T_1 (Figure 4b), only the objects p_2, p_3, and p_4 change their locations. Based on the new information, we report only the positive update $(Q, +p_2)$ and negative update $(Q, -p_3)$ that indicate that p_2 is considered now as part of the answer set of Q while p_3 is no

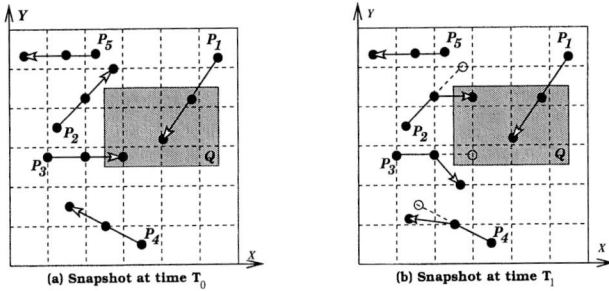

(a) Snapshot at time T_0 (b) Snapshot at time T_1

Fig. 4. Predictive queries

longer in the answer set of Q. Notice that no tuples are produced for object p_1 where it does not change its information from the previously reported result at time T_0.

3.3   Out-of-Sync Clients

Mobile objects tend to be disconnected and reconnected several times from the server for some reasons beyond their control, i.e., being out of battery, losing communication signals, being in a congested network, etc. This *out-of-sync* behavior may lead to erroneous query results in any incremental approach. Figure 5 gives an example of erroneous query

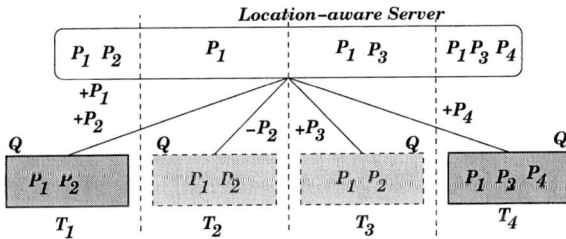

Fig. 5. Example of Out-of-Sync queries

result. The answer of query Q that is stored at both the client and server at time T_1 is (p_1, p_2). At time T_2, the client is disconnected from the server. However, the server keeps computing the answer of Q, and sends the negative update $(Q, -p_2)$. Since the client is disconnected, the client could not receive this negative update. Notice the inconsistency of the stored result at the server side (p_2) and the client side (p_1, p_2). Similarly, at time T_3, the client is still disconnected. The client is connected again at time T_4. The server computes the incremental result from T_3 and sends only the positive update $(Q, +p_4)$. At this time, the client is able to update its result to be (p_1, p_2, p_4). However, this is a wrong answer, where the correct answer is kept at the server (p_1, p_3, p_4).

    A naive solution for the out-of-sync problem is once the client wakes up, it empties its previous result and sends a *wakeup* message to the server. The server replies by the query answer stored at the server side. For example, in Figure 5, at time T_4, the location-aware server will send the whole answer (p_1, p_3, p_4). This approach is simple to implement and process in the server side. However, it may result in significant delay due to the network cost in sending the whole answer. Consider a moving query with hundreds of objects in its result that gets disconnected for a short period of time. Although, the query has missed a couple of points during its disconnected time, the server would send the complete answer to the query.

To deal with out-of-sync clients, we maintain a repository of committed query answers. An answer is considered committed if it is guaranteed that the client has received it. Once the client wakes up from the disconnected mode, it sends a *wakeup* message to the server. Then, the server compares the latest answer for the query with the committed answer, and sends the difference of the answer in the form of positive and negative updates. For example, in Figure 5, the server stores the committed answer of Q at time T_1 as (p_1, p_2). Then, at time T_4, the server compares the current answer with the committed one, and send the updates $(Q, -p_2, +p_3, +p_4)$. Once the server receives any information from a moving query, it considers its latest answer as a committed one. However, stationary queries are required to send explicit *commit* message to the location-aware server to enable committing the latest result. *Commit* messages can be sent at the convenient times of the clients.

4   Experimental Performance

In this section, we present a preliminary experiment that shows the promising performance of the continuous query processor. Figure 6 compares between the size incremental answer returned by utilizing the incremental approach and the size of the complete answer. We use the *Network-based Generator of Moving Objects* [3] to generate a set of 100K moving objects and 100K moving queries. The output of the generator is a set of moving objects that move on the road network of a given city. We choose some points randomly and consider them as centers of square queries.

The location-aware server buffers the received updates from moving objects and queries and evaluates them every 5 seconds. Figure 6a gives the effect of the number of moving objects that reported a change of location within the last 5 seconds. The size of the complete answer is constant and is orders of magnitude of the size of the worst-case incremental answer. In Figure 6b, the query side length varies from 0.01 to 0.02. The size of the complete answer increases dramatically to up to seven times that of the incremental

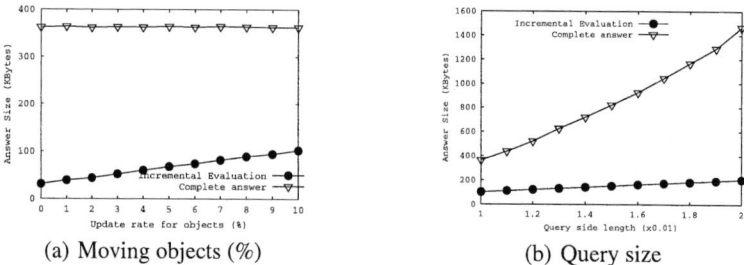

(a) Moving objects (%)   (b) Query size

Fig. 6. The answer size

result. The saving in the size of the answer directly affects the communication cost from the server to the clients.

5   Conclusion

In this paper, we presented a scalable and incremental framework for continuous query processing in location-aware servers as an application of spatio-temporal databases. Mainly, we emphasize on the scalability and incremental evaluation of continuous spatio-temporal queries. The applicability of the proposed framework to a wide variety of continuous spatio-temporal queries is discussed. A recovery mechanism for updating the results of clients that are disconnected from the server for a short period of time is presented. Preliminary results show that the size of the result of the incremental approach is around 10% of the size of a complete result. Thus, the proposed scalable and incremental framework has promising savings in both computational processing and network bandwidth.

References

1. Walid G. Aref, Susanne E. Hambrusch, and Sunil Prabhakar. Pervasive Location Aware Computing Environments (PLACE). http://www.cs.purdue.edu/place/.
2. Rimantas Benetis, Christian S. Jensen, Gytis Karciauskas, and Simonas Saltenis. Nearest Neighbor and Reverse Nearest Neighbor Queries for Moving Objects. In *IDEAS*, 2002.
3. Thomas Brinkhoff. A Framework for Generating Network-Based Moving Objects. *GeoInformatica*, 6(2), 2002.
4. Ying Cai, Kien A. Hua, and Guohong Cao. Processing Range-Monitoring Queries on Heterogeneous Mobile Objects. In *Mobile Data Management, MDM*, 2004.
5. Michael J. Carey et al. Shoring up persistent applications. In *Proceedings of the ACM International Conference on Management of Data, SIGMOD*, 1994.
6. Sirish Chandrasekaran and Michael J. Franklin. Streaming Queries over Streaming Data. In *Proceedings of the International Conference on Very Large Data Bases, VLDB*, 2002.
7. Jianjun Chen, David J. DeWitt, Feng Tian, and Yuan Wang. NiagaraCQ: A Scalable Continuous Query System for Internet Databases. In *Proceedings of the ACM International Conference on Management of Data, SIGMOD*, 2000.
8. Bugra Gedik and Ling Liu. MobiEyes: Distributed Processing of Continuously Moving Queries on Moving Objects in a Mobile System. In *Proceedings of the International Conference on Extending Database Technology, EDBT*, 2004.
9. Antonin Guttman. R-Trees: A Dynamic Index Structure for Spatial Searching. In *Proceedings of the ACM International Conference on Management of Data, SIGMOD*, 1984.
10. Marios Hadjieleftheriou, George Kollios, Dimitrios Gunopulos, and Vassilis J. Tsotras. On-Line Discovery of Dense Areas in Spatio-temporal Databases. In *Proceedings of the International Symposium on Advances in Spatial and Temporal Databases, SSTD*, 2003.
11. Susanne E. Hambrusch, Chuan-Ming Liu, Walid G. Aref, and Sunil Prabhakar. Query Processing in Broadcasted Spatial Index Trees. In *Proceedings of the International Symposium on Advances in Spatial and Temporal Databases, SSTD*, 2001.
12. Moustafa A. Hammad, Michael J. Franklin, Walid G. Aref, and Ahmed K. Elmagarmid. Scheduling for shared window joins over data streams. In *Proceedings of the International Conference on Very Large Data Bases, VLDB*, 2003.

13. Moustafa A. Hammad, Mohamed F. Mokbel, Mohamed H. Ali, Walid G. Aref, Ann C. Catlin, Ahmed K. Elmagarmid, Mohamed Eltabakh, Mohamed G. Elfeky, Thanaa M. Ghanem, Robert Gwadera, Ihab F. Ilyas, Mirette Marzouk, and Xiaopeng Xiong. Nile: A Query Processing Engine for Data Streams. In *Proceedings of the International Conference on Data Engineering, ICDE*, 2004.

14. Glenn S. Iwerks, Hanan Samet, and Ken Smith. Continuous K-Nearest Neighbor Queries for Continuously Moving Points with Updates. In *Proceedings of the International Conference on Very Large Data Bases, VLDB*, 2003.

15. Dongseop Kwon, Sangjun Lee, and Sukho Lee. Indexing the Current Positions of Moving Objects Using the Lazy Update R-tree. In *Mobile Data Management, MDM*, 2002.

16. Iosif Lazaridis, Kriengkrai Porkaew, and Sharad Mehrotra. Dynamic Queries over Mobile Objects. In *Proceedings of the International Conference on Extending Database Technology, EDBT*, 2002.

17. Mong-Li Lee, Wynne Hsu, Christian S. Jensen, and Keng Lik Teo. Supporting Frequent Updates in R-Trees: A Bottom-Up Approach. In *Proceedings of the International Conference on Very Large Data Bases, VLDB*, 2003.

18. Mohamed F. Mokbel, Walid G. Aref, Susanne E. Hambrusch, and Sunil Prabhakar. Towards Scalable Location-aware Services: Requirements and Research Issues. In *Proceedings of the ACM workshop on Advances in Geographic Information Systems, ACM GIS*, 2003.

19. Mohamed F. Mokbel, Thanaa M. Ghanem, and Walid G. Aref. Spatio-temporal Access Methods. *IEEE Data Engineering Bulletin*, 26(2), 2003.

20. Mohamed F. Mokbel, Xiaopeng Xiong, and Walid G. Aref. SINA: Scalable Incremental Processing of Continuous Queries in Spatio-temporal Databases. In *Proceedings of the ACM International Conference on Management of Data, SIGMOD*, 2004.

21. Mohamed F. Mokbel, Xiaopeng Xiong, Walid G. Aref, Susanne Hambrusch, Sunil Prabhakar, and Moustafa Hammad. PLACE: A Query Processor for Handling Real-time Spatio-temporal Data Streams (Demo). In *Proceedings of the International Conference on Very Large Data Bases, VLDB*, 2004.

22. Jignesh M. Patel and David J. DeWitt. Partition Based Spatial-Merge Join. In *Proceedings of the ACM International Conference on Management of Data, SIGMOD*, 1996.

23. Sunil Prabhakar, Yuni Xia, Dmitri V. Kalashnikov, Walid G. Aref, and Susanne E. Hambrusch. Query Indexing and Velocity Constrained Indexing: Scalable Techniques for Continuous Queries on Moving Objects. *IEEE Trans. on Computers*, 51(10), 2002.

24. Simonas Saltenis and Christian S. Jensen. Indexing of Moving Objects for Location-Based Services. In *Proceedings of the International Conference on Data Engineering, ICDE*, 2002.

25. Simonas Saltenis, Christian S. Jensen, Scott T. Leutenegger, and Mario A. Lopez. Indexing the Positions of Continuously Moving Objects. In *Proceedings of the ACM International Conference on Management of Data, SIGMOD*, 2000.

26. Timos K. Sellis. Multiple-Query Optimization. *ACM Transactions on Database Systems, TODS*, 13(1), 1988.

27. Praveen Seshadri. Predator: A Resource for Database Research. *SIGMOD Record*, 27(1):16–20, 1998.

28. Zhexuan Song and Nick Roussopoulos. K-Nearest Neighbor Search for Moving Query Point. In *Proceedings of the International Symposium on Advances in Spatial and Temporal Databases, SSTD*, 2001.

29. Jimeng Sun, Dimitris Papadias, Yufei Tao, and Bin Liu. Querying about the Past, the Present and the Future in Spatio-Temporal Databases. In *Proceedings of the International Conference on Data Engineering, ICDE*, 2004.

30. Yufei Tao, Dimitris Papadias, and Qiongmao Shen. Continuous Nearest Neighbor Search. In *Proceedings of the International Conference on Very Large Data Bases, VLDB*, 2002.

31. Yufei Tao, Dimitris Papadias, and Jimeng Sun. The TPR*-Tree: An Optimized Spatio-temporal Access Method for Predictive Queries. In *Proceedings of the International Conference on Very Large Data Bases, VLDB*, 2003.
32. Yufei Tao, Jimeng Sun, and Dimitris Papadias. Analysis of Predictive Spatio-Temporal Queries. *ACM Transactions on Database Systems, TODS*, 28(4), 2003.
33. Douglas B. Terry, David Goldberg, David Nichols, and Brian M. Oki. Continuous Queries over Append-Only Databases. In *Proceedings of the ACM International Conference on Management of Data, SIGMOD*, 1992.
34. Xiaopeng Xiong, Mohamed F. Mokbel, Walid G. Aref, Susanne Hambrusch, and Sunil Prabhakar. Scalable Spatio-temporal Continuous Query Processing for Location-aware Services. In *Proceedings of the International Conference on Scientific and Statistical Database Management, SSDBM*, June 2004.
35. Jun Zhang, Manli Zhu, Dimitris Papadias, Yufei Tao, and Dik Lun Lee. Location-based Spatial Queries. In *Proceedings of the ACM International Conference on Management of Data, SIGMOD*, 2003.
36. Baihua Zheng and Dik Lun Lee. Semantic Caching in Location-Dependent Query Processing. In *Proceedings of the International Symposium on Advances in Spatial and Temporal Databases, SSTD*, 2001.

Load Distribution
for Distributed Stream Processing

Ying Xing

Computer Science Department,
Brown University, Providence RI, USA
yx@cs.brown.edu

Abstract. Distributed steam processing is necessary for a large class of stream-based applications. To exploit the full power of distributed computation, effective load distribution techniques must be developed to optimize the system performance and cope with time-varying loads. When traditional load balancing or load sharing strategies are applied to such systems, we find that they either fall short in achieving good load distribution or fail to maintain good task partition in the long run.

In this paper, we study two important issues of dynamic load distribution in the context of data-intensive stream processing. The first one is how to allocate processing resources for push-based tasks such that the average end-to-end data processing latency can be minimized. The second issue is how to maintain a good load distribution dynamically for long running continuous queries. We propose a new hybrid load distribution strategy that addresses the above concerns by load clustering. To achieve scalability, our algorithm is completely decentralized and asynchronous.

1   Introduction

Stream based continuous query processing fits a large class of new applications, such as sensor networks, location tracking, network management and financial data online analysis. In these systems, data are pushed to a stream processing engine from external sources and then "flow through" the continuous query operators as they get processed. Stream-based applications usually involve large volumes of data and require timely response, which makes scalability a key requirement to such systems. Loosely coupled shared nothing distributed systems can provide high performance, scalability and extensibility with low cost. Furthermore, many stream-based applications are naturally distributed. For these reasons, distributed stream processing becomes important.

One of the biggest issues for distributed computing is the development of effective load distribution techniques that can fully exploit the potential power of available resources. However, this problem has not yet been fully studied in the context of push-based stream processing. In this paper, we focus on the dynamic load distribution problem for data-intensive continuous queries. In particular, we try to answer the following two questions:

- First, for push-based systems, how to distribute load so that the average end to end data processing latency can be minimized?

W. Lindner et al. (Eds.): EDBT 2004 Workshops, LNCS 3268, pp. 112–120, 2004.

– Second, as the load changes, how to maintain a good load distribution effectively and efficiently?

When traditional load balancing and load sharing approaches are applied in this setting, we find that they either fall short in achieving good load distribution or fail to maintain good task partitions dynamically. First, consider the load balancing strategy, which tries to equalize the load among all the processing nodes. Load balancing is commonly used in pull-based systems to achieve speed up, where data can be pulled faster if more resources are available. However, it can not achieve the same kind of speed up in push-based systems. This is because in such systems, the input data rates are decided by the external sources. After certain threshold, resource utilization is irrelevant to load distribution. On the other hand, if a task can be processed by n servers (also called nodes), then processing it on more than n nodes will incur extra data communication overhead unnecessarily. For systems with high input data rates, the inter-node data transfer delays can be significant compared to the intra-node data processing delays and queuing delays. Thus for such systems, we must try to minimize the data transfer cost instead of equally distributing load among all the servers. One simple way to do this is to run a task at a single node first, and then offload to other nodes if the node gets overloaded. Such an approach is load sharing based. However, a big potential problem for load sharing is that as the load varies, connected query graphs may get "cut" and "pasted" from node to node and thus results in long term bad task partition [12].

Based upon the above observations, we propose a new load distribution scheme that aims at minimizing the data communication delays for data-intensive tasks. Here we assume that the intra-node data processing and queuing delays are relatively small compared to intra-node data transfer delays. In particular, our algorithm tries to cluster load on a small set of nodes as long as no node gets overloaded. At the same time, to ensure long term partition quality, we constantly balance load between nodes with existing inter-node streams and only allow operators on the boundaries to be transferred between those nodes. Moreover, to minimize load re-distribution overhead, a load transfer process is only invoked if its benefit is larger than some threshold.

In the implementation of the above algorithm, we restrict our attention to decentralized schemes since a centralized load distributor creates a hot spot and limits the scalability of the system. Also, for this initial work, we only focus on inter-operator distributed processing. The smallest load transfer unit is each single operator.

The rest of this paper is organized as the following. Section 2 introduces the system model and some assumptions. Our basic algorithm is introduced in Sect. 3 and its implementation issues are discussed in in Sect. 4. Section 5 present the result of a preliminary experiment. Section 6 introduces the related works. Finally the conclusions and future directions are summarized in Section 7.

2   Problem Description

2.1   System Model

In this paper, we assume a cluster of loosely coupled homogeneous machines as the stream processing servers. Each processing node (server) has its private resources (CPU, memory and disks). All nodes are connected by a high bandwidth network. Assume network bandwidth is not a bottleneck but the network transfer delays are not negligible.

A task is represented by a directed loop free connected query graph. Each vertex of the graph represents a continuous query operator. Each arc represents a data stream flowing between the operators. Data streams are pushed to the cluster from external data sources. When a task is partitioned over multiple nodes, those nodes form a processing group. Each connected sub-query graph on a single node is also called an independent graph. An inter-node arc is also called a cutting edge if its direction is not important.

The operators considered in this paper are filters, unions, user defined functions, windowed aggregation and windowed join. They are also abstracted as unary or binary operators with or without internal states. We assume that any operator can be processed at any node. The cost to transfer those operators depends on the size of their states.

2.2   Domain Partition

To avoid message flooding by load information exchange, the whole system is divided into small overlapped load distribution domains. More specifically, each node will select certain number of nodes to form its own domain. Those selected nodes will report their load information to the selector node (also called listener node) periodically or upon change. The maximum number of listener nodes a node can have is fixed in the system. A node can only send load to or request load from nodes in its domain. Nodes with direct dataflow between them are called neighbors (or logical neighbors). The domain of a node includes all its neighbors and some non-neighbor nodes. Each node updates its domain periodically or based on need.

2.3   Load Representation

In our system, the loads of operators and nodes are represented by functions of time. We represent time as time intervals $(T_0, T_1, T_2, \dots)$. The load $l(T_k, O)$ of operator O at time interval T_k is the processing time of O during time interval T_k divided by the length of T_k. The load of a node is defined as the total load of all its operators. We assume that other system overhead (such as scheduling, statistics monitoring and load distribution overhead) can be controlled below certain threshold.

2.4   Problem Description

The optimization goal here is to find a dynamic load distribution algorithm that can minimize the average end-to-end latency for data-intensive stream processing. In addition, we require that the algorithm must be decentralized and the decisions should only depend on local information instead of global knowledge.

3   Algorithm Overview

In this section, we introduce the basic scheme of our dynamic load distribution algorithm.

As mentioned earlier, for data-intensive tasks, minimizing the average end-to-end latency can be achieved by minimizing network transfer delays (given no node is over-loaded). Thus, the main idea of our algorithm is to partition connected query graphs into minimum number of connected sub-query graphs and keep the nodes that are processing those sub-query graphs moderately loaded. In addition, when a node pushes load to other nodes, it selects operators that can minimize the number of cutting edges between the nodes.

We define four load states based on the load level of the nodes. They are under loaded, moderately loaded, heavily loaded and overloaded. The moderately loaded state is the desired state that we like the nodes to work at. When a node gets heavily loaded, it will try to offload independent query graphs to under loaded nodes. Such load transfers can prevent the node from getting overloaded without creating new cutting edges. When a node enters the overloaded state, it is allowed to partition its query graphs and offload to any nodes to its domain. An overloaded node will balance load with as fewer numbers of nodes as possible as long as none of them is over loaded. If a node is under loaded, it will merge adjacent sub-query graphs with its under loaded logical neighbors to minimize the number of cutting edges. This is called load coalescing.

To maintain good task partition dynamically, we only allow connected sub-query graphs along the border arcs to be transferred between logical neighbors. To minimize the change that a node gets overloaded and avoid "cut-and-paste" load transfer between non-neighbor nodes in the same processing group, we let all nodes constantly balance load with its logical neighbors. By this effort, the load levels of nodes in the same processing group can be roughly the same. Then, when an overloaded node offloads to other nodes, it will select nodes not in its processing group with high probability.

In summary, our strategy combines load sharing, load coalescing and logical neighbor load balancing in one scheme. We call it the hybrid dynamic load distribution approach. In the next section, we will discuss how to implement this algorithm in a decentralized asynchronous setting.

4   Implementation Issues

In a decentralized load distribution algorithm, each node has its own load distributor and all nodes follows the same algorithm. Our load distribution algorithm contains the following components:

- **Domain selection policy** that determines how to form and update a node's load distribution domain.
- **Load evaluation policy** that determines how to evaluate the load of a node and the operators on it.
- **Information exchange policy** that determines how to exchange load information between nodes.
- **Decision policy** that determines when to transfer load, to which node to transfer, and how much load to transfer.
- **Load selection policy** that determines which operators to transfer.
- **Load transfer policy** that determines how to send and receive load from other nodes.

Due to space limitation, we will skip the domain selection policy, information exchange policy and the load transfer policy. For the rest policies, some important issues are highlighted in the followings.

4.1   Load Evaluation and Forecasting

In order to make load distribution decision, a node must first know the load information of itself and of nodes in its domain. The load of a node is a function of time. Each node can measure its current load level and keep a history of its past load. However, the load distribution decisions should be based on the future load instead of the load level of current time. Otherwise, the nodes may overreact to temporary load fluctuations. Moreover, if future load is available and a node finds that it is going to get overloaded, it can pre-offload before its performance gets really bad. Unfortunately, in a push based system, the future load function is usually unavailable. In this paper, we propose a load forecasting scheme that uses the past loads to predict the future loads as the follows.

Using the history load $l(T_{n-i}), \ldots, l(T_{n-1}), l(Tn)$ at time T_n, certain forecasting algorithm can be used to estimate the future load $l(T_{n+1}), l(T_{n+2}), \ldots, l(T_{n+k})$. The average value of future load is then used for load distribution decision. A number of forecasting algorithms can be used here, for example, local extrapolation, exponential smoothing, moving average and auto-regression. Which one makes the best prediction is application dependent. When no prior knowledge is available, we run several simple predictors at the same time and compare their past predictors. The best predictor is then selected on the fly.

4.2   Asynchronous Decision Policy

A load transfer decision making is triggered whenever the load information of a node gets updated or if it receives a load update message from other nodes. The actual load transfer can be either sender initiated or receiver initiated. Here, we use different strategies for different kinds of load transfers. For load balancing between logical neighbors, we prefer a receiver initiated mode so that load distribution burden can be relieved from more loaded nodes. Thus, each time a node makes decisions, it checks whether it has logical neighbors whose load levels are higher than its own load level more than certain threshold. If so, the node will balance load among them and request load from the sender nodes. For load pushing by overloaded or heavily loaded nodes, we prefer sender initiate load transfer. This is because in those cases, only the sender nodes know to which nodes they should offload and how much load to transfer. For load coalescing, we would like the node with lowest load level among its neighborhood to push load to its under loaded neighbor with next lowest load level. Otherwise, if we allow an under loaded node to push load to a neighbor with lower load level, then conflict may happen if the neighbor node requests load from it at the same time by load balancing.

4.3   Load Selection

After the receiver node and the amount of load transfer are determined, a sender node must select appropriate operators to transfer so that the data communication cost and load transfer cost can be minimized. In addition, the load sum of selected operators should be as close to the desired amount as possible. Finding the optimal solution for such a problem is NP hard [7]. Here, we use a local greedy approach to expand connected sub-query graphs from border arcs.

The greedy algorithm will choose operators that introduce minimum number of cutting edges first. If there is a tie, the operator with smaller state size will be chosen to minimize load transfer cost. To avoid the situation that operator with large state size being transferred frequently, we require that those operators can only be transferred if its processing node is overloaded and there are no operators with small state size on the node.

4.4 Stability

Obviously, the total load of the selected operators will not be exactly the desired amount. To ensure stability, we require that a node cannot send load more than specified amount. But then, if a sender node cannot transfer enough load to a receiver node, they may constantly try to transfer load between each other. To avoid such situation, we require that a node can only make subsequent transfer decisions after certain amount of time or if its actual load level changes significantly.

4.5 Conflict Avoidance

Since the above load transfer decisions are made asynchronously, two or several nodes may send load to the same node at the same time. This is called a conflict problem. We use a simple scheme that randomizes the load decision-making time to avoid conflictions. It turns out to be very effective.

4.6 Sender Delayed Load Transfer

Even without conflicts, some loads can still be sent back and forth between nodes. To solve this problem, synchronous load balancing algorithms usually use two phases load transfer: the optimal amount of load transfer is determined in the first phase and the actual load transfer happens at the second phase. In our asynchronous implementation, we achieve similar result by letting the sender node delay the actual load transfer for certain amount of time. The delay time is decided from the sender node's load level.

5 Preliminary Experiment

To experiment on our algorithm, we implement a distributed stream processing simulator using the CSIM18 Simulation Engine. A simulated network and stream processing engines are implemented in the simulator. The operators tested are filters, unions, windowed aggregates and windowed joins. Here, we present a preliminary experiment that compares the performance of our hybrid algorithm with the traditional load balancing and load sharing algorithms.

In this experiment, three connected query graphs are assigned to a system with 20 nodes. Each query graph contains 20 operators. Each node uses a round robin scheduler to schedule the operators. At the beginning of the experiment, each connected query graphs is assigned to a random node. The input data rates increase slowly during a warm up period of 20 simulation second. In this period, the processing nodes gather the statistics of the query graphs and distribute load when necessary. During time period 30sec to 200 sec, we increase the input data rates to four times the original rates and then let them drop back . Figure 1 shows the average end to end latency of three different algorithms as functions of time after the warm up period.

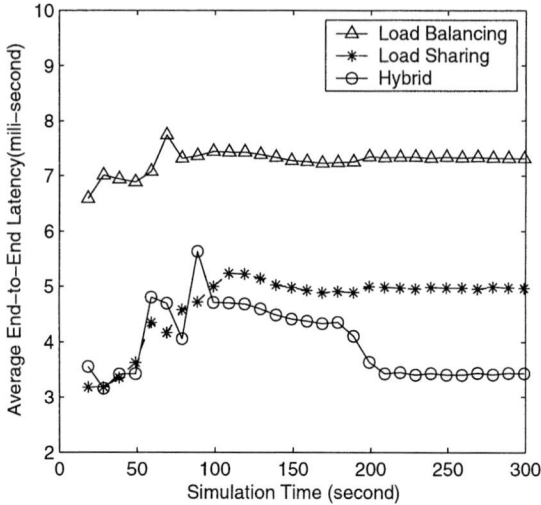

Fig. 1. Dynamic performance comparison for three algorithms

The experiment result shows that after the warm up period, both the hybrid algorithm and the load sharing algorithm converge to initial distributions with low average end-to-end latency. This is because they create cutting edges only when some node gets overloaded and thus results in small data transfer delay. On the contrary, the load balancing algorithm creates cutting edges even when it is not necessary.

Aside from static performance, the hybrid algorithm also achieves good dynamic performance. No matter the load increases or decrease, it can always adapt to the changes. In comparison to this, the load sharing strategy can not adapt well when load decreases. This is because it does not merge load among under loaded nodes.

6   Related Work

Our system model is based on the newly developed stream-based data processing engines. These systems mainly focus on efficient continuous query processing in a single server [2, 4, 10]. A scalable distributed stream processing model is introduced in [5]. Our work is an extension of [5], which focuses on the load distribution problem of this system. Nevertheless, our work is also general enough to be applied to other push-based distributed or parallel dataflow systems.

The load balancing problem for parallel continuous query processing has been studied in [13]. They consider a single operator processed by multiple servers and adjust data partitions adaptively using a centralized controller so that the workloads of different servers are balanced dynamically. Our work is complementary to theirs since we focus on inter-operator load distribution instead of intra-operator parallelism and our algorithm is decentralized.

Operator placement has been studied in traditional parallel database systems in the context of pipelined parallelism [6]. These works are mostly static or dynamic just before execution [1, 11]. Also, traditional database systems are pull-based. Thus load balancing are commonly used. In this paper, we study new dynamic load distribution schemes for long running push-based system instead.

Works on dynamic load distribution strategies for other distributed or parallel systems provide a lot of useful information for us. Former efforts either fall into the category of dynamic load balancing [8, 14, 15] or load sharing [9]. Load sharing strategies are usually used for load distribution without task partition. When data communication costs are considered, dynamic load balancing is commonly used. Due to the high overhead, their applications are often limited to large scientific computations and simulations. Most of the works are particularly targeted at mesh repartitioning. These tasks are also pull-based. As far as we know, none of them has combined different strategies in a push based setting.

7   Conclusions and Future Directions

The combination of push-based and long-running nature of continuous queries introduces new challenges to the load distribution problem. Our investigation has led to the development of a new dynamic load distribution scheme that is aimed at minimizing network transfer latency by load clustering. A scalable decentralized implementation of this algorithm is presented in this paper. We also propose initial solutions for different issues in this framework such as load forecasting, operator selection and conflict avoidance.

There are still a lot of works can be extended from the current scheme. First, in this paper, we assume that the data processing delays and queuing delays are relatively small in comparison to the network delays. In some cases, per tuple data processing delay can also be relatively large. For example, some operators may involve table lookup on disks and some operators may require complex computations. If the input rates for these operators are bursting, then queuing delay can become a major part of end-to-end latency. In these cases, only consider minimizing network transfer delay by load clustering will not be sufficient and appropriate. Thus, in our next step, we will expend our work to address the above problem using queuing analysis.

Secondly, we have only applied our algorithm on inter-operator level load distribution so far. Since intra-operator distributed processing usually requires centralized control, how to incorporate it in a decentralized peer to peer system is a very challenging problem. We would like to explore this problem in the future works.

Finally, it is worth mentioning that another advantage of load clustering is that it can provide more intra-node processing optimization opportunities. For example, some scheduling algorithm schedules connected sub-query graphs instead of each individual operator to minimize context switching overhead [3]. Studying load distribution strategies under such context is also challenging and interesting.

Acknowledgements

I am grateful to my advisor Stan Zdonik for the inspiration and guidance for this research, and to Ugur Cetintemel for valuable discussions. I also want to thank Jeong-Hyon Hwang for his contribution in the simulator implementation.

References

1. L. Bouganim, D. Florescu, and P. Valduriez. Dynamic load balancing in hierarchical parallel database systems. In *Int'l. Conf. on Very Large Data Bases (VLDB)*, pages 436–447, Bombay, India, September 1996.
2. D. Carney, U. Cetintemel, M. Cherniack, C. Convey, S. Lee, G. Seidman, M. Stonebraker, N. Tatbul, and S. Zdonik. Monitoring Streams – A New Class of Data Management Applications. In *Int'l. Conf. on Very Large Data Bases (VLDB)*, pages 215–226, Hong Kong, China, August 2002.
3. D. Carney, U. Cetintemel, A. Rasin, S. Zdonik, M. Cherniack, and M. Stonebraker. Operator scheduling in a data stream manager. In *Int'l. Conf. on Very Large Data Bases (VLDB)*, Berlin, Germany, September 2003.
4. S. Chandrasekaran, A. Deshpande, M. Franklin, J. Hellerstein, W. Hong, S. Krishnamurthy, S. Madden, V. Raman, F. Reiss, and M. Shah. TelegraphCQ: Continuous dataflow processing for an uncertain world. In *CIDR Conference*, pages 269–280, Asilomar, CA, January 2003.
5. M. Cherniack, H. Balakrishnan, M. Balazinska, D. Carney, U. Cetintemel, Y. Xing, and S. Zdonik. Scalable Distributed Stream Processing. In *CIDR Conference*, pages 257–268, Asilomar, CA, January 2003.
6. D. DeWitt and J. Gray. Parallel database systems: the future of high performance database systems. *Communications of the ACM*, 35(6):85–98, 1992.
7. M. R. Garey and D. S. Johnson. *Computers and Intractability: A Guide to the Theory of NP-Completeness*. W. H. Freeman and Co., 1979.
8. B. Hendrickson and K. Devine. Dynamic load balancing in computational mechanics. *Computer Methods in Applied Mechanics and Engineering*, 184:485–500, 2000.
9. O. Kremien, J. Kramer, and J. Magee. Scalable, adaptive load sharing for distributed systems. *IEEE Parallel and Distributed Technology: Systems and Applications*, 1(3):62–70, 1993.
10. R. Motwani, J. Widom, A. Arasu, B. Babcock, S. Babu, M. Datar, G. Manku, C. Olston, J. Rosenstein, and R. Varma. Query processing, approximation, and resource management in a data stream management system. In *CIDR Conference*, pages 245–256, Asilomar, CA, January 2003.
11. E. Rahm and R. Marek. Dynamic multi-resource load balancing in parallel database systems. In *Int'l. Conf. on Very Large Data Bases (VLDB)*, pages 395–406, 1995.
12. K. Schloegel, G. Karypis, and V. Kumar. *Graph Partitioning for High Performance Scientific Simulations. CRPC Parallel Computing Handbook*. Morgan Kaufmann, 2000.
13. M. A. Shah, J. M. Hellerstein, S. Chandrasekaran, and M. J. Franklin. Flux: An Adaptive Partitioning Operator for Continuous Query Systems. In *ICDE Conference*, pages 25–36, 2003.
14. M.H. Willebeek and A.P. Reeves. Strategies for dynamic load balancing on highly parallel computers. *IEEE Trans. on Parallel and Distributed Systems*, 4(9):979–993, September 1993.
15. C.Z. Xu, B. Monien, R. Luling, and F.C.M. Lau. Nearest neighbor algorithms for load balancing in parallel computers. *Concurrency: Practice and Experience*, 9(12):1351–1376, 1997.

XML Query Processing and Optimization

Ning Zhang

School of Computer Science,
University of Waterloo,
Ontario, Canada, N2L 3G1
nzhang@uwaterloo.ca

Abstract. In this paper, I summarize my research on optimizing XML queries. This work has two components: the first component is the definition of a logical algebra and logical optimization techniques. This algebra can be translated into different physical algebras such as native or extended-relational algebras. The second component is the design of physical storage structures and physical optimization techniques.

1 Introduction

XML has grown from a markup language for special-purpose documents to a standard for the interchange of heterogeneous data over the Web, a common language for distributed computation, and a universal data format to provide users with different views of data by transforming between different formats. All of these increase the volume of data encoded in XML, consequently increasing the need for database management support for XML documents. An essential concern is how to store and query potentially huge amounts of XML data efficiently.

There are generally two approaches to providing database support for XML data management: extended-relational approach and native XML approach. In the extended-relational approach, XML documents are transformed to relational data, and XQuery expressions are translated to SQL expressions. The space for XML query optimization is on the XQuery-to-SQL translation and the SQL expression itself. On the other hand, in the native XML approach, XML documents are managed without any relational database support. XML data are simply modeled as labeled, ordered, rooted trees. Any query on XML data is then translated into a series of operations on XML trees. The optimization is therefore on the translation and the operations themselves.

Both of these approaches have their own advantages and disadvantages. For example, the extended-relational approach is heavily dependent on the physical level representation (e.g., interval encoding [5]) of XML data. Existing translation schemes are either generally inefficient in processing tree structured data, or require significant amount of work on update. On the other hand, the native XML approach benefits from the fact that one can design new storage structures and define new operators to satisfy both query and update requirements. The downside of the native approach is its lack of maturity, especially in the optimization techniques.

In this paper, I propose a novel approach to compromise between the above two approaches by defining a logical algebra that captures the semantics of XQuery. The

W. Lindner et al. (Eds.): EDBT 2004 Workshops, LNCS 3268, pp. 121–132, 2004.

definition of the logical algebra should be general enough so that it can be implemented by the extended-relational or the native approach. A set of rewrite rules and a cost model should also be defined so that equivalent execution plans could be deduced and their costs could be estimated. Another major part of my thesis will be the development of physical optimization techniques that deal with storage structures and access methods. The aim of my Ph.D. research is, thus, to develop XML query processing and optimization techniques, in particular those techniques that are not only provably efficient in theory, but also empirically verifiably so in practice.

2 Significant Research Problems

In my Ph.D. research, I am concentrating on two research questions:

1. How to define a logical algebra and logical optimization rules that can be used by an extended-relational or native optimizer.
2. How to design physical storage structures and access methods in support of this logical algebra for efficient query processing.

XQuery is a functional programming language, thus it can be evaluated as any other functional programming language and enjoys their optimization techniques. However, since XQuery is designed as a database query language, one should bear in mind that the input data could be massive. To efficiently evaluate XQuery expressions against large amounts of data, we follow the traditional database query model:

- Define a logical algebra and rewrite rules for the query language.
- Design new physical storage structures if needed.
- For each logical operator, many physical operators (access methods) that implement the same functionalities could also be defined. These physical operators have different performances depending on the physical data distributions and the presence of auxiliary data (e.g., indexes).
- A cost model is also needed as a basis of choosing the optimal physical query plan.

In this paper, I shall present my preliminary study of the first three issues in the above list. The cost model is left as my future work.

3 Logical Algebra

3.1 Problem Definition

A logical algebra can be thought of as a specification that captures the semantics of XQuery expressions so that the primary concern of the physical operators is how to satisfy the specification. The algebra must be *sound* (the translation of XQuery expressions into algebraic expressions must be correct) and *complete* (*any* XQuery expression can be translated into an algebraic expression). There are several problems that need to be considered when defining the algebra:

Sorts: The data model defined by W3C is a sequence of tree nodes. This implies that at least two sorts, List and TreeNode, are needed as indicated by the W3C's XQuery Formal Semantics [6]. However, we shall see that more sorts, such as NestedList and Tree, are necessary or convenient.

Operators: As usual, the algebra includes a set of operators, defined by their signatures and semantics. These should be *closed* under the sorts we define. I shall investigate well-known operations on these sorts, as well as defining new operations, and rewrite rules based on them.

Completeness vs. Safety: The completeness property requires that any XQuery expression can be translated into an algebraic expression that returns the same result. However, since XQuery is Turing-complete [9], which introduces possibly non-terminating expressions, a complete algebra will be unsafe. To avoid this problem, I identify a subclass of XQuery that does not include recursive functions, and define a complete algebra for this subclass only. To expand to a larger subclass, one can define additional (maybe higher-order) operators based on this algebra.

Other issues such as type checking and error/exception handling are outside the scope of my thesis. The definition of rewrite rules is leaf as future work.

3.2   Preliminary Results

Sorts. The input and output of an XQuery expression defined by XQuery data model is a *flat* sequence of tree nodes. Since there are no nested sequences, it seems that it is sufficient to define operators over two sorts: List (representing flat list) and TreeNode, together with other primitive sorts such as Integer, Boolean and String. However, flat list operations are not efficient in manipulating trees, which can be thought of as nested lists. For example, Fig. 1(a) is an XQuery expression taken from XQuery Use Cases. The output of the expression conforms to the tree schema shown in Fig. 1(b), where the root is labeled as results, which has zero or more children labeled result, under which there are two children (subtrees) whose values depend on the value of $t and $a. The leaf nodes labeled with { } are placeholders that can be replaced by the value (subtree) of the enclosed expression.

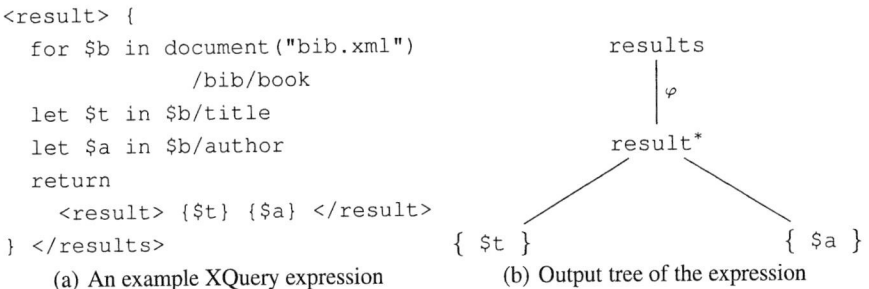

```
<result> {
  for $b in document("bib.xml")
              /bib/book
  let $t in $b/title
  let $a in $b/author
  return
    <result> {$t} {$a} </result>
} </results>
```

(a) An example XQuery expression

(b) Output tree of the expression

Fig. 1. An XQuery expression and its output schema

The edit label φ is an expression that evaluates the values for the variable(s) to replace the placeholder(s). It can be translated more formally into a list comprehension:

$$\varphi = \big[(\$t, \$a) \mid \$b \leftarrow \texttt{doc()/bib/book}; \$t \leftarrow \$b\texttt{/title}; \$a \leftarrow \$b\texttt{/author}\big]$$

The output of the comprehension is a list of 2-tuples (i.e., nested list), instead of a flat list of tree nodes. Relying on the W3C's data model over flat lists, the list comprehension can be evaluated either by iterating over each element in $\$b$, during which $\$t$ and $\$a$ are evaluated accordingly, or by first creating a long list for each $\$t$ and $\$a$ in a batch, then joining them based on their structural relationship. Both of these strategies are not optimal since the first (pipelining) approach suffers from exponential runtime (to the size of the query) in the worst case [7], while the join-based approach needs an additional structural join [13].

On the other hand, generalizing the input and output as nested lists enables a single operator to implement the above list comprehension as a whole. A physical tree pattern matching operator (introduced later), for example, could implement the list comprehension with a single scan of the input data without the need for structural joins. This efficiency benefit necessitates a new sort NestedList that allows arbitrary level of nestings. It is straightforward to convert a nested list to a tree. However, there are no labels on the converted tree nodes. Therefore, it is necessary to define another sort Tree that represents labeled trees. In our algebra, an input XML document is of sort Tree; while some of the intermediate results could be of sort NestedList.

In addition, we also need sorts such as PatternGraph and SchemaTree, which are used to translate path expressions and constructor expressions, respectively. The sort PatternGraph captures the constraints specified by one or more path expressions. For example, the path expression /a[b][c] can be modeled as a pattern graph that has four vertices labeled with root, a, b and c, and three directed edges (root,a), (a,b), and (a,c). The three edges are all labeled with "/", which means that the "from" and "to" vertices are in parent-child relationship. The vertex a is marked as returning vertex, which means that the tree nodes matched with this vertex should be returned.

Definition 1 (PatternGraph). *A PatternGraph is a labeled, directed graph, which is denoted by a 5-tuple $\mathcal{P} = \langle \Sigma, \mathcal{V}, \mathcal{A}, \mathcal{R}, \mathcal{O} \rangle$, where Σ is a finite alphabet representing element (attribute, etc.) names, $\mathcal{V}$ and $\mathcal{A}$ are the sets of vertices and arcs (directed edges) in the graph, respectively, $\mathcal{R}$ is the set of binary relations between vertices, and $\mathcal{O} \subseteq \mathcal{V}$ is a set of output vertices indicating that all matching vertices should be output as results.*

For each vertex $v \in \mathcal{V}$:

- *v is labeled with $*$ or a set of characters in Σ, where $* \notin \Sigma$.*
- *v is associated with a list (may be empty) of $\langle \prec, l \rangle$ tuples, where $\prec$ is a comparison operator and l is a numerical or string literal.*

Each arc $(s, t) \in \mathcal{A}$ is labeled with a relation $r \in \mathcal{R}$, which indicates that (s, t) is in relation r.

The sort SchemaTree (cf. Fig. 1(b)) represents a labeled tree that is extracted from XQuery constructor expressions. This labeled tree structure specifies the schema of an out XML document. Each node in the schema tree is labeled with an element name, with an optional wildcard symbol * or ?. A node could be marked as a placeholder, in which case its node label should be an algebraic expression. All arcs in the tree represent parent-child relationship, so there is no label on the arcs.

Definition 2 (SchemaTree). *An SchemaTree is a labeled tree structure, which is denoted by a 4-tuple $\mathcal{O} = \langle \Sigma, \mathcal{N}, \mathcal{A}, \mathcal{E} \rangle$, where Σ is a set of finite alphabet representing element/attribute names, $\mathcal{N}$ is a set of tree nodes, $\mathcal{A}$ is a set of tree arcs, and $\mathcal{E}$ is a set of (XQuery/algebraic) expressions.*

Each leaf-node in $\mathcal{N}$ is labeled with a character in Σ (in which case it is an empty element/attribute) or an expression in $\mathcal{E}$. For each non-leaf node, it is labeled with a character in Σ (in which case it is called a constructor-node*) or a boolean-valued expression in $\mathcal{E}$ (in which case it is called an* if-node*).*

Each arc in $\mathcal{A}$ may (or may not) be labeled with an expression in $\mathcal{E}$.

In addition to path expression and constructor expression, FLWOR expression is another type of major expression. The uniqueness of FLWOR expression is that it is the only kind of expression that can introduce new variables. Since variables can be referenced by other expressions in some scope, it is necessary to define a scope-wise sort Env to keep track of all the defined variables and their bounded values constitute. The sort Env can be thought of as a NestedList (or unlabeled tree) with additional variable bindings to each level in the nesting.

Definition 3 (Env). *An environment (Env) is a layered, balanced tree structure, which is denoted by a 3-tuple $\mathcal{E} = \langle \mathcal{N}, \mathcal{A}, \mathcal{V} \rangle$, where $\mathcal{N}$ is a set of nodes, $\mathcal{A}$ is a set of arcs, and $\mathcal{V}$ is a set of variables. All tree nodes at the same level from the root forms a layer. Each layer is either associated with a variable in $\mathcal{N}$, or a boolean formula. All nodes in the same layer have the same cardinality relationship, i.e., the parent-child relationship between layers x and $x + 1$ is either one-to-one or one-to-many, but not mixed. A path from the root to a leaf is called a* total variable bindings, *which include the bindings for all variables and boolean formula introduced in the* where-*clause.*

Example 1. The following FLWOR expression:

```
for $a in E1, $b in E2
   let $c := E3, $d := E4
      for $e in E5
         return E6
```

generates a nested list ($a, ($b, $c, $d, ($e))). Variables in this nested list from left to right are nested in different levels (as indicated in Fig. 2). Whether there is a opening parenthesis "(" between two variables determines how the tree is constructed. If there is a "(", every list item in the value bounded to the second variable is a child of the first variable binding. This corresponds to a for-clause style of binding values.

If there is no "(", the list value of the second variable as a whole is a child of the first variable binding. A possible environment instantiated from this nested list is shown in Fig. 2.

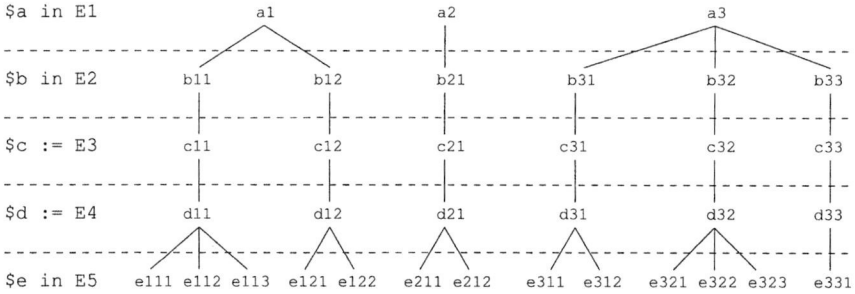

Fig. 2. An example environment by the schema ($a, ($b, $c, $d, ($e)))

The environment forms a forest, in which the number of trees is the number of values instantiating $a. The list of nodes at each level are generated by the expression at the left-hand-side, given the input nodes at its top levels: the first-level nodes are generated by the expression E1, and the second-level nodes are generated by the expression E2 given the input of the nodes at the first level, and so on. This environment actually specifies 13 possible value assignments (each corresponding to a path from a root the a leaf) to the five variables. Therefore, to obtain the final result, the expression E6 is evaluated once for each of these paths, and their results are concatenated together.

Operators. The XQuery data model has already defined functions and operations for each sort (data type). We can use these as the operators over the predefined sorts in our algebra. In addition, we need to define operators for the newly introduced sorts. In relational algebra, some operators are schema-related (π and ρ, etc.), and some operators are value-related (σ, $\bowtie$, sorting, etc.). In our XML algebra, we also define operators in these two categories, but some operators may examine both schema and value information (cf. Table 1).

The operators listed in the structure-based and value-based have extended but very similar semantics to the relational operators. For example, σ^s selects tree nodes whose tag names are "s", and $\bowtie^s$ join two lists of nodes if their structural relationships are "s".

The two hybrid operators involve both types of information and thus have more complex semantics. The tree pattern matching (TPM) operator (τ) takes an XML tree and a pattern graph as input, and produces a nested list as output. The semantics of τ operator is to find all nodes in the input tree that satisfy all the constraints specified by the pattern graph. The resulting nodes are output as a nested list according to their structural relationships in the input tree (i.e., two nodes are immediately nested in the

Table 1. Operators

Category	Operator	Signature	Short Description
	σ^s	List $\rightarrow$ List	selection based on tag names
structure-	$\bowtie^s$	List $\times$ List $\rightarrow$ List	structural join
based	π^s	List $\rightarrow$ NestedList	tree navigation along axis s
value-	σ^v	List $\rightarrow$ List	selection based on values
based	$\bowtie^v$	List $\times$ List $\rightarrow$ List	value-based join
hybrid	τ	List $\times$ PatternGraph $\rightarrow$ NestedList	tree pattern matching
	γ	NestedList $\times$ SchemaTree $\rightarrow$ Tree	tree construction operator

output nested list iff they are in immediate ancestor-descendant relationship in the input tree). This operator is particularly interesting and I shall introduce this physical optimization technique in Section 4.

The construction operator (γ) takes a NestedList and SchemaTree as input, and produce a labeled Tree (which represent an XML document). Among the parameters, the NestedList is the intermediate results (tree without node labels) obtained by other operators, and the SchemaTree is the schema information that indicates how the intermediate results should be labeled.

These two operators, τ and γ, reside on the bottom and top of the execution plan, respectively. The τ operators process the input XML documents and produce intermediate results (nested lists). The γ operator takes the intermediate results together with the output schema, and produces the resulting XML document. The other operators reside in the middle in the execution plan, and serve as transformation tools on the intermediate results.

4   Physical Storage and Operators

4.1   Problem Definition

Database query execution is I/O-expensive, and physical optimization concentrates on reducing I/O costs based on the physical storage scheme and data distribution. Unlike relational databases, XML data are ordered and hierarchically organized. More importantly, the XML schema is more flexible and allows mixed content. Existing extended-relational approaches shred XML documents into small pieces (elements) and store them without considering their structural relationships. To answer queries related to structural constraints, it is necessary to perform a structural join on each structural constraint, which could pose optimization difficulties. To efficiently answer such queries, we need to study the following problems:

Path Expressions: Path expression is arguably the most natural way to query tree-structure data. It deserves attention because, first, it is one of the most heavily used expressions in XQuery, and its performance will greatly affect the overall performance.

(a) An example XML document

(b) The string representation of the XML tree

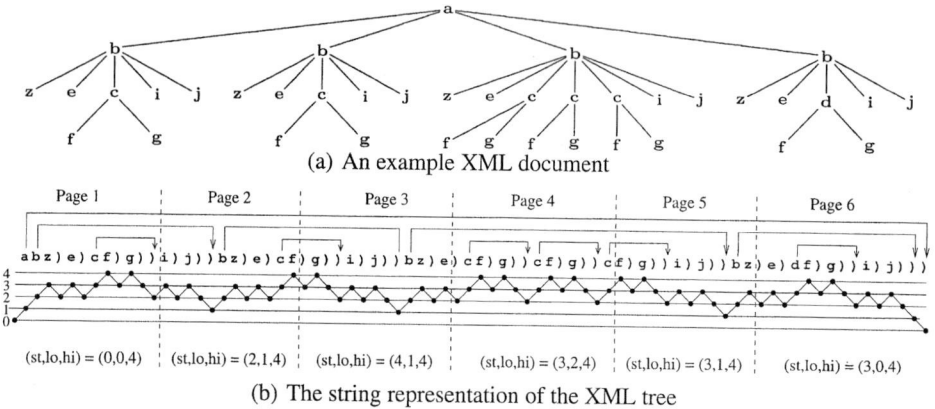

Fig. 3. Storing an XML tree as a string

Second, it is significantly different from relational query languages, so it may require new optimization techniques.

Physical Storage Structures: As discussed above, relational storage structure is invariant to ordering. Therefore, a new storage scheme taking into consideration the ordering of a an tree structure may be advantageous for relational storage structure.

4.2 Preliminary Results

Storage Systems. To answer path queries, we have designed a succinct XML physical storage scheme [15], in which schema information (tree structure consisting of tags) and data information (element contents attached to the leaves of the subject tree) are stored separately. The reason for the separation is that, first, the physical management issues are much easier when we consider only one type of data — the tree structure without variable-length element contents is more regular and can be managed more efficiently, and content-based indexes (such as B^+ trees and suffix trees) can be created only on the content information without worrying about its structure. Second, queries can be decomposed into operations that operate on these two types of information individually, and the final result can be composed by the partial results from the two classes of operators.

Another requirement for the storage structure design is to efficiently answer tree-structure related queries. The rationale is to *cluster* XML elements at the physical level based on one of the "local" structural relationships (say parent-child). The idea is to linearize the tree nodes in pre-order but keep balanced parentheses to denote the beginning and ending of a subtree. This clustering method makes update easier since each update only affects a local sub-string. Furthermore, pre-order of the tree nodes coincides with the streaming XML element arrival order. So the path query evaluation algorithm (outlined in Section 4.2) can also be used in the streaming context.

Fig. 3 illustrates the string representation of a tree. Each character in the string represents a node in the tree, and the characters are ordered by the pre-order traversal of the tree. During the per-order traversal, the end of a subtree is presented by a right parenthesis ')' in the string. It is well-known that any tree can be represented by such a string, and vice versa [10]. To conform to the paged I/O model, the string can be divided into pages as well. In each page, a page header keeps track of the lowest (lo) and highest (hi) levels of all nodes in the page. This information is used to save unnecessary I/O's when traversing the tree (See [15] for more details).

Path Expression Evaluation. We have also identified a subset of the path expression, which we call next-of-kin (NoK) expressions, consisting of only those local structural relationships (/ and following-siblings). The evaluation of NoK expressions (a.k.a. NoK pattern matching) can be performed efficiently based on our physical storage structures without the need for structural joins. The NoK pattern matching calls two primitive tree traversal operations (FIRST-CHILD and FOLLOWING-SIBLING as shown in Algorithm 1). It can be proved that only a single scan of the input data is needed for the NoK pattern matching.

Algorithm 1 NoK Pattern Matching

$\underline{\text{NPM}}(proot, snode, R)$

1   **if** $proot$ is the returning node
2   **then** LIST-APPEND$(R, snode)$;
3   $S \leftarrow$ all frontier children of $proot$;
4   $u \leftarrow$ FIRST-CHILD$(snode)$;
5   **repeat**
6   **for each** $s \in S$ that matches u with both tag
                    name and value constraints
7   **do**
8                       $b \leftarrow$ NPM(s, u, R);
9   **if** $b = $ **true**
10   **then** $S \leftarrow S \setminus \{s\}$;
11   delete s and its incident arcs
                                    from the pattern tree;
12   insert new frontiers caused by
                                    deleting s;
13              $u \leftarrow$ FOLLOWING-SIBLING(u);
14   **until** $u = $ NIL or $S = \emptyset$
15 **if** $S \neq \emptyset$
16   **then** $R \leftarrow \emptyset$;
17   **return false**;
18 **return true**;

Given a general path expression, we first partition it into interconnected NoK expressions, to which we apply the more efficient navigational pattern matching algorithm.

Then, we join the results of the NoK pattern matching based on their structural relationships, just as in the join-based approach. Experimental results show that our approach outperforms existing join-based approaches and a state-of-the-art commercial native XML management system [15].

5   Related Work

The definition of our algebra is inspired by previous algebras (in particular, YAT algebra [4] and TAX algebra [3, 8]). In YAT algebra, operators can be separated into three categories: (1) **Bind** operators take a collection of XML documents and produce a set of structures called *Tab*, which are ¬1NF relations, as output. (2) Then any standard relational operators (such as **Selection**, **Projection**, **Join**, and **Union**) can be applied to the *Tab* structure. (3) Finally, **Tree** operators are applied to *Tab* structures to generate new nested XML documents. In our algebra, we also define some "border" operators that insulate other more "relational-style" operators from the tree data model. Therefore, we can reuse the optimization techniques developed for relational databases. In addition, as discussed in Section 3.2, more sorts and operators are needed to support efficient query processing.

In TAX algebra [8], the input, as well as the output, of any operator is a collection of labeled trees. A great difficulty for this approach is that trees are more heterogeneous than tuples (relations). When defining operators, specifying the objects (tree nodes) to manipulate is therefore much more difficult than that for tuples. By comparison, relational algebra specifies attributes by their names or their positions in the tuple; while TAX algebra specifies tree nodes by a tree pattern (or generalized tree pattern in [3]), to specify certain nodes by giving the constraints that these nodes should satisfy. Therefore, TAX algebra generalizes relational algebra in terms of how to specify objects to manipulate, but also introduces complexity at the same time. We shall see that in some cases, a pattern tree is an overkill for some intermediate results, which can be represented by lists or nested lists and thus can be manipulated more efficiently by operations on these specialized data structures.

Previous research on the evaluation and optimization of path expressions fall into two classes. *Navigational* approaches traverse the tree structure and test whether a tree node satisfies the constraints specified by the path expression [12]. *Join-based* approaches first select a list of XML tree nodes that satisfy the node-associated constraints for each pattern tree node, and then pairwise join the lists based on their structural relationships [1, 2, 11, 14]. Compared to the navigational techniques, join-based approaches are more scalable and enjoy optimization techniques from the relational database technology. However, there are inevitable difficulties because join-based approach usually results in many structural joins. In Section 4, we follow a novel approach that combines the advantages of both navigational and join-based approaches.

6   Open Problems and Planned Work

In this paper, I have presented my preliminary work on the definition of algebra and design of physical storage and optimization techniques. What remains is to define a complete set of operators, prove the soundness and completeness properties in a large fragment of XQuery (basically XQuery without recursive functions), and develop logical optimization techniques. Another primary goal of my research is to demonstrate how extensively this algebra accommodates optimization techniques, and how effective these techniques are in practice. I will justify the efficiency of the algebra by defining rewrite rules and investigating different evaluating strategies such as lazy evaluation (or output-oriented) strategy. We have shown (as in Fig. 1(b)) that the output template (SchemaTree) can be extracted from an XQuery expression. The remaining work is to show how to further generate an execution plan by backward (from output to input) analysis.

References

1. Shurug Al-Khalifa, H. V. Jagadish, Nick Koudas, Jignesh M. Patel, Divesh Srivastava, and Yuqing Wu. Structural Joins: A Primitive for Efficient XML Query Pattern Matching. In *Proc. 18th Int. Conf. on Data Engineering*, pages 141–152, 2002.
2. Nicolas Bruno, Nick Koudas, and Divesh Srivastava. Holistic Twig Joins: Optimal XML Pattern Matching. In *Proc. ACM SIGMOD Int. Conf. on Management of Data*, pages 310–322, 2002.
3. Zhimin Chen, H. V. Jagadish, Laks V. S. Lakshmanan, and Stelios Paparizos. From Tree Patterns to Generalized Tree Patterns: On Efficient Evaluation of XQuery. In *Proc. 29th Int. Conf. on Very Large Data Bases*, 2003.
4. V. Christophides, S. Cluet, and J. Simeon. On Wrapping Query Languages and Efficient XML Integration. In *Proc. ACM SIGMOD Int. Conf. on Management of Data*, pages 141–152, 2000.
5. David DeHann, David Toman, Mariano P. Consens, and M. Tamer 'Ozsu. A Comprehensive XQuery to SQL Translation using Dynamic Interval Encoding. In *J. ACM*, pages 623–634, 2003.
6. Peter Fankhauser, Mary Fernandez, Ashok Malhotra, Michael Rys, Jerome Simeon, and Philip Wadler. XQuery 1.0 Formal Semantics. W3C Working Draft, World Wide Web Consortium, November 2004. Available at http://www.w3.org/TR/query-semantics/.
7. Georg Gottlob, Christoph Koch, and Reinhard Pichler. Efficient Algorithms for Processing XPath Queries. In *Proc. 28th Int. Conf. on Very Large Data Bases*, pages 95–106, 2002.
8. H.V. Jagadish, Lakes V. S. Lakshmanan, Divesh Srivastava, and Keith Thompson. TAX: A Tree Algebra for XML. In *Proc. 8th Int. Workshop on Database Programming Languages*, 2001.
9. Stephan Kepser. A Proof of the Turing-completeness of XSLT and XQuery. Technical report, University of Tübingen, 2002.
10. Donald E. Knuth. *The Art of Computer Programming*, volume 1. Addison-Wesley, Reading, MA, 3rd edition, 1997.
11. Dennis Shasha, Jason T. L. Wang, and Rosalba Giugno. Algorithmics and Applications of Tree and Graph Searching. In *Proc. 21st ACM SIGACT-SIGMOD-SIGART Symp. Principles of Database Systems*, pages 39–53, 2002.
12. Jerome Simeon and Mary Fernandez. Galax, 2004. Available at http://www-db-out.bell-labs.com/galax/.
13. Yuqing Wu, Jignesh M. Patel, and H. V. Jagadish. Structural Join Order Selection for XML Query Optimization. In *Proc. 19th Int. Conf. on Data Engineering*, 2003.

14. C. Zhang, J. Naughton, D. Dewitt, Q. Luo, and G. Lohman. On Supporting Containment Queries in Relational Database Management Systems. In *Proc. ACM SIGMOD Int. Conf. on Management of Data*, pages 425–436, 2001.
15. Ning Zhang, Varun Kacholia, and M. Tamer Özsu. A Succinct Physical Storage Scheme for Efficient Evaluation of Path Queries in XML. In *Proc. 20th Int. Conf. on Data Engineering*, 2004.

An Access Structure for Similarity Search
in Metric Spaces

Vlastislav Dohnal

Faculty of Informatics, Masaryk University,
Botanická 68a, 602 00 Brno, Czech Republic
xdohnal@fi.muni.cz

Abstract. Similarity retrieval is an important paradigm for searching in environments where exact match has little meaning. Moreover, in order to enlarge the set of data types for which the similarity search can efficiently be performed, the mathematical notion of metric space provides a useful abstraction of similarity. In this paper, we present a novel access structure for similarity search in arbitrary metric spaces, called D-Index. D-Index supports easy insertions and deletions and bounded search costs for range queries with radius up to ρ. D-Index also supports disk memories, thus, it is able to deal with large archives. However, the partitioning principles employed in the D-Index are not very optimal since they produce high number of empty partitions. We propose several strategies of partitioning and, finally, compare them.

1   Introduction

Searching has always been one of the most prominent data processing operations because of its useful purpose of delivering required information efficiently. However, exact match retrieval, typical for traditional databases, is not sufficient or feasible for present applications, such as multimedia information retrieval, data mining, machine learning, and genome databases. What seems to be more useful, if not necessary, is to base the search paradigm on a form of *proximity*, or *dissimilarity* of a query and data objects. Roughly speaking, objects that are near a given query object form the query response set. In this place, the notion of mathematical *metric space* provides a useful abstraction of nearness.

Several storage structures, such as [2, 3, 6, 9], have been designed to support efficient similarity search execution over large collections of metric data where only a distance measure of pairs of objects is possible to quantify. However, the performance is still not satisfactory. Though all of the indexes are trees, many tree branches have to be traversed to solve a query, because similarity queries are basically range queries that typically cover data from several tree nodes or some other content-specific partitions. In principle, if many data partitions need to be accessed for a query region, they are not *contrasted* enough and such partitioning is not useful from the search point of view. Recently, the *excluded middle vantage point* strategy for partitioning of metric data has been proposed to develop an index structure [12] called *Excluded Middle Vantage Point Forest*, which creates a forest of one path search trees.

In this article, we describe recently proposed similarity search structure, called D-Index [8], which uses this strategy. The organization stores data objects in buckets with

W. Lindner et al. (Eds.): EDBT 2004 Workshops, LNCS 3268, pp. 133–143, 2004.
© Springer-Verlag Berlin Heidelberg 2004

direct access to avoid hierarchical bucket dependencies. Such organization also results in a very efficient insertion and deletion of objects. Though similarity constraints of queries can be defined arbitrarily, the structure is extremely efficient for queries searching for very close objects. We point out issues related to the design of the D-Index. In particular, we propose three strategies to combine partitioning principles which lead to better behavior of D-Index.

2   Related Work

The urgent need of indexing techniques that support execution of similarity queries led to the application of *spatial access methods* (SAMs) such as R-Tree. Unsatisfactory performance of R-Trees on high dimensional vector spaces lead to the further development. New access structures for searching high dimensional spaces, e.g. iDistance [13] or Pyramid [1] were proposed and analyzed. They both outperform R-Trees and demonstrate significant speedup. However, SAMs are limited by the following assumptions on which they rely: i) objects are represented by vectors in a multidimensional vector space, ii) the similarity between a pair of objects is often based on an L_p metric, e.g. Euclidean distance, which does not introduce any kind of correlation. Moreover, SAMs assume that the distance function can be trivially evaluated by means of time, which is not always the case of multimedia data, e.g. the distance of strings is measured by the *edit distance*, which has the complexity $\mathcal{O}(n^2)$. Finally, SAMs usually optimize only the number of access to disk memories, not the number of distance evaluations.

A more general approach to the similarity based searching is an index structure that operates in metric spaces. Note that in metric spaces we can only state the distance between two objects and a metric function is often considered as a CPU demanding operation. Uhlmann [10] proposes *metric tree* that partitions the metric space using the relative distances of objects. This technique is improved in [11] and *vantage point tree* is proposed. A further improvement of this concept has recently been presented by Yianilos [12]. This approach is based on the *excluded middle vantage point strategy* and creates a forest of vantage point trees. This principle is also exploited in the D-Index. The main contribution of indexing methods based on metric spaces is that they are not limited to the usage on vector spaces, thus, they can be applied on other domains, such as text strings or XML documents, without any additional nontrivial transformation to a vector space.

Although the number of access structures for metric spaces is impressive, see a recent survey [5] most of them suffer from being intrinsically *static*, which limits their applicability in dynamic environments. Contrary to SAM, presented metric trees optimize only the number of distance computations. Zezula et al proposed M-Tree [6] that optimizes both CPU and I/O costs.

3   Searching in Metric Spaces

A convenient way to assess similarity between two objects is to apply metric functions to decide the closeness of objects as a distance, that is the objects' dissimilarity. A *metric space* $\mathcal{M} = (\mathcal{D}, d)$ is defined by a domain of objects (elements, points) $\mathcal{D}$

and a total (distance) function d – a *non-negative* ($d(x, y) \geq 0$ with $d(x, y) = 0$ iff $x = y$) and *symmetric* ($d(x, y) = d(y, x)$) function that satisfies the *triangle inequality* ($d(x, y) \leq d(x, z) + d(z, y)$, $\forall x, y, z \in \mathcal{D}$). We assume that the maximum distance never exceeds d^+, thus we consider a *bounded metric space*.

In general, the problem of indexing in metric spaces can be defined as follows: *given a set $X \subseteq \mathcal{D}$ in the metric space $\mathcal{M}$, preprocess or structure the elements of X so that similarity queries can be answered efficiently.* For a query object $q \in \mathcal{D}$, two fundamental similarity queries can be defined. A *range query* retrieves all elements within distance r to q, that is, the set $\{x \in X, d(q, x) \leq r\}$. A *nearest neighbor* query retrieves the h closest elements to q, that is a set $R \subseteq X$ such that $|R| = h$ and $\forall x \in R, y \in X - R, d(q, x) \leq d(q, y)$.

For the space constraints of this article, we consider only the similarity range search operations here. In the following, we first define partitioning principles and then outline the ideas of the D-index. Next, we provide the range search algorithms. Finally, we present a sketch of comparison with M-Tree.

3.1   General Approach: Separable Partitioning

To achieve the objectives, the partitioning principle of D-Index is based on a mapping function, which is called the *ρ-split function*, where ρ is a real number constrained as $0 \leq \rho < d^+$. In order to gradually explain the concept of ρ-split functions, we first define a first order ρ-split function and its properties.

Definition 1. *Given a metric space $(\mathcal{D}, d)$, a first order ρ-split function $s^{1,\rho}$ is the mapping $s^{1,\rho} : \mathcal{D} \rightarrow \{0, 1, -\}$, such that for arbitrary different objects $x, y \in \mathcal{D}$, $s^{1,\rho}(x) = 0 \land s^{1,\rho}(y) = 1 \Rightarrow d(x, y) > 2\rho$ (separable property) and $\rho_2 \geq \rho_1 \land s^{1,\rho_2}(x) \neq - \land s^{1,\rho_1}(y) = - \Rightarrow d(x, y) > \rho_2 - \rho_1$ (symmetry property).*

In other words, the ρ-split function assigns to each object of the space $\mathcal{D}$ one of the symbols 0, 1, or $-$.

The concept of ρ-split functions can, of course, be generalized by concatenating n first order ρ-split functions with the purpose of obtaining a split function of order n.

Definition 2. *Given n first order ρ-split functions $s_1^{1,\rho}, \ldots, s_n^{1,\rho}$ in the metric space $(\mathcal{D}, d)$, a ρ-split function of order n $s^{n,\rho} = (s_1^{1,\rho}, s_2^{1,\rho}, \ldots, s_n^{1,\rho}) : \mathcal{D} \rightarrow \{0, 1, -\}^n$ is the mapping, such that for arbitrary different objects $x, y \in \mathcal{D}$, $\forall i\ s_i^{1,\rho}(x) \neq - \land s_i^{1,\rho}(y) \neq - \land s^{n,\rho}(x) \neq s^{n,\rho}(y) \Rightarrow d(x, y) > 2\rho$ (separable property) and $\rho_2 \geq \rho_1 \land \forall i\ s_i^{1,\rho_2}(x) \neq - \land \exists j\ s_j^{1,\rho_1}(y) = - \Rightarrow d(x, y) > \rho_2 - \rho_1$ (symmetry property).*

An obvious consequence of the ρ-split function definitions is that by combining n first order ρ-split functions $s_1^{1,\rho}, \ldots, s_n^{1,\rho}$, which satisfy the separable and symmetric properties, we obtain a ρ-split function of order n $s^{n,\rho}$ which also demonstrates the separable and symmetric properties. We often refer to the number of symbols generated by $s^{n,\rho}$, that is the parameter n, as the *order* of the ρ-split function. In order to obtain an addressing scheme with direct access, another function that transforms the ρ-split strings into integers is defined as follows.

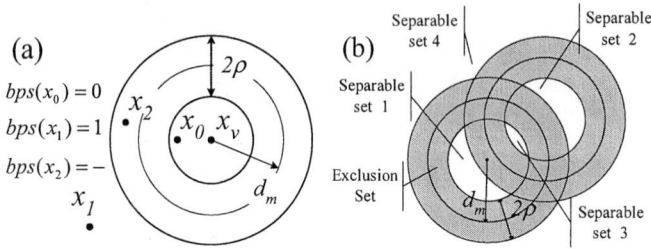

Fig. 1. The *bps* split function (a) and the combination of two *bps* functions (b)

Definition 3. *Given a string* $b = (b_1, \ldots, b_n)$ *of* n *elements 0, 1, or* $-$*, the function* $\langle \cdot \rangle : \{0, 1, -\}^n \to [0..2^n]$ *is specified as:*

$$\langle b \rangle = \begin{cases} [b_1, b_2, \ldots, b_n]_2 = \sum_{j=1}^{n} 2^{n-j} b_j, & \text{if } \forall j \; b_j \neq - \\ 2^n, & \text{otherwise} \end{cases}$$

When all the elements are different from '$-$', the function $\langle b \rangle$ simply translates the string b into an integer by interpreting it as a binary number (which is always $< 2^n$), otherwise the function returns 2^n.

By means of the ρ-split function and the $\langle \cdot \rangle$ operator, we can assign an integer number i ($0 \leq i \leq 2^n$) to each object $x \in \mathcal{D}$, i.e., the function can group objects from $X \subset \mathcal{D}$ in $2^n + 1$ disjoint subsets.

Though several different types of first order ρ-split functions are proposed, analyzed, and evaluated in [7], the *ball partitioning split* (*bps*) originally proposed in [12] under the name *excluded middle partitioning*, provided the smallest exclusion set. For this reason, this approach is also applied in the D-Index and can be characterized as follows.

The ball partitioning ρ-split function *bps* uses one reference object (pivot) x_v and the *medium distance* d_m to partition a data set into three subsets, see Figure 1a. The result of the *bps* function gives the unique identification of the set to which the object x belongs:

$$bps(x) = \begin{cases} 0 & \text{if } d(x, x_v) \leq d_m - \rho \\ 1 & \text{if } d(x, x_v) > d_m + \rho \\ - & \text{otherwise} \end{cases}$$

The subset of objects characterized by the symbol '$-$' is called the *exclusion set*, while the subsets of objects characterized by the symbols 0 and 1 are the *separable sets*, because any range query with radius not larger than ρ cannot find qualifying objects in both the subsets.

To obtain more separable sets we define higher order ρ-split function as a combination of several *bps* functions, where the resulting exclusion set is the union of the exclusion sets of the original split functions. Furthermore, the new separable sets are obtained as the intersection of all possible pairs of separable sets of the original functions. Figure 1b gives an illustration of this idea for the case of two split functions. Several strategies of combining ρ-split functions are discussed in Section 4.

3.2   D-Index

The basic idea of the D-Index is to create a multilevel storage and retrieval structure that uses several ρ-split functions, one for each level, to create an array of *buckets* for storing objects. On the first level, we use a ρ-split function for separating objects of the whole data set. For any other level, objects mapped to the exclusion bucket of the previous level are the candidates for storage in separable buckets of this level. Finally, the exclusion bucket of the last level forms the exclusion bucket of the whole D-Index structure. It is worth noting that the ρ-split functions of individual levels use the same ρ. Moreover, split functions can have different order, typically decreasing with the level, allowing the D-Index structure to have levels with a different number of buckets. In particular, from the structure point of view you can observe the buckets organized as the following two dimensional array consisting of $1 + \sum_{i=1}^{h} 2^{m_i}$ elements.

$$B_{1,0}, B_{1,1}, \ldots, B_{1,2^{m_1}-1}$$
$$B_{2,0}, B_{2,1}, \ldots, B_{2,2^{m_2}-1}$$
$$\vdots$$
$$B_{h,0}, B_{h,1}, \ldots, B_{h,2^{m_h}-1}, E_h$$

All separable buckets are included, but only the E_h exclusion bucket is present – exclusion buckets $E_{i<h}$ are recursively re-partitioned on level $i + 1$. Then, for each row i (i.e. the D-Index level), 2^{m_i} buckets are defined and are separable up to 2ρ, thus we are sure that there do not exist two buckets at the same level i both containing relevant objects for any similarity range query with radius $r \leq \rho$.

In order to deal with overflow problems and growing files, buckets are implemented as *elastic buckets* and consist of the necessary number of fixed-size blocks (pages) – basic disk access units.

Range Search. Given a range query $\mathcal{Q} = \mathcal{R}(q, r)$, we define a simple search algorithm. This algorithm, however, evaluates only limited queries with $r \leq \rho$.

Algorithm 1. *Search*

> **for** $i = 1$ **to** h
>   *return all objects x such that $x \in \mathcal{Q} \cap B_{i, \langle s_i^{m_i, 0}(q) \rangle}$;*
> **end for**
> *return all objects x such that $x \in \mathcal{Q} \cap E_h$;*

During the elaboration of the algorithm we manipulate the value of parameter ρ of split functions. When we use $\rho = 0$ the function $\langle s_i^{m_i, 0}(q) \rangle$ always gives a value smaller than 2^{m_i}. Consequently, one separable bucket on each level i is determined. Finally, the algorithm also accesses the exclusion bucket of the whole structure. The algorithm requires $h + 1$ bucket accesses, which forms the upper bound on the search.

Generic Range Search. Algorithm 1 requires to access one bucket at each level of the D-Index, plus the exclusion bucket. In the following two situations, however, the number of accesses can even be reduced: i) if the query region is contained in the exclusion partition of the level i, then the query cannot have objects in the separable buckets of this level and only the next level must be considered, ii) if the query region is contained in a separable partition of the level i the following levels, as well as, the exclusion bucket need not be accessed, thus the search terminates on this level.

Another drawback of the simple algorithm is that it works only for search radii up to ρ. However, with additional computational effort queries with $r > \rho$ can also be executed. Indeed, such queries can be executed by evaluating the split function $s^{r_q-\rho}$. In case $s^{r_q-\rho}$ returns a string without any '$-$', the result is contained in the single bucket $B_{\langle s^{r_q-\rho}\rangle}$ plus, possibly, the exclusion bucket.

Let us now consider that the string returned contains at least one '$-$'. We indicate this string as $b = (b_1, \ldots, b_n)$ with $b_i = \{0, 1, -\}$. In case there is only one $b_i = $ '$-$', we must access all buckets B, whose index is obtained by substituting '$-$' with 0 and 1. For this purpose, we define the function G that returns all identifications of buckets that must be accessed. For example, G returns the set $\{\langle 001\rangle, \langle 011\rangle\}$ for the string '0–1'. In the most general case, we must substitute in the string b all the '$-$' with zeros and ones and generate all possible combinations.

Given a query region $\mathcal{Q} = \mathcal{R}(q, r_q)$ with $q \in \mathcal{D}$ and $r_q \leq d^+$. An advanced algorithm can execute the similarity range query as follows.

Algorithm 2. *Range Search*

> *01.* **for** *i=1* **to** *h*
> *02.*   **if** $\langle s_i^{m_i,\rho+r_q}(q)\rangle < 2^{m_i}$ **then** (exclusively in a separable bucket)
> *03.*   *return all objects x such that $x \in \mathcal{Q} \cap B_{i,\langle s_i^{m_i,\rho+r_q}(q)\rangle}$;* **exit;**
> *04.*   **end if**
> *05.*   **if** $r_q \leq \rho$ **then** (search radius up to ρ)
> *06.*   **if** $\langle s_i^{m_i,\rho-r_q}(q)\rangle < 2^{m_i}$ **then**(not exclusively in an exclusion b.)
> *07.*   *return all objects x such that $x \in \mathcal{Q} \cap B_{i,\langle s_i^{m_i,\rho-r_q}(q)\rangle}$;*
> *08.*   **end if**
> *09.*   **else** (search radius greater than ρ)
> *10.*   **let**$\{l_1, l_2, \ldots, l_k\} = G(s_i^{m_i,r_q-\rho}(q))$
> *11.*   *return all objects x such that $x \in \mathcal{Q} \cap B_{i,l_1}, \ldots, x \in \mathcal{Q} \cap B_{i,l_k}$;*
> *12.*   **end if**
> *13.* **end for**
> *14.* return all objects x such that $x \in \mathcal{Q} \cap E_h$;

In general, Algorithm 2 considers all D-Index levels and eventually also accesses the global exclusion bucket. However, the test on the line 02 can discover the exclusive containment of the query region in a separable bucket and terminate the search earlier. Otherwise, the algorithm proceeds according to the size of the query radius. If $r \leq \rho$ there are two possibilities. If the test on line 06 is satisfied one separable bucket is accessed. Otherwise no separable bucket is accessed on this level because the query region is from this level point of view exclusively in the exclusion zone. Provided the search radius is greater than ρ, more separable buckets are accessed on a specific level. Unless terminated earlier, the algorithm accesses the exclusion bucket at line 14.

3.3 Comparison

We have compared the D-Index with other index structures, particularly, we considered M-Tree[1] [6] and a sequential organization (SEQ). According to [5], these are the only types of index structures for metric data that use disk memories to store objects. We have conducted the experiments on 45-dimensional vectors of image color features compared by the *quadratic distance* measure. The data set consisted of 11,000 objects and had practically normal distribution. We have measured average performance over 50 different query objects considering numerous similarity range queries. The results are shown in Figure 2.

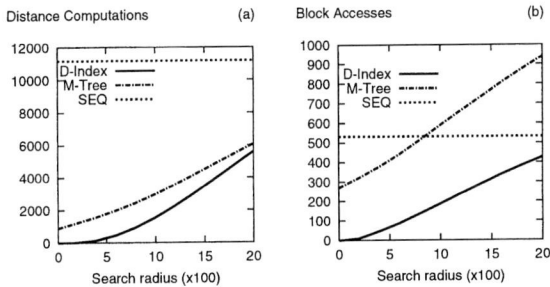

Fig. 2. Comparison of the range search efficiency in the number of distance computations (a) and the number of block accesses (b)

For all tested queries, i.e. retrieving subsets up to 20% of the database, the D-Index always needed less distance computations than the M-tree and the number of block accesses of the M-tree was significantly higher than for the D-Index. This is obvious since the M-Tree has nodes with fixed capacity[2] while the bucket in D-Index consists of necessary number of blocks (the size of blocks is fixed). The superior performance in the terms of distance computations can be attributed to the fact that the D-Index also applies the pivot-based filtering techniques, which significantly reduce the number of distance computation, for details see [8]. Moreover, the D-Index uses the same pivots in the partitioning, i.e. ρ-split functions, and in the filtering technique to further reduce the number of distance evaluations. Figure 2b demonstrates another interesting observation: to run the *exact match* query, i.e. range search with $r = 0$, the D-Index only needs to access one block. As a comparison, the M-Tree needs one half of the SEQ. Notice that the exact match search is used to locate an object to be deleted and forms the main cost of delete operations. In this respect, the D-Index is able to manage deletions much more efficiently than the M-tree. In this case, the advantage of the D-Index over the M-Tree is caused by its structure. The M-Tree must traverse the tree and access all internal nodes along the search path. However, the D-Index computes ρ-split functions, which does

---

[1] The software is available at http://www-db.deis.unibo.it/research/Mtree/

[2] Overflow problems are solved with node splits. Thus, after a split there is approximately 50% of space wasted in the new nodes, which need not be filled anymore.

not require any disk accesses and directly determines the bucket to access. Due to the applied pivot-based algorithm, all object in blocks of buckets are sorted according to the distance to a pivot. Consequently, the D-Index is able to locate a block in the bucket where the object to delete resides without any additional block accesses.

We have also performed scalability tests over the same data collection but ranging from 100,000 to 600,000 objects. For these experiments, the D-Index structure was defined by 37 pivots and 74 buckets.The D-Index was strictly linear, that is, the costs to evaluate a query grow linearly with the data size. The M-Tree was slightly better than the D-Index but this is attributed to the fact that M-Tree is incrementally reorganizing its structure while the D-Index structure is using a constant structure. The development of a dynamic structure of D-Index is our main research issue. This problem is partially discussed in the next section.

4   Improved Partitioning Strategies

In this stage, we emphasize the main drawback of the D-Index access structure and sketch some possible solutions. The experiments revealed that the D-Index is very efficient and outperforms the others nearly in all situations. However, its partitioning principles are not very optimal and produce unbalanced partitions. In particular, we concern the problem of selecting reference objects (pivots). Next, we deal with the issue of combining several rho-split functions into a single mapping function.

The problem of choosing pivots is important for any search technique in the general metric space, because all such algorithms need, directly or indirectly, some "anchors" for partitioning and search pruning. It is well known that the way in which pivots are selected affects the performance of proper algorithms. This has been recognized and demonstrated by several researchers [11, 2]. Recently, the problem was systematically studied in [4], and several strategies for selecting pivots have been proposed and tested. The generic conclusion is that good pivots are i) far away from the remaining objects of the metric space and ii) far away from each other pivot. In the D-Index, we also use this technique to select pivots.

The design of D-Index structure requires specification of several ρ-split functions which are usually combinations of bps functions. In general, the idealized split function should produce balanced buckets each containing nearly the same number of objects and minimize the size of the exclusion bucket. Figure 3 presents three possible strategies to combine two bps functions. The first technique, depicted in (a) is utilized in the D-Index and uses the pivot p_1 and $d_m = r_1$ to divide the space into two separable partitions. Next, these two partitions are repartitioned using a different bps function which applies a different pivot p_2 and $d_m = r_2$, however, the same for both the partitions. As a result, we obtain four separable buckets. We refer to this method as the *strict strategy*.

The second strategy in (b) differs from the first one in one aspect. It makes use of the pivot p_2 in the second function as well, but two different values of d_m, r_2^1 and r_2^2 are applied for the left and the right partition, respectively. The hypothesis behind is that by manipulations with the parameter d_m we can achieve better balanced buckets, diminish empty buckets and decrease the occupation of exclusion sets. We refer to this as the *variable d_m strategy*.

item (e.g., uncacheable data, compulsory misses) occurs that entails a round-trip to the database, performance will suffer. [2] provides a feeling for the performance penalty of relational databases with and without the technique of prefetching. According to the experiments described in [2], the retrieval time of data is up to 5.5 times faster to get rows in a batch of 100 rows than a row at a time. Simple prefetch mechanisms, which create read-ahead threads for certain queries that return large quantities of data sequentially from a single table, are already used in commercial data servers or application servers.

The prefetching technique of reading ahead of time, which we refer to as read-aheads in the rest of the paper, is used to reduce the number of database roundtrips either by augmenting the current query to include the answer to the next queries or to generate additional queries that are likely to come next. In current application servers, some read-ahead techniques are already used by object managers or containers. However, these techniques should be used systematically, because incorrect guessing reduces the throughput of the server, and the overhead examining the query for possible concatenations increases the latency. Current object managers that are responsible for accessing the database cannot efficiently benefit from the application's context descriptions. In this respect, we want to help such object managers to maximize the probability of correct guessing and to have efficient database interactions by finding the rules of thumb regarding what strategies to use to determine efficient sequences of SQL statements. We want to provide a systematic vision for state-of-the-art read-ahead techniques.

2   Motivation and Problem Formulation

Our goal is to bring the potentially accessible data to application's environment in the most efficient way in terms of maximal throughput and minimal database interaction cost. We use relational structure of data such as table relationships and data dependencies, and access patterns of the applications to predict the potentially accesssible data that has the lowest retrieval cost. We separate this original problem into two parts.

1. Design generic rules for determining the efficient sequences of SQL statements for read-ahead queries on relational databases, such that the rules would be useful across application domains and data-access patterns.
2. Develop efficient and scalable algorithms for fine-tuning the read-ahead access rules in each particular application.

We seek rules of thumb that would be applicable accross application domains and data-access patterns. To derive such *generic domain-independent rules*, we need to study the parameters that influence the costs of various combinations of read-ahead SQL statements that implement the generic access patterns. These generic domain-independent rules are then fine-tuned according to the data-access patterns of particular applications.

In the first phase of our project, we look for break-even points for efficient sequences of SQL statements by discovering new parameters and by exploring known parameters such as the size of data in the tables (number of rows and columns), the complexity of SQL calls (e.g., number of joins, presence of subqueries), presence of indexed columns, shape of the graph we are trying to retrieve (in a depth-first manner or breadth-first manner), and network latency (in later stages of the project). Break-even points correspond to parameter values that are used in constructing efficient sequences of SQL statements, which give maximal throughput with minimal database interaction cost including data-retrieval time. As an outcome of this phase, we will have rules of thumb applicable across applications regarding what strategies to use for efficient sequences of SQL statements. At present, we don't consider the caching aspects of the problem to answer subsequent queries from the results that were prefetched. In addition to this, we don't consider read-aheads for batch queries. For example, instead of focusing on queries such as *find the name of all customers*, we focus on queries such as *find the name of the customer with given ID* .

Example 2.1 We consider a simple financial services data model for our examples [10]. According to this model, there can be many banks, and each customer can have multiple accounts in different banks. Relations *Person* and *Organization* store detailed informa-tion about customers of the banks. The relation *Customer* stores the common attributes of persons and organizations. The relation *Account* stores account information for cus-tomers in various banks. In the first and second transactions, we consider a customer representative who issues three and two data-access requests, respectively for the same customer from the database (The data-access requests are abbreviated with uppercase letters).

Transaction 1:

A Find the city and SSN of (person) customer '0011111'.
B Find the total amount of money that customer '0011111' has in all his accounts.
C Find the routing numbers of the banks where customer '0011111' has accounts.

Transaction 2:

D Find the name of customer '0011111'.
C Find the routing numbers of the banks where customer '0011111' has accounts.

For Transaction 1, request **A** requires two joins on tables for Customer, Person and Address without any read-aheads as in Figure 1. With read-aheads, it will be a smart choice to also bring data from Account table as in Figure 2, because request **B** that comes after **A**, requires data in the Account table. So using just one SQL statement with three joins as in Figure 2, we answer the first two requests **A** and **B**. For request **C**, we need to access the Bank_Customers table, so we need another SQL statement to fetch the data. As a result, with two SQL statements as in Figure 2 (three joins for the first statement and no joins for the second statement), we are able to answer the requests in Transaction 1. As another option, we can bring all the graph data in just one SQL statement by joining all the required tables at once; but in this case we will have a more complex query shown in Figure 3. This example shows the trade off between some of the parameters, such as the cost of the join operation versus the number of database roundtrips. Although the SQL statement in Figure 3 requires one database roundtrip, we may choose to use two SQL statements as in Figure 2 because these statements need fewer join operations in total and thus may result in lower total roundtrip time for large databases.

```
select Address.city, Person.ssn
from Customer, Person, Address
where Person.customerId=Customer.customerId
and Customer.addressId=Address.addressId
and Customer.customerId= '0011111'
```

Fig. 1. SQL statement for Transaction 1: A

AB:
```
select  Person.ssn, Address.city, sum(amount)
from Customer, Account, Person, Address
where Person.customerId=Customer.customerId
and Customer.addressId=Address.addressId
and Customer.customerId=Account.customerId
and Customer.customerId= '0011111'
group by Person.ssn, Address.city
```

C:
```
select routingNumber
from Bank_Customers
where customerId='0011111'
```

Fig. 2. SQL statements for Transaction 1: AB and C

```
select Address.city, Person.ssn, Bank_Customers.routingNumber, sum(amount)
from Customer, Account, Person, Address, Bank_Customers
where Person.customerId=Customer.customerId and Customer.addressId=Address.addressId
and Customer.customerId=Account.customerId and Customer.customerId= '0011111'
and Customer.customerId=Bank_Customers.customerId
group by Person.ssn, Address.city, Bank_Customers .routingNumber
```

Fig. 3. SQL statement for Transaction 1: ABC

As the above example illustrates, our goal is not to find the minimal number of data-access statements, but to find the efficient number of simplest data-access statements. For example, one very complex data-access statement can bring all the data by reading ahead of time at one roundtrip, but this statement may not result in the maximal throughput due to the cost of the join operations. Also this data-access statement can bring the data that may never be needed by the application.

In subsequent phases of the project, we will explore the effect of object-to-relational mapping technique on our generic domain-independent rules and will develop and test learning algorithms to increase the efficieny of our generic rules for the data-access patterns of particular applications.

3   Related Work

In [11], various types of prefetching are characterized according to its short-term and long-term benefits. In short-term prefetching, future accesses to data are predicted according to the cache's recent access history. In long-term prefetching, global object access patterns are used to identify valuable objects that are worth prefetching (i.e., if an object is accessed by one client, it is likely that it will be accessed by other clients) [11].

Both prefetching techniques are mainly used in reducing the latency used in loading web pages [4]. In our work, we use long-term prefetching that also uses data-access costs to identify cheap and valuable prefething sequences.

Prefetching is used to either pre-load the data needed for the subsequent queries for the given workload or load a specific collection of objects related to the requested object. The former case requires a more complex mechanism to track the cache contents and an analysis of which parts of the previous query is contained in the subsequent query, is required. [5] addresses the former case as an optimization for computing overlapping queries that generate Web pages (e.g., online shopping, where users narrow down their search space as they navigate through a sequence of pages). Predicate-based caching also serves the same idea where current cache content is used to answer future queries [7]. The approach in [12] uses the transition probabilities for each query to find the most probable query that can appear after the current query. So while executing the current query, they also execute the most probable subsequent query by using probable parameters and query pattern. In our approach, we take into account the cost of the data-access statements and parameters that affect this cost, to find the efficient sequence SQL statements.

[9] proposes to use a predictive cache to recognize and exploit access patterns for applications by incorporating prefetching mechanism with cache replacement mechanism to eliminate erroneous or least-likely prefetches. [6] also aims to 'pre-cache' the objects that are likely to be subsequently accessed by the application. Haas et al. propose a heuristic approach to cache and prefetch the objects whose object identifiers were returned as part of the query, so they make prefetching decisions according to the object identifiers found in the result set of the query. However, instead of focusing on finding the most beneficial prefetches, their goal is to find the cost of caching the prefetched objects. They incorporate the prefetching process into query processing to find the best execution plan by considering the cost of caching the prefetched tuples.

[2] specifically addresses the prefetching technique on relational databases where persistent objects are implemented. They use the context of an object as a predictor for future accesses in navigational applications. This context describes the structure in which the object was fetched. Main prefetching methods are listed (e.g., prefetching all the attributes of the requested object(s)). The results are applicable accross application domains, because they use generic access patterns that are applicable across a wide range of applications. However, they only make one-level prefetching for referenced objects, so they don't actually answer the 'how deep' question for read-aheads. Their overall goal is to minimize database latency for future data-access statements, so they don't explore the cost of efficient sequence of data-access statements.

We explore the cost of data-access statements to find efficient generic data-access patterns. None of the previous work consider the prefetching problem both with query optimization parameters and navigational access patterns, such as following a relationship, at the same time. Also by providing a mechanism for merging simple data-access statements to find an efficient sequence of data-access statement, we actually use a different aspect for multi-query optimization [3] where dependencies or common subexpressions between the queries in a sequence are explored and computed.

4   Proposed Approach

Applications use objects, but these objects are mapped to tuples of the appropriate tables. In relational databases, the objects accessed by the applications are always associated with each other. Most of the time, the data in the database is accessed according to these associations, and again most of the time these associations are intuitive and work just as you would expect. This is an important observation for the first phase of our project in which we don't specifically use data-access patterns of particular applications. Instead, for the first phase of the project, our goal is to come up with generic read-ahead rules that are applicable across applications. An important property of applications for systems such as health-care, financial, or human resources is repetitive usage of the same query templates. For example, an application can request the due date of a credit card payment after requesting the balance, or it can request the transactions of the same card in the last billing period. The similar associations and dependencies that can be found in different domains form a basis for guessing the useful generic access patterns in our project.

Generic access patterns aren't enough to determine the most beneficial and efficient read-ahead scheme configuration. These patterns are helpful to determine the useful sequence of SQL statements. On the other hand, we need to find efficient sequences of (merged) SQL statements. Finding such efficient sequences includes answering the following questions:

1. How much to read ahead? This question requires figuring out which tables and table columns may be subsequently accessed, and how the structure of data (e.g., existence of an indexed attribute) and relational constraints affect the structure of a read-ahead query.
2. How deep to read ahead? This question requires figuring out the levels of the object hierarchy that may be subsequently accessed. How does the number of joins affect the efficiency of sequence of SQL statements?
3. In what direction to read ahead? In each level of the object hierarchy, each object can be associated with many different objects. This question requires figuring out the trade-off of typical directions of the traversal on the object hierarchy that is stored in the relational database.

5   Research Methodology

We construct a testbed to experiment with the parameters that affect the cost of SQL statements used while reading ahead of time. The focus of our case study is to discover and experiment with the data-access patterns of financial applications with parameters that are related to the structure of the data in the database. For this case study, we use a slightly modified version of the standard data model for financial services (e.g., banking and investment services) as described in [10]. Some of the main entities of this model are shown in Figure 4. We use Oracle 9i as our data server to implement the entire data model which has 55 tables and maximum fan-out of 7 relationships. After creating a sample database for this model, we list possible query templates for the model. Here, we list some query templates.

- Find the attributes of a given customer
- Find the accounts for a given customer
- Find the agreements to which a given financial product(s) is related
- Find the assets of a given customer that are used for loan agreements
- Find the account transactions of a given account
- Find the names of the customers that have more than a given number of accounts

The above list can be easily extended. By using these potential query templates, we can come up with meaningful generic access sequences for the database.

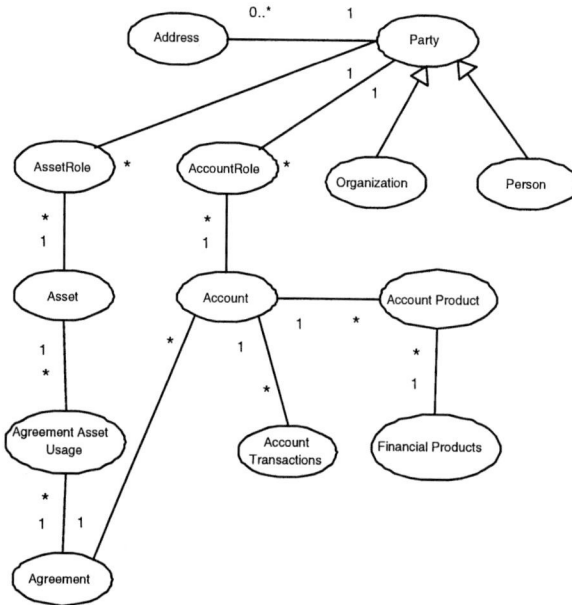

Fig. 4. Some entities in the financial services model

We generate SQL statements that implement access patterns, which are part of the given access sequence. To generate various combinations of SQL statements for the given access sequence with read-ahead functionality, we can use the following prefetch methods:

- Prefetch only primary keys of the associated objects
- Prefetch primary and non-primary foreign keys
- Prefetch key and non-key attributes, or only non-key attributes
- Prefetch via traversing the inheritance-extension, one-to-many association (i.e., aggregation), or many-to-many type of relationships

We model the data accesses as a directed graph. In this directed graph, vertices correspond to simple data-access statements and edges correspond to transition probabilities between the statements. These probabilities can be calculated and updated using access log files of the database server. For example, if we consider each data-access request used in Example 2.1 as simple data-access statement,we obtain the simple *data-access statement transition graph* in Figure 5. Based on this simple hypothetical transition graph, whenever A is accessed there is a 40% chance that B will be accessed next. We assume an acyclic graph that can have multiple sources and sinks for the first phase of the project.

To initialize large transition graphs for financial services applications, we generate vertices by using above query templates and generate edges with random probabilities by above prefetch methods that use generic associations and dependencies among relations.

We need to merge simple data-access statements to find optimal sequences of SQL statements for the given access sequence. There are two principle ways to combine two or more SQL statements. Either the statements are executed *at the same time* or they are executed *one after the other*. We call the first combination *merged execution* and denote it by operator *; the second combination represents *sequential execution* and is denoted by operator +. We can apply * repeatedly to describe access patterns, and apply + repeatedly to combine patterns to form the access sequence. By definition, * is commutative, while + is not, and * has precedence over +. For example, if we have an access sequence *ADEF* for a larger graph in Figure 6, we can come up with compound statements such as $A*D*E+F$, $A*D*E*F$, $A*C*D+E*F$, $A*B*D+E*F$, $A+D*E*F$ and so on. By using large acyclic graphs, we can consider more complex access patterns. To find efficient compound statements, we derive a benefit formula, which takes into account the processing cost and the probabilities of each simple and compound statements that can generate the given access sequence. This formula also includes a risk factor, which aims to balance the cost and usefullness of the generated sequence. According to the query workload or even type of applications, the risk factor can change.

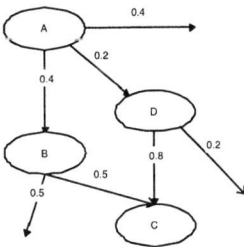

Fig. 5. Query transition graph for Example 2.1

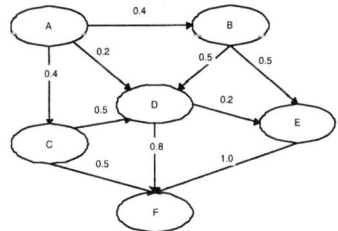

Fig. 6. A sample query transition graph

By using the results of the benefit formula and the computed cost of an access sequence, e.g., processing cost for $A+D+E+F$, we will determine rules of thumb regarding what strategies to use for efficient sequences of SQL statements for the financial services domain. Then, we will test and fine-tune the rules on other application domains.

6   Discussion

The results of our work can be used to effectively preload associated dataset of a requested object that may be subsequently accessed. Our work can also be integrated with query optimizers to find the efficient execution plans for compound SQL statements. This integration provides us another aspect for multi-query optimization.

This work can also be integrated with Container Managed Persistence containers or Java Data Object drivers as a performance tuning technique. Using this technique, we will be able to get ahead of time the working set of objects for the current transaction in very concurrent environments. Also this work can be helpful in determining the right cache size for systems that use prefetching.

One of the important implementation challenges is to merge simple SQL statements on-the-fly to experiment with the compound SQL statements. This isn't a trivial task, because it requires the detailed knowledge of the relational structure of data. Even for the statements that are syntactically similar, we can have different merged SQL statements.

We use applications' common behaviours and the cost of database interactions to generate read-ahead rules that can provide a significant performance gain for systems where many concurrent data-intensive read-only applications access huge databases.

Acknowledgements

I would like to thank Rada Chirkova and Munindar P. Singh for their guidance and suggestions. I would also like to thank Timo Salo for his helpful comments. This research is supported under NCSU CACC Grant 11019.

References

1. Sibel Adali, K. Selçuk Candan, Yannis Papakonstantinou, and V. S. Subrahmanian. Query caching and optimization in distributed mediator systems. In *Proc. 1996 ACM SIGMOD Conf. on Management of Data*, pages 137–148, 1996.
2. Philip A. Bernstein, Shankar Pal, and David Shutt. Context-based prefetch – An optimization for implementing objects on relations. *VLDB Journal*, 9(3):177–189, 2000.
3. Sunil Choenni, Martin Kersten, Amani Saad, and Johan van den Akker. A framework for multi-query optimization. In *Proc. 8th Int. Conf. on Management of Data (COMAD'97)*, pages 165–82, 1997.
4. Brian D. Davison. *The Design And Evaluation Of Web Prefetching and Caching Techniques*. PhD thesis, Department of Computer Science, Rutgers University, October 2002.
5. Daniela Florescu, Alon Levy, Dan Suciu, and Khaled Yagoub. Optimization of run-time management of data intensive Web sites. In *Proc. 25th VLDB Conf.*, pages 627–638, September 1999.
6. Laura M. Haas, Donald Kossmann, and Ioana Ursu. Loading a cache with query results. In *Proc. 25th VLDB Conf.*, pages 351–362, 1999.
7. Arthur M. Keller and Julie Basu. A predicate-based caching scheme for client-server database architectures. *VLDB Journal*, 5(1):35–47, 1996.
8. Tom M. Kroeger, Darrell D. E. Long, and Jeffrey C. Mogul. Exploring the bounds of Web latency reduction from caching and prefetching. In *USENIX Symposium on Internet Technologies and Systems*, 1997.

9. Mark Palmer and Stanley B. Zdonik. FIDO: A cache that learns to fetch. In *Proc. 17th VLDB Conf.*, pages 255–264, Barcelona, Spain, 1991.

10. Len Silverston. *The Data Model Resource Book*, volume 2. John Wiley and Sons, New York, 2001.

11. Arun Venkataramani, Praveen Yalagandula, Ravindranath Kokku, Sadia Sharif, and Mike Dahlin. The potential costs and benefits of long term prefetching for content distribution. In *Proc. of Web Content Caching and Distribution Workshop*, 2001.

12. Dazhi Wang and Junyi Xie. An approach toward Web caching and prefetching for database management systems. Technical report, Department of Computer Science, Duke University, 2001. http://www.cs.duke.edu/~junyi/cps216/report.pdf.

RAM: A Multidimensional Array DBMS

Alex R. van Ballegooij

CWI, Amsterdam, The Netherlands
alex.van.ballegooij@cwi.nl

Abstract. Application areas beyond (simple) administrative tasks are dominated by custom built solutions. Tasks like multimedia analysis require a view on data different from that offered by most database management systems: the set based data model may no longer suffice.

To address this issue we introduce RAM: a multidimensional array database system. The concept of an array database system is not new, however our approach differs from earlier work in that we realize this new view on data by mapping it onto a traditional relational schema. This approach unites the strengths of existing database systems with the added benefits of bulk array processing.

1 Motivation

Application areas beyond (simple) administrative tasks are dominated by custom built solutions, and, if used at all, database management systems are only used for persistent storage.

Past experience with the implementation of multimedia retrieval and analysis in a database setting, see e.g. [10, 11], have proved the potential value of set-oriented query processing techniques for multimedia analysis. However, the *efficient* manipulation of the (inherently ordered) media data requires non-trivial data storage schemes. The resulting query plans are rarely intuitive, while deriving such plans is a laborious and error-prone process: it is difficult to keep track of the relationship between the operations in the relational query and the steps in the original algorithms.

For these reasons, multimedia analysis applications are often implemented using specialized mathematical environments, such as Matlab [12]. While this provides an array data structure suited for the task, it is not ideal. The interface offered is an imperative programming language; this makes development error-prone, time consuming, and, resulting applications are not scalable beyond main memory capacity without explicit user intervention[1]. In addition, data-management facilities are limited to rudimentary use of files for persistent storage, lacking the features commonly provided by database management systems.

We seek a solution to these problems by introducing array data structures in a database environment.

---

[1] User intervention like explicit division of the data into separate chunks and alteration of algorithms to deal with fragmented data.

W. Lindner et al. (Eds.): EDBT 2004 Workshops, LNCS 3268, pp. 154–165, 2004.

1.1 Research Objective

The hypothesis behind our research is that the architecture of a relational database system is a suitable basis for the development of a multi-dimensional database system. The query optimization and storage layers provide the opportunities to construct a solution which in practice provides performance close to a dedicated implementation, while reducing the burden on the programmer: a DBMS allows application programmers to abstract from complex issues such as data management and efficient evaluation of complex queries.

The main research objective is summarized as follows: "How can support for storage and efficient processing of multi-dimensional arrays be integrated into a relational database management system?".

The first issue to address is the actual storage and manipulation of array structures in a relational database environment.

Second, scalability is a large challenge in the database community. In practice, current database systems fail on large data-sets. A typical system can hardly manage more than a few gigabytes, let alone the daunting volumes of large scale scientific problems and comprehensive multimedia archives. We belief that array processing helps to improve scalability of database systems because the clear structure and (more) predictable processing patterns allow for efficient memory management.

Finally, it can be expected that query evaluation over array structures performed in a foreign environment, the relational paradigm, comes at a cost. The efficiency of query evaluation is an important requirement for a usable system however, and must be maintained. While the existing query optimization layer in the database system itself contributes to the efficient processing of arrays, this may not be good enough. Therefore we explore suitable storage methods, specific array-query optimization, and, the possible addition of new low level operators.

The research is experimental: lessons learned in practice through the construction of a prototype system direct the research. Key elements, such as the query translators and optimizers, are being developed and tested on various real-world test cases. Additionally, the prototype is being deployed in the development of multimedia retrieval systems: practical performance is an essential part of result validation.

2 Related Work

Arrays have been defined as an operational data structure in many instances, ranging from low level programming language definitions to related work on query languages for arrays. Efforts that formalize arrays and array manipulation beyond simple operational descriptions include the *theory of arrays* [8] and *a mathematics of arrays* [9]. Both have close ties with array oriented programming languages, such as APL and FORTRAN.

Arrays have been popular for a long time for scientific and high-performance computing: their simple structure allows for automatic program parallelization on SIMD type parallel architectures. From a language theoretic point of view, arrays have been a popular topic in the functional language community: functional array operations can be elegantly expressed and are applicable in a wide variety of computational problems. Finally, the database community provided a steady supply of research results on array oriented databases, both in the context of specialized applications, such as multidimensional databases for OLAP, as in more general array oriented database systems. Examples of work on general purpose array database systems include: the array query language AQL [5], the RasDaMan DBMS [1], and, the array manipulation language AML [6].

3   The RAM System

The RAM system is a prototype system that is being developed as part of the research[2]. Instead of developing an array database system from scratch, we aim at adding arrays to an existing database system: mapping arrays to relations. This way the array extensions naturally blend in with existing database functionality.

To enable concise expression of array specific queries the RAM system implements a comprehension based array-query language (see [2]) similar to the language found in AQL [5]. Support for this language is isolated in a separate front-end that communicates to the DBMS itself through the native relational language it supports. This approach is consistent with the layered design of MonetDB [7], the principle target system for RAM, which allows for front-ends supporting different query languages to be placed on-top of a generic relational kernel.

The front-end does not translate the array comprehensions directly into the relational query language of the backend: queries are translated into an intermediate array-algebra before the final transformation to the relational domain. This array algebra is a simple language comprised of 6 basic operators.

This intermediate language is utilized by a traditional System-R style optimizer specifically geared towards optimization of array queries. Through application of rewriting rules the optimizer searches for a (more) optimal query plan by minimizing intermediate result sizes. In addition, the optimizer makes strategic decisions about data fragmentation, arrays are divided into chunks based on high-level access patterns, to streamline processing at the lower levels.

By adding the array functionality into a relational DBMS we can reuse existing storage and evaluation primitives. By storing array data as relations the full spectrum of relational operations can be applied to that array data. This indirectly guarantees complete query and data-management functionality: the RAM front-end focuses solely on problems inherent to the array domain.

Relational Storage. The obvious method to store an array in a relational database is to model the relation between indexes and values explicitly, as depicted in Figure 1. Unfortunately, the large storage overhead introduced by explicitly storing D index values for each value in a D-dimensional array makes this mapping generally impractical due to the induced processing cost in I/O and memory usage.

Development of a relational mapping for arrays, that is both suitable for efficient processing and space efficient, is part of our ongoing research. The current prototype compresses the multiple index columns into a single column by enumerating the array

---

[2] A discussion of the first prototype RAM implementation is presented in [13].

	0	1	2
0	A	B	C
1	D	E	F
2	G	H	I

X	Y	Value
0	0	A
1	0	B
2	0	C
0	1	D
1	1	E
2	1	F
0	2	G
1	2	H
2	2	I

f(x,y)	Value
0	A
1	B
2	C
3	D
4	E
5	F
6	G
7	H
8	I

a   b   c

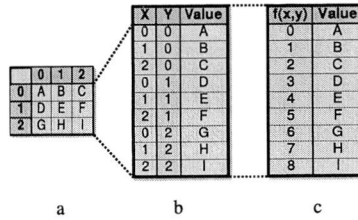

Fig. 1. An array(a), its relational equivalent(b), and, the relation with compressed index(c)

indexes in a row-major manner: also depicted in Figure 1. The storage scheme is compact, and, allows the reconstruction of the full index vector on demand when needed. Furthermore, the enumerated index values can be used directly in many cases, reducing the amount of data that to be processed, resulting in more efficient query evaluation.

3.1 Distinguishing Features of RAM

Previous efforts toward array oriented database systems were based on the development of complete array-DBMS from the ground up. The RAM system follows an alternative approach and is based on a standard layered approach: array support relies on an existing relational architecture.

A benefit of this approach is the time saved by not recreating functionality readily available, which leads to several distinct advantages. First, common DBMS functionality such as transactional control and data integrity is readily available. Second, existing query optimizers for set-based queries are reused and may offer the benefit of optimizations not directly associated with normal array processing. Third, it integrates data storage and query processing functionality for both domains, array and sets. Finally, it allows us to isolate the core array functionality in the array portion of the system while the relational engine ensures complete functionality.

Array manipulation is centered around the manipulation of index-values, bulk function application, and, array lookups. Isolation of this core array functionality in a separate unit allows for a clean model and hence a strict focus on array processing and query optimization. Additional functionality like the selection of a set of relevant values from an array can be left to the underlying relational system.

Similarly, it allows a clear separation of concerns regarding physical execution: whereas existing relational operator implementations and optimizers take care of physical execution, utilizing a computer systems resources at maximum efficiency, the RAM system development focuses on optimizations specific to array queries only. For example: determination of a high-level fragmentation strategy that focuses on avoiding (re-)computation based on array specific processing patterns. The DBMS layer takes care of scalability within the thus created array fragments.

3.2 Discussion

A concern with relational mapping of foreign data structures is the issue of efficiency: a (slight) loss of performance can be expected. Performance of the early prototype utilizing a commercial SQL based DBMS was problematic: partially due to the very large SQL queries generated, and, partially due to the lack of native support for our ordered array data.

Previous research in the database field has shown that when specialized support for sequences is added to relational systems, the performance of queries over ordered data can be dramatically improved, see e.g. [4].

We investigated ways to overcome the performance issues with MonetDB: the MonetDB database kernel offers native support for dense sequences. As expected this package performed significantly better, reasonably close to the efficiency of a specialized tool, see [13]. The datasets used are sufficiently large to force the system to resort to secondary storage. This supports the assumption that it is primarily the native support for sequences that provides the required performance and not MonetDB's design based on a main memory architecture.

4   Current Status

The current version of the prototype RAM system offers full query translation to SQL and MIL, the query language of MonetDB. Nevertheless, it is a work in progress: the array data model, high-level query language, and, the intermediate array algebra have been developed; whereas the query optimizer and relational translators are still being actively developed.

4.1   The Array

Mathematically, an array A is defined as a many-to-one function $A : \mathcal{D}_A \longrightarrow \tau_A$ over *array indexes*, multi-dimensional discrete numeric vectors. What distinguishes arrays from other classes of functions are the restrictions imposed on their *domain* (the set of values $\mathcal{D}$ for which a function is defined). An array's *range* (the range of a function f is defined as the set of all values that f can take as its argument varies over $\mathcal{D}$) plays a less prominent role in array theory.

The domain of an array, called its *shape* ($\mathcal{S}$), is a set of multi-dimensional discrete numeric vectors defined by a dense n-dimensional hyper rectangle in $\mathbb{N}_0^n$. For notational convenience we restrict this further by imposing that the lower bound of each of the hyper-cubes axes is 0. This allows unambiguous definition of the domain of an axis by its length alone. In array terminology: the *shape* of an array is determined by the combination of its *valence* $|\mathcal{S}|$ (the number of dimensions) and the lengths of each of its axes.

Definition 1 (Shape). *A n-dimensional* shape $\mathcal{S}$ *is a vector of n natural numbers, denoting axis lengths, that uniquely defines a compact hypercube in $\mathbb{N}_0^n$ located at the origin.*

In RAM array shape is deliberately not modeled as a one dimensional array of numbers: from a theoretical point of view an unessential restriction. However, modeling shape as an array introduces uncalled-for complexity in query processing.

Definition 2 (Index Value). *An index value is a vector* $\bar{\imath} \in S$ *(the notation $\bar{\imath}$ used for index vectors is shorthand for* $(i_0, i_1, \ldots, i_{(n-1)})$*).*

The shape is the domain of an array. An array relates each of the index values implied by its shape to some value. Following common collection-type terminology, we call these values an array's *elements*. The most important restriction imposed on an array's elements is that all elements in a single array must be of the same type.

Definition 3 (Element Type). *An array's element type, τ_A, defines the type of the elements of that array. Arrays contain elements of atomic type defined in the database layer, i.e. $\tau_E \in \{char, int, float, \ldots\}$, or arrays.*

The way in which RAM deals with nested array structures is omitted from this discussion for simplicity.

Definition 4 (Array). *An array A is a function $A : S_A \longrightarrow \tau_A$ which defines a many-to-one relation between the* index values *in a shape S_A and elements of a particular type τ_A.*

Note that these definitions allow for infinite structures: arrays with infinite valance, arrays with infinite length axes, and, even infinitely nested arrays. However, in practice, physical limitations restrict arrays to finite structures.

Definition 5 (Valence). *The* valence $|S_A|$ *of an array A is defined as the number of dimensions in its shape.*

Definition 6 (Size). *The* size $|A|$ *of an array A is defined as the number of elements it contains. Array size can easily be derived given its shape:* $|A| = \prod_{i=0}^{|S_A|} S_A^i$.

The regular structure of an array guarantees that a number of basic properties, such as *valence* and *size*, can be computed given the array's description only. Although trivial, the fact that these properties can easily be computed is valuable for the analysis (and optimization) of array expressions.

4.2 The RAM Query Language

The RAM query language is composed of two complementary components: methods to extract values from arrays, and, methods to construct arrays. Value extraction is supported through *array application*: arrays are functions that can be applied to index values to yield results. For array construction the RAM query language supports a generative comprehension style *constructor* and a constructive *concatenation* operator.

The query language presented to the user contains rudimentary data management primitives, e.g. primitives to persistently store arrays, or, permanently delete arrays. However, for clarity we focus solely on the core of the language: array expressions.

The RAM query language uses a functional paradigm: arrays are immutable once created, therefore functions (over arrays) have no side-effects. Effectively, this decision excludes update primitives from the language; arrays can be created once and subsequently queried, but never altered. This behavior seems reasonable, since the expected use of the query language is oriented toward computation (the use of existing arrays to compute completely new arrays containing new values), not data management.

Value Extraction. RAM allows value extraction from arrays through functional application: for a one dimensional array A, $A(x)$ yields the value associated with location x in the array. The language is flexible and allows arrays to be applied to any expression that results in an integer value. Such expressions typically contain integer variables, constants and arrays with $\tau = int$.

Arrays have a finite domain (its shape) and it is trivial to construct vectors beyond this domain. However, application of an array to an index vector beyond its domain is undefined. Two solutions for this problem are readily available: such an application can be considered invalid (either guaranteeing that they do not occur, or, producing runtime errors when they do), or, such an application could yield a undefined value. For RAM we have chosen the latter [3]: $\forall \bar{\imath} \notin S_A : A(\bar{\imath}) = nil$.

Array Generation. The RAM array constructor allows the definition of new arrays in terms of other arrays, functions over scalar values, and constant values. This is realized by defining both the shape of the array and a function that specifies the value of each cell given its array index. The constructor is based on a comprehension syntax which provides a simple, but nevertheless powerful, syntax to generate arrays.

It appears that comprehensions are a convenient and intuitive way of expressing queries (see [2]): most user languages for databases are based on (set-) comprehension. For example, the set-comprehension $\{x | x \in D, C_1, C_2, \ldots, C_n\}$ is easily recognized in the SQL variant SELECT * FROM D WHERE C_1 AND C_2 AND ... AND C_N;.

Array-comprehension is based on the same formalism as set-comprehension. However, the semantics of set-comprehension and array-comprehension are fundamentally different for two reasons. First, a set-comprehension $\{x | x \in D, C_1, C_2, \ldots, C_n\}$ specifies which elements from D are part of the result through *selection* conditions $C_1, C_2, \ldots, C_n$. The array constructor is a *generative* construct: it generates a new array through specification of its shape and the function over its index values. Second, a set-comprehension simply defines a set of values, whereas the result of an array-comprehension defines a (multi dimensionally) ordered and indexed collection of values.

The RAM array constructor syntax has the following form:

Definition 7 (Array Comprehension). *The comprehension:*

$$A = [f(i_0, \ldots, i_{(n-1)}) | i_0 < S_A^0, \ldots, i_{(n-1)} < S_A^{(n-1)}]$$

specifies an array A with shape S_A and $\forall (i_0, \ldots, i_{(n-1)}) \in S_A : A(i_0, \ldots, i_{(n-1)}) = f(i_0, \ldots, i_{(n-1)})$, *where* $n = |S_A|$.

An n-dimensional array is defined by specifying its shape S_A and associating its indexes $\bar{\imath} = (i_0, \ldots, i_{n-1})$ with their cell values $f(\bar{\imath})$. Function f may apply the operators defined on the base type in the database layer to values indexed in previously defined arrays, the index values themselves, as well as constant values. Since we defined the array indexes as consecutive ranges of natural numbers starting from 0, the shape of the array is defined completely by giving its *index generators*:

---

[3] In databases, the value nil has a variety of meanings, such as 'undefined' and 'unknown'. In this case nil denotes 'undefined'

Definition 8 (Index Generator). *An index generator $i_j < S_A^j$ defines a dense sequence of integers starting at 0: $\{i_j | i_j \in \mathbb{N}_0, i_j < S_A^j\}$. The expression S_A^j is a constant-expression using only standard integer mathematics, numerical constants, and, existing array-shapes.*

The RAM comprehension syntax is inspired by a similar construct in NRCA, the low level array language that supports the Array Query Language AQL [5]. The semantics of the comprehension syntax are simple and best explained through an example: consider the comprehension $[x + 3 * y | x < 3, y < 3]$. It defines an array with shape $[3, 3]$ and binds the (result of) function $x + 3 \cdot y$ to each of its cells. The resulting array can be visualized as follows:

0	1	2
3	4	5
6	7	8

Array Construction. The concatenation operator is a typical example of a 'constructive' operator: it makes larger arrays from smaller components.

The RAM concatenation operator $++$ operates over multi-dimensional arrays. It merges two arrays by appending the second array to the first. A prerequisite for applying the concatenation over two arrays A and B is that their value types match, $\tau_A = \tau_B$, and they have compatible shape: identical valence, and, all but the last (highest order) axes have the same length.

Definition 9 (Operator: Multi-Dimensional Concatenation). *A and B are arrays with the same element type.*

$$A ++ B = [if(i_n < S_A^n) \text{ then } A(\bar{\imath})$$
$$\text{else } B(i_0, \ldots, i_{n-1}, i_n - S_A^n) | \bar{\imath} < S_A \oplus S_B]$$

where: $\quad n = |S_A| - 1, S_A \oplus S_B = [S_A^0, \ldots, S_A^{n-1}, S_A^n + S_B^n]$

The concatenation operator is not commutative, i.e. $A ++ B \neq B ++ A$, a result of the order defined over array elements.

The following example demonstrates concatenating a $[2, 2]$- and a $[2, 1]$ array:

A	B
C	D

$++$

| X | Y |

$=$

A	B
C	D
X	Y

The fact that the concatenation operator operates over the highest order axis of arrays is an arbitrary choice. The impact of this choice is that concatenation of two arrays over a dimension other than the last one requires a preceding array transformation, e.g. transposing the source arrays to make the concatenation dimension the last one, and after concatenation transposing the result to reconstruct the dimension order of the source arrays:

$$\left(\boxed{\begin{array}{c|c} A & B \\ \hline C & D \end{array}}^{T} \mathbin{+\!\!+} \boxed{\begin{array}{c} X \\ \hline Y \end{array}}^{T} \right)^{T} = \boxed{\begin{array}{c|c|c} A & B & X \\ \hline C & D & Y \end{array}}$$

4.3   Intermediate Algebra

The RAM array algebra consists of a small set of operators, sufficient to express the query language. It contains functionality to generate new arrays given a shape, and, the functionality to manipulate existing arrays.

The first two operators generate new arrays given a shape. The *const* operator fills a new array with a constant value, whereas the *grid* operator creates an array with numbers taken from its index values.

Definition 10 (Algebra: Const). *The* const *operator creates a new array of a given shape filled with a constant value.*

$$const(\mathcal{S}, c) = [\, c \mid \bar{\imath} < \mathcal{S} \,]$$

Example 1 (Algebra: const).

$$const([3,2],0) = \boxed{\begin{array}{c|c|c} 0 & 0 & 0 \\ \hline 0 & 0 & 0 \end{array}}.$$

Definition 11 (Algebra: Grid). *The* grid *operator creates a new array of a given shape filled with values taken from its index values.*

$$grid(\mathcal{S}, j) = [\, i_j \mid \bar{\imath} < \mathcal{S} \,]$$

Example 2 (Algebra: grid).

$$grid([3,2],0) = \boxed{\begin{array}{c|c|c} 0 & 1 & 2 \\ \hline 0 & 1 & 2 \end{array}}, \qquad grid([3,2],1) = \boxed{\begin{array}{c|c|c} 0 & 0 & 0 \\ \hline 1 & 1 & 1 \end{array}}.$$

The next pair of operators deals with function application. The *map* operator applies a function (offered by the DBMS) to a set of aligned arrays, whereas the *apply* operator applies an array (which is a function) to a set of aligned index arrays. Aligned arrays are a representation of multi-valued attributes, this is needed since RAM does not support compound element types such as tuples.

Definition 12 (Aligned Array). *Aligned arrays are arrays with identical shape representing related data: in these arrays elements with corresponding index-vectors are related.*

Using aligned arrays, multiple arrays can be used to represent a single array with tuple-elements.

Example 3 (Aligned arrays).

$$\left(\boxed{\begin{array}{c|c} 0 & 3 \\ \hline 1 & 4 \\ \hline 2 & 5 \end{array}}, \boxed{\begin{array}{c|c} 0 & 1 \\ \hline 2 & 3 \\ \hline 4 & 5 \end{array}} \right) \Longleftrightarrow \boxed{\begin{array}{c|c} (0,0) & (3,1) \\ \hline (1,2) & (4,3) \\ \hline (2,4) & (5,5) \end{array}}.$$

Definition 13 (Algebra: Map). *The* map *operator creates a new array of which each element is the result of applying a given function to aligned elements in a set of arrays.*

$$map(f, A1, \ldots, Ak) = [f(A1(\bar{\imath}), \ldots, A(\bar{\imath}))| \bar{\imath} < \mathcal{S}_A] \; ,$$

where: $\quad \mathcal{S}_A = \mathcal{S}_{A1} = \ldots = \mathcal{S}_{Ak}$

Example 4 (Algebra: map).

$$map(+, \begin{array}{|c|c|}\hline 0 & 3 \\ \hline 1 & 4 \\ \hline 2 & 5 \\ \hline \end{array}, \begin{array}{|c|c|}\hline 0 & 1 \\ \hline 2 & 3 \\ \hline 4 & 5 \\ \hline \end{array}) = \begin{array}{|c|c|}\hline 0 & 4 \\ \hline 3 & 7 \\ \hline 6 & 10 \\ \hline \end{array}.$$

Definition 14 (Algebra: Apply). *The* apply *operator creates a new array of which each element is the result of applying a given array to aligned elements in a set of index-arrays.*

$$apply(A, I1, \ldots, Ik) = [A(I1(\bar{\imath}), \ldots, I(\bar{\imath}))| \bar{\imath} < \mathcal{S}_I] \; ,$$

where: $\quad \mathcal{S}_I = \mathcal{S}_{I1} = \ldots = \mathcal{S}_{Ik}, k = |\mathcal{S}_A|, \forall \bar{\imath} \notin \mathcal{S}_A : A(\bar{\imath}) = nil$

Example 5 (Algebra: apply).

$$apply(\begin{array}{|c|c|c|}\hline A & B & C \\ \hline \end{array}, \begin{array}{|c|c|}\hline 0 & 1 \\ \hline 2 & 0 \\ \hline \end{array}) = \begin{array}{|c|c|}\hline A & B \\ \hline C & A \\ \hline \end{array}.$$

The choice operator allows elements from two distinct sources (arrays) to be merged into a single result.

Definition 15 (Algebra: Choice). *The* apply *operator creates a new array of which each element is*

$$choice(C, A, B) = [if(C(\bar{\imath})) \; then \; A(\bar{\imath}) \; else \; B(\bar{\imath})| \bar{\imath} < \mathcal{S}_C] \; ,$$

where: $\quad \mathcal{S}_A = \mathcal{S}_B = \mathcal{S}_C, \tau_A = \tau_B, \tau_C = boolean$

Example 6 (Algebra: choice).

$$choice(\begin{array}{|c|c|}\hline T & F \\ \hline T & T \\ \hline F & T \\ \hline \end{array}, \begin{array}{|c|c|}\hline a & b \\ \hline c & d \\ \hline e & f \\ \hline \end{array}, \begin{array}{|c|c|}\hline A & B \\ \hline C & D \\ \hline E & F \\ \hline \end{array}) = \begin{array}{|c|c|}\hline a & B \\ \hline c & d \\ \hline E & f \\ \hline \end{array}.$$

Definition 16 (Algebra: Aggregate). *The* aggregate *operator applies an aggregation function over the first j axes of an array.*

$$aggregate(g, j, A) = [g([A(\bar{\imath})|i_0, \ldots, i_{j-1}])|i_j, \ldots, i_{n-1}] \; ,$$

where: $\quad n = |\mathcal{S}_A|$

Example 7 (Algebra: aggregate).

$$aggregate\left(sum, 1, \begin{array}{|c|c|}\hline 0 & 3 \\\hline 1 & 4 \\\hline 2 & 5 \\\hline\end{array}\right) = \begin{array}{|c|c|c|}\hline 3 & 5 & 7 \\\hline\end{array}.$$

These 6 operators are sufficient to express anything a user can specify in the RAM query language. In certain cases however, alternative operators may lead to more convenient solutions. An example of such an operation is concatenation. From a minimalistic point of view, the concatenation operation is superfluous (Definition 9 defines it using *choice*). However, concatenation is an operation that allows for an efficient mapping to the backend by exploiting the union operation offered by the relational paradigm.

Definition 17 (Algebra: Concat).

$$concat(A, B) = A + +B$$

Concatenation is only one example of a common operation granted direct mapping to the backend. Implementation of specialized mappings for other common operations is future work. However, the algebra will only be extended if there is sufficient evidence that doing so results in significant improvements.

5 Future Work

The RAM system in its current form is a fully functional prototype. However, some of its components are still under development, such as the RAM optimizer and the mapping to the relational backend.

The relational mapping component itself presents ample opportunities for the development of alternative mapping schemes and efficient relational query plans. However, our research focuses primarily on the problems associated with array processing itself. At present, the existing mapping appears to be sufficiently effective. Further exploration of alternative mappings is postponed in favor of addressing the array query optimization problem.

Early experiments have revealed several simple transformation rules that already result in effective optimizations, see [3]. One of the additional challenges to be tackled is effectively exploiting reoccurring patterns in subsequent queries, like those in the steps of an iterative analysis algorithm[4].

Another problem to be addressed is fragmentation. Whereas the underlying relational system can be trusted to handle large array fragments efficiently, arrays still have to be split into fragments that correspond with associated access patterns at a high level to maximize effectiveness. Such fragmentation opens a world of opportunities such as coarse-grained lazy evaluation and streamlined block based processing: investigation of these opportunities is planned.

---

[4] An example of such an algorithm, used in our own multimedia retrieval applications, is the EM algorithm.

References

1. P. Baumann. A database array algebra for spatio-temporal data and beyond. In *Next Generation Information Technologies and Systems*, pages 76–93, 1999.
2. P. Buneman, L. Libkin, D. Suciu, V. Tannen, and L. Wong. Comprehension syntax. *SIGMOD Record*, 23(1):87–96, 1994.
3. R. Cornacchia, A. R. van Ballegooij, and A. P. de Vries. A case study on array query optimisation. In *Proceedings of the First International Workshop on Computer Vision meets Databases (CVDB 2004)*, Paris, France, June 2004.
4. A. Lerner and S. Shasha. A Query Language for Ordered Data, Optimization Techniques, and Experiments. In *Proceedings of the 28th VLDB Conference*, 2002.
5. L. Libkin, R. Machlin, and L. Wong. A query language for multidimensional arrays: Design, implementation, and optimization techniques. In *Proceedings of ACM SIGMOD International Conference on Managing Data*, pages 228–239. ACM Press, June 1996.
6. A.P. Marathe and K. Salem. A language for manipulating arrays. In *Proceedings of the 23rd VLDB Conference*, pages 46–55, 1997.
7. MonetDB. Monet database management system. `http://monetdb.cwi.nl/`.
8. T. More jr. Axioms and theorems for a theory of arrays. *IBM Journal of Research and Development*, 17(2):135–157, March 1973.
9. L.M.R. Mullin. *A Mathematics of Arrays*. PhD thesis, Syracuse University, December 1988.
10. N. Nes. *Image Database Management Systems – Design Considerations, Algorithms and Architecture*. PhD thesis, University of Amsterdam, December 2001.
11. The Lowlands Team. Lazy users and automatic video retrieval tools in (the) lowlands. In *Proceedings of the Tenth Text REtrieval Conference, TREC*, Gaithersburg, Maryland, USA, November 2001. NIST, NIST.
12. The MathWorks Inc. Matlab. `http://www.mathworks.com`.
13. A. R. van Ballegooij, A. P. de Vries, and M. Kersten. RAM: Array processing over a relational DBMS. Technical Report INS-R0301, CWI, March 2003.

Handling Inconsistencies in Data Warehouses

Mónica Caniupán

Carleton University,
School of Computer Science,
Ottawa, Canada
mcaniupa@scs.carleton.ca

Abstract. Data warehouses (DWs) can become inconsistent when some dimensional constraints are not satisfied by the dimension instances. In this paper, we present preliminary results about the effects of the violation of partitioning constraints in homogeneous dimension instances over aggregation queries, and in particular over the summarizability property (SUMM) of the DWs. We are interested in finding ways to retrieve consistent answers even when the DW is inconsistent. We give a notion of repair for inconsistent instances based on a notion of prioritized minimization. We also describe a notion of consistent answer in DWs.

1 Introduction

Data warehouses (DWs) are data repositories that integrate data from different sources and also keep historical data. They can be queried by *OLAP* (On-Line Analytical Processing) systems, which in particular, require aggregation of data stored in the DW [4].

The DWs consist mainly of dimensions and facts. Dimensions reflect the way in which the data is organized. Some some typical dimensions are time, location, customers, etc. The facts correspond to quantitative data related with (a finite number of) dimensions, for example facts related with sales may be associated to the dimensions time, and location, and should be understood as the sales done by the locations in certain periods of time.

DWs can be modelled and implemented by using a relational (ROLAP) or a multidimensional (MOLAP) approach. The multidimensional approach is better than the relational one to support data aggregation, because aggregations can be computed in a straightforward way from the multidimensional structure. We base our work on the *multidimensional model* proposed in [7], where dimensions are modelled by hierarchy schemas together with a set of constraints, while the facts are represented by tables that refer to the dimensions. In this paper we only consider basic dimension schemas, called *strictly homogeneous dimension schemas* (cf. section 2).

Usually, dimensions are considered the static part of the DW, whereas the facts are considered the dynamic part, in the sense that the update operations affect mainly the fact tables. However, in [8, 9] the need to update dimensions is analyzed. They argue that dimensions have to be adapted to changes in data sources or in the business structure. They define a set of update operators for homogeneous dimension schemas and instances.

In the presence of such update operations, DWs may become inconsistent with respect to dimension constraints. We are interested in studying the effects of violations

W. Lindner et al. (Eds.): EDBT 2004 Workshops, LNCS 3268, pp. 166–176, 2004.

of a specific class of dimension constraints, the so-called *partitioning constraints* in homogeneous dimension instances (from now on, homogeneous instances) on aggregation queries. These constraints are fundamental for enforcing navigability properties in dimension schemas. One of the effects we will analyze in detail is how the violation of constraints affects the SUMM property of the DWs. The latter is the capability of correctly computing queries (*cube views*) using others pre-computed aggregate views. We will concentrate on queries with aggregation functions, which perform grouping of attributes and return a value for each group.

This analysis has been done on the basis of examples and theoretical work. We will use DB2 data warehousing technology to implement our concepts and mechanisms for CQA.

We also intent to retrieve consistent answers to queries even when the DW is inconsistent. Of course, a characterization of such answers becomes necessary. In order to do this, we use the concept of *repair* of a DW that is inconsistent wrt the dimension constraints. A concept of repair was first introduced in [1] in the context of relational databases and first order integrity constraints. In that framework, a repair is another database instance that minimally differs from the original instance (wrt inclusion of sets of tuples inserted or deleted into/from the original database) and satisfies the given set of integrity constraints. In [2] it is defined the set of consistent answers to aggregation queries with scalar functions (that return a single value for an entire relation). That set is defined as an optimal interval $[a, b]$ such that the evaluation of the query on every repair of the database returns a value v such that $a < v < b$.

We will show that these previous notions of repair are not suitable for the DW framework. In consequence, we give a new definition of repair and consistent answer for multidimensional DWs subject to a set of partitioning constraints and for queries with aggregation functions. DW repairs are used as an auxiliary concept to characterize the consistent answers.

We get dimension instances repairs wrt partitioning constraints by introducing minimal changes over the original inconsistent dimension instances. In order to achieve this, and given that we are considering hierarchical representations with multiple levels, we explore the notion of prioritized minimization (as given in [12]). After that, we give a preliminary definition of consistent answer for such kind of queries. Intuitively, a consistent answer to a query with aggregation function is a set of attributes grouped together with an interval, as defined in [2], for each aggregation function.

For future research we leave the development of a methodology for computing repairs (if necessary, because this should be avoided whenever possible due to its complexity) and consistent answers. In addition, we will extend this study to heterogeneous dimension schemas [7].

2   Preliminaries

A hierarchy schema is a directed acyclic graph $(C, \nearrow)$, where C is a set of categories, and $\nearrow$ is a child/parent relation between categories (edges in the graph), $\nearrow^*$ is the transitive and reflexive closure of $\nearrow$. For simplicity, categories do not have any attributes, and there is a distinguished top category named *All*, whose only element is $\{all\}$, that is reachable from all other categories. The category at the lowest level is named the *bottom* category.

Example 1. The figure 1(a) shows the *National Parks* hierarchy schema, with:

- $C = \{Park, Type, Location, Country, All\}$,
- $\nearrow$ consists of the edges $\{(Park, Type), (Park, Location), (Type, Country), (Location, Country), (Country, All)\}$; and
- $\nearrow^* = \nearrow \cup \{(Park, Park), (Type, Type), (Park, Country), ...\}$. □

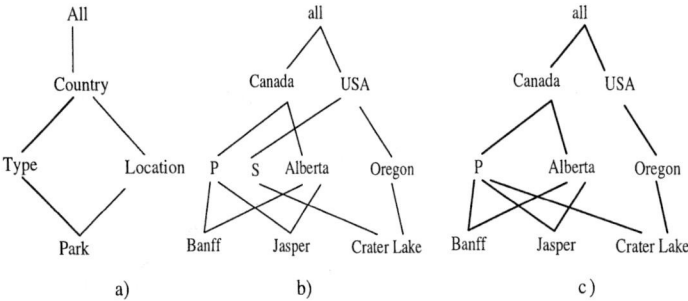

Fig. 1. a) Hierarchy schema b),c) Dimension Instances

The hierarchy schema has a domain D that can be infinite, whose elements have a unique name. An instance over a hierarchy schema is defined as a first order logic (FOL) structure of the form 1.

$$\mathcal{D} = \langle D, C_i^D, ..., C_m^D, All^D, all^D, A^D, <^D, <^{*^D} \rangle, \qquad (1)$$

where D is the domain of the herbrand structure [13], whose elements k must be interpreted with their own values. $C_i^D, ..., C_m^D, All^D \subseteq D$, are unary predicates that represent categories, and All^D is the top category, with element $\{all^D\}$. $A^D \subseteq \{p_{ij} \mid i, j = 1, ..., m\}$, where each p_{ij} represents an edge between the categories i and j on the hierarchy schema. $<^D \subseteq D \times D$ is the child/parent relation between elements of categories. $<^{*^D} \subseteq D \times D$ is the reflexive and transitive closure of $<^D$. In this sense, $<^{*^D}$ can be seen as an interpreted relation name, which has a fixed interpretation depending on the interpretation of $<^D$. A dimension instance $\mathcal{D}$ indicates relationships between elements of categories which must be connected in the hierarchy schema. This is achieved through the set of the p_{ij}, in the sense that: $\mathcal{D} \models p_{ij} \Leftrightarrow p_{ij} \in A^D$.

Example 2. $\mathcal{D} = \langle D, Park(\cdot)^D, Type(\cdot)^D, Location(\cdot)^D, Country(\cdot)^D, All(\cdot)^D, all^D, A^D, <^D, <^{*^D} \rangle$ is an instance for the hierarchy schema (a) in Figure 1, where D is composed by names for parks, types, locations, countries, and:

- $Park^D = \{Banff, Jasper, CraterLake\}$, $Type^D = \{P, S\}$,
- $Location^D = \{Alberta, Oregon\}$, $Country^D = \{Canada, USA\}$, $All^D = \{all^D\}$
- $A^D = \{p_{parktype}, p_{parklocation}, p_{typecounty}, p_{locationcountry}, p_{countryAll}\}$
- $<^D = \{(Banff, P), (Banff, Alberta), (Jasper, P), (Jasper, Alberta),$
    $(CraterLake, S), (CraterLake, Oregon), (P, Canada), (S, USA),$
    $(Alberta, Canada), (Oregon, USA), (Canada, All), (USA, All)\}$.
    Figure 1(b) illustrates this instance.
- $<^{*^D} = <^D \cup \{(Banff, Banff), (Banff, Canada)... \}$ □

A roll-up function is the mapping of the relation $<^*$ between elements of C_i, C_j categories. It is expressed by:

$$\mathcal{R}^{C_j}_{C_i}(\mathcal{D}) := \{(x, y) | C_i(x) \wedge C_j(y) \wedge x <^* y\} \qquad (2)$$

This function is fundamental for computing aggregation of data.

Dimension instances must satisfy a set of conditions [7]. The partitioning property is one of them. It is defined by:

$$\forall (x, y, z)(C_i(x) \wedge C_j(y) \wedge C_j(z) \wedge x <^* y \wedge x <^* z \rightarrow y = z) \qquad (3)$$

It enforces that roll-up functions are functional, and so they allow for the correct computation of aggregations. The SUMM property says that a category C can be computed from other category C' in a dimension instance $\mathcal{D}$ if and only if: $R^C_{Cbottom}(\mathcal{D}) = R^{C'}_{Cbottom}(\mathcal{D}) \bowtie R^C_{C'}(\mathcal{D})$ [7].

We call *specific dimensions constraints* those constraints that model hierarchy schemas [7]. Those constraints are used to specify paths and the existence of distinguished elements in the categories. Homogeneous schemas are those modelled by the *into constraints*, which establish all the paths as mandatory. In those schemas, roll-up functions are expected to be total between elements of categories. A schema is called strictly homogeneous when it has one bottom category.

Finally, we concentrate on queries with aggregation functions of the form 4.

$$SELECT A_1, \ldots A_m, af$$
$$FROM T, R_1, \ldots R_m$$
$$WHERE \ \{joins \ conditions \ and \ others \ conditions\}$$
$$GROUP BY A_1, \ldots A_m, \qquad (4)$$

where $A_1, \ldots A_m$ are attributes of the facts table T or of roll-up functions $R_i, \ldots R_m$ (they will be treated as tables), and af is one of: MIN, MAX, COUNT, SUM, AVG, COUNT, applied to one attribute $A_i \neq A_1, \ldots A_m$.

3   The Need for DW Repairs and Consistent Answers

In general, DWs are conceived as collections of materialized views whose main sources are operational databases. As consequence, much effort has been centered in keeping consistency between the sources and the DW [5, 6, 15, 17]. To the best of our knowledge, the first work related to consistency in dimension schemas in the sense of [7] is presented in [11]. They argue that a dimension schema is consistent if their instances satisfy the partitioning condition. That notion of consistency is used to guide the update operations on dimension schemas that keep that property satisfied. However, there has been no work so far that tackles the problem of already having an inconsistent dimension instance with respect to a specific class of constraints, but still being able to provide consistent answers, in a sense similar to the notion of consistent answer introduced in [1–3] for relational databases. In this regard, the work presented here is the first attempt to handle the problem of consistent query answering (CQA) in DWs.

The concept of repair was already defined in [1] in the context of relational databases. However, that notion does not capture the minimality required by the natural process of repairing multidimensional DWs. This is the case even if we represent the DW as an instance of a relational DB (the ROLAP approach). We show this with an example.

Example 3. Figure 2 shows a snowflake schema [4] for the *National Parks* dimension. "PK" indicates the primary key for each table, and the following first order integrity constraint enforce the partitioning property:

$$IC: \forall xyzwv \; Park(x, y, z) \wedge Type(y, w) \wedge Country(w) \wedge$$
$$Location(z, v) \wedge Country(v) \rightarrow w = v$$

Assume we have the following dimension instance r:

– *Park* ={*(Banff, P, Alberta), (Jasper, P, Alberta), (CraterLake, P, Oregon)*},
– *Type* = {*(P, Canada)*},
– *Location* = {*(Alberta, Canada), (Oregon, USA)*},
– *Country* = {*Canada, USA*}.

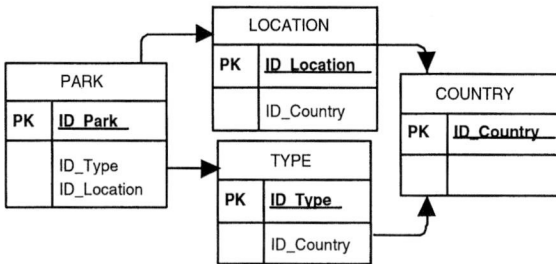

Fig. 2. Snowflake schema

Instance r does not satisfy the IC because $Canada \neq USA$, and:

$$r \models Park(CraterLake, P, Oregon) \wedge Type(P, Canada) \wedge Country(Canada) \wedge$$
$$Location(Oregon, USA) \wedge Country(USA)$$

The only possible repair in the relational sense of [1] is obtained by deleting *Park (CraterLake, P, Oregon)*. However, if we apply this change in the multidimensional representation it implies to delete the pairs *(CraterLake, P)* of the roll-up function R_{Park}^{Type} and *(CraterLake, Oregon)* of $R_{Park}^{Location}$, which is not a minimal repair since it is enough to reestablish consistence to delete just one of them. In section 4 we show that to delete both pairs is not a minimal change. $\qquad\square$

We will show that good repairs for DWs are obtained by doing minimal deletion of pairs in the roll-up functions involved in the violations of constraints. The problem in the relational model is that a tuple can contain many pairs of those functions (in example 3 a tuple contains two pairs). In that sense, relational model does not allow us to work on a granularity lower than a tuple. Our definition of repair (section 4.1) captures exactly the minimality of changes desired for DWs. We achieve this by identifying the roll-up functions involved in the violations of partitioning constraints, defining a prioritized set of roll-up functions (inspired by the notion of prioritized minimization given in [12]), then those set of functions are manipulated (deletion of pairs) in order to achieve consistence. The repairs are those that reestablish the consistence by doing minimal changes over the prioritized roll-up functions.

On the other side, the importance of the summarizability property of DWs has been analyzed [10, 14]. In [14] a particular class of heterogeneous hierarchies is transformed into homogeneous hierarchies to support summarizability. This is achieved by inserting null values, fusioning other values, and introducing new categories when partitioning constraints are violated. Although these operations, which allow us to get summarizability, could be used for repairing inconsistent DWs, they do not produce minimal repairs. In addition, the fusion of values may produce undesired changes in the semantic of the dimension instances.

4   Repairs and Semantically Correct Answers in DWs

Let us show by means of an example how the unsatisfied partitioning constraints (PC) may affect query answering.

Example 4. Let $\mathcal{D}$ be the instance in figure 1(c), and $PC : \forall (x, y, z)(Park(x) \wedge Country(y) \wedge Country(z) \wedge x <^* y \wedge x <^* z \to y = z)$. Here, $\mathcal{D} \nvDash PC$. As a consequence, the roll-up function: $R_{Park}^{Country} = \{(Banff, Canada), (Jasper, Canada), (CraterLake, Canada), (CraterLake, USA)\}$ is not functional.

Suppose the facts table *Sales*= $\{(Banff, 5000), (Jasper, 5000), (CraterLake, 10000)\}$ stores sales for national parks, and consider the aggregation query Q: "Give the SUM (sales) group by country". The answer for Q is: $\{(Canada, 20000), (USA, 10000)\}$. $\qquad\square$

Clearly, this result presents an anomaly, the sales of the park *Crater Lake* are added twice, as sales of Canada and also as sales of USA. Now, let us explore how that violation affects the summarization property.

Example 5. Consider the following materialized views and roll-up functions:

- *Sales-Type* = {(*P*, 20000)}, *Sales-Loc* = {(*Alberta*, 10000), (*Oregon*, 10000)}
- $R_{Type}^{Country}$ = {(*P, Canada*)}, $R_{Location}^{Country}$ = {(*Alberta, Canada*),(*Oregon, USA*)}

The answers to Q: "Give the SUM(sales) group by country" are {(*Canada*, 20000)} and {(*Canada*, 10000), (*USA*, 10000)}, using the respective views and roll-up functions. However, by the summarizability property, the answers must be similar, specially in homogeneous instances, where a category is summarizable from any of the categories below it [7].   □

Given an homogeneous instance $\mathcal{D}$ satisfying the basic properties of the graph structure [7], and a set of partitioning constraints PC, we claim:

Theorem 1. $\mathcal{D} \models PC$ *if and only if* $\mathcal{D} \models SUMM$.   □

This result is important because we can verify summarizability by testing satisfiability of partitioning constraints. This test could be easily performed by using views. In that way, we could identify the elements participating in violations and use that information to fix the dimension instance.

4.1 Dimension Instances Repairs

Partitioning constraints can be seen as functional dependencies (FD) in relational databases. The general way to repair inconsistent databases wrt to FDs is by deleting the tuples participating in the violations [2]. However, in dimension instances, there are no tuples in the sense of relational databases, but there exist dimension tuples [7], so we could consider as tuples the pairs in the roll-up functions between elements.

Dimension instances form a hierarchy of roll-up functions. In consequence, we should identify from which roll-up functions pairs are to be deleted in order to get a good repair. Inspired by the notion of prioritized minimization given in [12], we propose to minimize changes, but assigning higher priority to lower categories. For this purpose, we define first levels of categories on a dimension instance, and to each level we associate a set of roll-up functions. Specifically, given a dimension instance $\mathcal{D}$ of the form (1) with maximum distance n among the categories of the graph, we define

Definition 1. A level L_i with $0 \le i \le n$ is a set of elements belonging to categories with distance i (in the hierarchy schema) to the bottom category. For each level L_i there exists a set $R_i \subseteq <^1$ defined by: $R_i := \{(a,b) | a < b \wedge C_j(a) \in L_i \wedge C_k(b) \in L_{i+1}\}$, where $\{C_j, C_k\}$ are categories of $\mathcal{D}$.   □

Example 6. For the instances of the figure 3(a):

- L_0 = {*Banff, Jasper, CraterLake*},
- R_0 = {(*Banff, P*), (*Banff, Alberta*), (*Jasper, P*), (*Jasper, Alberta*),
  (*CraterLake, Oregon*)}.   □

---

[1] The child/parent relation among categories elements.

Definition 2. The distance Δ between two dimension instances $\mathcal{D}_1, \mathcal{D}_2$ on the set R_i with $0 \leq i \leq n$ is defined by: $\Delta_i(\mathcal{D}_1, \mathcal{D}_2) = \{(a, b) | (((a, b) \in R_{i,\mathcal{D}_1}) \wedge ((a, b) \notin R_{i,\mathcal{D}_2})) \vee (((a, b) \in R_{i,\mathcal{D}_2}) \wedge ((a, b) \notin R_{i,\mathcal{D}_1}))\}$.

Given a dimension instance $\mathcal{D}$, we define: $\mathcal{D}_1 \leq_{\mathcal{D},i} \mathcal{D}_2 \leftrightarrow \Delta_i(\mathcal{D}, \mathcal{D}_1) \subseteq \Delta_i(\mathcal{D}, \mathcal{D}_2)$. □

Example 7. Let $\mathcal{D}, \mathcal{D}_1, \mathcal{D}_2$ be the instances in figures 1(c), 3(a), and 3(c), respectively. It holds:

- $\Delta_0(\mathcal{D}, \mathcal{D}_1) = \{(CraterLake, P)\}$,
- $\Delta_0(\mathcal{D}, \mathcal{D}_2) = \{(CraterLake, P), (CraterLake, Oregon)\}$,
- $\mathcal{D}_1 \leq_{\mathcal{D},0} \mathcal{D}_2$, because $\Delta_0(\mathcal{D}, \mathcal{D}_1) \subseteq \Delta_0(\mathcal{D}, \mathcal{D}_2)$. □

Definition 3. Let $\mathcal{D}, \mathcal{D}_1, \mathcal{D}_2$ be dimension instances over the hierarchy schema H with domain D. It holds: $\mathcal{D}_1 \leq_{\mathcal{D}} \mathcal{D}_2$ iff: $\exists i \, ((\Delta_k(\mathcal{D}, \mathcal{D}_1) = \Delta_k(\mathcal{D}, \mathcal{D}_2), k < i) \wedge (\mathcal{D}_1 \leq_{\mathcal{D},i} \mathcal{D}_2))$. □

Definition 4. Given a dimension instance $\mathcal{D}$, and a set of partitioning constraints PC, a repair of $\mathcal{D}$ wrt PC is a dimension instance $\mathcal{D}'$, such that $\mathcal{D}' \models PC$, and $\mathcal{D}'$ is $\leq_{\mathcal{D}}$-minimal in the class of dimension instances that satisfy PC. The set of repairs of $\mathcal{D}$ is denoted by $Repairs_{PC}(\mathcal{D})$. □

Example 8. Figures 3(a),(b) show the repairs for the instances in figure 1(c). □

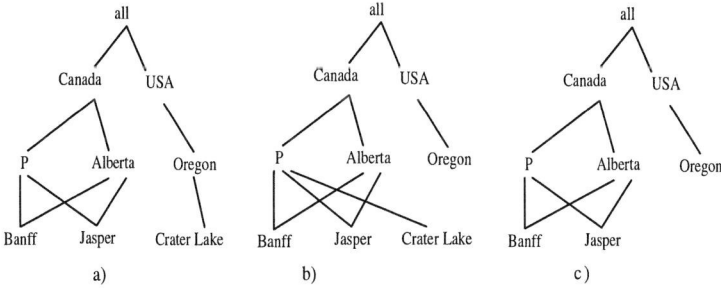

Fig. 3. Dimension Instances

4.2   Consistent Answers

Definition 5. Given a dimension instance $\mathcal{D}$, a set of partitioning constraints PC, and a set of repairs $Repairs_{PC}(\mathcal{D})$, the execution of the aggregation query Q over each $\mathcal{D}' \in Repairs_{PC}(\mathcal{D})$ generates a *set of pre-answers* for each $\mathcal{D}'$, $Pre_{PC}^Q \mathcal{D}' := \{Q(\mathcal{D}') \mid \mathcal{D}' \in Repairs_{PC}(\mathcal{D})\}$. □

The pre-answers are a set of tuples: $< A_1, \ldots, A_n, Aggr >$, where $A_1, \ldots, A_n$ are attributes of the group-by clause of Q, and $Aggr$ is the value for the aggregation function af on $\mathcal{D}'$.

Example 9. Consider the repairs in example 8, the sets of pre-answers for Q in example 4 are: $\{(Canada, 10000), (USA, 10000)\}$ and $\{(Canada, 20000)\}$, respectively.   □

Definition 6. A consistent answer to an aggregation query Q, over a dimension instance $\mathcal{D}$ wrt to a set of partitioning constraints PC, is a set of tuples $< A_1, \ldots, A_n, r(Aggr) >$, where $< A_1, \ldots, A_n >$ are the attributes of the group-by clause of Q, and $r(Aggr)$ is a range $[a, b]$ of values, a is the greatest-lower-bound (glb), and b is the least-upper-bound (lub) for $Aggr$ in $Pre^Q_{PC}(\mathcal{D}')$ for all $\mathcal{D}' \in Repairs_{PC}(\mathcal{D})$.   □

Example 10. A consistent answer in example 4 is: $\{(Canada, \{10000, 20000\}), (USA, \{0, 10000\})$.   □

5   Future Work

A repair is a minimal consistent dimension instance wrt to partitioning constraints. However, a repair is not an homogeneous instance (see figures 3(a), (b)), because some roll-up functions are modified and they are not total anymore. Furthermore, the summarizability property cannot be reestablished in the repairs. However, we could obtain total functions and also summarizability by introducing "dummy" elements in some categories in the repairs, as in [14]. We are analyzing the possible advantages of implementing this idea in the query answering process for DWs. We are also studying the method proposed in [14] to repair DWs and compute consistent answers. We want to see if we get the same consistent answers even when the concept of repair is different.

We could also improve the definition of repairs by using knowledge from equality atoms constraints [7], which impose the existence of certain distinguished elements in the categories. We could require those repairs to satisfy those constraints to get more accurate repairs.

We are developing a methodology for computing consistent answers. We have considered to use the knowledge from partitioning constraints and roll-up functions to compute them, avoiding the computation of all the possible repairs, which is known to be inefficient [1–3].

This is a preliminary study that we will extend to heterogeneous dimension schemas [7], where the situation could be a bit different; mainly because those schemas relax some conditions, becoming more vulnerable to inconsistencies. We already explored update operations over heterogeneous schemas, finding some differences wrt updating homogeneous schemas. Those results will be included in a future publication.

The problem of retrieving consistent answers to aggregation queries is not a new issue, it was already studied for scalar aggregation functions in [2] for relational databases under functional dependencies. We are working on the extension of this work to handle referential constraints in addition to the FDs. We think that future results for this kind of databases will be useful in the context of DWs, in particular, in the case where *OLAP* operators and DWs are implemented on top of relational databases (ROLAP).

On other side, we are interested in optimizing the query answering process in DWs by taking advantage of aggregation constraints [16]. Also the issue of CQA wrt to aggregation constraints is open. Experiments and implementations will be done on the DB2 platform.

Acknowledgment. I am grateful to my PhD supervisor Prof. Leo Bertossi for his support and technical conversations. Research supported by NSERC Discovery Grant 250279-02. We appreciate stimulating conversations with Prof. Alberto Mendelzon and Carlos Hurtado at a very early stage of this research.

References

1. M. Arenas, L. Bertossi, and J. Chomicki. Consistent query answers in inconsistent databases. In *Proc. ACM Symposium on Principles of Database Systems (ACM PODS'99, Philadelphia)*, pages 68–79. ACM Press, 1999.
2. M. Arenas, L. Bertossi, J. Chomicki, X. He, V. Raghavan, and J. Spinrad. Scalar aggregation in inconsistent databases. *Theoretical Computer Science*, 296(3):405–434, March 2003.
3. P. Barcelo, L. Bertossi, and L. Bravo. Characterizing and computing semantically correct answers from databases with annotated logic and answer sets. *Semantics of Databases (Springer LNCS 2582)*, pages 1–27, 2003.
4. S. Chaudhuri and U. Dayal. An overview of data warehousing and OLAP technology. *SIGMOD Rec.*, 26(1):65–74, 1997.
5. H. Garcia-Molina, W. J. Labio, and J. Yang. Expiring data in a warehouse. In *Proc. 24th Int. Conf. on Very Large Data Bases VLDB*, pages 500–511, 1998.
6. H. Gupta and I. S. Mumick. Selection of views to materialize under a maintenance cost constraint. In *Database Theory – ICDT'99: Proc. 7th International Conference, Jerusalem, Israel, January*, Springer LNCS 1540, pages 453 470, 1999.
7. C. Hurtado. *Structurally Heterogeneous OLAP Dimensions*. PhD thesis, Computer Science Dept., University of Toronto, 2002.
8. C. Hurtado, A. Mendelzon, and A. Vaisman. Updating OLAP dimensions. In *Proc. 2nd IEEE-DOLAP Workshop, Kansas City, Missouri, USA*, pages 60–66, 1999.
9. C. Hurtado, A. Mendelzon, and A. Vaisman. Maintaining data cubes under dimension updates. In *Proc. 15th IEEE-ICDE Conference, Sydney, Australia*, pages 346–357, 1999.
10. L. V. S. Lakshmanan, R. T. Ng, C. X. Wang, and Xiaodong. The generalized MDL approach for summarization. In *Proc. 28th Int. Conf. Very Large Data Bases, VLDB, Hong Kong, China, August 20-23*, pages 766–777, 2002.
11. C. Letz, E. T. Henn, and G. Vossen. Consistency in data warehouse dimensions. In *Proc. Int. Database Engineering and Applications Symposium, (IDEAS'02), July 17-19, Edmonton, Canada*, pages 224–232. IEEE Press, 2002.
12. V. Lifschitz. Circumscription. In *Handbook of Logic in AI and Logic Programming, Vol. 3, Oxford University Press*, pages 298–352, 1994.
13. J. W. Lloyd. *Foundations of Logic Programming*. Springer Verlag, 1984.
14. T. B. Pedersen, C. S. Jensen, and C. E. Dyreson. Extending practical pre-aggregation in online analytical processing. In *Proc. 25th Int. Conf. Very Large Data Bases, VLDB, Edinburgh, Scotland*, pages 663–674, 1999.

15. L. Schlesinger and W. Lehner. Extending data warehouses by semi-consistent views. In *Proc. 4th International Workshop of Design and Management of Data Warehouses (DMDW 2002, Toronto, Kanada, May 27), CEUR Workshop Proceedings, Technical University of Aachen (RWTH)*, pages 43–51, 2002.

16. D. Srivastava, K. Ross, P. Stuckey, and S. Sudarshan. Foundations of aggregation constraints. In *PPCP'94: Second Int. Workshop, Orcas Island, Seattle, USA*, Springer LNCS 874, pages 193–204, 1994.

17. D. Theodoratos and M. Bouzeghoub. A general framework for the view selection problem for data warehouse design and evolution. In *Proc. 3rd ACM int. workshop on Data warehousing and OLAP*, pages 1–8. ACM Press, 2000.

Data Sharing and Querying
for Peer-to-Peer Data Management Systems

Anastasios Kementsietsidis

Department of Computer Science,
University of Toronto, Canada
tasos@cs.toronto.edu

Abstract. In this work, we investigate mechanisms to support data sharing and querying in a *peer-to-peer data management system*, that is, a peer-to-peer system where each peer manages its own data. To support data sharing, we propose the use of mapping tables which list pairs of corresponding data values that reside in different peers. Our work illustrates how automated tools can help manage the tables between multiple peers by inferring new tables from existing ones and by checking their consistency. In terms of querying, we propose a framework in which users pose queries only with respect to their local peer. Then, we provide a rewriting mechanism that uses mapping tables to translate a locally expressed query to a set of queries over the acquainted peers.

1 Introduction

Peer-to-peer computing consists of an open-ended network of distributed computational peers, where each peer exchanges data and services with a set of other peers, called its acquaintances. The peer-to-peer paradigm, initially popularized by file-sharing systems such as Napster [1] and Gnutella [2], offers an alternative to traditional architectures found in distributed systems and the web. Distributed systems are rich in services but require considerable overhead to launch and have a relatively static, controlled architecture. In contrast, the web offers a dynamic, anyone-to-anyone architecture with minimum startup costs but limited services. Combining the advantages of both architectures, peer-to-peer offers an evolving architecture where peers come and go, choose with whom they interact, and enjoy some traditional distributed services with less startup cost.

Each peer-to-peer system provides two basic services to its peers. First, it offers to its peers the ability to share data with each other. Second, it offers the ability for peers to query each other's contents. Our objective is to investigate mechanisms that can be used to support these two services in the context of a *peer-to-peer data management system*, that is, a peer-to-peer system where each peer manages its own data. In the past, database research has dealt with similar issues in the context of multidatabase systems [10]. However, the solutions provided there are not directly applicable to peer-to-peer data management systems. This is mainly due to the following three features of the new paradigm: the lack of centralized control; the transience of the inter-peer connections; the limited cooperation among the peers.

Traditionally, in multidatabase systems, data integration and exchange between heterogeneous data sources is provided mainly through the use of inter-schema mappings

W. Lindner et al. (Eds.): EDBT 2004 Workshops, LNCS 3268, pp. 177–186, 2004.
© Springer-Verlag Berlin Heidelberg 2004

(generalized view definitions often called global-or-local-as-view (GLAV) mappings) that specify how the schemas of the sources are related [17, 21]. Given two sources S_1 and S_2, to construct a mapping m between them, the sources must be willing to share at least portions of their schemas and cooperate in establishing and managing the mappings. Management of mappings becomes an issue when the participating sources change their schemas [24]. Then, the mappings must be updated to reflect the changes. Our work considers peer-to-peer settings in which cooperation between sources to establish such schema mappings is either not desirable (perhaps for privacy reasons) or not feasible (since sources might belong to different worlds [18]). In such settings, we consider an alternative and more flexible form of mappings, called *mapping tables*. Mapping tables are data-level mappings which list pairs of corresponding values between two sources. Our work motivates the use of mapping tables in peer-to-peer environments and shows that the maintenance of these tables can be automated [15]. In terms of query answering, existing approaches assume that a query posed on source S_1 can be answered locally (using S_1's database) and in addition, it can be translated, using the schema-level mapping m, into a query on S_2. However, this environment makes the (implicit) assumption that the answer to the query that S_2 provides can be made to conform to the schema of S_1. Our work makes no such assumption but relies on mapping tables to translate structured queries between peer databases that may contain related data that overlaps little, if at all [14].

Contributions

To the best of our knowledge, our work is the first to address the problem of *data sharing* between heterogeneous sources. Data sharing deals with the exchange of data between heterogeneous sources whose data need not be interdependent and may represent different real world domains. It may not be possible or desirable to transform such data to fit a common schema. As such, data sharing differs from the well-studied problems of data integration [17] and data exchange [11]. Both of the latter two problems use schema-level mappings to express the relationships between source schemas. In data integration, these mappings are used, at run time, to conform the data of one source to the schema of another. In data exchange, the mappings are used to populate a target schema with the data of a source schema.

Our work investigates the use of mapping tables as the primary mechanism for data sharing between peers [15]. Currently, mapping tables provide the basis for data sharing in peer-to-peer data management systems such as the ones found in the domain of biological databases [9]. Still, the creation of mapping tables is a time-consuming and manual process performed by a set of expert curators. We are aware of no data management tools currently designed to facilitate the creation, maintenance and management of these tables. Our work illustrates how automated tools can help manage mappings between multiple sources by inferring new mappings and checking their consistency. In practice, inferring new mappings proves useful when two peers first become acquainted. The system is able to use existing mappings in the network of peers to associate the values of the newly acquainted peers. This task requires no human intervention and, thus, it alleviates the need for a human curator. Checking consistency of mappings is important in order to detect and report possible errors in existing mappings. Without automated support, curators edit, copy, or merge mappings that come from a variety of sources and it can be a cumbersome task to make sure that the associations of one mapping do not *conflict* with the ones expressed by another. Our approach offers an automated way to detect these inconsistencies.

In terms of query answering, we propose a framework in which users pose queries only with respect to their local peer schema. Then, we provide a rewriting mechanism that uses mapping tables to translate a locally expressed query to a set of queries that can be executed in the acquainted peers. Although the idea of query translation is not novel, the context in which it is applied is. Traditional views or schema mappings are queries (or pairs of queries), so query translation involves manipulating relatively small queries. Mapping tables however contain data and may be very large. Query translation in our environment involves manipulating these large tables.

An important contribution of our work is the use of a common formalism for both data sharing and for query answering. Through this formalism, we are able to represent both mapping tables and queries. This uniformity offers a number of advantages including the ability to store in a peer database both queries and their translations and the ability to reuse algorithms that were developed for our data sharing setting during query answering.

For the purposes of our work, and in order to test the applicability of our ideas, we have implemented our solutions on a prototype peer-to-peer data management system in which each peer is a data management system with its own schema and data. Peers communicate using a Gnutella-like protocol which is customized to our specific needs. For our experiments, we use two different domains, namely, biological databases and flight reservation information.

Outline

Section 2 offers an overview of the database literature on peer-to-peer systems. Section 3 presents an overview of our main results and the paper concludes in Section 4 with a discussion of our future work. The work presented in this article is part of the Hyperion project[1] [6] at the University of Toronto.

2   State of the Art

To put our work in perspective, it proves useful to introduce a classification of existing peer-to-peer systems. We classify such systems into two categories based on the behaviors and characteristics of the peers within each system. Distinguishing characteristic of the peers in the first system category is that these are *altruistic*. In more detail, systems in this category often rely on the architecture and the services of systems like CAN [22], CHORD [23] or Tapestry [25]. An example of such a system is OceanStore [3] while relies on Tapestry to provide distributed file storage. A peer that joins such systems offers its computational or storage resources to it. The system often decides the set of peers with which the new peer will be acquainted. Furthermore, the system can decide the data

---

[1] In Greek mythology, Hyperion [high-peer-ee-on] is the Titan of light. His name literally means "dweller on high" or "the one above". He was the father of Helius (the sun), Selene (the moon), and Eos (the dawn).

contents of the peer and where these data should be replicated (to increase availability). Due to this replication, the data stored in a peer are available even after the particular peer leaves the system. In term of research, some of the main issues here are the efficiency of the lookup and routing services, and how to maintain this efficiency in the presence of peer arrivals and departures.

In the second category of systems, peers are *selfish*. Here, each peer brings into the system its own data and decides independently with which of the other peers it will be acquainted. Once the peer leaves the systems, its data usually become unavailable to the other peers. Our own work in the context of the Hyperion project, is classified in this second category of systems. Our main focus is on the *data management* issues that arise in this environment. As an example, we are interested on the issue of heterogeneity. While in the previous category of systems, peers are assumed to have the same underlying format (or schema) to represent their data, here each peer might use a different data representation. We do not consider the efficiency of routing schemes and the scalability of our solutions to tens of thousands of peers. One reason for this is that the size, in terms of number of peers, of the systems we consider is considerably smaller.

In what follows we review some of the work in peer-to-peer data management which is the main focus of this thesis. Bernstein et al [7] introduce the Local Relational Model (LRM), a data model designed for peer-to-peer applications. The model's aim is to support semantic interoperability between relational databases in the absence of a global schema. The proposed model makes use of *domain relations* which are equivalent to the notion of mapping tables. However, no provision is described to manage these relations.

Lenzerini [17] describes a general framework for modeling data integration applications which can also be used to represent peer-to-peer applications. An important difference between this work and ours is that the former uses schema-level mappings between the peers, while our work relies mainly of data-level mappings. Thus, the two works are complimentary.

Our initial work on mapping tables shows how these can be used in support of keyword-based searches within peer-to-peer systems. Our current work extends these results to consider the use of mapping tables to support structured queries. The work of Huebsch et al [13] also supports structured queries but the assumption there is that all peers share the same schema.

In Piazza, associations between peers are expressed through either global-as-view (GAV) or local-as-view (LAV) mappings [12, 19]. During query answering, both types of mappings are used to translate queries between peers. Our work on query translation is complimentary to Piazza since our solutions do not rely on GAV/LAV mappings but assume that the only associations available between peers are in the form of mapping tables. An important distinction between the two proposals is that in Piazza the data retrieved from the peer-to-peer network always conform to the schema of the peer where the user-query is initiated. Our work, on the other hand, makes no such assumption.

Ng et al [20] propose an alternative approach to query translation in peer-to-peer environments. Initially, the authors assign a set of descriptive keywords to each schema element of a peer schema. Then, the schema elements of different peers are associated if they have a *similar* set of descriptive keywords. Once schema element associations are established, the translation of queries between different peers is performed by using associated schema elements. An important limitation of the approach is the underlying assumption that descriptive keywords are used consistently throughout the peer-to-peer network. Thus, unlike our work, their solutions cannot handle differences in the vocabularies of the peers.

The work of Chang and Garcia-Molina [8] deals with the translation of queries between heterogeneous sources. The authors use syntactic rules to map selection predicates from one database to that of another. At first glance, mapping tables look like *materializations* of these syntactic rules. However, the two constructs operate under different assumptions. As an example, a syntactic rule that maps two selection predicates ignores the intricacies of this mapping at the data level, that is, the fact that at that level the mapping between values might be incomplete or be many-to-many. Part of our work on mapping tables addresses exactly these issues. Our approach also offers a *uniform* representation both for the rules, i.e., the mappings at the data level, the queries, and for the mappings between translated queries.

Aberer et al [4] introduce a formal framework to assess the quality of peer mappings by measuring the quality of query rewritings that are obtained from these mappings. The mappings considered by the authors are similar, in spirit, to mapping tables since they have the form of functions that map the values of attributes belonging to acquainted peers. However, the focus of this work is more on the assessment of the quality of the mappings, and less on the mappings themselves and how these can be used to perform rewriting. Our work, on the other hand, focuses on these latter issues. Thus, the two approaches are complimentary.

3   Status of Current Work

This work was developed within the framework of the Hyperion project [6] at the University of Toronto. Thus, before we move on to the main topics of the thesis, we offer an overview of Hyperion and we present its main design principles. This, in turn, allows us to put our solutions in context since it shows the environment within which our solutions are designed to work.

3.1   The Hyperion Architecture

The objective of the Hyperion project is to facilitate data sharing between autonomous and heterogeneous sources that are organized in a peer-to-peer fashion. Source autonomy is an important requirement in practice. Sources that join a peer-to-peer network are usually not willing to compromise their autonomy while doing so. As an example, consider biological data sources where each peer source belongs to a different research group or institute. Although each group is willing, due to mutual benefit, to share its data with other groups, it is often not willing to alter its data representation or its internal naming scheme. Which brings us to the next issue, namely, heterogeneity, as a by-product of source autonomy.

In such settings, the approach taken by Hyperion to address the above issues is to augment each source with an interoperability layer. The layer, shown in Figure 1, consists mainly of three modules which we briefly describe here:

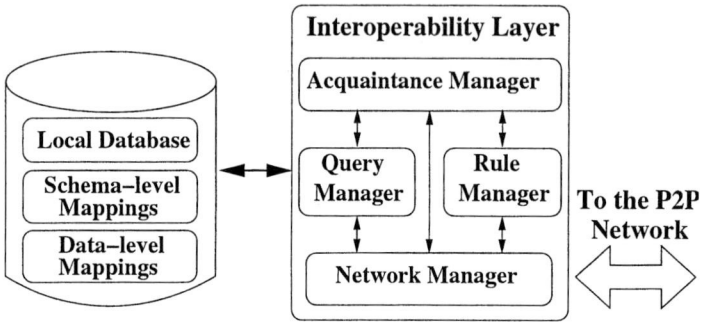

Fig. 1. The Hyperion interoperability layer

- **Acquaintance Manager:** The objective of the acquaintance manager is to resolve heterogeneity issues that arise between a pair of peer sources that are acquainted. To this end, the module maintains any possible schema-level (GLAV) mappings between the schemas of the sources. However, since such mappings are not always available, or possible, it also maintains possible data-level mappings, in the form of mapping tables. Mapping tables respect peer autonomy since they do not impose constraints on the peer schemas. They are minimally invasive in that they do not restrict the operation of peers in anyway beyond the agreement on values expressed in the tables. The first part of our thesis deals with the maintenance of these tables within the acquaintance manager.

- **Query Manager:** One of the guiding principles in Hyperion is that a user should only be aware and knowledgeable of her own local peer schema. As a result, all user queries are expressed with respect to this schema and it is the responsibility of the system to retrieve additional related results from the peer-to-peer network. The query manager is responsible for rewriting the locally expressed queries to ones that can be executed with respect to the schemas of other peers. The second part of our thesis focuses on how this translation can be performed through the use of mapping tables.

- **Rule Manager:** The objective of the rule manager is to provide mechanisms that can be used by peers in order to coordinate updates between them. Our proposal is to achieve such coordination through the use of Event-Condition-Action (ECA) rules. Providing update coordination in a peer-to-peer environment presents some interesting technical challenges. However, since this work in not part of our thesis, we will not elaborate any further.

In what follows, we provide more details about our solutions for the first two modules of Hyperion.

3.2   Mapping Tables

Mapping tables are the primary mechanism for data sharing between peers. In what follows we offer an overview of our work on mapping tables [15, 16].

Consider two peers S_1 and S_2 that expose attributes U and V respectively. Then, a mapping table m is a relation over the attributes $X \cup Y$, where $X \subseteq U$ and $Y \subseteq V$ are non-empty sets of attributes from the two peers. A tuple (x, y) in the mapping table indicates that the value x, in the domain of X, is associated with the value y, in the domain of Y. We impose no restrictions on the association between values, and thus the recorded associations can be one-to-one, one-to-many or many-to-many.

Starting from this simple idea of associating values between different domains, our framework offers a number of extensions including the ability to use variables. Variables offer a compact and convenient way to represent common associations between values, such as, the identity association. For example, a tuple (v_1, v_1) in mapping table m, where v_1 denotes a variable, represents the fact that every value in the domain of X is associated to itself in the domain of Y. The introduction of variables in mapping tables necessitates the use of valuations [5] in order to determine the set of Y-values with which a certain X-value is associated. Formally, given a valuation ρ of the variables of mapping table m, a value $x \in \pi_X(\rho(m))$ is associated with a certain set of values in the domain of Y, namely, with the set $\pi_Y(\sigma_{X=x}(\rho(m)))$.

Up to this point, we concerned ourselves only with the X-values appearing in the mapping table and how these are associated. What about the X-values that do not appear in the table? What can we say about their associations? Our work investigates alternative semantics for mapping tables to address these and related issues. Through the alternative semantics, we are able to specify whether the missing X-values can be associated either to any Y-value (open-world semantics) or to no Y-value (closed-world semantics).

3.3   Mapping Constraints

Mapping tables, by definition, represent value correspondences. Part of our contribution is the treatment of mapping tables as constraints on the exchange of information between sources. This is achieved by using the associations of values, recorded in the tables, to constrain the association of tuples in the two peers. Formally, consider again peers S_1 and S_2 and let $t_1[U]$ and $t_2[V]$ denote tuples of the two peers, respectively. Then, tuple t_1 with $t_1[X] = x$ can be mapped, with respect to mapping table m and valuation ρ, only to tuples t_2 in peer S_2 for which $t_2[Y] \in \pi_Y(\sigma_{X=x}(\rho(m)))$.

An important benefit of *mapping constraints* is our ability to automatically maintain and combine multiple constraints over a network of peers. Still, an obstacle that hinders the immediate deployment of our techniques is the high complexity of the inference and consistency problems for mapping constraints. Specifically, our investigation shows that the inference problem for mapping constraints is NP-complete even under restrictions that can be considered severe. To reduce the complexity of the problem, we provide a solution that applies over paths. We perform inference over these paths and we show experimentally that our algorithm works efficiently in practice. Furthermore, our experiments show that there is added benefit to consider alternative paths in a peer-to-peer network since we are able, in practice, to infer additional data associations.

3.4   Query Translation

Our work on peer-to-peer query answering starts with the investigation of the query answering semantics [14]. In brief, the proposed semantics allow for query answers that need not conform to a common schema. As such, our query semantics are consistent with the requirements of the data-sharing problem.

The execution of queries over the peer-to-peer network requires the translation of queries between peers. This translation relies solely on the use of mapping tables. Specifically, in our work we show how mapping tables can be used to translate select-project-join queries, where the selection formula is *positive*, i.e., it has no negation and it consists of conjunctions and disjunctions of atoms of the form $(A = B)$ and $(A = a)$, where A and B are attribute names and a is a constant. We consider both sound translations (which only retrieve correct answers) and complete translations (which retrieve all correct answers, and no incorrect answers). In this setting, we investigate the complexity of testing for sound translations and we show that the problem is Π_2^p-complete, in the size of the query. Since large queries rarely occur in practice, the high complexity is not an obstacle and as evidence we provide an implementation of the algorithm that works efficiently. We also propose and implement algorithms for computing sound and complete translations, and we offer experimental results that show the efficiency of these algorithms.

One of the advantages of our approach is that we use the same underlying formalism to represent both mapping tables and queries. Specifically, we introduce the notion of T-queries which is a tabular representation of queries and we show that for each select-join query, where the selection formula is positive, we can have an equivalent T-query. Our solutions deal with projection independently since we show that the issues involved in projection are orthogonal to those for the other two operators. The introduction of T-queries offers a number of advantages including simplicity of implementation of the proposed algorithms due to the uniformity of representation. Furthermore, by representing queries as tables, we are able to store as part of our database both the queries themselves, and the query translations. Our system attempts to take advantage of these past, stored, translations during the process of translating a new query. The objective is to reuse, if possible, the stored translations to reduce the time to compute a translation for the query under consideration. Our experiments prove that this technique is effective and results in considerable savings in terms of computation time.

4   Conclusions and Future Work

The objective of this thesis was to investigate mechanisms to support data sharing and querying in peer-to-peer data management systems. To this end, we proposed the use mapping tables as a mechanism to address the heterogeneity of the peers while respecting peer autonomy. We described briefly how automated tools can help manage the tables between multiple peers by inferring new tables from existing ones and by checking their consistency. In terms of querying, we proposed a framework in which users pose queries only with respect to their local peer. Then, we outlined our rewriting mechanism which uses mapping tables to translate a locally expressed query to a set of queries over the acquainted peers.

In terms of future work, there are a number of issues to address in the area of data sharing through the use of mapping tables. Specifically, our current semantics of mapping tables do not accommodate for NULL values and we intend to investigate how NULLs can be incorporated into these semantics.

In the current implementation, the mapping table inference algorithm accepts as input a path of peers and, by using the mapping tables along the path, it computes as output a set of inferred mapping tables. Since the peers on the path are autonomous, they can update their corresponding mapping tables independently and without notifying any other peer. These updates may influence the mapping tables that can be inferred along the path. Currently, to reflect the effect of the updates on the inferred mapping tables, one must re-execute the inference algorithm. Clearly, this approach is not optimal since a large portion of the previously inferred mapping tables remains unaffected by the updates. Thus, what is required is an incremental inference algorithm that detects the updates in the mapping tables of the path and determines which inferred mapping tables are affected by these updates and how these tables need to be updated.

Our query language currently does not support negation. As part of our future work, we intend to investigate how we can incorporate this operator. Such an extension will require a corresponding extension in the semantics of mapping tables. This is because our solutions rely on the same underlying formalism to represent mapping tables and queries.

References

1. Napster. http://www.napster.com/.
2. Gnutella. http://www.gnutelliums.com/.
3. OceanStore. http://oceanstore.cs.berkeley.edu/.
4. Karl Aberer, Philippe Cudré-Mauroux, and Manfred Hauswirth. The chatty Web: emergent semantics through gossiping. In *Proceedings of the Twelfth International Conference on World Wide Web*, pages 197–206. ACM Press, 2003.
5. Serge Abiteboul, Richard Hull, and Victor Vianu. *Foundations of Databases*. Addison-Wesley, 1995.
6. Marcelo Arenas, Vasiliki Kantere, Anastasios Kementsietsidis, Iluju Kiringa, Renée J. Miller, and John Mylopoulos. The Hyperion Project: From Data Integration to Data Coordination. *SIGMOD Record*, 32(3):53–58, 2003.
7. Philip Bernstein, Fausto Giunchiglia, Anastasios Kementsietsidis, John Mylopoulos, Luciano Serafini, and Ilya Zaihrayeu. Data Management for Peer-to-Peer Computing: A Vision. In *Proc. of the Int'l Workshop on the Web and Databases (WebDB)*, 2002.
8. Chen-Chuan K. Chang and Hector Garcia-Molina. Mind your vocabulary: Query mapping across heterogeneous information sources. In *ACM SIGMOD Int'l Conf. on the Management of Data*, pages 335–346, 1999.
9. Susan Davidson, G. Christian Overton, and Peter Buneman. Challenges in integrating biological data sources. *Journal of Computational Biology*, 2(4):557–572, 1995.
10. A. Elmagarmid, M. Rusinkiewicz, and A. Sheth. *Management of Heterogeneous and Autonomous Database Systems*. Morgan Kaufmann Publishers, 1999.
11. Ronald Fagin, Phokion G. Kolaitis, Renée J. Miller, and Lucian Popa. Data exchange: Semantics and query answering. In *Proc. of the Int'l Conf. on Database Theory (ICDT)*, pages 207–224, 2003.
12. Alon Halevy, Zack Ives, Dan Suciu, and Igor Tatarinov. Schema Mediation in Peer Data Management Systems. In *Proc. of the Int'l Conference on Data Engineering*, 2003.

13. Ryan Huebsch, Joseph M. Hellerstein, Nick Lanham Boon, Thau Loo, Scott Shenker, and Ion Stoica. Querying the Internet with PIER. In *Proc. of the Int'l Conf. on Very Large Data Bases (VLDB)*, pages 321–332, 2003.

14. Anastasios Kementsietsidis and Marcelo Arenas. Data sharing through query translation in autonomous sources. *(To appear in VLDB 2004)*.

15. Anastasios Kementsietsidis, Marcelo Arenas, and Renée J. Miller. Data mapping in peer-to-peer systems: Semantics and algorithmic issues. In *ACM SIGMOD Int'l Conf. on the Management of Data*, pages 325–336, 2003.

16. Anastasios Kementsietsidis, Marcelo Arenas, and Renée J. Miller. Managing data mappings in the Hyperion project. In *Proc. of the Int'l Conference on Data Engineering*, pages 732–734, 2003.

17. Maurizio Lenzerini. Data Integration: A Theoretical Perspective. In *Proc. of the ACM Symp. on Principles of Database Systems (PODS)*, pages 233–246, 2002.

18. Bertram Ludäscher, Amarnath Gupta, and Maryann E. Martone. Model-based mediation with domain maps. In *Proc. of the Int'l Conference on Data Engineering*, pages 81–90, 2001.

19. Jayant Madhavan and Alon Y. Halevy. Composing Mappings Among Data Sources. In *Proc. of the Int'l Conf. on Very Large Data Bases (VLDB)*, pages 572–583, 2003.

20. Wee Siong Ng, Beng Chin Ooi, Kian Lee Tan, and Ao Ying Zhou. PeerDB: A P2P-based system for distributed data sharing. In *Proc. of the Int'l Conference on Data Engineering*, pages 633–644, 2003.

21. Lucian Popa, Yannis Velegrakis, Renée J. Miller, Mauricio A. Hernandez, and Ronald Fagin. Translating web data. In *Proc. of the Int'l Conf. on Very Large Data Bases (VLDB)*, pages 598–609, 2002.

22. Sylvia Ratnasamy, Paul Francis, Mark Handley, Richard Karp, and Scott Shenker. A scalable content addressable network. In *ACM SIGCOMM Int'l Conf. on Data Communications*, pages 161–172, 2001.

23. Ion Stoica, Robert Morris, David Karger, Frans Kaashoek, and Hari Balakrishnan. Chord: A scalable Peer-To-Peer lookup service for Internet applications. In *ACM SIGCOMM Int'l Conf. on Data Communications*, pages 149–160, 2001.

24. Yannis Velegrakis, Renée J. Miller, and Lucian Popa. Mapping adaptation under evolving schemas. In *Proc. of the Int'l Conf. on Very Large Data Bases (VLDB)*, pages 584–595, 2003.

25. Ben Y. Zhao, Ling Huang, Jeremy Stribling, Sean C. Rhea, Anthony D. Joseph, and John D. Kubiatowicz. Tapestry: A resilient global-scale overlay for service deployment. *IEEE Journal on Selected Areas in Communications*, 22(1):41–53, January 2004.

Relevance Feedback in XML Retrieval

Hanglin Pan

Max-Planck-Institut für Informatik,
D-66123 Saarbrücken, Germany
pan@mpi-sb.mpg.de

Abstract. Highly heterogeneous XML data collections that do not have a global schema, as arising, for example, in federations of digital libraries or scientific data repositories, cannot be effectively queried with XQuery or XPath alone, but rather require a ranked retrieval approach. As known from ample work in the IR field, relevance feedback provided by the user that drives automatic query refinement or expansion can often lead to improved search result quality (e.g., precision or recall). In this paper we present a framework for feedback-driven XML query refinement and address several building blocks including reweighting of query conditions and ontology-based query expansion. We point out the issues that arise specifically in the XML context and cannot be simply addressed by straightforward use of traditional IR techniques, and we present our approaches towards tackling them.

1 Introduction

1.1 Motivation

Ranked retrieval systems for heterogeneous XML data with both structural search conditions and keyword conditions have been developed recently across digital libraries, federations of scientific data repositories, and hopefully portions of the ultimate Web (XRank [8], XIRQL [6], XXL [13, 14], etc.). These systems are based on pre-defined similarity measures for elementary conditions and then use rank aggregation techniques to produced ranked results lists. Due to the users' lack of information on the structure and terminology of the underlying diverse data sources, users can often not avoid posing overly broad or overly narrow initial queries, thus facing either too many or too few results.

For the user, it is much more appropriate and easier to provide a relevance judgment on the best results of an initial query execution, and then refine the query, either interactively or automatically by the system. This calls for applying relevance feedback technology [1, 2, 9, 11, 12, 16] in the new area of XML retrieval. The key question is how to generate a refined query appropriately based on a user's feedback in order to obtain more relevant results among the top-k result list.

As an example, suppose we have the following portion of XML document collection (Figure 1) with research activities and bibliographic information after crawling and indexing some scientists' homepages.

The user may submit the following query in order to find researchers who work in Germany on the field of Information Retrieval (IR). The query is expressed in the XXL

W. Lindner et al. (Eds.): EDBT 2004 Workshops, LNCS 3268, pp. 187–196, 2004.

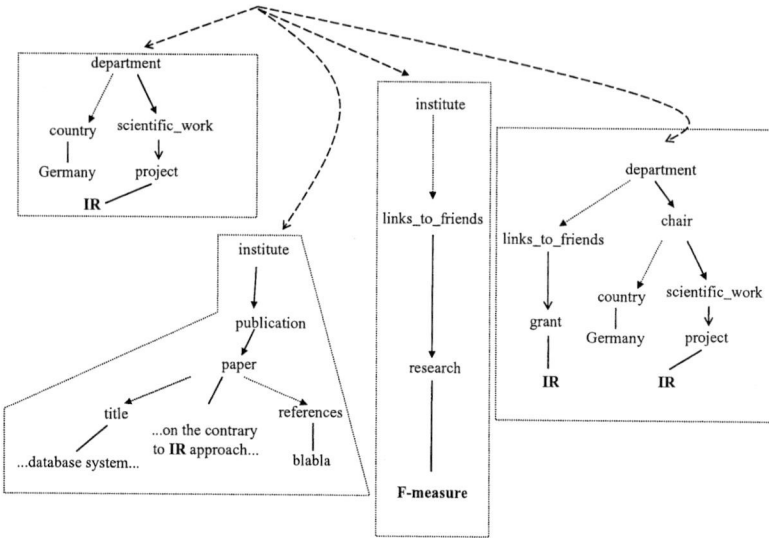

Fig. 1. Structurally diverse XML data graph

language [14], but could be posed in a similar way in other languages such as XIRQL [6] or XRank [8].

```
SELECT * FROM INDEX
WHERE ~department AS $H
AND $H/country = "Germany"
AND $H/#/~research AS $R
AND $R ~ "IR";
```

Here '/' stands for path concatenation, '#' for arbitrary paths of XML elements, '~' for semantic similarity conditions on XML element (or attribute) names as well as XML element (or attribute) contents, and '$H' for variable condition. We refer to [14] for details.

XXL queries contain exact and vague conditions. In the above query, the path-matching condition $H/country and the element-content condition ="Germany" are exact, the other four conditions are vague: 1) #, 2) ~department, 3) ~research, 4) ~ "IR". In the following we focus on the vague conditions.

The sample query is decomposed into four elementary sub-queries, each of which is binded with a *weight* indicating its relative importance. (see weight assignment in section 2.1 and architecture of XXL in section 4.)

Each of elementary sub-queries is evaluated by system locally and scored based on IR-style $tf * idf$ measures for element contents and general ontological similarity measure for element names. The total *score* of an XML path with regard to the entire query is computed in a simple probabilistic manner as the product of the local scores, (for all conditions are combined in a conjunctive manner. See section 2.1 for how to combine *weights* and *scores*.) Here using *maximum* is one option to avoid result redundancy. To give an impression on how overall scores are computed based on local scores, we show a sample result list:

```
Result 1: (overall=0.8)
 /department;1/(scientific_work/project);0.8/IR;1

Result 2: (overall=0.7)
 /institute;1/publication/paper;0.7/IR;1

Result 3: (overall=0.6*1*0.9=0.54)
 /institute;1/links_to_friends;0.6/research;1/F-measure;0.9

Result 4: (overall=max(0.48,0.42)=0.48)
 /department/chair;0.6/(scientific_work/project);0.8/IR;1
 /department/links_to_friends;0.6/grant;0.7/IR;1
```

In the result set from the first round of query execution, the attached numbers to each blocks of meta-data from index are *scores* given by the engine, either as local measurements on element path (some are shown as rectangle in Figure 2) and element content (shown as circle), or as overall.

In such a ranked retrieval model, the aggregation of, possibly weighted, scores of sub-queries is often subjective to the user and thus should be personalized at runtime. Relevance feedback can help to automatically tune weights and other options of the query execution engine to the user's specific information needs.

In an XML setting we have much richer opportunities for relevance feedback than in a traditional text-only IR environment. Consider the sample results for our example query shown in Figure 2. At the document level, the user may mark results 1, 2, and 4 as positively relevant. At the element level, the user has much more fine-grained control over positive and negative feedback. For example, in results 1 and 4, the path scientific_work/project is positive. In result 2, after zooming into the content, the user may find out that the paper is mainly about "Database Systems" instead of "Information Retrieval", so it is assessed as negative. Finally, in results 3 and 4, the tag name links_to_friends is assessed as negative.

Our opportunity now is to exploit this kind of feedback for automatically refining the initial query into a better suited query such as:

SELECT * FROM INDEX
WHERE (department;1.0 | institute;1.0 | chair;0.8) AS $H ::1.0
AND $H/country = "Germany" ::0.6
AND $H/(research;1.0 | (scientific_work/project);0.95 | project;0.8 | grant;0.7
| paper;0.7)/# AS $R ::0.8
AND $R ~ ("IR"|"F-measure") ::0.9;

Here the numbers after '::' that are attached to the various search conditions are *weights* that are used in the total scoring function (see section 2.1) to reflect the relative importance of the various conditions. The numbers after ';' are *weights* used for local

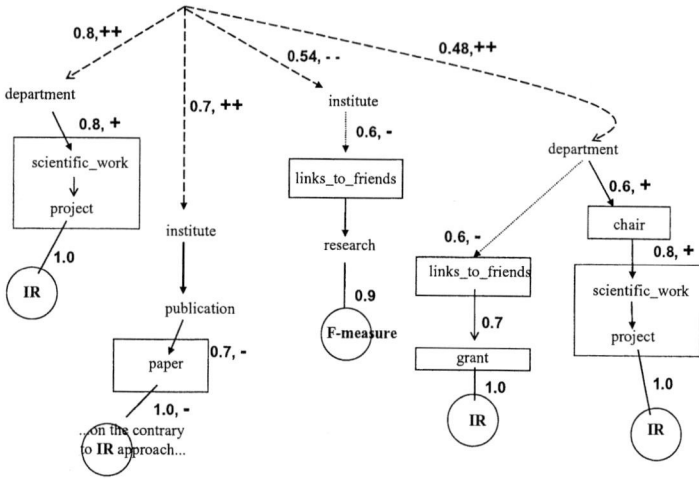

Fig. 2. Sample retrieval results, with computed similarity scores and user's feedback at both document level (marked with ++, − −) and element level (marked with +,−)

scoring function in query expansion. The symbol '|' denotes disjunction. Thus the new query uses query expansion to reach out for semantically relevant data that uses diverse terminology different from the terms in the original query. Query expansion is a standard technique in IR, but note that in our approach it is used not just for XML content terms, but also for XML element names and it is driven by query-specific ontological similarity measures [13].

1.2   Research Objectives

The objectives in this Ph.D. project are twofold:

Feedback Capturing: A systematic study is required on how to capture and exploit different kinds of feedback interactions like:

Binary feedback vs. non-binary feedback:

1. Binary feedback means (+), (−) are the only two values of feedback.
2. Non-binary feedback means using a multivalued relevance scale, e.g. (+2), (+1), and (−2) mean "highly relevant", "marginally relevant", and "not at all relevant" respectively.

Feedback for different granularities:

1. feedback only on entire documents,
2. feedback on documents as well as elements,
3. feedback on documents, elements, and also entire paths.

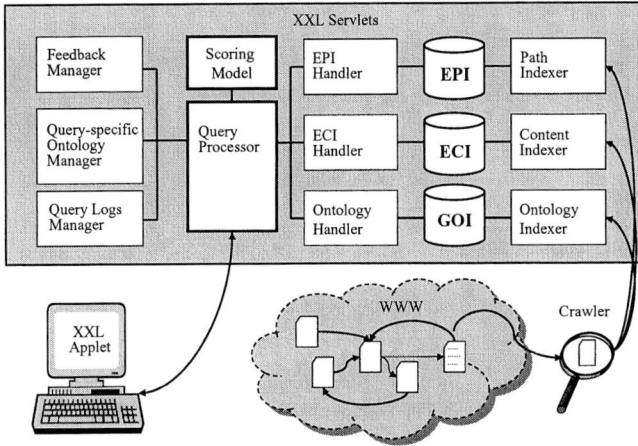

Fig. 4. Architecture of the XXL Search Engine with relevance feedback support

5   Evaluation Plan

Our evaluation plan is to participate in the proposed *Relevance Feedback Track* at INEX 2004 [7]. It will provide a benchmark for relevance assessment for further the relevance feedback process in XML retrieval, and handle both Content-Only (CO) queries and Content-And-Structure (CAS) queries.

Acknowledgments

I wish to express my gratitude to my advisor Gerhard Weikum for his guidance and encouragement, and to Ralf Schenkel for his helpful comments.

References

1. Ricardo Baeza-Yates and Berthier Ribeiro-Neto, editors. *Modern Information Retrieval.* Addison Wesley, 1999.
2. Chris Buckley and Gerard Salton. Optimization of relevance feedback weights. In *Proc. of the 18th ACM SIGIR*, pages 351–357. ACM Press, 1995.
3. Ugur Cetintemel, Michael J. Franklin, and C. Lee Giles. Flexible user profiles for large scale data delivery. Technical Report CS-TR-4005 (UMIACS-TR-99-18), University of Maryland, 1999.
4. Hang Cui, Ji-Rong Wen, Jian-Yun Nie, and Wei-Ying Ma. Query expansion by mining user logs. *IEEE Transaction on Knowledge and Data Engineering*, 15(4):829–839, 2003.
5. Ronald Fagin and Edward L. Wimmers. Incorporating user preferences in multimedia queries. In Foto N. Afrati and Phokion G. Kolaitis, editors, *Database Theory – ICDT '97, 6th Int. Conf., Delphi, Greece, 1997, Proceedings*, volume 1186 of *LNCS*, pages 247–261. Springer, 1997.

6. Norbert Fuhr and Kai Großjohann. XIRQL: A query language for information retrieval in XML documents. In *Research and Development in Information Retrieval*, pages 172–180, 2001.

7. Norbert Fuhr and Mounia Lalmas. Initiative for the evaluation of XML retrieval (INEX), 2003. http://inex.is.informatik.uni-duisburg.de:2003/.

8. Lin Guo, Feng Shao, Chavdar Botev, and Jayavel Shanmugasundaram. XRANK: Ranked keyword search over XML documents. In *Proc. of the 2003 ACM SIGMOD Int. Conf. on Management of Data*, pages 16–27. ACM Press, 2003.

9. E. Ide. New experiments in relevance feedback. In Gerard Salton, editor, *The Smart Retrieval System: Experiments in Automatic Document Processing*, pages 337–354. Prentice Hall, 1971.

10. John Lamping and Ramana Rao. Laying out and visualizing large trees using a hyperbolic space. In *ACM Symposium on User Interface Software and Technology*, pages 13–14, 1994.

11. Michael Ortega-Binderberger, Kaushik Chakrabarti, and Sharad Mehrotra. An approach to integrating query refinement in SQL. In *Extending Database Technology, EDBT*, pages 15–33, 2002.

12. J. Rocchio. Relevance feedback in information retrieval. In Gerard Salton, editor, *The Smart Retrieval System: Experiments in Automatic Document Processing*, pages 313–323. Prentice Hall, 1971.

13. Ralf Schenkel, Anja Theobald, and Gerhard Weikum. Ontology-enabled XML search. In Henk M. Blanken, Torsten Grabs, Hans-Jörg Schek, Ralf Schenkel, and Gerhard Weikum, editors, *Intelligent Search on XML Data, Applications, Languages, Models, Implementations, and Benchmarks*, volume 2818 of *LNCS*, pages 119–131. Springer, 2003.

14. Anja Theobald and Gerhard Weikum. The index-based XXL search engine for querying XML data with relevance ranking. In Christian S. Jensen, Keith G. Jeffery, Jaroslav Pokorný, Simonas Saltenis, Elisa Bertino, Klemens Böhm, and Matthias Jarke, editors, *Advances in Database Technology – EDBT 2002, 8th Int. Conf. on Extending Database Technology, Prague, Czech Republic, Proceedings*, volume 2287 of *LNCS*, pages 477–495. Springer, 2002.

15. Martin Theobald, Ralf Schenkel, and Gerhard Weikum. Exploiting structure, annotation, and ontological knowledge for automatic classification of XML data. In Vassilis Christophides and Juliana Freire, editors, *WebDB: International Workshop on Web and Databases, San Diego, 2003*, 2003.

16. Xiang Sean Zhou and Thomas S. Huang. Exploring the nature and variants of relevance feedback. In *Proc. of the IEEE Workshop on Content-based Access of Image and Video Libraries (CBAIVL'01)*, pages 94–101. IEEE CS Press, 2001.

XML Challenges for the Database Community: Past, Present, and Future

Daniele Braga, Alessandro Campi, and Stefano Ceri

Politecnico di Milano
Dipartimento di Elettronica e Informazione
Piazza Leonardo da Vinci 32, Milano, Italy I–20133
{braga,campi,ceri}@elet.polimi.it

Abstract. It is a common understanding that "the Web changes everything", and this applies to an increasing number of computer applications. In the last years, we also understood that "XML is the means" for this change to take effect, as XML has progressively become the basis on which Web applications are built. This corollary was the claim of [9], published four years ago, in which XML was pointed out as a prominent and promising research direction for the database community.

Indeed, among the many promises that followed the advent of XML, some have been fulfilled, some are still at the stage of promise. After four years, one of the authors was asked to "redo" the same exercise, reconsidering the challenges posed to the database community and making another assessment of the area checking whether the expectations and challenges of the year 2000 have been met in 2004. This paper compares the past and present status of several XML-related research activities, examining the "next steps" that should lead to further integration of XML with database technology in terms of language and system requirements.

1 Introduction: XML Mission

XML was initially designed as a simplification of SGML to provide a flexible instrument for publishing data on the Web as alternative to HTML; it has increasingly gained importance as a standard data representation format for information interchange between Web applications. In the early times of its specification, the mission of XML was meant to be manyfold, so as to address several issues at a time:

- Enabling *internationalized media-independent electronic publishing* and allowing people to *display information the way they want it*; this objective has been achieved in conjunction with XSLT [19] as the standard technology for mapping presentation-independent data structures to specific media-dependent markup languages and representation formats.
- Allowing industries to define *platform-independent protocols for data exchange*, especially in electronic commerce; this is probably the most active area at the moment, especially w.r.t. to the "Web Service revolution".
- Making it easy for people to *process data using inexpensive software*. This is achieved somehow "by construction", as XML is text-based and a plethora of free parsers are available, offering common tree-based abstractions and traversal APIs.

W. Lindner et al. (Eds.): EDBT 2004 Workshops, LNCS 3268, pp. 197–208, 2004.

- Providing *rich metadata* that will help people find information and help information producers and consumers find each other. Many XML-based standards are commonly used, both as direct metadata specification formats (Mpeg7 for multimedia, SCORM for education, ...) and as the basis for services specification and classification (WSDL, UDDI, ...).
- Delivering *information to user agents* in a form that allows automatic processing after receipt. And indeed, XML is an important ingredient for the new languages and formalisms marking the advent of Semantic Web and ontologies.

The effort to clarify and try reaching these objectives started several years ago with the first XML proposal; ad-hoc query languages came immediately after, even though the database community was not really involved in the early XML design process. The inherent complexity of querying semi-structured data makes the process much harder than defining XML itself. As an evidence of this problematic process, consider that XML was first introduced in 1997 and became a recommendation in 1998, while XQuery was first proposed in February 2001 (as heritage of several already established language proposals), and is still in the status of working draft.

2   The Past: XML Four Years Ago

Four years ago, we announced that XML was good news to the database community, and we meant it for at least three reasons.

First of all, XML is (and was) simple and powerful; XML data is easy to read for the human eye and for a parser at the same time, and maps hierarchies of concepts directly into hierarchies of data chunks. Indeed, XML is also very effective to represent *data semantics*. XML documents are self-describing and must comply with a document class specification (DTD [17] or XML Schema [23]) that dictates the structure of the document. XML is very effective in providing *data independence* as well, as XML documents are inherently specified independently from presentation.

Second, XML was winning the Data Interchange Standard War. There were several successful data interchange standards, such as SQL + JDBC (the "intergalactic data speak") or technologies like CORBA and DCOM, specifically targeted to represent and exchange distributed objects and components for distributed applications. However, they did not solve the interoperability problem, as they describe "computations" much more then "data" themselves; in other words, they don't help much in describing the semantics of the data being exchanged between systems.

Last, classical data abstractions from the theory of data representation and management do apply to XML: modeling, constraining, querying, viewing, updating, mining.

For these three reasons, it was easy to envision that *XML would be in the "core business" of the database community*; and indeed XML-related topics cover the majority of scientific sessions at VLDB, SIGMOD, EDBT and ICDE, the leading conferences of the area. However, not all the above data abstractions have been addressed with the same effort and success. The next sections address these issues.

2.1   XML Data Modeling and Constraining

Two standard formats are available for defining and constraining the structure of XML documents, *Document Type Definitions* (DTD) and *XML Schema Definitions* (XSD).

DTDs are simple but quite poor in their expressive power; they do allow to define the structure of a document as a sequence of elements, PCDATA content, and attributes; however, simple types are available only for attributes (ID, IDREF, NMTOKEN, CDATA, enumerations, ...), while PCDATA chunks are indistinguishable. Such a formalism can be thought of as a generative notation, such as a grammar.

XSDs are more expressive. They are based on the notion of data type, and offer the chance to define the type of each element using a very rich set of basic predefined types (44 different types); it is also possible to define ad-hoc data types, either as restrictions of the basic types, or building complex types as arrays, records, or unordered sequences of items of predefined data types. Furthermore, XSDs allow to define integrity constraints such as to state the exact number of subelements of a certain type. This higher expressive power is balanced by the fact that XSD is very verbose, probably too much.

2.2   XML Query Languages (Querying and Viewing)

The first languages such as Lorel [4], were variants of languages thought for generic semi-structured data and not specifically for XML. Given the emphasis on object-oriented data models, a huge emphasis was on references, represented by ID/IDREF couples, a feature that now is not regarded as crucial anymore.

Native XML query languages, from the very first XQL [14], to XML-QL [11], up to Quilt [10], which took some characteristics from many pre-existing languages, eventually resulted in the first XQuery proposal. It is also worth mentioning XSL [22], which is not exactly a query language, but is still capable of query-like transformations.

The ancestors of XQuery have diverse expressive powers; XSLT and XQuery, instead, are Turing complete (they both support recursion and composition of user-defined functions). Moreover, XQuery is a fully functional language, in which expressions can be substituted by their results and computations can be decomposed into partial transformations. Therefore, views are supported "by construction".

2.3   Updating and Mining

These directions were scarcely investigated in the past - at least not at a level of establishment comparable with that of the other dimensions - and they are still lagging behind. We will address such data managing abstractions again when dealing with the current perspectives on XML evolution.

3   The Present of XML

In moving to the assessment of the present of XML we separately consider the current strengths first, and then its major weaknesses.

3.1   Present XML Strengths

We observe that in several applications XML is particularly suited for being a sort of "glue" for distributed computations that need to cooperate or interoperate by exchanging data encoded in some standard format. Indeed...

...XML scales up...

XML turned from a document markup language into the standard abstraction for data interchange and for defining interfaces between co-operating software components. From being an instrument for enabling data publication by various cooperating applications, XML has become a key enabling technology for achieving data interoperability.

... to a programming abstraction ...

XML is also used as the representation format for the internal state of several software applications; so it is also a key enabling technology for building applications, assisted by powerful tools and combined with other well-matching technologies.

... to Web Services enabler ...

Web Services are the dominant paradigm for building *distributed* applications. All major Web Service standards (e.g. SOAP [24], WSDL [21], UDDI, BPEL) use XML for data representation and service description and classification.

... and even further!

XML is adopted in many application domains, such as education (SCORM [5] and IMS [13] are XML based standard for classification of Learning Objects), multimedia (Mpeg-7 [1] has XML metadata), e-commerce protocols for negotiation and binding, genetics, mathematics (MathML [20]), chemistry.

3.2   Present XML Weaknesses

One major shortcoming regards the fact that XQuery is far too complex for unskilled users. Consider the following query, taken from the W3C XQuery Use Cases, that extracts pairs of books with different titles but the same authors:

```
<bib> {
    for $book1 in doc("www.bstore.example.com/bib.xml")//book,
        $book2 in doc("www.bstore.example.com/bib.xml")//book
    let $aut1 := for $a in $book1/author
                 order by $a/last, $a/first
                 return $a
    let $aut2 := for $a in $book2/author
                 order by $a/last, $a/first
                 return $a
    where $book1 << $book2 and not($book1/title = $book2/title)
          and deep-equal($aut1, $aut2)
    return <book-pair>
               { $book1/title }
               { $book2/title }
           </book-pair>
} </bib>
```

Such a statement is readable only for experienced IT professionals, with some background concerning queries, functions, and variables representing sets of elements; it goes beyond the classical abilities which are required in order to write the same query in SQL, and in general XQuery programmers must go beyond the classical abstractions required to write SQL-embedded applications on top of relational databases. We acknowledge that XQuery is inherently more complex than SQL, as it must deal with an inherently more complex data model. Such greater complexity of XQuery, however, should be dealt with by language designers, who so far have concentrated on the expressive power of XQuery and given little attention to the methodological and pedagogical aspects of teaching the language so as to make it accepted.

One useful way to address the problem is to identify progressive programming abstractions within XQuery and to associate to each abstraction a level of language complexity. In such construction, the first level could include XPath, FLWOR expressions, basic XML constructors and joins, while recursive user-defined functions would probably belong to the highest level. The advantage of a layered approach to XQuery would be:

- Ease of staging the learning of the language (by levels).
- Scaled deployment of XQuery implementations and of their respective development environments (by layers).
- Greater compatibility and comparability of XQuery implementations.

We strongly believe that it would be highly beneficial for XQuery implementors to be able to indicate that their product supports a given level of XQuery.

Another shortcoming of XML is that if DTDs are too poor, XML Schema is too verbose and complex. As an example, just consider the following scary specification of an arbitrarily long list of productName/quantity couples:

```
<xsd:complexType name="Items">
 <xsd:sequence>
  <xsd:element name="item" minOccurs="0" maxOccurs="unbounded">
   <xsd:complexType>
    <xsd:sequence>
     <xsd:element name="productName" type="xsd:string"/>
     <xsd:element name="quantity">
      <xsd:simpleType>
       <xsd:restriction base="xsd:positiveInteger">
        <xsd:maxExclusive value="100"/>
       </xsd:restriction>
      </xsd:simpleType>
     </xsd:element>
    </xsd:sequence>
   </xsd:complexType>
  </xsd:element>
 </xsd:sequence>
</xsd:complexType>
```

As already suggested for XQuery, a possible approach to this issue might be to introduce *levels*; the first level could include few basic data types, support for the specification of key constraints, and referential integrity. A different approach, still driven by a simplification effort, might be to introduce user friendly interfaces to enable the representation and design of schemas in a visual environment (e.g. in a way similar to that described in section 5.1).

Another major shortcoming regards the fact that XML updates are missing. A long debate took place on the fields of the W3C specification: not only it seems to be questionable how updates should be specified, how they should be implemented, and which is the semantics of updates addressing hierarchical structures; even the need for an update language is not certain yet, and at the time a W3C proposal is still missing.

Indeed, two different schools of thought regard XML differently: either as a data storage format or as a format for representing data streams. Only those adopting the former perspective can perceive the need for an update language, while the latter viewpoint hardly allows to conceive such an extension.

However, the need for updates became strong for all the vendors that have implemented XQuery together with a native XML storage systems (and not only as a query interpreter for data stored in textual files in a regular file system). According to our experience, there are three main kinds of requirements for updates:

- Supporting bulk insertions and deletions (as implemented in Xyleme [3]). This is the simplest approach, as the only required capability is that of uploading and deleting entire documents.
- Supporting insertions and deletions of some specified fragments in specified positions, as implemented in XUpdate [2], which exploits the expressive power of XPath for accessing the involved fragments.
- Supporting a full fledged language, with nested statements and that exploits the expressive power of XQuery, as proposed in [16]. As far as we know, such a language hasn't been implemented yet.

4 The Future: XML Challenges

4.1 XML Query Languages

Despite the lengthy standardization process, XQuery is far from being complete and satisfactory according to all viewpoints; much work can still be done to formalize, enrich, enhance, and disseminate XQuery as a standard, so as to substantially contribute to its success and diffusion among the widest audience; to this end, the language is supposed to address diverse and even contrasting expectations and needs.

A first set of possible evolutions is somehow *language-independent*. The formalization of the basic query features in terms of an XML algebra is a good example of something that is already available but could be improved. A minimal set of orthogonal algebraic operators was not determined yet; such a result could be exploited to define nontrivial equivalence properties and therefore to perform high-level nontrivial optimizations, in a way similar to the exploitation of algebraic transformations for optimizing access plans within relational database systems.

Recalling that the XML data model is semi-structured, is also possible to envision several extensions to enhance querying capabilities or integrating functionalities that are typical of other domains, such as information retrieval and graph matching. Among several possibilities, we point to the following as the most interesting ones:

- Proximity search. Quite often in XML documents "physical" proximity implicates "semantic" proximity, as data are often clustered according to precise criteria and the document order is often meaningful; imprecise (fuzzy) queries might cover all cases in which users only have a vague idea about the structure of the target documents or about what they are looking for. Uncertainty can also be traded with efficiency whenever a fast estimate is preferable to long computations for exact results (synopsis, histograms, pre-computation of aggregates, ...).
- Combining queries and keyword-based search. XML data can contain large excerpts of free text; integrating free text analysis and searching functionalities may substantially improve the impact of XQuery outside the community of database experts.

Of course such extensions require an effective and unambiguous syntax, but in principle these are language-independent extensions, as the most crucial point is to devise suitable metrics and algorithms rather than to invent sweet syntactic sugar.

Another orthogonal language evolution opportunity regards XML data streams, which might be crucial in all scenarios in which XML is the means for distributed applications to cooperate. Message flows may be processed on the fly, and the extracted (condensed) data can be stored in repositories. Applications may range from log analysis to security checks on the fly. We know of an XQuery implementation done by BEA exclusively for this purpose.

4.2   Native XML Repositories

Some more technical and quite classical challenges are directly posed to "core DB" researchers:

- Support for XML queries by means of ad-hoc efficient data storage and indexes
- Use of schema knowledge to optimize queries
- Support for parallel and distributed query processing
- Dealing with replicas and order (quite new w.r.t. the relational knowhow)
- Dealing with irregular data and heterogeneous data sources (as contrasted to efficient storage and indexing)
- Support for views and view materialization
- Support for irregular schema specifications (DTDs and XSDs)

However, many native XML repositories have already been implemented, and several new commercial products and open source initiatives are intensively developed. This poses a pressing need for independent and effective benchmarks to compare the performances of different repositories. According to [15], the target of a benchmark should be to test the capability of managing:

- Bulk loading and (dually) full document reconstruction.
- Path traversal (ubiquitous access methods).
- Casting (always switching to and from text).

- Missing elements and structural uncertainty: absences are more frequent than nulls.
- Order (*within* the data model, unlike RDBs).
- References (as dual to path traversal).
- Joins (typical bottleneck + hierarchical data).
- Handling large data volumes.

4.3   XML and Semantic Web

The Semantic Web is a recent attempt to win one of the most interesting challenges on the field of automated reasoning: to add intelligence to data management and computations in general. More specifically, the Semantic Web is commonly meant as the possibility to achieve semantic interoperability by means of accurate modeling of conceptual domains. A recent slogan to indicate the relevance of XML for the Semantic Web is:

XML + ontologies = semantic interoperability

Ontologies are a formal and consensual specifications of conceptualizations that provide a shared and common understanding of a domain, an understanding that can be communicated across people and application systems. After all, technologies that support access to unstructured, heterogeneous and distributed information might become as essential as programming languages were in the 60's and 70's [12]. Typical XML based ontology formats are RDF [18] and OWL [25]. XML tools enable editing and manipulating ontologies quite easily.

5   Ongoing Research at Politecnico di Milano

We now turn our focus to some ongoing research at Politecnico di Milano, exploring the chance of applying to XQuery some of the extensions applied in the past to SQL. In the following we will refer to a scenario based on the XML document sketched below (bib.xml), containing a list of bibliographic entries:

```
<bib refNumber="45">
  . . .
  <book id="AO97" year="2000">
    <author> J. Acute </author>
    <author> J. Obtuse </author>
    <title> Applying Triangular Inequalities </title>
    <publisher> Addison-Wesley </publisher>
  </book>
  . . .
</bib>
```

5.1   XQBE

XQBE (XQuery By Example [8]) is a visual dialect of XQuery inspired by the QBE language (Query By Example, [26]). QBE was initially proposed as alternative to SQL

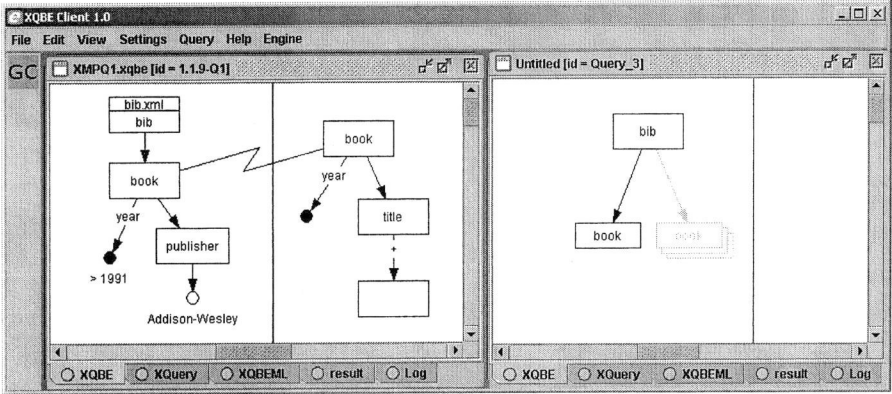

Fig. 1. A query in XQBE and the visual support for schema specifications

and then became popular as the user-friendly language supported by MS Access. The success of QBE demonstrated that a visual query language is effective and intuitive when the basic graphical constructs of the language are close to a visual abstraction of the underlying data model. Accordingly, while QBE is a relational query language, based on a tabular representation of data, XQBE is based on the use of annotated trees, so as to adhere to the hierarchical nature of the XML data model.

XQBE supports most of the expressive power of XPath, the construction of new XML elements, and nontrivial restructuring of existing documents. However, its expressive power is limited w.r.t. XQuery; as an example, XQBE does not support disjunction and user defined functions (a user confident with functions can directly use XQuery). These limitations are precise design issues: a complete but too complex visual language would fail both in replacing the textual one and in addressing most users' needs.

To exemplify XQBE, Figure 1 shows a query that reads *"List books published by Addison-Wesley after 1991, including their year and title"*. The *source* part (on the left) describes the source data, matching the book elements with a year attribute greater than 1991 and a publisher subelement equal to "Addison-Wesley". In the *construct* part (on the right), an example of the query result is visually sketched. The binding edge between the book nodes states that the query result shall contain *as many* book elements *as* those matched in the source part. The paths that branch out of the node with a binding edge indicate which of its contents are to be retained (thus "projecting" the bound node - in our example only the title and publication year are retained).

XQBE is targeted to unskilled users, without knowledge of query languages, so usability is a critical success factor. The set of visual constructs, i.e. the XQBE syntax, is a trade off between a neat graphical characterization, with different shapes for different concepts, and the fact that an unreasonably large set of symbols would be rather confusing. XQBE also supports a visual environment for exploiting available schema specifications, so as to facilitate the formulation of queries towards documents whose schema is unknown; Figure 1 also shows that a bib may contain a sequence of books.

5.2   Fuzzy XPath

FXPath is a fuzzy extension of XPath 1.0 addressing the following characteristics: *fuzzy predicates*, specifying flexible selection conditions, *fuzzy subtree matching*, providing a ranked list of retrieved items rather than the usual document-ordered list, *fuzzy quantification*, allowing the specification of linguistic quantifiers as aggregation operators. In order to allow for vague specification of selection conditions, we extended the XPath syntax with the specification of fuzzy predicates. An FXPath expression can contain several fuzzy conditions, and each of them is satisfied to a degree in [0,1]. We shall rank FXPath query results according to these degrees. To keep the new language features separate from the standard specification, non-standard expressions are enclosed into curly braces, so that a simple parsing algorithm can ignore them and translate an expression into corresponding crisp expressions.

The following query extracts articles published as close to year 2000 as possible:

```
/bib/book[{@year NEAR 2000}]
```

The results are ranked according to the distance of the value of `year` from 2000, and its crisp equivalent is obtained ignoring the condition; a standard XPath processor then returns all the books in document order.

The next example shows how fuzzy conditions can be imposed upon the *structure* of XML data. The keyword NEAR can also be used as an XPath axis such that the degree of matching is stronger for those elements that are closer in the containment hierarchy:

```
/bib{/NEAR}/book
```

The list of the result nodes will be ranked w.r.t. to the increasing number of steps to be descended. Note that the keyword NEAR is used in the previous examples with a different meaning, but in all cases it expresses 'proximity'; such overloading is meant to help the user's intuition.

5.3   Active XQuery

Active XQuery is a trigger specification language for XML repositories, based on a predefined XQuery update model; the syntax and semantics of our language are inspired by the SQL3 specification. This active extension of XQuery arises nontrivial problems related to the interleaving of updates and triggers, which led us to define an algorithm for update reformulation and to devise a compact semantics. More details are in [7].

A simple example of update will give an intuition of our proposal at work: the "bulk" insertion of new bibliographic references. In this scenario, the attribute `refNumber`, which represents the number of books, is automatically maintained by triggers responsible for its decrement or increment after each deletion or insertion respectively. For sake of brevity, we only show only the trigger that reacts to insertions.

```
CREATE TRIGGER IncrementCounter
AFTER INSERT OF //book
LET $Counter := NEW_NODE/../@refNumber
DO ( FOR $bib IN /bib
       UPDATE $bib
       { REPLACE $Counter WITH $Counter + 1 } )
```

5.4   XMine Rule

Knowledge can be represented in many different ways, such as clusters, decision trees, association rules, etc.; in particular, *association rules* have proved to be an effective tool to discover interesting and unexpected relationships in massive amounts of data [6].

XMine Rule is an XML-specific operator that extends XQuery to the declarative specification of association rules for XML data; it allows to express complex mining tasks compactly and intuitively. The operator can indifferently (and simultaneously) target both the content and the structure of the data, since the distinction in XML is subtle. XML association rules are implications of the form $B \Rightarrow H$ where the rule *body B* and *head H* are sub-fragments of a set of fragments of interest (the set of *transactions*). Rules are also characterized by two measures: the *support*, which measures the percentage of transactions that contain both B and H, and the *confidence*, which measures the percentage of transactions that contain H within the transactions that also contain B. As an example, we consider the problem of mining frequent associations among people who appear as *coauthors*. The mining task can be formulated as:

```
XMINE RULE IN doc("bib.xml")
FOR ROOT IN //bib/book/
LET BODY := ROOT/author,
    HEAD := ROOT/author
EXTRACTING RULES WITH SUPPORT = 0.1 AND CONFIDENCE = 0.2
```

In the FOR clause, the special variable ROOT specifies the set of fragments which represents the set of transactions. Next, two special variables, BODY and HEAD, identify the fragments which should appear respectively in the rule body and in the rule head. Note that both BODY and HEAD are defined w.r.t. the *context* of the ROOT variable, since confidence and support values have meaning only w.r.t. the context defined by the set of transactions. The EXTRACTING RULES WITH clause specifies the minimum support and confidence thresholds for the output association rules to be considered.

6   Conclusions

In the last decade, the Web has become the uniform paradigm for end-user interaction with computer applications, and XML has been key for supporting such revolution. The database community has played a prominent role in XML development. The community has addressed both "fully original" XML-centred research and has also performed a solid transfer of its background knowledge to XML-based solutions. We expect that this trend will further grow in the years to come.

References

1. MPEG-7. http://www.mpeg.org/MPEG/index.html.
2. XUpdate Use Cases. http://www.xmldatabases.org/projects/XUpdate-UseCases/.
3. Xyleme. http://www.xyleme.com/.
4. S. Abiteboul, D. Quass, J. McHugh, J. Widom, and J. L. Wiener. The Lorel query language for semistructured data. *International Journal on Digital Libraries*, 1(1):68–88, 1997.

5. ADL. SCORM. http://www.adlnet.org/.
6. R. Agrawal, T. Imielinski, and A. N. Swami. Mining association rules between sets of items in large databases. In *Proc. of the 12th ACM SIGMOD Int'l Conf. on Management of Data*, pages 207–216, Washington, D.C., 1993.
7. A. Bonifati, D. Braga, A. Campi, and S. Ceri. Active XQuery. In *Proc. of the 18th Int'l Conf. on Data Engineering, IEEE Computer Society Press, San José, California*, Feb. 2002.
8. D. Braga and A. Campi. A graphical environment to query XML data with XQuery. In *Proc. of 4th Int'l Conf. on Web Information Systems Engineering (WISE)*, December 2003.
9. S. Ceri, P. Fraternali, and S. Paraboschi. XML: Current develoments and future challenges for the database community. In *Proc. of the 7th EDBT*, pages 3–17, 2000.
10. D. Chamberlin, J. Robie, and D. Florescu. Quilt: an XML Query Language for Heterogeneous Data Sources. In *Proc. of Webdb 2000 The Web and Databases Workshop*, May 2000.
11. A. Deutsch, M. Fernandez, D. Florescu, A. Levy, and D. Suciu. A Query Language for XML. In *Proceedings of the Query Languages Workshop*, Cambridge, (MA), December 1998.
12. D. Fensel and M. L. Brodie. *Ontologies: A Silver Bullet for Knowledge Management and Electronic Commerce*. Springer Verlag, 2003.
13. IMS Global Consortium. IMS. http://www.imsglobal.org.
14. J. Robie, J. Lapp, and D. Schach. XML Query Language (XQL). In *Proceedings of the Query Languages Workshop*, Cambridge, (MA), December 1998.
15. A. Schmidt, F. Waas, M. Kersten, D. Florescu, M. J. Carey, I. Manolescu, and R. Busse. Why and how to benchmark xml databases. *SIGMOD Record*, 30(3):27–32, 2001.
16. I. Tatarinov, Z. G. Ives, A. Y. Halevy, and D. S. Weld. Updating XML. In *Proc. of the 20th ACM SIGMOD Int'l Conf. on Management of Data*, 2001.
17. W3C. Document Type Definition. http://www.w3.org/TR/REC-html40/sgml/dtd.html, 1999.
18. W3C. Resource Description Framework (RDF). http://www.w3.org/RDF/, 1999.
19. W3C. Extensible Stylesheet Language (XSL). http://www.w3c.org/TR/xsl/, October 2001.
20. W3C. MathML. http://www.w3.org/Math, February 2001.
21. W3C. Web Services Description Language (WSDL). http://www.w3.org/TR/wsdl20, 2001.
22. W3C. XML Query (XQuery). http://www.w3.org/XML/Query, June 2001.
23. W3C. XML Schema. http://www.w3.org/XML/Schema, May 2001.
24. W3C. SOAP. http://www.w3.org/TR/soap, June 2003.
25. W3C. OWL Web Ontology Language. http://www.w3.org/TR/owl-features/, February 2004.
26. Moshé M. Zloof. Query-by-example: A data base language. *IBM Systems Journal*, 16(4):324–343, 1977.

L-Tree: A Dynamic Labeling Structure
for Ordered XML Data

Yi Chen[1], George Mihaila[2], Rajesh Bordawekar[2], and Sriram Padmanabhan[2]

[1] University of Pennsylvania
yicn@seas.upenn.edu
[2] IBM T.J. Watson Research Center
{mihaila srp bordaw}@us.ibm.com

Abstract. With the ever growing use of XML as a data representation format, we see an increasing need for robust, high performance XML database systems. While most of the recent work focuses on efficient XML query processing, XML databases also need to support efficient updates. To speed up query processing, various labeling schemes have been proposed. However, the vast majority of these schemes have poor update performance. In this paper, we introduce a dynamic labeling structure for XML data: L-Tree and its order-preserving labeling scheme with O(log n) amortized update cost and O(log n) bits per label. L-Tree has good performance on updates without compromising the performance of query processing. We present the update algorithm for L-Tree and analyze its complexity.

1 Introduction

With the advent of XML as a data representation format, we see an increasing need for robust, high performance XML database management systems which support efficient queries and updates processing. There has been great interest in storing XML data in RDBMS [1, 3, 11, 14, 15], in order to leverage the power of RDBMS for data management. However, since XML data is fundamentally different from relational data encountered in typical business applications, there are several challenges for storing XML data into relational database.

First, XML is the successor of earlier document markup languages such as SGML and HTML, primarily a *document* format. The implicit order among data elements, the so called *document order*, is important. An XML database needs a mechanism to record the relative position of data elements. Recently [15] presented how to store XML data in RDBMS preserving the document order. However, how to maintain the order upon updates is not clear.

Second, an XML database must be able to efficiently retrieve XML fragments by some XML query language, like XPath or XQuery. The edge table approach [11] treated an XML document as a tree, and generated a tuple for every XML node with its parent node identifier in the relation. To process queries with structural navigation, one self-join is needed to obtain each parent-child relationship. [1, 14] proposed to inline the information of leaf nodes into the tuple for their parents, such that the joins between a node and its leaf children are eliminated. However, to answer descendant-axis "//" or ancestor-axis in XML query, many self-joins are needed.

W. Lindner et al. (Eds.): EDBT 2004 Workshops, LNCS 3268, pp. 209–218, 2004.

One popular method for maintaining the document order, which assigns ordered labels to data items, turns out be very helpful to answer ancestor-descendant queries. Specifically, an XML document, treated as an ordered tree, is traversed in depth-first order and ordered labels are assigned to element nodes. Each node x receives two numbers, the first one, B_x, when it is first visited, and the second one E_x, when it is exited. For example, Figure 1 shows an XML tree where every node is labeled by two numbers. Using this scheme, a navigation query can be converted to an interval containment test by using the following observation: for any two nodes x and y, x is an ancestor of y if and only if the interval (B_x, E_x) includes the interval (B_y, E_y), or equivalently $B_x < B_y$ and $E_y < E_x$. Now, to answer a query "book//title" over the example, one only needs to find the nodes with tag "book" and the nodes with tag "title", then test their labels to check the ancestor-descendant relationship. When XML data is stored in RDBMS, the ancestor-descendant queries can be processed by exactly one self-join with label comparisons as predicates, which is as efficient as child-axis. The effectiveness and efficiency of XQuery processing with the labeling scheme in comparison with other XQuery implementations is discussed in [7].

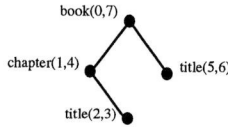

Fig. 1. An example of an XML labeling scheme

While very advantageous for queries and preserving the document order, most of the proposed labeling schemes [2, 12, 13, 17] incur large relabeling costs. Consider the labeling scheme in Figure 1 which assigns labels from the integer domain, in sequential order. This leads to relabeling of half the nodes on average, even for a single node insertion. Alternatively, one can leave gaps in between successive labels to reduce the number of relabelings upon updates. As proved in [5], an order-preserving labeling scheme without any relabelings upon updates requires $O(n)$ bits per label, which leads to large space requirements and costly label comparisons during query processing. It is not clear how to assign the gaps between labels such that we can find a good trade-off between the number of bits used to encode the labels and the number of node relabelings each update will cause. The paper addresses this problem.

The contributions and the structure of this paper are:

1. We introduce a dynamic structure called L-Tree to maintain an order-preserving labeling scheme for XML data in the presence of updates in Section 2.
2. We analyze the amortized update cost of an L-Tree and the label size. We derive exact functions for the update complexity and the label size, and discuss how the optimal results can be achieved by choosing different tree parameters in various application settings. This is presented in Section 3.

3. We discuss how an L-Tree can accommodate XML subtree updates to achieve better performance compared to single node updates as well as a variant of the main labeling scheme in Section 4.

Related work is discussed in Section 5 and Section 6 concludes the paper.

2   L-Tree and XML Labeling Scheme

When designing an XML labeling scheme, we need to answer the following two questions: 1) how to assign labels to elements in an XML document D to reflect the document order? and 2) when a new node is inserted, what label should be assigned to it, and which existing labels need to change to preserve the order?

For the purpose of the discussion, it is helpful to view the XML document in its textual representation as a linear ordered list of begin tags, end tags, and text sections, $L_D = (a_1, a_2, \ldots, a_n)$. Our problem is similar to the maintenance of an ordered list. A label from an integer interval $[0, M)$ is assigned to each tag to reflect its order in the list. Intuitively, we would like to distribute these n labels over the whole interval evenly. However, random updates will cause some areas in the interval to become much more dense than others. If a new tag is inserted at a position where the difference between the labels of its neighbors is 1, we have to redistribute some labels to make room for the newly inserted tag.

The basic idea of our algorithm is that we divide the whole interval $[0, M)$ into many intervals of equal size, each of which are further divided to smaller intervals, and so on. Then we set a limit on the number of labels in each interval such that we can control the density of each interval. In this way relabelings upon an update are localized. The nested relationship of intervals and subintervals suggests a tree structure. So we build a tree and associate each interval to an internal node in the tree to maintain the labels for XML data. This tree is called a *L-Tree* (short from *label tree*).

2.1   Labeling Scheme of the L-Tree

An L-Tree is an ordered balanced tree with n leaves. We attach the tags in the XML document to these n leaves in order, starting from the leftmost leaf. The shape of the L-Tree is determined by two parameters f and s, which control the number of leaf descendants of internal nodes. Specifically, the maximal fanout of any internal node in an L-Tree is $f - 1$, and the minimal fanout is f/s. We will discuss how to choose the values of these parameters in Section 3.

For any node x in the L-Tree, we assign a number $N(x)$, recursively in a top-down fashion as follows:

1. $N(root) = 0$
2. Let x be the ith, $(0 \leq i < f - 1)$ child of y, $N(x) = N(y) + i \cdot (f - 1)^{h(x)}$

Here the height $h(x)$ of any node x is defined as the number of edges on the longest path from x to any leaf node in the subtree rooted in x (in particular, leaf nodes have height 0). Let us also denote by h the height of the L-Tree ($h = h(root)$). The number

$N(x)$ is the smallest integer in the interval corresponding to x, and the difference between the numbers of two siblings are the space reserved for future insertions.

Finally, the labels of the XML tags are the labels assigned to their corresponding leaves in the L-Tree. It is easy to see that the above labeling scheme preserves the order of the XML tags.

Proposition 1. *Let x be a leaf in an L-Tree corresponds to an XML tag a_i and y corresponds to a a_j, a_i appears before a_j in the XML document if and only if $N(x) < N(y)$.*

The label of an XML element node is composed by a pair: the numbers of two leaves in the L-Tree which correspond to that XML node's begin tag and end tag, respectively. The order-preserving property of this labeling scheme allows us to convert the XML navigation queries into interval containment tests as illustrated in Section 1.

2.2   Bulk Loading

Initially, we build an L-Tree for some existing XML document in a bulk loading mode. To maximize the capability to accommodate further insertions, we build a complete f/s-ary tree initially (the height of this tree is the smallest number h for which $(f/s)^h \geq n$). Figure 2(a) shows an XML tree and its corresponding L-Tree ($f = 4$, $s = 2$).

2.3   Incremental Maintenance

Now let us examine how to maintain the balance of an L-Tree in the presence of insertions and assign labels to the inserted XML tags (see Algorithm 1).

For example, we would like to insert an XML node with tag "D" as the preceding sibling of the node tagged by "C" in the XML tree in Figure 2(a). We need to insert two leaves into L-Tree, corresponding to the begin tag and end tag of the XML node, respectively. Next we illustrate how to insert two leaves into L-Tree one after another.

For every internal node t in the L-Tree, denote by $c(t)$ the number of children of t and by $l(t)$ the number of leaves in the subtree rooted at t. In order to keep the labels

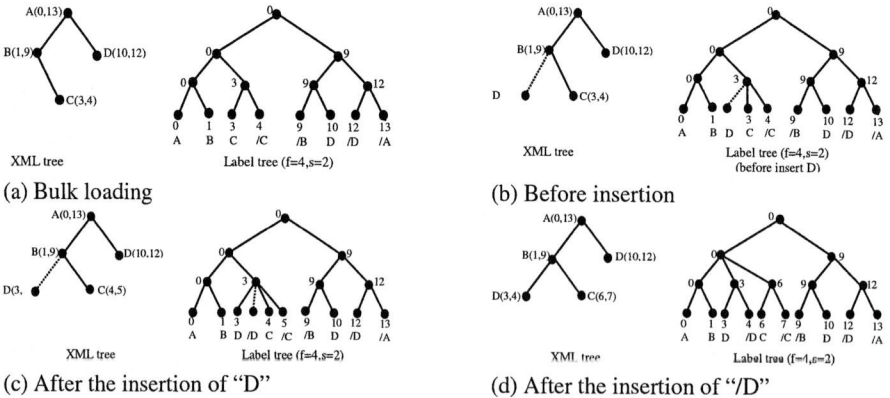

(a) Bulk loading

(b) Before insertion

(c) After the insertion of "D"

(d) After the insertion of "/D"

Fig. 2. An example of L-Tree

Algorithm 1 Label Tree Incremental Maintenance Algorithm

1: **function** $insert - after(x, y)$
2:   $z = parent(y)$
3:   insert x as the right sibling of y
4:   **while** $z \neq NULL$ **do**
5:     $l(z) + +$
6:     **if** $l(z) = s \cdot (f/s)^{h(z)}$ **then**
7:       $t = z$
8:       $z = parent(z)$
9:   **if** $t = NULL$ **then**
10:     let x be the kth child of its parent
11:     call $label(parent(x), N(parent(x)), k)$
12:   **else**
13:     let t be the kth child of its parent
14:     split t into s complete f/s-ary trees with the same sequence of leaves
15:     **if** $t = root$ **then**
16:       create a new root with the s top-level nodes as children;
17:       call $label(root, 0, 0)$
18:     **else**
19:       replace subtree rooted at t with the s subtrees
20:       call $label(parent(t), N(parent(t), k)$
21:   **return**
22: **function** $label(x, num, k)$
23:   $N(x) = num$
24:   **if** x is not a leaf **then**
25:     **for** $i = k$ to $c(x)$ **do**
26:       $y = i$-th child of x
27:       call $label(y, num + i \cdot (f - 1)^{h(y_i)}, 0)$
28:   **return**

---

distributed in a balanced manner, we impose a limit $l_{max}(t) = s \cdot (f/s)^{h(t)}$ on the maximum number of leaves that each internal node t may have in its subtree.

When we insert a leaf x in the L-Tree, $l(z)$ increases by one for every ancestor z of x. We look for the highest ancestor t satisfying $l(t) = l_{max}(t)$.

If no such t exists, we relabel x and its right siblings. In our insertion example, assuming that we maintain the links between an XML node to its corresponding leaves in the L-Tree, we can get the label of the XML node tagged by "C": (3,4). First we insert a leaf to the L-Tree, corresponding to the begin tag "D", before the leaf with number "3". Figure 2(b) shows the intended insertions as dotted lines. The L-Tree after the insertion is shown in Figure 2(c).

Otherwise, if such a node t does exist, we need to rebalance the L-Tree. We split t into s nodes and replace t with s complete f/s-ary subtrees of the same leaf sequence. This causes the relabeling of the subtrees of these s nodes as well as their right siblings.

As an example, now we insert another L-Tree leaf, which corresponds to the end tag "/D", right after the leaf which corresponds to "D". The intended insertion is represented by dotted lines in Figure 2(c). This insertion results in a split of the node numbered "3" of height 1 as shown in Figure 2(d).

The key idea behind the L-Tree splitting and subsequent relabeling upon an insertion is the following: if the insertion causes the number of leaves of some subtree to increase to a large number, this means that the labels of these leaves have become very dense. To remedy the situation we split the subtree and relabel it to provide more slack for this portion, in order to better accommodate further insertions in this portion. Since the number of leaves of any subtree is controlled and the density of the labels is also controlled, the number of nodes involved in relabelings amortized over several insertions will also be controlled.

In this paper we focus on the XML insertions since for deletions we can just mark as deleted the corresponding leaves in the L-Tree without any relabeling.

2.4 Structure Properties

In this section we examine the properties of an L-Tree and compare it with a B^+-tree.

Proposition 2. *For any internal node x, we have (1) $(f/s)^{h(x)} \leq l(x) < s \cdot (f/s)^{h(x)}$; (2) $f/s \leq c(x) < f$; and (3) All leaves are at the same level of the tree.*

Proposition 3. *Cascade splitting in an L-Tree is not possible, that is, one node splitting will not cause another node split.*

An L-Tree is similar to a B^+-tree in that it guarantees certain occupancy of the tree such that the tree is balanced dynamically and the height is bounded by $O(\log n)$, where n is the number of nodes in the tree. The differences are:

1. The goals of a B^+-tree and an L-Tree are different. The purpose of a B^+-tree is to enable fast lookups given XML labels. Though B^+-tree can adjust its structure dynamically if the labels change their values, it is not able to determine how the labels should be changed. An L-Tree is built to maintain the labels for XML nodes in the presence of updates. It helps us to determine what labels to be assigned to newly-inserted XML nodes and how the labels of existing nodes should be changed.
2. The splitting criterion of an L-Tree is based on the number of leaves of a node, rather than the number of children, therefore it will not cascade split as a B^+-tree.
3. For each internal node x in L-Tree, $f/s \leq c(x) < f$. For B^+-trees, $s = 2$.

3 Complexity Analysis

3.1 Query and Maintenance Costs

In this section we compute an upper bound on the amortized cost of queries/updates and the number of bits used per label as functions of an L-Tree parameters f and s. The query and maintenance cost of an L-Tree is measured as the number of disk accesses. Since the XML nodes are recommended to be clustered by their tags rather than labels [17], and we don't make any assumptions about nodes being cached, the cost is measured in terms of the number of nodes accessed for searching or relabeling.

For queries, an L-Tree does not incur any additional cost. In fact, if we store the label along with the XML node itself, we can retrieve the label of a given node for free.

Now we analyze the amortized cost of maintaining an L-Tree upon an insertion of leaf x using the accounting method. The cost consists of three parts: First, cost h to update $l(z)$ for every ancestor z of x. Second, if there are no nodes satisfying the splitting criterion, we pay at most f to relabel the right siblings of x. Otherwise, we split the highest one t into s nodes and relabel these s subtrees as well as t's right siblings. The number of nodes relabeled is bounded by the number of descendants of t's parent: $2s \cdot (f/s)^{h(v)}$.

We charge the cost of relabeling to the $(s-1) \cdot (f/s)^{h(t)}$ insertions, which make $l(t)$ grow from $(f/s)^{h(t)}$ to $s \cdot (f/s)^{h(t)}$. So an insertion is charged $2f/(s-1)$ for each relabeling, and charged $2f \cdot h/(s-1)$ for all the relabelings.

Let n be the number of tags in the current XML tree, and M be the maximal number we use to label all the nodes in the corresponding L-Tree. Since each XML tag corresponds to a leaf in the L-Tree, we have $n = l(root) \geq (f/s)^h$.

The amortized cost for an insertion to an XML tree of size n is

$$cost(f, s, n) \leq \frac{(1 + 2f/(s-1))}{\log(f/s)} \cdot \log n + f$$

Since $M \leq (f-1)^h$, the maximum number of bits to encode a label is:

$$bits(f, s, n) = \log M = \frac{\log(f-1)}{\log(f/s)} \cdot \log n$$

Since f and s are some constant parameters, we can maintain the labels of XML data with $O(\log n)$ bits and $O(\log n)$ amortized insertion cost.

3.2 Tuning the L-Tree

As discussed in [10], $O(\log n)$ is the tight worst case lower bound for update cost to maintain an ordered list, if the query cost is 1. Since the cost is measured as the number of disk accesses even a reduction by a constant factor is helpful for a system implementation. Hence, we are interested in minimizing the precise insertion cost. We approximate the current XML tree size as the initial tree size n_0. We would like to set the values of parameter f and s according to different application needs to optimize the constant factors of the cost and bits.

Minimize the Update Cost
In some applications, our goal is to set the values of parameters f and s, such that the amortized cost of insertion is minimal. This is an optimization problem:

$$Object : min(cost)$$

We can find the solution by solving the following equations:

$$\frac{\partial cost}{\partial f} = 0 \text{ and } \frac{\partial cost}{\partial s} = 0$$

For a given n_0, we can solve the above equations to get the values of f_0 and s_0.

Minimize the Update Cost for Given Number of Bits
If we are constrained on the number of bits we are allowed to use to encode a label as B, the math model we build is the following:

$$Object : min(cost) \quad Subject\ to : bits \leq B$$

This is a problem of optimization under inequality constraints. First we minimize function $cost$ unconstrained. If the minimum point (f_0, s_0) satisfies the inequality constraints, it's the minimum point in the interior of the region under consideration.

We also investigate the function on the boundary of the region. That is, we convert the optimization problem under inequality constraints to the optimization problem under equality constraints as follows:

$$Object : \min(cost) \quad Subject\ to : bits - B = 0$$

We solve this problem by introducing a Lagrange multiplier μ and form:

$$g(f, s, n, \mu) = cost + \mu \cdot bits$$

The values of f, s and μ which give the conditional minima of $cost$ can be found by solving the following equations:

$$\frac{\partial g}{\partial f} = 0 \text{ and } \frac{\partial g}{\partial s} = 0 \text{ and } bits - B = 0$$

We compare the solutions of the above equations with (f_0, s_0) to determine the values of f and s which result in minimal cost given label size B.

Minimize the Overall Cost of Query and Updates
When the number of bits to encode a label is less than the machine word size, the label comparison for query can done by hardware, otherwise it must be done by software. In this case, the query cost is proportional to the number of bits used. For this situation, we want to find optimal f and s to get the minimal overall cost for queries and updates. To achieve it, we need to know the query/update workload and some characteristics of the document. Due space limitation, we defer the details to [4].

4   Discussion

4.1   Multiple Node Insertions

Usually, insertions to XML documents are subtrees. Although a subtree insertion can be implemented as a sequence of leaf insertions, the question is whether we can improve the update cost by inserting multiple leaves to a L-Tree at the same time.

Without loss of generality, let p be the number of leaves to be inserted to the L-Tree. To see how the subtree insertion affects the amortized update cost, we notice that the update cost consists of three parts:

1. The cost h for updating $l(z)$ for all the ancestors z of inserted nodes. This cost now is charged to p inserted nodes.
2. The cost f for relabeling right siblings if no nodes satisfy the splitting criterion. Now it is charged to p inserted nodes.
3. The amortized cost $2f/(s - 1)$ for each insertion to relabel the subtrees rooted at the splitting node as well as its right siblings. Since it is an amortized cost, it makes no difference that nodes are inserted one after another, or at one time. However, a node which is inserted by itself may need to pay this cost for up to h ancestors' splits. Will this be affected if the insertion size is p?

For simplicity, assume $p = (s-1) \cdot (f/s)^{h_0}$, for some $h_0 \geq 1$. Each subtree insertion causes the split of an ancestor x whose height $h(x) = h_0$. Also, these inserted nodes may later on pay for the splits of other ancestors y with $h(y) > h_0$. The total amortized cost for all the ancestors' splits is bounded by $2f \cdot (h - h_0 + 1)/(s-1)$. So the amortized cost of each inserted node is bounded by:

$$cost(f, s, n, p) \leq \frac{\log n}{p \cdot \log(\frac{f}{s})} + \frac{f}{p} + \frac{2f}{s-1} \cdot (\frac{\log n - \log(\frac{p}{s-1})}{\log(\frac{f}{s})} + 1)$$

To generalize, if the bulk insertion size p is not exactly $(s-1) \cdot (f/s)^{h_0}$, we will have similiar result above. Due space limitation, we defer the details to [4].

As we can see, the larger the size of inserting subtree is, the lower the amortized cost each inserted node need to pay for. However, the decrease of the cost is roughly logarithmic in the increase of insertion size.

4.2 Virtual L-Tree

As an alternative to storing the L-Tree on disk, we can store only the leaf labels (with the XML nodes) because all the structural information of the L-Tree is implicit in the labels themselves. Indeed, if we examine closely the way labels are computed, we see that any leaf label is of the form:

$$N(x) = i_0 + i_1 \cdot (f-1)^1 + \cdots + i_{h-1} \cdot (f-1)^{h-1}$$

where i_0 is x's relative position in its siblings list, i_1 is x's parent's position among its siblings, and so on. In other words, the base $(f-1)$ digits of $N(x)$ provide an encoding of all the ancestors of x. Based on this observation, we can run the L-Tree incremental maintenance algorithm without the L-Tree. For example, in order to check if an internal node y satisfies the splitting criterion, it suffices to count how many leaf labels are in the range $[N(y), N(y) + (f-1)^h(y))$. If the leaf labels are maintained in a B-tree whose internal nodes also maintain counts, such range queries can be executed efficiently (in logarithmic time). Furthermore, once a splitting (virtual) node has been identified, the leaf labels corresponding to the s complete f/s-ary (virtual) trees can be computed easily and updated in place, on the labels identified by the range query. There is clearly a tradeoff between the extra computation required by the range queries and the storage space necessary for materializing the L-Tree.

5 Related Work

The problem of order-preserving labeling of an ordered list in the presence of random updates has been studied previously [8, 9, 16]. Our work has been inspired by these works, and extends to parameterize the problem, and propose a solution that can adjust the parameters according to different application requirements. Furthermore, we support batch insertions in L-Tree to improve the performance. [6] proposed a multi-level labeling scheme, which trades query cost to get better update cost.

Recently Cohen et al. [5] addressed the problem of designing persistent labels upon updates, by studying the minimum number of bits required to encode such a label, without considering the order of siblings. We approach the problem in a different perspective: we minimize the number relabelings upon updates given a label size of $\Theta(\log n)$.

Recently, several researchers have investigated various approaches for using labeling schemes to facilitate XML query processing [7, 12, 13, 17]. None of these schemes consider label maintenance in presence of updates.

6 Conclusions

We have presented a labeling scheme for maintaining the order of data items of an XML document. An L-Tree is introduced to assign and update labels of data items. An L-Tree can automatically adapt to uneven insertion rates in different areas of the XML document: in the areas with heavy insertion activity, the L-Tree adjusts itself by creating more slack between labels to better accommodate future insertions. We analyzed the amortized cost of incremental updates and derived a cost formula that enabled us to tune the tree parameters to achieve optimal performance in various application settings.

References

1. P. Bohannon, J. Freire, P. Roy, and J. Simeon. From XML-Schema to Relations: A Cost-Based Approach to XML Storage. In *Proc. ICDE*, 2002.
2. N. Bruno, N. Koudas, and D. Srivastava. Holistic twig joins: Optimal XML pattern matching. In *ACM SIGMOD*, 2002.
3. Yi Chen, Susan Davidson, Carmem Hara, and Yifeng Zheng. RRXS: Redundancy reducing XML storage in relations. In *Proc. VLDB*, 2003.
4. Yi Chen, George Mihaila, Sriram Padmanabhan, and Rajesh Bordawekar. Labeling your XML. Technical report, 10 2002.
5. E. Cohen, H. Kaplan, and T. Milo. Labeling dynamic XML trees. In *ACM PODS*, June 2002.
6. Shunsuke Uemura Dao Dinh Kha, Masatoshi Yoshikawa. An XML Indexing Structure with Relative Region Coordinate. In *Proc. of the 17th ICDE*, pages 313–320, 4 2001.
7. David DeHaan, David Toman, Mariano Consens, and M. Tamer Ozsu. A comprehensive XQuery to SQL translation using dynamic interval encoding. In *ACM SIGMOD*, 2001.
8. P. F. Dietz. Maintaining order in a linked list. In *Proc. 14th ACM STOC*, pages 62–69, 1982.
9. P. F. Dietz and D. D. Sleator. Two algorithms for maintaining order in a list. In *Proc. 19th ACM STOC*, pages 365–372. Springer, 1987.
10. Paul Dietz, Joel Seiferas, and J. Zhang. A tight lower bound for on-line monotonic list labeling. In *In Proc. 4th Scandinavian Workshop on Algorithm Theory (SWAT)*, pages 131–142, 1994.
11. Daniela Florescu and Donald Kossmann. Storing and querying XML data using RDMBS. *IEEE Data Engineering Bulletin*, 22(3):27–34, 1999.
12. T. Grust. Accelerating XPath location steps. In *ACM SIGMOD*, 2002.
13. Q. Li and B. Moon. Indexing and querying XML data for regular path expressions. In *VLDBJ*, pages 361–370, 2001.
14. J. Shanmugasundaram, K. Tufte, C. Zhang, G. He, D. J. DeWitt, and J. F. Naughton. Relational databases for querying XML documents: Limitations and opportunities. In *VLDBJ*, pages 302–314, 1999.
15. I. Tatarinov, E. Viglas, K. Beyer, J. Shanmugasundaram, E. Shekita, and C. Zhang. Storing and querying ordered XML using a relational database system. In *ACM SIGMOD*, 2002.
16. Athanasios K. Tsakalidis. Maintaining order in a generalized link list. *Acta Informatica*, 21, 1984.
17. C. Zhang, J. Naughton, D. DeWitt, Q. Luo, and G. Lohman. On supporting containment queries in relational database management systems. In *ACM SIGMOD*, 2001.

Implementation of XPath Axes in the Multi-dimensional Approach to Indexing XML Data*

Michal Krátký[1], Jaroslav Pokorný[2], and Václav Snášel[1]

[1] Department of Computer Science, VŠB – Technical University of Ostrava,
{michal.kratky,vaclav.snasel}@vsb.cz
[2] Department of Software Engineering, Charles University in Prague,
pokorny@ksi.ms.mff.cuni.cz
Czech Republic

Abstract. XML (Extensible Mark-up Language) has been recently understood as a new approach to data modelling. An implementation of a system enabling us to store and query XML documents efficiently requires the development of new techniques which make it possible to index an XML document in a way that provides an efficient evaluation of a user query. Most XML query languages are based on the language XPath and use a form of path expressions for composing more general queries. XPath defines a family of 13 axes, i.e. relationship types in which an actual element can be associated to other elements in the XML tree. Previously published multi-dimensional approaches to indexing XML data use paged and balanced multi-dimensional data structures like UB-trees and R*-trees. In this paper we revise the approaches and introduce a novel approach to the implementation of an XPath subset.

Keywords: indexing XML data, XPath axes, multi-dimensional data structures, UB-tree, R*-tree, BUB-forest, Signature R*-tree.

1 Introduction

XML [18] has been recently understood as a new approach to data modelling. A collection of *well-formed* XML documents is an XML database and the associated *DTD* or *XML Schema* is its database schema. An implementation of a system enabling us to store and query XML documents efficiently (so called *native XML databases*) requires the development of new techniques.

An XML document is usually modelled as a graph the nodes of which correspond to XML elements and attributes. The graph is mostly a tree (we suppose that none of the attributes is of IDREF/IDREFS type). To obtain specified data from an XML database, a number of special query languages have been developed, e.g. *XPath* [17] and *XQuery* [16]. A common feature of these languages is the possibility to formulate paths in the XML graph. In fact, most XML query languages are based on the XPath language that uses a form of path expressions for composing more general queries. The

---

* Work is partially supported by Grant of GACR No. 201/03/0912.

W. Lindner et al. (Eds.): EDBT 2004 Workshops, LNCS 3268, pp. 219–229, 2004.
© Springer-Verlag Berlin Heidelberg 2004

XPath defines a family of 13 *axes*, i.e. relationship types in which an actual element (*context node*) can be associated with other elements in the XML tree. The family of axes is designed to allow a set of graph traversal operations which are seen to be atomic in XML document trees.

In the past, there were many considerations about the straightforward use of existing relational or object-relational DBMSs for storing and querying XML data. Since a tree is accessed during the evaluation of a query, conventional approaches through the conventional database languages SQL or OQL fail or they are not enough efficient. Recently there have been several approaches to indexing XML data. Some of them are based on a traditional *relational technology* (e.g. *XISS* [12]), other use special data structures for the representation of XML data as a *trie* (e.g. *Index Fabric* [4] and *DataGuide* [14]) or multi-dimensional data structures (e.g. *XPath Accelerator* [6]). The latter approach uses R-trees but also B-trees as database indices in the environment of a relational DBMS. As expected, R-trees outperform B-trees in that proposal. The work [4] presents an index over the prefix-encoding of the paths in an XML document tree. A more complete summary of various approaches to indexing XML data is e.g. [3].

Previously published multi-dimensional approaches (e.g. [8,9]) to indexing XML data use paged and balanced multi-dimensional data structures like *UB-trees* [1], *R-trees* [7], *R*-trees* [2], and *BUB-trees* [5]. In this paper we revise these approaches and combine them in such a way that an implementation of an XPath subset is possible. Our proposal is more general and enables an efficient accomplishment of querying text content of an element or attribute value as well as queries based on regular path expressions and axes of the XPath specification. We compared BUB-trees with R*-trees and their respective signature variants. The results confirm that our signature extension of multidimensional data structures is significantly better than the R*-tree. As these structures are paged and balanced, they are appropriate for indexing a huge amount of large XML documents and can serve as an alternative to the implementation of a native XML database.

In Section 2 we describe and revise a multi-dimensional approach to indexing XML data. This approach enables an efficient implementation of XPath axes (Subsection 2.3). We mainly focus on a class of queries employing exact matching for an element content or an attribute value. Section 3 describes multi-dimensional data structures *BUB-forest* [10] and *Signature R*-tree* [11], which are employed for indexing XML data. Section 4 provides some information about the complexity of query evaluation with multi-dimensional indexing. Section 5 reports on experimental results for selected XPath queries. In conclusion we summarize the results and outline future research directions.

2   Multi-dimensional Approach to Indexing XML Data

In [8,9] a multi-dimensional approach to indexing XML data was introduced. We revise this approach in a way, which allows an efficient implementation of XML query languages based on the XPath.

2.1   Model of XML Documents

As far as an XML document modelled by a tree is concerned, we can view it as a set of paths from the root node to all leaf nodes. Suppose the unique number $id_N(u_i)$ of a

```
<!DOCTYPE books [
  <!ELEMENT books(book)>
  <!ELEMENT book(title,author)>
  <!ATTLIST book id CDATA #REQUIRED>
  <!ELEMENT title(#PCDATA)>
  <!ELEMENT author(#PCDATA)>
]>
```

```
<?xml version="1.0" ?>
<books><book id="003-04312">
  <title>The Two Towers</title>
  <author>J.R.R. Tolkien</author></book>
<book id="001-00863">
  <title>The Return of the King</title>
  <author>J.R.R. Tolkien</author></book>
<book id="045-00012">
  <title>Catch 22</title>
  <author>Joseph Heller</author></book>
</books>
```

Fig. 1. (a) DTD of documents which contain information about books and authors. (b) Well-formed XML document valid w.r.t. DTD

node u_i (element or attribute) which is obtained by counter increments according to the document order [6].

Let $\mathcal{P}$ be a set of all paths in a XML tree. A *path* $p \in \mathcal{P}$ in an XML tree is a sequence $id_N(u_0), id_N(u_1), \dots, id_N(u_{\tau_P(p)-1}), s$, where $\tau_P(p)$ is the length of p, s is PCDATA or CDATA string, $id_N(u_i) \in D = \{0, 1, \dots, 2^{\tau_D} - 1\}$, τ_D is the chosen length of binary representation of numbers from the domain D. Node u_0 is always the root node of the XML tree. Since each attribute is modelled as a super-leaf node with CDATA value, nodes $u_0, u_1, \dots, u_{\tau_P(p)-2}$ always represent elements. A *labelled path* lp for a path p is a sequence $s_0, s_1, \dots, s_{\tau_{LP}(lp)}$ of names of elements or attributes, where $\tau_{LP}(lp)$ is the length of lp, and s_i is the name of the element or attribute belonging to the node u_i. Let us denote the set of all labelled paths by $\mathcal{LP}$. A single labelled path belongs to a path, one or more paths belong to a single labelled path. If the element or attribute is empty, then $\tau_P(p) = \tau_{LP}(lp)$, else $\tau_P(p) = \tau_{LP}(lp) + 1$.

Signatures for coding of all strings, path and path content were used in the approach [8, 9]. Here, we use path, labelled path and term index.

Definition 1 (Point of n-dimensional Space Representing a Labelled Path).
Let $\Omega_{LP} = D^n$ be an n-dimensional space of labelled paths, $|D| = 2^{\tau_D}$, and $lp \in \mathcal{LP}$ be a labelled path $s_0, s_1, \dots, s_{\tau_{LP}(lp)}$, where $n = max(\tau_{LP}(lp), lp \in \mathcal{LP}) + 1$. **Point** t_{lp} **of n-dimensional space** Ω_{LP} **representing labelled path** is defined as $(id_T(s_0), id_T(s_1), \dots, id_T(s_{\tau_{LP}(lp)}))$, where $id_T(s_i)$ is a unique number of term s_i, $id_T(s_i) \in D$. A unique number $id_{LP}(lp)$ is assigned to lp. ∎

Definition 2 (Point of n-dimensional Space Representing a Path).
Let $\Omega_P = D^n$ be an n-dimensional space of paths, $|D| = 2^{\tau_D}$, $p \in \mathcal{P}$ be a path $id_N(u_0), id_N(u_1), \dots, id_N(u_{\tau_{LP}(lp)}), s$, and lp a relevant labelled path with the unique number $id_{LP}(lp)$, where $n = max(\tau_P(p), p \in \mathcal{P}) + 2$. **Point** t_p **of n-dimensional space** Ω_P **representing path** is defined as $(id_{LP}(lp), id_N(u_0), \dots, id_N(u_{\tau_{LP}(lp)}), id_T(s))$. ∎

Example 1 (Decomposition of the XML Tree to Paths and Labelled Paths).
In Figure 2 we see an XML tree modelling the XML document in Figure 1(b). This XML document contains paths:
$-0, 1, 2, '003-04312'; 0, 5, 6, '001-00863';$ and $0, 9, 10, '045-00012'$
belong to the labelled path books, book, id,

−0,1,3,'The Two Towers';
0,5,7,'The Return of
the King';   and   0,9,
11,'Catch 22' belong to
the labelled path books,
book,title,

−0,1,4,'J.R.R. Tolkien';
0,5,8, 'J.R.R. Tolkien';
and   0,9,12,'Joseph
Heller' belong to the labelled
path books, book, author.

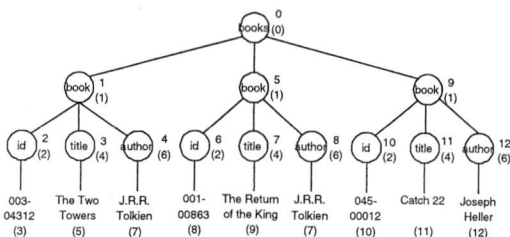

Fig. 2. Example of an XML tree with the unique numbers $id_N(u_i)$ of elements and attributes u_i and the unique numbers $id_T(s_i)$ of names of elements and attributes and their values s_i (values in parenthesis)

We define three indexes:

1. Term Index. This index contains a unique number $id_T(s_i)$ for each term s_i (names and text values of elements and attributes). Unique numbers can be generated by counter increments according to the document order. We want to get a unique number for a term and a term for a unique number as well. This index can be implemented by the B-tree.

In Figure 2 we see the XML tree with unique numbers of terms in parenthesis.

2. Labelled Path Index. Points representing labelled paths together with labelled paths' unique numbers (also generated by incrementing a counter) are stored in the labelled path index.

For three labelled paths in Figure 2 we create three points (0,1,2); (0,1,4); and (0,1,6) using id_T of element's and attribute's names. These points are inserted into a multi-dimensional data structure with id_{LP} equal to 0, 1, and 2, respectively.

3. Path Index. Points representing paths are stored in the path index.

In Figure 2 we see unique numbers of elements. Let us take the path to the value The Two Towers. The relevant labelled path book,book,title has got id_{LP} 1 (see above). We get the point (1,0,1,3,5) after inserting a unique number of the labelled path id_{LP}, unique numbers of elements id_N and the term The Two Towers. This point is stored in a multi-dimensional data structure.

An XML document is transformed to points of vector spaces and XML queries are implemented using queries of multi-dimensional data structure. The multi-dimensional data structures provide a nature processing of *point* or *range queries* [1]. The point query probes if the vector is or is not present in the data structure. The range query searches all points in a query box $T_1 : T_2$ defined by two points T_1, T_2. Consequently, we can create the queries in the same way as the XML tree is decomposed to vectors of multi-dimensional spaces.

2.2 Queries for Values of Elements and Attributes

Now, we describe an implementation of a query for values of elements and attributes as well as a query defined by a simple path based on an ancestor-descendent relation. Query processing is performed in three phases which are connected:

1. **Find unique numbers id_T of the query's terms in the term index.**
2. **Find labelled paths' id_{LP} of the query in the labelled path index.** We search the unique numbers in a multi-dimensional data structure using point or range queries.
3. **Find points in the path index.** We find points representing paths in this index using range queries. Now, the result is formatted using unique numbers $id_N(u_i)$ of nodes u_i from these points.

Example 2 (Evaluation Plan of the XPath Query /books/book[author="Joseph Heller"]*).*

1. Find id_T of terms books, book, author, and Joseph Heller in the term index.
2. Find a unique number id_{LP} of the labelled path books, book, author in the labelled path index, which was transformed to the point representing the labelled path. We retrieve $id_{LP} = 2$ of labelled path by the point query (0,1,6).
3. Create two points defining a query box, which searches points relevant to this query. The query box is defined by the points (2,0,0,0,12) and (2,max_D,max_D,max_D, 12), where max_D is the maximal value of the domain D of space Ω_P. id_{LP} of the labelled path retrieved during the last phase is located in the first points' coordinates. id_T of term Joseph Heller is located in the last points' coordinates. Since, we search points with arbitrary values of 2nd–4th coordinates, the first point contains the minimal values of a multi-dimensional space's domain and the second point contains the maximal values of the domain.

We need to distinguish between labelled paths and paths belonging to an element or attribute. We deal with this using flags added to points. Similarly, we can deal with the indexing of more XML documents, which can be valid w.r.t. different schemas.

2.3 Implementation of XPath Axes

The basic XPath query expression in non-reduced notation is axis::tag[filter], which provides by evaluation on the context node u a set of nodes u', where the relation given by the axis contains (u, u'), tag for u' is tag, the condition assigned by filter assumes the value TRUE on u'.

Let us denote the context node by u, the level of a node u_i in the XML tree by $l(u_i)$. Obviously, $l(u_0) = 0$. Without loss of the generality we denote l as $l(u)$. The query result in the path index contains points representing paths from the root to leafs. These points contain the unique numbers of all ancestors $u_0, \ldots, u_{l-1}$ of the current node u, i.e. $id_N(u_0), \ldots, id_N(u_{l-1})$.

Implementation of Axes:
– ancestor – nodes lie on the path from u to the root node. So far as we want to retrieve the ancestors of a node from the point representing path, we retrieve relevant id_N from this point. Unique numbers $id_N(u_0), \ldots, id_N(u_{l-1})$ are obtained for the axis ancestor, $id_N(u_0), \ldots, id_N(u_{l-1}), id_N(u)$ for ancestor-or-self (u and nodes lie on the path from u to the root node), and $id_N(u_{l-1})$ for parent (first node on the path from u to the root node).
– descendant – all nodes, which the node u is the parent for. Now, we use unique numbers of u node's ancestors: $id_N(u_0), \ldots, id_N(u_{l-1})$, as well as $id_N(u)$ and $l(u)$. During the range query's points creation we use the knowledge that all descendants have

got the same ancestors as the node u and their parent is the node u. We search all descendants of the node u by the range query in the path index: $(0, id_N(u_0), \ldots, id_N(u_{l-1}),$ $id_N(u), 0, \ldots, 0) : (max_D, id_N(u_0), \ldots, id_N(u_{l-1}), id_N(u), max_D, \ldots, max_D)$.
– child – direct descendants of the node u. A naive approach is to perform axis descendant and id_N of children to obtain in $(l(u)+3)^{th}$ coordinates of the result's points. Let us imagine inefficient searching of the root node's children for example. A more efficient implementation is based upon finding one point, which contains id_N of a child, redefinition of the range query and processing of this query.

Algorithm:
1. Perform range query $(0, id_N(u_0), \ldots, id_N(u_{l-1}), id_N(u), 0, \ldots, 0) : (max_D,$ $id_N(u_0), \ldots, id_N(u_{l-1}), id_N(u), max_D, \ldots, max_D)$. Processing of this query will be finished after the acquisition of one or no relevant point. The identified point contains id_N of a child in $(l(u)+3)^{th}$ coordinate.
2. Since we do not know which child was retrieved (from document order point of view) we must define two queries for the acquisition of both preceding and following children.

Denote the acquired child as u_c ($id_N(u_c) = id_N(u_{l+1})$), the child with the highest identified id_N, but smaller than $id_N(u_c)$ as u_{pc}, the child with the lowest identified id_N, but greater than $id_N(u_c)$ as u_{fc}. Definition of two range queries ($id_N(u_{pc}) = -1$ and $id_N(u_{fc}) = max_D + 1$ after finding the first child):

a) $(0, id_N(u_0), \ldots, id_N(u_{l-1}), id_N(u), id_N(u_{pc}) + 1, 0, \ldots, 0) : (max_D, id_N(u_0),$
    $\ldots, id_N(u_{l-1}), id_N(u), id_N(u_c) - 1, max_D, \ldots, max_D)$
b) $(0, id_N(u_0), \ldots, id_N(u_{l-1}), id_N(u), id_N(u_c) + 1, 0, \ldots, 0) : (max_D, id_N(u_0),$
    $\ldots, id_N(u_{l-1}), id_N(u), id_N(u_{fc}) - 1, max_D, \ldots, max_D)$

Processing the simple queries will be finished after the acquisition of one or no relevant point. In the case that the first/second query retrieves no point, the first/last child was identified in the former query.
3. We continue with step 2 until these range queries retrieve some points.

– preceding-sibling – siblings of node u preceding in the document order. We search all points representing paths pertaining to elements with the same ancestors as node u and $(l(u)+2)^{th}$ coordinate $< id_N(u)$. A naive approach to finding the preceding-siblings of node u is to perform the range query: $(0, id_N(u_0), \ldots, id_N(u_{l-1}), 0, 0, \ldots,$ $0) : (max_D, id_N(u_0), \ldots, id_N(u_{l-1}), id_N(u) - 1, max_D, \ldots, max_D)$. An efficient implementation is similar to the implementation of the child axis.
– following-sibling – siblings of node u following in the document order. We search all points representing paths pertaining to elements with the same ancestors as node u and $(l(u)+2)^{th}$ coordinate $> id_N(u)$. A naive approach to finding the following-siblings of node u is to perform the range query: $(0, id_N(u_0), \ldots, id_N(u_{l-1}), id_N(u) +$ $1, 0, \ldots, 0) : (max_D, id_N(u_0), \ldots, id_N(u_{l-1}), max_D, \ldots, max_D)$. An efficient implementation is similar to the implementation of the child axis.
– preceding – nodes preceding to node u (except ancestors) in the document order. We search the nodes preceding the node u by the range query: $(0, 0, \ldots, 0) : (max_D,$ $id_N(u_0) - 1, \ldots, id_N(u_{l-1}) - 1, id_N(u) - 1, max_D, \ldots, max_D)$.

– following – nodes following to node u (except descendants) in the document order. We search the nodes following the node u by the range query: $(0, id_N(u_0) + 1, \ldots, id_N(u_{l-1}) + 1, id_N(u) + 1, 0, \ldots, 0) : (max_D, \ldots, max_D)$.

In the above described range queries no restrictions were given to the unique numbers of labelled paths. In practice, the first coordinates of range query's points contain a particular id_{LP} instead of an interval $\langle 0; max_D \rangle$.

3   Index Data Structures

Due to the fact that an XML document is represented as a set of points in the multi-dimensional approach, we use multi-dimensional data structures like UB-tree, BUB-tree, R-tree, and R*-tree for their indexing. (B)UB-tree data structure uses *Z-addresses* (*Z-ordering*) [1] for mapping a multi-dimensional space into a single-dimensional one. Intervals on *Z-curve* (which is defined by this ordering) are called *Z-regions*. (B)UB-tree stores points of each Z-region on one disk page (tree's leaf) and a hierarchy of Z-regions forms an index (inner nodes of tree). In the case of indexing point data, an R-tree and its variants cluster points into *minimal bounding boxes* (*MBBs*). Leafs contain indexed points, super-leaf nodes include definition of MBBs and remaining inner nodes contain a hierarchy of MBBs. (B)UB-tree and R-tree support *point* and *range queries* [1], which are used in the multi-dimensional approach to indexing XML data. The range query is processed by iterating through the tree and filtering of irrelevant tree's parts (i.e., regions) which do not intersect a query box.

One more important problem of the multi-dimensional approach is the unclear dimension of spaces of paths and labelled paths. Documents with the maximal length of path being 10 exist, but documents with the maximal path length 36 may appear as well (see [13]). A naive approach is to align the dimension of space to the maximal length of path. For example, points of dimension 5 will be aligned to dimension 36 using a blank value (often zero number) in 6th–36th coordinates. This technique increases the size of the index and the overhead of data structure as well. In [10] *BUB-forest* data structure was published. This data structure deals with the problem of indexing points of different dimensions. BUB-forest contains several BUB-trees, each of them indexes a space of different dimension. We can index points representing paths and labelled paths regardless of worsening efficiency by indexing XML documents with very different length of paths. We can use the same approach for other data structures, e.g. R-trees.

The range query used in the multi-dimensional approach is called the *narrow range query*. Points defining a query box have got coordinates for some dimensions the same, whereas the size of interval defined by the coordinates of the first and second point for other dimensions nears to the size of space's domain. Notice, regions intersecting a query box during processing of a range query are called *inter-sect regions* and regions containing at least one point of the query box are called *relevant regions*. We denote their number by N_I and N_R, respectively. Many irrelevant regions are searched during processing of the narrow range query in multi-dimensional data structures. Consequently, a ratio of relevant and intersect regions, so called *relevance ratio* c_R, becomes much lower than 1 with an increasing dimension of indexed space. In [11] the *Signature R-tree* data structure was depicted. This data structure enables the efficient processing of the narrow range query. Items of inner nodes contain a definition of (super)region and n-dimensional signature of tuples included in the (super)region (see Figure 2). A superposition of tuples' coordinates by operation OR creates the signature. Operation AND is used for better filtering of irrelevant regions during processing of the narrow range query. Other multi-dimensional data structures, e.g. (B)UB-tree, are possible to extend in the same way.

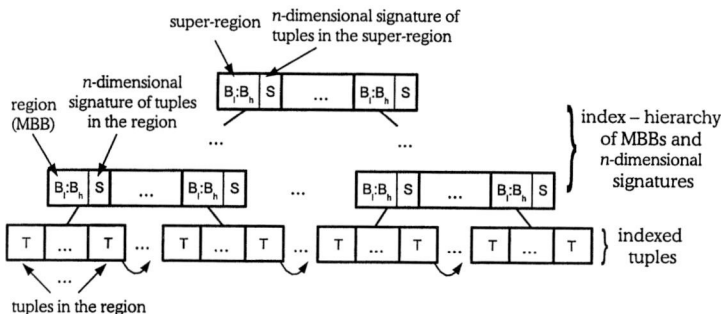

Fig. 3. A structure of the Signature R-Tree

4   Cost Analysis

A point query is often used for searching in the term and the labelled path index. The complexity of the point query is $O(log(m))$, where m is the number of the indexed objects. The efficiency of the multi-dimensional approach mainly depends on the efficiency of range query processing in the path index. Complexity of the general range query algorithm is $O(N_I \times \log_c m)$, where c is the node's capacity. It holds $c_R \ll 1$ (see previous section) for the narrow range query, particularly for increasing dimension of indexed space. In the case of the Signature R-tree (and (B)UB-tree as well) is the complexity $O(N_{RQ} \times \log_c m)$, where N_{RQ} is the number of searched regions (leaf nodes). Our experiments show $N_I \gg N_{RQ} \geq N_R$. In other words, the space complexity of the algorithm is enhanced for the reduction of the time complexity. Some XML queries are implemented by a sequence of q range queries. The complexity of the sequence is $O(\sum_{i=1}^q N_{RQ} \times log_c(m))$.

Conventional approaches, like XISS [12] and XPath Accelerator [6], index particular elements (and attributes). Simple query for values of elements as well as a query defined by a simple path based on an ancestor-descendent relation is processed using a consecutive filtering of elements which are not in relation ancestor-descendent as long as the result is retrieved. In Section 2.2 we can see that, in our approach, such a query is processed using one query in a data structure and the filtering of a large number of irrelevant elements does not approach.

5 Experimental Results

In our experiments[1], we used Protein Sequence Database XML document [15]. The document size is 683 MB. It includes 21,305,818 elements and 1,290,647 attributes. Approximately 17 mil. paths were obtained from this document. With respect to the frequency of the path lengths, the multi-dimensional forests with two trees indexing spaces of dimension $n = 7$ and $n = 9$ were created for indexing XML data. We used BUB-tree, R*-tree, and their signature variants with the length of n-dimensional signature $n \times 64$. The underlying table summarizes the index characteristics, square brackets indicate an increase of index volume for signature multi-dimensional trees. The average utilisation 62% was reached.

Dimen-sion n	Number of points	Index size [MB]				Number of inner leaf nodes (BUB-tree)	
		BUB-tree	Sig. BUB-tree	R*-tree	Sig. R*-tree	inner	leaf
7	8,268,357	440.9	471 [+7%]	478.6	512.2 [+7%]	10,917	214,842
9	8,739,522	562.1	635.2 [+13%]	603.1	680.7 [+13%]	17,751	270,065

First, queries for values of elements and attributes as well as a query defined by a simple path based on an ancestor-descendent relation similar to `ProteinDatabase/ProteinEntry[reference/refinfo/authors/author = 'Smith, E.L.']` were tested. For each space, queries with smaller (bellow 10) and larger (10^3–10^4) size of results were selected. In all cases, the ratio of number of searched leaf nodes and number of all leaf nodes, disk access cost (DAC), and query processing time were measured. The results of query processing are presented in Table 1. Evidently, the R*-tree proves to have better properties than BUB-trees during the narrow range processing. Signature variants of these data structures provide better efficiency than classical data structures. In the case of Signature R*-tree only 0.14% of all leaf nodes were searched and the average time of query processing turns out to be 70 ms.

Table 1. Results of queries for values of elements and attributes as well as a query defined by a simple path based on an ancestor-descendent relation in the path index

	Searched leaf nodes [%]				DAC				Time [s]			
	BUB tree	Sign. BUB-tree	R* tree	Sign. R*-tree	BUB tree	Sign. BUB-tree	R* tree	Sign. R*-tree	BUB tree	Sign. BUB-tree	R* tree	Sign. R*-tree
Avg.	1.15	0.22	0.29	**0.14**	7,566	794	917	**445**	2.9	0.5	0.12	**0.07**

Second, the efficiency of XPath axes implementation was tested. In all cases, DAC and query processing time for the Signature R*-tree were measured. The results of query processing are presented in Table 2. Ancestors axes are processed by no disk access.

---

[1] The experiments were executed on an Intel Pentium®4 2.4Ghz, 512MB DDR333, under Windows XP.

Table 2. Results of XPath axes queries in the path index

Axis	Number of resultant		Searched leaf nodes [%]	DAC	DAC for simple range query	Time [s]
	elements	points				
descendant	1,121	982	0.20	621	-	0.06
child	9	9	0.05	225	25	0.1
descendant-or-self	1,245	1,015	0.23	648	-	0.05
parent	1	-	-	-	-	-
following	2,487	2,017	0.45	1,387	-	0.1
preceding	2,312	1,803	0.39	1,124	-	0.09
following-sibling	5	5	0.04	187	27	0.09
preceding-sibling	7	7	0.03	165	24	0.09
Avg.	**1,026.6**	**585**	**0.20**	**622.4**	**25.3**	**0.08**

Since some axes (child, following-sibling, and preceding-sibling) are implemented by a sequence of range queries, DAC for one range query are presented in Table 2 as well. The volume of searched leaf nodes is again very low.

6   Conclusion

In this paper the multi-dimensional approach to indexing XML data and an efficient implementation of XPath axes were described. The BUB-forest was employed for indexing heterogeneous XML data with the root to leaf paths of widely differing lengths. Our experiments prove that the approach can serve as an alternative to implementing native XML databases. In our future work, we would like to further improve the abilities and the efficiency of the multi-dimensional approach. In particular we will develop an implementation of another complex XML queries which are defined by XML query languages such as XPath and XQuery.

References

1. R. Bayer. The Universal B-Tree for multidimensional indexing: General Concepts. In *Proceedings of WWCA'97, Tsukuba, Japan*, 1997.
2. N. Beckmann, H.-P. Kriegel, R. Schneider, and B. Seeger. The R*-tree: An efficient and robust access method for points and rectangles. In *Proceedings of the 1990 ACM SIGMOD International Conference on Management of Data*, pages 322–331.
3. A. B. Chaudhri, A. Rashid, and R. Zicari. *XML Data Management: Native XML and XML-Enabled Database Systems*. Addison Wesley Professional, 2003.
4. B. Cooper, N. Sample, M. J. Franklin, G. R. Hjaltason, and M. Shadmon. A Fast Index for Semistructured Data. In *Proceedings of the 27th VLDB Conference*, 2001.
5. R. Fenk. The BUB-Tree. In *Proceedings of 28th VLDB Conference*, 2002.
6. T. Grust. Accelerating XPath Location Steps. In *Proceedings of ACM SIGMOD 2002, Madison, USA*, June 4-6, 2002.

7. A. Guttman. R-Trees: A Dynamic Index Structure for Spatial Searching. In *Proceedings of ACM SIGMOD 1984, Boston, USA*, pages 47–57, June 1984.

8. M. Krátký, J. Pokorný, T. Skopal, and V. Snášel. The Geometric Framework for Exact and Similarity Querying XML Data. In *Proceedings of First EurAsian Conferences, EurAsia-ICT 2002, Shiraz, Iran*. Springer–Verlag, LNCS 2510, 2002.

9. M. Krátký, J. Pokorný, and V. Snášel. Indexing XML data with UB-trees. In *Proceedings of ADBIS 2002*, volume Research Commmunications, pages 155–164.

10. M. Krátký, T. Skopal, and V. Snášel. Multidimensional Term Indexing for Efficient Processing of Complex Queries. *Kybernetika, Journal of the ACR, accepted*, 2004.

11. M. Krátký, V. Snášel, J. Pokorný, and P. Zezula. Efficient Processing of Narrow Range Queries in the R-Tree. Technical Report ARG-TR-01-2004, *http://www.cs.vsb.cz/arg*, 2004.

12. Q. Li and B. Moon. Indexing and Querying XML Data for Regular Path Expressions. In *Proceedings of 27th VLDB International Conference*, 2001.

13. L. Mignet, D. Barbosa, and P. Veltri. The XML Web: a First Study. In *Proceedings of Twelfth International World Wide Web Conference, WWW 2003*. ACM, 2003.

14. J. W. R. Goldman. DataGuides: enabling query formulation and optimization in semistructured databases. In *Proceedings of 23rd VLDB Conference*, 1997.

15. University of Washington's database group. The XML Data Repository, 2002, http://www.cs.washington.edu/research/xmldatasets/.

16. W3 Consortium. XQuery 1.0: An XML Query Language, W3C Working Draft, 15 November 2002, http://www.w3.org/TR/xpath/.

17. W3 Consortium. XML Path Language (XPath) Version 2.0, W3C Working Draft, 15 November 2002, http://www.w3.org/TR/xpath20/.

18. W3 Consortium. Extensible Markup Language (XML) 1.0, 1998, http://www.w3.org/TR/REC-xml.

Dynamic Range Labeling for XML Trees

Takeharu Eda[1], Yasushi Sakurai[1], Toshiyuki Amagasa[2],
Masatoshi Yoshikawa[3], Shunsuke Uemura[2], and Takashi Honishi[1]

[1] NTT Cyber Space Laboratories, Japan
{eda.takeharu,yasushi.sakurai,takashi.honishi}@lab.ntt.co.jp
[2] Graduate School of Information Science,
Nara Institute of Science and Technology, Japan
{amagasa,uemura}@is.aist-nara.ac.jp
[3] Information Technology Center, Nagoya University, Japan
yoshikawa@itc.nagoya-u.ac.jp

Abstract. Structural joins based on range labeling schemes are considered as one of the most important topics in studies on XML query processing. When an XML data set is updated, however, the nodes have to be relabeled in order to keep their order relationship. Costly bulk node relabeling should be avoided to allow for continuous processing of queries for dynamic XML trees that are updated often. In this paper, we propose two dynamic node labeling schemes to avoid "gap shortfalls". One is simple local relabeling scheme and the other is more sophisticated in that it uses approximate histograms that keep the statistics of the update operations. These two techniques allow node labels to be managed dynamically and locally. Experiments show that they can avoid bulk relabeling while still permitting update operations.

1 Introduction

Many query languages that can exploit the structure of XML trees have been developed using database techniques [2, 7]. To avoid costly searches, *structural joins* [1] were developed around *range labeling schemes* [5]. Specifically, nodes in an XML tree are labeled with pairs of numbers which represent the pre- and postorder of the tree. Queries that includes *regular path expressions* [10] are transformed into *structural joins* using node labels. By building indexes on names, values, and given labels, such queries can be evaluated without having to do costly searches of the entire XML data set.

The rapidly increasing popularity of XML as a data exchange format has led to there being a huge amount of frequently updated XML data on the Internet. However, to date, the update problems of range labeling schemes have not been studied to a sufficient degree. The naive range labeling scheme, without "gaps", requires complete relabeling after the insertion position even if only one node is inserted. We can improve on naive labeling by counting nodes sparsely [4]. However, if we consider only static and persistent labels, as the updates continue, the number of available positions would eventually become smaller than the number of nodes in the subtree to be inserted and we would end up relabeling of all nodes in the XML data set. Thus, persistent range labeling schemes are not suitable for data-oriented XML that changes a lot [8].

W. Lindner et al. (Eds.): EDBT 2004 Workshops, LNCS 3268, pp. 230–239, 2004.

Four kinds of labeling schemes, range labeling, prefix labeling [8], computable identifier [9], and prime labeling [11], have been developed in the context of XML databases. Each of the schemes has some drawback and advantage. However, it is not realistic to label XML nodes with all types of the labels to obtain all of the advantages owing to storage limitations. Its update capability has not still been developed, but range labeling scheme is the most well-studied, simplest, and the best from the viewpoint of query performance [11].

To ensure fast query processing using *structural joins* while updates occur, we need to avoid costly bulk node relabeling. This study deals with a dynamic form of range labeling. That is, we label nodes sparsely to reduce the number of relabelings, and if the number of nodes in the subtree to be inserted is larger than the number of available positions, or if an update deviation uses up the available positions, we relabel only the neighbour nodes around the updated position without relabeling all nodes in the database. The idea of *dynamic range labeling* is derived from the observation that the structural conditions of range labeling schemes are based on only the order relations of the label numbers, not their values. Furthermore, we can introduce an approximate histogram to hold information on update operations; it can handle growing XML data, unlike the simple dynamic technique. Experimental results show that our minimal dynamic relabeling approach keeps the balance among the nodes labels' numerical distribution and can avoid extensive bulk relabeling.

The rest of this paper is organized as follows. Section 2 explains range labeling schemes. Section 3 considers how to deal with update operations and shows that naive static labeling schemes cannot cope with continuous update operations. Section 4 describes the relabeling methods that we developed. Section 5 shows experimental results, and Section 6 concludes this paper.

2   Range Labeling Schemes

We can define the node label in a range labeling scheme as follows.

Definition 1 (Node Label): Given an XML tree T and a node $v(\in T)$, the label of v whose preorder is i and postorder is j is (a_i, b_j) on the condition that a_i and b_j are strictly increasing sequences of positive integers to i and j, respectively.

We call a_i and b_j the *extended preorder* and *extended postorder* and $(a_1, a_2, a_3, \ldots, a_{n-1}, a_n)$ and $(b_1, b_2, b_3, \ldots, b_{n-1}, b_n)$ the *extended preorder series* and *extended postorder series*, respectively. By using a stack, we can label all nodes in an XML file in one pass.

Lemma 1 [Structural Condition]: Let the label of node v be (a_i, b_j) and the label of node w be (a_k, b_l). v is an ancestor of w if and only if

$$a_i < a_k, \text{ and } b_j > b_l.$$

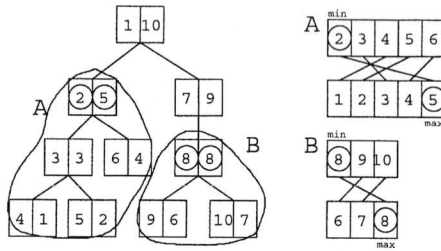

Fig. 1. Range Labels: Pre- and Post-order Schemes

3   Considering XML Tree Update

XML Trees Update: We considered only insertion and deletion of XML subtrees like A and B in Figure 1. Each subtree contains the root node and all its descendants. Therefore, its preorder and postorder series are consistent (i.e. well-ordered, depth-first) and independent of one another. We call this kind of subtree which is the object of insertion or deletion a *unit tree* of update operation.

Bulk Load: We bulk load a XML tree by labeling the nodes with sparse numbers like Figure 2 to try to provide enough gaps for insertions[1]. The bulk load interval is determined

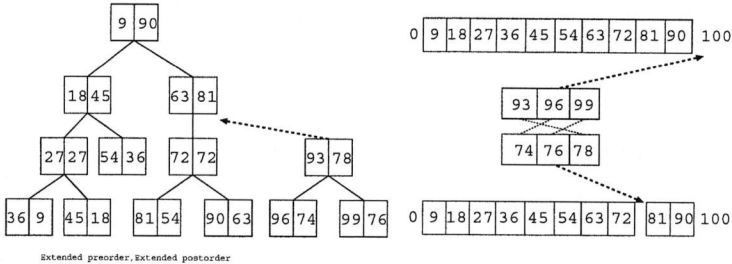

Fig. 2. Inserting a Unit Tree

by dividing the maximum label value by the number of nodes. In the example shown in Figure 2, the maximum value is 100 and the interval is 9.

Insertion: The position inserted into is one interval since the both of order of a unit tree are continuous. Then a unit tree is labeled with the numbers which divide the inserted position space equally in order to use available space efficiently as shown in Figure 2.

Deletion: Let T be the XML tree and d be the root node of a unit tree to be deleted. Since the postorder of d is the maximum of all the postorders of nodes in the unit

---

[1] Sparse labeling of *interval scheme* is introduced in [4].

tree, the range of postorders for the descendants of d is known. Thus, we can delete these labels of descendants in the extended preorder and extended postorder series of T

However, we believed that static sparse labeling is not good enough for XML trees that are frequently updated, because the intervals between nodes are of finite length. Eventually, there will be a unit tree whose size exceeds the interval at the insertion position, at which time, the XML tree would have to be completely relabeled.

Preliminary Experiments: To check whether "gap shortfall" problems occur, we conducted experiments using a series of numbers to represent the extended preorder (or postorder) series of an XML tree. We created test synthetic operation sequences composed of insertions and deletions.

Test Operation Sequences and Data Sets: Table 1 shows the parameters of each test data set. We choose three patterns for distributing the update: uniform and two normal. The distributions of the insertions and deletions were independent of each other. In the case of the normal distribution, we experimented with 30% or 70% as the average update position for the whole extended preorder series. The standard deviation of both normal distributions was 10%. The ratio of insertion and deletion was 1:1 or 2:1; 2:1 was obtained by analyzing the actual growing XML data, go.xml [6]. 2:1 is close to the ratio of Gene Ontology vocabulary data. The number of nodes in each unit tree was randomly generated, with 2, 10, or 30 as the maximum number. The number of operations was 30000, and 32-bit positive integers were used for the label numbers. The number of nodes was initially 10000.

Table 1. Parameters of The Test Data

Distribution of updated positions	uniform, normal (30%), normal (70%)
Insertion : deletion	1:1, 2:1
Max. num. of nodes in unit tree	2, 10, 30

Experimental Results: We counted the frequency of bulk loads while continuing the update operations. The results are shown in Table 2. The number of bulk loads increases substantially as the number of nodes in the unit tree increases.

If XML data are rather static, that is update operations are rare and not queried so often, we can relabel all of the nodes in the database while the traffic to the database is low. However, XML is recently adopting new roles and is being used not only

Table 2. Ave. Num. of Bulk Loads in 30000 Operations

Num. of nodes in unit tree	Bulk loads (average)
2	1.0
10	14.2
30	68.3

for data exchange but also as the basic structure for expressing data. Accordingly bulk loading is serious problem since the system must be suspended for some time. To avoid this and continue to process XML queries efficiently, we propose two dynamic range labeling schemes that keep the balance of label numbers and avoid bulk loading.

4   Dynamic Range Labeling Schemes

The first dynamic range labeling scheme uses a simple approach that is based on the observation that narrower intervals should be expanded and larger ones should be shrunk. The second scheme improves on the naive *balanced* condition of the first one by using approximate histograms. It keeps the information on the updated positions and can reflect the deviation of updates in the distribution of label numbers. We have two number series; the extended preorder series and extended postorder series. Since the order relations of the series are independent of each other, we can relabel each series independently. Thus here, we explain only the extended preorder series of T. We assume that $Width$ is the maximum integer available for labels and, for the purposes of illustration, assume that $a_0 = 0$ and $a_{n+1} = Width$.

Simple Dynamic Labeling: Let X be the unit tree to be inserted, $|X|$ be the number of nodes in X. We define the $BestInterval$ as follows,

$$BestInterval := \left\lfloor \frac{Width}{|T| + |X| + 1} \right\rfloor$$

If X partitions x into equal-length intervals and the interval is larger than $BestInterval$ times min, the neighbor nodes are not relabeled.

Definition 2 (*Balanced* for insertion): Let min be a constant less than 1. If an interval x satisfies $min \cdot BestInterval \cdot (|X| + 1) < x$, x is **balanced**.

Definition 2's condition checks whether x is large enough for X. If not, we expand the interval of the inserted position a little so that the interval satisfies this condition.

The insertion algorithm is shown in Table 3. First, it checks whether x is **balanced** or not (line 2). If not, x is expanded by traversing **T** both (or either) ways and the number of nodes the in unit tree is increased by two (lines 3-12). These steps are repeated until x becomes **balanced**. Figure 3 shows simple dynamic relabeling of the tree in Figure 2. If $min = \frac{1}{2}$, $x = 10$ is too small for the insertion of three nodes (a). The interval is expanded by two from the beginning endpoint and the number of nodes in the unit tree is increased by two (b). In (c), $x = 46$ becomes enough for the insertion of 7 nodes. x is divided by $7 + 1$, and the 7 inserted nodes are labeled at that intervals. Next, we show the definition **balanced** for deletion.

Definition 3 (*Balanced* for deletion): Let max be a constant larger than 1. If x satisfies $x < max \cdot BestInterval$, x is **balanced**.

Table 3. Insertion Algorithm

──**Algorithm** *Insert*

input: extended preorder series: $\mathbf{T} = (a_1, \ldots, a_n)$, the number of nodes in a unit tree to be inserted: $|X|$, the preorder of inserted position: k

output: extended preorder series with $n + |X|$ nodes

```
1    x := a_{k+1} - a_k;
2    if (x is not balanced)
3        if(k = 1)
4            T := (a_3, ..., a_{n-1}, a_n);
5            Insert(T, |X| + 2, 1);
6        else if(k = |T|)
7            T := (a_1, a_2, ..., a_{n-3});
8            Insert(T, |X| + 2, |T|);
9        else
10           T := (a_1, a_2, ..., a_{k-1}, a_{k+2}, ..., a_n);
11           Insert(T, |X| + 2, k - 1);
12       endif
13   else
14       Δx := ⌊ x/(|X|+1) ⌋;
15       return T := (a_1, a_2, ..., a_k, a_k + Δx, a_k + 2Δx, ..., a_k + |X| · Δx, a_{k+1}, ..., a_n);
16   endif
```

In the case of deletion, we first delete nodes from T, then use the insertion algorithm (Table 3) so that the interval of the inserted position satisfies the condition in Definition 3. When using the insertion algorithm for deletion, we consider the number of nodes in X to be 0 (*i.e.* $|X| = 0$). The lopsided intervals generated after deletion can be depolarized by using the same algorithm because we define the permissible zone of *balanced* as the labels not less than $BestInterval \times min$ and not larger than $BestInterval \times max$.

Dynamic Labeling Using Approximate Histograms: If insertions frequently occur at one place, the intervals around that place should be wider than at other places and vice versa in the case of deletion. By recording the update positions and the times of updates, we can expand the intervals where insertions occur frequently and narrow the intervals where deletions occur frequently.

Approximate Histograms: We create two approximate histograms; one counts the update operations at approximate positions of the extended preorder series and the other independently counts the operations on the extended postorder series. Each histogram is an array of size $size$ and has the parameter $delta$, which is the limit for counting update operations. If the XML data set is updated more than $delta$ times, we can renew the update information by erasing all histogram values and count from the beginning. Let us consider a histogram $H = (h_1, h_2, \cdots, h_{size})$. Initially, $h_i = 0 (1 \leq i \leq size)$. In addition, the variables h_{min}, sum and $count$ are maintained to keep the state of the histogram. h_{min} is the minimum value in the histogram, sum is the summation of $h_i(1 \leq i \leq size)$, and $count$ is the number of update operations.

```
                        Width: 100              |X| = 3
                        min  : 1/2       BestInterval: 100/13=7

        x = 100-90 = 10      0 9 18 27 36 45 54 63 72 81 90              100
(a)     1/2*7*(3+1)=14 > x
        Not balanced.                                  X

                 ↓

        x = 100-72 = 28      0 9 18 27 36 45 54 63 72                    100
(b)     1/2*7*(5+1)=21 > x
        Not balanced.

                 ↓

        x = 100-54 = 46      0 9 18 27 36 45 54                          100
(c)     1/2*7*(7+1)=28 < x
        Balanced.

                 ↓

        (100-54)/(7+1)=5     0 9 18 27 36 45 54 59 64 69 73 77 81 85    100
(d)     delta = 5

                        Extended Preorder Series
```

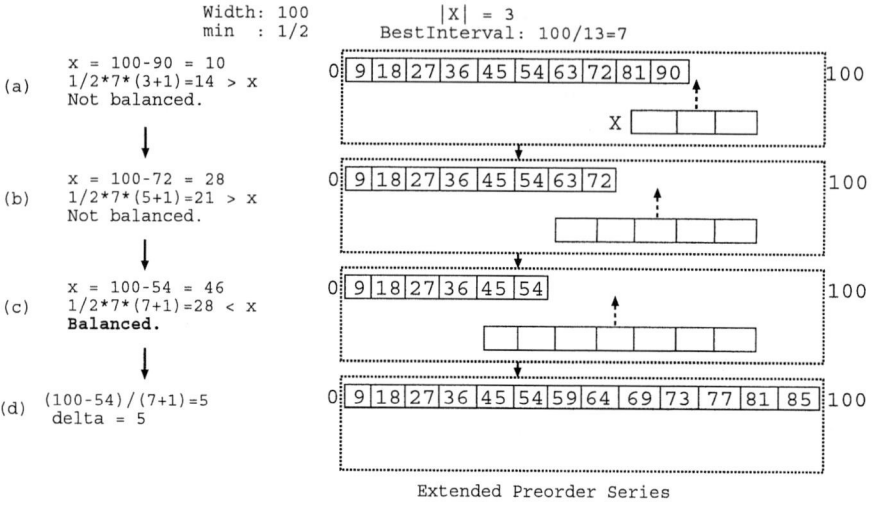

Fig. 3. Example of Simple Dynamic Labeling

Updating Histograms: Let $(a_1, a_2, \cdots, a_n)$ be extended preorder series. If the insertion occurs between $a_k (1 \leq k \leq n)$ and a_{k+1}, $0 < \frac{a_k}{Width} \cdot size \leq size$. Let $p = \lceil \frac{a_k}{Width} \cdot size \rceil$. h_p is incremented because one insertion happened at a_k[2]. In the case of deletion from a_k to a_{k+m}, the positions are determined in the same way as for insertion, h_p is decremented and sum is updated. $count$ is the counter of update operations. While sum and $count$ can be updated without accessing the histogram values when an update operation occurs, h_{min} cannot be updated without accessing the histogram values. Thus we scan the histogram to update h_{min}. In our experiments, we set $size$ as 1000, 3000, or etc. , and $delta$ as 5000, etc. , due to the limitations of the computer used to create the histograms. The data structure is small and easy to implement. We can record approximate information about the update operations in fixed-length histograms even if the size of the XML database varies.

Improving The Relabeling Algorithm: The idea of using histograms is to reflect the distribution of update operations in the extended preorder series and extended postorder series independently. The following two techniques are used to achieve this. One is translation. Since the values in a histogram can be negative or 0 due to deletion, we translate all the values in the histogram into positive values virtual histogram using h_{min} ((a) and (b) in Figure 4).

$$(h_1, h_2, \cdots, h_{size}) \Longrightarrow (h_1 - h_{min} + 1, h_2 - h_{min} + 1, \cdots, h_{size} - h_{min} + 1)$$

sum is also translated into $sum - size \times (h_{min} - 1)$. Then, we get the percentage of position p in the virtual histogram, $\frac{h_p}{sum}$. Clearly, $0 < \frac{h_p}{sum} < 1$ and $\sum_{p=1}^{size} h_p = sum$. The other technique involves approximate correspondence between histograms and the

---

[2] The number of nodes in the unit tree to be inserted or deleted is not retained in our method.

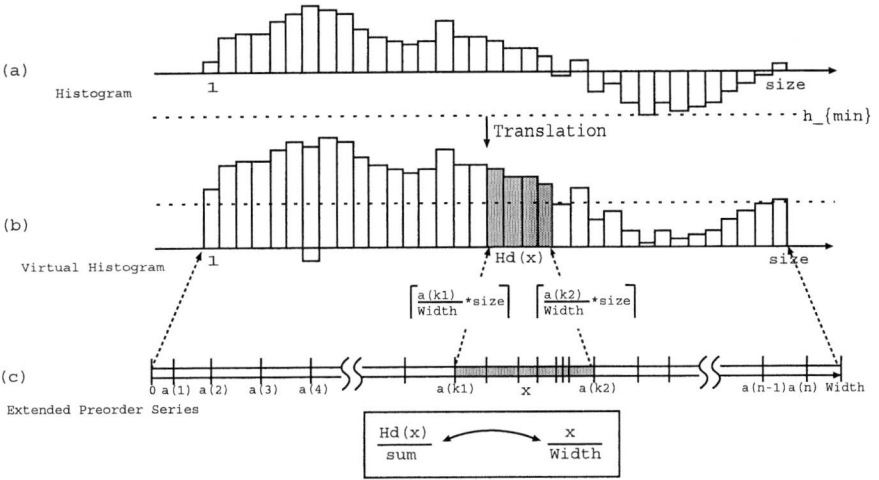

Fig. 4. Translation and Approximate Correspondence

extended preorder series. The interval from the beginning number to the end number to be updated in an extended preorder series corresponds to an updated part in a histogramThe corresponding histogram position p_k of node a_k is $p_k = \left\lceil \frac{a_k}{Width} \cdot size \right\rceil$. Next, we define the corresponding interval in the histogram of $x = a_{k2} - a_{k1}$ in the extended preorder series as $Hd(x) = \sum_{k=k1}^{k2} h_{p_k}$. Then, we get the approximate correspondence, $\frac{x}{Width} \Longleftrightarrow \frac{Hd(x)}{sum}$. If the corresponding values are close to each other, the position in the extended preorder series can be considered to reflect the statistical information in the corresponding values in a histogram. Thus, we can redefine what it means for x to be **balanced** as follows,

Definition 4 (*Balanced* using histogram for insertion): If $x = a_{k2} - a_{k1}$ satisfies $\frac{Hd(x)}{sum} \cdot min < \frac{x}{Width}$, where min is a constant less than 1, x is **balanced**.

Definition 5 (*Balanced* using histogram for deletion): If $x = a_{k2} - a_{k1}$ satisfies $\frac{x}{Width} < \frac{Hd(x)}{sum} \cdot max$, where max is a constant larger than 1, x is **balanced**.

These conditions check whether the percentage of the x in the extended preorder series reflects the percentage of the corresponding intervals in histogram. We use the same insertion algorithm in Table 3 in the case of both insertion and deletion by using the appropriate definition of **balanced**.

5 Experimental Results

The simple and histogram-based schemes were evaluated using the same data set shown in Table 1 from the following two aspects; One is the frequency of bulk loading. Our definition of bulk loading is that at least 80% of nodes must be relabeled. The other is the average number of local relabeling operations per update operation. Even if bulk loading occurs only rarely, it is useless if the cost of each local relabeling is high[3]. The average number of bulk loads is shown in Table 4. When the maximum number of nodes in a unit

Table 4. Ave. Num. of Bulk Loads

Num. of nodes in a unit tree	Static	Simple	Histogram
2	1.333	0	4.833333
10	8.5	1067.5	0
30	30	2233.167	0.166667
total	13	1100.222	1.665

tree is 2, the simple scheme can avoid bulk loading. With 10 or 30 nodes per unit tree, bulk loading occurs often. With the histogram-based scheme, when the number of nodes in the unit tree is 2, bulk loading occurs more than with the static scheme. However, even if the number of nodes in the unit tree increases, the number of bulk loads does not increase much.

We analyzed the average and maximum costs by dividing the data set into two types; stable data and growing data. The insertion:deletion ratio for stable data is 1:1 and for growing data it is 2:1. Table 5 shows the average and maximum cost for each update operation in the case of stable data. The simple scheme keeps the number of relabeling nodes quite small, unlike the histogram-based scheme. We can say that the simple scheme is better than the histogram-based scheme in the case of stable XML data. Table 6 shows

Table 5. Stable data set (1:1)

	Simple	Histogram
Ave.	17	38
Max.	1035	5110

Table 6. Growing data set (2:1)

	Simple	Histogram
Ave.	35336	327
Max.	103118	95091

the results for growing data set. While the simple scheme fails to handle the growing data set efficiently, the histogram-based scheme reduces the cost significantly. When the data is growing, the histogram-based scheme is better than the simple scheme.

6   Conclusion

This paper proposed dynamic range labeling schemes for data-oriented dynamic XML trees. Experiments showed that the simple scheme can efficiently manage stable data sets, and the histogram-based scheme can manage growing data sets. The dynamic range labeling schemes do not keep a *durable reference* [4] of labels. Instead of persistence, they provide efficient query processing in which XML data sets can be continuously updated.

---

[3] **Cost** is the number of nodes to be relabeled when an update operation occurs.

If the persistence of labels is essential and update operations occur frequently, we need another kind of persistent labels. Our relabeling algorithms can be implemented the most efficiently if there exist linked lists of preorder and postorder series. These simple data structures can be maintained more easily than complex tree structures proposed in [3].

References

1. Shurug Al-Khalifa et al. Structural Joins: A Primitive for Efficient XML Query Pattern Matching. In *Proc. ICDE*, 2002.
2. Scott Boag et al. XQuery 1.0: An XML Query Language.
3. Yi Chen et al. L-Tree: a Dynamic Labeling Structure for Ordered XML Data. In *Proc. DataX (in conjunction with EDBT2004)*, 2004.
4. Shu-Yao Chien et al. Storing and Querying Multiversion XML Documents using Durable Node Numbers. In *Proc. WISE*, 2001.
5. Edith Cohen et al. Labeling Dynamic XML Trees. In *Proc. PODS*, 2002.
6. Gene Ontology Consortium. http://www.geneontology.org/.
7. Jonathan Robie. XQL FAQ. http://www.ibiblio.org/xql/.
8. Haim Kaplan et al. A comparison of labeling schemes for ancestor queries. In *Proc. SODA*, 2002.
9. Dao Dinh Kha et al. A Structural Numbering Scheme for XML Data. In *Proc. XMLDM (in conjunction with EDBT2002)*, 2002.
10. Quanzhong Li et al. Indexing and Querying XML Data for Regular Path Expressions. In *The VLDB Journal*, 2001.
11. Xiaodong Wu et al. A Prime Number Labeling Scheme for Dynamic Ordered XML Trees. In *Proc. ICDE*, 2004.

FliX: A Flexible Framework for Indexing Complex XML Document Collections

Ralf Schenkel

Max-Planck-Institut für Informatik, Saarbrücken, Germany
schenkel@mpi-sb.mpg.de

Abstract. While there are many proposals for path indexes on XML documents, none of them is perfectly suited for indexing large-scale collections of interlinked XML documents. Existing strategies lack support for links, require large amounts of time to build or space to store the index, or cannot efficiently answer connection queries. This paper presents the *FliX* framework for connection indexing that supports large, heterogeneous document collections with links, using the existing path indexes as building blocks. We introduce some example configurations of the framework that are appropriate for many important application scenarios. Experiments show the feasibility of our approach.

1 Introduction

1.1 XML on the Web

Some years ago, XML documents have mostly been used for exchanging data between different applications, hence the complete information was contained in a single document. Nowadays, as XML is increasingly used as a replacement for HTML on the Web or intranets, documents usually have XLinks or XPointers to data in other documents. In addition to such inter-document links, the XML standard allows intra-document links between elements of a single document.

While this increases the expressiveness of XML in intranets, in digital libraries, and on the Web, it is on the other hand one of the big challenges for XML retrieval. With information spread over several linked documents, an XML search engine should treat elements that are referenced through links similarly to "normal" child elements when evaluating path expressions in queries, which is typically done using some path indexing technique. However, two problems arise when taking links into account: (1) Links change the structure of XML documents, so they are no longer trees, but form a directed graph; (2) links generate interconnections of previously unconnected XML documents, yielding large sets of connected elements with long paths between them. While the latter problem can lead to path indexes that grow extremely large and take very long to build, the former even renders some of the established and highly efficient path indexes unusable. The framework that we are presenting in this paper can cope efficiently with large, heterogeneous collections of linked documents.

The second major challenge for XML retrieval is raised by the heterogeneity of data on the Web, but also in heterogeneous collections of data from different sources. As there is no universal standard for representing data in XML (and it is unlikely that there will

W. Lindner et al. (Eds.): EDBT 2004 Workshops, LNCS 3268, pp. 240–249, 2004.

ever be such a standard), schemas used to represent data widely vary across different data sources, and some do not provide a schema at all. Existing query languages for XML like XPath and XQuery are no longer appropriate for searching in such an environment as they cannot cope with the diversity of data. As an example, consider the query

```
/movie[title="Matrix: Revolutions"]/actor/movie
```

(i.e., find movies whose actors were also in the cast of "Matrix: Revolutions") may not give any result at all: One of the data sources may use the tag name science-fiction instead of movie, it may reflect the title of the movie as "Matrix 3", or the path between the elements may be longer than 1. To find as many relevant elements as possible (i.e., to get good recall), the system should automatically relax the query, which may yield the following extended query:

```
//~movie[~title~"Matrix: Revolutions"]//~actor//~movie
```

This extended query has semantic vagueness for content and tag names (using the similarity operator $\sim$ as in the XML search language XXL [10]) as well as structural vagueness (by relaxing all child axes to descendants-or-self axes). Here, the $\sim$ operator means that elements whose tag names are semantically similar to the name in the query qualify for the result, too, but possibly with a lower relevance that is derived from the degree of semantic similarity. In the XXL search engine [8, 11], similar words as well as similarity scores for them are extracted from an ontology.

Adding structural vagueness is motivated by the following example: A query like movie/actor can only be an approximation of what the user really wants, because the user cannot know the exact structure of the data. We therefore consider not only children as matches, but also descendants; the relevance of a result decreases with increasing path length. It is evident that evaluating queries with such structural vagueness requires the efficient evaluation of path expressions with the descendants-or-self axis, which is a weakness of most path indexes for linked XML documents. The FliX framework that we present in this paper is specifically optimized for this setting.

There have been some proposals for indexing connections in collections of XML documents; see Section 2 for an overview. However, the choice of the "best" indexing strategy for a given collection of XML documents depends on a number of parameters: the size of the XML collection, the structure of the XML data (e.g., presence of links, link density, max depth of a document, number and distribution of the tag names), and the query load (e.g., children or descendants queries, query patterns, locality). Therefore, there typically is no single "best" index for large, heterogeneous document collections. Instead, one index may be better suited for one part of the collection, while another may be best for another part. The existing indexes are not flexible enough to adapt to such a setting.

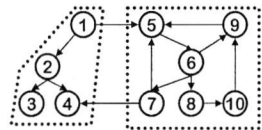

Fig. 1. Heterogeneous collection of 10 XML documents)

The FliX[1] framework that we present in this paper overcomes this problem by combining indexes for parts of the collection, using the "best" index for each part. As an

---

[1] Framework for indexing large collections of interlinked XML documents.

example, consider the document collection shown in Figure 1. It is easy to see that it consists of a part consisting of documents one to four that forms a tree, while the rest is closely interlinked. FliX partitions the document collection into the so-called meta documents as shown in the figure and chooses, depending on its configuration, for example a pre/postorder based index [5] for the tree-like partition, and a HOPI index [9] for the partition with many links. This optimal choice of the index for a meta document allows faster evaluation of queries as well as more compact indexes. Using these indexes, queries are executed by first evaluating the query within a meta document and then following the links between meta documents at run time. This approach highly reduces the time required to return the most relevant results to the client.

1.2   Contribution and Outline of the Paper

The paper presents a solution to the highly relevant problem of connection indexing in large, heterogeneous collections of XML documents. Specifically, we make the following important contributions:

- We present the FliX framework to index large, heterogeneous collections of interlinked XML documents and, ultimately, the Web, that reuses existing indexing strategies as building blocks. FliX is extensible and can be tailored to the needs of the application and to the structure of the data to be indexed. It efficiently supports XPath's `descendants-or-self` axis, but can handle other query types, too.
- We show instantiations of the framework that strongly improve path index performance for practically relevant cases. This includes an extension of the well-known pre-/postorder index [5] to documents with links.
- We have implemented the framework and carried out preliminary experiments on real XML data from DBLP. The results indicate that our framework outperforms existing indexing strategies in terms of query performance as well as index size.

2   Indexing the Structure of XML Documents

2.1   XML Data Model

We consider a graph $G_d = (V_d, E_d)$ for each XML document d in the collection, where 1) the vertex set V_d consists of all elements of d plus all elements of other documents that are referenced within d and 2) the edge set E_d includes all parent-child relationships between elements as well as links from elements in d to other elements of d or external elements. Then, a collection of XML documents $X = \{d_1, \ldots, d_n\}$ is represented by the union $G_X = (V_X, E_X)$ of the graphs $G_1, \ldots, G_n$ where V_X is the union of the V_{d_i} and E_X is the union of the E_{d_i}.

2.2   Existing Path Indexes

Pre/Postorder Scheme (PPO). This path index proposed by Grust [5] computes the *pre order* and the *post order* for each element e of a single XML document without links, by traversing the document in depth-first order. Thus, building the index takes time $O(|E_X|)$, and space consumption is $O(|V_X|)$. All XPath axes can be evaluated using these numbers. This index structure is highly efficient for reachability queries and can, with slight additions, also provide the distance between two nodes.

HOPI. This index [9] makes use of a compact representation of reachability and distance information in graphs proposed by Cohen et al. [2]. The index maintains for each element e two sets of elements $L_{in}(e)$ and $L_{out}(e)$ (so-called *labels*) such that there is a path from x to y iff $L_{out}(x) \cap L_{in}(y) \neq \emptyset$. These labels can also be augmented with distance information to compute the distance of two elements. HOPI provides a divide-and-conquer algorithm for index creation that is reasonably fast as long as the document collection is not too large. Querying the index for reachability of two elements is very fast for most elements. Experiments [9] indicate that the HOPI index is usually an order of magnitude more compact than the transitive closure.

Others. There have been a number of other proposals for path indexes, among them Dataguides [4], APEX [1], Index Fabric [3], and the Index Definition Scheme [6] that can be used to define special indexes (e.g. 1–Index, A(k)–Index, D(k)–Index [7], F&B–Index) with k being the maximum length of supported paths. However, none of these approaches is explicitly optimized for the `descendants-or-self` axis, and therefore none of them efficiently supports them.

As discussed in Section 1, the choice of the "right" index for a structurally homogeneous document collection (like a meta document in FliX) depends on a number of parameters. As a first rule of thumb, if there are no links, PPO will typically be the best choice; if all paths are short or do not contain wildcards, APEX or an instance of the Index Definition Scheme will do fine; if we expect to evaluate long paths and queries with wildcards which is the case when we add structural vagueness to queries, we may want to use HOPI. However, HOPI's size may grow large for large document sets and, more importantly, the time to build HOPI superlinearly increases with increasing number of documents.

3   Flexible Indexing of XML Documents with FliX

3.1   FliX Concepts

As we pointed out in Section 2, the existing path index structures cannot efficiently support descendant queries on large collections of interlinked XML documents. Additionally, index size and the time to build the index grow enormously for some of the index structures if the document collection is huge, and it is usually impossible to find an "optimal" indexing strategy for a heterogeneous collection.

The FliX framework presented in this paper aims to solve these problems. It first divides the document set into carefully chosen fragments (so-called meta documents) where each meta document contains some or all of the links between its documents. Additionally, FliX maintains the set of remaining inter- or intra-document links that are not contained in any meta document. After that, an index is built for each meta document, using the "best" available indexing strategy given the characteristics of the meta document. A descendant query is then evaluated first on the local indexes (which will probably return the "best" results, i.e., elements that are connected with short paths).

After that, results spanning multiple meta documents are evaluated by following links between meta documents at run-time.

FliX returns results approximately ordered by ascending distance. As soon as a new result is found, it is returned to the client for further processing. This is especially important as users are typically not interested in seeing all results of a query (which often would be way too many with documents from the Web), but may be satisfied with the top k results, with k usually less than 100. A search engine using FliX for indexing can therefore return the best results early to the user and may even stop the execution when it can determine that it has produced the top k results.

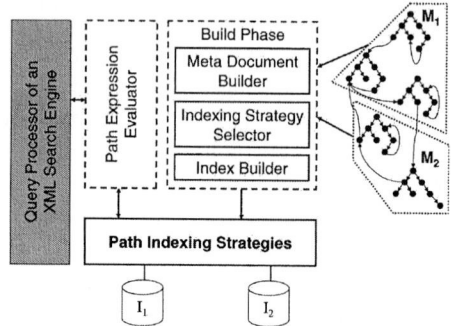

Fig. 2. Architecture of our framework for XML indexing

3.2 FliX Architecture

FliX consists of the following core components (see Figure 2):

- Several *Path Indexing Strategies*, among them PPO, APEX and HOPI, that support the XPath axes and return results in ascending order of distance.
- The *Meta Document Builder MDB* that automatically builds an "optimal" set of meta documents $M = \{M_1, \ldots, M_m\}$, where each meta document consists of a distinct subset of the set X of interlinked XML documents to be indexed.
- The *Indexing Strategy Selector ISS* that automatically selects, for each meta document, the "optimal" indexing strategy, based on structure, size and other properties of the meta documents.
- The *Index Builder IB* that builds *index structures* for each of the meta documents, using the selected indexing strategy for each meta document.
- The *Path Expression Evaluator PEE* that evaluates the `descendants-or-self` axis and returns results approximately ordered by ascending path length.

The Meta Document Builder, the Indexing Strategy Selector, and the Index Builder are used in the *Build Phase*, while the Path Expression Evaluator is used in the *Query Evaluation Phase*.

4 The Build Phase

4.1 Meta Document Builder and Index Strategy Selector

Building the meta documents and selecting the best indexing strategies for them are closely intertwined. Both heavily depend on 1) the structure of the document collection, e.g., the number of documents, the distribution of the document sizes, link structure, and the average number of links per document, and 2) on the query load, e.g., which axes dominate the load, how long the typical result paths are, how often do result paths cross document borders, and so on. Additionally, certain algorithms to build meta documents may rule out the usage of some index strategies. As an example, if the meta documents are built to form graphs, not trees, then PPO can no longer be used. To overcome these problems in FliX, we have predefined several *configurations* of the framework, i.e., a strategy to build meta documents together with a set of indexing strategies that can be applied. Each configuration fits a certain kind of collection structure. The ultimate goal is that FliX can itself determine the "optimal" configuration for the actual application or, if the collection is too heterogeneous, automaticaly build homogeneous partitions of the collection. However, in our current implementation, an administrator must decide which configuration to use.

When the configuration to use has been fixed, the problem of finding the "best" meta documents can be stated as follows: Given the set of interlinked XML documents X, an upper bound for (disk or main) memory available for index structures, and an upper bound for index creation time, find an "optimal" set of meta documents $M = \{M_1, \ldots, M_m\}$, where each meta document consists of a distinct subset of X. Here, the optimality of M means that, when indexing each M_i with the best possible indexing strategy, the average time for evaluating an arbitrary path expression over the complete document collection X is minimized. Additionally, total space consumption of all indexes and accumulated time to build the indexes must not exceed the respective upper bound. This optimization problem is hard to solve exactly, because the set cover problem is NP-hard, therefore each configuration comes with its own approximation algorithm.

When the selection of the meta documents has been finished, we explicitly construct the meta documents as input for the Index Builder. To do this, we join the XML data graphs of all the documents within a meta document into the data graph of the meta document (i.e., we unify the sets of nodes and the sets of edges). Additionally, we (conceptually) replace each document-internal link within one of the documents as well as each inter-document link between two documents with a corresponding new edge in the XML data graph of the meta document. For nodes of the meta element that have links to elements of other meta documents, we store this information with the element together with the target elements of the links.

4.2   Index Builder (IB)

When the choice of the meta documents and of the corresponding indexing strategies has been made, we build all the index structures. Additionally, we maintain, for each meta document M_i, the set L_i of elements with outgoing links that are not reflected in the index. For a given element a of the meta document, the set $L(a)$ denotes all elements in the same meta document that are descendants of a and have such an outgoing link. The index structures are extended to support querying for $L(a)$ of a given element a, which is (conceptually) computed by intersecting the set of descendants of a and L_i.

4.3   Example Configurations of FliX

Naive. The naive, albeit useful configuration of FliX considers each document in the XML document collection as a separate meta document. Depending on the structure of each document, either a PPO index is built if the document does not contain any intra-document links, or a HOPI index is built. This approach can be useful if documents are relatively large, the number of inter-document links is small, and queries usually do not cross document boundaries.

Maximal PPO. The most efficient path index is PPO, but it cannot be used with linked documents. However, a closer analysis shows that in some cases, the resulting XML graph G_X forms still a tree even in the presence of links, because the graph of the documents and the links between them is a tree and all links point to root elements. In other cases, removal of a small number of links leads to this situation. Figure 3 shows an example for this: If we removed the edge between documents 5 and 4, the resulting graph would form a tree. This opens up two possible configurations of FliX: (1) remove edges until the remaining graph forms a single tree and index it with PPO, or (2) using a greedy algorithm, build partitions of the graph of the documents such that each partition forms a tree, is as large as possible, and the number of partition-crossing edges is small; each partition then forms a meta document that is indexed with PPO.

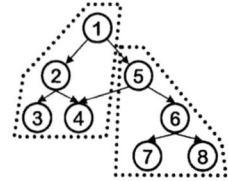

Fig. 3. Efficient partitioning of a document graph that is almost a tree

Unconnected HOPI. In the first step of the divide-and-conquer algorithm to build HOPI [9], partitions of the XML graph are built such that each partition does not exceed a configurable size and the number of partition-crossing edges is small. The second step then builds HOPI indexes for the partitions, and the last step then joins the subindexes to the index for the complete graph. It is straightforward to stop the algorithm after the second step and use the partitions as meta documents. This approach is useful when most documents contain links.

5   Query Execution with FliX

Our index framework is optimized for the descendants-or-self axis used in path expressions of the form a//B [2], i.e., find all successors of element a that are of type B. This includes wildcard queries of the form a//* to find all successors of element a. A special case of this is to decide if two given elements a and b are connected, i.e., evaluating the reachability query a//b, and to determine the length of the shortest path between these elements. It also supports the immediate evaluation of a path expression like A//B where only the type of the starting element is fixed, but slightly less efficiently. The algorithms can be adapted easily for other cases, e.g., to support the child axis as in a/B, or to support the corresponding reverse axes like ancestors-or-self.

5.1   Finding Descendants in Approximate Order

In the Query Execution Phase, the *Path Expression Evaluator (PEE)* computes the answer to reachability or distance queries of type a//B or a//*, for a start element a and some

---

[2] This is an XPath syntax where lower case letters represent fixed elements, upper case letters represent element types, and // represents XPath's descendants-or-self axis.

element type B. To calculate the result of the query, it makes use of the indexes built for the meta documents. The PEE returns a stream of result elements $e_1, e_2, \ldots$ that satisfy the query, approximately ordered by their distance to the start node a.

The PEE maintains a list IE of intermediate elements, ordered by ascending distance to the start element a of the query. The priority of an element in the queue denotes the minimal distance that any descendant of the element may have to the start node a. We denote the distance of two elements u and v by $\text{dist}(u, v)$. IE is initialized with a at priority 0. In the main loop of its algorithm, the PEE picks the first element e from IE and determines the meta document M in which e resides. Using the index for M, the PEE then computes the set R of all elements in M that are reachable from e and satisfy the search condition, sorted by ascending distance to e; the elements of R are returned to the client. Additionally, the set L of elements with outgoing links that are reachable from e is computed using the index for M. This step ignores all links that are already represented in the index for M. For each element $l \in L$, the destination(s) of its outgoing link(s) are then inserted into IE with priority $\text{dist}(a, e) + \text{dist}(e, l) + 1$, and the main loop continues until either IE runs empty or, if the client has specified a distance threshold, if the first entry in the queue has a larger distance than this threshold.

This algorithm does not return the result elements in perfectly ascending distance to a, because it returns the results within a single meta document as one block, regardless of their distance. However, this algorithm maintains a reasonably good approximation by processing the intermediate elements in ascending distance to a.

The maximum time to evaluate a query heavily depends on the selection of the meta documents. In an ideal setting, the MDB will have prepared the meta documents such that processing time is minimized for most queries and only a few queries require many hops across meta documents.

5.2   Evaluation of Other Expressions

Connection Test. Testing if two elements a and b are connected is straight-forward: The priority queue is initialized with a at priority 0, and the algorithm proceeds until finds b. As this may result in a traversal of the complete document collection at worst, the maximal depth of the search should be limited by the client. Because the client uses the length of the path between a and b to compute the relevance of this pair of elements, it can compute a threshold for the path length beyond which the resulting relevance is negligible.

Evaluating A//B Expressions. To evaluate queries like A//B where only the type of the starting element is fixed, only the initial step of the PEE has to be modified: The PEE determines all elements of type A and inserts them into the priority queue with priority 0, then the evaluation algorithm is run.

6   Preliminary Experiments

In this section, we present the results of some preliminary experiments on a small set of data with our current implementation of FliX that has not yet been optimized. Even though these experiments are far from being exhaustive, they strongly indicate the viability of our indexing framework.

We compared our approach to two other indexing strategies: an extended version of HOPI that supports distance information and a database-backed implementation of APEX (without optimizations for frequent queries), both applied to the complete data collection. We tested four configurations of FliX: The naive configuration where a PPO index is built for each document (PPO-naive), a simple implementation of Maximal PPO, and two variants of Unconnected HOPI with partition sizes set to 5,000 (HOPI-5000) and 20,000 nodes (HOPI-20000). We implemented all strategies as multithreaded, Java-based applications.

The data collection used for the experiments was extracted from the DBLP collection. We generated one XML document for each second-level element of DBLP (article,inproceedings,...) and chose the corresponding documents for publications in EDBT, ICDE, SIGMOD and VLDB and articles in TODS and VLDB-Journal. The resulting collection consisted of 6,210 documents with 168,991 elements and 25,368 inter-document links with an overall size of 27 megabytes.

The HOPI index is huge (about 266 MB), but it is still more than an order of magnitude smaller than storing the complete transitive closure. HOPI-20000 requires about 18 MB space, HOPI-5000 requires only about twice as much space as the APEX index (about 2.2 MB), and naive PPO and Maximal PPO are even smaller (about 1.9MB). So using FliX can save a lot of space over the HOPI index, and the Maximal PPO configuration is as space efficient as PPO.

To assess the performance of FliX, we submitted a query to determine the first 100 article descendants of Mohan's VLDB '99 paper about ARIES. HOPI was clearly the fastest to return the results, with an almost constant time of 0.6 seconds. However, the FliX configurations HOPI-5000 and HOPI-20000 outperformed HOPI in the time needed to return the first results, and they clearly improved on APEX by a factor of at least 2. Maximal PPO returned the first results even faster than the other indexes because these results were in the first, large trees MaximalPPO considered, but its performance for later results was not as good because, unlike the unconnected HOPIs, it had to follow many links at run-time. The error rate (i.e., fraction of all results that were returned in wrong order) was 8.2% for HOPI-5000, 10.4% for HOPI-20000, and 13.3% for Maximal PPO, which is tolerable for most applications. Naive PPO was constantly slower than the other indexes, because documents were so small that the quick index lookup per document with PPO could not compensate for the additional overhead of following all links at runtime. Other experiments with different start elements and different tag names showed similar results.

These experimental results have shown that FliX can increase performance of answering descendants or connection queries, at the price of a moderate increase in storage cost and some error in the order of results.

7 Future Work

Our future work will aim to improve FliX in the following regards:

- We plan to investigate more sophisticated algorithms for building meta documents, including automatic methods that analyze the document collection and identify homogeneous subcollections.

- We are looking into further optimizing FliX's query evaluation algorithm, e.g., returning results exactly sorted instead of approximately and eliminating unnecessary link traversals when checking connectivity of two nodes.
- We consider adding self-tuning functionality: If it turns out in the query evaluation engine that most queries have to follow many links, then the choice of meta documents is no longer optimal for the current query load. In this case, meta documents should be rebuilt, taking the query load into account.
- We will carry out additional experiments to test the scalablity of FliX with larger sets of documents and to test the adaptivity of FliX with more heterogeneous document collections.

References

1. C.-W. Chung et al. APEX: An adaptive path index for XML data. In *SIGMOD*, pages 121–132, 2002.
2. E. Cohen et al. Reachability and distance queries via 2-hop labels. In *SODA*, pages 937–946, 2002.
3. B. Cooper et al. A fast index for semistructured data. In *VLDB*, pages 341–350, 2001.
4. R. Goldman and J. Widom. DataGuides: Enabling query formulation and optimization in semistructured databases. In *VLDB*, pages 436–445, 1997.
5. T. Grust. Accelerating XPath location steps. In *SIGMOD*, pages 109–120, 2002.
6. R. Kaushik et al. Covering indexes for branching path queries. In *SIGMOD*, pages 133–144, 2002.
7. C. Qun et al. D(k)-index: An adaptive structural summary for graph-structured data. In *SIGMOD*, pages 134–144, 2003.
8. R. Schenkel, A. Theobald, and G. Weikum. Ontology-enabled XML search. In H. Blanken, T. Grabs, H.-J. Schek, R. Schenkel, and G. Weikum, editors, *Intelligent Search on XML Data*, volume 2818 of *LNCS*, pages 119–131. Sept. 2003.
9. R. Schenkel, A. Theobald, and G. Weikum. HOPI: An efficient connection index for complex XML document collections. In *EDBT*, pages 237–255, 2004.
10. A. Theobald and G. Weikum. Adding Relevance to XML. In *WebDB*, pages 105–124, 2000.
11. A. Theobald and G. Weikum. The index-based XXL search engine for querying XML data with relevance ranking. In *EDBT*, pages 477–495, 2002.

A Statistical Approach for XML Query Size Estimation

Mong Li Lee, Hanyu Li, Wynne Hsu, and Beng Chin Ooi

School of Computing, National University of Singapore
{leeml,lihanyu,whsu,ooibc}@comp.nus.edu.sg

Abstract. The increasing number of XML repositories has intensified research activities in the optimization of XML queries. The success of any optimization approach hinges on an accurate query size estimation. This paper presents a statistical method for estimating the result size of XML queries. Our estimation system extracts two summarized information, namely, node ratio and node factor, from every distinct parent-child path in the XML files. Experiment results indicate that our approach requires small memory footprint, and yet proves to be sufficient in estimating the result size of queries under the data-independent assumption.

1 Introduction

As XML emerges as the standard of data representation and exchange on the Internet, many query languages have been proposed for it. A common feature among XML query languages such as XPath and XQuery is the specification of query patterns in the form of path expressions. Consider the query "$//Article[Title = `XML']/Authors$" that returns all the Authors of Article with title 'XML'. This query pattern can be viewed as a tree structure with Authors as the target node. As in conventional query processing, the estimation of selectivity affects query evaluation plans and query processing costs.

Existing XML query estimators support a limited class of query patterns. Markov based models [5,7] estimate linear path queries since they capture only information on path frequencies. [6] utilizes path frequencies to estimate the size of simple twig queries. In [9], the *position histogram* is used to describe the element distribution and a position histogram join is employed to estimate the query size. This approach does not distinguish between ancestor-descendant and parent-child relationships. [8] propose the *XSketch* framework that utilizes summarized graph structures to estimate queries.

In this work, we develop a comprehensive solution to estimate the result size of general XML query patterns. We extract highly summarized information, namely, node ratio NR and node factor NF from every distinct parent-child basic path. When evaluating an XML query, this statistical information is recursively aggregated to estimate the frequency of the target node. Compared with existing solutions, our method utilizes statistical data that is compact, and yet proves to be sufficient in estimating the result size of queries under the data-independent assumption.

The paper is organized as follows. Section 2 gives a taxonomy of paths in XML queries. Section 3 describes the proposed estimation system. Section 4 gives the experiment results and we conclude in Section 5.

W. Lindner et al. (Eds.): EDBT 2004 Workshops, LNCS 3268, pp. 250–259, 2004.

2   Taxonomy of Paths

This section provides a taxonomy of XML path queries used in the paper.

Linear Path: Given an XML query P, if all the nodes in P are connected sequentially, then P is called a linear path. The relationship between any two adjacent nodes can be an ancestor-descendant or a parent-child relationship.

Basic Path: A linear path with only two nodes is called a basic path.

Twig: If the root node of an XML path P has more than one immediate children nodes, then P is called a twig.

Simple Twig: Given a twig P, if every branch of P is a linear path, then P is known as a simple twig.

General Path: A general path is all the possible combinations of *linear paths* and *twigs*.

Figure 1 illustrates the different query paths. The solid line and dotted line denote the parent-child and ancestor-descendant relationship respectively.

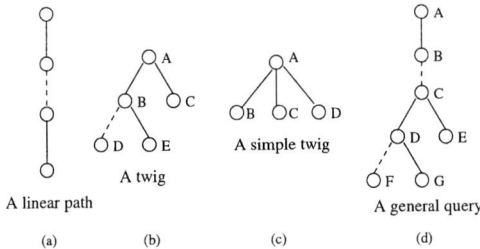

Fig. 1. Examples of path queries

3   Estimation System

This section describes the proposed estimation system. We introduce the statistical information captured in Section 3.1. Section 3.2 discuss several basic methods of aggregating statistical information. Finally we present the algorithm in Section 3.3.

3.1   Summary Statistics

Given a path P in an XML data set X, we denote the root node in the path as R and the target node in P as T. The target node T refers to the node whose size we want to estimate. We define $f(node)$ as the frequency of *node* in X and $f(node|path)$ as the frequency of *node* with respect to *path* in the dataset. For example, in Figure 2, we have $f(C) = 4$ and $f(C|\text{'}A/B/C/D\text{'}) = 2$.

Two important summary variables are captured, namely *Node Ratio* (NR) and *Node Factor* (NF). The variable NR indicates the ratio of the occurrence of a root node R in some path P to the total occurrence of R in an XML dataset, while the variable NF gives the average number of nodes T for a given root node R in a path P.

Definition 1: Node Ratio (NR). Let X be an XML dataset and P a path in X. If R is the root node in P, we define the ratio of the frequency of R in P to the frequency of R in X as the node ratio NR of R in P, which is given by

$$NR(R|P) = f(R|P)/f(R)$$

Definition 2: Node Factor (NF). Let X be an XML dataset and P a path in X. If R and T are the root node and target node in P respectively, then we define the ratio of the frequency of T in P to the frequency of R in P as the node factor NF of T in P. That is,

$$NF(T|P) = f(T|P)/f(R|P)$$

From the above definitions, we obtain

$$f(R|P) = f(R) * NR(R|P); f(T|P) = f(R) * NR(R|P) * NF(T|P)$$

We use the equation above to estimate the query result size. Symbol " $'$ " is adopted to distinguish the estimated result from the actual value, then we have

$$f'(R|P) = f(R) * NR'(R|P); f'(T|P) = f(R) * NR'(R|P) * NF'(T|P) \quad (1)$$

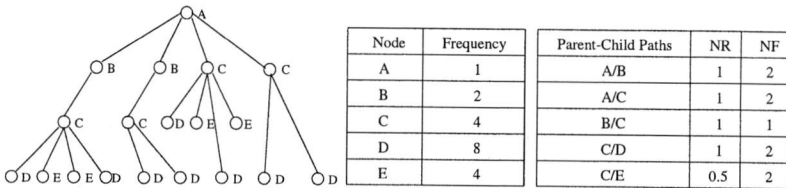

Node	Frequency		Parent-Child Paths	NR	NF
A	1		A/B	1	2
B	2		A/C	1	2
C	4		B/C	1	1
D	8		C/D	1	2
E	4		C/E	0.5	2

Fig. 2. An XML instance and corresponding NR,NF for parent-child paths

We capture the frequency of every distinct name node, the node ratio NR and node factor NF for every distinct basic parent-child path as shown in Figure 2. For parent-child paths, the root node R and the target node T are the parent node and the child node in the path respectively. Note that from the definitions, $NR \leq 1$ and $NF \geq 1$.

Our estimation solution contains two main operations, decomposition and aggregation. The decomposition operation is straightforward, that is, we decompose an given path into a set of basic paths, each of which contains two adjacent nodes in the original query pattern. For example, if we decompose the query shown in Figure 1(b), the basic paths in the result set are 'A/B', '$B//D$', 'B/E' and 'A/C'. The aggregation operation is the key of our estimation method, which computes NR' and NF' of the given query path from all NR and NF of the parent-child basic paths.

3.2   Path Selectivity

Next, we explain how the NR and NF information of basic parent-child paths can be aggregated to estimate the size of the various path queries. The estimation formulae are based on the following assumption.

Basic Path Independent Assumption: The distribution of a basic path b in an XML document is independent of the distribution of its incoming paths and sibling paths.

In Figure 2, the distribution of basic path 'C/D' is independent of its incoming paths, 'B/C' (or '$A/B/C$') and 'A/C'. Similarly, 'C/D' is also independent of its sibling path 'C/E'.

Serialized Linear Paths. Suppose we have two linear paths b_1, b_2 and their corresponding $NR(R_1|b_1)$, $NF(T_1|b_1)$, $NR(R_2|b_2)$ and $NF(T_2|b_2)$, where R_i and T_i are the first and last nodes in path b_i. If the target node T_1 has the same label as that of the node R_2, we can connect these two paths b_1 and b_2 sequentially and eliminate R_2. The result is also a linear path, denoted as $b_1 \cdot b_2$. For example, if $b_1 =$ 'A/B', $b_2 =$ 'B/C', then $b_1 \cdot b_2 =$ '$A/B/C$'.

To calculate $NR'(R_1|b_1 \cdot b_2)$ and $NF'(T_2|b_1 \cdot b_2)$, we first compute $NF'(T_1|b_1 \cdot b_2)$. The value of $NF'(T_1|b_1 \cdot b_2)$ is estimated as $NF(T_1|b_1) * NR(R_2|b_2)$. From the definition of NR and NF, the accurate value of $NF(T_1|b_1 \cdot b_2)$ should be $NF(T_1|b_1) * (f(T_1|b_1 \cdot b_2) / f(T_1|b_1))$. Taking into consideration the Basic Path Independent Assumption, we use $(f(T_1|b_2)/f(T_1))$, which is $NR(R_2|b_2)$, to replace $(f(T_1|b_1 \cdot b_2)/f(T_1|b_1))$.

We will use two examples in Figure 2 to explain how to obtain $NR'(R_1|b_1 \cdot b_2)$ and $NF'(T_2|b_1 \cdot b_2)$.

Example 1: Estimate $f'(D|'B/C/D')$.
We have $NF'(C|'B/C/D') = NF'(C|'B/C') * NR'(C|'C/D') = 1$.
Here, the purpose of $NR'(C|'C/D')$ is to filter out those elements C which are under B but do not contain D. If the result $NF'(C|'B/C/D')$ is greater than or equal to 1 (as shown in this case), then $f(C|'/B/C/D')$ is greater than or equal to $f(B|'B/C/D'')$. Assuming that C is uniformly distributed under B, we can deduce that $f(B|'/B/C/D')$ should remain unchanged as $f(B|'/B/C')$. As a result, we set $NR'(B|'B/C/D') = NR'(B|'B/C')$.
Similarly, $NF'(D|'B/C/D') = NF'(C|'B/C/D') * NF'(D|'C/D')$.
Note that $NR'(B|'B/C/D') = 1$ and $NF'(D|'B/C/D') = 2$.
Finally, we have $f'(B|'B/C/D') = f(B) * NR'(B|'B/C/D') = 2$ and
$f'(D|'B/C/D') = f(B) * NR'(B|'B/C/D') * NF'(D|'B/C/D') = 4$.

Example 2: Estimate $f'(E|'B/C/E')$.
We have $NF'(C|'B/C/E') = NF'(C|'B/C') * NR'(C|'C/E') = 0.5$.
In this case, $NF'(C|'B/C/E')$ is less than 1, which violates the definition of NF (the number of target node must be greater than or equal to the number of root node). In this example, $NR'(C|'C/E')$ filters out not only those C under B, but also elements B as shown in Figure 2. To handle this situation, we set
$NR'(B|'B/C/E') = NR'(B|'B/C') * NF'(C|'B/C/E')$ and $NF'(C|'B/C/E') = 1$.
This is because we assume that the remaining C elements are uniformly distributed under B. Thus, the number of B should be reserved as many as possible and $NF'(C|'B/C/E')$ must be 1.

Similarly, $NF'(E|'B/C/E') = NF'(C|'B/C/E') * NF(E|'C/E') = NF(E|'C/E')$.
Finally we estimate $f'(B|'B/C/E') = f(B) * NR'(B|'B/C/E') = 1$ and
$f'(E|'B/C/E') = f(B)* NR'(B|'B/C/E') * NF'(E|'B/C/E') = 2$.

From the two examples above, we summarize the following formula.

Given two paths b_1 and b_2 where $T_1 = R_2$

$$NF'(T_1|b_1 \cdot b_2) = NF(T_1|b_1) * NR(T_1|b_2)$$
$$if \ (NF'(T_1|b_1 \cdot b_2) \geq 1)$$
$$NR'(R_1|b_1 \cdot b_2) = NR'(R_1|b_1)$$
$$NF'(T_2|b_1 \cdot b_2) = NF'(T_1|b_1 \cdot b_2) * NF(T_2|b_2) \qquad (2)$$
$$else$$
$$NR'(R_1|b_1 \cdot b_2) = NR'(R_1|b_1) * NF'(T_1|b_1 \cdot b_2)$$
$$NF'(T_2|b_1 \cdot b_2) = NF(T_2|b_2)$$

Similarly, we can sequentially connect more than two linear paths and compute corresponding NR and NF. Consider the scenario that P_i is composed by $b_1 \cdot b_2 \cdot b_3 \ldots \cdot b_i$ with the corresponding $f(R_i)$, $NR(R_i|b_i)$ and $NF(T_i|b_i)$. We first calculate $NR'(R_1|P_2)$ and $NF'(T_2|P_2)$, then in turn compute the next NR' and NF' until we reach $NR'(R_1|P_i)$ and $NF'(T_i|P_i)$. In practice, if the linear path b_i contains more than two nodes, it would be decomposed into a set of basic paths which hold only two nodes. The NRs and NFs of parent-child paths can be directly retrieved from the estimation system. The processing of ancestor-descendant paths are discussed later in this section.

Parallelized Linear Paths. Given a set of linear paths $l_i, (1 \leq i \leq n)$ and the corresponding $NR(R_i|l_i)$, where R_i is the first node in path l_i, if $R_i = R_j = R(i \neq j; 1 \leq i, j \leq n)$, we can combine all the l_i into a simple twig where R is the root node and every l_i is a branch. For example, the simple twig in Figure 1 is constructed from linear paths 'A/B', 'A/C' and 'A/D'.

There are two possible relationships among the branches in the path obtained: intersection and union. In the case of intersection, we need to estimate the size of R that appear in all the l_i. Otherwise, the path condition is satisfied if R is the root node of any one of the l_i. We denote the intersection and union associations in the paths as $l_1 \cap l_2 \ldots \cap l_n$ and $l_1 \cup l_2 \ldots \cup l_n$ respectively.

If P is given by $l_1 \cap l_2 \ldots \cap l_n$, then the node ratio $NR'(R|P)$ is computed from the intersection of all l_i:

$$NR'(R|P) = \prod_{i=1}^{n} NR(R|l_i) \qquad (3)$$

On the other hand, suppose P is given by $l_1 \cup l_2 \ldots \cup l_n$. Given the values of the corresponding node ratios $NR(R|l_i)$ where R is the root node of P, we have the following formula that is based on set theory.

$$NR'(R|P) = \sum_{i=1}^{n} NR(R|l_i) - \sum NR(R|l_{i_1})NR(R|l_{i_2}) + \ldots +$$
$$(-1)^{(k-1)} \sum NR(R|l_{i_1})NR(R|l_{i_2})\ldots NR(R|l_{i_k}) \qquad (4)$$
$$(1 \leq i_1, i_2 \ldots i_k \leq n; i_a \neq i_b \ where \ a \neq b)$$

Ancestor-Descendant Basic Paths. Next, we compute the NR' and NF' of an ancestor-descendant basic path. Suppose we issue the query '$A//C$' over the XML instance in Figure 2. The result of this query is the union of the results of linear path queries '$A/B/C$'$\cup$'A/C'. The NR' and NF' of these linear paths can be determined as described before. Note that the path '$A/B/C$' and 'A/C' are obtained by searching the table shown in Figure 2. Since we combine all the possible paths, our solution cannot process recursive XML instance.

Let s and l_i denote an ancestor-descendant basic path and linear paths that comprises s respectively. Let R and T be the parent and child nodes in s. Then we can use Formula 4 to estimate $NR'(R|s)$ since it essentially is a union case. $f'(T|s)$ is a summary of $f'(T|l_i)$ which can be computed by

$$f'(T|s) = f(R) * \sum_{i=1}^{n} (NR'(R|l_i) * NF'(T|l_i))$$

$NF'(T|s)$ is equivalent to $f'(T|s)/f'(R|s)$ and $f'(R|s)$ is equal to $f(R) * NR'(R|s)$, then we have

$$NF'(T|s) = \frac{\sum_{i=1}^{n} (NR'(R|l_i) * NF'(T|l_i))}{NR'(R|s)} \tag{5}$$

General Paths. A general path query typically has two structures: a twig, and a linear path followed by a twig (see Figure 1(b) and (d)).

A set of general paths $g_i (1 \le i \le n)$ that have the same root node R can be parallelized into a larger general path (or a twig) as shown in Figure 1(b). Using the Formula 3 or 4, we can easily compute $NR'(R|G)$ as parallelizing linear paths.

Suppose we have a linear path L, a general path G and the corresponding $NR'(R_L|L)$, $NF'(T|L)$ and $NR'(R_G|G)$ where T is the last node in L, T and R_G have same label, we can join L with G at node T. The resulting path, denoted by $L \cdot G$, is a general path with the structure as shown in Figure 1(d). Formula 2 can be employed to estimate the size of T in such a general path by computing $NR'(R_L|L \cdot G)$ and $NF'(T|L \cdot G)$. The reason is similar to serializing linear paths.

3.3 Estimation Algorithm

Based on the summary statistics and the various methods to aggregate them, we develop an algorithm to estimate the frequency of a target node in a given general path query. Our generalized estimation technique (see Algorithm 1) employs a bottom-up approach to compute the NR' and NF' of the nodes, before calculating the node frequency in a top-down manner. This essentially implies that we first decompose a general query tree pattern into a set of basic parent-child paths, then recursively aggregating the NR' and NF' information using the methods described in Section 3.2.

Algorithm 1 calls a function $PathStat$ which returns an object containing the values of NR' and NF'. Suppose P is a general path query with root node $Root$ and target node TG. We call the path from $Root$ to TG the *primary path*. The variable $NF'list$, initially set to empty, stores the NF' values of the sub-paths in the primary path.

Lines 2-5 in $PathStat$ checks whether TG is contained in the trunk of the current path p. If it is, we decompose p into a linear path l' (the path from R to TG), and a general path g' (the subtree rooted at TG). In order to obtain $NR'(R|p)$ and $NF'(TG|p)$, we recursively call $PathStat$ to determine the NR' and NF' of l' and g' respectively. A special case occurs when p is a linear path and TG is the last node in p, then g' is a single node. Note that this part is only executed once.

In Lines 6-24, p may be decomposed or instantiated into a set of sub-paths depending on its type. To compute the NR' and NF' of p, it is necessary to know the NR' and NF' of its sub-paths. Hence, $PathStat$ is invoked recursively to determine the NR' and NF' of every sub-path until a parent-child basic path or a single node is reached. The NR' and NF' of every sub-path is then aggregated to obtain the final result size. Note that only the NF' of nodes that occur in the primary path will be stored (lines 22-23) since the rest of the NF' information does not contribute to the final frequency estimation.

Algorithm 1 Estimate Query Result Size

Input: path P, target node TG;   **Output**: frequency count $f'(TG|P)$

1: Initialize $NF'list = \{\}$, $cursor = 0$
2: $s_P = PathStat(P)$,
3: $f'(TG|P) = f(Root) * s_P.NR' * \prod\limits_{i=0}^{cursor} e_i (e_i \in NF'list)$

Function $PathStat(p)$

1: Let R be the root node in p, and T be the last node of p if p is a linear Path
2: **if** $isLinearGenearal(p)$ and TG in linear part **then**
3:    Let l' be the linear path from R to TG, g' be the general path rooted from TG
4:    $s_p.NR' = NR'(R|l' \cdot g')$, $s_p.NF' = NF'(TG|l' \cdot g')$
5:    $e_0 = s_p.NF'$; return s_p
6: **if** $isNode(p)$ **then**
7:    $s_p.NR' = 1$, $s_p.NF' = 1$; return s_p
8: **if** $isParentChild(p)$ **then**
9:    $s_p.NR' = NR(p)$, $s_p.NF' = NF(p)$; return s_p
10: **if** $isAncestorDescendant(p)$ **then**
11:    Instantiate p into a set of $l_i (1 \leq i \leq n)$
12:    $s_p.NR' = NR'(R|l_1 \cup l_2 \cup ...l_n)$, $s_p.NF' = NF'(T|l_1 \cup l_2 \cup ...l_n)$; return s_p
13: **if** $isLinear(p)$ **then**
14:    Decompose P into a set of basic path $b_i (1 \leq i \leq n)$
15:    $s_p.NR' = NR'(R|b_1 \cdot b_2 \cdot ...b_n)$, $s_p.NF' = NF'(T|b_1 \cdot b_2 \cdot ...b_n)$; return s_p
16: **if** $isTwig(p)$ **then**
17:    Decompose P into a set of general path $g_i (1 \leq i \leq n)$, every branch of P is a g_i
18:    $s_p.NR' = NR'(R|g_1 \cap ...g_n)$(or $\cup$), $s_p.NF' = null$; return s_p
19: **if** $isLinearTwig(p)$ **then**
20:    Let l and t be the linear and twig parts of p. Let C be the common node.
21:    $s_p.NR' = NR'(R|l \cdot t)$, $s_p.NF' = (C|l \cdot t)$
22:    **if** $inPrimaryPath(C)$ **then**
23:       $cursor + +$, $e_{cursor} = s_p.NF'$
24:    return s_p

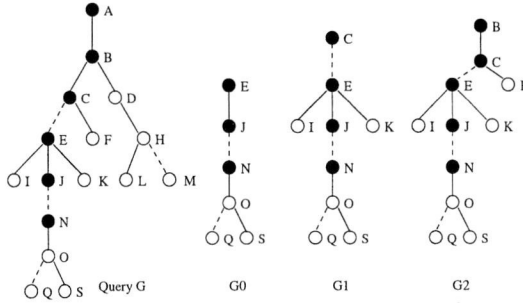

Fig. 3. Estimating the frequency of N in G

Consider the general query G in Figure 3. If N is the target node, then the path from A to N is the primary path (indicated by the shaded nodes in G). Since N does not lie in the linear portion of G, which is 'A/B', we recursively decompose G until we obtain the path G_0. We store $e_0 = NF'(N|G_0)$ in the $NF'list$. On backtracking, we will encounter path G_1 that comprises of a linear path and a twig, which have node E in common. Since E lies in the primary path, we store node $e_1 = NF'(E|G_1)$. Similarly, we will put $e_2 = NF'(C|G_2)$ and $e_3 = NF'(B|G)$ in the $NF'list$. Finally, the e_i in the $NF'list$ are used to compute the frequency of node N in G.

4   Experimental Studies

In this section, we examine the accuracy of the proposed estimation approach on both real-world and synthetic datasets. Our method are implemented in Java and the experiments are carried out on a Pentium IV 1.6 GHz PC with 512 MB RAM running on Windows XP.

The datasets used are IMDB [1], Shakespeare's Plays (SSPlays) [2], DBLP [3] and XMark20 generated by XMark [4]. The synthetic dataset XMark20 is more skewed compared to the real datasets. Table 1 gives the characteristics of the various datasets.

Table 1. Characteristics of datasets

Dataset	Size (MB)	♯(Distinct Nodes)	♯(Distinct Paths)	Memory Usage for Statistics
IMDB	1	12	11	0.23KB
SSPlays	7.5	21	38	0.63KB
DBLP	22	26	35	0.63KB
XMark20	20	83	114	2.04KB

When implementing our proposed method, we encode every distinct node and distinct path. Thus, the total memory usage is given by

$$MemoryUsage = \sharp DistinctNodes * 8 + \sharp DistinctPaths * 12$$

where 8 bytes are used to represent the node ID and frequency, and 12 bytes are used to represent the path ID, NR, and NF.

4.1 Sensitivity Experiments

This set of experiments investigates the accuracy of positive queries. We generate 12 positive queries on both real and synthetic datasets. These queries comprise of parent-child linear queries, ancestor-descendant linear queries, parent-child twigs. The query size (number of nodes) varies from 2 to 5, and the relative error is employed to measure the estimation accuracy. Table 2 shows the performance of using the proposed compact statistical information to estimate positive queries.

Table 2. Error rates for positive queries

Queries	Dataset	Estimated size	Actual size	Error
//Play/Act/Prologue/Speech	SSPlays	12	12	0
//Play/Act[Epilogue/Stagedir]/Title	SSPlays	5	4	25.0%
//Play//Scene	SSPlays	750	750	0
//Play/Personae[Pgroup]/Title	SSPlays	33	33	0
//Movie/Directed_By/Director	IMDB	520	520	0
//Cast/Actor/LastName	IMDB	6886	6886	0
//Movie//Genre	IMDB	1475	1475	0
//Proceedings//Editor	DBLP	1892	1892	0
//Dblp/Inproceedings/Title	DBLP	58077	58077	0
//Australia/Item/Description/Text	XMark20	310	315	1.6%
//Open_auction/Annotation//Listitem	XMark20	2052	2148	4.5%
//Listitem/Text/Emph[Keyword]/Bold	XMark20	15	41	63.4%

Overall, the memory usage for the statistical information is low (see Table 1), and the error rates for the queries on real-life datasets (SSPplays, IMDB, DBLP) are within acceptable range since these data are typically uniformly distributed. The error rate for the synthetic dataset (XMark20) is considerably higher since the dataset is much more skewed compared to the real-life datasets.

4.2 Comparative Experiments

We also implement *XSketch* [8] using f-stabilize method and evaluate its accuracy and memory usage with our method. 50 positive queries are generated on IMDB, SSPlays and XMark20 respectively using the template described in [8], i.e., queries with linear branches, and the target node is the leaf node. Only parent-child relationship is used here. The length of the query path ranges from 3 to 12 nodes.

Figure 4 shows the memory usage and average relative error of the two techniques for the various datasets. We observe that both techniques utilize a smaller amount of memory for real-life datasets compared to that required by the synthetic dataset XMark20. This is largely because of the relatively regular structures of the real-life datasets. The uniform data distribution in the real-life datasets also leads to a lower error rate for both methods compared to the synthetic dataset.

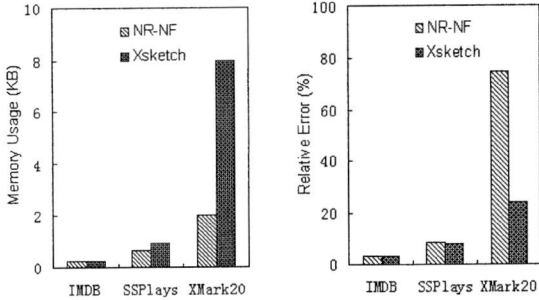

Fig. 4. Comparative experiments

For the synthetic dataset, our approach requires a smaller memory footprint compared to *XSketch*. The latter requires more memory in order to achieve a lower relative error. This is because *XSketch* uses a summarized graph to describe the XML data. For skewed data, it naturally results in higher memory space consumption while yields more accurate estimated results. Given the trade-off between memory usage and estimation accuracy, our approach complements existing techniques.

5   Conclusion

In this paper, we have presented a comprehensive solution to estimate the result size of a general XML query. Our system captures highly concise information, NR and NF, for every distinct parent-child path in an XML dataset. We have described how the statistical information can be aggregated to estimate XML query sizes. Experiments on both real and synthetic data sets indicate that our proposed method is able to achieve reasonably low error rates with a small amount of memory. In future work, we plan to investigate the usage of the proposed estimator in XML query optimization systems.

References

1. http://www.imdb.com.
2. http://www.ibiblio.org/xml/examples/shakespeare.
3. http://www.informatik.uni-trier.de/ ley/db/.
4. http://monetdb.cwi.nl/.
5. A. Aboulnaga, A. R. Alameldeen, and J. F. Naughton. Estimating the Selectivity of XML Path Expressions for internet Scale Applications. In *VLDB*, 2001.
6. Z. Chen, H. V. Jagadish, F. Korn, and N. Koudas. Counting Twig Matches in a Tree. In *ICDE*, 2001.
7. L. Lim, M. Wang, S. Padmanabhan, J. S. Vitter, and R. Parr. XPathLearner: An On-Line Self-Tuning Markov Histogram for XML Path Selectivity Estimation. In *VLDB*, 2002.
8. N. Polyzotis and M. Garofalakis. Statistical Synopses for Graph-Structured XML Database. In *SIGMOD*, 2002.
9. Y. Wu, J. M. Patel, and H. V. Jagadish. Estimating Answer Sizes for XML Queries. In *EDBT*, 2002.

Summarizing XML Data
by Means of Association Rules

Elena Baralis[1], Paolo Garza[1], Elisa Quintarelli[2], and Letizia Tanca[2]

[1] Dip. di Automatica e Informatica,
Politecnico di Torino (Italy)
Corso Duca degli Abruzzi, 24 — 10129 Torino (Italy)
{baralis,garza}@polito.it
[2] Dip. di Elettronica e Informazione,
Politecnico di Milano (Italy)
Piazza Leonardo da Vinci, 32 — 20133 Milano (Italy)
{quintare,tanca}@elet.polimi.it

Abstract. XML is a rather verbose representation of semistructured data, which may require huge amounts of storage space. We propose several summarized representations of XML data, which can both provide succinct information and be directly queried. These representations are based on the extraction of association rules from XML datasets.

Keywords: Semistructured Data, Data Mining, Association Rules, Intensional Answers

1 Introduction

The eXtensible Markup Language (XML) [21] was initially proposed as a standard way to represent, exchange and publish information on the Web, but its usage has recently spread to many other application fields (e.g. for publishing legacy data, for storing data that cannot be represented with traditional data models and for ensuring interoperability among software systems).

However, XML is a rather verbose representation of data, which may require huge amounts of storage space. We propose several summarized representations of XML data, which can both provide succinct information and be directly queried. In particular, we propose *patterns* as abstract representations of the constraints that hold on the data, and their use for (possibly partially) answering queries, either when fast (and approximate) answers are required, or when the actual dataset is not available, e.g., it is currently unreachable. In this last case the service of a "semantic" proxy, which caches patterns instead of actual data pages, can be provided. In this paper we focus on *instance patterns* which represent actual data summaries.

Our summarized representations are based on the extraction of association rules from XML datasets. Association rules describe the co-occurrence of data items in a large amount of collected data [1]. Rules are usually represented as implications in the form $X \Rightarrow Y$, where X and Y are two arbitrary sets of data items, such that $X \cap Y = \emptyset$.

W. Lindner et al. (Eds.): EDBT 2004 Workshops, LNCS 3268, pp. 260–269, 2004.

In our framework, a data item is a pair *(data-element,value)*, e.g. (Author,Smith). The quality of an association rule is usually measured by means of support and confidence. Support corresponds to the frequency of the set $X \cup Y$ in the dataset, while confidence corresponds to the conditional probability of finding Y, having found X and is given by $sup(X \cup Y)/sup(X)$. Association rule mining is a well-known problem, extensively dealt with (see, e.g., [1, 12]), and we do not address it in this paper.

Once rule extraction has been performed, an intuitive and effective language is needed both to represent and query the extracted knowledge. In this work, we extend the graphical graph-based XML query language GSL [8], with the twofold aim to represent in an intuitive way both summarized information (i.e., patterns), and queries over it. Graphical query expressions in GSL can be easily translated into X-Query expressions [3].

Patterns can be exploited to provide intensional query answering. An intentional answer to a query substitutes the actual data answering the query (the extensional answer) with a set of properties characterizing them [17]. Thus, our intensional answers are in general more synthetic than the extensional ones, but usually approximate.

The paper is organized as follows. Section 2 introduces the different types of patterns we propose and describes how we represent them in our graph-based language. In Section 3 we propose an approach to provide intensional answers to user queries, as well as optimization possibilities for ordinary query processing. Section 4 shows some preliminary experimental results on pattern extraction from XML data. Previous work is discussed in Section 5, while conclusions and possible lines for future work are presented in Section 6.

2   Pattern Based Representations of an XML Dataset

Patterns are classified in two orthogonal ways. The first type of classification refers to the accuracy with which the pattern represents the dataset.

— An *exact* pattern expresses a property which holds on *any* instance of the dataset. Thus exact patterns represent *constraints* (e.g. functional dependencies between schema elements by means of schema patterns).
— A *probabilistic* pattern holds only on a given (large) fraction of the instances in the dataset. It is a weak constraint on the dataset, characterized by a quality index describing its reliability.

The second classification dimension corresponds to the different level of detail (i.e., summarization level) of the represented information. In particular:

Schema patterns are expressed on the structure of the dataset. They are used to describe general properties of the schema, which apply to all instances. A schema pattern may be derived as an abstraction of a set of association rules, all relating the same elements. Because of space constraints, we do not consider schema patterns in this work.

Domain patterns express constraints on the values of the instances of a dataset. For example, domain constraints restrict the admissible values of a given element.

Instance patterns are expressed on the instances of the dataset. In particular, in this paper they are used to summarize the content of a dataset by means of the most relevant (frequent) association rules holding on the dataset. We use them to derive an approximate answer to a query, without requiring to actually access the dataset to compute the answer. The answer may contain a subset or a superset of the required information, depending on the form of the query and of the considered instance pattern.

2.1   Representing XML Datasets

While plain XML is still used for many applications, the XML standard data model, called *Infoset* [20], is gaining a wide diffusion. It represents both XML schemata and documents as *multi-sorted trees*, i.e. trees including nodes (called *information items*) belonging to a variety of types. In other words, an XML document's information set consists of a number of information items; the information set for any well-formed XML document will contain at least a document information item (the root of the tree) and several others. An information item is an abstract description of some parts of an XML document: each information item has a set of associated *properties*[1]. In particular, in this work we consider the *element-only* Infoset content model, which allows an XML nonterminal tag to include only other elements and/or attributes, while the text is confined to terminal elements. Furthermore, without loss of generality, we do not consider some features of the Infoset that are not relevant to the present work, such as namespaces, the ordering label, the referencing formalism through ID-IDREF attributes, URIs, and Links.

Following the Infoset conventions, we represent an XML document by a labeled tree[2] $\langle N, E, r \rangle$ where N is the set of nodes, $r \in N$ is the root of the tree (i.e. the root of the XML document), E is the set of edges. Moreover, the following properties on nodes and edges hold: **1)** Each node n_i has a tuple of labels $NL_i = \langle Ntag_i, Ntype_i, Ncontent_i \rangle$; the type label $Ntype_i$ indicates whether the node is the root, an element, text, or attribute[3], whereas the label $Ncontent_i$ can assume as value a PCDATA or $\perp$ (undefined, for nonterminals). **2)** Each edge $e_j = \langle (n_h, n_k), EL_j \rangle$, with n_h and n_k in N, has a label $EL_j = \langle Etype_j \rangle$, $Etype_j \in \{attribute\ of, sub\text{-}element\ of\}$. Note that edges represent the "containment" relationship between different items of a XML document, thus edges do not have names.

In this work we are interested in finding relationships among elementary values of XML documents. Thus, we do not distinguish between textual content of leaf elements and value of attributes. As a consequence, in order to draw graphical concepts in a more readable way, we do not report the edge label and the node type label.

The Infoset tree (with the considered labels for nodes and edges) of (a portion of) a well-formed XML document, which will be used as running example in the rest of the paper, is pictorially represented in Fig. 1. The document reports information about

---

[1] In the Infoset specification, property names are shown in square brackets, [thus]. We do not follow this convention in this paper.

[2] Note that XML documents are here tree-like structures (and not generic graphs) because we do not introduce referencing formalism.

[3] XML documents may also contain ENTITY nodes (not unlike macro calls that must be expanded when parsing) or processing instructions or comments. We do not consider such elements in this paper.

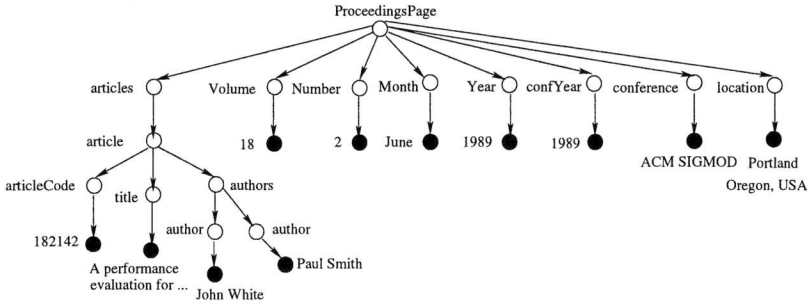

Fig. 1. A simplified labeled tree of a portion of the XML SIGMOD Record document in [15]

Conference Proceedings, based on a slight variation of the SIGMOD Record XML document [15] (e.g., information about abstracts has been added). Attributes and elements are characterized by empty circles, whereas the textual content of elements and the value of attributes is reported as a black-filled circle (denoted as *content node* in the following).

2.2 GSL Language

The graphical representation of XML patterns is based on the syntax of the GSL language [8]. In general, a GSL query is represented by a colored *graph*, which is used to identify the subgraphs (i.e., the portions of a semistructured document) where the query is to be applied, and an optional set of *formulae*[4], representing restrictions imposed on those subgraphs. Queries are represented as graphs with colored nodes and edges. A query is characterized by two colors: *red* (R) specifies positive conditions, while *green* (G) indicates a desired situation in the resulting instance. Using black and white, we represent the R color by thin lines and the G color by thick lines. Informally, an instance satisfies a query if, whenever the red part of the rule query matches (i.e., it is in some way similar to) a part of the instance, the whole query matches it too. Note that at the node level matching corresponds to the well-known concept of *unification* [19].

In general, a GSL query is applied to an instance that does not satisfy it. Query application consists in a change to that instance, so that the query is satisfied by the resulting instance. In other words, query semantics is given as a set of pairs of instances (I, I'), where I' is the result of applying the query to I. For example, the query in Figure 3.(a) requires to find *articles written by the author Paul Smith*. We point out that the green part of the graph (thick line) is used to add to the original XML document an element with tag `result` (for example, a sub-element of the root node) that contains a copy[5] of the subtrees similar to the red part (thin line) of the pattern. As will be seen in the sequel, GSL colored trees are used also to graphically represent patterns.

In order to apply queries to XML trees we need to define a notion of similarity between graphs, to compare trees (or more in general graphs) representing queries to trees

---

[4] We do not discuss this feature further, since we do not exploit it in this paper.

[5] Recall that we use references formalisms in this paper. Thus, since arcs can only represent containment, the *result* tag contains a copy of the required information.

representing document instances. We formalize the concept of similarity between graphs through *bisimulation* [16]. Our choice to use bisimulation for performing the matching between graphs is motivated by the fact that the algorithm for testing the equivalence (w.r.t. bisimulation) between two labeled graphs has a polynomial time complexity (even for cyclic graphs)[6]. Instead, the Graph Isomorphism problem is NP. These general considerations on complexity must be more specifically applied to our case, where trees, instead of generic graphs, are used. In this case, matching via bisimulation has linear time complexity.

In essence, two labeled graphs are bisimilar (we denote with the symbol $\sim$ the bisimulation relation) iff they contain the same sequential paths. Note that bisimulation is an equivalence relation and though it is implied by graph isomorphism (i.e., two isomorphic.graphs are also bisimilar), it is easy to see that the vice versa does not hold. This is why the pure notion of bisimulation does not help us to give the semantics to queries where conditions on pairs of nodes are included. Thus we need to further refine it by introducing additional conditions: given two labeled graphs G_0 and G_1, we say that b is a *functional bisimulation* or *embedding*[7], denoted by $G_0 \xrightarrow{b} G_1$, iff $G_0 \overset{b}{\sim} G_1$ and the relation b is a function.

Consider an XML tree G and a GSL query Q. Intuitively, G satisfies Q if for any subgraph G_1 of G matching (with respect to $\xrightarrow{b}$) the red part of the query (i.e. the precondition), there is a way to 'complete' G_1 into a subgraph G_3 of G such that the whole query Q (i.e. with the green part) matches G_3.

2.3   Representing Patterns

In this section we adapt the notion of GSL colored tree to represent instance patterns.

Definition 1. *A (probabilistic) instance pattern is a pair $\langle G, c \rangle$, such that: 1) G is a rooted GSL tree; 2)$G_{\{R\}} \neq \emptyset$, $G_{\{G\}} \neq \emptyset$, and the root r of G is in $G_{\{R\}}$; 3)each leaf of G is a content node with a defined content label (i.e. a value); 4)c is the confidence of the instance pattern and $0 < c \leq 1$. Note that when $c = 1$ the instance pattern is exact and c may be omitted.*

For example, the instance pattern in Figure 2.(a) represents an association rule. In the graphical representation we indicate the confidence of the instance pattern on the root of the graph. A more complex instance pattern expressing an association rule with more than one path in the green part of the graph (i.e., in the association rule head), is depicted in Figure 2.(b). Note that here the confidence is associated to the conjunction of the two conditions in the green part (i.e., the consequent) of the instance pattern.

It is also interesting to combine instance patterns and represent them in a compact way (i.e., by a unique GSL tree). When considering instance patterns whose green part is composed by a unique path, we call *index* a colored tree which summarizes a set of instance patterns which differ only in the content node of the green path. For example, in Figure 2.(c) we represent an index summarizing the relationships between the author Paul Smith and the conferences where he published a paper: the new instance pattern

---

[6] See [9] for an algorithm for verifying bisimulation equivalence between graphs.

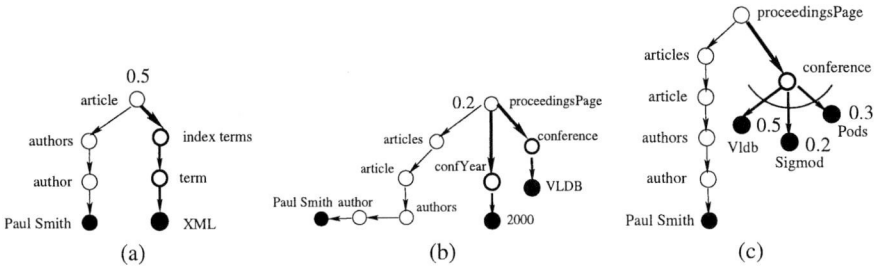

Fig. 2. (a) An instance pattern: *with a confidence* 0.5 *the author Paul Smith is likely to have XML as term in the index terms* (b) A more complex instance pattern: *with a confidence* 0.2 *the author Paul Smith is likely to have a publication to the Conference VLDB 2000* (c) An index that summarizes some similar instance patterns

contains more paths in the consequent, graphically linked by an arc, with each confidence reported on the leaf (note the difference with Figure 2.(b), reporting instead a conjunctive condition in the green part).

In general, instance patterns can have more than one path both in the red and in the green part. This means that multiple elements or attributes are considered simultaneously when extracting association rules.

3   Using Patterns to Answer Queries

Graph-based instance patterns can be used to provide intensional answers to users' queries, i.e., to compute answers without actually accessing XML datasets. The problem of providing intensional answers by means of integrity constraints has been initially addressed in [17] in the relational databases context. In this work we extend the approach to graph-based probabilistic patterns and XML documents.

We consider in this paper only Very Simple Queries (VSQ) composed by a unique green node with an outgoing green edge pointing to a red tree. The green node (usually an XML element) yields as query result a node containing as sub-elements the subtrees of the original XML document satisfying the query (see Figure 3.(a) for an example of this kind of query).

In this work we give only the intuitive idea of the semantics of queries when applied to patterns; applying queries to patterns has the effect of producing other patterns, which represent a summarized description of the resulting instance. In the case of instance patterns the resulting pattern corresponds to (a fraction of) the actual data instances.

We now show how intensional answers are actually provided by means of several examples. Consider the instance pattern included in the index of Figure 2.(c) specifying that, with a confidence of 0.5, the author Paul Smith published a paper to VLDB Conference. If we consider Query 3.(a) asking for all proceedings pages of Paul Smith, we can answer that with a confidence of 0.5 (i.e. 50% of Paul Smith's publications) Paul Smith published in VLDB conference (the query matches with the red part of the instance pattern in Fig.2(a)). If we consider the index in Figure 2.(c) (reporting for the author Paul Smith the conferences where he published), we provide a partial (but more

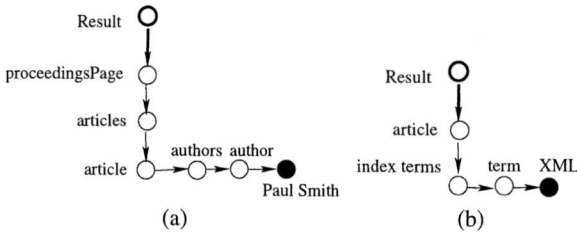

Fig. 3. (a) A query: *find information on the author Paul Smith* (b) A query: *find information about the article with XML in the index terms*

complete) answer to Query 3.(a). The answer may be partial because instance patterns are extracted enforcing support and confidence thresholds.

Consider now Query 3.(b) asking for information about articles with the keyword XML in the index terms. If we exploit the instance pattern of Figure 2.(a)), a (partial) answer is that the author Paul Smith (with probability 1) published on the XML topic (note that here the query matches the green part of the instance pattern in Figure 2.(a)). The reliability value tells us that in Smith's publications the term XML has a probability of occurrence of 0.5 (w.r.t. all others possible terms).

In the first case, where the query matches the red part of the instance pattern, we obtain an answer that has the meaning of an implication. In the second case, where the query matches the green part of the instance pattern, the answer is a set of items, each with its own reliability value.

4   Preliminary Experiments

Proposed algorithms for mining association rules (e.g., [1, 12]) consider a collection of transactions, each containing a set of items. In our framework, to define the concept of transaction, we select as *transaction root* the appropriate node in the labeled graph representing the structure of the XML document. A transaction can now be defined as a collection of pairs *(data-element,value)*. *Data-element* is the label of an element with a content rooted in the transaction root and defined as a complete sub-path from the transaction root to the element. *Value* is the content of the considered element. For example, in our experiments on the SIGMOD Record XML document, each transaction is associated to an article, and includes all the pairs (data-element,value) which characterize it (e.g., (authors/author,Paul Smith), (indexterms/term,XML), etc.).

The *(data-element,value)* representation for data items yields a single item when the XML element contains a single data value. When instead the XML element has a textual content, in principle, each word of the text, coupled with the element label, can yield a data item. In practice, before transformation into data items, textual elements are subject to stopword elimination (i.e., elimination of very frequent and "useless" words such as articles) and stemming (i.e., reduction of words to their semantic stem) [18]. Both operations are commonly performed in textual data management.

In this section we analyze the result of extracting instance patterns from the XML SIGMOD Record collection in Section 4.1. However, since the approach is general and applicable also to structured data, to further characterize instance and schema patterns, we have also considered a small collection of structured datasets (see [4]). In this work, we restrict our experiments to patterns with a single element both in the red and in green part. Hence, we adopted for association rule extraction the levelwise approach of Apriori [1][7].

4.1   SIGMOD Record Dataset

In the SIGMOD Record dataset, all instance patterns have been extracted, without enforcing any support threshold and using the article element as transaction root element.

Table 1. Number of instance patterns for the SIGMOD Record dataset

Min. Supp.	Size (KB)	Num. of instance patterns	Extraction time
20%	76	2390	0.21s
10%	260	8424	0.53s
5%	932	30634	1.21s
0%	70000	2497958	43.18s

To analyze the degree of compression obtained by the instance pattern representation, we compare the size of the original dataset (764KB) with the size of the pattern set. Table 1 shows the number of instance patterns, the size in KB of the instance pattern set and the extraction time, for different values of minimum support threshold. Any support threshold above 10% yields a pattern set that provides a good compact representation of the original dataset, while lower support values yield an excessively detailed summarization. However, instance patterns with a support greater than 10% should be able to answer to a wide range of questions, because each pattern represents summarized information holding on at least 10% of the articles.

5   Previous Work

Several papers [5, 6, 10, 11] address the problem of defining constraints for XML data. In [6] it is argued that, analogously to traditional databases, also XML data need a formal definition of constraints, and an effort to define the most important categories of constraints for XML data is performed. In particular path constraints, keys and foreign keys are considered. [5] proposes a deeper analysis of the definition of absolute and relative keys and describes a new key constraint language for XML, which can handle keys with a complex structure.

In [11], adopting the key definition proposed in [5], a technique is proposed to obtain a compact set of keys from an XML document. In particular only a minimal set of keys is mined, representative keys. To identify representative keys, two interest measures similar

---

[7] Only two scans of the dataset are needed for the extraction of itemsets composed by at most two items.

to support and confidence are associated to a key, and precise (confidence=100%) and valid (confidence $\geq$ 95%) keys are mined.

The discovery of functional dependencies in XML documents is still an open problem. [2, 14] have devoted some efforts to the definition of XML functional dependencies, but, to the best of our knowledge, automatic extraction of XML functional dependencies from an XML corpus has not been addressed. On the other hand, discovery of functional dependencies from relational databases has been extensively explored (e.g., [13]), but these techniques cannot be straightforwardly applied to XML documents.

6   Conclusions and Future Work

In this work we have described a graph-based formalism for specifying instance patterns on XML documents and we have shown how to exploit patterns to provide intensional answers to user queries. We have also performed a preliminary experimental evaluation of the characteristics of the proposed patterns, which yield positive results.

As an ongoing work we are studying how to combine constraints and association rules to improve the precision of intensional answers. We are also considering extensions of our language to deal with more complex queries and patterns (e.g., containing negative information and multiple paths both in the red and green part).

References

1. R. Agrawal and R. Srikant. Fast algorithm for mining association rules. In *Proceeding of VLDB'94*, 1994.
2. M. Arenas and L. Libkin. A normal form for xml documents. *ACM TODS*, 2002.
3. E. Augurusa, D. Braga, A. Campi, and S. Ceri. Design and implementation of a graphical interface to xquery. In *SAC'03*, 2003.
4. E. Baralis, P. Garza, E. Quintarelli, and L. Tanca. Answering Queries on XML Data by means of Association Rules. Technical Report 2004.3, Politecnico di Milano. http://www.elet.polimi.it/upload/quintare/Papers/BGQT-RR.ps.
5. P. Buneman, S. Davidson, W. Fan, C. Hara, and W. Tan. Reasoning about keys for XML. In *DBLP'01*, 2001.
6. P. Buneman, W. Fan, J. Siméon, and S. Weinstein. Constraints for semistructured data and XML. *ACM SIGMOD Record*, 30(1):47–54, 2001.
7. A. Cortesi, A. Dovier, E. Quintarelli, and L. Tanca. Operational and Abstract Semantics of a Query Language for Semi–Structured Information. *Theoretical Computer Science*, 275(1–2):521–560, 2002.
8. E. Damiani, B. Oliboni, E. Quintarelli, and L. Tanca. Modeling Semistructured Data by using graph-based constraints. Technical Report 27/03, Politecnico di Milano. Dipartimento di Elettronica e Informazione, July 2003.
9. A. Dovier, C. Piazza, and A. Policriti. An efficient algorithm for computing bisimulation equivalence. *To appear in Theoretical Computer Science*.
10. W. Fan and L. Libkin. On XML integrity constraints in the presence of DTDs. In *Symposium on Principles of Database Systems*, 2001.
11. G. Grahne and J. Zhu. Discovering approximate keys in XML data. In *Proceedings of CIKM'02*, pages 453–460. ACM Press, 2002.

12. J. Han, J. Pei, and Y. Yin. Mining frequent patterns without candidate generation. In *Proceeding of SIGMOD'00*, 2000.
13. Y. Huhtala, J. Kärkkäinen, P. Porkka, and H. Toivonen. TANE: An efficient algorithm for discovering functional and approximate dependencies. *The Computer Journal*, 42(2):100–111, 1999.
14. M.L. Lee, T.W. Ling, and W. L. Low. Designing functional dependencies for xml. In *EDBT*, 2002.
15. P. Merialdo. SIGMOD RECORD in XML, 2003. http://www.acm.org/sigmod/record/xml.
16. R. Milner. A Calculus of Communicating System. In *Lecture Notes in Computer Science*, volume 92. Springer-Verlag, Berlin, 1980.
17. A. Motro. Using Integrity Constraints to Provide Intensional Answers to Relational Queries. In *In Proceedings of VLDB'89*, pages 237–245. Morgan Kaufmann, 1989.
18. M. F. Porter. *An algorithm for suffix stripping*. Program, 1980.
19. J. Staples and P. J. Robinson. Unification of quantified terms. In Robert M. Keller Joseph H. Fasel, editor, *Proceedings of a Workshop on Graph Reduction*, volume 279 of *LNCS*, pages 426–450, Sante Fé, NM, 1986. Springer.
20. World Wide Web Consortium. XML Information Set, 2001. http://www.w3C.org/xml-infoset/.
21. World Wide Web Consortium. Extensible Markup Language (XML) 1.0, 1998. http://www.w3C.org/TR/REC-xml/.

Prune XML Before You Search It:
XML Transformations for Query Optimization

Stéphane Bressan[1], Zoé Lacroix[2], Ying Guang Li[1], and Anna Maddalena[3]

[1] National University of Singapore (Singapore)
{steph,liyng}@comp.nus.edu.sg
[2] Arizona State University (USA)
zoe.lacroix@asu.edu
[3] University of Genoa (Italy)
maddalena@disi.unige.it

Abstract. In this paper, we present a query optimization approach for XML document management environments loosely-coupled with the storage system. Our technique is based on two main steps: first, based on the query, input documents are transformed, by pruning parts that are irrelevant with respect to the query; then the query is executed on the pruned documents. An index structure is also provided to further optimize the pruning process. Experimental results show that, by using our pruning strategy, query execution time can be significantly reduced.

1 Introduction

XML documents management requires the usage of specific tools for storing and managing XML documents in an effective and efficient way. To this end, several techniques have been recently developed to store XML documents in native [6] or relational format [12], to index paths [7] or individual document components [9], as well as to process more or less complex XML queries [3]. These techniques can be effectively used by query processors in integrated environments, in which XML documents are first stored in a specific format, then processed according to the indexing and optimization methods developed for the chosen storage format.

Despite this traditional approach, some organizations may not want to disrupt their information management strategy and may not need or wish to store and manage native XML data but rather only process transient XML data received from other organizations. Others may prefer to keep the integrity of the XML document sources as ASCII files to be able to use the numerous and sophisticated existing authoring tools and to avoid the usage of expensive and complex XML-based systems. All these organizations may benefit of the usage of a query processor which is only loosely coupled with the XML storage system.

Loosely coupled processors operate on an internal representation of XML documents and thus leverage neither the XML storage structure nor the possible access methods supported by dedicated XML management systems. Kweelt [11] is an example of such processors. It loads the entire XML document from an external source (e.g. a file, a

W. Lindner et al. (Eds.): EDBT 2004 Workshops, LNCS 3268, pp. 270–279, 2004.

stream, or a database management system), creates a Document Object Model (DOM) representation, and evaluates the query on the DOM, which, usually, is entirely held in main memory, thus preventing the manipulation of large documents. Although a loosely-coupled approach may be less efficient than the one relying on integrated XML data management systems, it exists and is widely used, since it is simple to deploy and quite economical.

To achieve good query performance in loosely-coupled environments and to make them more scalable, an important issue consists in reducing the size of the input documents before querying execution. The basic idea is to cut off (i.e., to prune) parts of the input XML documents that are irrelevant with respect to a query. Input documents are transformed into other documents smaller in size, but equivalent to the input ones with respect to the query to be executed. Thus, query execution over such smaller documents produces the same result than query execution over input ones but is faster.

The pruning operation can be seen as a sort of projection over XML documents. Projection operations have been proposed in several algebras for XML documents, such as, for instance, the TAX algebra [8]. Moreover, a projection strategy for XML documents has been introduced in [10], to support main-memory XQuery evaluation over XML documents.

In this paper, we propose an approach for query optimization in loosely-coupled environments, based on a pruning strategy for XML documents. Under the proposed approach, query processing is performed in two steps: first, based on the query, input documents are transformed on the fly, at query execution time, by pruning document portions that are irrelevant with respect to the query, then the query is executed on the pruned document. Our transformation generates documents equivalent to the original ones with respect to the query to be executed but, since irrelevant parts are cut off, it guarantees better query execution performance. To further optimize the pruning process, an index structure is proposed, corresponding to an inverted index of tag offsets in the source documents, whose directory consists of document DataGuides [7]. We executed several experiments using Kweelt as a testbed for our performance analysis and the XOO7 benchmark [2]. The obtained results show that, by using the proposed index structure and transformations, query execution time can be significantly reduced, even when considering the pruning time as part of the query processing time. Our approach differs from the one presented in [10] in three main aspects. First of all, we introduce a compact representation for XQuery queries, called *structural pattern*, used to guide the pruning process. Moreover, the proposed pruning strategy generates documents that are in general smaller than those generated by the technique in [10], due to the special treatment of nodes for which no content or descendant information is required to answer the query. Finally, the usage of the index structure further improves the pruning performance.

The paper is organized as follows. Section 2 presents a motivating example to clarify the proposed approach. Section 3 introduces the notion of structural pattern, used to identify relevant paths in the query, whereas the pruning strategy is discussed in Section 4. Experimental results are then presented and discussed in Section 5. Finally, Section 6 presents some concluding remarks and outlines future work. Due to space constraints, proofs of the presented results have been omitted (see [1] for additional details).

2 Preliminaries and Motivating Example

In this paper, XML documents are represented as rooted, unordered, and labeled trees where each node corresponds to an element (with attribute and value information associated), and each edge represents a parent-child relationship. Thus, when no otherwise stated, XML documents and XML trees are used as synonymous. For the sake of simplicity, we also assume that an XML dataset corresponds to a single document, eventually generated by adding a dummy root to all the existing documents. We then consider single-block canonical queries in XQuery [4], that is, queries do not containing nested queries in the RETURN clause [8]. Furthermore, although our approach is not limited to this case, the queries we consider are all based on root-to-element path expressions. In the following, Q denotes the set of single-block canonical queries in XQuery and a generic query $q \in Q$ is simply called query.

To explain the approach we propose, consider the XML tree D_1 corresponding to document my.xml, presented in Fig.1 and the following query q:[1]

```
FOR $a IN DOC("my.xml")/A, $g IN $a/B/D/G,
    $h IN $g/N/H, $i IN $g/I
LET $v := DOC("my.xml")/A/V, $e := DOC("my.xml")/A/B/C/E
WHERE $h/@price > avg($e/@price) AND $i/@year > 2000
RETURN $h
```

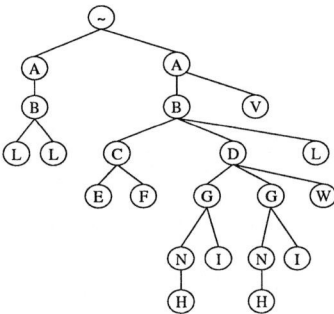

Fig. 1. XML tree of document my.xml

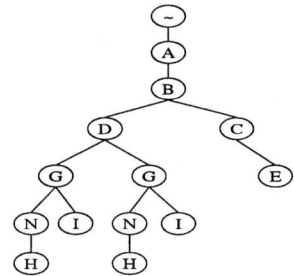

Fig. 2. XML tree of document D2

To execute q against $D1$, the basic idea of our approach is to transform $D1$ into a new tree $D2$ such that: (i) the results of the evaluation of q against $D1$ and $D2$ coincide; in this case, we say that D_1 and D_2 are *query equivalent* with respect to q; (ii) $D2$ is *smaller* in size than $D1$, i.e., it has been obtained from $D1$ by pruning parts of the document that are not needed to answer q.

The XML tree in Fig.2 corresponds to a document satisfying these requirements. Indeed: (i) D1 and D2 differ only on elements not involved in the query. For instance, $D2$ does not contain nodes V, L, F and W since they are not mentioned in q; moreover it contains only once nodes for which no attribute or content information is checked in

---

[1] A node labeled with ˜ represents the XML document root.

q (i.e., A, B, and C); (ii) D2 is smaller in size than D1 (it contains less nodes). As a consequence, executing q against $D2$ takes less time but it generates the same result than against $D1$. We refer to $D2$ as the *image* of $D1$ with respect to q.

In the following, we first introduce a tree-based representation of a query q, that we call *structural pattern*, which will simplify the definition of our pruning strategy. In general, we are interested in pruning transformations such that, given an XML document D and a query q, the time to generate the image I of D with respect to q plus the time to execute q against I is lower than executing q against D. This property is not theoretically guarantee by the proposed transformation. However, we introduce an index structure, supporting the pruning process, and we show that quite often this result is experimentally achieved.

3   XML Query Representation

A *structural pattern* is a tree representation of the interesting portion of a query. It codifies, in a compact way, all paths involved in the query together with information concerning which document elements have to be accessed to retrieve content information. More precisely, the structural pattern is a tree containing one node for each XML element tag name and one edge for each parent-child (i.e., /) or ancestor-descendant (i.e., //) relationship between XML elements appearing in a path definition of a variable binding in the query. A structural pattern may contain two types of nodes: (i) *existential nodes*, corresponding to elements that must be present in the document but for which no information (#PCDATA, attribute, children or descendants information) has to be checked; (ii) *evaluation nodes*, corresponding to elements on which conditions have been posed or that will belong to the result. Such nodes can be either *"access-content nodes"*, for which only attribute or children information of the corresponding elements is relevant to query processing, or *"access-subtree nodes"*, for which the sub-tree rooted by their corresponding elements must be considered to solve the query. This happens for nodes having an out-going ancestor-descendant edge, nodes appearing in the RETURN clause without attributes and nodes for which #PCDATA information has to be checked. Note that also in the last case we need to access the entire subtree since, in general, positions of #PCDATA content inside an element is unknown. Typically, a query condition (the WHERE clause) involves access-content nodes, whereas the query output (the RETURN clause) may contain either access-content or access-subtree nodes.

Given a query q, the structural pattern sp of q is computed in four steps.

1: Removal of Useless Variables. Useless variables (i.e., variables such that no query condition depends on them) are discarded. A variable is useless if it satisfies the following conditions: i) it appears only once in the LET clause, and ii) it does not appear in the WHERE or RETURN clause or in the definition of a variable appearing in such clauses. Non useless variables are said to be *essential*. We call S the set of essential variables.

Example 1. Consider the query q presented in Section 2. The set of essential variables is $S = \{\$a, \$g, \$h, \$i, \$e\}$. In details, $\$h$, $\$i$, and $\$e$ are essential because they appear either in the WHERE or RETURN clause. On the other side, $\$a$ and $\$g$ are essential because they are used to define variable $h, which appears in the RETURN clause. Note that $v does not belong to S since it appears just once in the LET clause, thus it is useless.   □

2: Construction of the Raw Structural Tree. Once we have identified all essential variables, a *raw structural pattern* is generated, containing all paths associated with each variable $w \in S$. Binding information between variables is represented in the raw structural pattern by adequately representing the corresponding paths. Nodes with the same label are maintained distinct at this step. More precisely, to construct the raw structural pattern, first of all, we replace each variable $w \in S$ with its definition. Let p_w be the path associated with a variable $w \in S$. Then, we build the raw structural tree according to one of the following rules: (i) if the definition of w does not depend on other variables, we insert p_w in the raw structural pattern; (ii) if the definition of w depends on $v \in S$, let $p_w = p_v/p$, we append p to p_v in the raw structural pattern.

Example 2. Consider Example 1. The raw structural pattern is shown in Fig. 3(a). We start by introducing the root node. Then, for each path p_w associated with a variable $w \in \{\$a, \$g, \$h, \$i, \$e\}$, we append p_w in the raw structural pattern. For instance, consider path $\tilde{\ }/A$ associated with variable $a. In the raw structural tree we append a node A to the root. Furthermore, to represent path $a/B/D/G$, associated with variable $g, we append path $B/D/G$ to node A.   □

3: Annotation. A node with tag name tg in a raw structural pattern is an *access-content node* if and only if: (i) q contains an attribute condition over tg elements, or (ii) its fan-out is greater than 1 and only parent-child edges start from that node.[2] A node with tag name tg in a raw structural pattern is an *access-subtree node* if and only if one of the following conditions holds: (i) at least one ancestor-descendant edge starts from that node, (ii) there exists a #PCDATA condition over elements having tg as tag name, or (iii) the node ends a path in the RETURN clause. Access-content nodes are annotated with 'c' and access-subtree nodes with 's'. Moreover, we define an ordering relationship $\preceq$ between annotations, such that $\bot \preceq c \preceq s$, where $\bot$ denotes the null annotation. Greater annotations mean that more information is required for the annotated node. Thus, each node of the raw structural pattern is annotated with its strongest annotation.

4: Generation of the Structural Pattern. All nodes with the same tag name are collapsed and the strongest annotation is assigned to the resulting node. Subtrees rooted by an s-annotated node are then removed (since they are implicitly represented by the s-annotation).

Example 3. During the annotation phase, nodes G, E and I are annotated with label c, since they correspond to access-content nodes. In particular, the fan-out of node G is greater than 1 and no ancestor-descendant edge starts from it; on the other hand, attribute information is required for nodes E and I. Two annotations are assigned to node H. Indeed, attribute information is required for it and the corresponding subtree is then accessed in the RETURN clause. The strongest annotation, i.e., s-, is retained. The resulting raw tree for query q is shown in Fig. 3(b). Nodes labeled with A, B, C, D, and N are existential nodes. The resulting structural pattern for query q is shown in Fig. 3(c).   □

---

[2] The last condition characterizes nodes for which sibling information is relevant.

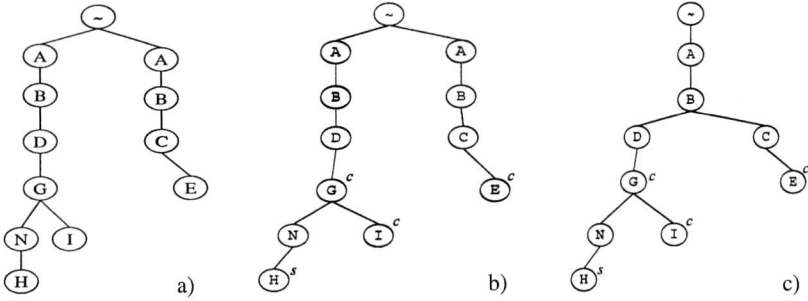

Fig. 3. The raw structural tree before and after annotation, and the structural pattern

In the following, given a query q, we denote the corresponding structural pattern with $sp(q)$. Starting from a structural pattern $p = sp(q)$ and a document D it is possible to generate a new document $rs(p, D)$, that we call *result set* of p against D, such that D and $rs(p, D)$ are equivalent with respect to q. Thus, $rs(p, D)$ corresponds to an XML tree containing all the elements and all the structural relationships required to answer q but smaller than D. Informally, this tree is generated by selecting from D only those elements that for sure are needed to answer the query (see [1] for formal details). In particular: (i) all element tags not appearing in p are not present in $rs(p, D)$; (ii) all existential nodes appear in $rs(p, D)$ only once since their content and their children information are not required to answer the query; (iii) all the document elements corresponding to annotated nodes must be retained in $rs(p, D)$. For access-subtree nodes, the subtrees rooted by them must also appear in $rs(p, D)$.

Example 4. Consider the structural pattern p in Fig. 3(c) and the XML tree $D1$ in Fig. 1. Fig.4 presents $rs(p, D)$. Note that nodes labeled F, V, W, L do not appear in $rs(p, D)$ since they do not appear in p. Moreover, existential nodes ($A, B, C, D,$ and N) appear only once. Finally, all nodes corresponding to annotated nodes in p still appear in $rs(p, D)$, together with all their attribute or content information. This is the case of nodes labeled E, G, I and H. In Fig. 4, dashed nodes represent nodes without attribute information. □

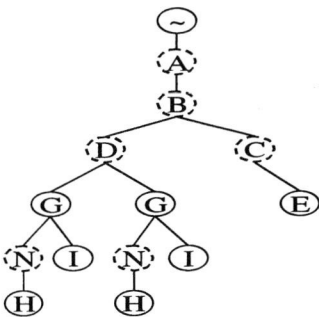

Fig. 4. Result set of a structural pattern

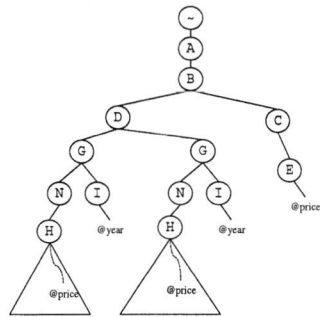

Fig. 5. The document image

```
1:   Procedure PRUNE
2:   Parameters
3:       sp(q) : Structural Pattern; D : XML tree; /* input parameters */
4:       p : path /* path from the root to the current visited node*/
5:       I: XML document tree /* the current image */
6:       Lₙ: list of nodes in I /* father nodes for the new image nodes*/
7:   p := p/root(sp(q));
8:   Create_Image(p,I, Lₙ)
9:   if ( I ≠ empty tree AND n_subtrees(S) > 0 ) then {
10:      /* n_subtrees(S) returns the number of subtrees of S*/
11:      for i = 1,..,n_subtrees(S) do { Prune(subtree(sp(q),i,D,p,Lₙ,I) }    }
12:  return I
```

Fig. 6. Procedure Prune

4   The Pruning Strategy

Given a structural pattern $sp(q)$, representing a query q, and a tree-based representation of a document D, the pruning strategy constructs an XML image corresponding to the result set of $sp(q)$ against D (i.e., $rs(sp(q), D)$), by recursively visiting the structural pattern.[3] Fig. 6 presents the recursive procedure Prune for generating $rs(sp(q), D)$, based on a depth first search (DFS) of $sp(q)$. For each visited node, depending on the node type, a portion of the image is generated calling procedure Create_Image (Fig. 7).

– If the node is not annotated, a dummy node is inserted in the image.
– If the node is c-annotated, the document is accessed to retrieve all elements reached by the path from the root to that node. Such elements, together with their attributes, are inserted into the image.
– If the node is s-annotated, the document is accessed to retrieve the sub-trees rooted by the path from the root to that node.

The complete image is obtained by calling procedure Prune with the considered structural pattern, the XML document, an empty list of nodes, and an empty image. In procedure Create_Image (Fig. 7), function label returns the label associated with a node whereas function pos returns the position of a node in the original document, if it is not a dummy node, or the position of its first non-dummy ancestor otherwise. This is needed to attach children to the right father. Finally, function descendant takes two positions and checks if the node at the first position is a descendant of the node at the second one in the input document.

Example 5. Consider the XML tree $D1$ and query q presented in Section 2. A DFS visit of the structural pattern of q (Fig. 3) starts from the root. Since nodes A, B, C and D are not annotated, the corresponding dummy nodes are created in the image. When node G is reached, since it is c-annotated, $D1$ is accessed to retrieve all elements G having an incoming path ˜$/A/B/D$. Then, a node is appended in the current image I, as child of node D, for each of the retrieved elements. Since in $D1$ there are exactly two G elements, two children labeled G are appended to D in the image I. Then, the search

---

[3] The proposed algorithm can be easily rewritten to directly deal with XML data.

```
 1:  Procedure Create_Image
 2:  Parameters
 3:      p : path; I: XML document tree; L_n: list of nodes in I;
 4:  let p = p'/m
 5:  let L_n =< u_1, ..., u_k >
 6:  if m is c-annotated then {
 7:      L_e = ordered list of nodes in D reached by p
 8:      if L_e ≠ λ then {
 9:          let L_e =< v_1, ..., v_h >
10:          for i = 1, .., h do
11:              for j = 1, .., k do
12:                  if descendant(pos(v_i), pos(u_j)) then append v_i as child of u_j
13:          L_n := L_e }
14:      else { I := empty tree }    }
15:  else if m is s-annotated then {
16:      L_s = ordered list of subtrees in D reached by p
17:      if L_s ≠ λ then {
18:          let L_s =< s_1, ..., s_h >
19:          for i = 1, ..., h do
20:              for j = 1, ..., k do
21:                  if descendant(pos(s_i), pos(u_j)) then append s_i as child of u_j
22:          L_n := L_s }
23:      else { I := empty tree }    }
24:  else { for i = 1, .., k do { create a new node m_i
25:                              let label(m_i) = label(n)
26:                              append m_i to u_i }    }
27:      L_n :=< m_1, ..., m_k >
```

Fig. 7. Procedure Create_Image

moves to node N of the structural pattern, which is not annotated. Thus, a new dummy node is appended to the image I, under any element G. When node H in the structural pattern is reached, because it is s-annotated, all subtrees rooted by H are retrieved and appended to the corresponding father nodes labeled with N.

Image portions corresponding to the other nodes are created accordingly. Fig. 5 shows the resulting image, reporting also the attributes used for the query evaluation. A triangle rooted by a node means that its subtree is inserted in the image. Note that for some nodes (H) the triangle also contains an attribute. This is to point out that such nodes were both c- and s- annotated. Furthermore, even if G is c-annotated in the structural pattern, no G attribute is required by the evaluation. However, the annotation was inserted since, according to the query, we must maintain sibling information between nodes N and I and this is possible only by inserting their corresponding father.   □

The most expensive operation performed by procedure Create_Image consists in retrieving the list of elements (actually, of positions) belonging to D reached by a certain path p (Fig.7 line 7), and the list of subtrees associated with p (Fig.7 line 16) Without any additional structures, to execute these operations, the entire file should be scanned since no special storage format is assumed for XML documents.

To improve the execution of these operations, we propose an index, consisting of: (i) a structural directory indexing paths, and (ii) an inverted index of tag offsets, listing for each path in the structural directory the position of elements reached by that path in the document. Positions are based on document offsets and they are assumed to be ordered. The structural directory can be realized by a structural summary, such as DataGuides [7] (for further details concerning the indexing technique see [1]).

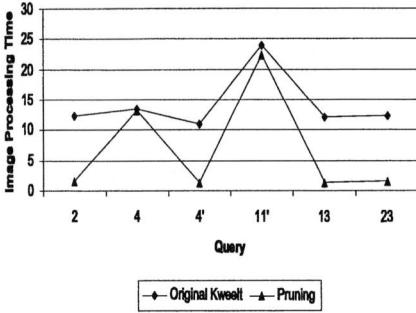

Fig. 8. Image Processing Time

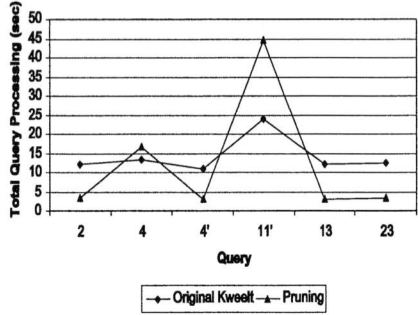

Fig. 9. Total response time

5   Experimental Results

We use Kweelt, which implements Quilt [5] one of the ancestors of XQuery, as a testbed for our performance analysis. The experimental hardware platform is a SUN-SPARC with Solaris-7, two 480MHz CPUs, and 256MB out of 4GB of RAM available for the experiment. We measured the performance of the algorithm using the XOO7 benchmark [2]. In particular, since the pruning strategy and the index are designed at the element level, we choose a specific subset of the XOO7 workload suitable to illustrate our proposal, forgetting, for example, queries which emphasize attributes. In the following, we report the results obtained by using one dataset, of size 8.62MB. Similar results have been obtained by using other datasets, with different size.

Image Processing. To emphasize the good performance achieved by generating an image before query execution, in Fig. 8 we compare query processing times obtained by executing input queries over the generated images with respect to the processing time of using Kweelt without any optimization. Since XML images are smaller than the original documents, processing queries over XML images is always faster than processing the same queries over the original documents.

Total Query Processing. The total query processing time is determined by the sum of the image generation time and the query execution time over the image. Fig.9 shows the experimental results. In general, pruning performs better than Kweelt. Indeed, when the query is high selective, the image is much smaller than the original document. On the other side, when the query is low selective (queries 4 and 11') the image size almost corresponds to the input document size. In such cases, since Kweelt does not construct any image, it performs better.

6   Concluding Remarks

We have proposed an optimization technique for query evaluation over XML documents in loosely-coupled environments, which prunes document parts irrelevant to query execution. A two-level index structure has also been proposed to further optimize the pruning step. By using the pruning strategy along with the index we propose, query execution time can be significantly reduced. Besides the presented pruning strategy, we have also implemented a simplified pruning technique performing just one data access, guaranteeing a faster pruning process but generates a larger document image (see [1] for further details).

From the experiments, it follows that the choice of the best strategy depends on the characteristics of the input document and query. Thus, as a future work, we plan to investigate how the knowledge or estimation of the characteristics of XML documents and the prediction of the characteristics of the result can be used to guide the optimizer in the choice of applying a transformation or not before query execution.

Acknowledgments

The authors wish to thank Barbara Catania for her valuable comments on this paper.

References

1. S. Bressan, B. Catania, Y.G. Li, Z. Lacroix, and A. Maddalena. Equivalence-Preserving Transformations for XML Documents. Technical Report DISI-TR-03-05 S, DISI, University of Genova, Italy.
2. S. Bressan, *et al.* XOO7: Applying OO7 Benchmark to XML Query Processing Tools. In *Proc. of the 10th ACM Int. Conf. on Information and Knowledge Management (CIKM)*, pages 167-174, Atlanta, Georgia, 2001.
3. N. Bruno, N. Koudas, and D. Srivastava. Holistic Twig Joins: Optimal XML Pattern Matching. In *Proc. of the ACM SIGMOD Int. Conf. on Management of Data*, pages 310-321, Madison, Wisconsin, 2002.
4. S. Boag, *et al.* XQuery 1.0: An XML Query Language. W3C Working draft, 2003.
5. D. Chamberlin, J. Robie, and D. Florescu. Quilt: An XML Query Language for Heterogeneous Data Sources. In *Proc. of the Int. Workshop on Web and Databases (WebDB)*, pages 1-25, Dallas, Texas, 2000.
6. R. Goldman, J. McHugh, and J. Widom. From Semistructured Data to XML: Migrating the Lore Data Model and Query Language. In *Proc. of the 2nd Int.l Workshop on the Web and Databases (WebDB '99)*, pages 25-30, 1999.
7. R. Goldman and J. Widom. DataGuides: Enabling Query Formulation and Optimization in Semistructured Databases. In *Proc. of the 23th Int. Conf. on Very Large Data Bases*, pages 436-445, Athens, Greece, 1997.
8. H. Jagadish, *et al.* TAX: A Tree Algebra for XML. In *Proc. of the 8th Biennial Workshop on Data Bases and Programming Languages (DBPL '01)*, pages 149-164, Frascati, Italy, 2001.
9. Q. Li and B. Moon. Indexing and Querying XML Data for Regular Path Expressions. In *Proc. of the 27th Int. Conf. on Very Large Databases*, pages 361-370, Roma, Italy, 2001.
10. A. Marian and J. Siméon. Projecting XML Documents. In *Proc. of the 29th VLDB Conference*, pages 213-224, Berlin, Germany, 2003.
11. A. Sahuguet. Kweelt: More Than Just Yet Another Framework to Query XML! In *Proc. of the ACM SIGMOD Int. Conf. on Management of Data*, 2001.
12. I. Tatarinov, *et al.* Storing and Querying Ordered XML Using a Relational Database System. In *Proc. of the ACM SIGMOD Int. Conf. on Management of Data*, 2002.

Keeping Pace with Evolving XML-Based Specifications

Marvin Tan and Angela Goh

School of Computer Engineering,
Nanyang Technological University, Singapore
{ps7726426d,asesgoh}@ntu.edu.sg

Abstract. Standards and specifications are essential to organizations that require exchange of information with other parties. XML is poised to be the definitive language of choice in Internet and Intranet applications and IT specifications are increasingly adopting XML schema. However, many specifications are still evolving. In order to cope with such rapid changes, extensions to the XML Schema Language are proposed. The objective is to ensure compatibility between different versions of standards. A framework which utilizes the XML Schema Language extensions is further proposed.

1 Introduction

In the past, standards and specifications for exchange of information between information systems were defined in proprietary languages and formats. The advent of the Internet has changed this trend. Today, specifications and standards used in information systems, within domains ranging from the financial sector to automobile industries, are increasingly formatted as XML documents. More significantly, many of these standards are described by XML schemas[10]. In the ideal world, commercial partnerships and alliances remain unchanged and final specifications of standards are indeed "final". In reality, commercial alliances grow and change; partnerships evolve and "final" specifications of a standard often have different versions.

With the ready availability of parsers and XML's extensible nature, XML is arguably the most popular data interchange language today. With the increasing adoption of XML Schema, it will be viewed as a natural way to resolve versioning issues for XML-based specifications. Examples of specifications that utilise XML Schema include W3C (World Wide Web Consortium) standards and OASIS's ebXML[7] for Supply Chain B2B transactions and WfMC's standards[8] in workflow systems. It was estimated in February 2000 that already more than 200 XML-based specifications exists [9]. Many new specifications would have been created since then.

The main problem with standards and interoperability today is the presence of multiple versions and variants of the same standard. In many domains, a universal common standard will never be possible. Hence, it is necessary to cope with changing standards as well as provide some means for similar standards to interoperate. To resolve the need to modify existing systems due to evolving standards, we propose to extend the XML Schema language to include elements and functionalities. Firstly, these extensions will provide a means to highlight the changes and differences between a preceding version or a variant and the original standard. Secondly, the new functionalities will establish

W. Lindner et al. (Eds.): EDBT 2004 Workshops, LNCS 3268, pp. 280–288, 2004.

a common version management definition so that frameworks or middleware may be developed to bridge the differences between different versions and variants of the standards/specifications.

In this paper, a common framework is proposed that allows objects or 'data exchanges' to be converted to a supported version based on the extensions found in them. The proposed extensions and framework will help manage compatibility issues with XML-based standards. The objectives of the work are fundamentally different from the version management solutions, proposed in document management[2] in system specification[3] and in documentation and software management[6]. These version management approaches focuses on the content while this work addresses changes in the meta-data, namely, schema evolution.

The organization of this paper is as follows. The next section will provide an example that highlights the benefits of the proposed extensions. Section 3 contains a description of the proposed extensions while Section 4 will present the proposed framework to aid and enforce the implementation of the proposed extensions. Section 5 discusses the possible issues arising from the use of the extensions. The last section concludes this paper and highlights possible future work.

2   An Example of Evolving Specifications and Standards

2.1   IMS Content Packaging Specifications

Chosen as example due to the rapid evolution and the availability of comprehensive revision history, eLearning standards have undergone tremendous change over the recent years. Take the example of the IMS Content Packaging (IMS CPS) Specifications version 1.1.3 and 1.1.2 [5]. The IMS CPS allows development of eLearning content in any format and to package it up with accompanying metadata so that other compliant systems may reuse the learning content.

As seen in Table 1, the Content Packaging Specifications contain numerous minor changes, such as 'renaming of an element', 'removal of an element' or 'shifting of a sub-element from one element to another'. These might not have a major effect on the logical definition of the Schema document. However, implementation-wise, it would mean that the developer has to recode portions of the module, which handle the standards. Some systems may even need to maintain separate modules to ensure backward compatibility with the previous versions. This is a major problem with most standards. Systems adhering to previous versions of standards will not be able to read objects created using the later versions. A software upgrade is required.

3   Proposed Extensions to XML Schema

Most "changes" to standards specifications may be captured formally using a modeling language. However, some changes are either too complex to be modeled clearly or are unimportant. Examples of the former include the 'overhaul' of existing documents and the expression of these elements in a different manner. An example of unimportant changes is the inclusion of comments, which have no technical implications to the

Table 1. Revision History Excerpt- IMS Content Packaging Specifications Ver 1.1.2 [4]

Version No.	Release Date	Comments
0.92	20 March 2000	Format updated with following changes: a) Move "isvisible" attribute from \<resource\> element to \<item\> element b) Add \<title\> to \<tableofcontents\> c) Revert back to the \<resource type="webcontent"\>approach introduced in the v0.9 document d) Rename \<organization\> to \<organizations\>
Public Draft 1.1	8 Dec. 2000	Made minor text changes and updated document to address the following issues: a) Replaced \<tableofcontents\> element with the \<organization\> element. b) Made \<title\> a sub-element of \<item\> rather than an attribute of it. c) Changed resource \<item\> element attribute "identifieref" to "resourceref". d) Made sub-level \<manifest\> a sub-element of \<manifestref\>, rather than \<manifest\>. e) Changed references from URL Base to XML Base. f) Reworded parts of section 2.1 in clarifying the definition of \<organizations\> and package. g) Added \<dependency\> element as a sub-element of \<resource\>. h) Updated XML samples.
Final 1.1	19 April 2001	Updated document to address the following open issues: a) Clarified the use of the \<organization\> and \<item\> elements. b) Added statement of recommendation to use PKZip v2.04g as the default Package Interchange File format in Section 1.2. c) Extended meta-data functionality to \<organization\>, \<item\>, and \<file\>. d) Changed the type attribute on \<organization\>to structure with a default value of hierarchical. e) Changed the href attribute on the \<resource\> element from Mandatory to Optional.

processing of the XML document. The updates or changes are formally declared through a language like XML Schema. These annotations are incorporated manually within the schema to reflect changes that have taken place. In other words, the revision history as illustrated in Table 1 are embedded in the schema.

3.1   Categorization of Changes

The possible changes that may occur between revisions of standards are categorized in Table 2.

Table 2. Three categories of version-to-version changes

Migratory Changes	Structural Changes	Sedentary Changes
• Morphing of an element to an attribute. • Migration of a sub-element from one element to another. • Modification of an attribute or element.	• Addition of new elements, sub-elements and attributes. • Removal of elements, sub-elements and attributes.	• Renaming of elements. • Renaming of attributes • Change of simple data type.

Migratory changes deal with the movement of elements or attributes to some other part of the document. This means that the elements or attributes existed in the previous version and are physically relocated within the current version. These changes also include the transformation of elements to attributes and vice versa. Such changes could require considerable modifications to be made to the original program reading the document, since the retrieval of attributes is fundamentally different from that of the elements.

Structural changes affect the document through the addition or removal of attributes or elements. Such changes mean that implementation of existing systems will have to be modified to support the new elements or developers must ensure that the removed elements will not have an impact on their system.

Sedentary changes, as the name suggests, involve no movement and have no effect on the structure of the XML standards document. It refers to the possible renaming of elements and attributes. Such changes can also be semantic in nature as the change in the attribute or element name might alter the original meaning completely.

One category of change that is difficult to model is **"semantic change"**. This category may not affect the structure of the schema at all. Such changes involve the change in the interpretation or the meaning of a term or terms used within the specification. For example, in a preceding version, the term **"entity"** in a "legal markup specification" may refer to businesses and companies and the recent version could expand the scope of **"entity"** to include people. Sometimes, semantic changes affect the transition between two versions of a specification or standard and sometimes they do not. There is no foolproof method of representing semantic changes convincingly with the aid of XML and XML Schema. However, the evolution of the Semantic Web [1] will greatly improve the representation of semantically-enriched information and provide possible means to indicate semantic changes within specifications. Section 5 highlights various means to alleviate the problem of representing semantic changes.

It is assumed that the original XML Schema avoids duplicate element names appearing in different local segments of element definition. As "duplicate names under different parent elements" is permitted in the declaration of an XML Schema, it makes the referencing of elements by their names impossible since they are sharing the same namespace. To work around this, the qualified path of the element may have to be used when referencing any particular element to avoid conflicts.

3.2   Identifying XML Schemas for Specifications

One of the key concepts in the use of these proposed extensions is the identity of the schema. The version and namespaces of the same family of specifications must be clearly specified along with information on the previous versions. There are many ways to do this. One way is to use attributes within the **XSD** tag. Parsers may easily access these attributes in order to determine the information. Subsequently, all new attributes or tags added will carry the 'vm' or 'version-management' namespace. Another namespace, 'pv', must also be declared for the previous version XSD.

3.3   Migratory Changes

In the version 1.1 (public draft) of the IMS Content Packaging Specifications, the element, '<manifest>' was moved out from the '<manifestref>' element to become a sub-element under the '<manifest>' element (nested self reference). This update should be reflected in the manner shown in Fig. 1. The original location in the previous version is stated with the type of the moved item in the previous version. This is to avoid confusion since attributes and elements may be given the same name. This category of changes could also involve modifications to attributes or elements and are more complex. Not

```
<xsd:complexType name="manifestType">
  <xsd:sequence>
    <xsd:element ref="metadata" minOccurs="0" />
    <xsd:element ref="manifest" minOccurs="0" maxOccurs="unbounded"
      vm:movedFrom="pv:manifestreftype" vm:type="sub-element"/>
    ... ...
  </xsd:sequence>
</xsd:complexType>
```

Fig. 1. An Example of the Migration of a Sub-element from One Element to Another

only may the name be altered but the structure and composition of the object in question may change including element occurrences and their use (optional or required).

Other changes in this category involve the transformation from an element to an attribute and vice versa. This entails the 'transformation' of the basic type of a tag (from an element to an attribute or vice versa). While the name of the tag may remain the same, the fundamental properties of the tag have changed. These changes should only involve elements of 'simple' type since the transformation of 'complex' elements or 'mixed content' elements to attributes is complicated and cannot be performed without excessive loss of information. Instead, they may be modeled as a series of removal and modification changes. In addition, during the change from a simple element to an attribute, the data type defined for the element will be lost as attributes may only contain literal string values. These changes may result in incompatibility problems or information loss as the information expressed in one version may not be relevant in another version.

3.4   Structural Changes

Structural changes add to or remove from the overall structure of the Schema. Additions are simply represented with **"vm:newAddition='true"** tags. Removal of elements and attributes will be reflected differently since the removed items will not exist in the new specifications. To cater for this, a new segment of XML elements must be declared in the XML Schema. The definition in Fig. 2 highlights the removal of both elements as

```
<vm:nonVisibleChanges>
  <vm:change type="removal">
    <vm:object type="element" name="pv:InLineBlock"/>
  </vm:change>
  <vm:change type="removal">
    <vm:object type="inner attribute" name="maxOccurs" from="pv:Activities"/>
  </vm:change>
</vm:nonVisibleChanges>
```

Fig. 2. An Example of the Removal of Elements

well as attributes. In this case, the attribute being a standard attribute is identified as an 'inner_attribute' and the parent element is stated. The namespace for the previous version is adopted to distinguish the elements.

3.5   Sedentary Changes

In the transition from IMS CPS Public Draft 0.91 to 0.92 (as seen in Table 1), the element '<organization>' was renamed to '<organizations>'. To reflect the renaming, the declaration will be updated as shown in Fig. 3.

```
<xsd:element name="organizations" type="organizationsType" vm:renamedFrom="pv:organization"/>
```

Fig. 3. An Example of the Renaming of an Element

How can these extensions be used in the real world? There are two possible scenarios. Firstly, there may be a wish to upgrade existing specifications and incorporate these extensions to enable version compatibility. One may start with the most recent version of the XML Schema document and insert the relevant extensions. Previous versions may be updated in an iterative manner. These extensions will not affect the existing data exchanges and applications. The existing compliant systems will simply ignore the extensions. The second scenario deals with the fairly straightforward establishment of new specifications from scratch. When a later version is created, the developers of the standards Schema 'translate' these changes from the previous version into the relevant extensions. Table 3 summarizes the proposed XML extensions.

Table 3. Extensions to XML Schema

Version identification	vm:familyId
	vm:version
	vm:previousVersionCompatible
	vm:previousVersionURI
Migratory Changes	vm:movedFrom
Structural Changes	vm:newAddition
	vm:nonVisibleChanges
	vm:changetype
Sedentary Changes	vm:renamedFrom

However, these extensions alone are insufficient unless some form of implementation is provided to support their use. Hence, Section 5 proposes a framework to employ these extensions.

4   Proposed Framework to Utilise Compatibility Extensions

Since these extensions do not employ the standard XML Schema namespace, applications will be unable to read these extensions. Hence, it is necessary to ensure that existing systems make use of the proposed extensions to achieve effective compatibility between versions and variants of standards specifications.

With reference to the elearning example, most learning content is packaged in XML documents (known as learning objects). These learning objects may be available over the Internet or even via electronic mail. As shown in Fig. 4, this proposed framework has the following functions:

- Reads the incoming XML documents and retrieves the relevant schemas (may be a iterative process depending on the number of versions elapsed between the two versions: stated in the XML document and the referenced Schema)
- Reads all the schemas and consolidates the 'compatible' segments of the documents based on the presented extensions.

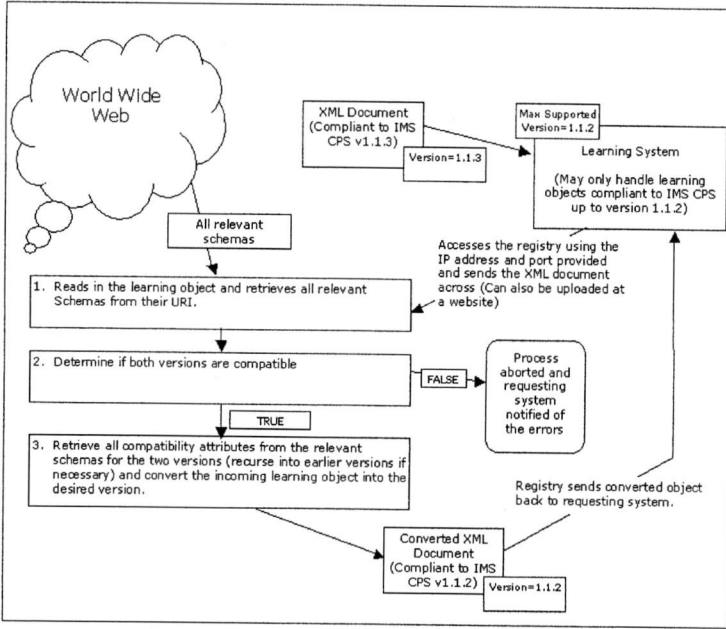

Fig. 4. Overview of Proposed Framework to provide Compatibility in the eLearning Domain

Based on the 'compatibility report' produced in the previous step, convert the document to the desired version and send it back to requesting system. The most feasible way is to provide a generic online registry (preferably by a standards body) that receives standards-based XML documents and instructions on the particular version desired. The registry may then retrieve the relevant schemas, do a check on the extension tags found in both versions and based on the compatibility instructions, convert the received XML document to a version desired by the initiating system. The document is then sent back to the system. This centralized solution may not be feasible in the long run because distributing APIs (Application Programming Interfaces) is a slow and tedious process. However, it is a necessary overhead. It is also necessary to avoid additional implementation work before existing systems can use the framework. With the aid of this framework and the proposed extensions, different versions of standards specifications will be more easily managed at a machine level.

5   Possible Problems and Issues

5.1   Representing Semantic Changes

As mentioned in Section 3.1, 'Semantic changes' cannot be represented in the proposed extensions using XML and XML Schema. However, some effects produced by 'Semantic Changes' may be simulated using the existing extensions. For example, if the meaning of a particular element has completely changed and there is no mapping between that element in a preceding version and the current one (even though the name is unchanged), we could model this effect by using the "removal change" as demonstrated in Fig. 2 and "addition" extension. This series of changes has the effect of removing the element from the current version and adding back an element with the same name. In that way, that particular element will not be treated the same way across the two versions.

5.2   Incompatibility Issues

As mentioned in Section 3.3, there will be problems if segments of different versions are incompatible, resulting in information loss. One scenario is as follows: a given document contains an element of a complex type. However, the number of components within the element has been reduced from 10 to 3. Therefore, there is redundant information provided in the original version. The conversion process will completely remove traces of such information.

Another scenario is the reverse. A later version can contain elements, which are not present in an earlier one. Therefore, the conversion of a document from a later to earlier version will result in the loss of information.

Additional extension tags for such information mismatch are required. To retain information from the preceding version that were removed in the current one, a new element must be included within XML Schema and a new attribute is placed within the element to indicate it as an element to store the incompatible information. The list of incompatible elements can be obtained from the "removal" change information (shown in Fig. 2). The incompatible information will be stored as a block of string type (inclusive of the name tags).

Often it is the lack of information that will cause immediate problems, since the missing information may be critical to the system functions. Though uncommon, this situation may occur during the conversion of an earlier version to a later one. The lack of information may not be resolved at a machine level until full-fledged semantics are available. In addition, backward compatibility is frequently not supported in most upgrades of applications and systems.

5.3   Effects of a Version Management Mechanism

Even though changes to standards and specifications are occurring rapidly, there is still a lapse between two versions of a specification. Changes usually arise from the continual research and analysis performed by the standards working groups. Feedback from usage within a specific domain is also extremely important in improving standards and specifications. With the proposed mechanism, changes can be more easily applied to specifications, leading to a higher adoption of specifications and standards. The time required to formulate the next version through feedback and analysis is significantly higher than the time required to incorporate the specifications to the application domain.

6   Conclusion

XML-based specifications may evolve relatively quickly over a short period of time. Even though some changes may be minor, systems which exchange information based on these specifications will still have to be modified. These systems may have to carry multiple legacy modules for backward compatibility. Hence, a proper version management framework is necessary to reduce the efforts required to ensure compatibility. Since an increasing number of standards are drafted in the form of XML Schemas, it would be natural to extend the XML Schema to provide constructs for compatibility between different versions of standards documents. The proposed extensions and framework will help to ease compatibility problems as standards and specifications evolve. Future work involves the building of a prototype to prove this concept of version management. The scalability and feasibility of such a solution will also be evaluated.

References

1. T. Berners-Lee. Semantic web road map, 1998. Internal note, World Wide Web Consortium, http://www.w3.org/DesignIssues/Semantic.html.
2. S. Chien, V. Tsotras, and C. Zaniolo. A comparative study of version management schemes for xml documents, 2000.
3. Franz Huber, Bernhard Schatz, Alexander Schmidt, and Katharina Spies. Autofocus: A tool for distributed systems specification. In *FTRTFT*, pages 467–470, 1996.
4. IMS Global. *IMS Content Packaging Specification Version 1.1.2 (Final Specification)*. IMS Global, http://www.imsglobal.org/content/packaging/cpv1p1p2/imscp_infov1p1p2.html, 2001.
5. IMS Global. *IMS Content Packaging Specifications*. IMS Global, http://www.imsglobal.org/content/packaging/index.cfm, 2002.
6. S. Mauw, M.A. Reniers, and T.A.C. Willemse. Message Sequence Charts in the software engineering process. In S.K. Chang, editor, *Handbook of Software Engineering and Knowledge Engineering*. World Scientific, 2000.
7. OASIS. ebxml. http://www.ebxml.org/.
8. WFMC. Workflow standards. http://www.wfmc.org/standards/docs.htm.
9. Mike Willis. Vertical industry standards: Legal xml and xfrml. In *The DIXON Conference 2000*, 2000.
10. World Wide Web Consortium (W3C), http://www.w3.org/TR/xmlschema-0/. *XML Schema part 0: Primer*, 2000.

Knowledge Management Framework for the Collaborative Distribution of Information

Jérôme Godard[1]⋆, Frédéric Andrès[1], William Grosky[2], and Kinji Ono[1]

[1] National Institute of Informatics, The Graduate School,
Hitotsubashi 2-1-2, Chiyoda-ku, Tokyo 101-8430, Japan
{jerome,andres,ono}@nii.ac.jp
[2] University of Michigan - Dearborn,
4901 Evergreen Road, Dearborn, Michigan 48128, USA
wgrosky@umich.edu

Abstract. The management of multimedia documents, which includes storage, indexing, query optimization, and distribution, requires very strong frameworks and policies in order to ensure its efficiency and reliability. There has been much work done in the fields of databases, information retrieval, relevance evaluation, and transaction processing for any kind of data; but these four domains are too often considered separately. This definitely causes a lack of comprehensive distributed information management. We are convinced that much benefit can be obtained by apprehending a global vision of the whole management process through XML. In fact, we want to provide technologies that improve the access to heterogeneous and distributed sources of information for people sharing common interests. In order to deal with detailed and consistent information, we have to consider several layers of metadata related to users, communities, devices, and data sources. This categorized information has thereafter to be handled and efficiently used by applications combining processes from the four operative domains. Then, we claim that it is possible to offer users an appropriate viewpoint of the data, i.e. a personalized, effective, and very accurate access to the information.

1 Introduction

Knowledge management is a wide area where many domains are merging; thus, it appears to be a key issue in more and more applications. But it still lacks global approaches that consider the knowledge management from the acquisition to the dissemination, in particular for the shared information within users communities. We aim at building an Information Engine, i.e. a system offering global management services adapted to categories of users having specific behaviors and expectations. We are involved in the Digital Silk Roads project (DSR [15]), which is focused on the management of multilingual documents related to cultural aspects; it is handling all kinds of multimedia documents (including text-based, image, audio, video formats). The services to be proposed to the

---

⋆ This research is partially supported by a grant (*bourse Lavoisier*) from the French Ministry of Foreign Affairs (*Ministère des Affaires Etrangères*) and the Joint Studies Program of The Graduate University for Advanced Studies (*Sokendai*).

W. Lindner et al. (Eds.): EDBT 2004 Workshops, LNCS 3268, pp. 289–298, 2004.

users by our Information Engine cover the usual database functions, user-personalized automated processes, and the management of transactions in order to ensure the capability of the system to work in heterogeneous distributed mobile environments. Personalized services are based on contexts such as localization, environmental variables (e.g. bandwidth), user's age, languages abilities, professional activities, hobbies, communities' involvement, etc. that give clues to the system about users' expectations and abilities. As text obviously is still (and indeed for many more years) the only reliable basis to build generic and portable strategies for the management of heterogeneous data, we chose to use metadata (through annotations) within XML about multimedia documents as a knowledge capture requirement. This *information about the data* has to cover four layers: users, communities, devices, and resources (which are homogeneous pieces of data, i.e. mono-type). Our goal, using well-structured knowledge management, is to precisely manipulate resources via the metadata we have about them. First, it is important to keep safely all the information we get about the resources. Then, we have to ensure the quality and the validity of the information we are storing. The third step is to properly disseminate the resources depending on the information we have about users. This approach is based on combined manual and automated processes for all the following services: annotation, storage, distributed back-up, data placement, information sharing, and relevance feedback. The main contribution of this paper is to provide a global *resource description* and manipulation framework that fits XML and enables us to enhance the collaborative distribution of information, by capturing all the knowledge that might be useful for improving the relevance of distributed semi-automated processes. In the second section, we will give an overview of the related work. Then we will present our *resource categorization model*, which allows us to identify and describe any kind of *resource*. The fourth section describes advanced services based on our model for the distribution of knowledge. In the last section, we will point out our contribution and introduce the forthcoming issues.

2 Related Work

Knowledge Distribution. The number of applications using ontologies to improve information retrieval processes and to deal with semantic heterogeneity is growing very fast; web services in particular already have several standards (e.g. DAML/OIL, ebXML) to describe service related information. Web-based Information systems have a typical structure which consists of three layers: semantic, application, and presentation. The Hera design methodology [19] considers integration and user support as aspects to be included within these three layers, which is a very relevant strategy according to us. Nevertheless, Hera uses a RDF-based ontology model which is very convenient but lacks context management support. Ontologies are also part of many semantic management frameworks for multimedia documents (e.g. audiovisual resources [18]); but most of the time, these frameworks are dedicated to a precise type of data and/or to a specific domain. Knowledge sharing is a wide area made up of many fields; moreover it covers different kinds of application, going from common memory space access to collaborative project management. It has been deeply investigated for many years and a lot of work has been produced (e.g. for software development teams [6]). As a matter of fact, most of the ontology-based applications are influenced by initiatives for the definition of interoperable metadata standards (such as Dublin Core). We also would like to point out that XML, with its large set of tools and extensions is commonly recognized as the best framework to build ontologies. The distribution of data within communities can be partially automated in order to reduce the query workload [10]; indeed, it is possible to evaluate what kind of data might be interesting or useful for a class of user (community), and for a specific user. It is very important to choose an appropriate heuristic [12] depending on the requirements related to users and environments in order to perform data placement. Then it becomes realistic to create automated data placement processes; an example of scheduled data placement [13] indicates that much benefit can be obtain without any human interaction.

Context-Dependence. The significance of context-aware computing is dramatically increasing and promises strong improvements in human-machine interaction. Indeed, autonomous interactivity performed by an application or agents [2] can successfully be based on active and passive context-aware features [1]. But in all cases, it is important to balance the degree of autonomy in order not to bother users. According to Hess and Campbell [11], context is one of the factors that differentiates ubiquitous computing from traditional distributed computing. Many approaches for context management are available in the literature and various theories have been proposed to formalize context [5]. The range of fields using context-dependence is quite wide. It goes from very abstract analysis [4] to Artificial Life applications. Our understanding of context-dependence is slightly different as we consider contexts as dimensions; this approach has been deeply investigated for the definition of Multidimensional XML [17] (MXML) which is an extension of XML including the management of context-dependent information. Versioning, which is vital in a collaborative project, is also a context-dependent issue. In order to avoid the drawbacks of the two casual versioning schemes (store last version + backward deltas, and store all versions), an adaptive document version management scheme [3] enables the system to continuously evaluate if it is pertinent to keep each version of a document. However, this strategy does not allow us to take fully advantage of the context-dependence. A very complete versioning management of XML documents has been proposed [7] but it does not consider distribution issues. XML versioning using MXML has been defined [8] and so represents a nice opportunity to deal with versioning through XML. Another possible interpretation of distributed knowledge versioning is adaptive point of view, i.e. personalized data access. This issue is very interesting to us since it is similar to the kind of query optimization we want to provide. Giving a formal approach of a multidimensional logic, [20] defines a set of contexts with properties that seems to be very convenient for MXML.

3 Our Knowledge Management Model

Our goal is to define a generic model for the management of distributed knowledge related to any kind of multimedia document. This approach is strongly relying on XML-based annotations, which imply for users to spend a certain amount of time and to be quite precise about the information they are adding. We have the great opportunity with

DSR (which aims at creating a global repository that enables us to validate, preserve, and disseminate cultural resources) to work with more than 300 specialists in various fields who are *motivated* and *able* to annotate documents very accurately. Building such a system is a great challenge, and requires to ensure the storage, the accessibility, and the retrieval of large volumes of multilingual multimedia contents related to the silk roads through XML. In this part, we present the model we use to identify, describe, and access any kind of resources with the aim to integrate them to DSR.

3.1   Contextual Data and Model

Cultural information is very difficult to handle. Since it includes aspects such as politics, art, or history, it is impossible to consider it as a fully representative information, even when the sources are the most reliable ones. This is the kind of contextual issue we want to address. The considerable amount and diversity of information we are dealing with entails building a strong and powerful knowledge tree (ontology like) with contextual features, which fits MXML or XML namespace. We are using a *Resource Categorization Tree* (RCT) so we are able to offer a coherent model with efficient operators. The *resource* is the basic element of our model; it can be any kind of unmixed multimedia document, i.e. a monotype document (pure text, picture, video. . .). Then we add knowledge through metadata to the *resources* and obtain the atomic element of our knowledge management: *resource & annotation*. We define here our algebraic structure. Let us first give a few notations which will be used throughout the paper:

- α is a node of the tree; Ω is the set of nodes of the RCT.
- A *resource* is denoted r and is a leaf of the RCT; $\mathcal{R}$ is the set of *resources*.
- If we consider a branch of the RCT, the nodes α_{i-1} and α_{i+1} are respectively called immediate predecessor and any of the immediate successors of the node α_i. The root node of the RCT is denoted α_0.
- For any of the nodes α_i of the tree (except the leaf nodes), $\tau(\alpha_i)$ is the label of the node α_i (i.e. the label on the branch between α_i and α_{i+1}).

The primary contextual element in our approach is the *descriptor*, which brings structured and precise information about the resources:

Definition 1 (Descriptor). *A descriptor is a contextual attribute (dimension), which gives information about resources. It is denoted δ and is related to a specific node of the RCT. The set of descriptors is denoted Δ. The ordered set of descriptors of α_i is a label: $\tau(\alpha_i) = (\delta_{i,1}, \ldots, \delta_{i,p})$ where $\delta_{i,j}$ is the jth descriptor of the ith node and p the number of descriptors contained in label $\tau(\alpha_i)$.*

An important property of the RCT is that for any of its immediate successors α_{i+1}, the node α_i has the same label $\tau(\alpha_i)$ and so has the same set of descriptors:
$\forall i \in [0, m-1], \tau(\alpha_i) = <\delta_{i,j}>_{j=1,\ldots,p}$, where m is the number of nodes contained in the full branch (path) from the root to the leaf representing the *resource r*.

The description of the resources through the *descriptors* is integrated in the RCT in order to perform effective operations on the information stored in a community repository. This is done with the *resource categorization*:

Definition 2 (Resource Categorization). *A Resource Categorization is a branch of the RCT, which is the path extending from the root to the considered resource (i.e. leaf node). A Resource Categorization R_r of a resource r is a tuple (N_r, T_r) where N_r is the non-void ordered set of nodes of r and T_r is the ordered family of labels on N_r. The set of ordered families of labels is denoted T.*

The deeper a label is (from the root), the more precise the information about the resource is. Since $T_r = (\tau(\alpha_0), \ldots, \tau(\alpha_{m-1}))$, where $(m-1)$ is the number of arcs the *Resource Categorization* R_r contains, we write R_r as $(N_r, \tau(\alpha_0), \ldots, \tau(\alpha_{m-1}))$ or $(N_r, <\tau(\alpha_i)>_{i=0,\ldots,m-1})$. A *descriptor* can appear in several labels of the RCT, except the *descriptors* contained in the root label $\tau(\alpha_0)$; indeed, a property of *descriptors* is that they can be used only once in a *Resource Categorization*.

All the knowledge we have about a *resource* is contained in the *resource description*; it is basically designed to structure the annotations, but it also aims at supporting the versioning of annotations:

Definition 3 (Resource Description). *A Resource Description is the complete instance of a Resource Categorization for a resource r.*

A Resource Description D_r of a resource r is a tuple (R_r, S_r) where R_r is a Resource Categorization and S_r is the ordered set descriptors values $<\sigma_{i,j,k}>$ of the resource r. It is obvious that R_r has to be equal to $(N_r, <\tau(\alpha_i)>_{i=0,\ldots,m-1})$ so we have:

$$D_r = \left(\ <\alpha_i>, \ <\delta_{i,j}>, \ <\sigma_{i,j,k}> \ \right)_{\substack{i=0,\ldots,m-1 \\ j=1,\ldots,p \\ k=1,\ldots,q}}$$

An extract of the RCT used for the DSR repository, and examples of labels and descriptors related to this RCT have been given in [9]. DSR *resource descriptor* list (defined by UNESCO & NII) has been influenced by the *production based attributes* of Dublin Core and by Getty's Art & Architecture Thesaurus.

3.2 Resources Comparison

Our model allows us to provide effective casual database-like operators (e.g. create, edit, insert) ; since their definition is trivial, we focus on the more complex comparative operators. The two following operators (used for the comparison of two *resources* r_1 and r_2) have in common to be made of two levels; they are first applied to sets of nodes N_{r_1} and N_{r_2}, and then, depending on this first result, to the sets of labels T_{r_1} and T_{r_2} (we use the following notation: $\tau(\alpha_i)_{r_j}$ is the label of ith node of the *resource categorization* R_{r_j}):

Operator 1 (Resources Difference). *$r_1.diff(r_2)$: the diff operator returns a tuple denoted (N_{diff}, T_{diff}), which is the result of a two-steps analysis. Indeed, in order to optimize the operative costs, we first check the nodes lists and notify the nodes contained in one of the Resource Categorizations R_1 and R_2 only. Then, we apply the same kind of operation to the descriptors (notation: $N^* \equiv N \setminus \alpha_0$):*

– *diff on nodes:*
- • *if $\tau(\alpha_1)_{r_1} = \tau(\alpha_1)_{r_2}$, then the operator returns N_{diff} being the list of nodes appearing only once in $\{N_1, N_2\}$: $N_{diff} = N_1 \cup N_2 \setminus N_1 \cap N_2$*
- • *if $\tau(\alpha_1)_{r_1} \neq \tau(\alpha_1)_{r_2}$, then the operator returns N_{diff} being the list of all nodes in N_1 and N_2: $N_{diff} = N_1^* \cup N_2^*$; it is possible in this case to generalize the diff operator for n resources $(r_1.diff(r_2, \ldots, r_n))$; thus:*

$$if \quad \tau(\alpha_1)_{r_1} \neq \tau(\alpha_1)_{r_i} \ \forall i \in [2, n], \ then \ N_{diff_{1,(2,\ldots,n)}} = \bigcup_{i=1}^{n} N_i^* \subset \Omega$$

– *diff on descriptors:*
- • *if $N_{diff} = \emptyset$, then obviously, the operator returns: $T_{diff} = \emptyset$*
  This case implies $(N_1, T_1) = (N_2, T_2)$, and means that $R_{r_1} = R_{r_2}$
- • *if $N_{diff} \neq \emptyset$, we have to take into account a property of RCT; indeed, since a descriptor can appear in several RCT's labels, we do not only consider the non-similar labels to look for redundancies. This is the reason why we check the common descriptors between D_1 and D_2:*
  $T_{diff} = \left\{ <\tau(\alpha_i) \setminus \{\delta_{i,j}\}>, \forall \alpha_i \in N_{diff} \mid \exists \delta_{p,q} = \delta_{i,j}, \ \delta_{p,q} \in D_1 \cap D_2 \right\}$

Operator 2 (Resources Intersection). $r_1.inter(r_2)$: *As mentioned earlier, the inter operator has the same structure as diff. This time, the two-steps analysis is not required to identify different cases, but it is interesting to perform a test on the second label in order to save some processing time. The inter operator returns a tuple (N_{inter}, T_{inter}):*

– *inter on nodes:*
- • *if $\tau(\alpha_1)_{r_1} \neq \tau(\alpha_1)_{r_2}$, then obviously the operator returns: $N_{inter} = \alpha_0$*
- • *if $\tau(\alpha_1)_{r_1} = \tau(\alpha_1)_{r_2}$, then the operator returns: $N_{inter} = N_1 \cap N_2$*
– *inter on descriptors:* $T_{inter} = \left\{ <\tau(\alpha_i), <\delta_{j,k}>> \mid \alpha_i \in N_{inter}, \exists \alpha_j \in N_1 \cup N_2 \setminus N_{inter} \mid \delta_{j,k} \in D_1 \cap D_2 \right\}$

From both previous operators, we evaluate the similarity between two *resources*:

Operator 3 (Resources Similitude). $r_1.sim(r_2)$: *This operator is based on the operators diff and inter (notation: $Card(T_a)$ is the number of descriptors contained in the ordered family of labels T_a); it returns: $\rho = (\rho_N, \rho_T) \in [-1, 1]^2$*

with $\rho_N = \dfrac{Card(N_{inter}) - Card(N_{diff})}{Card(N_1 \cup N_2)}$, $\rho_T = \dfrac{Card(T_{inter}) - Card(T_{diff})}{Card(T_1 \cup T_2)}$

- – *ρ_N gives a global idea about the similarity between the types of r_1 and r_2.*
- – *ρ_T gives a more precise evaluation about r_1 and r_2 similarity. It also allows us to find similarities between documents having different types.*

It is obvious that the sim operator provides an interesting support for advanced indexing of *resources* as it allows us to record relationships between *resources* each time a new entry is performed in the repository. We plan to add some variables in the sim operator in order to record the descriptors occurrences and then to return a weight related to the number of occurrences.

4 Adaptive Services

4.1 Environmental Knowledge

Advanced services for collaborative distribution of information must rely on knowledge related to the data (in our case through the RCT); but they also need to consider all elements that are involved in the process and might influence the access to the information. We clearly need a representation of all the useful information about the contextual entities (i.e. users, communities, and devices); this is the motivation of the profile:

Definition 4 (Profile). *A profile is a set of descriptors and values that are related to one environmental entity; it is a tuple denoted:*

$$\pi = (<\delta_i>, <\sigma_{i,j}>)_{\substack{i=1,\ldots,k \\ j=1,\ldots,l}} \text{ where k is the number of descriptors and l the number}$$

of ordered values for each descriptor. The set of profiles is denoted Π.

The values can be constants (birthdate, CPU...) or variables (localization, job...); it is important to specify types in order to manage efficiently history records (a profile is time-stamped). The possible number of values for each descriptor is bounded. Moreover, the list of values for one descriptor is ordered; from the most relevant to the less one. e.g. in the case of languages, the first one must be the user's mother-tongue and then decreasingly regarding his skills.

4.2 Offering Multi-viewpoint

The word *viewpoint* has various interpretations. It can be *a perspective of interest from which an expert examines a knowledge base* [14] or *an interface allowing the indexation and the interpretation of a view composed of knowledge elements* [16]. Our approach is slightly different. Indeed, we focus on the interaction between the data and the querying environment: we use all available knowledge to extract and to provide the most relevant set of data for the user. Then, the *viewpoint* becomes the characterization of an association *resource-environment*:

Operator 4 (Viewpoint). *A Viewpoint is expressed as a function returning an ordered set of Resource Descriptions. We use ν to denote a Viewpoint:*

$$\nu = \xi \circ \psi : \mathcal{R}^p \times \Delta^p \times \Sigma^p \times \Pi \longrightarrow \mathcal{R}^q \times \Delta^q \times \Sigma^q$$

$$\left(<D_i>_{i=1,\ldots,p}, \pi_e\right) \xmapsto{\Xi \circ \Psi} <D_k>_{k=1,\ldots,q}$$

$$with \ \psi : \mathcal{R}^p \times \Delta^p \times \Sigma^p \times \Pi \longrightarrow \mathcal{R}^q \times \Delta^q \times \Sigma^q \times \Pi$$

$$\left(<D_i>_{i=1,\ldots,p}, \pi_e\right) \xmapsto{\Psi} \left(<D_j>_{j=1,\ldots,q}, \pi_e\right)$$

$$and \ \ \xi : \mathcal{R}^q \times \Delta^q \times \Sigma^q \times \Pi \longrightarrow \mathcal{R}^q \times \Delta^q \times \Sigma^q$$

$$\left(<D_j>_{j=1,\ldots,q}, \pi_e\right) \xmapsto{\Xi} <D_k>_{k=1,\ldots,q}$$

where p is the number of considered Resource Descriptions and q the number of returned Resource Descriptions ($q \leq p$), π_e is the profile of the environment e (with $\pi_e = \pi_u \cup \pi_d$, u denotes a user and d a device), and Ξ and Ψ are two sets of rules:

- Ξ contains acceptation rules. If a descriptor value of D_r does not respect a rule in Ξ, then the set returned by ξ does not contain D_r.
- Ψ contains transformation rules. If a descriptor of D_r is involved in any rule of Ψ, its value might be modified depending on π_e.

Each rule is a test on a pair of descriptor values; one from the *Resource Description* and the other one from the profile. Both sets of rules are deeply dependent on the type of domain the Viewpoint is applied to. ψ and ξ also allow us to rearrange in order the *Resource Description* sets by classifying decreasingly the elements respecting the larger amount of rules.

Example 1. We give here two examples for multi-viewpoint support (different from the obvious multilingual one) using the two types of rules for DSR:

- Ξ: if a *resource* of the set $<D_i>$ is a video using a codec which is not available on the user's system, then the *resource* is removed from $<D_i>$.
- Ψ: map focus points might depend on the users' location if no specific information appears in the query; in the case of DSR, querying a silk roads map would first return maps focused on the area the user is located in.

We can also consider Ψ's rules results as commands for *resources* transformation; for instance, an image, that has a bigger resolution than the one of the user's screen, would be reduced to the screen resolution. Our viewpoint definition can be seen as a query optimizer. This strategy is very useful for distributed systems and heterogeneous environments (especially mobile devices). It is of course important to define the transformation rules according to the server software environment; in the DSR case, we use some applications providing image management, text summarization... Then it becomes trivial to manage the information, and to apply the modifications depending on the descriptor values.

4.3   Data Placement

The architecture of the DSR platform deals with communities of users. The data is basically stored on a main central server, with back ups on local servers. But as most of the countries that are involved in the project have low computing and bandwidth capacities, it is important to optimize the distribution of the *resources*; this is the aim of the data placement. Indeed, using automated processes, we can dispatch efficiently and accurately the *resources* for communities and users. We have here to specify that the DSR platform has a 3-layers architecture: *servers*, *access-point*, and *devices*. Indeed, each community has a device called *access-point*, i.e. a machine that has enough computing power, storage capacity, and connect-ability to be a kind of sub-server for the other devices of the community. This architecture requires the information about a layer to be kept on the upper layer. In fact, the *server* must contain a record of all *access-points*'s profiles, and an *access-point* has details about all the *devices* and users involved in the community that the *access-point* is representing. We define the operator Dispatch (disp), which is applied to the *Resource Description* of any new *resource r* added (or updated) on the servers:

Operator 5 (Dispatch Resource). $r.disp$: *Let us consider the resource description of r denoted $D_r = (N_r, T_r, S_r)$, the profile of the ith community $\pi_{c_i} = (T_i, S_i)$, the total number of communities denoted C, the profile of the jth user of the ith community denoted $\pi_{u_{i,j}}$, and the total number of users in the ith community denoted U_i; disp is first applied on communities and then on users:*

$$\forall \pi_{c_{i=1,...,C}}, \text{ we define } \rho_{D_c} = \frac{Card(T_{inter})}{Card(T_r \cup T_i)}, \rho_{D_c} \in [0,1]$$

- *if $\rho_{D_c} \geq s_{c_1}$, then the resource r is copied on the access-point.*
- *if $s_{c_2} \leq \rho_{D_c} < s_{c_1}$, then a link pointing on the resource r in the server is created on the access-point (index table).*
- *if $\rho_{D_c} < s_{c_2}$, then $\forall \pi_{u_{i,j}}$, we define $\rho_{D_u} = \frac{Card(T_{inter})}{Card(T_r \cup T_{i,j})}, \rho_{D_u} \in [0,1]$*

  - *if $\rho_{D_u} \geq s_{u_1}$, then the resource r is copied on the device of the jth user that has the larger storage capacity.*
  - *if $s_{u_2} \leq \rho_{D_u} < s_{u_1}$, then a link pointing on the resource r in the server is created on the user local index table.*
  - *if $\rho_{D_u} < s_{u_2}$, no information is sent from the server to lower layers.*

where $s_{c_1}, s_{c_2}, s_{u_1}, s_{u_2}$ are thresholds. One of the main issues is to fix these values. We are currently defining some criteria to calculate them; by the way, we already know that the values will have to be arbitrarily adjusted after experimental results. It is also clear to us that some descriptors are more important than others; we are including a weighting factor to make the operator more effective.

Example 2. It is easy to notice the interest of disp if you consider a DSR member being an architect, and so who is part of the architect community within DSR. This person would get an easier and faster access to the data related to architecture from the access-point (e.g. many *resources* containing the buildings label). Then, according to his own profile (location, other topics of interest. . .), he would receive on his device some *resources* or links that are relevant to him.

5   Conclusion

This paper proposes a generic framework to address contextual problems in the case of annotated multimedia documents management within communities. We have investigated the related issues and solutions, presenting our model and showing concrete examples from DSR. Our aim is to efficiently offer the most appropriate information to the users. We introduced a proposal for a global management of distributed heterogeneous *resources* based on *categorization* and *description*, and an adaptive access model. We must point out that the services proposed are not only useful is the case of DSR; they can be applied to any collaborative project, and are promising to compensate the lack of knowledge management and drawbacks of data distribution in a P2P and mobile environment. Much work still has to be done to provide a complete framework and experimental results. We have to improve the *resources* comparison and placement operators in order to fully take advantage of our model. We also started adding transactions processing for each layer of our architecture (using JXTA-Javaspaces-JMX)... There is objectively no limit for services to be added; indeed, it is impossible to provide a complete management of distributed knowledge, but there are many significant improvements to be achieved with our model.

References

1. L. Barkhuus and A. K. Dey. Is Context-Aware Computing Taking Control away from the User? Three Levels of Interactivity Examined. In *Proc. of Ubicomp*, pages 149–156, Seattle, WA, USA, October 12-15 2003.
2. T. Bauer and D. B. Leake. Real Time User Context Modeling for Information Retrieval Agents. In *Proc. of CIKM*, pages 568–570, Atlanta, Georgia, USA, November 5-10 2001.
3. B. Benatallah, M. Mahdavi, P. Nguyen, Q. Z. Sheng, L. Port, and B. McIver. Adaptive Document Version Management Scheme. In *Proc. of CAiSE*, pages 46–62, June 16-18 2003.
4. M. Benerecetti, P. Bouquet, and C. Ghidini. On the Dimensions of Context Dependence: Partiality, Approximation, and Perspective. In *Proc. of CONTEXT*, pages 59–72, Dundee, UK, July 27-30 2001.
5. P. Bouquet and L. Serafini. Two Formalizations of Context: A Comparison. In *Proc. of CONTEXT*, pages 87–101, Dundee, UK, July 27-30 2001.
6. T. Chau, F. Maurer, and G. Melnik. Knowledge Sharing: Agile Methods vs. Tayloristic Methods. In *Proc. of WETICE*, pages 302–307, Linz, Austria, June 9-11 2003.
7. S.-Y. Chien, V. J. Tsotras, and C. Zaniolo. XML Document Versioning. *SIGMOD Record*, 30(3):46–53, September 2001.
8. M. Gergatsoulis and Y. Stavrakas. Representing Changes in XML Documents using Dimensions. In *Proc. of XSym*, pages 208–222, Berlin, Germany, September 8 2003.
9. J. Godard, F. Andrès, and K. Ono. Management of Cultural Information: Indexing Strategies for Context-dependent Resources. In *Proc. of DSR Symposium*, pages 369–374, Nara, Japan, December 10-12 2003.
10. S. D. Gribble, A. Y. Halevy, Z. G. Ives, M. Rodrig, and D. Suciu. What Can Database Do for Peer-to-Peer? In *Proc. of WebDB*, pages 31–36, Santa Barbara, CA, USA, May 24-25 2001.
11. C. K. Hess and R. H. Campbell. A Context-Aware Data Management System for Ubiquitous Computing Applications. In *Proc. of ICDCS*, pages 294–301, USA, May 19 - 22 2003.
12. M. Karlsson and C. Karamanolis. Choosing Replica Placement Heuristics for Wide-Area Systems. In *Proc. of ICDCS*, Tokyo, Japan, March 23-26 2004.
13. T. Kosar and M. Livny. Scheduling Data Placement Activities in Grid. Technical Report 1483, Computer Sciences Department, University of Wisconsin, USA, July 2003.
14. O. Marino, F. Rechenmann, and P. Uvietta. Multiple Perspectives and Classification Mechanism in Object-Oriented Representation. In *Proc. of ECAI*, pages 425–430, 1990.
15. K. Ono, editor. *Proc. of DSR Symposium*, Tokyo, Japan, December 11-13 2001.
16. M. Ribière and R. Dieng-Kuntz. A Viewpoint Model for Cooperative Building of an Ontology. In *Proc. of ICCS*, pages 220–234, Borovets, Bulgaria, July 15-19 2002.
17. Y. Stavrakas, M. Gergatsoulis, and P. Rondogiannis. Multidimensional XML. In *Proc. of DCW*, pages 100–109, Quebec City, Canada, June 19-21 2000.
18. C. Tsinaraki, E. Fatourou, and S. Christodoulakis. An Ontology-Driven Framework for the Management of Semantic Metadata Describing Audiovisual Information. In *Proc. of CAiSE*, pages 340–356, Klagenfurt, Austria, June 16-18 2003.
19. R. Vdovjak, P. Barna, and G.-J. Houben. Designing a Federated Multimedia Information System on the Semantic Web. In *Proc. of CAiSE*, pages 357–373, June 16-18 2003.
20. R. K. Wong, F. Lam, and M. A. Orgun. Modelling and Manipulating Multidimensional Data in Semistructured Databases. In *Proc. of DASFAA*, pages 14–21, Hong Kong, April 18-20 2001.

XML-Based Revocation and Delegation in a Distributed Environment

Konstantina Stoupa[1], Athena Vakali[1], Fang Li[2], and Ioannis Tsoukalas[1]

[1] Department of Informatics, Aristotle University, Thessaloniki, Greece
{kstoupa,avakali,tsoukala}@csd.auth.gr
[2] Department of Computer Science, Shanghai Jiao Tong University, China
Fli@mail.sjtu.edu.cn

Abstract. The rapid increase on the circulation of data over the web has high-lighted the need for distributed storage of Internet-accessible information due to the rapid increase on the circulation of data over the web. Thus, access control mechanisms should also be distributed in order to protect them effectively. A recent idea in the access control theory is the delegation and revocation of rights, i.e. the passing over of one clients rights to the other and vice versa. Here, we propose an XML-based distributed delegation module which can be integrated into a distributed role-based access control mechanism protecting networks. The idea of X.509v3 certificates is used for the transfer of authorization information referring to a client. The modules are XML-based and all of the associated data structures are expressed through Document Type Definitions (DTDs).

1 Introduction

Role-based access control [11] seems to be the ideal model for large-scale heterogeneous networks since they organize clients into categories according to their duties (in an organization or enterprise). Moreover, large-scale environments require a level of self-administration [1, 2, 7, 9]. If a client is off duty, (s)he should pass over her/his authorizations to another client without the interference of a central administrator. Such an opportunity is given through delegation of roles and authorizations. A system that supports delegation of rights, should also support their revocation. Each delegation demands auditing in order to have the ability to return to the initial condition.

Distributed systems require a medium for transferring access control information concerning a user. This can be achieved through the use of certificates which are electronic documents containing basically identity (and other information) about their owners [3]. The most well-known proposals covering this functionality are the X.509v3 certificates and the Attribute Certificates (an overview is presented in [5, 6, 10]. The public-key certificates X.509v3 is an ISO/IETF standard which certifies both the identity and the attributes of a client and they are digitally signed by a certification authority. An X.509v3 certificate except for the core fields (issuer, licensee, public keys, etc.), it also contains some fields for extension. Here we adopt the X.509v3 certificates and we use the extension fields to store all of the needed access control information (including the delegation and revocation information). Those certificates are signed by internal or

W. Lindner et al. (Eds.): EDBT 2004 Workshops, LNCS 3268, pp. 299–308, 2004.

external authorities and they are updated each time an access control procedure modifies the characteristics of clients.

In the context of delegation earlier research efforts have focused on centralized delegation. RDM2000 (Role-based Delegation Model 2000) is a centralized role-based delegation model supporting hierarchical and multi-level delegation [12]. The main idea of this system is that it allows users acting in a specific role to delegate roles to other users. The series of PBDM (Permission-based Delegation Model) models extends this idea. PBDM0 also allows the user-to-user delegation of permissions while PBDM1 and PBDM2 supports role-to-role delegation [13]. In order to satisfy such a need, PBDM uses a central security administrator controlling the permission flow by defining separately delegatable roles. SQL also supports a kind of delegation since it uses the GRANT-REVOKE commands. It is about a user-to-user or user-to-role approach.

All of the above models are centrally administered and therefore, not adequate for large-scale distributed environments because the delegation mechanism would become a bottleneck. The major characteristics of our approach are:

1. the distributed orientation, i.e. there are several local delegation and revocation modules supporting local requests and a global module for servicing clients requests.
2. the support of both user-to-user and role-to-role delegation by employing the idea of administrative roles which can modify the features of regular roles. Therefore, each user is assigned both regular and administrative roles. In case the delegatee (whom the authorizations or roles are delegated to) is a role the delegator should be or act in an administrative role.
3. the support of delegated object which may be either role or authorization.
4. the ability to be integrated into a distributed access control mechanism having a central authorization certificate issuing authority.

Since there is great research interest in building XML-expressed access control policies (such XACML, XrML, ODRL), XML was our choice in implementing the module. Moreover, XML is appropriate for expressing semi-structured data and metadata (e.g. the format of the protected resources, the policies, etc). Such a module can be integrated into existing access control mechanisms or modern frameworks (such as XACML, XrML) able to protect the resources of large heterogeneous organizations in order to extend their functionality (so as to support delegation and revocation).

We believe that our contribution is significant since there is little been done in distributed delegation of authorizations or roles. Moreover, we have decided to use XML to express the major entities of our models since there are already standardized XML-based access control languages, a feature that will help us in integrating our module into existing access control frameworks. Our work advances the current state of the art since we introduce the idea of delegation into Internet-accessed distributed protected networks. Moreover, we have tried to design a both user-to-user and role-to-role delegation of authorizations or roles in order to complete the functionality of such a module.

The remainder of the paper is as follows: Section 2 describes the appropriate environment and access control mechanism where our delegation/revocation modules can best be integrated. Section 3 describes the general function of the delegation and revocation modules. Section 4 elaborates on delegation and revocation requests and their XML format is given. Moreover, we relate the delegation/revocation procedure with the Authorization Certificates by focusing on the modifications made on them in case a delegation or a revocation takes place.

2   Resource Accessing Over a Distributed Topology

The distributed environment consists of several servers (forming a local network or a Virtual Private Network (VPN)) protecting repositories and supporting a number of *internal clients*, i.e. clients accessing the system form inside the local network (Fig. 1). One of the servers is characterized as *master server* since it is also the one connecting the local environment with the Internet. The rest of servers are characterized as *slaves*. Every internal client sends his/her access control request to the server it is connected to (slave or master).

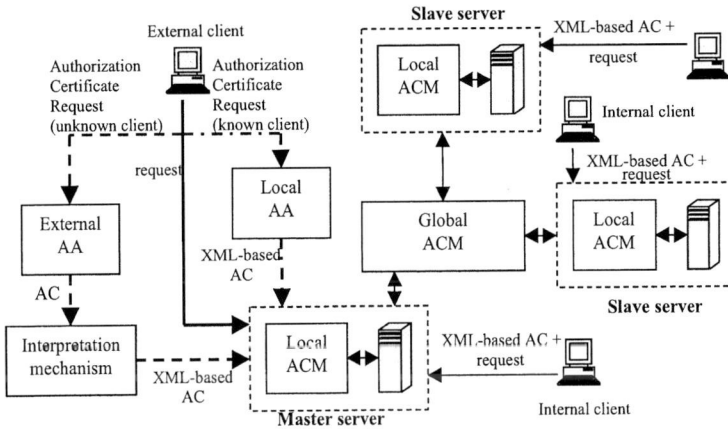

Fig. 1. Function of the distributed access control environment

In case of *external clients*, (i.e. clients trying to enter the local environment through Internet), every access control request is sent to the master server which decides which slave server should forward the request to. Of course, since master server is also supporting a repository, it may fulfill the request itself if the request refers to it.

This Internet-accessible distributed environment can be employed in a large-scale organization or enterprise (e.g a geographically distributed multinational enterprise) whose network can also be accessed by external partners through Internet. Consider the scenario of a national bank having many branches along the country. Every branch forms a sub-network supported by a local server. Of course, all of these sub-networks are connected to form the whole network of the bank. In this case a client may try to enter the network from outside (e.g. from his/her home) in which case acts like an external user, or (s)he may try to gain access from inside the main network (e.g. through a machine connected to the sub-network of Athens branch). Internal users can send requests to the server (either master or slave) supporting their location. External users' requests pass through the master server, which processes them or redirect them to the appropriate slave server.

Each server contains a local access control mechanism whose rules have power only in the local network it supports. Moreover, there is a global access control mechanism which is placed in the "center" of the environment and contains some general rules or policies governing the function of all the servers. Since, the proposed environment is role-based, both subjects and objects are organized into roles [8] both *local* and *global* ones. Local roles have effect only in a sub-network. For example there may be a role named "employee" in the Athens branch which characterizes only the employees of this branch. A global role could be the general manager of the bank whose authorizations have effect in the whole network. XML is used for expressing roles, policies, authorizations and certificates which are associated with each user and contain his/her features.

Every access control mechanism (ACM) needs (a) a request (either access request or delegation request) and (b) authorization information about a client (which is sent through an XML-based authorization certificate (AC)).

External users can be both known and unknown. According to the case the request is fulfilled through two distinct routes.

1. In case the client is unknown to the system, a trusted Authorization Authority (AA) is asked to issue an Authorization Certificate (AC). Due to the miss of a general standard for such certificates, their format may vary according to which authority has issued them. Therefore, the certificate should be interpreted in an XML-expressed AC recognizable by the access control mechanism (dashed line route).
2. In case the client is known, a local Authorization Authority issues directly the XML-based certificate which is passed to the access control mechanism (dash dot line route).

3   Delegation and Revocation Modules

Delegation and revocation processes are part of the access control mechanism. Therefore, these processes have to be included in a distributed access control system (as the one depicted in Fig. 1).

3.1   The Delegation Module

Fig. 2 depicts the format of the proposed delegation module. The client sends a delegation request escorted by its XML-based authorization certificate (AC) to the local delegation mechanism (which is part of the local Access Control Mechanism–ACM). This mechanism can fulfill delegation concerning local entities (roles and authorizations). In case, the delegation request concerns local entities and it is valid, the local delegation mechanism satisfies the request and updates the authorizations certificate which is sent back to its owner. On the other hand, when the delegation request refers to global entities, it is passed over to the global delegation mechanism (which is part of the global ACM), which is in charge of sending the updated authorization certificate to the client. Moreover, there is a database storing copies of the authorization certificates required for the revocation procedure.

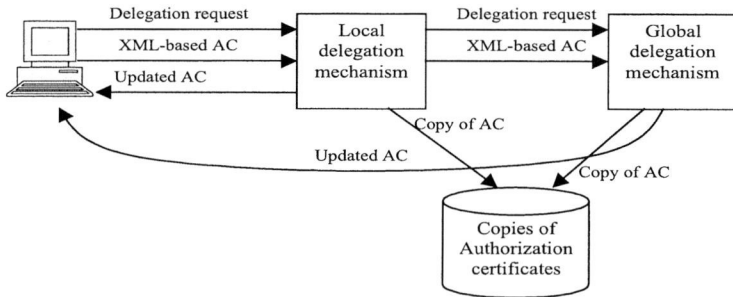

Fig. 2. Function of delegation module

3.2 The Revocation Module

The revocation procedure is always conducted by both global and local modules in unison. The reason is that a delegation of roles or authorizations which initially concerned local entities may also be propagated to global entities through cascading delegation. For example, consider the general manager delegates his role to the manager of Athens branch, who in his turn delegates it to the financial manager of his branch. In case, the general manager wants to revoke his role, the revocation mechanism should scan the base with the copies of ACs and communicate with all of the local mechanisms servicing roles that have been granted the revoked role or authorization, in our case the Athens branch. A revocation request is always sent from the interested client to the connected local module and typically revocation is practiced as:

1. **One-Level**: in case the delegation was one-level. This type of revocation may concern:
   (a) *Delegation of a local role*: the revocation request is fulfilled by the local revocation module. (dash lines)
   (b) *Delegation of a global role*: the revoked object is a global role or authorization and therefore the request is passed to the global module which fulfills it (dash lines+dash dot lines).
2. **Cascading**: in case of cascading delegation. This type of revocation may concern:
   (a) *Cascading into local roles*: the revocation request is fulfilled by the local module by revoking the object from every role where it is delegated. (dash lines)
   (b) *Cascading into both local roles of the same subnetwork and global roles*: the local mechanism revokes the object from the local roles and afterwards it sendsa revocation request where the revocator is a local role and the revocatee a global one (dash lines+dash dot lines).
   (c) *Cascading into global and local roles of another subnetwork*: the local mechanism upon receiving the request tries to fulfill it to the point the revoked object

has not be delegated to global roles. In this case it passes over the updated request (with the new revocator and revocatee) to the global mechanism which in its turn revokes the object from the global roles. In case the revoked object has been delegated to local roles empowered into other sub-networks, the global module sends an appropriate request to the appropriate local revocation module (dashed lines+dash dot lines+round dot lines).

Every time a revocation request is serviced, both the client and the copies base is informed.

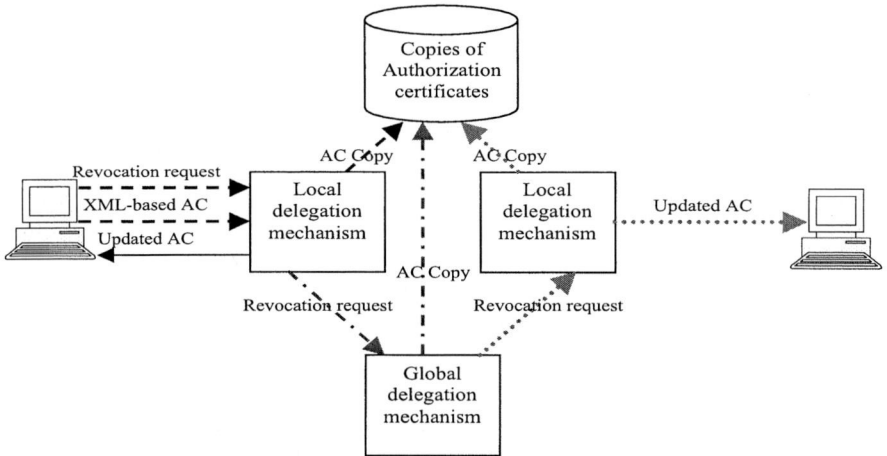

Fig. 3. Function of revocation module

4   Delegation and Revocation Requests

Delegation is triggered through delegation requests which define which *delegator* (users acting in a certain role, or a role) wants to delegate which *delegation object* (certain authorizations or whole roles) to which *delegatee* (user or role).

Each delegation request is represented by the following ELEMENT (in DTD[1]).

```
<!ELEMENT delegation_request (delegation_structure,
                              delegation_constraints)>
```

where (a) the delegation structure part defines the delegator and the delegate, as well as the roles (or authorizations) that are to be delegated (i.e the delegation object) and (b) the delegation constraints part describes the features of the delegation.

---

[1] The reason we use DTD instead of XML Schema is brevity in presentation. In the implmentation XML Schema will be used.

4.1   Delegation / Revocation Structure

Delegation structure is expressed with the following element:

```
<!ELEMENT delegation_structure (delegator,delegatee+,
            delegated_object,scope)>
```

The *delegator* may be a user acting in a regular role or an administrative role (either local or global), the *delegatee* may be a user or a regular role and the *delegated_object* may be a regular role or a set of authorizations. When users act in regular roles, they cannot delegate roles or authorizations to other roles since they are not allowed to modify a role. Such a task is allowed only to administrative roles (forming the administrative hierarchy). Thus, the following cases arise in a delegation request:

1. For delegators acting in regular roles
   (a) Delegate role to user. When a user u_1 acting in regular role r_1 delegates his regular role r_2 to user u_2 (of course $r_2 \leq r_1$ in the role hierarchy, which means that since u_1 possesses r_1 (s)he also possesses r_2)
   (b) Delegate authorizations to user. When user u_1 acting in regular role r_1 delegates his/her authorization a to user u_2.
2. For delegators acting in administrative roles
   (a) Delegate role to role. When user u_1 acting in administrative role r_1 delegates his/her regular role r_3 to regular role r_2.
   (b) Delegate authorizations to role. For example, administrative role r_1 delegates authorization a to regular role r_2.

```
<!ELEMENT revocation_request (revocator, revocatee,
            revocated_object,scope)>
<!ELEMENT revocator (user?, revocator_role)>
<!ELEMENT user (#PCDATA)>
<!ELEMENT revocator_role (#PCDATA)>
<!ATTLIST revocator_role type (regular|administrative)>
<!ATTLIST revocator_role id ID #REQUIRED>
<!ELEMENT revocatee (#PCDATA)>
<!ATTLIST revocatee type (user|role)>
<!ELEMENT revocated_object (#PCDATA)>
<!ELEMENT scope (rrh1_identity, (arh_identity, rrh2_identity)?)>
<!ELEMENT rrh1_idenity (#PCDATA)>
<!ELEMENT arh_identity (#PCDATA)>
<!ELEMENT rrh2_idenity (#PCDATA)>
```

Fig. 4. Function of revocation module

Since an organization may contain many roles and administrative hierarchies, we should define the *scope* of the delegation, i.e. to which hierarchies it refers. Thus, the request structure should be enriched with two more fields defining the identity of the regular role and the administrative role hierarchy.

Similarly, the revocation request (since it is "opposite" to the delegation request) occurs when a client acting in a role revokes all or part of the rights (s)he has delegated in the past. Therefore, a revocation request should include the information shown in Fig. 4, where (a) *revocatee* is the role or person the delegated object has been given to, (b) *revocated object* is the target of revocation (which may be an authorization or a whole role), (c) *rrh1_identity* is the scope of the revocator role, (d) *arh_identity* is the scope of the revocator role in case it is an administrative one and, (e) *rrh2_identity* is the scope of the revocatee.

4.2 Delegation Constraints

Typically, the main delegation constraints are:

1. *Permanence*: in case a delegation is permanent, the delegator permanently passes on his(her) authorizations to the delegatee.
2. *Monotonicity*: this feature refers to the "power" that the delegator possesses after the delegation. In a monotonic delegation, the delegator maintains his(her) authorizations.
3. *Totality*: this feature refers to the extent with which authorizations assigned to a role are delegated to another. In case of a total delegation the delegator passes over all of his(her) authorizations.
4. *Levels of delegation*: it defines whether a role can be further delegated and for how many times.
5. *Activation/de-activation condition* : every delegation should take place when a condition is fulfilled and it should be cancelled according to a de-activation condition. Those conditions can be anything, e.g. temporal ones (June 6th 2004).

A delegation request may or may not contain constraints, or it may contain a part of them. Therefore, the final format of the delegation request tuple is shown in Fig. 5.

After the completion of a delegation (or revocation) the AC of the delegator and the delegatees (or revocator and revocatees) should be informed. Such authorization certificates contain the characteristics of their owners. When a certificate is initially issued (both by the local and external authorization authorities) should include the following information: (a) the *licensee id*, (b) the *issuer id*, (c) the regular roles of the licensee, (d) the administrative roles, (d) the valid period, which depicts the life duration of the certificate and (e) some extension fields which include the following delegation/revocation information:

1. *Denied authorizations*: this list is expanded every time the licensee acting in a role delegates monotonically an authorization.
2. *Delegated objects*: this is a list consisting of the roles and authorizations that have been delegated to the licensee.
3. *Revocable objects*: a list containing the roles and authorizations that the licensee has delegated but (s)he has the right to revoke them at some time. Of course, this list contains only those subjects that have been temporary delegated.

```
<!ELEMENT delegation_request (delegation_structure,
            delegation_constraints)>
<!ELEMENT delegation_structure (delegator,delegatee+,
            delegated_object,scope)>
<!ELEMENT delegator (user?, role)>
<!ELEMENT user (#PCDATA)>
<!ELEMENT role (#PCDATA)>
<!ATTLIST role id ID #REQUIRED>
<!ATTLIST role type (regular|administrative)>
<!ELEMENT delegatee (#PCDATA)>
<!ATTLIST delegatee type (role|user)>
<!ELEMENT delegated_object (#PCDATA)>
<!ELEMENT scope ((rrh1_identity, arh_identity,rrh2_identity)?)>
<!ELEMENT rrh1_idenity (#PCDATA)>
<!ELEMENT arh_identity (#PCDATA)>
<!ELEMENT rrh2_idenity (#PCDATA)>
<!ELEMENT delegation_constraints (permanence,
            monotonicity, delegation_levels,
            activation_condition, deactivation_condition)>
<!ELEMENT permanence empty>
<!ATTLIST permanence type (permanent|temporary)>
<!ELEMENT monotonicity empty>
<!ATTLIST monotonicity type (monotonic|non_monotonic)>
<!ELEMENT delegation_levels (#PCDATA)>
<!ELEMENT activation_condition (ANY)>
<!ATTLIST activation_condition type (temporal|event_driven)>
<!ELEMENT deactivation_condition (ANY)>
<!ATTLIST deactivation_condition type (temporal|event_driven)>
```

Fig. 5. Function of revocation module

5   Conclusions

In this paper we introduced a distributed delegation/revocation mechanism supporting Internet-accessible distributed environments consisting of several local networks. The most appropriate access control model seemed to be the role-based one. Roles were mainly introduced to organize the subjects (clients requesting access). We have also tried to use them for the categorization of protected resources. XML has been adopted to express requests and other access control issues (roles, policies, etc.). The medium proposed for transferring access control (and delegation) information about a user is the Authorization Certificate. Since there is not yet a standard format of such certificates we have introduced an interpretation mechanism which accepts every external certificate and translates it into an XML format recognizable by the access control mechanism. Here we have mainly focused on the delegation and revocation procedures. The future goal is to implement the proposed structures and algorithms in a prototype environment in order to evaluate their usage mainly over the Internet-accessed resources.

References

1. E. Barka and R. Sandhu. Framework for Role-Based Delegation Models. In *Proc. 16th Annual Computer Security Applications Conference*, pages 168–176, 2000.
2. E. Barkaand R. Sandhu. A role-based Delegation Model and Some Extensions. In *Proc. 23rd National Information Systems Security Conference*, 2000.
3. J. Dai and J. Alves-Foss. Certificate Based Authorization Simulation System. In *Proc. 25th Annual Int. Computer Software and Applications Conference*, pages 190–195, 2001.
4. C. Goh and A. Baldwin. Towards a more Complete Model of Role. In *Proc. 3rd ACM Workshop on Role-Based Access*, pages 55–61, 1998.
5. A. Herzberg, Y. Mass, L. Mihaeli, D. Naor, and Y. Ravid. Access Control Meets Public Key Infrastructure, Or: Assigning Roles to Strangers. In *Proc. Symposium on Security and Privacy*, pages 2–14, 2000.
6. J. Linn and M. Nystrom. Attribute Certification. An Enabling Technology for Delegation and Role-Based Control in Distributed Environments. In *Proc. 4th ACM Workshop on Role-based access control*, pages 121–130, 1999.
7. P. Michiardiand R. Molva. Inter-domain authorization and delegation for business-to-business e-commerce. In *Proc. 1st E-business and E-work Conference*, 2002.
8. M.J. Moyer and M. Ahamad. Generalized Role-Based Access Control. In *Proc. IEEE 21st Int. Conference on Distributed Computing Systems*, pages 391–398, 2001.
9. S. Na and S. Cheon. Role Delegation in Role-Based Access Control. In *Proc. 5th ACM Workshop on Role-Based Access Control*, pages 39–44, 2000.
10. J.S. Park and R. Sandhu. Binding identities and attributes using digitally signed certificates. In *Proc. 16th Annual Computer Security Applications Conference*, pages 120–127, 2000.
11. R.S. Sandhu, E.J. Coyne, and H.L. Feinstein. Role-Based Access Control Models. *IEEE Computer*, 29(2):38-47, 1996.
12. L. Zhang, G.-J. Ahn, and B.-T. Chu. A Rule-based Framework for Role-Based Delegation and Revocation. *ACM Trans. on Information and System Security*, 6(3):404–441, 2003.
13. X. Zhang, S. Oh, and R. Sandhu. PBDM: A Flexible Delegation Model in RBAC. In *Proc. 8th Symposium on Access Control Models and Technologies*, pages 149–157, 2003.

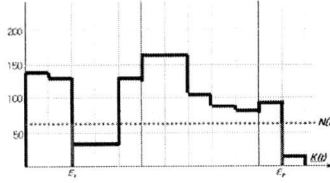

Fig. 3. EPOB(End Point of Over Bandwidth

Algorithm 3 E-based prefetch technique

1. Divide a presentation into segments based on E.
2. Calculate the amount of prefetching after comparing the required bandwidth from zero to E_i and network bandwidth until E_i.
3. Compare the amount of prefetch calculated in Step 2 and the mobile buffer size.
4. If the buffer size in Step 3 is bigger than the prefetching data size, the presentation is determined as playable and prefetching is implementing according to the prefetch policy.
5. If the buffer size is smaller than the prefetching data size, the presentation is determined as unplayable and is transferred to the transcoding phase.

Buffer Size for Mobile Terminals. The buffer size for mobile terminals directly indicates the prefetching size and is calculated using the definitions below:

Definition 2

B :Buffer size, B_{max}: Maximum buffer size, MB_{max}: Maximum buffer size of a mobile terminal, MB_{req}: Buffer size of the mobile terminal for stable playing

P_i :ith prefetch of segment E_i (P_{is}: Prefetching start, P_{ie}: Prefetching end).

$K_i(t)$:ith Required bandwidth of playing segment E_i(K_{is}: Required bandwidth start, K_{ie}: Required bandwidth end).

$N_i(t)$:ith Network bandwidth of segment E_i, Γ: Consumption amount of data when playing X, Ω: Required amount of data required when playing X

The buffer size for prefetching can be calculated by using the Required amount function and Consumption amount function. First, the function which deals with the Required amount needed to play a presentation at the time of t is defined as Ω.

$$\Omega(P_i, t) = N_i(t) \bullet (t - P_{is}) \text{ if } P_{is} < t < P_{ie} \tag{2}$$

And the function regarding the Consumption size of the time segment *t*, while playing a presentation is defined as Γ.

$$\Gamma(K_i(t), t) = K_i(t) \bullet (t - K_{is}) \text{ if } K_{is} < t < K_{ie} \tag{3}$$

From the Required amount of data, which is the result of function $\Omega(P_i, t)$ of X, it is possible to deduct the Consumed data amount by $\Gamma(K_i, t)$ and the remaining B required at *t*.

$$B(P_i, K_i(t), t) = \Omega(P_i, t) - \Gamma(K_i, t) \tag{4}$$

At the maximum point of B, the required bandwidth starts and B_{max} should be the size that is acceptable for a mobile terminal. Thus, the acceptable buffer size acceptable of a mobile terminal can be calculated as follows:

$$MB_{req} = B(P_i, K_i(t), t) \; in \; other \; words \; MB_{max} \geq MB_{req} \tag{5}$$

If the data size to be prefetched in X is bigger than the maximum buffer size of the mobile terminal, it should be determined as unplayable and transferred to the transcoding phase.

3.2   Transcode Technique

The PC server, which composes and sends the X, is called the Source, and the part which receives and plays the X is called the Destination. In this case, there can be a situation where $QoS(X_{sour}) \neq QoS(X_{dest})$. Thus it is called transcoding, which is a Δ function to achieve a balance of service quality, like $QoS(X_{sour}) = \Delta[QoS(X_{dest})]$. Transcoding has two attributes, the transcoding ratio per hour (ratio of data transcode) and the transaction ratio per hour. The transcoding ratio indicates the original data size and transcoded data size after transcoding, and the transaction ratio is the amount of data that can be transcoded per second. The criterion for this was set in [13], and transcoding is conducted according to this.

Determining Playability for E-Based Transcode Scheduling. On the basis of the definition of EPOB, namely E, it becomes possible to determine playability by applying the transcode technique to X. In X from [Fig. 3], there exists 2 Es, namely E_1 and E_2. The integrated value from 0 to E in the **N(t)** graph indicates the amount of data that a terminal can receive until E time. In the same way, the integrated value from 0 to E_i in **K(t)** indicates the amount of data that X requires until E_i time. Therefore, [Formula 1] is calculated by choosing one stream from 0 to E_1 if X has over 2 Es and by applying the transcoding afterwards. If the value is bigger than the network bandwidth, another stream is chosen within E_1 and transcoding is applied again. If the calculated value is smaller than the network bandwidth, calculate [Formula 1] by expanding the segment division from the starting of 0 to E_2.

Formula 1 Playability Test Formula for E-Based Transcoding

K(t) : Required bandwidth of the playing segment, N(t) : Network bandwidth
Δ : Transcoding, E_i : Every point of EPOB (End Point Over Bandwidth)

$$\Delta[\int_0^{E_i} K(t)dt] \leq \int_0^{E_i} N(t)dt \tag{6}$$

A presentation that satisfies formula (6) is playable if it is transcoded.

As in [Formula 1], [Algorithm 4] explains the how XML contents are playable. Here, the value transcoded after integrating **K(t)** should be smaller than the value of **N(t)**.

Algorithm 4 Algorithm to Determine Playability After Transcoding Application

---

1. Divide XML contents into E-based segments.
2. Stream for transcoding belongs to the XML contentsE.
3. After applying transcoding to the XML contents, the result is playable in the form of XML contents if it satisfies the analysis model. If not, it is unplayable.

The playability of the XML contents with transcoding can be determined in [Formula 1] by comparing the amount of data attainable through the network with the amount of data the XML contents require.

E-Based Transcode Scheduling. The technique for E-based transcode scheduling, as well as the characteristics of the technique and an algorithm to apply transcoding, are suggested as follows. The algorithm will check whether [Formula 1] and the time for transcoding are both satisfied during each transcoding step. The transcoding time of the step, as in [Formula 1], is the total transcoding time calculated by the given scheduling - that is, the initial delay time. Thus, the algorithm, which satisfies these conditions, is [Algorithm 5]. Stream selection policy on [Algorithm 5] is [Policy 1].

Algorithm 5 Stream Selection Algorithm for E-Based Transcode Scheduling

---

1. In compliance with the given selection policy, choose stream α for transcoding.
2. Convert stream α, selected at Step 1, into α' by applying a transcoding standard table [5].
3. Replace α with α' in the XML contents and compose a new XML contents'.
4. Complete if XML contents' satisfies [Formula 1].
5. If the result does not satisfy Step 4, start from Step 1 again.

Definition 3

α :Selected Stream, S: Playing Segments , $DPS_i = D_i$ / sec: Data per Second

Δ :Transcoding($\Delta_{.tf}$: Transfer Rate , $\Delta_{.ta}$: Transaction Rate)

Policy Stream Selection Policy

---

1. The Stream Requiring the Highest bps in XML contents, First
$$\alpha_{\max\_DPS} = Max_{j \in E_i}(DPS_j)$$
2. The Stream Requiring the Highest Transcoding Ratio in XML contents, First
$$\alpha_{\max\_\Delta_{.tf}DPS} = Max_{j \in E_i}(\Delta_{.tf}DPS_j)$$
3. The Stream Requiring the Largest Data Transcoding Ratio among all the data in XML contents, First $\alpha_{\max\_\Delta_{.ta}DPS} = Max_{j \in E_i}(\Delta_{.ta}DPS_j)$
4. The Stream Across Maximum number of Playing Segment in XML contents, First
$$\alpha_{\max\_S} = Max_{j \in E_i}(S_j)$$
5. The Stream having the Maximum Data size among all the data in XML contents, First
$$\alpha_{sumD_i} = Max_{j \in E_i}\left(\sum_{k=1}^{n} D_{jk}\right)$$

---

4   Experiments and Results

4.1   Aims and Methods of the Experiments

The aim of the experiment is to suggest a superior stream policy which can reduce early delay time to play XML contents on mobile terminals by 1) analyzing stream composition in XML contents; 2) measuring the time to prefetch and transcode streams that belong to the XML contents. As shown in the experiments, the number of selected streams and transcoding times are closely related. Even though the frequency and time of transcoding have a significant interrelationship, this paper gives priority to the time factor. The experiment has been implemented as follows: 1) The input value undergoes an early playability test to check whether the XML contents are playable on mobile terminals. 2) In this process, if the result is negative, the playability test utilizes prefetching. 3) Find the EPOB and try prefetching per segment, and then compare this value with the mobile buffer size to determine playability. 4) If the result is negative, the XML contents are sent to the transcoding phase. 5) Transcoding is selected by the stream selection policy existing in segments. 6) After converting the selected streams, it is determined whether the streams are playable or not. If the result is affirmative, the process is finished, but if not, the transcoding should be repeated until the streams become playable. The experiments have been conducted 90 times with sample XML contents under different network environments (14Kbps, 28Kbps, 56Kbps, 144Kbps).

4.2   Experimental Results

The results of the experiments show that there were slight changes in the stream selection policy to network bandwidth. As [Fig. 4] and [Fig. 5] show, transcoding the maximum amount of data per second (Policy 1) and the maximum total of data among the existing XML contents (Policy 5) resulted in a better policy selection. Consequently, the elapsed time to transcode all the XML contents is 4 seconds (144Kbps) and the time using the superior stream selection policy (Policy 1) is 0.66 seconds (144Kbps), which shows that using the superior stream selection policy is much more effective in terms of early delay times and secured stability to play XML contents on mobile terminals.

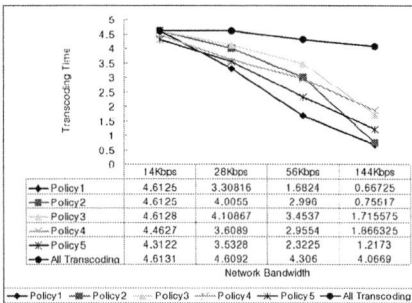

	14Kbps	28Kbps	56Kbps	144Kbps
Policy1	4.6125	3.30816	1.6824	0.66725
Policy2	4.6125	4.0055	2.996	0.75517
Policy3	4.6128	4.10867	3.4537	1.715575
Policy4	4.4627	3.6089	2.9554	1.866325
Policy5	4.3122	3.5328	2.3225	1.2173
All Transcoding	4.6131	4.6092	4.306	4.0669

Fig. 4. Selection Policy Transcoding Time Result

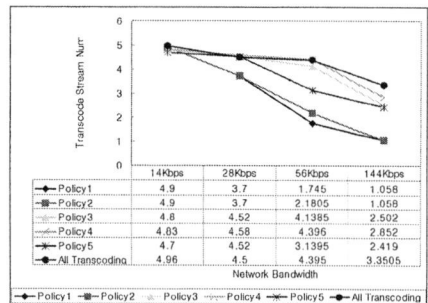

	14Kbps	28Kbps	56Kbps	144Kbps
Policy1	4.9	3.7	1.745	1.058
Policy2	4.9	3.7	2.1805	1.058
Policy3	4.8	4.52	4.1385	2.502
Policy4	4.83	4.58	4.396	2.852
Policy5	4.7	4.52	3.1395	2.419
All Transcoding	4.96	4.5	4.395	3.3505

Fig. 5. Selection Policy Transcoding Stream Number Result

5   Conclusion

This paper aims at proposing methods to minimize the initial delay time occurring in playback of XML contents in mobile terminals. For this, the method of transcoding various streams included in XML contents in accordance with selection policy has been suggested. In this method, the transcoding time is regarded as the initial delay time occurring in mobile terminals. Thus, the method was proposed as a means of minimizing the initial delay time. In addition, a prefetch technique has also been suggested to suit the restricted memory space in mobile terminals. The fact that adopting of the two above-suggested methods, rather than transcoding all data included in XML contents when playback in mobile terminal, is more effective in terms of initial delay time has been verified in a testing procedure.

References

1. Niklas Bjork and Charilaos Christopoulos. Trans-coder Architectures for Video Coding. *IEEE Transactions on Consumer Electronics*, 44(1), 1998.
2. Won-hee Choi. Buffer Prefetch Method for Playing Multimedia in Mobile Terminals. Master's thesis, Soongshil University, pages 1–25, 2003.
3. Rita Cucchiara, Massimo Piccardi, and Andrea Prati. Temporal Analysis of Cache Prefetching Strategies for Multimedia Applications. *IEEE International Conference on Performance, Computing, and Communications*, pages 311–318, 2001.
4. Frank H.P. Fitzek. A Prefetching Protocol for Continuous Media Streaming in Wireless Environments. *IEEE Journal on Selected Areas in Communications*, 19(10):2015–2028, October 2001.
5. Maria Hong, Joon-Sung Yoon, Young-Hwan Lim. A Transcode Scheduling Technique to Reduce Early-Stage Delay Time in Playing Multimedia in Mobile Terminals. *Journal of Electrical Engineering and Information Science* 10-B(6):695–704, 2003.
6. Sung-Mi Jeon. Converting Path Creation Methods to Play Multimedia with Different Service Quality between Vertical Sections. Ph.D. dissertation, Soongshil University, pages 2–31, 2003.
7. Taeil Jeong, JeaWook Ham, and Sungo Kim. A Pre-scheduling Mechanism for Multimedia Presentation Synchronization. In *Proc. of IEEE International Conference on Multimedia Computing and Systems*, pages 379–386, June 1997.
8. Eui-Sun Kang. Guided Search Method Research to convert MPEG2 P frame into H.263 P frame under Compressed Condition. Master's thesis, Soongshil University, pages 1–15, 2001.
9. Javed I. Khan and Qingping Tao. Prefetch Scheduling for Composite Hypermedia. *IEEE International Conference on Communication*, volume 3, pages 768–773, 2001.
10. Jo-Won Lee. Study on improving transcoder efficiency in reducing image size in compressed segments. Ph.D. dissertation, Soongshil University, pages 1–18, 2001.
11. Young-Hwan Lim, Sun-Hye Lee, and Myung-Soo Lim. Study on Real Time Presentations of Multimedia Mail on the Internet. *Journal of Korea Information Processing Society*, 6(4):877–889, 1999.
12. In-Ho Lin and Bih-Hwang Lee. Synchronization Model and Resource Scheduling for Distributed Multimedia Presentation System. *IEICE TRANS. INF. & SYST.*, 83-D(4), April 2000.
13. Dae-Won Park, Maria Hong, Kyu-Jung Kim, and Young-Hwan Yim. Study on Sending Image Streams to Mobile Phones without Additional Software. *Journal of Korea Information Processing Society*, 3(3):55–66, 2001.

What's Next in XML and Databases?

Minos Garofalakis[1], Ioana Manolescu[2], Marco Mesiti[3],
George Mihaila[4], Ralf Schenkel[5],
Bhavani Thuraisingham[6], and Vasilis Vassalos[7]

[1] Bell Labs, USA
minos@research.bell-labs.com
[2] INRIA, France
ioana.manolescu@inria.fr
[3] University of Milan, Italy
mesiti@dico.unimi.it
[4] IBM Watson Research Center, USA
mihaila@us.ibm.com
[5] Max Planck Institute, Germany
schenkel@mpi-sb.mpg.de
[6] NSF, USA
bthurais@nsf.gov
[7] Athens University of Economics and Business, Greece
vassalos@aueb.gr

1 Introduction

Since the time XML became a W3C standard for document representation and exchange over the Web, many efforts have been devoted to the development of standards, methodologies, and tools for handling, storing, retrieving, and protecting XML documents. The purpose of this panel, held during the international EDBT'2004 workshop on "*database technologies for handling XML information on the Web*" [3], is to discuss the current status of the research in XML data management and to foresee new trends towards the XML-ization of database research.

The panel included Minos Garofalakis (Bell Labs, USA), Ioana Manolescu (INRIA, France), George Mihalia (IBM Watson Research Center, USA), Ralf Schenkel (Max Planck Institute, Germany), Bhavani Thuraisingham (NSF, USA), and Vasilis Vassalos (Athens University of Economics and Business, Greece). Marco Mesiti (University of Milano, Italy) served as moderator.

This paper reports the main research topics discussed during the panel. It is opinion of the panelists that many efforts should be devoted to the definition and implementation of retrieval systems that cope with both the XQuery query language and the emerging requirements of identifying fast, approximate and ontology-based answers for Web users' queries. Moreover, the use of XML as main means for the representation and exchange of information on the Web introduce novel issues for the security and privacy communities. Finally, a lot of attention should be devoted to the issues of XML data integration, schema versioning and stream processing.

The panel conclusions are reported along with the answers to the following "controversial" questions posed to the panelists:

W. Lindner et al. (Eds.): EDBT 2004 Workshops, LNCS 3268, pp. 318–324, 2004.

1. *"Is it always so relevant XML data management for the database community?"*.
2. *"Are Xschemas really used or DTDs are still predominant?"*
3. *"Will native databases have market in the next future? In which application areas?"*
4. *"There is a great emphasis on 'approximate queries for XML documents'. What are real applications that take advantages from this research?"*

2   Approaches for XML Documents Retrieval

Retrieval of XML information is a broad field of research that range from the definition and implementation of query languages for XML databases, to the definition of mechanisms for the retrieval of approximate results and the use of ontologies for the retrieval of documents distributed over heterogenous sources on the Web. Ioana, Minos and Ralf discussed key research directions on this research field.

Development and Implementation of XQuery Language.   Ioana sees that research should target the XQuery language. XQuery has evolved into a very complex language. By now, it fully subsumes XPath; covers all SQL-style data transformations; allows for ordered and unordered querying, is being extended for text search, and is based on a functional-style data model. This complexity caters to widely different requirements, and makes XQuery useful in many contexts, such as: application integration, persistent database management, stream processing, document database management, information retrieval etc. This richness of application domains is likely to promises XQuery a long and fruitful future.

XQuery is soon to be issued as a W3C standard. This opens up new issues on XQuery implementations: defining storage and execution models, optimization techniques, and cost models. Among the promising applications of XML data management, warehousing of XML data and Web services deserve significant attention, due to the increase of XML data on the Web.

Data Reduction and Approximation.   Minos sees the issue of XML data reduction and approximation as a promising direction for future research. With the rapid growth of available XML data, one can expect a proliferation of on-line decision support systems that enable the interactive exploration of large-scale XML repositories. In a typical exploratory session, a domain expert poses successive queries in a declarative language (such as XQuery or XSLT), and uses an appropriate visualization of the results in order to detect interesting patterns in the stored data. Obviously, the successful deployment of decision-support systems depends crucially on their ability to provide timely feedback to users' queries. This requirement, however, conflicts with the inherently expensive evaluation of XML queries which involve complex traversals of the data hierarchy, coupled with non-trivial predicates on the path structure and the value content.

Generating *fast, approximate answers* based on precomputed, concise synopses of the XML data is a cost-effective solution for offsetting the high evaluation cost of XML queries. (Of course, another natural application for such XML-data synopses is as an effective tool for generating *approximate, compile-time selectivity estimates* during the optimization of complex user queries over XML databases.) Ideally, such approximate answers are computed very fast (since they only use concise summaries of the data) and are also accurate, in the sense that they preserve the key statistical traits of the true result with low error. Users can then examine this approximate "preview", assess the information content of the true answer, and decide whether it needs to be retrieved by executing the query over the base data. Overall, by providing users with fast and accurate feedback on the form of the results, the system can reduce the number of queries that need to be evaluated in order to effectively support the data exploration task.

Clearly, the effectiveness of such an approximate XML-query answering system hinges upon the existence of accurate synopsis structures that capture the key statistical characteristics of the base XML data and can thus produce low-error approximate answers to user queries. Data-reduction and approximation problems are now fairly well understood in the context of flat, relational databases, and a number of proposals exist for building relational-data synopses (based, for example, on histograms, wavelets, or random samples) and using them to approximate SQL query results. The proposed techniques and summarization methods, however, are suitable only for flat, relational data and do not easily extend to the case of general XML hierarchies. More recent work has proposed novel, effective synopsis mechanisms for large XML documents, in the context of both XPath selectivity estimation and approximate answering of XML "twig" queries (see, for example, [2, 5–7]). Still, these proposals only represent the first steps of the database community in this exciting research area, and several important problems remain wide open. Examples of directions for future work in this area follow.

- *Summarizing XML-Document Values.* Thus far, the primary focus of XML-synopsis proposals has been on summarizing the *label-path structure* of the underlying document, typically paying little attention to the *value content* of XML elements. Some initial ideas on summarizing both structure and value content are described in [5], but only for the case of numeric values. The problem of designing effective synopsis mechanisms for XML documents with *textual values* remains open. This domain opens up many interesting research questions and possibilities for cross-fertilization of ideas and concepts from Information Retrieval.
- *Generic Framework for Characterizing XML Data Synopses.* The goal here is to identify the key dimensions of the design space for XML data synopses, and classify existing proposals along these dimensions. Such a generic framework has already been proposed for the case of relational histogram summaries and, in fact, has directly led to identifying novel, effective classes of histograms (representing unexplored "points" in the underlying design space) [8]. Of course, the design-space characterization problem becomes significantly more complex in the case of XML data synopses, since such synopses need to effectively capture *the structure as well as the values* in an XML database.

Ontology-Based Retrieval of XML Documents on the Web. Ralf moved the discussion to querying XML on the Web. Such a case is radically different from querying XML databases consisting of XML with a fixed and known schema. As there is no universal standard for representing data in XML (and it is unlikely that there will ever be such a standard), schemas used to represent data widely vary across different Web sites, and some do not provide a schema at all. Widely adopted query languages for XML like

XPath and XQuery are no longer appropriate for searching in such an environment as they cannot cope with the diversity of data. This opens up some very interesting and important research questions.

Instead of the existing query languages, Ralf thinks that we need a new query paradigm with an expressiveness between the powerful, but complex and schema-dependant XQuery and the limited, keyword-based search that today's Web search engines provide. As users don't know (and typically don't care about) how the schema looks like, queries should not explicitly specify the structure of the data, but express the "information need" of users, a kind of "find what I mean" approach. Queries should express the user's guess how the data may be structured, and it is the system's task to find documents that match this guess.

From a research point of view, this leads to the application of both structural and ontological similarity measures to match documents and queries. Additionally, as the system's notion of good results may not coincide with the user's, relevance feedback must be a core part of a system to establish user-based instead of system-induced similarity measures. Finally, as the introduction of similarities highly increases the number of potentially relevant results, any efficient system must apply algorithms for query evaluation that are optimized to compute the most relevant results first.

3   XML Data Integration, Versioning and Stream Processing

XML Data Integration. Vasilis argues that XML is uniquely well-suited to contribute to the solution of the large problem of data integration and web services integration. With the proliferation of information and the increased connectivity, the problem of putting together information from disparate, heterogeneous, autonomous data sources is ever more pressing. XML is uniquely qualified to act as the global data model for heterogeneous information: it is self-describing, which allows information from different sources to encapsulate its description, it natively supports missing or duplicate information elements, and it has a less rigid structure than the object-oriented or relational data model. This last feature is critical, as flexibility is needed to combine rich data from different sources, even if each source is rigidly structured. At the same time, flexible schema languages, most notably XML Schema, have evolved, which provide the benefits of schema-based processing to XML data without sacrificing the flexibility necessary to put together disparate information.

The use of XML for integration has been predicted since the invention of XML. Jon Bosak in [1] explains that XML will be used for "applications that require the Web client to mediate between two or more heterogeneous databases" and "applications ... which ... tailor information discovery to the needs of individual users". But the evolution of XML use followed the evolution of XML processing software. Very quickly after its introduction XML gained wide acceptance as a message exchange format. XML message exchange needs little technical infrastructure and standards beyond the XML definition and an XML parser. XML messages need to be filtered and XML data transformed, so XPath and XSLT evolved to satisfy these needs along with XPath and XSLT processors.

The underlying infrastructure for supporting ad-hoc queries and views on distributed heterogeneous data is taking longer to develop, due to the complexity of the query processing problems involved, but Jon Bosak's prediction is slowly becoming a reality, with the introduction of products such as Enosys Software's Integration Server (which now powers BEA's Liquid Data product). The whole family of XML standards, such as XQuery for querying, XML Schema for defining the structure of the views and the underlying heterogeneous information, RDF to define semantics, and WSDL to define and call remote computational services, come into play to solve the integration problem.

As for XML as a native storage and retrieval format, it has significant benefits for data that have strong semistructured characteristics such as (most importantly) bioinformatics data, and therefore a significant opportunity to take hold in such domains.

Versioning and Stream Processing. George highlighted several areas of XML research that still require considerable work. Thus, in the area of data federation, the ability to define XML views over distributed collections of both XML and relational data will be very important, since a great deal of the world's data will continue to be stored in relational databases. For this vision to become a reality, efficient algorithms for distributed XML query processing need to be developed.

In the same context, that of distributed systems and specifically of Web services-based architectures, it is also increasingly important to be able to efficiently process streaming XML data. One promising direction for improving the performance of applications based on streaming XML data is converting the data to a binary message format. In addition to dramatically reducing the parsing time, a carefully designed binary format can also embed query processing hints that will enable applications to effectively skip irrelevant portions of large messages.

Another aspect that will become critical as Web services become widespread, is the ability to reason about evolving schemas of XML messaging formats. Robust versioning schemes, with built-in provisions for backward compatibility will be essential in a world where applications designed for different versions of a messaging standard will have to interoperate seamlessly.

Finally, and probably most important, as XQuery is becoming the query language of choice for XML data, a lot of attention will need to be given to efficient indexing structures for XML data, efficient structural join algorithms, as well as advanced query optimization algorithms for XQuery.

4   Security and Privacy in the Semantic Web

Bhavani addressed open issues in the protection of XML documents in the semantic web. The major components for the semantic web include web infrastructures, web databases and services, and ontology management and information integration. A lot of work has been done in these three areas, but little consideration has been devoted to security. Since XML is used for the representation of information, and RDF as a language for describing ontology, a lot of work should be devoted to securing XML and RDF information in the these three areas.

Furthermore, XML and RDF could be used to specify policies. We also need to examine the Web Rules Language to specify security policies. Closely related to security is privacy. We also need to examine the specification and enforcement of privacy policies.

Finally we need to develop trust mechanisms for the semantic web. This also includes developing a trust negotiation language as well as developing mechanisms for enforcing trust. In summary, security, privacy and trust for the semantic web are important research areas.

5 Conclusion

A general consideration, arisen from the panel discussion (that also answer the first trivial question), is that XML data management is a relevant research direction for the database community and it will become more and more relevant in the future. This is also perceived by the increase in the number of XML or XML-ized application data sets. Application-generated data is usefully structured in XML; Web service messages follow XML syntax; business standard formats are in XML. These various XML data sources need to be organized, queried, stored, analyzed, mined for information.

The second question has been addressed by Ioana. Relying on her experience, DTDs are still predominant, due to the perceived important complexity of XSchemas (thus high learning cost). A recent study [4] shows that 40% of the XML documents on the Web have a DTD, and less than 1% have an XSchema, most of which are WAP documents. So, it seems that DTDs are there to stay.

For what concern the third question, native databases are likely to have a market in enterprise-wide warehousing of various documents, which may or may not have been initially XML, but which are amenable to an XML format reflecting their internal structure. Also, native XML databases are a precious tool when the data is highly textual (e.g. news contents, documentary databases) and/or of very complex and variable structure (e.g. biological data). Finally, it could be guessed that in some years, all the XML querying market will belong to native databases - as it seems more and more clear that the complexity of current XML query languages exceeds the capability of RDBMSs.

Ioana addressed the last question. She claims that the approximation of the document structure is useful as it allows the users to deal with a lower cognitive overhead: it is easier to "think of a simpler object", thus document. In this direction, techniques and tools from the field of Knowledge Representation and Information Retrieval are likely to be useful. Also, fuzzy querying (by means of text search-like queries) is currently getting a lot of attention, within the framework of the XQuery language.

References

1. J. Bosak. XML, Java and the Future of the Web. *WWW Journal* 2(4): 219-227, 1997.
2. J. Freire, J. Haritsa, M. Ramanath, P. Roy, and J. Simeon. StatiX: Making XML Count. *ACM SIGMOD Conf.*, 2002.
3. M. Mesiti, B. Catania, G. Guerrini, and A. Chaudhri. *DataX: International Workshop on Database Technologies for Handling XML information on the Web*. In conjunction with Int'l Conference on Extending Database Technology (EDBT 2004). March 14, 2004, Heraklion (Crete) Greece. http://www.disi.unige.it/person/MesitiM/dataX/
4. L. Mignet, D. Barbosa, and P. Veltri. The XML Web: a first study. *WWW Conf.*, 2003.
5. N. Polyzotis and M. Garofalakis. Statistical Synopses for Graph-Structured XML Databases. *ACM SIGMOD Conf.*, 2002.

6. N. Polyzotis and M. Garofalakis. Structure and Value Synopses for XML Data Graphs. *VLDB Conf.*, 2002.

7. N. Polyzotis, M. Garofalakis, and Y. Ioannidis. Approximate XML Query Answers. *ACM SIGMOD Conf.*, 2004.

8. V. Poosala, Y. Ioannidis, P. Haas, and E. Shekita. Improved Histograms for Selectivity Estimation of Range Predicates. *ACM SIGMOD Conf.*, 1996.

Modeling Contextual Information Using Active Data Structures

Kevin Goslar and Alexander Schill

Dresden University of Technology,
Chair for Computer Networks
{goslar,schill}@rn.inf.tu-dresden.de

Abstract. In this paper, we present some ideas how to represent, handle, and integrate semantically expressive contextual information. Our approach enhances topic maps by more topic and association types and embedded code. Our data model is a comprehensive picture combining the knowledge of many context-aware applications. It is capable of performing automatic updates of the contained contextual information, computes higher-level information by itself, and routes context events to client applications. We present a context-aware front end of a car navigation system that uses our data model.

1 Introduction

The motivation of our work is to provide a semantically expressive information model for contextual data. Handling of contextual data is a crucial component for the success of Pervasive Computing (PervComp). The research community currently discusses some interesting approaches, but we still see unexploited potentials for the use of contextual information. Imagine the possibilities of all applications sharing their knowledge to create a large knowledge database about the users and their situation. Such scenarios require a contextual database (CDB), which stores and integrates contextual information from different applications. With such a CDB at hand, many problems and issues of PervComp would be implementable with justifiable effort. As *real world* we define the physical world, in which the humans live. A context-aware computer application, existing in the *computer world*, is aware of relevant aspects of the real world by monitoring *entities* (things) in the real world using sensors.

Sect. 2 provides the requirements for a contextual data model. Current approaches to model context information are reviewed in Sect. 3. Sect. 4 provides the basic concepts of our approach and Sect. 5 gives the details. Sect. 6 concludes this paper.

2 Requirements for a Representation Format for Contextual Data

In this section, we describe the characteristics of pervasive environments and contextual data and show the resulting requirements for a specialized contextual data model.

W. Lindner et al. (Eds.): EDBT 2004 Workshops, LNCS 3268, pp. 325–334, 2004.

2.1   Characteristics of Pervasive Computing

Pervasive computing scenarios have a number of specific characteristics, which need to be considered by a CDB. They are:

Heterogeneity: PervComp involves different devices, runtime environments, programming languages, paradigms, and applications. A CDB should be independent from those heterogeneous characteristics.

Individuality: Not all aspects of pervasive scenarios can be foreseen by the programmer of a pervasive application [10]. Individual requirements of individual users have to be maintained by the end user [7].

Offline Use: Parts of the CDB need to be replicated to mobile devices for disconnected operation. Functioning replicas of CDBs need the data, semantic information about the data and logic to handle it.

Indirect Addressing: Entities are mostly identified by a circumscription like *set the temperature of all rooms with no person inside to 15° C* instead of directly naming them with *set the temperature of room 123 to 15°C*, regardless of what is currently going on in that room, because this would be no context-aware behavior at all.

Many Applications: PervComp scenarios involve many simultaneously running applications [6], which need to operate autonomously. Otherwise, the user would be disturbed with plenty of messages and questions.

Community: Many applications possess information about the context, which could also be useful to other applications and therefore should be integrated into the CDB [5]. This information should be integrated semantically into the database rather that "stolen" from applications using software sensors.

2.2   Characteristics of Contextual Data

Many researchers agree to the notion that the *context* of something is a collection of relevant parameters from the environment, which describe the situation of that entity [2, 4, 13]. This is a sufficient definition for our work. Contextual data has some unique characteristics, which need to be taken into account by a contextual data model.

Heterogeneity: Heterogeneous real world situations involve many types of entities, which must be modeled and handled efficiently by the CDB. Frequently used approaches, such as the relational data model [1], have limitations w. r. t. that aspect.

Complexity: Contextual data structures are highly interconnected graphs of objects, which can be too complex to be understood by human users and for the limited capabilities of mobile devices. It is necessary to break down the graph into smaller parts.

Distribution: Entities and sensors to monitor them are spread all over the real world. Contextual data emerges in different computer systems, making it necessary to integrate different data sources semantically into one ontology.

Data quality: Contextual information always represents imperfect assumptions about the real world [6]. We estimate the validity of contextual data based on data-specific quality indicators as it is proposed by [6, 14].

Dynamics: To avoid permanent update operations, a CDB should store the information how to read the current value of fast changing contextual data from the environment rather than storing the current values themselves.

Mutability: The real world evolves and changes permanently [6, 8]. Data types change and new data types occur. The data model should be extensible at runtime without the need to change, recompile or restart the database engine.

Unavailability: Higher-level knowledge is based on very detailed low-level information, which is not always immediately visible to the sensors. It is necessary to observe the user for a while until all necessary data is available in the CDB.

Privacy: Pervasive technology will capture and store confidential and private information. Therefore, we need security mechanisms as well as a data model, which is simple enough to be inspected by the human end users.

2.3   Requirements for a Representation Format for Contextual Information

In addition to the requirements that were derived from the characteristics of pervasive environments and contextual data we identified the following requirements for contextual data.

Formality: Only a well-defined data model allows non-ambiguous representations, which can be translated into the ontology of other applications or used by reasoning mechanisms [6].

Globality: Although a consistent model of all existing data is hard to implement and maintain [12], we need at least an unambiguous identification schema for contextual data. We model data in small modules, but address it globally.

Modularity, Reusability: Application specific data should be maintained and provided by the respective applications. Generic data structures should be reused to avoid structural redundancy.

Extensibility: Adaptation of the contextual data model to the changing environment is done permanently. The contextual database must be flexible enough to be extensible at any point with many new concepts.

History: Reasoning mechanisms need previous values of contextual data to recognize trends and extrapolate prospective values. The CDB should be able to reproduce snapshots of previous moments.

3   Related Work

The early context-aware research provided frameworks for pervasive infrastructure, i.e. sensors and communication issues. More recent research is becoming aware of the problem how to represent contextual information.

3.1   Object-Oriented Approaches

Many earlier context-aware approaches like the *Context Toolkit* [3] model contextual information as classes in an object oriented programming language. These application-oriented frameworks encapsulate context-aware functionality like dealing with sensors. They mostly use static models of context with simple data types, which cannot be changed at runtime, and do not allow to compose a context model out of modules that are provided by different applications.

3.2   Topic maps

Power [10] suggests the use of topic maps to integrate contextual data located in different contextual databases. Topic maps allow defining relations between physical or logical objects located inside or outside the computer world. Power keeps the data stored at their original location and uses a metadata structure (the topic map) to interconnect them. He also mentions the idea to store context data inside the topic map itself, but he doesn't discuss this idea in detail. While realizing the need for more dynamic topic maps in order to handle the characteristics of contextual data, no details are provided how such an extension could look like.

3.3   Henricksen et al.

Henricksen et al. [6] propose a data format for contextual information based on semantic networks. Several types of associations are defined, e.g. distinguishing associations to data obtained from sensors or data provided by the user. This is relevant metadata for contextual information, but we need more precise information about the source of contextual data, e.g. if it was obtained from hardware or software sensors. Higher-level information is inferred by derived associations, which contain a derivation function that performs algorithms to compute new knowledge out of existing data. This is a powerful concept, but it is not determined where the algorithm of the derivation function is defined and when and how it is invoked. We see the data derivation function as a part of the data model and therefore store its code or its invocation inside the data model. Association types with quantitative qualifiers are also defined. Collection associations can occur more than once for each entity, a set of alternative associations represents alternative possibilities in the graph, and from a set of temporal associations only one association is valid in a given time interval. This allows modeling the past and the present together in one representation, but leads to very complex data structures, which show plenty of irrelevant information. The data quality is modeled using data-specific quality attributes.

This model provides useful concepts for a contextual data representation format. It provides means to visually represent logic in the data model, but only for very basic operations. This leads to complex circumscriptions of the intended structures. A modular concept is missing to break down the data structure in simple, reusable pieces as well as a concept to semantically integrate data from different contextual applications and databases. The model integrates several dimensions of contextual data (i.e. history, adaptability, dependency), in one representation, which will lead to complicated representations in large application scenarios.

4   Basic Concepts of our Approach

In this section we present ideas how to represent contextual data, which is used by more than one application. Individual context-aware applications in well-defined scenarios are implemented more effectively using existing approaches like [3].

Semantic Net: A context model should reflect the real world without unnecessary abstractions. Opposed to AI approaches, which mostly depict the world as a collection

Context- and Situation-Awareness
in Information Logistics

Ulrich Meissen, Stefan Pfennigschmidt, Agnès Voisard, and Tjark Wahnfried

Fraunhofer Institute for Software and Systems Engineering (ISST),
Mollstrae 1, 10178 Berlin, Germany
{ulrich.meissen,stefan.pfennigschmidt,agnes.voisard,
tjark.wahnfried}@isst.fraunhofer.de

Abstract. In order to deliver relevant information at the right time to its mobile users, systems such as event notification systems need to be aware of the users' context, which includes the current time, their location, or the devices they use. Many context frameworks have been introduced in the past few years. However, they usually do not consider the notion of characteristic features of contexts that are invariant during certain time intervals. Knowing the current situation of a user allows the system to better target the information to be delivered. This paper presents a model to handle various contexts and situations in information logistics. A context is defined as a collection of values usually observed by sensors, e. g., location or temperature. A situation builds on this concept by introducing semantical aspects defined in an ontology. Our *situation awareness* proposal has been tested in two projects.

1 Introduction

Information logistics aims at providing a subscriber with the right information at the right time and at the right place (see for instance [4]). Two of its representative applications are ongoing projects at Fraunhofer ISST, namely *Personalized Web Services for the Olympic Games 2008 in Beijing* [10] and *MeLog* ("Message Logistics") [13], which consists in delivering mobile users their personal electronic messages according to their relevance with respect to the users' current *situation*. In such applications, beyond the classical dimensions of time and place, content represents a major challenge. Indeed, the information need that will turn into delivered content is a dynamic concept, i. e., a function of time, space, and preferences of the user, among other parameters.

Location-based services have emerged a few years ago to allow end users to obtain information based on some location, usually the position of the user [16]. Such services, for instance mechanisms to answer a query such as "Where is the nearest subway station?" or "What are the exhibitions in the city today?" are currently receiving a great deal of interest. They manipulate the common aspects of location and time but also more complex notions such as the profile of a user. In most event notification systems (ENS) designed so far, the profile of a user consists of more or less static definitions of personal data such as name and address as well as preference data (cf. [9]). With the dynamic incurred by the time and location components, the profile of the user has to be defined

W. Lindner et al. (Eds.): EDBT 2004 Workshops, LNCS 3268, pp. 335–344, 2004.

in a highly dynamic way, i. e., as a function of the other dimensions. In other words, the user demand may change rapidly according to such dimensions. A type of user demand can be gathered in time intervals. For instance, if a user is in the car, he or she would like to be kept updated on the (current) traffic situation in some area. *Situation awareness* is a solution to this problem; the fact of being in the car represents a certain *situation*.

This paper focuses on a model to handle user situations as well as the surroundings of the user – including time and current location – and other attributes referred to as the *context* of the user. The idea is to abstract from sensors and derive semantics as much as possible. Only then the user demand may be satisfied, i. e., information filtered and personalized. Even though some of these notions have been studied in the past few years, we are not aware of any model that encompasses all these notions in a unified framework. The notion of situation has been studied in different fields of computer science such as computational linguistics (situation theory [2, 3]) and robotics (situation calculus [11, 12]). Although there are similarities to our situation definition, the scope of application of these approaches is different. Our situation model complements the area of information logistics [4] by a formal description of the user's environment and its influences on the information need of the user. The definition of our situation model is based on definitions that had been established in the fields of artificial intelligence [12] and context awareness [1, 14]. Especially the interpretation of context data and their aggregation as studied in [8] is closely related to our work. Research done in the field of semantic networks and ontologies [6, 7] plays an essential role in our model, in order to interpret real situations.

This paper is organized as follows. Section 2 gives the example of a typical application in information logistics (MeLog). This example serves as a reference throughout the paper. Section 3 presents our model of context and situation. In Sect. 4, we get back to the application and we describe it using our model. Finally, Sect. 5 draws our conclusions and presents future perspectives.

2   An Example Scenario

In order to illustrate our needs and motivate our approach towards an integrated model on situations, let us consider a real world scenario: Mr. Busy is a project manager in a large scale distributed enterprise. He spends half of is working time out of his office on business travel. Due to his traveling activities he has a logistic problem with messages: In the average, an amount of about 60 e-mail messages, 5 faxes and 5 voice messages are usually addressed to his office every day. Some of these messages are very important for him to get during his travel, because they might contain useful information for the next business meeting or just for traveling purposes. To solve this problem he has to check these messages regularly which is often rather inconvenient and sometimes impossible.

Let us consider a small snapshot of the business travel plan of Mr. Busy in order to make the task clear. Based on various information sources like his organizer or the travel management unit we can describe his travel in a sequence of situations:

```
until 12:00 at the office, working
12:00 - 12:30 taking a taxi to the airport 12:30 - 13:30 at the
airport Berlin Tegel 13:30 - 15:00 flight 452 to London Heathrow
```

```
15:00 - 15:20 at the airport London Heathrow 15:20 - 16:30 in a
car with Ms. Miller 16:30 - 19:00 project meeting in London 19:00
- 19:30 taking a taxi to Hotel Comfort ... 10:30 - 07:00 flight
608 to Bejing
```

From the time he left several messages arrived in his office. Now let us presume that Mr. Busy has a perfect virtual assistant who selects only the messages that are relevant to the known situations during his travel. This perfect assistant decides the relevance to the incoming messages as follows:

```
voice:    the car is repaired and
ready to collect              (not yet relevant) e-mail:  report on
project P1                           (relevant for meeting)
e-mail:  virus alert from IT support                      (not
yet relevant) e-mail:  invitation to a birthday party (not yet
relevant) e-mail:  report on project P3 (not yet relevant) e-mail:
better connecting flight from Bejing available      (relevant for
travel) fax:       night events in London from Hotel Comfort
(relevant for leisure) e-mail: letter from the board about last
year activities    (not yet relevant)
```

Being aware of the current and preferably the future situations of his client is essential for such a perfect assistant. The *MeLog* application described in Sect. 4 utilizes situation awareness by comparing situation patterns with observed situation sequences in order to provide the functionality of such an assistant. This approach is based on a situation model described in the following section.

3   Situation Model

This section is concerned with our situation model, the kernel of our approach. We introduce the concept of a situation and describe its associated operators. These operators allow to handle many real-life situations and to use them in order to deliver the right information at the right time.

3.1   From Context to Situations

A situation is defined in [12] as "the complete state of the universe at an instant of time". However, in order to describe someone's individual situation we do not need the whole state of the universe but rather use a subset that is considered relevant [5]. A state – called *context* in our model – is a collection of *context variables*, each representing one relevant observable real world parameter, e. g.,

$$\texttt{gpsLocation} = (52.5264, 13.4172) \ ,$$
$$\texttt{velocity} = 1.8 \, \text{km/h} \ .$$

A context can be considered as a snapshot or instantiation of all context variables at some point in time. The observation may physically be done via any kind of sensor function which do not play any role here. The value of a context variable (e. g., gpsLocation) will slightly change from time to time, i. e., from context to context, whereas we would not say that a slight movement of a participant within the conference room really affects the situation of the people attending the meeting. We use the notion of *characteristic features* of a context to get properties that are more stable over time. A characteristic feature – or *characteristic* for short – is a logical proposition about a context or a subset of its components, i. e., its context variables:

$$\texttt{organizationalLocation (conferenceRoom) ,}$$
$$\texttt{kindOfMovement (slow) .}$$

The mapping between context variables (e. g., velocity) and characteristic features (e. g., kindOfMovement) is defined using application-dependent aggregation rules which are also not discussed in detail here. From the examples used in the previous sections one can see the possible existence of a generalization/specialization relation. That means, one characteristic feature can be inferred when knowing another one. If we know, for example, that a project meeting takes place Tuesday, we can say also that it takes place weekdays. To utilize this, we use concept graphs (directed acyclic graphs), where the nodes are connected by *subsumes*-relations (Fig. 1). We utilize these kind of graphs or taxonomies because they are simple and reflect common ways of human thinking and structuring. Throughout this paper we will refer to such kind of graphs as *dimension structures*. Context and its characteristics encompass many *dimensions* or aspects [14], e. g., time, location, activities, or kind of movement, which should be handled separately. A dimension can be viewed as the type of a characteristic feature and is represented by a predicate and a dimension structure. For many of these aspects ontologies representing common knowledge already exist and can be used to express context characteristics.

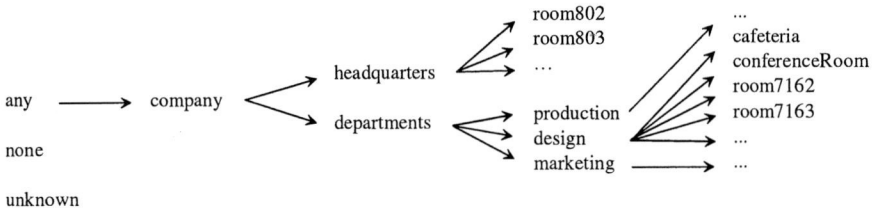

Fig. 1. Example of a dimension structure

We are now able to give a more formal definition of situation. We use the concept of characteristic features described previously. A situation in our model will be formed by a sequence of contexts with invariant characteristics and is described as a triple

$$S = (t_{\text{beg}}, t_{\text{end}}, cs)$$

where
t_{beg} is the starting time of the situation (i. e., the time of the first context of the sequence),
t_{end} is its end time (i. e., the time of the last context of the sequence), and
cs is a set of characteristic features which are invariant throughout the sequence. cs is interpreted as the conjunction of all characteristic features: $cf_1 \wedge \ldots \wedge cf_n$.

This definition offers a rich concept that enables us to describe the activity and the location of the user, such as being "at home", "at the office", "in the train", or "on the phone". We would like to emphasize two major features. First, the notion of situation may encompass many dimensions as one can be both in a taxi and on the phone. To handle this aspect efficiently we chose not to mix dimensions and to consider them separately. Second, the generalization/specialization notions of our characteristics enable the description of situations on different levels of granularity. It can be general, e. g., "traveling", or more precise, e. g., "in a taxi going down the Champs Elysees".

Situation Awareness. Recognizing and identifying situations is a central requirement for applications in information logistics. Applications that make use of situations and are able to handle changes such as entering or leaving a situation are denoted *situation-aware applications*. There are two ways for such an application to utilize the situation model: (1) Analysis of past and current situations, where context information is available. (2) "Situation construction" or planning of situations with assumed characteristics, where context information is not available, but where the characteristics (which are propositions about the contexts) impose restrictions on context variables. These restrictions can be used afterwards to check whether the planned situation actually takes or took place, or not. In addition, one can define *typical situations* and check whether an actual situation complies with a certain definition. This last point will be further discussed as an example in Sect. 4.2. To define typical situations we additionally use the notion of *situation patterns*, as logical propositions about situation characteristics.

3.2 Operators

The situations defined above are handled through operators. We distinguish operators that manipulate whole situations from the ones that work on characteristics of situations.

Operators on Characteristics. The following three operators have in common that they deal with similarities or analogies between characteristics:

$\texttt{generalize}\,(cs_1, cs_2) \to cs_r$

This operator takes two sets of characteristics cs_1, cs_2, and finds the most specific set of characteristics cs_r that is common for both. In order to do that it utilizes the subsumes relation of the dimension structures used and finds the least common ancestor.

$\texttt{fulfills}\,(cs, p) \to \{\texttt{true, false}\}$

This operator determines whether a set of characteristics cs complies to the conditions of a situation pattern p.

$\texttt{compare}\,(cs_1, cs_2) \to [0, 1] \subset \mathbb{R}$

This operator computes the similarity between two given sets of characteristics cs_1, cs_2 by applying a similarity metric on the subsumes-paths within the dimensions (e. g., semantic distance [15]).

Operators on Situations. We use the notion of *situation sequences* to denote a series of directly subsequent situations.

$\texttt{previous}\,(s) \to s_p$

This operator determines the predecessor s_p of a given situation s (*nil* if there is no situation known).

$$\texttt{next}\ (s) \rightarrow s_\mathrm{s}$$

This operator determines the successor s_s of a given situation s (*nil* if there is no situation known).

$$\texttt{combine}\ (seq) \rightarrow s_\mathrm{r}$$

This operator tries to find a generalized situation s_r covering the whole time interval of a situation sequence *seq*. The resulting situation will be built such that, the begin time equals the begin time of the first situation and the end time equals the end time of the last situation of the sequence. The characteristic of the resulting situation will be the most specific generalized characteristic of all situations. If the sequence contains no situations the result will be *nil*. If the sequence contains only one situation the result will be this situation.

4   Application

In this section, we present the *MeLog* system as a functional prototype of a situation-aware application in information logistics. MeLog is short for "message logistics" and was developed within the scope of a research project at Fraunhofer ISST in 2002 and 2003.

4.1   The MeLog System

MeLog gives automatic decision support in order to deliver electronic messages such as e-mail, converted fax, or voice messages at the right time. Based on user situations such as "at the airport", "eating at a restaurant", and "during the project meeting", the system recognizes the most relevant topics and delivers messages that have high information value for these or the following situations. In order to do that, MeLog in a first step calculates the *relevance* between a message and the user's situations via his or her topics of interest. Based on relevance, time-dependent *utility* and *acceptance* functions are then taken into account in order to calculate the time of highest information value. The strategies and algorithms of these calculations are not discussed here in detail.

The MeLog system consists of several components. As shown in Fig. 2 they can be divided into components of the system kernel layer and components of the data model layer. The kernel layer encompasses all functional components. That is, this layer is responsible for the recognition of context data, the aggregation of that data, and the derivation of situations.

The data layer manages all information sources necessary for predicting the information value, such as dimension ontologies, situation history, etc. One concrete example of dimension data we used is the user's address book. The set of topic descriptions known as overall "interesting" to the user also belongs to the data layer. Examples of topic structure sources are the user's e-mail folder structure or similar structures found in document management systems.

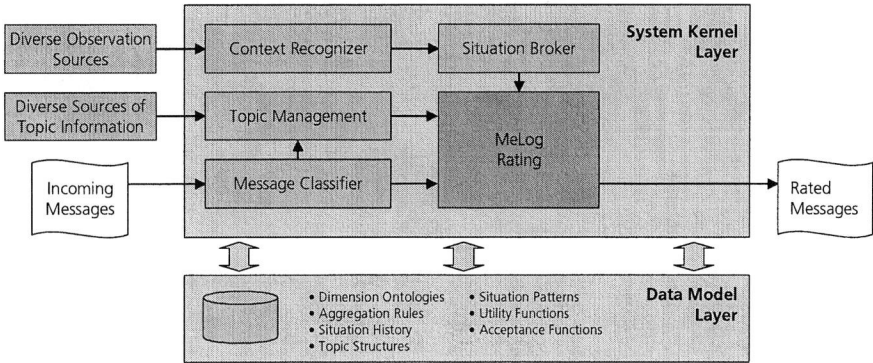

Fig. 2. MeLog system architecture

Another category of input is context data, gathered by different observation sources. Besides other sources MeLog takes advantage of the entries in the user's electronic diary, such as appointments. These entries serve as information about situations that are planned by the user. Any kind of sensor data incorporated by the system is also an observation source in this view. Thus it is a major capability of the approach to consider aspects of planned situations as well as real world sensor data.

4.2   Back to the Example Scenario

In the following short example we want to find out whether actual situations, in this case the flight to London and the project meeting, fit to typical situations defined by the user, in this case traveling and meetings for project P1. Afterwards the relevance of messages can be calculated on the basis of these typical situations and their associated information demand.

In our example context data is available from the following sensors: (1) location sensors; decimal geo coordinates (type: WGS84), (2) electronic organizer; entry keywords (type: string), (3) laptop; used documents (type: string).

Our situation characteristics are described by the following dimensions: (1) transportation in use, (2) organizational location, (3) kind of movement, (4) person in presence, (5) document in use.

Behind each of these dimensions a domain-dependent dimension structure is used in order to describe meta knowledge about the values within the dimension. In our example Mr. Busy has defined characteristics of two typical situations as well as the information demand associated with these patterns:

```
p("traveling")  =
[transportationInUse(any), kindOfMovement(any/../significant)]
p("meeting P1") =
[organizationalLocation(any/../company/departments/design)
              OR organizationalLocation(any/../company/headquarters),
          personInPresence(any/../staff/design/project teams/team P1)
           OR personInPresence(any/../partners/companyX/marketing),
          kindOfMovement(none),
          documentInUse(any/../work/projects/project P1)]
```

The first one means *"when Mr. Busy is traveling, he uses transportation and he is moving significantly"*. The second means *"when Mr. Busy is in a meeting about Project P1 he is either in the headquarters or design department, people from the project team or marketing partners are in presence, he is not moving, and he uses documents for project P1"*. The *generalize* operator can be used to derive such patterns from past situations, e. g., if several "traveling" situations already took place the common characteristics of a typical situation can be derived from generalizing these observed situations.

Table 1. Context data gathered during business travel

Time	Coordinates from location sensor	Keywords from electronic organizer	Documents from laptop
...	...	...	...
11:57:45	(52.5264, 13.4172)	office, working	design-plan-alpha-2b.tex
11:57:46	(52.5263, 13.4171)	office, working	none
...	...	...	...
15:42:01	(52.4259, 12.6045)	flight, berlin, london	project-P4-report.pdf
...	...	...	...
17:35:21	(51.5851, 0.0351)	meeting, miller, turner	project-P1-milestone.ppt
...	...	...	...
19:31:22	(51.5626, 0.0687)	hotel	none
...	...	...	...

Table 1 shows a part of the raw sensor data the application gets before and during the business travel. According to predefined aggregation rules, nodes within the dimensions structures can be derived from that data. Based on that the characteristics of an observed situation can be inferred. Such rules tell the application, for instance, which of the observed coordinates correspond to which node within the organizational location ontology (cf. Fig. 1). Based on this aggregation MeLog derives two situations from the sensor data, situation s_1 (*flight*, 13:30 - 15:00) and situation s_2 (*meeting*, 16:30 - 19:00). The characteristics of these situations are shown below.

```
cs(s1) =
[transportationInUse(any/../airplane),
        kindOfMovement(any/../significant),
        documentsInUse(any/../work/projects/project P4/project-P4-report.pdf)]
cs(s2) =
[organizationalLocation(any/../company/departments/design/room7163),
        personInPresence(any/../staff/design/project teams/team P1/Ms. Miller),
        personInPresence(any/../staff/design/project teams/team P1/Mr. Turner),
        kindOfMovement(none),
        documentInUse(any/../work/projects/project P1/project-P1-milestone.pdf)]
```

Now the application uses the *fulfills* operator in order to decide whether these observed situations fit to the predefined situation patterns. Checking whether the characteristics of the "flight" situation fulfill the characteristics of the "traveling" pattern gives the following term:

```
fulfills(cs(s1), p("traveling"))
 = fulfills(transportationInUse(airplane), transportationInUse(any)) AND
   fulfills(kindOfMovement(significant), kindOfMovement(significant))
 = TRUE
```

Analogically follows:

```
fulfills(cs(s2), p("traveling"))  =
FALSE fulfills(cs(s1), p("meeting P1")) = FALSE fulfills(cs(s2),
p("meeting P1")) = TRUE
```

According to the outcome of the operations above the information demand associated with a typical "travel" situation can be also associated with the observed "flight" situation. The demand associated with a typical "project P1 meeting" situation can be associated with the observed "meeting" situation.

5   Conclusion

This paper presented a model to handle various contexts and situations in information logistics. A context is defined as a collection of values extracted from the environment at a certain time (e. g., location and speed extracted by sensors). A situation builds on this concept by introducing propositions about context data, which form characteristic features that are stable over a time interval. Semantical aspects in form of ontologies are used to enable interpretation of situations by applications. When the system is able to deduce situations from the context, it is implicitly able to infer the user's information demand. This enables the delivery of information relevant at a certain point in time.

Currently we focus on the prediction of situations. By mining situation sequences, one is able to find patterns in situations and to predict future situations, hence anticipate the information that will be of interest to the user in the future. A second research direction is to use our model as a means to precisely describe and analyze scenarios in information logistics, in order to derive application needs in that field. Grouping people according to the situation they share combined with the analysis of appropriate levels of individualization are points of particular interest in such applications.

Acknowledgements

We wish to thank the anonymous reviewers for their useful comments, as well as Andreas Billig, Stefan Decker, Rüdiger Gartmann, and Norbert Weißenberg for interesting discussions.

References

1. G. D. Abowd, A. K. Dey, P. J. Brown, N. Davies, M. Smith, and P. Steggles. Towards a better understanding of context and context-awareness. In H.W. Gellersen, editor, *Handheld and Ubiquitous Computing: First International Symposium, HUC'99*, volume 1707 of *LNCS*, Berlin/Heidelberg/New York, 1999. Springer Verlag.
2. V. Akman and M. Surav. The use of situation theory in context modeling. *Computational Intelligence*, 13(3):427–438, 1997.
3. R. Cooper, K. Mukai, and J. Perry, editors. *Situation Theory and its applications*, volume I of *CSLI Lecture Notes No. 22*. CSLI: Center for the Study of Language and Information, Stanford University, California, 1990.

4. W. Deiters, T. Löffeler, and S. Pfennigschmidt. The information logistics approach toward user demand-driven information supply. In D. Spinellis, editor, *Cross-Media Service Delivery*, pages 37–48, Boston/Dordrecht/London, 2003. Kluwer Acadamic Publishers.

5. A. K. Dey. *Providing architectural support for building context-aware applications.* PhD thesis, College of Computing, Georgia Institute of Technology, 2000.

6. T. R. Gruber. Towards principles for the design of ontologies used for knowledge sharing. In N. Guarino and R. Poli, editors, *Formal Ontology in Conceptual Analysis and Knowledge Representation*, Boston/Dordrecht/London, 1993. Kluwer Academic Publishers.

7. M. Gruninger and Jintae Lee. Ontology applications and design. *Communications of the ACM*, 45(2):39–41, 2002.

8. S. Haseloff. Context gathering – an enabler for information logistics. In P. Chamoni, W. Deiters, N. Gronau, R.-D. Kutsche, P. Loos, H. Müller-Merbach, B. Rieger, and K. Sandkuhl, editors, *Multikonferenz Wirtschaftsinformatik (MKWI) 2004, Band 2*, pages 204–216, Berlin, 2004. Akademische Verlagsgesellschaft.

9. A. Hinze. *An Adaptive Integrating Event Notification Service.* PhD thesis, Free University of Berlin, Computer Science Institute, 2003.

10. B. Holtkamp, R. Gartmann, and Y. Han. Flame2008: Personalized web services for the Olympic Games 2008 in Beijing. In *e-2003, e-Challenges Workshop*, 2003.

11. Y. Lespérance, H. J. Levesque, Fangzhen Lin, D. Marcu, R. Reiter, and R. B. Scherl. A logical approach to high level robot programming – a progress report. In B. Kuipers, editor, *Working notes of the 1994 AAAI fall symposium on Control of the Physical World by Intelligent Systems*, New Orleans, LA, 1994.

12. J. McCarthy and P. J. Hayes. Some philosophical problems from the standpoint of artificial intelligence. Report Memo AI-73, Department of Computer Science, Stanford University, Stanford, California, 1968.

13. U. Meissen, S. Pfennigschmidt, K. Sandkuhl, and T. Wahnfried. Situation-based message rating in information logistics and its applicability in collaboration scenarios. In *Proceedings of the 30th Conference on EUROMICRO*. IEEE Computer Society, 2004 (to appear).

14. D. Petrelli, E. Not, M. Zancanaro, C. Strapparava, and O. Stock. Modelling and adapting to context. *Personal Ubiquitous Computing*, 5(1):20–24, 2001.

15. P. Resnik. Using information content to evaluate semantic similarity in a taxonomy. In Chris Mellish, editor, *Proceedings of the 14th International Joint Conference on Artificial Intelligence*, pages 448–453, San Francisco, 1995. Morgan Kaufmann.

16. J. Schiller and A. Voisard, editors. *Location-based Services.* Morgan Kaufmann, San Francisco, 2004.

An Indexing Scheme for Update Notification in Large Mobile Information Systems*

Hagen Höpfner[1], Stephan Schosser[1], and Kai-Uwe Sattler[2]

[1] Otto-von-Guericke University of Magdeburg, Department of Computer Science,
P.O.Box 4120, D-39016 Magdeburg, Germany
{hoepfner@iti.cs.uni-magdeburg.de| schosser78@arcor.de}

[2] Technical University of Ilmenau, Department of Computer Science and Automation,
P.O.Box 10 0565, D-98684 Ilmenau, Germany
kus@tu-ilmenau.de

Abstract. Due to the increasing usage of small and low footprinted devices like mobile phones as clients of mobile information systems a new problem arises: "How to determine the relevance of updates for a large number of mobile clients?" In this paper we present an indexing scheme that represents conjunctive queries posed by the mobile clients in a trie. So, IDs of the clients are referenced by their queries and checking the relevance of an update can be efficiently done by a trie lookup.

1 Introduction and Motivation

Most mobile information system are designed as an add-on to existing classical, fixed network based information systems. The mobile clients have to connect to the fixed network via a base station. But, normally such systems do not consider the extremely increasing number of mobile devices that are usable for accessing the data. In fact, mobile phones, smart phones and networked PDAs will be used as information system clients. So, a new central challenge for supporting mobile devices on the server site arises: *How to handle interest of a large number of mobile clients efficiently?*

The light-weightiness of the mobile clients and the classical problem of incrementally updating materialized views prohibit to transfer all updates directly to the mobile clients. So, client queries have to be stored and evaluated on the server. Now, if an update occurs it is obviously inefficient to check all stored queries sequentially.

An alternative, which is presented in this paper, is a query index based update evaluation approach that allows to look up such mobile devices which are potentially interested in updated information. At this, queries are represented as paths in a trie [2] whereby each path references a set of mobile client IDs.

The remainder of the paper is structured as follows. In Section 2 we discuss related work and point out the differences between our work and overlapping research areas. Section 3 describes the query index and how it is used to look up mobile clients efficiently. The evaluation of our approach can be found in Section 4. Finally, the paper closes with conclusions and an outlook on ongoing research in Section 5.

---

* This research is supported by the DFG under grant SA 782/3-2

W. Lindner et al. (Eds.): EDBT 2004 Workshops, LNCS 3268, pp. 345–354, 2004.
© Springer-Verlag Berlin Heidelberg 2004

2   Related Work

Our work is embedded into the context of mobile databases and information systems. We do not support completely wireless systems but systems that allow mobile clients to connect via a base station to a fixed network as discussed in [11]. Furthermore, several works regarding the replication and synchronization of data between a static server and mobile clients has been done. But these approaches, that can be classified as data centric (e.g. [9]) and transaction centric (e.g. [3, 10]), consider the integration of offline executed update operations from the mobile clients to the server. However, we currently do not take into account the synchronization of such updates but focus on performance aspects of notifying mobile clients about updates on the server.

Beside this, our research can be interpreted as profile handling. That means, that the stored queries describe the profiles of mobile users as it is done in [1] or [14]. But profiles are based on a semantic based selection of needed data. We plan to support also semantic queries regarding user contexts in our future work.

Another related research area concerns the query containment problem that is considered in many publications, e.g. [4, 12]. [13] comprises the complexity issues of various kinds of queries that are represented as conjunctively connected predicates. However, we have to deal with query containment only when we use semantic information for query indexing. Here, we focus on an approach using syntactical information which could be extended to use semantic information.

Last but not least we have to point out, that there exist relationships between the problems that are focused in our work and the common problem of incrementially updating materialized views [8]. If we consider stored queries as view definitions we have also to decide which "view" is affected by an update. But we do not have to materialize the update on the mobile clients as yet.

3   Indexing Mobile Clients Using a Trie

As already mentioned, a sequential check of all registered queries is inefficient. Therefore, we introduced in [6] first ideas on a trie-based indexing of mobile clients. Database queries are represented as conjunctively connected predicates that are ordered in an alpha-numerical predicate order. We currently support three[1] different kinds of predicates *relation predicates*, *join predicates*, and *selection predicates*. A relation predicate r is comparable to the projection operator of the relational algebra. A projection $\pi_X(r(R))$ with $X \subseteq R$ can be written as the relation predicate $r(R)(x_1, \ldots, x_n)$ with $\{x_1, \ldots, x_n\} = X$. In a similar manner, join predicates j_n are comparable to the equijoin operator of the relational algebra. That means that a equijoin $r(R_1) \bowtie_{a=b} r(R_2)$ with $R_1, R_2 \subseteq R, a \in R_1$ and $b \in R_2$ can be written as the join predicate $r(R_1).a = r(R_2).b$. Finally, a selection predicate p_l represents the selection operator of the relational algebra. A selection $\sigma_F(r(R))$ with the selection condition F is written as the selection predicate

---

[1] The context predicates that where introduced in [6] are not considered in this paper but will be included in our approach in the future.

$r(R).F$. The selection condition F is restricted to comparisons with constants of the form `attribute` γ `constant` with $\gamma \in \{\leq, <, =, \neq, \geq, >\}$.

Thus, database queries are given in a standardized calculus notation, i.e. in conjunctive form. Predicates are ordered in a lexicographic manner: at first relation predicates r_i, then the join predicates j_k and the selection predicates p_l.

Definition 1. *A database query* $Q = \{r_1 \wedge \ldots \wedge r_m \wedge j_1 \wedge \ldots \wedge j_n \wedge p_1 \wedge \ldots \wedge p_o\}$ *can be represented as a sequence of predicates* $\langle r_1, \ldots, r_m, j_1, \ldots, j_n, p_1, \ldots, p_o \rangle$, *where* $\forall i, k \in 1 \ldots m, i < k \Rightarrow r_i \triangleleft r_k$ *and* $\forall i, k \in 1 \ldots n, i < k \Rightarrow j_i \triangleleft j_k$ *as well as* $\forall i, k \in 1 \ldots o, i < k \Rightarrow p_i \triangleleft p_k$ *holds. Here,* $\triangleleft$ *means "lexicographically smaller".*

Obviously, this query language is *not* strong relational complete, but is restricted to a subset of calculi which is sufficient for the realization of typical applications of mobile information systems.

Now, the trie can be described as follows: Each query predicate is represented as an edge and leaves represent links to mobile device ID-lists. Thus a database query $Q_P = \{r_1 \wedge r_2 \wedge \ldots \wedge r_m \wedge j_1 \wedge j_2 \wedge \ldots \wedge j_n \wedge p_1 \wedge p_2 \wedge \ldots \wedge p_o\}$ is included in the trie in form of the complete path $P = r_1 r_2 \cdots r_m j_1 j_2 \cdots j_n p_1 p_2 \cdots p_o$ from the root of the trie. A mobile device ID-list contains all IDs of mobile devices having registered the query represented by the corresponding path.

3.1 Physical Transformation of Database Queries into Trie-Paths

Due to optimization issues regarding the implementation of this index approach, we have to refine the theoretical description given above. Relation predicates r_i consist of the name of considered relation $r(R_i)$ and a set of projected attributes $(x_1, \ldots, x_n)$. As the relation name can be used by various queries that project different sets of attributes, we store the relation name and the attribute set separated as $k_{r_i} \hat{=} r(R)$ and $k_{p_i} \hat{=} (x_1, \ldots, x_n)$, respectively.

Join predicates j_i are stored undivided as $k_{j_i} \hat{=} r(R_1).a = r(R_2).b$, but we have to add relation nodes for relations, that are used in the join predicates but not in the projection predicates.

Selection predicates p_i consist of an attribute name `attribute`, a comparison operator $\gamma \in \{\leq, <, =, \neq, \geq, >\}$ and a comparative value `constant`. Obviously, an attribute name can be used in different selection predicates with various comparison operators and various comparative values. So, we represent selection predicates as two separated parts $k_{a_i} \hat{=}$ `attribute`γ and $k_{v_i} \hat{=}$ `constant`.

Furthermore, implementing a trie requires to encapsulate the information logically represented by the edges into the nodes[2]. So we have six different kinds of nodes: the root of the trie, *relation nodes* k_r, *projection nodes* k_p, *join nodes* k_j, *attribute nodes* k_a and *attribute value nodes* k_v. Figure 2 illustrates the physical implementation of the example shown in Figure 1. Furthermore, the last join node contains a list of all attributes that are used in selection predicates. This is necessary for minimizing the space consumption while checking their relevance (see Section 3.2). In order to minimize the number of nodes that are checked per update, the node order is based on the following restrictions:

---

[2] Nodes are implemented in form of Java classes.

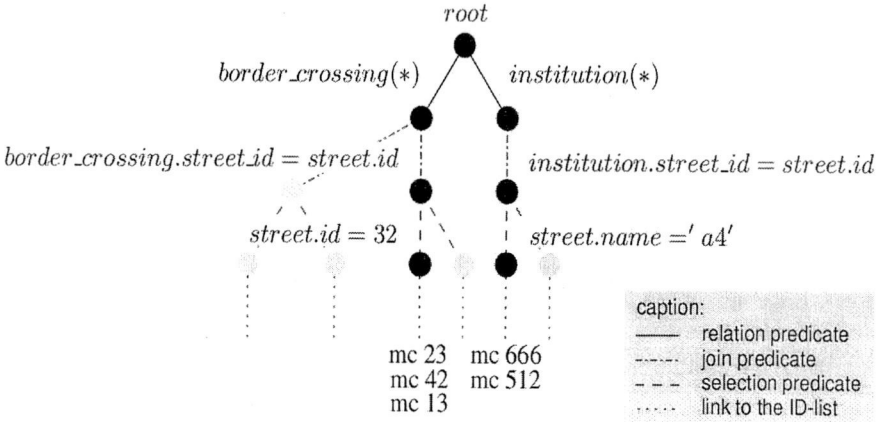

Fig. 1. Logical trie representation of queries

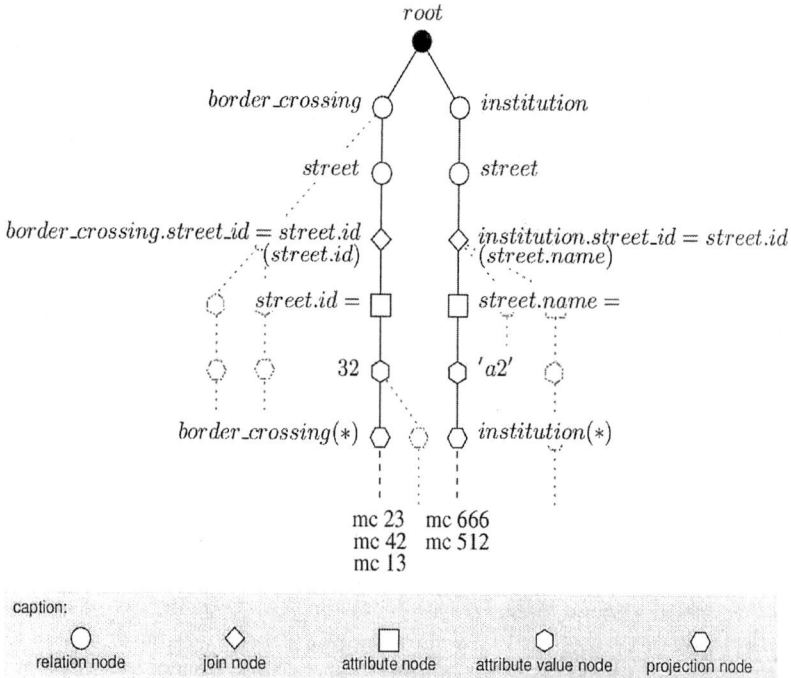

Fig. 2. Physical trie representation of queries

- Most of all relation nodes restrict the search space for an incoming update. If an update is based on relation R_1 we do not have to check queries that do not use R_1. So, relation nodes are stored directly below the root.

- As mentioned above, join predicates are used similar to the equijoin operator. So, if a registered query uses join predicates it is inevitable to compute the join. Surely, this operation is quite expensive but without executing the join, a correct check of selection predicates is impossible. So, the join nodes follow the relation nodes in a path.
- The position of the projection nodes at the bottom is motivated by the fact, that the relevance of a projection can be reduced to update operations. If we first check join predicates and selection predicates we can fully check the relevance of insert and delete operations, at this. Now, projection predicates are only relevant if the projected attribute is neither used as join attribute nor is included in the selection predicates. But, to check this we first need to look at the join nodes as well as at the attribute and attribute value nodes.

Definition 2. *The node order in a trie path is given as* $k_{r_1}, \ldots, k_{r_m}, k_{j_1}, \ldots, k_{j_n}, k_{a_1},$ $k_{v_1}, \ldots, k_{a_o}, k_{v_o}, k_{p_1}, \ldots, k_{p_q}$, *where* $\forall i, l \in 1 \ldots m, i < l \Rightarrow k_{r_i} \triangleleft k_{r_l}, \forall i, l \in$ $1 \ldots n, i < l \Rightarrow k_{j_i} \triangleleft k_{j_l}, \forall i, l \in 1 \ldots o, i < l \Rightarrow k_{a_i} \triangleleft k_{a_l}$ *and* $\forall i, l \in 1 \ldots q, i < l \Rightarrow$ $k_{p_i} \triangleleft k_{p_l}$ *holds. At this,* $\triangleleft$ *means lexicographically smaller.*

3.2 Looking up the Trie

A trie look-up is performed for each incoming update *before* this update is performed on the database. The aim is to compute a list of client IDs of the mobile clients that had registered a query which is affected by this update. We distinguish between three different kinds of updates: (1) insert, (2) update and (3) delete operations. All these can only be relevant for registered queries that use the same relation as the update. So, we first compare the relation nodes with the given relation name (see Algorithm 1). At this, we benefit from the lexicographical order of the relation nodes (see line 10). The result is a set of pointers to the found relation nodes. These pointers are used as starting points for the following steps. Because of the physical structure of the trie, this step also checks the "hidden" relations that are used for join-predicates only.

Algorithm 1: *Checking relation predicates*

---

01 **OUTPUT:** RN // a set of pointers to the found relation nodes in the path
02 **INPUT:** r // name of the relation affected by this update
03   trie with $root$ node
04
05 $RN = \{\}$
06 *checking_relation_predicates(node, r, RN)*
07 **for each** child c_i of *node* **do**
08   **if** $c_i.value = r$ **and** $c_i.type = k_r$ **then** $RN = RN \cup \{c_i\}$; return
09   **else**
10   **if** $c_i.type \neq k_r$ **or** $r \triangleleft c_i.value$ **then** return
11   **else** call *checking_relation_predicates(c_i, r, RN)*

Relation predicates can be followed in a path by a join node, by an attribute node or by a projection node. After calling Algorithm 1 we have to find out the kind of the next node. Because of the space limitations we skip a detailed description of this here but assume that the algorithm returns the following three sets: (1) FJ is a set of the first join nodes in paths that are represented in RN, (2) FA is a set of the first attribute nodes in paths that are represented in RN but not in FJ and (3) FP is a set of the first predicate nodes in paths that are represented in RN but not in FJ and not in FA.

Unfortunately, checking the join predicates in a uniform way, similar to the relation predicates, is not efficiently possible because updates, deletes and inserts modify join results in various ways. Furthermore, we have to compute the joins on the database because the relevance of the selection predicates, that is checked later on, depends on the join results. But, we do not have to consider all attributes. In fact, the temporary join result contains only the join attributes and the attributes used in the selection predicates.

Checking Join Nodes. Checking the relevance of an update operation regarding join nodes is done for each element of the set FJ. The return value of each call is a set AJ_i of pointers to the nodes below the join nodes and PR_i a set of temporary join results, that are needed for checking selection predicates. All paths that are not represented in the union of all AJ_i are not considered in the following steps. As mentioned above join nodes contain join predicates of the form $r(R_1) \bowtie_{a=b} r(R_2)$ with $R_1, R_2 \subseteq R$, $a \in R_1$ and $b \in R_2$. The algorithm first collects all join nodes of a path. So, we get a join-statement for each path of the form $r(R_1) \bowtie_{a_1=a_2} r(R_2) \bowtie_{a_3=a_4} r(R_3) \cdots r(R_j) \bowtie_{a_{2j-1}=a_{2j}} r(R_{j+1})$ with $j \in \mathbb{N}$ and $a_{2j-1} \in R_j$. Checking the relevance of such a statement for the update is done in the following way:

Insert Operation: We assume inserts in standard SQL-notation: INSERT INTO table_name (column_list) VALUES (value [, ...]).

$A = (a_1^i, \ldots, a_n^i)$ is the attribute list of relation used for inserting data. $V = (x_1^i, \ldots, x_n^i)$ is the tuple of inserted values. Furthermore, $r(R_{j+1})$ is the relation that is used for inserting the data, $a_1^i = a_{2j}$ is the according join attribute and x_1^i is the inserted value of a_1^i. So the join predicates are affected by the update if $\pi_{a_1}(r(R_1)) \bowtie_{a_1=a_2} \pi_{a_2,a_3}(r(R_2)) \ldots (\sigma_{a_{2j-1}=x_1^i}(r(R_j)))$ is not empty.

Delete Operation: Delete operation affect a join predicate if the tuples that have to be deleted are included in the join result. We assume delete operations in SQL-notation[3] as DELETE FROM table_name WHERE clause. Because this can affect more than one tuple in the database we first have to look up the according values of the join predicate. With the updated relation $r(R_{j+1})$, we can use the clause that was given by the statement: $r(R_T) = \pi_{2j}(\sigma_{\texttt{clause}}(r(R_{j+1})))$. Now, the join is affected by the update if $\pi_{a_1}(r(R_1)) \bowtie_{a_1=a_2} \pi_{a_2,a_3}(r(R_2)) \cdots \pi_{a_{2j-2}, a_{2j-1}}(r(R_j)) \cap r(R_T)$ is not empty.

Update Operation: Currently we handle update operations as combination of delete and insert operations.

As aforementioned, we need the result of the joins to check the selection predicates. Therefore, attributes that are not used as join attributes may be required. So, we have to guarantee that these attributes are included into the temporary result. In fact, we do not

---

[3] Currently we forbid the usage of cascading delete operations.

use the minimal join presented above but add all attributes of selection predicates, that are included in the last join node, to the projections.

Checking Attribute Nodes and Attribute Value Nodes. First we look up the selection predicates with a recursive algorithm. It returns for each relevant path a set of selection predicates P_Q. An insert operation affects a query Q if it satisfies at least one selection predicate. Formally, that means for an inserted tuple $A = (a_1^i, \ldots, a_n^i)$ with the values $V = (x_1^i, \ldots, x_n^i)$ that $\exists p \in P_Q | \sigma_p(r(R_A)) \neq \emptyset$ must hold. In order to check the relevance of delete operations we have to distinguish between queries, that use join nodes and queries without join nodes. In the first case, we have to check whether the delete affects the part of the according temporary join result that is covered by the selection predicates. Therefore, with an SQL-notated delete, the temporary join result $TJ \in PR_i$ and the disjunction $D = p_1 \vee p_2 \vee \ldots \vee p_o$ with $o = |P_Q|$ that means, that $\sigma_{clause}(\sigma_D(TJ)) \neq \emptyset$ must hold. In the second case we have to use the base relation instead of TJ. Therewith, the selection predicates of queries without join predicates are affected by a deletion operation if $\sigma_{clause}(\sigma_D(r(R_{table\_name}))) \neq \emptyset$ holds. Updates are handled as combination of delete and select operation, again.

Checking Projection Nodes. We do not have to check projection nodes or projection attributes, respectively, if the update operation is an insert or an delete because these operation increase or decrease the cardinality of the query result. So, the relevance of such updates is already recognized by checking the selection predicates and/or join predicates. But, in the case of updates it can occure, that the update modifies join attribute values and a selection attribute values but not the projected attributes. Such updates are not relevant for a registered query if the projected attributes are not contained in the list of updated attributes.

Fetching the IDs of the Mobile Clients. If all checks result in a relevance of an update operation we fetch the IDs of the mobile clients and notify them about the update. However, we do not consider the update of the data that is managed on the mobile clients but will do this in future work.

4   Evaluation

To evaluate our approach we implemented a small driver support systems that provides traffic information about road works, traffic jams as well as additional information about public utilities in a location depended manner. Here, we do not consider updating the trie by fast moving cars but approximate journeys by locating cars on a street. That means, that streets are implemented as a line between two coordinates. In fact, the benefit of our approach is not the complete realization of such a system but we use it for evaluating the update notification. Typical queries are: "Where is the next parking block with available parking lots?", "Is there a road block on my current road?" or "Where is the next garage?". The corresponding database[4] is realized using PostgreSQL and contains three cities and

---

[4] See [7] for details.

about 200 fictitious streets. Some streets cross cities. Furthermore we inserted about 9000 public utilities distributed among the cities. We assume 20 permanent traffic jams and five border crossings that hamper the traffic.

Queries are generated automatically and contain 1-3 projection predicates, 0-2 join predicates and 0-3 selection predicates. Two examples for such queries are:

- $\langle border\_crossing(*), border\_crossing.street\_id = street.id, street.id = 32 \rangle$
- $\langle institution(id), institution.street\_id = street.id, street.name =' A4' \rangle$

As mentioned in Section 3.2 we use updates in standard SQL notation, like:

- DELETE FROM R_WORKS__T_JAMS WHERE street_id=22 AND gps_start_y=1700
- UPDATE BORDER_CROSSING SET w_t_freight_vehicles='03:54' WHERE name='Mittenwald'

Figure 3(a) illustrates height and width of an example trie that represents 15,000 queries whereby 12,766 queries are different from each other. At this, we also included the values for a compressed representation that utilizes the fact, that values of nodes with only one child node can be stored in one node. While processing our algorithms that only means, that checks regarding this two values use the same node pointer but the space consumption is much lower.

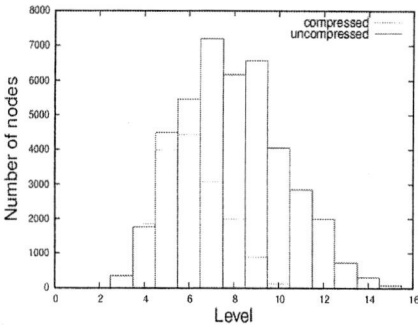

(a) Number of trie-nodes per trie-level (15,000 queries; 12,766 different queries)

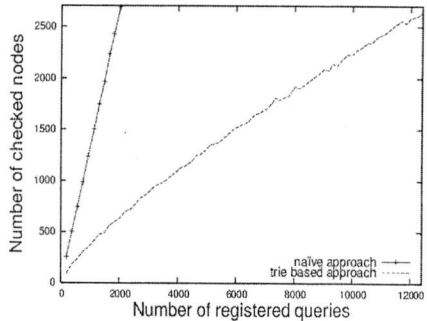

(b) Comparison between naïve approach and the trie based approach

Fig. 3. Space consumption and performance evaluation

At first we compare our approach to the naïve approach that represents the queries in a list. That means, the naïve algorithm sequentially scans the registered queries. The result of this comparison is shown in Figure 3(b). The predictable large number of nodes checked in the naïve approach depends on the fact, that such approaches typically do not consider predicate overlapping between the queries of different users. The result of our approach for this test depends on the trie representation used for storing the queries. So, we can point out that - in this test - our approach performs better than the naïve approach.

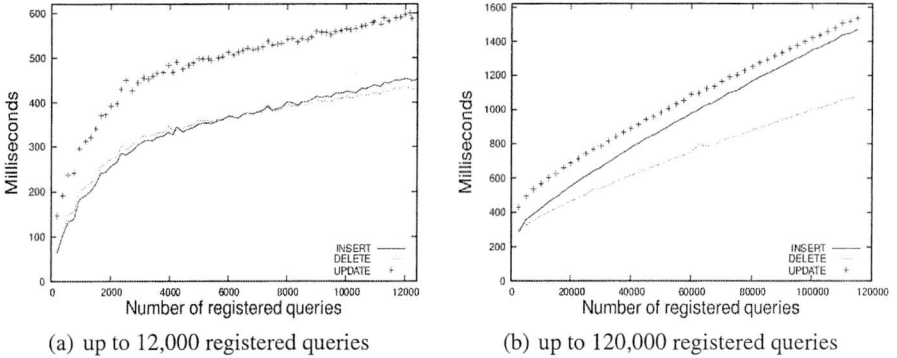

(a) up to 12,000 registered queries   (b) up to 120,000 registered queries

Fig. 4. Correlation between duration of updates and number of registered queries

The trie and its algorithms are implemented under Windows XP in Java. The communication between Java and PostgreSQL is realized with the standard PostgreSQL-JDBC-driver. For the experiments we used a standard PC with an AMD Athlon^{TM}XP 2100+ processor and 768 MB Ram. The duration of handling an update on this configuration is illustrated in Figure 4. At this, Figure 4(a) shows, that insert and delete operations are not as expensive as update operations. But in Figure 4(b) we see that the curves of insert and update operations converge with an increasing number of registered queries.

5   Conclusions and Outlook

In this paper we presented an indexing scheme for update notification in large mobile information systems. Queries posed by mobile clients are represented as paths in a trie at the server. We first discussed the used query representation that uses queries in form of conjunctively connected relation, selection and join predicates. Afterwards, the implementation and the physical representation of the trie was introduced. We illustrated how nodes are fetched and how the relevance of an update is checked regarding the different predicates. Finally, we presented and evaluated our approach and pointed out its benefit.

In spite of the acquired good results, there is a lot of future work. First of all, the used query language is not relational complete. We currently do not support unions. In addition to this, aggregation functions are not supported because of the used calculus. We also skipped the context predicates that are mentioned in [6]. In fact, first steps to support large context based mobile information are done. In [5] we introduced a general model that is not limited to location based queries but allows to specify more context elements like time relevance, task dependency, et cetera. Moreover, we plan to optimize the query index. For example, selection predicates are currently represented in a redundant manner, so we hopefully benefit from storing them in a clustered way or as intervals similar to 1-dimensional R-Trees.

References

1. Peter W. Foltz and Susan T. Dumais. Personalized Information Delivery: An Analysis of Information Filtering Methods. *ACM CACM*, 35(12):51–60, December 1992.
2. E. Fredkin. *Trie memory*. Information Memorandum, Bolt Beranek and NewMan Inc., Cambridge, MA, 1959.
3. J. Gray, P. Helland, P. O'Neil, and D. Shasha. The Dangers of Replication and a Solution. *SIGMOD Record*, 25(2):173–182, 1996.
4. Sha Guo, Wei Sun, and Mark Allen Weiss. Solving Satisfiability and Implication Problems in Database Systems. *ACM TODS*, 21(2):270–293, 1996.
5. H. Höpfner and K.-U. Sattler. Semantic Replication in Mobile Federated Information Systems. In A. James, S. Conrad, and W. Hasselbring, editors, *Proc. of the Fifth Workshop EFIS*, pages 36–41. Akademische Verlagsgesellschaft Aka GmbH, Berlin, July 2003.
6. Hagen Höpfner and Kai-Uwe Sattler. SMoS: A Scalable Mobility Server. In Anne James and Muhammad Younas, editors, *Poster Proc. of BNCOD20* , pages 49–52. Coventry University, jul 2003.
7. Hagen Höpfner, Stephan Schosser, and Kai-Uwe Sattler. Toward Trie-based Indexing of Mobile Clients in Large Mobile Information Systems. Preprint 02, Otto-von-Guericke-University of Magdeburg, Department of Computer Science, January 2004. http://wwwiti.cs.uni-magdeburg.de/iti_db/publikationen/preprints/2004/HoeSchSat.html.
8. Ken C. K. Lee, Hong Va Leong, and Antonio Si. Incremental View Maintenance for Mobile Databases. *Knowledge and Information Systems*, 2(4):413 – 437, nov 2000.
9. S. H. Phatak and B. R. Badrinath. Multiversion Reconciliation for Mobile Databases. In *Proc. of the 15th ICDE, Sydney, Austrialia*, pages 582–589. IEEE Computer Society, March 1999.
10. Shirish H. Phatak and B.R. Badrinath. Transaction-centric Reconciliation in Disconnected Databases. *ACM Monet Journal*, 53, 1999.
11. Evaggelia Pitoura and George Samaras. *Data Management for Mobile Computing*. Kluwer Academic Publishers, Dordrecht, 1998.
12. X-H. Sun, N. N. Kamel, and L. M. Ni. Processing Implications on Queries. *IEEE Transactions on Software Engineering (SE)*, 15(10), October 1989.
13. C. Türker. *Semantic Integrity Constraints in Federated Database Schemata*. Akademische Verlagsgesellschaft Aka GmbH, Berlin, 1999.
14. Ugur Cetintemel, Michael J. Franklin, and C. Lee Giles:. Self-Adaptive User Profiles for Large-Scale Data Delivery. In *Proc. of the 16th ICDE*, pages 622–633. IEEE Computer Society, March 2000.

A Mobile Agents Based Architecture for the Distributed Processing of Continuous Location Queries in a Wireless Environment: Performance Evaluation*

Sergio Ilarri[1]**, Eduardo Mena[1], and Arantza Illarramendi[2]

[1] IIS Dept, Univ. of Zaragoza, Maria de Luna 1, 50018 Zaragoza, Spain
{silarri,emena}@unizar.es
[2] LSI Dept, Univ. of the Basque Country, Apdo. 649, 20080 Donostia, Spain
jipileca@si.ehu.es

Abstract. With the current advances of mobile computing technology, we are witnessing an explosion in the development of applications that provide mobile users with a wide range of services. Of special interest are those applications that exploit the particular features of mobile environments to provide the user with context-aware information. In particular, we focus on location-dependent queries, which are still a subject of research mainly due to the lack of an architecture that is well-adapted to deal with continuous location queries in an efficient way.

In this paper we present the distributed architecture, based on mobile agents, that we propose to process continuous location-dependent queries in mobile environments. We then evaluate our proposal, showing that the system achieves a good precision and scales up well.

Keywords: location-dependent querying, tracking moving objects, continuous querying, mobile agents.

1 Introduction

With the current advances of mobile computing technology, we are witnessing an explosion in the development of applications that provide mobile users with a wide range of services. While most of these services are the counterpart of those available in desktop computers, there exist other applications that exploit the special features of mobile environments to supply more relevant information. For example, the answer to a location-dependent query depends on the locations of moving objects. A sample location-dependent query is "show me the available taxi cabs within three miles of my current location", which could be very useful, for example, for a user looking for an available taxi cab while walking home in a rainy day [14].

Nowadays there exist commercial applications that deal with location-dependent aspects. However, they present many disadvantages, among which we would like to

---

* This work was supported by the CICYT project TIC2001-0660, the DGA project P084/2001, and the research institute I3A.
** Work supported by the Aragón Government and the European Social Fund (ref. B132/2002).

W. Lindner et al. (Eds.): EDBT 2004 Workshops, LNCS 3268, pp. 355–364, 2004.

point out the lack of a general architecture that is well adapted to deal with continuous queries in an efficient way. This implies that current solutions are only suitable for the specific context for which they were developed and they do not work in a global, large-scale and heterogeneous environment.

In this paper we present and evaluate an architecture for the processing of location-dependent queries [6] that is based on mobile agents. Mobile agents are autonomous software entities that can stop its execution and resume it at a different computer, carrying their state information [11]. Thus, they execute in certain contexts (*places*) within a computer, and can travel from one place to another. They are very useful to build mobile computing applications [5], as they offer great advantages over the traditional client/server approach in environments with limited or unreliable bandwidth, and also allow disconnected operations.

In our approach, we use mobile agents to support our distributed query processing, track interesting moving objects, and optimize the wireless communications without the need of installing servers specialized in different tasks. Mobile agents are very convenient for this context, not only from a design and implementation point of view: it also has been proved that the overall performance of a system based on mobile agents is, at worst, similar to that of the equivalent system based on remote communications, as shown, for example in [10].

The rest of the paper is as follows. In Section 2 we describe the underlying infrastructure that we consider for the processing of location-dependent queries, approach that we describe in Section 3. The empirical evaluation of our query system appears in Section 4. In Section 5 we present some related works. Finally, conclusions and future work are included in Section 6.

2   Underlying Infrastructure

As framework of our work, we consider an infrastructure composed of moving objects and proxy computers that provide location information.

Moving objects are entities provided with a wireless device (e.g., a car or a person with a wireless communication device) and a mechanism that obtains their location. Several positioning methods with different precision [3] can be used to get the location of a moving object (e.g., methods based on GPS or methods that require network assistance). In our work, we do not make any assumption about the specific technique used.

Proxies are computers that provide location information about objects located within a certain area, that we call *proxy area*. In a cellular network [2, 12], a proxy area is obtained as the union of the coverage areas of one or more base stations. Although our concept of proxy is similar to that of *Location Server* [9], we decided to use a different term to fit it to the specifics of our decentralized query processing approach: 1) proxies provide the software infrastructure needed for the execution of mobile agents, and 2) there is a module called *Data Management System* (*DMS*) at the proxy.

The DMS handles location data about moving objects within its proxy area in order to answer SQL queries about them. We do not focus here on the problem of how the DMS is aware of the location of moving objects, but we would like to highlight some interesting alternatives: 1) it could receive GPS data from moving objects and use a DOMINO database [15] to update efficiently these data, 2) it could use data stream technology [1] to process the incoming location data regarding the queries currently submitted to the proxy, 3) it could obtain the location data by using a network-based positioning method, 4) it could query the moving object themselves about their location, or 5) any hybrid approach is also possible.

3   Distributed Query Processing Approach

We first explain our approach for the processing of location-dependent queries [6]. For that purpose, we first introduce some terminology related to location-dependent queries, and then describe the (mobile) agent-based architecture that we use to process the queries in a distributed way.

Location queries are composed of *location constraints* that express location-dependent conditions that moving objects must satisfy to be included in the answer to the query; e.g., the constraint "Inside(5 miles, 'car38', policeCar)" selects the police cars (the *target class*, whose instances are termed *target objects*) within five miles around the moving object identified as "car38" (the *reference object*).

1: location-dependent query ⇒ parameterized SQL queries
2: **while** (not cancel) **do**
3:      Obtain the locations of the *reference objects*
4:      Update the SQL queries with the locations of the reference objects
5:      **for** each SQL query **do**
6:          execute the query
7:          **if** there are several SQL queries about the same *target class* **then**
8:              Join the result of such queries
9:          **end if**
10:     **end for**
11:     Present the answer to the user
12: **end while**

Fig. 1. Basic algorithm for location query processing

In Figure 1 we present the basic algorithm to obtain an answer to a location query. The query is transformed into standard SQL queries about the locations of target objects. These queries are parameterized with the location of the reference objects, that must be consequently obtained before executing the queries. We will explain in the following how this algorithm is executed in a distributed way; thus, for example, the line 6 in Figure 1 involves several proxy computers. The steps performed in our distributed query processing approach are:

1. *Analysis of the user query and translation into SQL queries* (line 1 in Figure 1). The *Query Processor* is the application executed on the user device (that we call *monitor*) that allows the user to issue queries. It first transforms the user query into an intermediate specification. Specifically, it obtains, for each constraint in the query,

its *reference object*, its *target class*, and an *area of interest*. Then, from this representation, one SQL query is obtained for each constraint, which is parameterized with the location of the reference object.

2. *Deployment of a network of agents*, that consists of three steps (see Figure 2):

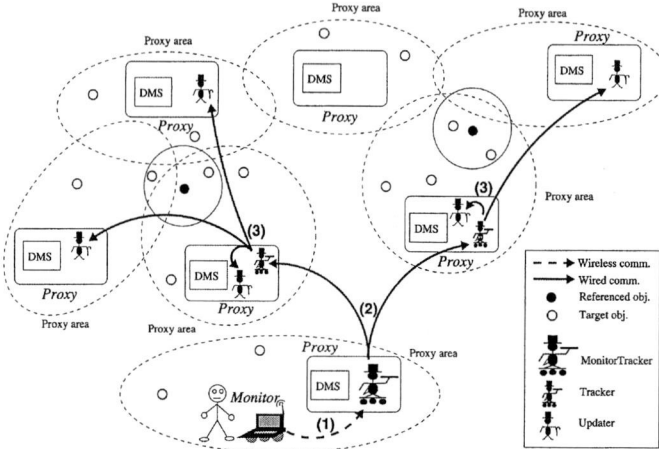

Fig. 2. Deployment of the network of agents

- The Query Processor sends a *MonitorTracker agent* to the proxy in charge of the monitor's location (step 1 in Figure 2). This agent performs three main tasks: a) to follow the monitor wherever it goes (moving from proxy to proxy), b) to store the data requested by the user in case of disconnection of the monitor, and c) to refresh the data presented to the user in an efficient manner, minimizing the wireless communications with the monitor (it will send only the necessary information).

- For its last task, the MonitorTracker sends a *Tracker agent* to the proxy that manages the location information of each reference object, initialized with the SQL queries related to such a reference object (step 2 in Figure 2). A Tracker agent performs three main tasks: a) to keep itself "close" to the proxy that manages the location of its reference object, traveling from proxy to proxy when needed in order to minimize the communication costs of tracking the reference object, b) to detect and process new locations of its reference object by querying the corresponding DMS at its proxy (line 3 in Figure 1), and c) to detect and process the location of target objects inside the area of interest around its tracked reference object.

- For its third task, a Tracker agent obtains for each SQL query in which its reference object appears, the proxies whose area intersects the area of interest of such an SQL query. Then, it creates one *Updater agent* on each of these proxies (step 3 in Figure 2). The Updaters are static agents whose goal is to retrieve relevant target objects from the DMS at their proxy. They are initialized with the SQL query that they must execute; such query is based on the current location of the reference object[1].

3. *Execution of standard queries* (line 6 in Figure 1). Each Updater agent executes its SQL query over the DMS of the proxy where it resides, with the goal of retrieving the location of relevant target objects and communicate the necessary data to its Tracker agent.

4. *Obtaining an answer.* Data obtained by Updater agents are sent to its corresponding Tracker agent. The Tracker agent performs the union of the results obtained by its Updater agents. Each Tracker agent sends its results to its MonitorTracker, which combines the results coming from the different Trackers (lines 7-9 in Figure 1) and sends the final answer to the monitor. Finally, the monitor presents the answer to the user (line 11 in Figure 1).

5. *Keeping the answer up-to-date.* The proposed architecture have been designed with the goal of processing continuous location-dependent queries efficiently. The answer to a continuous query must be refreshed with a certain *refreshment frequency* [7], specified by the user according to his/her needs and the allowed cost of wireless communications[2].

While a continuous query is executing, the deployed network of agents must adapt to changes in the locations of moving objects. For example, as a reference object moves, its associated area of interest moves too. Therefore, the related Tracker agent must rearrange its network of Updater agents and update their SQL queries with the new location of the reference object (line 4 in Figure 1). Similarly, if a reference object disappears from its current proxy[3], the Tracker agent needs to identify the new proxy in charge of the location of the reference object. Besides, the Tracker will also travel there, with two purposes: 1) remote requests about the location of the reference object are avoided, and 2) when the reference object changes of proxy it will be easier for the Tracker to locate its new proxy, as most location databases schemes are more efficient when the searches imply nearby proxies[12]. It is not the purpose of this paper to describe how the agents synchronize in order to provide timely answers (see [7] for more details of our approach).

Notice in Figure 2 that the only wireless data transfer occurs when the Query Processor sends the MonitorTracker to the proxy of the monitor and when the MonitorTracker sends a new answer to the Query Processor: any other communication occurs among proxies using a fixed network.

4   Experiments

In this section, we describe some tests that we have performed to evaluate experimentally[4] the reliability, accuracy and scalability of our prototype. The prototype has been

---

[1] Such location parameters will be updated by the Tracker whenever necessary.

[2] Alternatively, the system could adjust itself to the maximum frequency that it can achieve [8].

[3] This is detected by the Tracker agent because the current proxy cannot provide the location of the reference object anymore.

[4] We have also modeled our system with Petri nets, which is out of the scope of this paper.

developed using Java as programming language and Grasshopper [13] as mobile agent system. We consider a scenario composed of six proxies; six Pentium IV 1.7 GHz with Linux have been used to play the role of such proxies. DMSs have been implemented as MySql databases, one on each proxy.

4.1   Tracking the Location of a Single Moving Object

We evaluate here our system with a query that tracks the location of a single object that moves at 5 du/sec (distance units per second; e.g., 1 du = 1 mile or 1 du = 1 meter).

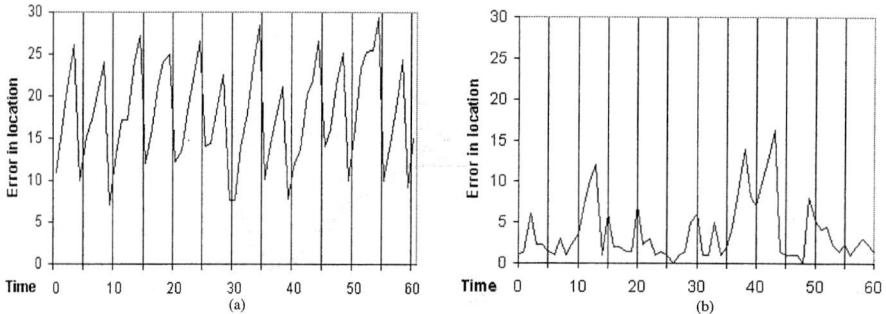

Fig. 3. (a) Monitoring an object at 5 du/sec); (b) using an estimator

In Figure 3.a we show the imprecision (error in distance) committed by the Query Processor for a query that simply tracks the location of such an object with a frequency of 1 answer refreshment every five seconds. We show the error in distance, i.e., the difference between the real location of the object and the location shown to the user at each time instant. Notice that the minimum imprecision occur every five seconds, corresponding to refreshments of the query answer, where the error is only due to the time elapsed since a location is queried until that information is presented to the user[5]. Figure 3.b was obtained by using a simple location estimator based on the last known orientation and speed of the moving object. This estimator allows us to increase the frequency of answers while keeping the same frequency of accesses to proxies and wireless communications; in this case, we estimate one answer every second instead of refreshing the answer every five seconds. The increase in the location error committed by the query processor between seconds 35-45 in Figure 3.b is due to a wrong estimation of locations caused by unexpected changes of the direction of the moving object. We have tested the system with different speeds for the moving object and observed, in all the cases, an improvement in the results when using an estimator.

4.2   Real Answer vs. Obtained Answer

In Figure 4 we evaluate the query processor in terms of expected answers for a continuous query (refreshment period of five seconds) that retrieves a set of objects moving at

---

[5] Moving objects are moving in the meanwhile!

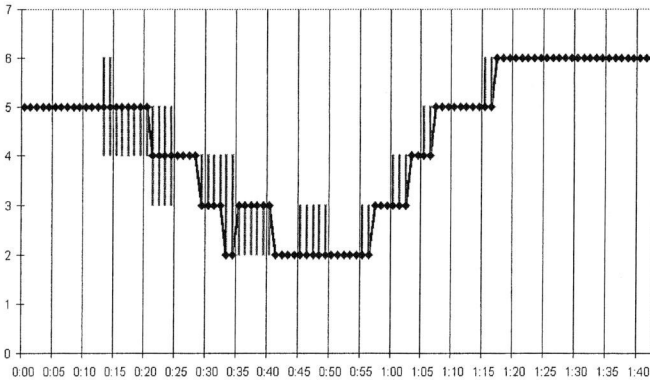

Fig. 4. Accuracy in the answer presented to the user

three du/sec. The X-axis shows several time instants (continuous vertical lines represent refreshments of the answer) and the Y-axis indicates a number of objects. The continuous dark line indicates the number of objects in the ideal answer at each moment (we measure the errors in the answer every second). Short vertical lines mean how many extra objects (lines above the continuous line) and missing objects (lines below the continuous line) were obtained by the query processor as answer to the issued query. For instance, between 0:35 and 0:40 there is one missing object in the answer presented to the user, and between 1:00 and 1:03 the answer shown by the query processor is presenting one extra object. Thus, short vertical lines represent temporal imprecision of the query processor, due to the time that it needs to detect a relevant change in the information provided by proxies. This error becomes bigger due to the movement of moving objects.

Notice that several objects can move at the same time in a way that the query processing mechanism can incur in imprecision. Please see the interval 0:45-0:50, when imprecision arises because one object exited the area of interest at 0:44 (which was detected by Updaters) and another object entered the area of interest at the same time (the number of objects in the ideal answer is still the same). However, the exiting object was not immediately detected by the system as one Tracker agent was traveling between BSs at that moment.

4.3 Scalability

We show in this section how the reliability of the query processor decreases when the number of (users issuing) continuous queries increases. The more queries, the more agents on the system (see Figure 5.a). However, notice that the environment is highly distributed, and therefore many queries are needed to overload a single proxy[6], as shown in Figure 5.b.

---

[6] Unfortunately, the communication mechanism in the agent platform used (Grasshopper) becomes unreliable as the number of mobile agents increases, so we are currently evaluating other alternatives.

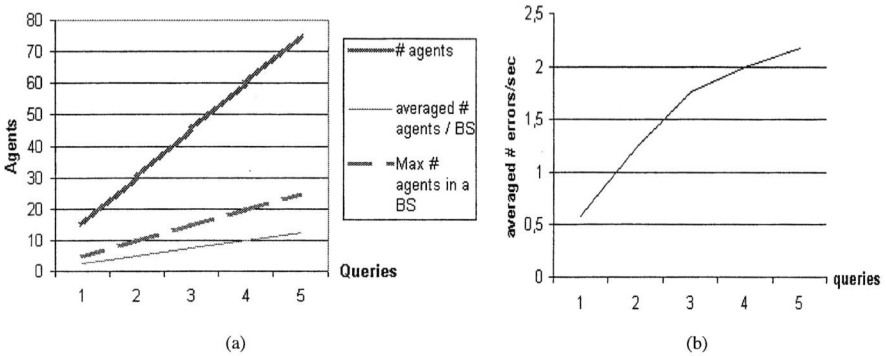

Fig. 5. Scalability of the Query Processor

Notice that increasing the number of moving objects does not affect the performance of our system because of two reasons: 1) The query processor is not interested in all the moving objects of the system, only in those belonging to a target class inside a certain area, 2) if the number of target objects increases, more objects could belong to the answer and therefore Updaters will retrieve more objects, but this issue does not affect the performance. Moreover, if the number of proxies increases, the system becomes more distributed but this does not negatively affect our system either (the overload at each proxy could decrease!). The real bottleneck of the system is the number of agents deployed, and this parameter only depends on the number of concurrent queries.

Apparently, we could improve the performance of the system by sharing agents among queries. For example, the same Updater could execute SQL queries concerning different location queries. However, we would need several threads, since the answers for such location queries could need to be refreshed at different time instants (e.g., the refreshment frequencies could be different). As the performance of several agents performing a single task is comparable to that of a single agent with several threads (one for each task), we do not advocate this solution.

5   Related Work

The DOMINO project [15] proposes a model to represent moving objects in a database. They focus on the problem of how to store location information about moving objects in a database with the goal of processing spatial and temporal queries in an efficient way. However, they consider a centralized architecture (the location data of moving objects are available at a single data repository).

In MobiEyes [4] a distributed approach for the processing of location queries is also proposed. However, in contrast to our proposal, the query processing is performed on the moving objects themselves, with the following main disadvantages: 1) moving objects must have certain "intelligence" as they must be aware of a geographic grid and be able to process queries, 2) the processing and communication load of a moving object depends on the number and type of queries issued into the system, 3) the approach is not completely distributed, as all the moving objects must communicate with a single centralized computer (the mediator), and 4) they assume that the user is not interested in a precise location of target objects.

In [16] the main concern is how to provide an up-to-date answer to the user while minimizing communications, by deciding when to transmit results to a mobile host. However, it is not well-adapted to deal with continuous queries that ask for locations of moving objects (e.g., monitoring a truck fleet). It is based on predicted paths and also considers a centralized architecture.

6 Conclusions and Future Work

In this paper we have presented an architecture for the processing of continuous location-dependent queries in wireless environments. We have then evaluated experimentally the performance of our prototype, showing the precision and scalability of the system. The main features of our approach are:

- We consider queries whose answer can depend on the movement of any relevant object.
- We propose a distributed architecture based on mobile agents that obtain the answer for a query by getting information from a distributed collection of DMSs with the goal of tracking relevant moving objects in an efficient way.
- No assumptions are made regarding how the locations of moving objects are obtained. Thus, our system works for different granularities of location information (e.g., GPS locations). Similarly, we do not overload moving objects with query processing tasks.

As future work, we plan to research the advantages that data stream technology can provide in this context. Another important issue is to extend our query language (management of new spatio-temporal constraints).

References

1. B. Babcock, S. Babu, M. Datar, R. Motwani, and J. Widom. Models and issues in data stream systems. In *Proceedings of 21st ACM Symposium on Principles of Database Systems (PODS 2002)*, 2002.
2. D. Barbará. Mobile computing and databases - a survey. *IEEE Transactions on Knowledge and Data Engineering*, 11(1):108–117, Jan-Feb 1999.
3. Harvey M. Deitel, Paul J. Deitel, Tem R. Nieto, and Kate Steinbuhler. *Wireless Internet and Mobile Business -How to Program-*. Prentice Hall, 2001.
4. Bugra Gedik and Ling Liu. Mobieyes: Distributed processing of continuously moving queries on moving objects in a mobile system. In *9th Conference on Extended Database Technology (EDBT 2004), Heraklion-Crete (Greece)*, March 2004.
5. Robert S. Gray, David Kotz, Saurab Nog, Daniela Rus, and George Cybenko. Mobile agents for mobile computing. Technical Report TR96-285, Dartmouth College. Hanover, NH, USA, 1996.

6. S. Ilarri, E. Mena, and A. Illarramendi. A system based on mobile agents for tracking objects in a location-dependent query processing environment. In *Twelfth International Workshop on Database and Expert Systems Applications (DEXA'2001), Fourth International Workshop Mobility in Databases and Distributed Systems (MDSS'2001), Munich (Germany)*, pages 577–581. IEEE Computer Society, ISBN 0-7695-1230-5, September 2001.

7. S. Ilarri, E. Mena, and A. Illarramendi. Monitoring continuous location queries using mobile agents. In *Sixth East-European Conference on Advances in Databases and Information Systems (ADBIS'2002), Bratislava (Slovakia)*, pages 92–105. Springer Verlag LNCS, ISBN 3-540-44138-7, September 2002.

8. S. Ilarri, E. Mena, and A. Illarramendi. Dealing with continuous location-dependent queries: Just-in-time data refreshment. In *First IEEE Annual Conference on Pervasive Computing and Communications (PerCom), Dallas Fort-Worth (Texas)*, pages 279–286. IEEE Computer Society, ISBN 0-7695-1895, March 2003.

9. Location Interoperability Forum (LIF). Mobile location protocol specification. http://www.openmobilealliance.org/tech/affiliates/lif/lifindex.html, [Accessed: May 19, 2004].

10. E. Mena, J.A. Royo, A. Illarramendi, and A. Goñi. Adaptable software retrieval service for wireless environments based on mobile agents. In *2002 International Conference on Wireless Networks (ICWN'02), Las Vegas, USA*, pages 116–124. CSREA Press, ISBN 1-892512-30-0, June 2002.

11. D. Milojicic, M. Breugst, I. Busse, J. Campbell, S. Covaci, B. Friedman, K. Kosaka, D. Lange, K. Ono, M. Oshima, C. Tham, S. Virdhagriswaran, and J. White. MASIF, the OMG mobile agent system interoperability facility. In *Proceedings of Mobile Agents '98*, September 1998.

12. E. Pitoura and G. Samaras. Locating objects in mobile computing. *IEEE Transactions on Knowledge and Data Engineering*, 13(4):571–592, July/August 2001.

13. IKV++ technologies. Grasshopper - a platform for mobile software agents. http://www.grasshopper.de/download/doc/GrasshopperIntroduction.pdf, , [Accessed: May 19, 2004].

14. Jari Veijalainen and Mathias Weske. *Modeling Static Aspects of Mobile Electronic Commerce Environments, Chapter 7 in Advances in Mobile Commerce Technologies*. IDEA Group Publishing, 2002.

15. O. Wolfson, A. P. Sistla, B. Xu, J. Zhou, S. Chamberlain, Y. Yesha, and N. Rishe. Tracking moving objects using database technology in DOMINO. In *Fourth International Workshop Next Generation Information Technologies and Systems (NGITS'99), Zikhron-Yaakov, Israel. Lecture Notes in Computer Science, Vol. 1649, Springer, ISBN 3-540-66225-1*, pages 112–119, July 1999.

16. Kam yiu Lam, Özgür Ulusoy, Tony S. H. Lee, Edward Chan, and Guohui Li. An efficient method for generating location updates for processing of location-dependent continuous queries. In *Database Systems for Advanced Applications*, pages 218–225, 2001.

Improving Usability of Location-Based Services with User-Centric Data Querying

Artem Katasonov

Information Technology Research Institute, University of Jyväskylä,
P.O.Box 35 (Agora), FIN-40014, Jyväskylä, Finland
artem.katasonov@titu.jyu.fi

Abstract. In this paper, we describe a computational model that produces a dataset which we consider to be an appropriate response for "give me a description of my neighborhood" type of queries in location-based services. Our attempt is to reflect the abstraction ability of a specific user, and in this way to maximize the usability of the service under restrictions on data volume posed by technical, economical and cognitive factors of mobile environments. We also present the results of instantiating the model for a simple LBS.

1   Introduction

Development of mobile networks and terminals provides basis for advanced mobile services and applications. Voice capabilities of mobile networks have been augmented with data capabilities of increasing speed, mobile phones have already reached considerable complexity and performance, got Java-support and color displays. One of the important new features is support for determining the location of a mobile terminal. The location data can be transmitted to third parties offering various services, including services for personal information and navigation (yellow-pages, route guidance), finding and tracking services (friends, children, property), and physical services (taxi, emergency services). While all of those are considered to be Location-Based Services (LBS), in this paper we restrict consideration to the first group only.

Overviews of LBS enabling technologies and technical issues can be found in books devoted to LBSs, e.g. [4], or numerous journal and conference papers, e.g. [3, 14]. LBSs have been a hot topic for both researchers and practitioners for a decade already, pushed forward by various players including mobile operators expecting LBSs to form an important revenue-generating class of mobile services, mobile phone manufacturers, Geographic Information Systems (GIS) community, and other content providers (e.g. publishers of yellow-pages directories). However, LBSs are still, in 2004, in a very early stage; commercially available services are few and rather simple.

Since the main value of LBSs comes from providing the user with some relevant information at appropriate place and time, data management is a major LBS concern. In addition, peculiarities of the mobile computing environment make communication of data to the users (one of the data management activities) a non-trivial problem. Mobile networks have limited bandwidth and high latency for transmitting data. Mobile devices have limited memory for storing, limited performance for processing and small displays

W. Lindner et al. (Eds.): EDBT 2004 Workshops, LNCS 3268, pp. 365–374, 2004.

for representing data. In addition, mobile users are typically in an unstable environment in varying conditions, where their cognitive capacity is demanded for other tasks as well. The mobile users have less "mental bandwidth" - capacity for absorbing and processing content - than a stationary user in front of a PC since the interaction with the mobile phone often is reduced to a secondary task that must not interfere with their primary task (e.g., driving or walking) [2].

Failing to address those issues may lead to situations when information does not arrive to the user in time, or when the user is unable to access or comprehend it in time, thus making the service undependable. There is also an economic aspect – in practice, a user has to pay for every byte of transmitted data, for connection time in GSM or for data volume in GPRS and above. Therefore, there is an obvious need for limiting the amount of data transmitted and presented to the user. However, doing that in a straightforward way may render the service useless (see example below).

In recent years, researchers from the database field have been actively attacking LBS data management issues. As [7] lists, the range of the studied questions includes data placement (centralization vs. distribution), data replication, indexing, query scheduling, data caching, broadcast (push) strategies, and combination of broadcast with on-demand access. The relevant research also includes indexing of moving objects [12], and multi-dimensional data modeling [5] for LBSs.

All those investigations should collectively contribute to optimization of processing of location-dependent queries, reduce response times and cost of data delivery in LBSs. However, the database researchers seem to have made so far little attempt to extend the notion of "location-dependent query" beyond basic spatial queries, i.e. range or nearest-neighbors search. So, query classification in [7] includes only local vs. nonlocal (current vs. specified location), and simple vs. general queries (equality conditions vs. spatial or nonspatial constraints). Very recently however, the discussion is started also of queries that would take the transportation network into account [6, 11], thus increasing the utility of LBSs.

However, one of the common queries in LBSs is the indefinite "give me a description of my neighborhood". Such a query is traditionally executed with one or a series of range queries; the user is presented therefore with all the data items (using selective inclusion based on their theme or other attributes) linked to locations within a certain distance from the user. In other words, only the total data extent and maybe granularity is affected. Even if the network distance is used, the result is probably too simplistic. For example, some of the existing LBSs provide the user with a map depicting his neighborhood. Usability of this function is usually quite low, in part because as in the traditional or web cartography only the extent (spatial and thematic) and granularity of the map are controlled. An overview map fitting into a mobile phone display (or small enough to be transmitted in reasonable time) loses most of the detail and is therefore of a little use. But a map detailed enough can show only, say, a few city blocks. Given that accessing other portions of the map and zooming operations take considerable time (new queries have to be made), it is difficult to put that information into use either.

On the other hand, in Mobile Human-Computer Interaction (HCI) and GIS fields, it is common to speak about the need for using context-aware user-adapted data representations [1, 2, 10, 15]. The talk goes beyond controlling the total extent/granularity;

in general, removing any detail that is unnecessary and presenting only relevant is advocated. For example, [15] proposes using "focus maps" in LBSs, where areas that are farther away from the current user location are represented with less detail than those in the close vicinity. [1] discusses "context mediation", in which selection for presentation amongst different map elements and amongst their variants is based on a set of utility functions defined on elements attributes and spatial distances. HCI and GIS studies, however, usually only describe general principles and heuristics for creating such data representations; we did not encounter in literature descriptions of formal algorithms or models that would give means for doing this automatically and efficiently.

We consider it to be a strange situation that those technical and cognitive aspects of the mobile environment (see above) tend to be attacked separately (technical by the database researchers and cognitive by the HCI researchers), even while both have a common denominator – amount of information.

In this work, we make a step towards an integrated solution. We describe a computational model that automatically produces a dataset which we consider to be an appropriate response for "give me a description of my neighborhood" type of queries. The dataset is both focused (as in [15]) and user-centric, it includes only those details that are believed to be relevant for the specific user in the specific context. The objective we pursue is to maximize the usability of the service under some posed restrictions on data volume. We also present an example of implementing the model in simple LBS.

2 Novel Type of Location-Dependent Queries

Our attempt is to mimic the abstraction ability of a human. Humans instinctively know how to filter out unnecessary detail, this is an important survival trait, since we cannot possibly save in our brain all the detail around us. An abstraction can be understood as a selection of a set of objects, attributes or processes out of a larger set of objects, attributes and processes, according to certain criteria determined by the current task [13].

Let us consider what happens, for example, when a human looks at a printed map. A map is an abstraction of reality aimed to serve needs of some group of users. However, it is still a multi-purpose instrument while it is not designed for one specific user in one specific context. Therefore, every user of a map conducts abstraction further, filtering out unnecessary details.

The area of interest for the user is around his current location. If he has a destination then the area of interest includes also all the way from the current location to that point. The area of interest does not have a strict border. The user pays primary attention to objects that are close to his current location and to the way to the destination, objects that are farther away are noticed also, but less attention is paid to details (this leads to the idea of "focus maps", as in [15]). Only some types of objects represented on the map are relevant for the user. For example, he may be interested in restaurants but not in hotels or interested only in motorways but not in footpaths. Different groups of objects have different regions, inside which they are of interest for the user. For example, the user may be interested in hotels that are anywhere in the city, and restaurants only if they are quite close to the current location or the way (this is noticed in [1] proposing that different utility functions for distance could defined for different object types). Different groups of objects have different relative importance. The same might be true even for objects inside one group. Depending on the current goals, the user could be interested in maps at different scales and overall detail levels. If the user is driving at a high speed then a low-detailed map is usually enough, whereas if the user is walking then he could need a detailed one.

These observations are quite general and apply to any kind of location-dependent data. We conclude that LBSs call for a novel type of location-dependent queries, which would be (1) spatio-contextual, i.e. implement range search in a multidimensional space, (2) focused, and (3) motion-adaptive. In the next section, a computational model is described realizing such a query.

3   Computational Model

For every object (data item), our model estimates its relative importance, based on its spatial distance from the user and the context of the user. Given that the total allowed amount of details (data volume) is set, the relative importance of objects define whether they will be represented in the result dataset and also the levels of detail, with which they will be represented.

The model calculates the relative importance of an object based on the distance from the user to this object in some metric "importance" space. This space is multidimensional. Two of its axes are obviously the spatial X and Y coordinates (or longitude and latitude). However, all the other coordinate axes depend on the specific implementation and information that the service has about objects and about the user. Therefore, developers of a specific LBS need to define all these axes and decide about methods for transformation of the available data into values of these coordinates. All the coordinates are to be metric; this means that the distance d between any two values of a coordinate can be calculated.

Both users and objects are modeled as points (or regions if appropriate) in this space. Besides X and Y, the meaning of a coordinate values is different for a user and for an object. For an object, a coordinate value represents the value of an object property, for the user, it represents the preferred value of this property – the closer the value of the property for the object to the preferred value, the more important the object is for the user. Those preferred values could be requested directly from the user. Another approach is to estimate them based on information the service may have about the user, including permanent properties (e.g. gender), relatively permanent properties (e.g. age, preferences), and context parameters (e.g. driver/pedestrian, current needs). While providing obvious advantages, use of this approach may restrict the possible set of coordinates.

For calculating the distance between a user and an object, our choice is use of the Manhattan metrics that defines the overall distance D as a simple sum of distances with respect to individual coordinates $D = d_1 + d_2 + ... + d_N$. The Manhattan metrics has some advantages in comparison with, e.g. the Euclidean metrics. First, it is computationally simpler. Second, it allows treating coordinates in groups. We could define, for example, $D = d_{spatial} + d_{nonspatial}$ and use then another method for calculation of the spatial distance (the Euclidean metrics or take into account the transportation network). Third, it allows considering coordinates in fully separate way, e.g. the overall average distance $\overline{D}$ is equal to the sum of average distances $\overline{d_i}$ with respect to individual coordinates, i.e. $\overline{D} = \overline{d_1} + \overline{d_2} + ... + \overline{d_N}$ (see below).

Since we cannot use the same units for all the coordinates, there is a question about coordinates ratio. Our choice is to define some weights k_i for all of the coordinates and therefore have $D = k_1 d_1 + k_2 d_2 + ...k_N d_N$. Ideally, coefficients k_i should be user-dependent (estimated or requested directly). However, in practical applications, they could be predefined by designers of the system.

The user of an LBS is mobile. The objects could also be mobile (e.g. taxi cars). Additionally, mobility may be also considered with respect to other coordinates, not only the spatial location. Therefore, we use predicted average distance over some period (it could be, e.g., the average time between consequent requests). With respect to one coordinate we define it as

$$\overline{d} = \frac{\int_0^T k(t)d(t)dt}{\int_0^T k(t)dt} \tag{1}$$

T is the period, $d(t)$ is the distance at time t, $k(t)$ is a function of t describing the degree of determinacy of the user and the object motions. If we are sure that the distance between the user and the object will change by the $d(t)$ rule, we can assign $k(t)$ to one. More practically, when $d(t)$ is only a prediction, $k(t)$ could be selected as $k(t) = \frac{T-t}{T}$ defining continuous linear fade from one to zero.

The simplest case (however, the most probable) is the following. For both the user and the object, the values of the coordinate, x_u and x_o, as well as the speeds of change of the coordinate, v_u and v_o, at time zero are only known. Therefore, the prediction for d(t) is $|(x_u + v_u t) - (x_o + v_o t)|$. In such a case, $\overline{d}$ could be easily computed.

As mentioned above, using the Manhattan metrics, average distances with respect to individual coordinates can be combined as

$$\overline{D} = k_1 \overline{d_1} + k_2 \overline{d_2} + ... + k_N \overline{d_N}. \tag{2}$$

Based on $\overline{D}$, the relative importance I of the object is calculated. We can use various equations, for example linear or quadratic

$$I = \frac{1}{\overline{D}} \quad or \quad I = \frac{1}{\overline{D}^2} \tag{3}$$

Based on I, the level of detail LOD is calculated, which the object will have in the result dataset. On designing the system, some $\widehat{I}$ value is to be selected. If an object has I equal to or greater than $\widehat{I}$ then it is represented with all the available details, i.e. its LOD is assigned to one. We assume also that we have the total volume of details V fixed (could come from data volume restrictions). Therefore, for all of the objects included into the result we have $\sum_i LOD_i \leq V$. Formally, this means that there is some lowest importance value I_0, under which objects are not included into the result, i.e. their LOD are assigned to zero. Consequently,

$$LOD = \begin{cases} 1, & \text{if } I \geq \widehat{I}, \\ I/\widehat{I}, & \text{if } I_0 \leq I < \widehat{I}, \\ 0, & \text{if } I < I_0 \end{cases} \tag{4}$$

Algorithmically, we need to select objects from the top of the descending-order list until $\sum LOD$ reaches V. There is no need to calculate I_0 directly.

The level of detail for an object, as we defined above, is a value in the interval between zero to one. If LOD is equal to zero the object is not represented at all; if LOD is equal to one the object is represented with all the available details. With LOD in between, a simplified representation of the object is included into the result dataset. Simplification affects both spatial and nonspatial properties.

The task of simplification of an object representation is similar to what is called generalization in cartography and GIS [9]. Generalization is a complicated process which is difficult to automate. We, however, advocate for simplification of each object separately and use of simple operations only removing some data and not introducing new, i.e. against e.g. data aggregation. The reason is not only to allow automatic generalization, but also to provide for simple join of datasets, if continuous querying or progressive data transmission is used. We advocate also for generalization that would fulfill the requirement that if $LOD_2 < LOD_1$ then the dataset representing an object at LOD_2 is a subset of the dataset at LOD_1. Then, knowing the set of LOD values for all the objects present in the user device memory, we could calculate what exactly data is there, regardless of how many queries and updates have contributed to it.

For nonspatial properties, generalization therefore involves only omitting some of them. We assume that for every property, a threshold value is defined. When LOD of an object is greater than or equal to this value, the property is included into the simplified representation of the object. In selection of thresholds, naturally, the importance of different properties and amount of data needed for encoding them is to be considered.

Generalization of a spatial geometry involves omitting some of its points. One simple approach is the following procedure. We calculate the number of points to be retained $m = round(M * LOD)$, where M is the number of points in the geometry. If geometry is a line and $m < 2$ then we assign m to 2 (end points are retained). If geometry is a polygon and $m < 3$ then we assign m to 1 (collapse to a point). For geometry simplification, an appropriate approach is use of the classical Douglas-Peucker algorithm (see [9]). Among other advantages, this algorithm has the important feature that the produced set of points for m_1 is always a subset of the set for m_2 if $m_1 < m_2$. The sequence of critical points could even be computed beforehand and stored. Then in run time, one needs only to select m first points from this sequence.

4   Example of Implementation

In this section, we present a simple example of implementing the described model. User-centric data querying functionality was added to the MultiMeetMobile LBS pilot system [8, 14]. The system is a mobile service for navigation and location-based information in a city environment, aimed for Java-enabled PDAs and smart-phones.

The system is based on two datasets. The first dataset on the street network of the city Jyväskylä was provided by the National Land Survey of Finland. A basic unit in this dataset is a street segment, which endpoints are either street crossings or dead ends. Segments are characterized with a large set of attributes; however, we use only some of them. Based on the type attribute, we divided the network into three sub-networks:

highways, streets, and footpaths. The other relevant attributes are: name of the street to which the segment belongs, allowed direction of traffic, length of the segment, address range on both sides of the segment, and spatial geometry consisting of at least two endpoints and possibly a number of vertices. The coordinate system used is the Finnish National Map Grid Coordinate System known as KKJ. This system uses rectangular map projection coordinates X and Y with meter as the measurement unit. This simplifies calculation on such data and makes it more human understandable.

The second dataset on points of interest in the city Jyväskylä has been artificially produced. We selected three important groups of points of interest: shops, restaurants, and hotels. We defined the following attributes for these points of interest: name, address, description, and spatial location.

The following metric coordinates were defined. X and Y are the rectangular map projection coordinates with meter as the measurement unit. For a street segment, we calculate the average of all its points and take coordinates of this average point as X and Y of the segment. Z is abstract elevation. All the objects have $Z = 0$. For a user, it can be any non-negative value (in meters). Therefore, the user experiences the area from a vantage-point, as if he were, for example, in an airplane. $iHighways$, $iStreets$, $iFootpaths$, $iShops$, $iRestaurants$, and $iHotels$ are coordinates with real values in the interval 0...1 encoding the relative importance of different data themes for the user. For an object, only one of these coordinates is applicable (that corresponds to its own type) and is equal to one.

X and Y coordinates of the user, as well as the current speeds of their change, are retrieved from the emulator of the location service. Z and the preferences coordinates are requested from the user directly (by the client application) and included as parameters into a query to the server.

For this demonstrative implementation, we did not consider the question of selection of model parameters very carefully. Some of parameters were thoughtfully selected, appropriate values for other were found in series of trials. The ratio coefficients k for X, Y and Z were assigned to one, for the preferences variables to 1000. $\hat{I}$ was assigned to 0.005, V to 45, and T to 60. Calculation of I applied linear formula $1/\overline{D}$. The following threshold values were selected for the segment attributes: street name - 0.2, direction of traffic - 0.4, length of segment - 0.6, address range - 0.8; for the attributes of points of interest: name - 0.25, address - 0.5, description - 0.75.

Since making calculations for all the objects, for which we have data, is very time consuming, we use pre-selection based on X and Y coordinates, with the size of pre-selection window estimated based on Z. All the data is stored in an Oracle database with Spatial extension. Pre-selection is performed with Spatial native range queries. Consequent processing is performed by in-house software.

A few figures follow demonstrating what kind of output described instance of the model produces. Since a graphical representation may depict only the spatial component of data, we decided not to present screenshots of the client terminal display, and generated instead pictures conveying a little more information. The pictures have white background and the color of objects (street segments and points of interest) ranges from almost white (that means that their LOD is close to zero) to black (LOD is equal to one). Thin lines in the pictures represent footpaths, thicker ones correspond to streets, and even thicker to highways. The larger black circle in the center of each picture shows the position of the user. The area covered by each picture is 700 by 700 meters square.

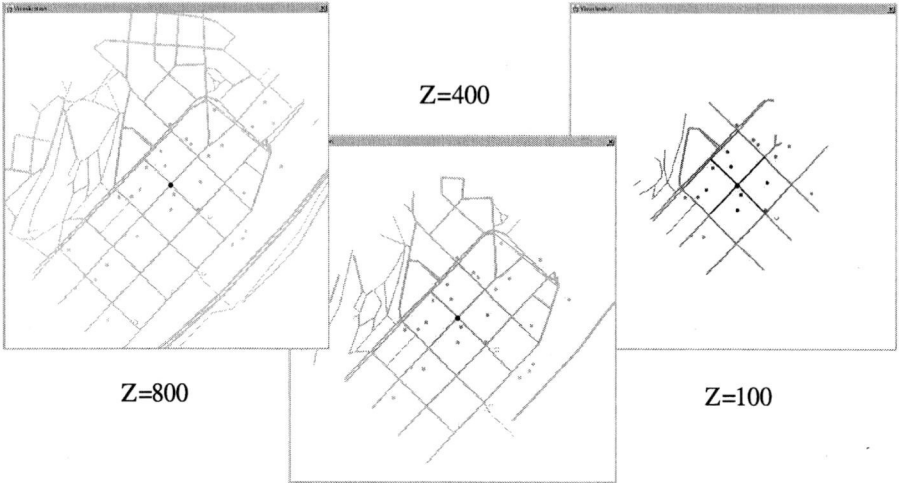

Fig. 1. Different overall detail levels

Figure 1 presents the same city area for different values of Z coordinate (800, 400 and 100 meters correspondingly). As can be seen, with reduction of Z the represented area decreases; however, the levels of detail of all the objects grow (scale change effect). Especially in the picture for $Z=100$, it can be noticed (by color difference) that the dataset is focused – the objects in the user's close vicinity are represented with more detail than those farther away. Change in segments' vertices number is probably difficult to notice. However, recall that, most importantly, LOD affects also nonspatial data – so, segments

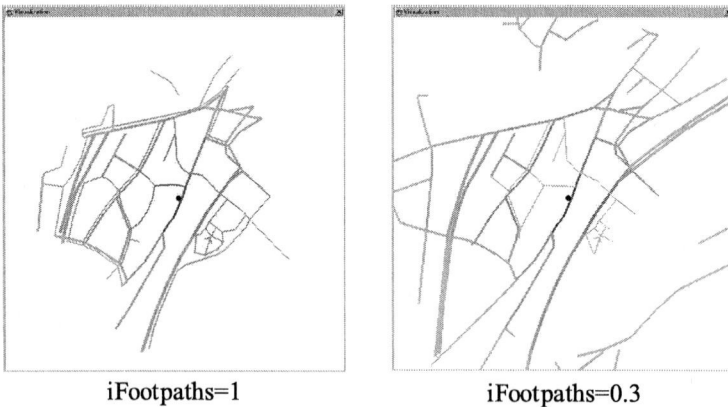

Fig. 2. When streets are more important than footpaths

shown as black include all the properties up to the address range, while those light-gray may have even the street name omitted.

In 2, both pictures depict the same area; however, while the picture on the left is for the case $iFootpaths = 1$, the picture on the right shows the case when $iFootpaths = 0.3$ ($iHighways = 1$ and $iStreets = 1$ for both pictures). As can be seen, there are many footpaths in the picture on the left, and their extent is equal to that of bigger roads. However, when their relative importance has been reduced, footpaths left only in the close vicinity of the user, and level of detail of those left was greatly reduced. This also enabled representing additional objects of other types (in this case streets and highways).

Figure 3 compares the cases when the user is stationary and when the user is moving in the southwest direction ($v_x = v_y = -8$ m/sec). As can be seen, the selection window has shifted to the direction of motion. The most detailed region now is not around the current user location. Additionally, the average level of detail of objects has reduced and the extent of the representation has slightly increased.

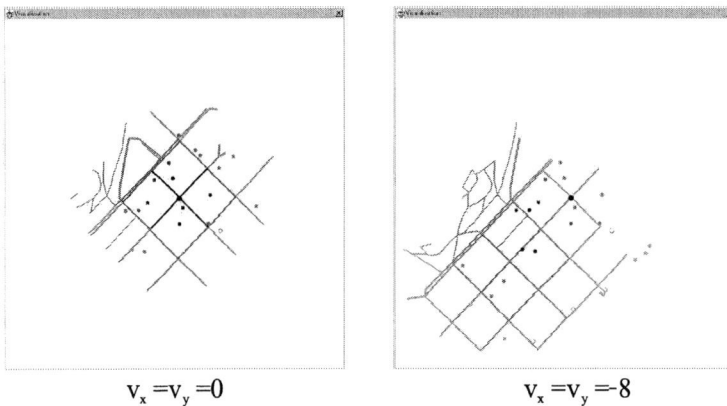

$$v_x = v_y = 0 \qquad v_x = v_y = -8$$

Fig. 3. When user is moving southwest

5 Conclusions

In this paper, we described a computational model that produces a dataset which we consider to be an appropriate response for "give me a description of my neighborhood" type of queries in location-based services. Our attempt is to reflect the abstraction ability of a specific user, and in this way to maximize the usability of the service under restrictions on data volume posed by technical, economical and cognitive factors of mobile environments. As can be seen from our example of instantiating the model, its simple mathematics allows achieving quite complex effects, such as data focusing, controlling the balance of different data themes, taking mobility into account, and other.

The technical performance of the model is yet to be validated. Anyway, we see our work as rather the first step towards a solution that will actually be applied in practice. Our work can be considered to belong mainly to the Mobile HCI field. However, a formal presentation of HCI ideas in the form of a computational model provides for continuation of the work from the database perspective, towards further formalization and optimization.

The questions related to criteria/algorithms for selecting model parameters are left outside the scope of the present paper and belong to future work. We believe that our approach in general is viable. However, empirical usability evaluation with real users and for different LBS types is another important direction of future work.

Acknowledgements

The greater part of this work was done in MultiMeetMobile project, which was financially supported by the National Technology Agency of Finland (TEKES) under contracts 40599/99, 40779/99, 40640/00, and industrial partners Hewlett-Packard, Nokia Networks and Yomi.

References

1. D. Chalmers, N. Dulay, and M. Sloman. A framework for contextual mediation in mobile and ubiquitous computing applied to the context-aware adaptation of maps. *Personal and Ubiquitous Computing*, 8(1):1–18, 2004.
2. D. Chincholle, M. Goldstein, M. Nyberg, and M. Eriksson. Lost or found? A usability evaluation of a mobile navigation and location-based service. In *Proc. Mobile HCI 2002*, volume 2411 of *LNCS*, pages 211–224, 2002.
3. D. Dao, C. Rizos, and J. Wang. Location-based services: Technical and business issues. *GPS Solutions*, 6(3):169–178, 2002.
4. J. Hjelm. *Creating Location Services for the Wireless Web*. John Wiley & Sons, 2002.
5. C. S. Jensen, A. Kligys, T. B. Pedersen, and I. Timko. Multidimensional data modeling for location-based services. *The VLDB Journal*, 13(1):1–21, 2004.
6. C. S. Jensen, J. Kolar, T. B. Pedersen, and I. Timko. Nearest neighbor queries in road networks. In *Proc. 11th ACM Int. Symposium on Advances in GIS*, pages 1–8, 2003.
7. D. L. Lee, J. Xu, B. Zheng, and W.-C. Lee. Data management in location-dependent information services. *IEEE Pervasive Computing*, 1(3):65–72, 2002.
8. J. Markkula, A. Katasonov, and A. Garmash. Developing MLS location-based service pilot system. In *Proc. IFIP 7th Conf. on Intelligence on Networks*, pages 229–244, 2002.
9. R. B. McMaster and K. S. Shea. *Generalization in digital cartography*. Resource Publication of the Association of American Geographers, Washington, D.C., 1992.
10. A.-M. Nivala and L. T. Sarjakoski. Need for context-aware topographic maps in mobile devices. In *Proc. 9th ScanGIS Conference*, pages 15–29, 2003.
11. D. Papadias, J. Zhang, N. Mamoulis, and Y. Tao. Query processing in spatial network databases. In *Proc. 29th VLDB Conference*, pages 802–813, 2003.
12. S. Saltenis and C. S. Jensen. Indexing of moving objects for location-based services. In *Proc. 18th Int. Conf. on Data Engineering*, pages 463–472, 2002.
13. S. Timpf. Abstraction, levels of detail, and hierarchies in map series. In *Proc. Int. Conf. Spatial Information Theory - Cognitive and Computational Foundations of Geographic Information Science*, volume 1661 of *LNCS*, pages 125–139, 1999.
14. A. Tsalgatidou, J. Veijalainen, J. Markkula, A. Katasonov, and S. Hadjiefthymiades. Mobile E-commerce and location-based services: Technology and requirements. In *Proc. 9th ScanGIS Conference*, pages 1–14, 2003.
15. A. Zipf. User-adaptive maps for location-based services (LBS) for tourism. In *Proc. 9th Int. Conf. for Information and Communication Technologies in Tourism*. Springer, 2002.

MITOS: A Smart Spaces System for Pervasive Computing

George Alyfantis, Stathes Hadjiefthymiades, and Lazaros Merakos

University of Athens, Department of Informatics and Telecommunications,
Communication Networks Laboratory, Panepistimioupolis, Ilisia,
Athens 15784, Greece

Abstract. The popularity of wireless networks has increased in the recent years, as they become a common addition to fixed LAN infrastructures. In this paper we introduce a novel use for a wireless network based on the IEEE 802.11 standard: a smart spaces system that proposes to wireless users to assume optimum locations in order to obtain a satisfactory QoS level when the wireless hot-spot becomes saturated. The system, being kept up to date with the traffic across the network and the location of each user, is capable of making the appropriate proposal urging users to move to new locations at reasonable distances. In that way, user perceived QoS and wireless network load-balancing can be both achieved. MITOS is the name of the developed smart spaces system. We discuss the general system architecture and operation as well as the optimum proposal algorithm. The operation of the system was verified in the wireless infrastructure of our department.

1 Introduction

According to M. Weiser [13], the father of ubiquitous computing, also called pervasive computing [5, 7, 10, 11], computers must disappear from conscious thought, in a way that they are integrated in the every day life. Over the recent years, we have experienced great penetration of wireless LANs. Especially, IEEE 802.11 LANs are met everywhere: in University departments, corporate facilities, factories, even at airports and public places. We can safely state that wireless LANs constitute a ubiquitous technology.

In such environments, where the population of wireless users is dense, it is possible that users experience poor wireless connectivity. This is reasonable if we consider a situation where a lot of users are gathered in an area covered by an access point (AP), and many of them are downloading large files. As a consequence, the wireless bandwidth is exhausted in that area, because the local AP gets congested. Hence, users harm one another and everybody experiences significant network delays resulting to a rather annoying situation. At the same time, there may be other APs in the building not congested at all, as they are installed at places where few users are usually present.

Thus, we can see that traffic among the APs in a building may not be evenly balanced. That is to say, the users do not take advantage of the overall wireless bandwidth; in contrary they use (or better abuse) certain portions of it. In that context it would be very interesting if there were a system that in first place could load-balance the traffic across the wireless network, and finally help users improve their wireless connection experience.

W. Lindner et al. (Eds.): EDBT 2004 Workshops, LNCS 3268, pp. 375–384, 2004.
© Springer-Verlag Berlin Heidelberg 2004

Given that the position of an AP and the area of its coverage are well defined after installation, there is no other way to succeed load-balancing than to balance the user population across the building. In other words, in case congestion occurs, users have to move to other locations to maintain a satisfactory QoS level.

1.1   Motivation

The motivation of our work originates at a hypothetical scenario presented by M. Satyanarayanan in [11]. According to this scenario, a lady is waiting for her connecting flight at the airport and while waiting she is editing several large documents. While she is waiting for her boarding time she wants to send them via e-mail using the wireless network of the airport. Unfortunately, there are many other users surfing the Web at her gate and the adjacent gate. Thus, her wireless connectivity is poor and she will not have adequate time to send all her messages until she boards the plane. The pervasive computing system of the airport observes the situation and gathers information from various sources. It discovers that only a few gates away, 3 minutes on foot, bandwidth availability is excellent. The system also knows there will be no departures or arrivals for half an hour. Hence, it consults the lady to get there, where she will manage to send her documents before her boarding call. So does the lady and she successfully sends all her messages and gets back in time for her departure.

2   The MITOS Architecture

MITOS is a Smart Spaces System (SSS, S3) developed after the scenario discussed above, but has a much wider scope. Specifically, its purpose is to balance the traffic load across a wireless network within a certain building. The S3, by observing the traffic distribution in the wireless network, is capable of discovering whether congestion takes place in a certain segment of the network. At the same time, it is kept up to date with the current location of each mobile user and the AP he is attached to. If congestion occurs, the S3 locates each affected user and urges him to move to another location, where the S3 has observed that bandwidth reserves are higher. The S3 sends also instructions necessary for the transition from the current to the proposed location.

2.1   System Naming

The word "mitos" has its origins in the ancient myth of Theseus, the son of King Aegeas (after whom the Aegean Sea is named) who went into the den of the half-man, half-bull beast, the minotaur, to kill it. Previous attempts had failed because of the maze in which the minotaur lived. Theseus girlfriend, Ariadne, had the clever idea of giving Theseus a silken thread ("mitos", in Greek) that he could unwind and use to find his way out of the maze. Since the purpose of the *MITOS* S3 is to find ways in which users with poor connectivity can lead themselves in other locations with better bandwidth, the *mitos* of Ariadne is a very representative symbol for that objective.

2.2   Architecture and Technologies

The MITOS S3 was designed to maintain continuous knowledge of the location of each mobile user and to be aware of the traffic load for every AP in the infrastructure. Moreover, when congestion is observed, an alerting message must appear to the user presenting the S3's Relocation Proposal (RP).

In order for these requirements to be fulfilled, the adopted architecture is composed of three basic entities (Fig.1):

- *Location Manager* - this component is in charge of user management and maintains relevant information (user identification data, current location, handling AP, proposed location and navigation information). Moreover, it manages wireless network traffic information and is responsible for advising users in the case of congestion. All information is maintained in a properly structured database.
- *SNMP Manager* - this component is in charge of gathering data from the APs, in order to compute load metrics, which allow detection of possible congestion. In case that one or more APs are found congested, SNMP Manager sends a full report to the Location Manager to take all the necessary steps.
- *Terminal Client* - this component is installed on the user's machine and actually comprises the interface between the user and the S3. It is constantly connected with the Location Manager to communicate location and connection information. Conversely, the Location Manager transmits messages asynchronously, in order to update the Terminal Client on the S3's RPs. The latter has to present that information to the user in a friendly way.

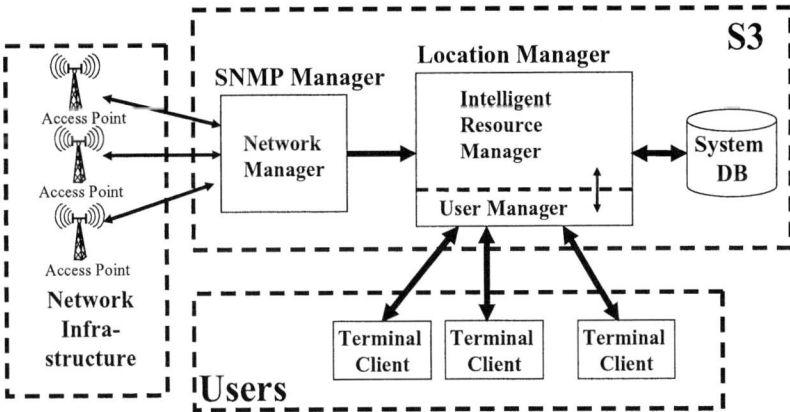

Fig. 1. MITOS S3 architecture and entity-level communication

The Terminal Client connects to the Location Manager through TCP. For the connection between the SNMP Manager and the Location Manager, we have also adopted TCP, as it is connection oriented, and the exchanged traffic reports are of great significance to the S3. Finally, the SNMP Manager, using the SNMP protocol (over UDP) queries the APs for the MIB (Management Information Base) variables necessary for traffic metric estimation. In order to implement the architecture presented above, we have adopted the following technological basis:

- *IEEE 802.11* - the IEEE standard for wireless local area networks [6]
- *Simple Network Management Protocol (SNMP)* - is defined in [2] and is the most prevalent management protocol for IP networks [12]
- *Nibble* - it is an indoor location system developed in UCLA [3, 1]. Its utility to the S3 is obvious, since the location of each user must be always known [8]
- *Java* - it is the "glue" that links together the aforementioned technologies

2.3   System Operation

The Location Manager is responsible for processing data coming from different system layers and resides on a node with increased computing power. All the information is kept in the S3's database and can be distinguished into:

- User information (e.g., current location, handling AP, relocation proposal and navigation information),
- Network traffic information, and
- Network-building information (e.g., different building locations and topological relationship between them, and locations each AP covers)

The information processed by the Location Manager is provided partly by the Terminal Client and partly by the SNMP Manager. The SNMP Manager sends to the Location Manager detailed traffic reports, in the case of congestion. Subsequently, the Location Manager, updates the database with the recently received report, and takes appropriate actions (described below). The Terminal Client regularly sends signal quality data so that the Location Manager can estimate the current location of the mobile device as well as the AP it is connected to.

2.4   Nibble Indoor Positioning

Nibble is a Java-based system capable of recognizing locations (rooms, corridors, etc) by their signal quality pattern obtained by the WLAN card. It maintains a properly trained XML-formatted Bayesian network and returns symbolic information [4]. Nibble is a stand-alone application [9] and adopts a decentralized architecture. However, for scalability, network change resilience and client flexibility, we enhanced Nibble so that it runs under the control of the Location Manager and estimates location on behalf of the client. Thus, it can be guaranteed that the Bayesian network will be always up to date and the Terminal Client application is lighter and more practical for a variety of mobile devices running Java.

2.5   Terminal Client User Interface

In case the S3 decides that a user should move to a certain location, in order to keep a satisfactory wireless QoS level, the Location Manager sends to the corresponding Terminal Client an appropriate message. Various messages are exchanged between the entities of the S3 by means of an application level protocol devised for this reason.

As soon as the Terminal Client receives this message, an alert indication is provided to the user urging him to move to the proposed location. In Fig. 2 and Fig. 3, we present a prototype implementation of the Graphical User Interface (GUI) provided through the Terminal Client. Such GUI was not designed according to the distraction-free perspective of pervasive computing but assisted us in validating the functionality of the S3.

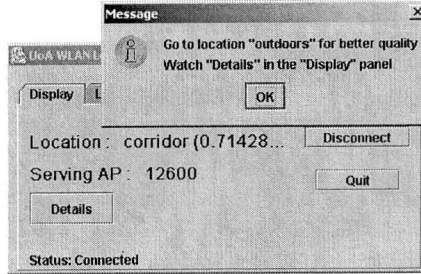

Fig. 2. Message box displaying the MITOS RP to the user

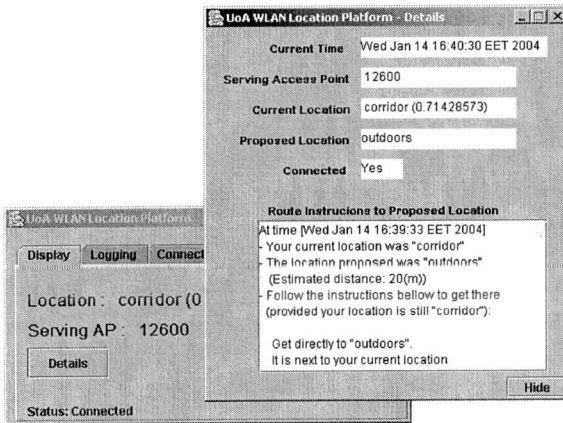

Fig. 3. Instructions for the transition from the current to the proposed location

2.6   Traffic Load Measurements

At the current implementation, the SNMP Manager computes the utilization factor of the wireless interfaces. The load threshold value beyond which we consider that the AP becomes saturated is set to 90, which corresponds to 90% link utilization. We have adopted this value in order to minimize the RP transmission frequency and the user distraction caused, keeping though the desired properties, as will be shown bellow.

The SNMP Manager updates every 500ms (period T) the load metric value (M_k) for every wireless interface k. As a result, the metric values exhibit great fluctuation, since

IP networks are typically subject to bursty traffic. For that reason, we apply a low pass filter in the metric values of each wireless interface taking the average over a number (W) of successive samples in a time window $W \times T$). The load value, L_t^k, of AP k at time t, is calculated as follows:

$$L_t^k = \frac{1}{W} \sum_{i=0}^{W-1} M_k(t - T \cdot i) \tag{1}$$

$M_k(t)$ denotes the metric value for wireless interface k at time t. It is obvious that there is a trade-off between larger and smaller values of W. A small value of W would render the S3 very sensitive to traffic fluctuations, and rather annoying to users who would receive RPs very frequently. On the other hand, if W assumed large values, the S3 would exhibit reduced responsivity in congestion situations. In our system, W assumed the value of 16. This value was selected after a series of experiments and was found capable of smoothing transient traffic load picks (attributed to HTTP requests), while maintaining the responsivity of the system to congestion occurrences.

If, at some time, the SNMP Manager finds the load of one or more interfaces exceeding the aforementioned threshold value, we consider that congestion has occurred. In that case, the SNMP Manager sends a report to the Location Manager indicating the situation.

As soon as the Location Manager receives that report, it knows exactly the traffic distribution among the wireless interfaces in the network. Then, it is responsible of taking action, exploiting the traffic information received, along with the user location information already acquired.

2.7   Location Representation

For the location representation in the S3 we used a graph-based model (Location Graph, LG). The locations identified by Nibble are mapped to LG nodes, and arcs denote the topological relation between such locations. Weights assigned to arcs denote the physical distance or cost for the transition from one location to another. Shortest paths (useful for navigation instructions) are calculated using the Dijkstra algorithm.

2.8   Optimum Location Proposal

In case of congestion, the objective of the S3 is to decongest the most loaded APs and distribute traffic (i.e. users) to neighboring APs. For the determination of the optimum location of each user, two are the factors that must be considered to issue a safe RP to the user: traffic load and distance. For each relocation ($A \rightarrow B$) considered by the system, we have adopted a cost function as follows:

$$
\text{Cost}(A \rightarrow B)
= \begin{cases} a \cdot \frac{100 \cdot \text{distance}(A,B)}{\text{maxDistance}} + (1-a) \cdot \text{load}(B), & \text{distance}(A, B) \leq \text{maxDistance} \\ \infty, & \text{otherwise} \end{cases} \tag{2}
$$

$$a = 0.6, \quad \text{maxDistance} = 200 \text{ m}$$

The system suggests to the user the location (B) with the lowest calculated cost value. Locations that are more than 200m apart are excluded from the feasible set. Distance is measured in meters, while load is measured in a percent scale, from 0 to 100. The weight factor, a, assumed the value of 0.6 that was arbitrarily selected. Alternatively, the weight factor could be user-specific, contained in user profiles, indicating preference for bandwidth abundance or geographically restricted relocations. The weight factor, a, takes value from the interval [0.05...0.95] in order to always take into account both factors.

The issued RP, apart from the name of the proposed location, contains relevant navigation details, derived from the pre-computed shortest paths. Users can follow the RPs and take advantage of the extra bandwidth available. The S3 sends RPs, indiscriminately, to all users connected to congested APs. However, if all affected users followed the advice of the system it is evident that load balancing across the wireless network would fail.

3   MITOS Assessment

To prove the aforementioned anticipation we performed a series of simulations. We assumed a complex floor layout with fifty locations (corridors, offices and an atrium), 10 APs covering these locations and 100 mobile users. Each AP covers an area of 5 locations. The relocation of users between locations is performed stochastically according to a state transition matrix, resulting in an environment of high mobility. In the building there are areas frequently visited and others that are not popular (defined stochastically).

Table 1. Application Characteristics

Application Type	Session activation probability	Bandwidth requirements (Kbps)	Session duration (sec)
WWW	0.4	500	5
Voice over IP	0.025	64	180
Video	0.005	1000	240

We considered three different types of applications with specific bandwidth and duration characteristics. Each application is invoked independently, according to the probabilities shown in Table 1.

We assumed that all users have the same application activation probabilities, as shown in Table 1, hence, their bandwidth requirements are similar. A RP is adopted stochastically by the receiving user, with probability P. It is also assumed that if a user adopts the RP, he follows the shortest path indicated to him. Furthermore, as soon as he reaches the proposed location, he avoids a new relocation for a certain period of time.

3.1   Simulation Metrics

To assess the MITOS system we defined the following metric:

$$\overline{D}(t) = \frac{1}{N} \sum_{i=1}^{N} D_i(t), \qquad t \in \{1, 2, \dots, C\} \tag{3}$$

C denotes the simulation time (i.e., the total number of simulation cycles, namely 2000 - cycle duration=5sec), N is the number of APs (namely 10), and $D_i(t)$ the instantaneous bandwidth demand on AP_i. $\overline{D}(t)$ is the instantaneous, average bandwidth demand for all APs (i.e. the desired balanced bandwidth demand). We have also introduced $dev_i(t)$, as shown in (4), to denote the instantaneous deviation of the bandwidth demand on AP_i from the desired balanced demand, $\overline{D}(t)$.

$$dev_i(t) = \left[D_i(t) - \overline{D}(t) \right]^2, \qquad i \in \{1, 2, \ldots, N\} \text{ and } t \in \{1, 2, \ldots, C\} \quad (4)$$

$dev(t)$, as shown in (5), is the total instantaneous deviation normalized over the desired bandwidth demand, $\overline{D}(t)$.

$$dev(t) = \frac{1}{[\overline{D}(t)]^2} \sum_{i=1}^{N} dev_i(t), \qquad t \in \{1, 2, \ldots, C\} \quad (5)$$

Our assessment was based on the metric given in (6). Dev is the time average of the deviation given in (5) over the entire simulation duration.

$$\text{Dev} = \frac{1}{C} \sum_{i=1}^{C} dev(t) \quad (6)$$

3.2   Simulation Results

In Fig. 4 we can see the Dev metric, as the RP acceptance probability (Pa) increases in the range [0.05...1.0] for the MITOS architecture. As the probability of RP acceptance increases over 0.90, MITOS exhibits a very large deviation, higher than that of the RP-free scheme. This behavior renders MITOS inappropriate for use in a real situation.

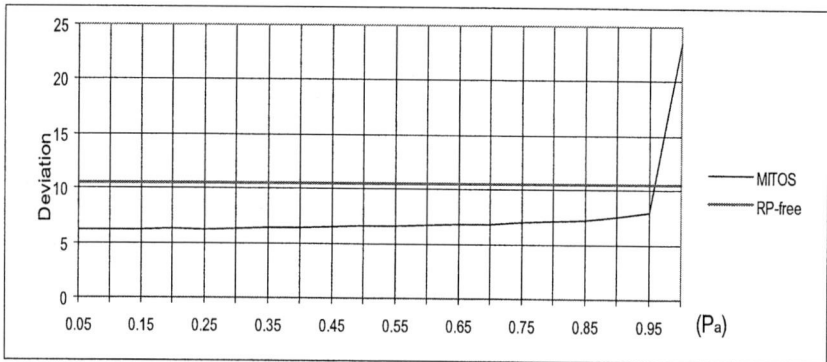

Fig. 4. MITOS simulation results as the probability of RP acceptance increases

To solve the problem of similar user treatment we decided to assign a bias term to each user, assuming random values in the range [-1.0...1.0]. The weight factor, a, in (2) is then modified as shown in (7).

$$a'(\text{bias}) = \begin{cases} 0.95, & a + \text{bias} > 0.95 \\ 0.05, & a + \text{bias} \leq 0.05 \\ a + \text{bias, otherwise} \end{cases} \qquad (7)$$

With this MITOS enhancement, it was found that the problem mentioned earlier was resolved. The simulation results for the enhanced scheme are shown in Fig. 5. We performed simulations for various load thresholds, namely 10%, 50% and 90%. The resulting trend-lines (fourth degree polynomial regression) represent the trend of traffic load deviation for the different thresholds.

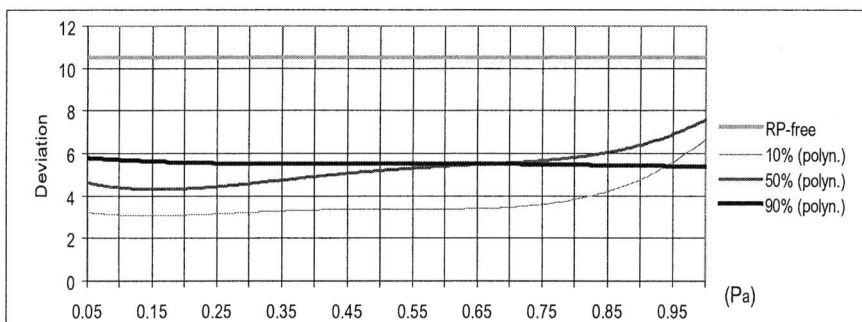

Fig. 5. Enhanced MITOS simulation results

From Fig. 5 we observe that the enhanced MITOS system exhibits significantly better behavior than the RP-free scheme under circumstances.

4 Conclusions

The implemented Smart Spaces System proposes to the users of a wireless network infrastructure, ways to improve their connectivity, being kept up to date with the traffic distribution among the wireless APs, the current location of each user and the AP he is attached to. In case of congestion, affected users are urged to move to a new location in the broader area, if they are willing to keep a satisfactory QoS level. Each RP is accompanied by navigation instructions for the transition from the current to the proposed location. The interest of the implementation lies in the fact that the system is capable of gathering and combining information from diverse layers (low-level congestion data, current location data, distance information, etc.) by using different technologies, according to the objectives of the pervasive computing paradigm. Furthermore, the problem of common user reaction to RPs was addressed.

In the future, we plan to extend MITOS capabilities to integrate game theoretic models or economic models as an overlay component to the S3 architecture, in order to further improve its performance.

References

1. The Nibble location system, May 2001. http://mmsl.cs.ucla.edu/nibble.
2. J. Case, M. Fedor, M. Schoffstall, and J. Davin. A simple network management protocol (snmp), ietf rfc 1157. *Networking Working Group*, 1990.
3. P. Castro, P. Chiu, T. Kremenek, and R. Muntz. A probabilistic room location service for wireless networked environments. In *Proc. of Ubicomp 2001*, 2001.
4. D. Fox, J. Hightower, L. Liao, D. Schulz, and G. Borriello. Bayesian filtering for location estimation. *IEEE Pervasive Computing*, July 2003.
5. D. Garlan, D. Siewiorek, A. Smailagic, and P. Steenkiste. Project aura: Toward distraction-free pervasive computing. *IEEE Pervasive Computing*, April 2002.
6. M. Gast. *802.11 Wireless Networks: The Definite Guide*. O'Reilly, April 2002.
7. U. Hansmann, L. Merk, M. Nicklous, and T. Stober. *Pervasive Computing Handbook. The Mobile World (Second Edition)*. Springer, 2003.
8. J. Hightower and G. Borriello. Location systems for ubiquitous computing. *IEEE Computer*, August 2001.
9. G. Papazafeiropoulos, N. Prigouris, G. Marias, S. Hadjiefthymiades, and L. Merakos. Retrieving position from indoor wlans through gwlc. In *Proc. of the IST Mobile & Wireless Communications Summit*, 2003.
10. D. Saha and A. Mukherjee. Pervasive computing: A paradigm for the 21st century. *IEEE Pervasive Computing*, March 2003.
11. M. Satyanarayanan. Pervasive computing: Vision and challenges. *IEEE Pervasive Computing*, August 2001.
12. M. Sidnie and D. Feit. *SNMP: A Guide to Network Management*. McGraw-Hill Professional, 1993.
13. M. Weiser. The computer for the twenty-first century. *Scientific American*, September 1991.

Service Allocation in Selfish Mobile Ad hoc Networks Using Vickrey Auction

Jinshan Liu and Valérie Issarny

INRIA - Rocquencourt,
Domaine de Voluceau, Rocquencourt, BP 105, 78153 Le Chesnay Cedex, France
{Jinshan.Liu,Valerie.Issarny}@inria.fr
http://www-rocq.inria.fr/arles/

Abstract. Incentive scheme for stimulating service provision in Mobile Ad hoc NETworks (MANET) has been under intensive investigation due to its significance to the operation of MANET. This paper applies distributed algorithmic mechanism design and utilizes Vickrey auction for service allocation in mobile ad hoc networks. We show that our method stimulates service provision and achieves desired system-wide service allocation in spite of each agent's selfish behavior, while introducing challenges from the inherent shortcomings of Vickrey auction and characteristics of MANET. We discuss the challenges, the existing solutions for wireline networks and propose a system model for service allocation in MANET.

1 Introduction

The popularity of light-weight terminals (e.g., handhelds, PDAs and cell phones) with integrated communication capabilities facilitates the ambient intelligence vision of service access anytime, anywhere. Mobile distributed systems that provide access to information and services spread among autonomous devices is of paramount importance to the vision. To realize the above system, cooperation among autonomous devices is a necessity. Unfortunately, cooperative behavior implies resource consumption (e.g., battery), which is not in the interest of the autonomous devices. How to stimulate service provision in mobile ad hoc networks has thus drawn intensive research activities [4, 12, 17, 26].

Not only do we need to stimulate service provision in ad hoc networks, we also need to allocate services in an efficient manner. More specifically, the allocation result should be a social, system-wide choice instead of an individual one. "Service", an instantiated configured system that is run by a providing organization [21], here not only refers to services like packets routing in network layer, but also to services in application layer, e.g., Web services [9]. Current directory-based service repositories (e.g., Jini) require centralized storage scheme and do not address the incentive issues of service allocation. Even with distributed service discovery (e.g., Service Discovery Protocol (SDP) for bluetooth), it is not as trivial as adding a price field in the service description record: (1) one issue is autonomous entities are normally unwilling to reveal their prices, which are considered private; (2) another issue is selecting the least expensive service and

W. Lindner et al. (Eds.): EDBT 2004 Workshops, LNCS 3268, pp. 385–394, 2004.

pay the lowest price does not serve a service most economically[1]. Mechanism design, especially *Distributed Algorithmic Mechanism Design* (DAMD) [6], is emerging as a suitable approach for solving the above mentioned problem. DAMD addresses the design of *incentive compatible* mechanisms (i.e., mechanisms that result in desired system-wide outcome from selfish behavior by the system's agents) at *tractable computational and communication expense*. It lies in the intersection of economics science and computer science.

DAMD is suitable for *Mobile Ad hoc NETworks* (MANET) because: (1) MANET is distributed by nature; (2) MANET can only afford tractable computational and communication complexity. However, DAMD for MANET is challenged by MANET's resource-constraints, infrastructureless and unpredictable nature: (1) The inherent mobility of MANET requires the designed mechanism to be robust; (2) Many existing DAMD-based mechanisms for wireline networks assume perfect connectivity between nodes, which is arguable in MANET; (3) Thin devices' limited *computational and communication* (C2) capability makes C2-saving a desirable property for mechanisms, as tractable complexity (i.e., polynomial computational complexity) can still be too heavy in many scenarios. Therefore, DAMD employed on wireline networks cannot be applied directly in the context of MANET, which demands specific consideration.

In this paper, we more specifically discuss application of Vickrey auction [23] for service allocation in mobile ad hoc networks. Vickrey auction is a well-known incentive compatible mechanism for solving service and resource allocation problems in multi-agent systems in an efficient, distributed and autonomy-preserving manner. Design of algorithmic Vickrey auction falls into DAMD. This paper has three goals: (1) introduce DAMD as a possible tool for designing incentive schemes for MANET; (2) discuss the challenges of applying Vickrey auction in MANET; (3) propose a viable model for service allocation via Vickrey auction in MANET. The paper is organized as follows. The next section introduces mechanism design and various auctions, explains how to apply Vickrey auction as a valuable tool for optimizing service allocation in MANET and outlines the accompanying challenges. Section 3 gives existing solutions in wireline networks for each challenge, and proposes a system model for service allocation via Vickrey auction in MANET. Finally, Section 4 concludes with discussion on future work.

2   Mechanism Design for Service Allocation in MANET

The field of mechanism design studies how to design systems so that agents' selfish behavior results in desired system-wide goals. "Agent" here refers to a software entity representing and working for the interests of the host node. However, the game-theory literature on mechanism design neglects computational and communication complexity, which makes mechanism-design approach unpractical in a lot of settings (e.g., Internet). This is addressed by DAMD (Sect. 2.1). Distributed algorithmic auctions, especially Vickrey auction, are a valuable tool for service allocation (Sect. 2.2). After justifying

---

[1] As analyzed in Sect. 2.2, it is actually a first-price, sealed-bid auction, in which bidders' bids are affected by their belief of peers' valuation.

Vickrey auction as the most suitable auction setting for our purpose, we detail the application of Vickrey auction to MANET with confronted challenges (Sect. 2.3).

2.1 Distributed Algorithmic Mechanism Design

In essence, Distributed Algorithmic Mechanism Design (DAMD) studies how to design incentive compatible mechanisms with tractable computation (i.e., algorithmic mechanism design [16]) in a distributed setting such as Internet computing [6]. DAMD takes into account communication overhead in addition to the local computational burden on agents.

More formally, consider a distributed system in which there is a set of possible outcomes $\mathcal{O}$ (e.g., result of resource allocation)[2]. A *strategy* for an agent is a complete contingency plan, i.e., a plan describing what decision the agent should make under each possible situation that might occur. Each of the n autonomous strategic agents[3] has a utility function $u_i: \mathcal{O} \rightarrow \mathcal{R}$, where $u_i \in \mathcal{U}$ ($\mathcal{U}$ defines the set of utility functions of agents) expresses an agent's preferences over these outcomes. The desired system-wide goals are specified by a *Social Choice Function* (SCF) $F : \mathcal{U}^n \rightarrow \mathcal{O}$ that maps the (actual) utility functions of agents to a particular outcome. However, each agent is usually reluctant to publicize its actual utility function, thus making it impossible to achieve any global goal.

For a given mechanism M, let S denote the *strategy space* of one agent, i.e., a set of strategies that can be taken by the agent, and $C_M(u) \subseteq S^n$ denote all possible strategy vectors that could reasonably result from selfish behavior. The goal of mechanism design is to define a mechanism M that implements the SCF, i.e., $M(C_M(U)) = F(U)$, for all $U \in \mathcal{U}^n$. With such a mechanism qualified as being *incentive compatible*, selfish behavior by agents will result in desired system-wide outcomes.

In game theory, the strategy that is always in the best interest of one agent, no matter how other agents act, is named *dominant strategy*. A mechanism with dominant strategy is very desirable for scenarios featuring interactions among autonomous, automated agents, compared to those without dominant strategy: (1) the behavior of agents is much simpler – following the dominant strategy regardless of other agents' behavior; (2) it saves the complex knowledge representation and logic evaluation for counterspeculating how other agents will behave. Thus, it is very desirable to have an incentive compatible mechanism with dominant strategy. The emphasis of mechanism design is put on the implementation of various types of auctions [16], which has been an efficient means for resource allocation [13], service assignment [24] and conflict resolution [5]. In the following, we investigate what kind of auction settings is suitable for our purpose.

2.2 Auctions

An auction consists of an auctioneer and potential bidders. The commonly seen auctions include English auction, first-price sealed-bid auction, Dutch auction and Vickrey auction.

---

[2] We rely mostly on [6] for definitions and notation.
[3] Since even random behavior can be considered as one kind of strategy, every agent is a strategic agent, strictly speaking.

English Auction. In English auction, the auctioneer starts with the reserve price and proceeds to solicit successively higher bids from the bidders until no one raises the bid. The highest bidder is the winner and pays the price she bids. The dominant strategy for one agent in English auction is to continuously raise its bid until it wins or it reaches the maximum price it is willing to pay for that item. A noticeable feature of English auction is that it is usually multi-round and the time and communication overhead is proportional to the difference between the starting price and the price at which the item is sold. However, it does allocate the item to the bidder with the highest valuation, who is the only bidder willing to outbid all other bidders.

First-Price, Sealed-Bid Auction. In first-price sealed auction, each bidder submits one bid in ignorance of all other bids to the auctioneer, who determines the highest bid and sells the item to that bidder for the bidding price. This kind of auction can be executed in one-round and thus is communication-saving. However, since each agent's bid is based on her private valuation *and* prior beliefs of others' valuations, the item is not always awarded to the party who values it most.

Dutch Auction. In Dutch auction, bidding starts at an extremely high price and is progressively lowered until a buyer claims an item by calling "mine". The winner pays the price at the current price. Dutch auction preserves maximal privacy: only the highest bid is revealed. However, like English Auction, it is multi-round, and like first-price, sealed-bid auction, one agent's bid is strategically based on its private valuations and its beliefs of others' valuation.

Vickrey Auction. Similar to the first-price sealed auction, Vickrey auction is sealed and executed in one-round. The highest bidder is the winner, but pays a price that is equal to the second-highest bid [23]. Vickrey auction has a very fundamental feature: the dominant strategy for every bidder is to bid her true valuation[4]. Thus Vickrey auction always rewards the item to the bidder who values it most, i.e., realizes SCF.

Table 1. *Various Auction Settings*

Auction Type	Communication Complexity	Existence of Dominant Strategy	Optimal Item Allocation
English Auction	Multi-Round	Yes	Yes
First-price, Sealed Auction	One-Round	No	No
Dutch Auction	Multi-Round	No	No
Vickrey Auction	One-Round	Yes	Yes

From Table 1 that lists the features of the four previously mentioned auctions, we can see that only Vickrey auction and English auction both have dominant strategy and realize SCF. Furthermore, Vickrey auction only requires single-round execution. Thus,

---

[4] Readers are referred to [22] for the proof.

from the perspective of both economic incentive and communication overhead, Vickrey auction is the best mechanism for service allocation in MANET.

2.3 Service Allocation via Vickrey Auction in MANET

It is worth noting that although an auction hosted by a service provider does find the service seeker that values a service most, it does not contribute to our purpose of social service allocation, i.e., serving a service request least expensively, which is essentially to allocate the service request to the service provider that can do so. Therefore, auctions are hosted by service seeking agents, leading to *reverse Vickrey auction*: the bidder (i.e., service provider) with the lowest instead of the highest bid is the winner.

Bids submitted by service providers are determined by the cost for serving a service, which depends on factors like capabilities of a bidder (e.g., computation power), the load of a bidder (e.g., how many services it has already been serving), the service to be served and some other factors. As the cost reflects suitability of a service provider serving a service better than simply the load, auction-based service allocation is better than non auction-based counterpart because it finds the cheapest way to serve a service via economic payoff. Auction based service allocation also achieves load balancing because heavy load leads to higher bid and thus less possibility of winning the auction.

As mentioned above, service allocation via reverse Vickrey auction in MANET has three desired properties:

1. It has a dominant strategy, thus it is simple to implement.
2. The agents are motivated to bid. The winner gets a payoff which equals to the difference between its valuation and the second lowest bid; the losers lose nothing (i.e., *payoff* = 0).
3. The service is always allocated efficiently: service (request) is allocated to the provider that serves it least expensively.

Despite Vickrey auction's impressive theoretical properties, Vickrey auction has the following two major shortcomings [19, 20]: the *fear of dishonest auctioneer* and the *reluctance of bidders to reveal their true valuation*. Since it is sealed, the winner has every reason to doubt the price the auctioneer tells her to pay is actually the second highest price. Thus, fair execution of auctions needs to be guaranteed. Moreover, the valuation of goods or tasks are sensitive and private information that bidders are unwilling to reveal [3, 19].

3 Design Issues for Service Allocation in MANET

The design of Vickrey auction for MANET is confronted with challenges posed by the limitation of Vickrey auction and the characteristics of MANET. Below, we investigate the resulting design issues that decompose into: *Currency versus Reputation*, regarding the remuneration types in auctions for MANET (Sect. 3.1); *Fair Execution*, on how to solve the problem of dishonest auctioneer, and assure fair execution of Vickrey auction; and *Privacy*, about how to keep the loser bids private (Sect. 3.2). In the end of this section, we propose a system model for carrying out Vickrey auction for service allocation in MANET (Sect. 3.3).

3.1 Currency Versus Reputation

All incentive schemes, including auctions implement a remuneration scheme to incentivize agents' cooperative behavior. Remuneration assumes a specific form that is called *renumeration type*. Digital currency and reputation are the two most common remuneration types [17].

Digital currency is used to reward cooperative agents; each agent owns some amount of digital currency and the amount is either resident on some security module executed on some tamper resistant hardware [4] or available via some on-line bank service [26]. However, the digital currency scheme does not imply any trust information[5]. Thus, the only way to punish misbehaving agents is to make them lose money (e.g., bidders' put some deposits before the auction [7]).

Alternatively, reputation, which is a perception of an agent's trustworthiness, is resident on other agents based on their previous experience with it. In some systems such as [12], the node can monitor neighbors' activity via promiscuous mode. In that case, experience not only includes direct interaction experiences (e.g., participate in the same auction), but also indirect experiences (e.g., being neighbors but never interact with each other). Experience can even be extended to include other agents' experience via exchange of reputation information [10].

However, because there is no way to bid "reputation" for some service, digital currency is preferred over reputation for a Vickrey auction system. But, reputation can be a supplementary reference for a seller or bidder, e.g., bidders can avoid disreputable auctioneer.

3.2 Fair Execution and Privacy Preserving of Auctions

In traditional models of centralized auction (e.g., eBay), there exists a trustworthy party that everybody trusts. It is trivial to conduct an auction in such scenarios, when every bidder can safely submit bids to the trusted party, which determines the winner of the auction. The existence of a trustworthy party is almost impossible in MANET, which makes "fair auction execution" and "privacy preserving" problems even more severe.

The most seen approach for solving the above problems is to transform a single point of trust into *a jury of trust*; every jury member does not have to be as trustworthy as in traditional models. There are currently two variations of this approach: (1) Jury members can include multiple auctioneers, most of which are assumed to be trustworthy. After each bidder sends shares of their bid to each auctioneer, only a majority of the auctioneers can open the bid with threshold computation (e.g., Verifiable Secret Sharing (VSS) [18]); (2) Jury members can also include a semi-trusted third-party and an auctioneer. Fair execution of auctions and privacy of loser bids are guaranteed if the third-party does not collude with the auctioneer [15], or with any bidder [1].

Executing the above secret sharing protocols requires expensive cryptographic operations, which can hinder the deployment on thin devices. *Elliptic Curve Cryptography* (ECC) [14] is an alternative to establish public keys, like RSA and DSA. The attraction of ECC is that significantly smaller keys can be used in ECC than other systems like RSA and DSA, but with same level of security (e.g., 160-bit ECC and 1024-bit RSA).

---

[5] You cannot tell one person is trustworthy simply because he/she is rich.

Hence, ECC is preferable for wireless communication due to its bandwidth saving with smaller key size and smaller digital signature [25].

An alternative way to speed up cryptographic operations on mobile devices is to introduce some dedicated hardware for the operations. Compared to the software approach, it is much faster and more physically secure. Low-end chips such as CDL-82™ has been planted into PDAs and biometric verification devices[6]. Additionally, dedicated hardware can also function as "nuglet counter" as mentioned in [4]. The plugging of custom hardware into computation-bounded mobile devices is proving to be a viable approach.

3.3 Service Allocation System

Having discussed the issues for applying reverse Vickrey auction for service allocation, we present a system model for conducting such auctions in mobile ad hoc networks. Our approach is essentially based on VSS and uses both remuneration schemes – digital money and reputation. Below is how reverse Vickrey auction for service allocation is carried out after the agents have formed a neighborhood via group management [2].

Service Discovery. For discovering services, we adopt a distributed "pull" multi-hop service discovery scheme. Every service seeking agent can advertise its request, which includes information of service properties (e.g., functional and QoS properties), the auction protocol (Vickrey auction in our case) and an optional list of jury members[7], by broadcasting it to peers bounded by number of hops. Jury members are chosen by the service seeker according to their reputation of being trustworthy, and are paid by the service seeker for their service[8].

Reputation Checking. On receiving a service request, each interested service provider first checks whether a jury list is included in the request. If the jury list is absent, potential bidders check whether the service seeker is trustworthy enough for revealing their bids. If the jury list is provided, potential bidders check whether at least two thirds of the members are trustworthy enough for being a jury member because, as to be stated in the next subsection, the auction protocol we use tolerates up to one third of the total shares to be faulty. Therefore, providing a jury list normally increases the possibility of bidding from bidders, which is to the interest of the service seeker.

If reputation checking is passed, potential bidders execute conformance checking with respect to service properties. And, if it does satisfy the request, it estimates the resource consumption for serving such a service. Thereupon, it calculates a bid based on the estimated resource consumption [11], and thus how much it wants to get paid for that service.

Service Allocation. If the jury list is absent, the bidders submit the bids directly to the service seeker and auction is conducted in a traditional centralized way. Alternatively, if

---

[6] Readers are referred to http://www.cdlusa.com/press/press.shtml for further details.

[7] Absence of this list indicates that the auction is to be conducted in a "traditional" mode, i.e., every bidder submits its bid directly to the service seeker.

[8] The allocation of jury member service can also be conducted via Vickrey auction, except that the very first juries for finding jury members may have to be located with the help of some third party.

the jury list is provided, each bidder conducts a secret sharing scheme and submits the shares of the bid to the jury members. The resolution of winner and the price to be paid is done among jury members with an elegant protocol proposed by Harkavy. *et. al.* [8], which: (i) preserves privacy of bids and anonymity of losers by only revealing the winner and the price to be paid; (ii) tolerates up to one third of missing or faulty shares; and (iii) introduces affordable computation cost. The winner will then get paid with the second lowest bid after completion of service. After each auction, any participant including service seeker, jury members and service provider can update the reputation of any other according to its degree of satisfaction after the auction (e.g., if it is convinced that the auction is fair, or it suspects of any dishonesty). And, the newly update reputation serves as a reference for future encounters.

Note that bidders can have different strategies for submitting bids. An aggressive provider can submit bids to more service requests than it can serve if it wins all the auctions, while a less aggressive provider makes sure that it will be able to serve all the service bids if it wins them all. The strategy very much depends on the current workload of the bidder and the punishment for defaulting a winner bid. As the amount of bids are partially determined by the load of the bidder, it is also affected by the bidder' bidding strategies. The bidders' strategies and their effect on bids is part of our future work.

As for the impact of mobility on our system model, one obvious observation is that our system is robust to leaving of up to one third of the jury members during the auction. However, since our model assumes connectivity among service seekers, jury members and bidders, the auction may be interrupted if mobility disrupts the connectivity.

The overhead of our model lies in the execution of bid resolution protocol. Assume the number of bidders is n, number of jury members is m, the threshold number is t (i.e., t jury members can not reveal the bids and $3t < m$), and the number of bits to represent a bid is V, the communication cost for the auction protocol is $O(t^2 * m * n * logV)$ [8].

4   Conclusion and Future work

In this paper, we have discussed issues that arise during design of a Vickrey auction system for service allocation in MANET. The motivation of Vickrey auction for MANET lies in its value for efficient service allocation in a social way. We have shown that although intensive study has been done to solve the problems raised by the limitation of Vickrey auction, additional challenges are confronted due to the infrastructureless and unpredictable nature of MANET. We further have proposed a system model for service allocation via Vickrey auction in MANET.

A possible extension of the current work is to base service allocation on offered QoS together with the amount of bids. One instinctive approach is to base selection on bid divided by client's QoS-dependent utility. But it is problematic because QoS dimensions require normalization since they are in different units [11]. Standard normalization among bids makes bidder's normalized bid dependent on other bids, which makes the existence of dominant strategy doubtful. Additionally, the amount of payment needs careful consideration since the winner is not always the lowest bidder.

In addition to bidders' strategies, as mentioned in the end of last section, our future work also includes adding deposit support for enforcing non-repudiation during the auction. This is necessary to guard against winners' defaulting behaviors and enforce honest participation of the auction. Note that the deposit in our work is provided by the service providers (i.e., sellers), contrary to buyers in normal cases. Another extension is to add support for ensuring the fair exchange of service and digital currency between the service seeker and the service provider.

Acknowledgments

This research is partially supported by the European Commission via IST OZONE (New Technologies and Services for Emerging Nomadic Societies) project[9] (IST-2000-30026).

References

1. O. Baudron and J. Stern. Non-interactive private auctions. In *Proc. of Fifth Int'l Conf. on Financial Cryptography* (FC), 2001.
2. M. Boulkenafed, J. Liu, D. Sacchetti, and V. Issarny. Group Management in Mobile Ad Hoc Networks: Design, Implementation and Experiments. INRIA Research Report 5060, December 2003.
3. F. Brandt and G. Weiß. Vicious strategies for Vickrey auctions. In *Proc. of the Fifth Int'l Conf. on Autonomous Agents*, ACM Press, 2001.
4. L. Buttyan and J.P. Hubaux. Stimulating cooperation in self-organizing mobile ad hoc networks. *ACM/Kluwer Mobile Networks and Applications*, 8, 2003.
5. L. Capra, W. Emmerich, and C. Mascolo. CARISMA: Context-Aware REflective mIddleware System for Mobile Applications. *IEEE Transactions of Software Engineering*, November 2003.
6. J. Feigenbaum and S. Shenker. Distributed algorithmic mechanism design: Recent results and future directions. In *Proc. 6th Int. Workshop on Discrete Algorithms and Methods for Mobile Computing and Communications*, ACM Press, 2002.
7. M. Franklin and M. Reiter. The design and implementation of a secure auction service. *IEEE Transactions on Software Engineering* 5:302–312, 1996.
8. M. Harkavy, J.D. Tygar, and H. Kikuchi. Electronic auctions with private bids. In *Proc. of the 3rd USENIX Workshop on Electronic Commerce*, 1998.
9. V. Issarny, D. Sacchetti, F. Tartanoglu, F. Sailhan, R. Chibout, N. Levy, and A. Talamona. Developing Ambient Intelligence Systems: A Solution based on Web Services. *Journal of Automated Software Engineering*, 2004, to appear.
10. J. Liu and V. Issarny. Enhanced reputation mechanism for mobile ad hoc networks. In *Proc. of the 2nd Int'l Conf. on Trust Management* (i'Trust 2004), March 2004.
11. J. Liu and V. Issarny. QoS-aware service location in mobile ad hoc networks. In *Proc. of 2004 IEEE Int'l Conf. on Mobile Data Management*, January 2004.
12. S. Marti, T.J. Giuli, K. Lai, and M. Baker. Mitigating routing misbehavior in mobile ad hoc networks. In *Proc. of the 6th ACM International Conf. on Mobile Computing and Networking*, August 2000.
13. M. McMillan. Selling spectrum rights. *Journal of Economic Perspectives*, 1994.

---

[9] http://www.extra.research.philips.com/euprojects/ozone

14. V. Miller. Uses of elliptic curves in cryptography. In *Proc. of CRYPTO 85*, 1985.
15. M. Naor, B. Pinkas, and R. Sumner. Privacy preserving auctions and mechanism design. In *Proc. of ACM Conference on Electronic Commerce*, 1999.
16. N. Nisan and A. Ronen. Algorithmic mechanism design. In *31st ACM Symp. on Theory of Computing*, pages 129–140, 2001.
17. P. Obreiter, B. König-Ries, and M. Klein. Stimulating cooperative behavior of autonomous devices: An analysis of requirements and existing approaches. In *Proc. of the 2nd Int'l Workshop on Wireless Information Systems*, 2003.
18. T. Pedersen. Non-interactive and information-theoretic secure verifiable secret sharing. In *Advances in Cryptology – CRYPTO 1991*, pages 129–140, 1991.
19. M.H. Rothkopf, T.J. Teisberg, and E.P. Kahn. Why are Vickrey auctions rare? *Journal of Political Economy* 98:94–109, 1990.
20. T.W. Sandholm. Limitations of the Vickrey auction in computational multiagent systems. In *Proc. of the 2nd Int'l Conf. on Multi-Agent Systems*, 1996.
21. C. Szyperski. Component Technology – What, Where and How? In *Proc. of the 25th Int'l Conf. on Software Engineering* (ICSE'03), 2003.
22. H.R. Varian. Economic mechanism design for computerized agents. In *Proceedings of the First Usenix Conference on Electronic Commerce*, 1995.
23. W. Vickrey. Counter speculation, auctions, and competitive sealed tenders. *Journal of Finance* 16:8–37, 1961.
24. N. Vulkan and N.R. Jennings. Efficient mechanisms for the supply of services in multi-agent environments. *International Journal of Decision Support Systems*, 2000.
25. M.J. Wiener. Performance comparison of public-key cryptosystems. *CryptoBytes, Technical Newsletter of RSA Laboratories*, 4, 1998.
26. S. Zhong, J. Chen, and Y.R. Yang. Sprite: A simple, cheat-proof, credit-based system for mobile ad-hoc networks. In *Proceedings of IEEE Infocom 2003*.

Engineering Incentive Schemes
for Ad hoc Networks
A Case Study for the Lanes Overlay[*]

Philipp Obreiter[1], Birgitta König-Ries[2], and Georgios Papadopoulos[1]

[1] Institute for Program Structures and Data Organization,
Universität Karlsruhe (TH), 76128 Karlsruhe, Germany
obreiter@ipd.uni-karlsruhe.de, diane@zorz.de
[2] Faculty for Computer Science,
Technische Universität München, 85747 Garching, Germany
koenigri@in.tum.de

Abstract. In ad hoc networks, devices have to cooperate in order to compensate for the absence of infrastructure. Yet, autonomous devices tend to abstain from cooperation in order to save their own resources. Incentive schemes have been proposed as a means of fostering cooperation under these circumstances. In order to work effectively, incentive schemes need to be carefully tailored to the characteristics of the cooperation protocol they should support. This is a complex and demanding task. However, up to now, engineers are given virtually no help in designing an incentive scheme. Even worse, there exists no systematic investigation into which characteristics should be taken into account and what they imply. Therefore, in this paper, we propose a systematic approach for the engineering of incentive schemes. The suggested procedure comprises the analysis and adjustment of the cooperation protocol, the choice of appropriate incentives for cooperation, and guidelines for the evaluation of the incentive scheme. Finally, we show how the proposed procedure is successfully applied to a service discovery overlay.

1 Introduction

In ad hoc networks, devices have to cooperate in order to make up for the absence of infrastructure. However, each participating device is under the control of its user and, thus, aims at maximizing its utility. This means that devices will only cooperate if this is profitable for them. Most often, cooperation is not profitable in itself. Therefore, distributed schemes have been proposed which offer incentives for cooperation, thereby making it attractive for devices to cooperate.

Such incentive schemes make use of incentive mechanisms in order to foster cooperation. Yet, the choice and configuration of appropriate incentive mechanisms is highly non-trivial. This is partly due to the dependency on the specifics of the application

[*] The work done for this paper has been partly funded by the Deutsche Forschungsgemeinschaft (DFG) in the context of the priority program (SPP) no. 1140.

W. Lindner et al. (Eds.): EDBT 2004 Workshops, LNCS 3268, pp. 395–404, 2004.

domain. Currently, there is no systematic procedure that supports the developer of an incentive scheme by managing the complexity of his task. As a result, the conception and evaluation of incentive schemes is still more approached as an art than a engineering principle. This situation is especially harmful since each of the various cooperation protocols of ad hoc networks demands for a specific incentive scheme that takes its characteristics into account.

Our approach is to systematically engineer incentive schemes. In Section 2, we discuss the state of the art for the development of incentive schemes. In Section 3, we take a closer look at appropriate models of cooperation. This provides the foundation for presenting and discussing a systematic procedure for engineering incentive schemes in Section 4. We exemplify such engineering for the cooperation protocol *Lanes* in Section 5 and, finally, conclude the paper in Section 6. An extended version of this paper is available as technical report [12].

2   Related Work

In this section, we discuss the state of the art for the development of incentive schemes in ad hoc networks. Furthermore, we discuss incentive engineering as an approach that is used in economics for the conception of appropriate incentives.

Existing Incentive Schemes in Ad hoc Networks.   In the absence of any systematic procedure for their development, the design of the existing incentive schemes [2, 3, 9, 10, 14] is characterized by the ex ante choice (and configuration) of incentive mechanisms [11]. For the development of further incentive schemes, the usefulness of the existing incentive schemes is limited. **(1)** They are bound to specific cooperation protocols, often without making this explicit. **(2)** Their conception is monolithic and, thus, hinders the reuse of their components. **(3)** Their evaluation is not performed on the basis of comparable criteria.

This means that it is unlikely that a developer can simply reuse one of the existing schemes in order to enhance cooperation in a given situation. On the other hand, he is given little if any help in designing his own incentive scheme. Thus, despite the fact that incentive schemes need to be tailored to the cooperation protocol used, little is known on how to achieve this tailoring.

Incentive Engineering.   In economics, incentive engineering [4] has been proposed as a means of systematically developing incentive schemes. It assumes an incentive mechanism that is arbitrarily quantifiable and provides full incentive compatibility. For example, the use of money provides such an incentive mechanism. For each action of the cooperation protocol, the engineer determines the quantification of the incentive mechanism that yields a maximization of some utility. This approach has been applied in [8] for an incentive scheme on the link layer.

However, incentive engineering is not suitable for the development of incentive schemes in ad hoc networks. This stems from the following reasons: **(1)** In [13], we have shown that, in ad hoc networks, it is impossible to conceive an incentive mechanism that it is both arbitrarily quantifiable and fully incentive compatible. **(2)** The exogenous determination of the quantification is contradicted by the autonomy of the devices. Consequently, the devices do not adhere to the developed scheme. **(3)** In ad hoc networks, it might be reasonable to adjust the cooperation protocols in order to facilitate the development of the incentive scheme. However, incentive engineering does not make use of this means.

3   Cooperation Models and Incentive Schemes

In previous work [11, 13], we proposed a transaction-centric cooperation model. It assumes that cooperation is composed of transactions among autonomous protocol entities. Each entity may commit to participate in one or several transactions.

The transaction-centric model makes sense for the provision and consumption of application services. However, it is difficult to apply the transaction-centric model to cooperation in networks and overlays. This stems from difficulties of capturing continuous cooperation among several entities into the transaction-centric model. We conclude that a more generic cooperation model is needed.

According to the commitment-centric cooperation model, an entity *enters into a commitment* if it commits to exhibit certain behavior. An entity *adheres to its commitment* if it actually exhibits the behavior it committed to. The transaction-centric model is a specialization of this cooperation model since it confines commitments to single transactions. More specifically, participating in a transaction means entering in a commitment, whereas adhering to a commitment refers to refraining from defecting in the course of a transaction.

4   The Procedure for Engineering Incentive Schemes

The systematic design of incentive schemes comprises several steps. As a first step, the engineer analyzes and adjusts the cooperation protocol that requires an incentive scheme. Subsequently, crucial design decisions have to be made regarding the choice of incentives and the means of implementing them. Finally, the engineer evaluates the resulting cooperation protocol by applying an appropriate evaluation method. In the following, we give an in-depth discussion of these steps. The discussion will be exemplified by the case study of Section 5.

4.1   The Cooperation Protocol

Analysis. A thorough understanding of the cooperation protocol is required for the design of an appropriate incentive scheme. Therefore, an analysis has to be conducted in order to answer the following questions: **(Q1)** What kinds of inter-entity cooperation exist? The answer to this question is determined by the cooperation protocol that the entities run. **(Q2)** Which steps of the cooperation protocol are not beneficial to the executing entity? The engineer focusses on influencing behavior regarding detrimental protocol steps. **(Q3)** Is behavior perceptible? If yes, how costly and reliable is such perception? It is clear that a rational entity only exhibits cooperative behavior if other entities are able to perceive such cooperativeness.

Adjustment. Before turning to the incentive scheme, the engineer has to consider whether the protocol should be adjusted. Such adjustment aims at ameliorating the properties of the protocol. More specifically, the protocol should be extended by mechanisms that make behavior more perceptible (Q3).

The engineer may choose among several perception mechanisms. If *digital signatures* are appended to protocol messages, the receiver of a message is able to verify the authenticity of the sender and to check whether the entities of the forwarding path altered the message. *Redundancy* enhances the perceptibility of specific protocol steps. For example, the cooperation protocol could be extended in order to accommodate the issuance of *receipts*. If a receipt is a non-repudiable evidence, it may be transferred to other entities. Consequently, these entities are able to perceive the behavior that is described by the receipt. A cost-effective perception mechanism is *overhearing*. An overhearing entity perceives which packets or messages are sent by other entities. However, due to physical or topological restrictions, the overhearing entity might not receive the same transmissions or messages as the intended receiver. *Probing* is based on the idea that an entity behaves similarly under certain conditions. Therefore, it suffices to perceive only parts of the behavior in order to conjecture which behavior is typically exhibited. Probing is attractive for behavior that is costly to perceive.

4.2   The Choice of Appropriate Incentives

Based on the analysis and adjustment of the cooperation protocol, the engineer has to choose incentives that effectively stimulate cooperative behavior. The definition of commitments sets the scope of the respective incentive mechanisms. Some of these mechanisms provide incentives for entering into commitments, whereas others provide incentives for adhering to them.

Definition of Commitments. A major design decision for incentive schemes consists of determining which type of behavior should be remunerated and which type should be taken as granted. Only misbehavior regarding the latter type has to be punished since, for the first type of behavior, the absence of remuneration constitutes a disincentive for misbehavior. It seems promising to remunerate if an entity commits to specific behavior. Accordingly, failure to adhere to such a commitment should be punished. The two extremes of defining commitments are as follows: **(a)** Participation in the system is the only commitment. This means that, upon participation, each entity has to adhere to the predefined protocols and transactions. This extreme fits best to cooperation protocols that require unconditional cooperativeness in order to be effective. Furthermore, this extreme allows for rather simple incentive schemes. Yet, the incentive compatibility of adhering to the own commitment is difficult to achieve if behavior is not perceptible. Then, the lack of adherence cannot be identified and punished. Consequently, imperceptible behavior should be exempted from commitments. **(b)** Each transaction is separately committed to. In this regard, a rational entity only participates in beneficial transactions. This extreme is suitable if cooperation can be decomposed into transactions.

Incentives for Entering into Commitments. In previous work [13], we have proposed incentive patterns as a means of rendering commitments mutually beneficial. This is necessary if a commitment appears to be beneficial only for some of the concerned

Table 1. Overview of incentive patterns and their properties

Pattern \ Properties	Trust based		Trade based	
	Collective pattern	Community pattern	Barter trade pattern	Bond based pattern (eg.: note pattern)
Roles	asymmetric		symmetric	asymmetric
Type of remuneration	*none*	reputation	service in return	note
Enforcement of remunerat.		-	+	o
Overhead	small	medium	small	high
Scalability	- -	-	+	o

entities. An incentive pattern induces that an entity enters into a otherwise detrimental commitment. The incentive patterns and their most important properties are summarized in Table 1. It provides a foundation for the choice of incentives that remunerate for entering into commitments. Incentive patterns fall into two classes: On the one hand, an entity may believe that its peers will reciprocate by entering into future commitments. This approach is based on *trust* and is applied by the collective pattern and community pattern. On the other hand, an entity is convinced to enter into a commitment if its peers enter into commitments that are beneficial for itself. Such a *trade* based approach is applied by the barter trade pattern and the bond based incentive patterns. For the barter trade, the temporal scope of the respective commitments coincides. Hence, the committing entities assume symmetric roles. In contrast, a bond is a commitment regarding behavior at some future point in time. The most relevant type of bonds are notes. A note contains a commitment of its issuer.

Incentives for Adhering to Commitments. Bilateral or multilateral commitments often refer to the mutual provision of services. From an abstract point of view, such mutual provision of services represents an exchange of items. Exchanges are processed according to *exchange protocols* [1]. The considerable overhead of existing exchange protocols has to be matched by the value of the items that are exchanged. For the repeated exchange of items, the sliding window mechanism provides a promising alternative solution. It limits the number of outstanding items. This means the entities' balance of delivered items is coupled.

If exchange protocols are not viable, there exists another means of inducing the adherence to commitments, namely *distributed reputation systems* [5]. They keep track which entities adhere to their commitments and which do not. An entity may defect by refraining from adhering to the own commitment while the peers adhere to theirs. However, the betrayed peers may disseminate their view of the defector to other entities so that other entities are aware of the defection. As a result of such awareness, other entities (and the defected peers) may refrain from entering into commitments with the defector or they may even refuse to adhere to their outstanding commitments. Such punishment provides an incentive for adhering to one's own commitments. The choice of the distributed reputation system is contingent upon the characteristics of the considered cooperation protocol. Distributed reputation systems make differing assumptions regarding the perceptibility of behavior and find different tradeoffs between the benefits and costs of keeping track of the entities' behavior.

4.3 Evaluation

After the design of the incentive scheme, the engineer has to evaluate her work. In general, simulations provide the only cost-efficient means for such evaluation. In the following, we discuss how such simulations can be conducted.

Evaluations of existing incentive schemes are focussed on the total utility of the participating entities. In addition, we propose to evaluate the fairness of the incentive scheme with respect to the individual utility/costs that arise from cooperation. High degrees of fairness indicate that entities have to exhibit cooperative behavior in order to benefit from the behavior of other entities.

The entities' behavior regarding the cooperation protocol has to be modelled appropriately in order to obtain meaningful simulation results. Such modelling consists of assigning strategies to each entity. For stateless strategies, the model defines the probability of exhibiting specific behavior. Stateful strategies are based on the trust mechanisms of the distributed reputation system and, thus, consider the past behavior of other entities.

Behavioral models are parameterizable and, thus, provide for some of the simulation parameters. The second type of simulation parameters is derived from the configuration of the incentive scheme. Finally, the specifics of the cooperation environment constitute the third type of simulation parameters.

According to the objectives of the evaluation, the engineer has to measure the total utility u and the total costs c that arise from cooperation. If the objectives of the evaluation include fairness, the individual utility u_i and individual costs c_i have to be measured separately for every entity. The coefficient of correlation between the (u_i, c_i) pairs is called the fairness coefficient. A straightforward means of correlation is the calculation of a regression line between the individual utilities and costs. In case of good linear correlation, the slope of the regression line indicates the magnitude of the incentive effects.

5   A Case Study: Lanes

In this section, the procedure of engineering incentive schemes is exemplified for a service discovery overlay.

5.1   The Lanes Protocol

Because of the lack of infrastructure in ad hoc networks, decentralized trading of application services becomes necessary. The *Lanes* [7] approach provides such a cooperation protocol for the announcement and search of services. The Lanes overlay is shown for three lanes in Figure 1. Services are announced along a lane across the proactive vertical overlay links, whereas services are searched via anycast across several lanes. By this means, the Lanes overlay ensures that any participating entity is able to find the services that are offered in the network.

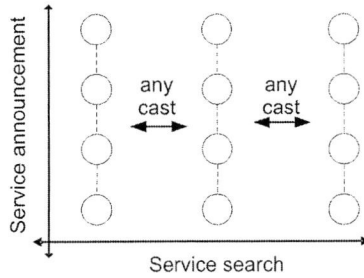

Fig. 1. The Lanes service discovery overlay

Analysis. Let us consider the questions introduced in Section 4.1. (**Q1:** *Kinds of Transactions*) The Lanes protocol is composed of five sub-protocols, i.e., service announcement, service request, overlay login, intra-lane and inter-lane maintenance. (**Q2:** *Non-Beneficial Steps*) Processing and (unaltered) sending of service announcements, searches and maintenance messages are all non-beneficial under certain circumstances. (**Q3:** *Perceptibility*) Behavior regarding the overlay maintenance can only be perceived by some of the immediate neighbors. Parts of the behavior for the announcement and search of services is not perceptible at all.

Adjustment. Lanes is conceived as an efficient service discovery overlay. Therefore, the complete protocol (including the non-beneficial protocol steps) is necessary for the effectiveness of the service discovery. Due to the imperceptibility of most behavior, several perception mechanisms have to be applied. We introduce redundancy by double linking overlay nodes. Further redundancy is added by promoting the uppermost entity of a lane to the coordinator of maintenance decisions. Furthermore, the sub-protocols that involve several entities are extended with the transmission of receipts. Finally, digital signatures are appended to those messages that are likely to be altered by misbehaving entities. The adjustment of the protocol cannot cope with the imperceptibility of some protocol steps. For instance, an entity is still able to return negative results for service searches without actually processing them.

5.2   The Choice of Appropriate Incentives

Definition of Commitments. If participation in the overlay was the only commitment, the design of the incentive scheme would become simple. However, in such a case, the imperceptible parts of the service announcement/search protocols are not executed. Therefore, participation in service announcements and searches should be separately committed to. In order to log into a lane, a newcomer commits to comply with the remaining sub-protocols. This means that each lane member has to participate in the maintenance protocols. Entities that do not adhere to their commitments are treated as outlaws. This means that the other entities opt to exclude them from the overlay. Such step is executed locally within a lane.

Incentives for Entering into Commitments. For logging in a new entity into the overlay, both the newcomer and the remaining entities have to commit to participate in the maintenance protocol. Therefore, the barter trade pattern provides appropriate incentives for this type of commitment. The second type of commitment refers to answering a service search of an other entity. For this purpose, we have to choose an incentive pattern that supports asymmetric roles. According to Table 1, the note pattern appears most appropriate. This is because the note pattern provides better enforcement of remuneration than the community pattern. Such enforcement is needed since the costs of processing service searches are considerable. Since we apply the note pattern, the issuer of a service search has to hand over a note to the entity that finds a matching service.

Incentives for Adhering to Commitments. Conventional exchange protocols are too expensive for the operation of the maintenance protocols. However, the sliding window mechanism could be applied in order to limit the number of outstanding notes. This means that every entity is only willing to accept a certain number of notes from other entities. The size of such *note credit* corresponds to the window size of the sliding window mechanism. If the note credit is reached, the bearer of the notes refrains from processing service searches of the notes' issuer. The lack of exchange protocols demands for the application of a distributed reputation system. For this purpose, we make use of the *Buddy System* [5].

5.3   Evaluation

In the following discussion of the evaluation, we will refer to the combination of the adjusted Lanes protocol and the incentive scheme as the *S-Lanes* protocol.

The *objective* of the evaluation is to assess the efficiency and fairness of the S-Lanes protocol. For the *behavioral modelling*, we distinguish between three types of entities. Altruists always cooperate, whereas uncooperative entities never cooperate. Cooperative entities only cooperate with those entities that have exhibited cooperative behavior towards themselves before. The behavior is further parameterized by the note credit that an entity accords to other entities. Further *simulation parameters* are the type of cooperation protocol (Lanes versus S-Lanes) and the cooperation environment. The system consists of *20* devices that participate in the overlay. Each of them provides a unique service and looks for services in an uniformly distributed manner. The cooperation environment is parameterized by the number of service searches that are initiated by each entity. The *measurement categories* consist of the number of found services (utility) and the number of sent messages or matching operations[1] (costs).

The simulation has been conducted with DIANEmu [6]. Figure 2 shows the individual utilities and costs[2] of 15 cooperative entities and 5 uncooperative entities. The uncooperative entities are able to profit from cooperation in the Lanes protocol as much as the cooperative entities. However, they do so with a minimum of costs. Therefore, the Lanes protocol is not fair. In contrast, uncooperative entities profit much less from co-

---

[1] A matching operation processes an incoming service search by testing whether it matches one of the hoarded service advertisements.

[2] For clarity reasons, the costs only refer to the number of matching operations.

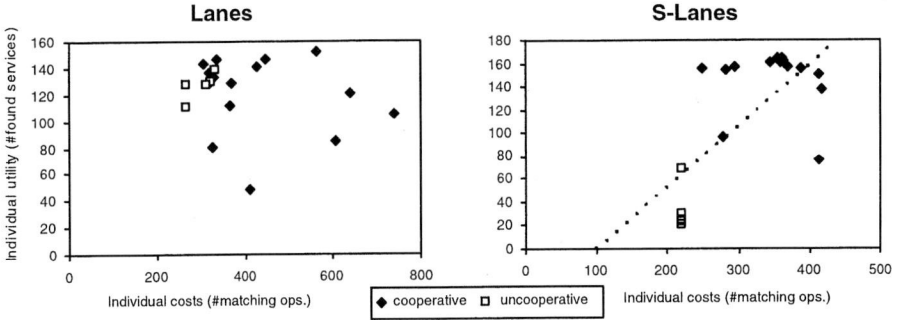

Fig. 2. The individual utilities and costs of 15 cooperative and 5 uncooperative entities

operation in the S-Lanes protocol than cooperative entities do. As a result, the respective utility/cost-pairs correlate well with the regression line. The correlation coefficient is *0.69*. The slope *b* of the regression line is *0.54*. This means that an entity has to perform approximately two matching operations in order to find a service. We have obtained similar results for other parameterizations[3]. The simulation results clearly demonstrate that the S-Lanes protocol complies with the demand for fairness. According to the results, the more searches are conducted and the tighter the note credit is, the higher the fairness coefficient and the incentive effect is.

6   Conclusion

In ad hoc networks, devices have to cooperate in order to compensate for the absence of infrastructure. Incentive schemes have been proposed as a means of fostering cooperation among self-interested devices. However, it is difficult to conceive an effective and efficient incentive scheme for a given cooperation protocol. Therefore, in this paper, we have proposed a systematic approach for the engineering of incentive schemes. For this purpose, we suggested a procedure for the design of incentive schemes. It comprises the analysis and adjustment of the cooperation protocol, the choice of appropriate incentives for cooperation, and guidelines for evaluation of the incentive scheme. The procedure has been exemplified for the Lanes protocol. The design and evaluation of an incentive scheme for this cooperation protocol is performed according to the steps of the proposed procedure. The simulation results have shown that the engineered cooperation protocol S-Lanes complies with the demand for fairness.

In the future, we aim at engineering incentive schemes for other service discovery overlays and for application layer cooperation protocols. In addition, we have to provide an enhanced guideline regarding the choice of appropriate incentives for the adherence to commitments.

---

[3] The simulation results are presented for various parameterizations in the technical report [12]. Results regarding total utility and costs are also included in the report.

References

1. N. Asokan. Fairness in Electronic Commerce. PhD thesis, University of Waterloo, 1998.
2. S. Buchegger and J.Y.L. Boudec. Performance Analysis of the CONFIDANT Protocol: Co-operation Of Nodes — Fairness In Distributed Ad-hoc NeTworks. In *Proc. of the MobiHOC, Lausanne, Switzerland*, pages 226–236, IEEE CS Press, 2002.
3. L. Buttyan and J. Hubaux. Stimulating cooperation in self-organizing mobile ad hoc networks. *ACM/Kluwer Mobile Networks and Applications* (MONET), 8, 2003.
4. K.E. Drexler and M.S. Miller. Incentive Engineering for Computational Resource Management. In B. Huberman (editor), *The Ecology of Computation*, 1988.
5. S. Fähnrich and P. Obreiter. The Buddy System – A distributed reputation system based on social structure. Technical Report 2004-1, Universität Karlsruhe, Faculty of Informatics, 2004.
6. M. Klein. DIANEmu – A java-based generic simulation environment for distributed protocols. Technical Report 2003-7, Universität Karlsruhe, Faculty of Informatics, 2003.
7. M. Klein, B. König-Ries, and P. Obreiter. Lanes – A lightweight overlay for service discovery in mobile ad hoc networks. In *Proc. of the 3rd Workshop on Applications and Services in Wireless Networks* (ASWN2003), Berne, Switzerland, 2003.
8. R.F. Liao, R.H. Wouhaybi, and A. Campbell. Incentive engineering in wireless LAN based access networks. In *Proc. 10th International Conference on Network Protocols* (ICNP), Paris, France, 2002.
9. S. Marti, T.J. Giuli, K. Lai, and M. Baker. Mitigating routing misbehavior in mobile ad hoc networks. In *Mobile Computing and Networking*, pages 255–265, 2000.
10. P. Michiardi and R. Molva. Core: A collaborative reputation mechanism to enforce node cooperation in mobile AD HOC networks. In *Proceedings of the 6th IFIP Communications and Multimedia Security Conference*, Portorosz, Slovenia, 2002.
11. P. Obreiter, B. König-Ries, and M. Klein. Stimulating cooperative behavior of autonomous devices – An analysis of requirements and existing approaches. In *Proceedings of the 2nd Intl. Workshop on Wireless Information Systems*, pages 71–82, 2003.
12. P. Obreiter, B. König-Ries, and G. Papadopoulos. Engineering incentive schemes for ad hoc networks – A case study for the Lanes overlay. Technical Report 2004-4, Universität Karlsruhe, Faculty of Informatics, 2004.
13. P. Obreiter and J. Nimis. A taxonomy of incentive patterns - the design space of incentives for cooperation. In *Proceedings of the Second Intl. Workshop on Agents and Peer-to-Peer Computing* (AP2PC'03), volume 2872 of LNCS, Springer, 2003.
14. S. Zhong, J. Chen, and Y.R. Yang. Sprite: A simple, cheat-proof, credit-based system for mobile ad-hoc networks. In *Proceedings of IEEE Infocom'03*, 2003.

The Case for Mobile OLAP

Andreas S. Maniatis

National Technical University of Athens,
Department of Electrical and Computer Engineering,
Knowledge and Database Systems Laboratory
andreas@dblab.ece.ntua.gr

Abstract. On-Line Analytical Processing (OLAP) is a trend in database technology, based on the multidimensional view of data. Numerous applications and development environments exist, offering OLAP analysis to developers, analysts and end users. Further more, mobile devices find their way into almost all aspects of every day life, ranging from cellular phones with advanced capabilities (smart phones) for personal use to professional PDA's used for numerous wireless applications – OLAP included – and thus generating the need for convergence of the two technologies. In this paper we introduce the term *Mobile OLAP* to express the porting of requirements and specifications for OLAP applications into the wireless and mobile computing world. More specifically, we examine the requirements posed for OLAP visualization applications on mobile devices, both in terms of presentation and usability. We then proceed by investigating the state of the art of the broader wireless computing community, focusing in the specifications more close to OLAP. Finally, we demonstrate how a "lightweight" presentation model for OLAP can significantly contribute towards mobile OLAP.

1 Introduction

In the last years, On-Line Analytical Processing (OLAP) and data warehousing (DW) have become major research areas in the database community [3, 19]. Although the *modeling of data* [18, 20] has been extensively dealt with, an equally important issue of the OLAP domain, the *visualization of data* has not been adequately investigated. In the context of OLAP, data visualization deals with the techniques and tools used for presenting OLAP specific information to end-users and decision makers. The database community expects visualization to be of significant importance in the area, during the next years [19], and although research has provided results dealing with the presentation of vast amounts of data [2, 4, 5, 15], OLAP has not been part of advanced visualization techniques so far.

Moreover, mobile and wireless devices are becoming widely used in various aspects of everyday life. The bust is driven mainly by vendors, who keep on producing more and more wireless products with increased capabilities and power. What is more important, numerous applications find their way into this new technology framework, applications either ported from traditional computer systems or novel ones, while most vendors devoted to Data Warehousing and OLAP have issued light versions of their solutions to run on PDAs with wireless capabilities. Academia, on the other hand has significant

W. Lindner et al. (Eds.): EDBT 2004 Workshops, LNCS 3268, pp. 405–414, 2004.

work to demonstrate for OLAP, as well as for wireless and mobile computing. However, there is very minimum work to be presented from the academia on the convergence of the two worlds, with [1, 16, 17] being notable exceptions.

In this paper we introduce the term *mobile OLAP*, attempting to bring together notions and functionality from the two domains, OLAP and Mobile Computing. We will present the state of the art concerning OLAP specific models and systems to work on mobile devices and based on them we will prepare a basic list with the minimum requirements of a system offering Mobile OLAP functionality. Further on and based on the requirements set before, we will describe a proposed architecture of a prototype system to seamlessly support Mobile OLAP, based on highly aggregated data stored locally on the mobile device and encapsulating our recently presented work concerning the *Cube Presentation Model (CPM)* and its mapping into a visualization technique, namely Table Lens and its adaptation for mobile OLAP, *OLAP Lens*.

The remainder of this paper is structured as follows: In Section 2, we briefly present the state of the art in mobile computing, with references in trends, architectures and systems in general and with a number of hints concerning important aspects as far as the convergence of OLAP and mobile Computing is concerned. In Section 3, we enumerate the most important specifications and requirements for a system supporting Mobile OLAP and in Section 4 we present the general architecture of such a system, based on the *Cube Presentation Model (CPM)* for the tabular visualization of OLAP screens and its mapping into *OLAP Lens*, an advanced visualization technique from the Information Visualization area. Finally in Section 5 we conclude our results and present topics for future work.

2   State of the Art in Mobile Computing for OLAP

With the tremendous recent growth of the mobile market and the availability of numerous mobile devices to huge numbers of end users, the need for applications working on these devices became increasingly pressing. OLAP applications were also affected by this trend, especially since Decision Support Systems (underlying OLAP) are crucial to high end users and executives who are – as a rule – using PDAs or mobile phones with advanced technical characteristics and capabilities.

So, initially, almost all of the vendors offering data warehousing and OLAP tools and platforms have included into their products special modules running on mobile devices and offering OLAP analysis possibilities to mobile decision makers. Nevertheless, this OLAP specific functionality for mobile devices provided by the vendors does very little towards exploiting the specific characteristics and power of the mobile devices on which these applications run. Rather, they base their solutions in migrating the desktop OLAP interface of their tools to the mobile device, employing WAP and the WML but fail to take into account recent, improved facts about mobile devices, such as increased system memory, clearer color screens, increased processing power or their limitations, such as small screen size, different usability and user interface requirements, often off line work etc.

To fill this gap, numerous approaches coming mainly from the academia and from various research areas have been proposing solutions and frameworks that address this problem. Many of them propose novel approaches to cope with the case of mobile OLAP and – what is more important – many of them have been actually implemented and used in real case scenarios. We will briefly present some of the most notable – to our judgment – approaches.

MOCHA [14] was an early, more generic approach for a database middleware for distributed data sources which, although not specifically addressing the case of mobile devices and OLAP, it incorporates many of the notions present in *"Mobile OLAP"*, such as the distributed nature of the system, the scaling to a larger environment along with the novel approach of deploying application specific functionality from one point of the system to all the others through the middleware itself.

A more specific approach is presented in [1], namely Hand-OLAP, a system specifically designed for bringing OLAP functionality to users of mobile devices. This proposal focuses mainly on a number of the drawbacks of handhelds devices, with emphasis in the small storage space and the usual discontinuance of the connection to the Wireless LAN. To cope with this issue, this approach focuses in presenting a solution for storing locally, in the mobile device, a compressed and highly summarized view of the data that can be more efficiently transmitted from the OLAP server than the original ones.

Finally, the work of [16, 17] focused more on matters of wireless network and power consumption on the mobile devices, proposing a suitable mobile OLAP model, along with an on-demand scheduling algorithm to minimize access time and energy consumption on mobile agents. This approach in based on summary tables too, along with the functionality of simple OLAP front-end tools to execute simple SQL queries. What is more, this proposal maximizes the aggregated data sharing between clients and reduces the broadcast length.

3   Requirements for Mobile OLAP

In this section we will introduce a number of requirements for mobile OLAP, based on all the aspects involved in the problem: *mobile devices, OLAP, user interface aspects, Wireless LAN* etc. From these general requirements the most important ones will be carefully selected to form the basis for a proposed architecture a system providing mobile OLAP functionality should have.

3.1   User Interface Design Requirements for Mobile OLAP

User interfaces and visual presentation designs for mobile devices are subject to a number of constraints, when compared to their desktop counterparts [10]. These include:

- *Small Display Size*: The small display of the devices is a central constraint to take into account, especially since OLAP presentation screens usually incorporate huge amounts of data to be displayed using a suitable – usually a tabular or other graphical – technique;
- *Limited Screen Resolution*: In close link to the previous constraint, the typical resolutions of mobile devices range from 100×80 pixels for mobile phones to 240×320 pixels for PDAs thus imposing specific care to be taken by the interface designers;

– *Limited Number of Available Colors*: Many mobile devices still offer only gray scale displays and available color displays are limited to a few thousand colors (when compared to their true-color desktop counterparts, offering millions of colors). So information encoding, differentiation and separations based on color are also another key trick for interface designers.

Further more, as far as usability and user interaction mechanisms are concerned, input devices offered by mobile devices differ significantly from the desktop computing domain. Key differences include:

– *No Standardization*: Various manufacturers often offer their own, device specific interaction facilities and input mechanisms. A typical keyboard and 2D pointing device are usually not present and if they are, their usability is significantly inferior to those of their desktop counterparts;
– *No Keyboard – No Mouse*: These input devices are the ones most known to end users and mobile devices offering even at a minimum such devices are the ones mostly welcome by the end users. Some similar input device should be available to users for mobile OLAP front-ends to run on their mobile devices.

3.2   Wireless LAN Requirements for Mobile OLAP

Another important issue is the bandwidth of the Wireless LAN (especially GPRS, but the same logic can be applied to WIFI as well) and its availability. Contemporary OLAP Analysis usually takes place on wired networks with a high throughput, but their wireless counterparts suffer from usual loss of connection and significantly lower available bandwidth. Thus, when a mobile user performs OLAP analysis on his device, he should be able to work off-line and with enough aggregated and summary data that will help him make the right decisions even without accessing detailed data stored on an OLAP server somewhere in the network.

Still, the system should provide with updated information from the server to the mobile device – through some sort of synchronization or replication technique – whenever a connection is available and new queries are posed by the user concerning data not stored in the device yet.

3.3   Performance Requirements for Mobile OLAP

Apart from the user interface and usability aspects described before having to do with the device capabilities and power, a couple of more requirements are hardware specific. These include:

– *Processing Power*: Although recent advances in mobile devices architecture and power have introduced PDAs and phones with better processing power, this feature still falls behind when compared with desktop systems on which OLAP takes place. Nevertheless, the OLAP front-end tools running on mobile devices do require some minimum processing power to perform simple queries or other ad-hoc analysis on the locally stored aggregated data, along with presentation and visualization techniques suitably designed and implemented for mobile devices;

– *Local Storage*: Memory is another important issue when huge volumes of data need to be processed for the purpose of OLAP. In this case too, mobile device memory is significantly increased in every new release but it still lacks behind when compared to servers or even desktop systems. Due to this limitation but also due to the fact that a user performing OLAP analysis does not really need access to the detailed data sets and fact tables of the DW he is accessing, highly aggregated and summary data can be safely stored on the mobile device for off line browsing and minimum processing.

3.4 An Overall Requirements List for Mobile OLAP

From the previously described issues to be dealt by a system offering mobile OLAP features and functionality to mobile users, we can extract the minimum issues to be dealt with and implemented in such a system. The requirements list is as follows:

– *Seamless and Uninterrupted Analysis*: The user should be able to perform basic mobile OLAP analysis even when he is off line the WLAN;
– *Local Storage of Highly Aggregated Data*: To ensure the previous requirement and to offer reduced access to the network, limited only to updates and data refreshment;
– *Perform Minimum Analysis*: The front-end tools on the mobile device should offer basic analysis and processing capabilities, such as simple SQL queries on the data stored locally;
– *Basic OLAP Presentation and Visualization*: At least a typical, tabular format presentation of a pivot table to visualize the OLAP data should exploit the existing limited screen and color features of the used mobile devices;
– *Basic Navigation and User Interface Interaction*: The user should be able to use typical navigational and interaction devices on mobiles (stylus, simple keyboard, jog keys etc) to pose new queries, perform standard OLAP operations and to navigate through the aggregated data;
– *Mobile OLAP Specifications*. The user views highly aggregated OLAP data – as contradicted to the detailed OLAP analysis accessing actual fact data on a conventional desktop system – but with the complete dimension hierarchy of the application available. Data refresh takes place on a demand basis, with activation of the GSM connection once a query posed cannot be answer using the locally stored aggregated data.

4 Architecture for Mobile OLAP

In this section we will describe a prototype system under development, supported by a suitable architecture for Mobile OLAP. The system is composed of three discrete and autonomous modules: A traditional *OLAP Server Module*, a *Middleware Application Server* and the mobile *Front-End Applications*.

The system incorporates and is largely based on two academic proposals concerning the modeling of OLAP presentational aspects, suitable both for traditional desktop OLAP applications and for mobile OLAP Front-Ends. The first [8] is the *Cube Presentation Model (CPM)*, a novel – and unique to the best of our knowledge – recommendation for an autonomous and concrete presentational model for OLAP. The second [7] is a recommendation on how CPM can be naturally mapped into specific, advanced visualization techniques from the Human Computer Interaction and Information Visualization areas, particularly tailored for cross-tab reports and incorporating usability and interaction features for the automated proactive user support on OLAP screens in general, but suitable for mobile devices as well.

4.1   The Cube Presentation Model

In [8] (and in [6] for an extended version), we have presented the *Cube Presentation Model (CPM)*, a novel proposal towards a presentation model for OLAP screens, based on two previous approaches, one from the academia [2] and one from the industrial field [9]. CPM is composed of two parts: (a) a *logical* layer which involves the formulation of cubes and (b) a *presentational layer* that involves the presentation of these cubes (normally, on a 2D screen). The main idea behind CPM lies in the separation of *logical data retrieval* (which we encapsulate in the logical layer of CPM) and *data presentation* (captured from the presentational layer of CPM). This duality provides the flexibility of possibly replacing one of the two layers with an alternative proposal smoothly. The logical layer that we propose is based on an extension of a previous proposal [21] with additional functionality that allows us to incorporate more complex cubes. In a nutshell, the logical model involves (a) *dimensions* defined as lattices of dimension *levels*, (b) *ancestor functions* (in the form of anc()) mapping values between related levels of a dimension, (c) *detailed data sets*, practically modeling fact tables at the lowest granule of information for all their dimensions and (d) *cubes*, defined as aggregations over detailed data sets.

Following, we give an intuitive and informal description of the *presentation layer* of CPM that provides a formal model for OLAP screens. The most important entities – as far as display aspects are concerned – of the presentation layer of CPM include:

- **Points:** A *point over an axis* resembles the classical notion of points over axes in mathematics and geometry. Still, since we are grouping more than one attribute per axis (in order to make things presentable in a 2D screen), formally, a point is a pair comprising of a set of attribute groups (with one of them acting as primary key) and a set of equality selection conditions for each of the keys;
- **Axis:** An axis can be viewed as a set of points. We introduce two special purpose axes, Invisible and Content. The Invisible axis is a placeholder for the levels of the data set which are not found in the "normal" axis defining the multicube. The Content axis has a more elaborate role: in the case where no measure is found in any axis then the measure which will fill the content of the multicube is placed there;
- **Multicubes:** A multicube is a set of axes, such that (a) all the levels of the same dimensions are found in the same axis, (b) Invisible and Content axes are taken into account, (c) all the measures involved are tagged with an aggregate function and (d) all the dimensions of the underlying data set are present in the multicube definition;
- **2D-Slice:** Consider a multicube MC, composed of K axes. A *2D-slice over MC* is a set of (K-2) points, each from a separate axis. Intuitively, a 2D-slice pins the axes of

the multicube to specific points, except for 2 axes, which will be presented on the screen (or a printout);

- **Tape:** Consider a 2D-slice SL over a multicube MC, composed of K axes. A *tape over SL* is a set of (K-1) points, where the (K-2) points are the points of SL. A tape is always parallel to a specific axis: out of the two "free" axes of the 2D-slice, we pin one of them to a specific point which distinguishes the tape from the 2D-slice;
- **Cross-Join:** Consider a 2D-slice SL over a multicube MC, composed of K axes and two tapes t1 and t2, not parallel to the same axis. A cross-join over t1 and t2 is a set of K points, where the (K-2) points are the points of SL and each of the two remaining points is a point on a different axis of the remaining axes of the slice;
- **Content Function:** At the schema level, we assume a function assigning the computation of measures to the Content axis of the multicube, along with ordering and other restrictions. We also assume a function, mapping combinations of multicube coordinates, one from each of the coordinate axis of the multicube to the measure axis. Each such assignment is practically a row in the result set of one of the queries/expressions/... computing the multicube, which we call *cell*.

4.2   A Prototype Platform for Mobile OLAP

A simple Architecture for Mobile OLAP is depicted in Figure 1. The general idea is that the user of the mobile device (PDA, mobile or smart phone with GPRS connectivity to a network, or even remote desktop) employs a suitable user interface on his device to navigate on his screen and perform OLAP analysis in general, based on data stored locally on his device in a highly aggregated and summarized format.

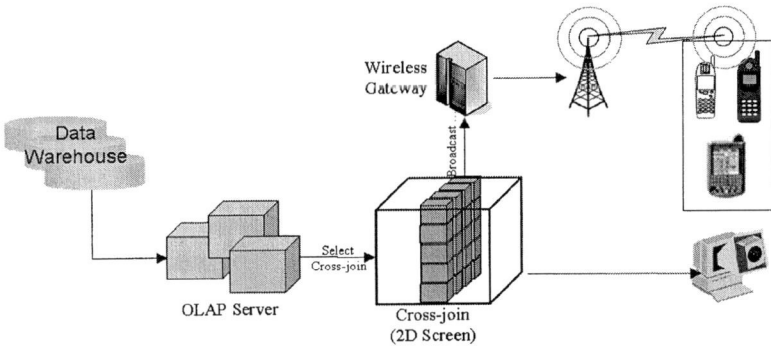

Fig. 1. A Simple Architecture for Mobile OLAP

This is generally quite adequate for a decision maker as aggregated data capture enough information for the user to get the answers he needs. Should there be a need for more data or a different set of data to be processed, the *front-end tool* passes the command for a new query to the *Application Server Module* and this in turn to the underlying *OLAP Server Module*, where the query is processed, data are returned to the Application Server Module where it is organized into a suitable presentational and exchange format according to CMP characteristics (aggregated data of *Cross-joins* of a 2D-Screen) and the results are retrieved by the mobile device and stored locally, in a suitable database schema, for further processing and manipulation, depending on the processing power of the device.

A more detailed design of the above architecture for a real system to support Mobile OLAP brings up a number of points and issues to be taken under consideration. Some of them are:

- **Local Storage:** For the mobile device to have adequate independence from the OLAP Server and for the user to be operative even when a WLAN in not available an amount of highly aggregated data need to be stored locally on the device. This can be done using some lightweight footprint database system for mobile devices, or other – simpler – storing mechanism;
- **Caching:** Since an Application Server middle layer is employed in the architecture, the option of caching should be taken into account to reduce eventual access to the fact data on the OLAP Server;
- **User Interface:** This is the most crucial issue since it refers to the core of OLAP, which is the presentation of data. The user interface must take into account all the limitations and special features of the mobile device on which it runs and it must be designed in such a way so as to proactively support the user to perform OLAP analysis and visualize the results in a comprehensible and meaningful way. In the following subsection we will briefly present an example of how specific queries can be visualized with a tabular format on a typical PDA screen.

Of course, other issues will arise as the detailed design and implementation of the system advances, but still the above will be the most significant ones, decisively affecting the performance and functionality of the whole architecture.

4.3 An Exemplary Front End UI for Mobile OLAP Applications

In our recent work [7] we have demonstrated how CPM can be combined with Table Lens [11, 12], a traditional cross-tabular presentation technique from the Human Computer Interaction area. This technique can be used for the visualization of tabular, multivariate and multidimensional data and appears to be quite appropriate for OLAP purposes too. Table Lens is based on the "Focus + Context" technique also known as "Fisheye distortion", that allows visualizing and manipulating large 2-D tables [12]. We extend this technique, based on the work of [13], and adopt it accordingly for the visualization of OLAP specific data, embedding the flexibility of both the standard fisheye distortion techniques of the typical Table Lens and the suitable exploitation of coloring schemes. We call this adapted visualization technique, the *OLAP Lens*.

The figures in Table 1 below depict an example of how a user can use his mobile device – running Pocket PC – to perform OLAP specific analysis with OLAP Lens.

In this example, let us assume that when the user activates this OLAP screen, he would like to be informed on three particular cross-joins: one involving the maximum sales, another involving the lowest and a third involving the cross-join closest to the average of the whole screen, along with a suitable coloring scheme for the rest of the displayed cells

Table 1. A Mobile OLAP Prototype Front-End using OLAP Lens for Pocket PC

	Venk	USA_S	Japan	Netz	USA_S
QTR1	147	172	328	203	191
QTR2	119	150	253	120	280
QTR3	117	147	200	117	270
QTR4	158	208	350	176	246

SalesCube over Products, Time, and G... (http://localhost/olap.asp — 6:06)

	Venk	USA_S	Japan	Netz	USA_S	Japan
QTR1	147	172	328	203	191	35
QTR2	119	150	253	120	280	50
QTR3	117	147	200	117	270	50
QTR4	158	208	350	176	246	222

...ube over Products, Time, and Geograp... (http://localhost/olap.asp — 6:08)

to show whether values are between lowest and average (light red) or between highest and average (light green). In this particular case, the cross-join QTR1/Netz/Japan is the one with the lowest summary of values (yellow color), QTR4/Venk/Japan is the one with the highest sum (green color) and QTR2/Venk/Japan is the one closest to the average sales per cross-join (red color). A number of user interface facilities can be implemented to assist the user in performing OLAP analysis, such as pop-up panes with aggregation functions to use on his screen, OLAP navigation (Drill-Down, Roll-Up, Slice and Dice, Pivot etc) and even structuring of new, ad-hoc queries.

5   Conclusions and Future Work

In this paper we introduced the notion of Mobile OLAP, a term used to describe the porting of contemporary OLAP analysis practices into mobile devices and systems. First we gave a selective overview of the state of the art concerning relative work and experience concerning systems and architectures supporting OLAP on mobile devices. We then proceeded with preparing a detailed list with requirements to be met by any system supporting Mobile OLAP. We then went on with the description of the proposed architecture of such a prototype system supporting Mobile OLAP, based on the presentational modeling aspects introduced in the CPM and its mapping into advanced visualization techniques such as OLAP Lens. We illustrated our proposition with a suitable example of OLAP analysis on a Pocket PC mobile device.

Next steps in our research include the full design and implementation of the prototype system supporting Mobile OLAP, called *CubeView*. This system will include at minimum the specifications and requirements set in this paper but it will also include additional features and options. In parallel, we are working on the introduction of suitable, novel visualization techniques for CPM, complying with current recommendations as far as usability and user interface design is concerned and its extension to address the specific visualization requirements of mobile devices.

References

1. A. Cuzzocrea, F. Furfaro, and D. Sacca. Hand-OLAP: A system for delivering OLAP services on handheld devices. *ISADS 2003*, pages 213–224, Pisa, Italy, April 9–11, 2003.
2. M. Gebhardt, M. Jarke, and S. Jacobs. A toolkit for negotiation support interfaces to multi-dimensional data. *ACM SIGMOD*, pages 348–356, 1997.
3. W.H. Inmon. *Building the Data Warehouse*. John Wiley & Sons, 1996.
4. Alfred Inselberg. Visualization and knowledge discovery for high dimensional data. 2nd *Workshop Proceedings UIDIS*, IEEE, 2001.
5. D.A. Keim. Visual data mining. *Tutorials of the 23rd International Conference on Very Large Data Bases*, Athens, Greece, 1997.
6. Andreas Maniatis et al. *CPM: A Cube Presentation Model for OLAP.* http://www.dblab.ece.ntua.gr/~andreas/publications/CPM_dawak03.pdf (long version)
7. A. Maniatis, P. Vassiliadis, S. Skiadopoulos, and Y. Vassiliou. Advanced visualization for OLAP. *DOLAP 2003*, New Orleans, Louisiana, USA, November 2003.
8. A. Maniatis, P. Vassiliadis, S. Skiadopoulos, and Y. Vassiliou. CPM: A cube presentation model for OLAP. *DaWaK 2003*, Prague, Czech Republic, September 3–5, 2003.
9. Microsoft Corp. OLEDB for OLAP. February 1998. Available at: http://www.microsoft.com/data/oledb/olap/
10. V. Paelke, C. Reimann, and W. Rosenbach. A visualization design repository for mobile devices. *Proceedings of the 2nd ACM International Conference on Computer Graphics, Virtual Reality and Interaction in Africa*, pages 57–62, Cape Town, South Africa.
11. Peter Pirollo and Ramana Rao. Table lens as a tool for making sense of data. *Proceedings of the AVI '96 Workshop*, Gubbio, Italy, June 1996.
12. R. Rao and S.K. Card. The Table Lens: Merging graphical and symbolic representations in an effective focus + context visualization for tabular information. *ACM SIGCHI* (CHI '94), Boston, Massachusetts USA, April 24-28, 1994.
13. R. Rao and T. Tenev. Extending Table Lens to multidimensional data and OLAP operations. *CODATA Euro-American Workshop on Data and Information Visualization*, Paris, France, June 24-25, 1997.
14. M. Rodriguez-Martinez and N. Rossopoulos. MOCHA: A self-extensible database middle-ware system for distributed data sources. *ACM SIGMOD*, pages 213–224, Dallas, Texas, USA, 2000.
15. Thomas Ruf, Juergen Georlich, and Ingo Reinfells. Dealing with complex reports in OLAP applications. *DaWaK '99*, Florence, Italy, August 30th – September 1st, 1999.
16. M.A. Sharaf and P.K. Chrysanthis. On-demand broadcast: New challenges and algorithms. *Proceedings of the 1st HDMS*, Athens, Greece, July 22nd, 2002.
17. M.A. Sharaf and K. Chrysanthis. Semantic-based delivery of OLAP summary tables in wireless environments. *Proceedings of the 11th CIKM*, McLean, Virginia, USA, 2002.
18. Aris Tsois, Nikos Karayannidis, and Timos Sellis. MAC: Conceptual data modeling for OLAP. *Proc. of the International Workshop on DMDW*, pages 28–55, 2001.
19. Various Authors. *The Lowell Database Research Self Assessment*. Lowell, MA, USA, May 4-6, 2003. Available at: http://research.microsoft.com/~Gray/lowell/
20. P. Vassiliadis and T. Sellis. A survey on logical models for OLAP databases. *SIGMOD Record* 28(4), December 1999.
21. Panos Vassiliadis and Spiros Skiadopoulos. Modeling and optimization issues for multidi-mensional databases. *Proc. of CAiSE-00*, Stockholm, Sweden, 2000.

On Constructing Small Worlds in Unstructured Peer-to-Peer Systems*

Yannis Petrakis and Evaggelia Pitoura

Department of Computer Science, University of Ioannina, Greece
{pgiannis,pitoura}@cs.uoi.gr

Abstract. Peer-to-peer systems have evolved as a means to share large amounts of data among autonomous nodes. A central issue in this context is locating nodes with data matching a user query. In this paper, we consider building peer-to-peer systems with small-world properties, that is, connecting the nodes to each other so that: (i) the distance between any two nodes is small and (ii) relevant nodes are connected to each other. Relevance between nodes is defined based on the probability that the two nodes match similar queries. We propose decentralized procedures for constructing small worlds based on routing indexes that describe the content of neighboring nodes. Our experimental results show that small-world peer-to-peer systems built with these procedures increase recall, that is, the percentage of relevant results returned.

1 Introduction

The popularity of file sharing systems such as Napster, Gnutella and Kazaa has spurred much current attention to peer-to-peer (P2P) computing. Peer-to-peer computing refers to a form of distributed computing that involves a large number of autonomous computing nodes (the peers) that cooperate to share resources and services. A central issue in P2P systems is identifying which peers contain data relevant to a user query.

In this paper, we propose building small worlds based on the content of the peers. Small worlds are networks with (i) a small distance between any two nodes (small diameter) and (ii) a large number of connections among relevant nodes (large clustering coefficient) [16]. We define the relevance of two nodes (peers) based on the probability of them matching the same set of queries. Intuitively, the topology of a small-world network represents a number of smaller networks (groups) that are rich in links between their peers (short-range connections), while they are linked to each other with a few random connections (long-range connections). The motivation for such small-world P2P networks is that once in the appropriate group, all relevant to a query peers are a few links apart. Long-range links are used for routing among groups.

We present an approach for building small worlds based on a fully decentralized procedure. Our construction is based on using local indexes. A local index is a characterization of the content of a peer. By aggregating local indexes of neighboring nodes, we create small worlds in a fully distributed manner.

---

* Work supported in part by the IST programme of the European Commission FET under the IST-2001-32645 DBGlobe project

W. Lindner et al. (Eds.): EDBT 2004 Workshops, LNCS 3268, pp. 415–424, 2004.

To demonstrate our approach, we implemented routing indexes using Bloom filters [3]. Bloom filters are bit vectors used for probabilistic representation of a set to support membership queries. Our performance results show that networks constructed by our procedures have the small-world properties. Moreover, they maximize recall and precision, that is, for a given query they increase the number of matching data returned while maintaining the number of peers visited small.

The remainder of this paper is structured as follows. In Section 2, we put our work in context with related research. In Section 3, we present the model of our system, while in Section 4, we describe how small worlds are built. In Section 5, we present experimental results. Section 6 concludes the paper.

2   Related Work

There are two basic types of P2P systems: structured and unstructured ones. In *structured P2P* systems, documents (or indexes of documents) are placed at specific nodes (peers) usually based on distributed hashing (DHTs) such as in CAN [11] and Chord [6]. With distributed hashing, each document is associated with a key and each peer is assigned a range of keys and thus documents. Peers are interconnected via a regular topology where peers that are close in the identifier space are highly interconnected. Very recently, researchers have proposed extending DHTs (e.g. Chord) with long range links towards creating small worlds [10]. In addition, recent extensions propose instead of associating keys to documents based on just the identifier of the document, to associate with each document (or peer) a vector describing its content extracted using IR algorithms and then use this vector as input to the hashing functions [13, 14]. However, this creates a dimensionality reduction problem, since the dimension of the vectors should match the dimension of the DHT.

These proposals can collectively be seen as an approach of building content-based small worlds in DHT-based P2P systems. In this case, the usual problems with structured P2P systems arise, since although DHTs provide very efficient searching, they compromise peer autonomy. The DHT topology is regulated since all peers have the same number of neighboring peers and the selection of peers is strictly determined by the DHTs semantics. Furthermore, sophisticated load balancing procedures are required.

We propose building small worlds in unstructured (non DHT-based) P2P systems. Unstructured P2P systems can be further distinguished between systems that use indexes and those that are based on flooding and its variations. With flooding (such as in Gnutella), a peer searching for a document contacts its neighbor peers which in turn contact their own neighbors until a matching peer is reached. Flooding incurs large network overheads. In the case of indexes, these can be either centralized (as in Napster), or distributed among the peers (as in routing indexes [4]) providing for each peer a partial view of the system. We show how by using such indexes, we can organize the peers in small worlds in a fully decentralized manner. Small-worlds in non DHT P2P systems are also discussed in [1] in the context of searchable querical data networks; however, this work does not include a concrete decentralized small-world construction procedure.

Finally, many recent research efforts [2, 5, 15] are focusing on organizing peers in clusters which in a sense are similar to groups in small worlds. In this setting, the number or the description of the clusters is fixed and global knowledge of this information is required. The clustering of peers in [9] is based on the schemes of the peers and on predefined policies provided by human experts.

3   Content-Based Small Worlds in P2P Systems

We assume a P2P system with a set N of peers n_i. Each peer stores a set of data items (such as documents or relations). Each peer is connected to a small number of other peers called its *neighbors*. A query q may be posed at any of the peers. We denote by $match(n_i, q) = true$ the fact that peer n_i has data items satisfying query q; otherwise $match(n_i, q) = false$. Peers with data satisfying a query are called *matching* peers. In the following, we use the notation $|S|$ to denote the number of elements of a set S.

3.1   Small Worlds in P2P Systems

The *distance* between two peers n_i and n_j, $dist(n_i, n_j)$, is the length of the shortest path from n_i to n_j. The *diameter* of the network is the maximum distance between any two peers in the network. The *clustering coefficient* of a network captures the probability that two neighbors of a peer are also neighbors themselves; it is the average fraction of pairs of neighbors of a peer that are neighbors of each other. Small world networks are characterized by: (i) a small diameter and (ii) a large clustering coefficient [16].

Intuitively, the topology of a small-world network represents a number of smaller networks that are rich in links between their peers (short-range connections) and these smaller networks are linked between them with a few connections (long-range connections). The small-world phenomenon finds many applications in real life [7, 16]. Friendship networks are a good example of this. Consider the friendship graph, where each peer corresponds to a person and two people are connected with an edge if they know each other. Such a graph consists of smaller sub-graphs (which are rich in short-range connections) each one representing a community and there are a few long-range links between peers of different communities (if A knows B and B knows C, then A is more likely to know C than some other random person).

Our goal is to organize peers into groups based on some characteristics, where there are many structured inter-group (short-range) links and a few random intra-group (long-range) links. The short range links are created based on a common characteristic of the peers that are connected, while the long range links are constructed randomly between peers of different groups. These links serve to reduce the average path length between any two peers in the network.

More specifically, we want to group together the peers that match the same set of queries. The motivation for building such small worlds in P2P systems is to increase the number of matching peers that are returned. This is because, if peers that match similar queries are linked together, once we find one matching peer, all others are nearby. In particular, we want the probability that n_i and n_j are neighbors to depend on their similarity. We define the similarity among two peers based on the probability that they match the same set of queries:

Definition 1 (Similarity Among Peers). *For two peers n_i and n_j, we define their similarity as follows: $psimilar(n_i, n_j) = min(a_1, a_2)$ over all queries q, where $a_1 = Probability\{match(n_i, q) \Rightarrow match(n_j, q)\}$ and $a_2 = Probability\{match(n_j, q) \Rightarrow match(n_i, q)\}$.*

Figure 1 shows a ramdom and a small world P2P network. In a small-world network, peers that match a query are nearby.

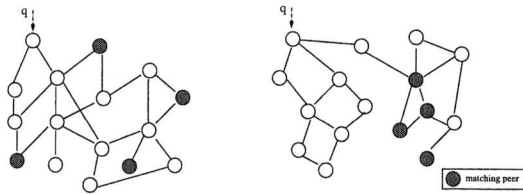

Fig. 1. (left) Random and (right) small-world P2P network

3.2 Content Summaries

Our approach is based on using local indexes to describe the content of each peer. We take the following generic approach: we assume that there is an "index" or summary called a local index $LI(n)$ that describes the content of each peer n. For instance, the index may be an inverted list of keywords, a B-tree, or a Bloom filter (as in our case study). A property of the "index" is that we can determine, with high probability, whether a peer satisfies a query based on its index, that is, without looking at the actual content of the peer. In particular, each index supports a predicate *imatch* such that: $\forall$ query q and peer $n \in N$, if $match(n, q) = true$ then $imatch(LI(n), q) = true$. The inverse also holds with a high probability. The case in which the inverse does not hold is called a *false positive*.

Besides its local index, each peer n maintains one routing index $RI(n, e)$ per link e, that describes the content of all peers that are reachable from n using link e at a distance at most R.

Definition 2 (Horizon and Radius). *A peer n_i has a horizon of radius R, if for each edge e, it maintains a routing index $RI(n_i, e)$ such that: $\forall$ query q and $n_j \in N$, such that if, using link e, $dist(n_i, n_j) \leq R$ and $match(n_j, q) = true$ then $imatch(RI(n_i, e), q) = true$.*

The index is representative of the content. In particular, we define a similarity metric between indexes, denoted as *similarity*, such that the more similar the peers, the more similar their indexes.

4 Building and Querying Small Worlds

Our goal is to create groups of similar peers. We distinguish between two types of links: *short-range* or short links that connect similar peers and *long-range* or long links that connect non-similar peers. Two peers belong to the same *group* if and only if there is a path consisting only of short links between them.

4.1 Query Routing

Our goal is to locate all matching peers. Assume that a query q is posed at peer n. First, n checks whether its own local index matches the query (whether $imatch(LI(n), q) = true$). Then, it propagates the query only through one or more of those links e whose routing indexes match the query ($imatch(RI(n, e), q) = true$). Analogously, each peer that receives the query first checks its own local index and propagates the query only through those links whose routing indexes match the query. This procedure ends when a maximum number of peers ($MaxVisited$) is visited or when the desired number of matching data items (results) is attained.

Note that following this procedure, it is possible to reach a situation in which no matching peers are found. This can happen for example if the peer n that poses a query has no matching outgoing links ($imatch(RI(n, e), q) = false \ \forall$ link e of n), which means that the matching peers (if any) are outside the radius R of n. To handle this case, we use a variation of the above procedure until we find the first matching link. Specifically, if no matching link has been found yet during the routing of the query, and the current peer has no matching outgoing links, then the long link of this peer is followed (even if it does not match the query). The idea is that we want to move to another group of the network, since the current group (bounded by the horizon) has no matching peers.

4.2 Small World Construction

Each new peer that enters the system tries to find a relevant group of peers and links with SL of them through short links. Also, it may link with a peer that does not belong to this group through a long link. Short links are inserted so that the peers with relevant information are located nearby and a large clustering coefficient is attained. Long links are used for keeping the diameter small. The idea is that we want to be easy to find both all the relevant results once in the right group, and the relevant group once in another group, thus reducing the number of hops that are needed to answer a query.

Specifically, when a new peer n joins the system, a join message that contains its local index $LI(n)$ is posed as a query to a well known peer in the system. This message maintains two lists (initially empty): (i) a list with peers of the same group with peer n, denoted *clist*, and (ii) a list with peers of different groups, denoted *dlist*. Whenever the message reaches a peer p, the similarity between the local indexes $LI(n)$ and $LI(p)$ is calculated. If the similarity is below a threshold t ($similarity(LI(n), LI(p)) < t$), peer p is added to the list *dlist* which means that p and n should belong to different groups. Otherwise, p is added to *clist*.

The join message is propagated using a query routing procedure that exploits the routing indexes as follows. The similarity between the local index $LI(n)$ of the new peer n and the routing indexes $RI(p, e)$ that correspond to each of the outgoing links e of peer p is calculated. The message is propagated through the most similar link e (for which $similarity(RI(p, e), LI(n))$ is the maximum) because there is higher probability to find the relevant group through this link. This routing procedure is followed until either

SL peers n_i with $similarity(LI(n_i),LI(n)) \geq t$ are found or a predefined number of peers (denoted $JMaxVisited$) is visited. Then a peer u is selected from the list *dlist*. The new peer connects to the peers of *clist* with short links and to peer u with a long link. If *dlist* is empty, which means that the message has not reached any peer from another group, the join message is also routed through the link for which the probability to reach a peer with similarity below the threshold t is the highest. That is, the message is propagated through the link e for which the routing index is less similar with the local index of the new peer $(similarity(RI(p,e), LI(n))$ is the smallest). The procedure stops when such a peer is found.

One disadvantage of the above algorithm is that it is difficult to define an appropriate value for the threshold. Furthermore, this value may need to change as the content of the peers changes. To address these issues, we also consider the following procedure that does not use threshold: the routing of the join message continues until the maximum number of peers visited $JMaxVisited$ is reached. The message is always propagated through the link that is most similar with the local index of the new peer. The message maintains a list $MaxMinList$ of all the visited peers and the corresponding similarities between their local indexes and the local index of the new peer. When the routing stops, the new peer selects to be linked to the SL most similar peers in $MaxMinList$ through short links, and randomly to one of the other peers in the list through a long link. We call the algorithm that uses a threshold, *threshold algorithm*, and the algorithm that does not use threshold *MaxMin algorithm*.

5   Experimental Evaluation

We use Bloom filters as indexes [8, 12]. Bloom filters are compact data structures for probabilistic representation of a set that support keyword queries ("Is keyword a in set A?"). We associate a document with each node. Each document has a number of elements (keywords). Every 10% of the documents are 50% similar to each other in terms of elements in common.

The size of the network is set to 500 peers and the horizon radius varies from 1 to 3. Each new peer creates one short link ($SL = 1$) and one long link with probability $P_l = 0.4$. The routing of the join message stops when a maximum number ($JMaxVisited$) of peers has been visited, varying from 5% to 20% of the existing peers. Analogously, the routing of the query stops when a maximum number ($MaxVisited$) of peers has been visited. This number remains constant to 10% of the network peers. In the first set of experiments, we show that our network satisfies the small-world properties. In the second set of experiments, we examine the performance of such a network, considering as performance metrics: (i) recall (i.e., the percentage of results found) and (ii) the number of hops until the first result is found. Table 1 summarizes our input parameters.

We examine the influence of the *join radius* (i.e., the radius used during the creation of the network). Note that we vary the radius used by a peer when joining the network, while we keep the radius used in query processing constant and equal to 3. Our objective is to show how the radius used *during the construction* of the network affects the quality of the constructed small-world network. We also perform experiments varying the percentage of peers visited during the join procedure ($JMaxVisited$) between 5% and 20%. We

Table 1. Input parameters

Parameter	Default Value	Range
Number of peers	500	
Radius of the horizon	3	1-3
Number of short links (SL)	1	
Probability of long link (P_l)	0.4	
Percentage of peers visited during join ($JMaxVisited$)	10	5-20
Percentage of peers visited during query ($MaxVisited$)	10	
Number of hits per peer	1	
Index (Bloom filter) size	6000 bits	
Number of elements per document	80	
Percentage of hits (matching peers per query)	7%	

compare networks constructed using the $MaxMin$ and the $threshold$ algorithms with a random (non small-world) network.

5.1 Network Properties

Diameter. We calculate the diameter of the network constructed following our procedures for creating a small world (Fig. 2). Our goal is to show that the network we build satisfies the small-world property of a small diameter O(log$N$) where N is the number of peers. We calculate the diameter for different values of the join radius. The value of the diameter is about 10 which means that it satisfies the property.

Quality of Clustering. We use two measures for evaluating clustering: join errors (the percentage of peers that fail to find an appropriate group to attach) and the average distance between peer groups.

The percentage of peers that cannot find the appropriate group to attach affects the quality of grouping. The number of join errors decreases as the join radius increases (Fig. 3). This is because, with a larger join radius, the join message is propagated more efficiently, since each routing index summarizes the content of more peers in the network. The benefit of increasing the radius above 2 is negligible (or there is no benefit), which means that a small radius suffices. Also, the number of join errors increases as the percentage of the peers visited during the join procedure increases. Again, increasing this percentage over 10% gives a small benefit, and thus, a small number of visited peers is required for achieving a good grouping. With the $threshold$ join algorithm, the new peer connects to the first SL peers it finds that have similarity larger than the threshold t, whereas with the $MaxMin$ algorithm, the join procedure continues until the maximum number of visited peers is reached. Thus, the $MaxMin$ algorithm achieves a better grouping of the peers.

We define the group peers distribution as the average distance among the peers in the same group GR: $db(GR) = \frac{\sum_{v \in GR} \sum_{u \in GR, u \neq v} dist(u,v)}{(|GR|(|GR|-1)}$. Figure 4 depicts the average distance for the groups created using the two join procedures and a random network. The networks built using our join algorithms have a smaller value for the distribution of the

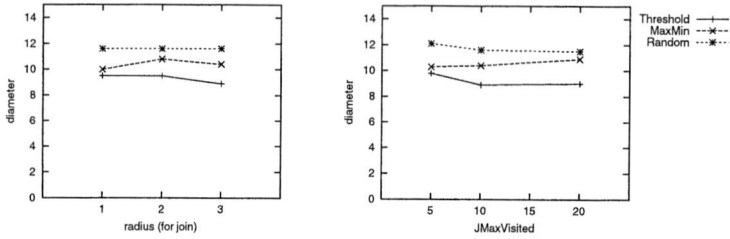

Fig. 2. Network diameter

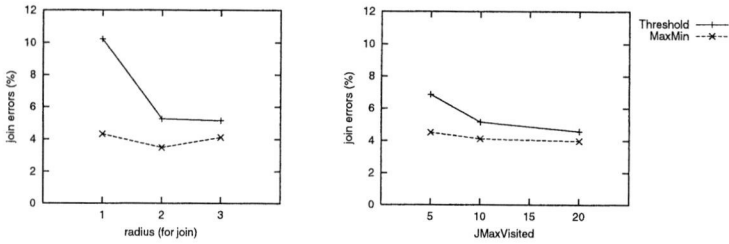

Fig. 3. Join errors

group peers than the random network. We achieve a small distribution for the group peers despite the fact that a new peer connects to only one relevant peer through a short link. Comparing the $MaxMin$ and the $threshold$ algorithms, we notice that for small values of the radius (1 and 2), the $MaxMin$ algorithm outperforms the $threshold$ algorithm. In all the other cases, the distribution value is nearly the same. Also variations of the radius and the percentage of peers visited during the join procedure have negligible influence to the distribution of the group peers for networks created by the $MaxMin$ algorithm (in contrast to the $threshold$ algorithm). The reason is that, even for small values of the radius and peers visited, the number of join errors for the $MaxMin$ algorithm remains very small (Fig. 3).

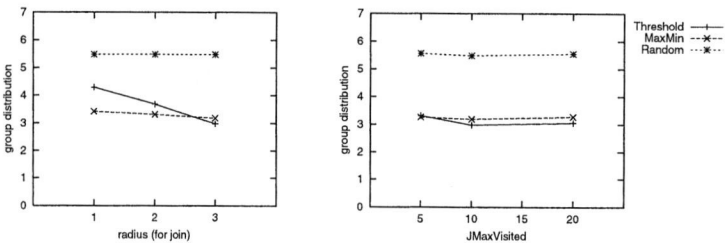

Fig. 4. Average distance between peers in each group

Comparison of the Two Join Algorithms. Following the $threshold$ algorithm, the join procedure ends when the first SL relevant peers are found, whereas with the $MaxMin$

algorithm, it stops only when the maximum number of visited peers has been reached. The result is that the *threshold* algorithm requires less hops during the join procedure. Our experiments show that the number of peers visited using the *threshold* algorithm is around 85% for $JMaxVisited = 5$ and 35% for $JMaxVisited = 10$ of the peers visited in the $MaxMin$ algorithm. Besides the fact that defining an appropriate value for threshold is hard, another drawback is that the *threshold* algorithm results in more join errors and a slightly worse performance (recall).

5.2 Performance of Querying

Recall. The networks created by the two join algorithms perform better than the random network due to the grouping of the relevant peers (Fig. 5). The $MaxMin$ algorithm performs a little better than the *threshold* algorithm since it achieves better clustering. The performance is good for radius 1 and a small percentage of visited peers (5%), Increasing either the radius or the percentage results in improving performance. However, in most cases, increasing the radius over 2 and the percentage over 10% gives nearly constant performance on average.

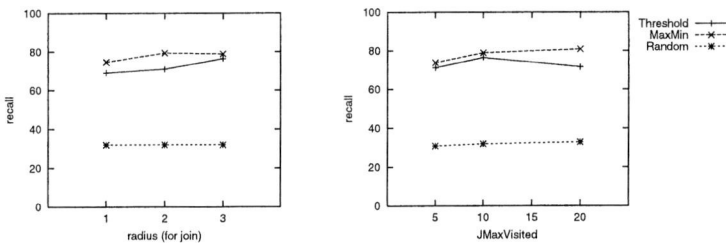

Fig. 5. Recall, i.e. percentage of matching peers found

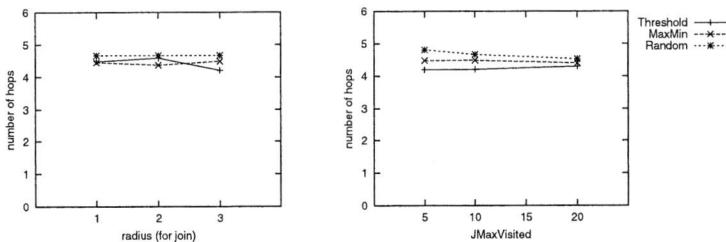

Fig. 6. Number of hops for locating the first matching peer

Hops for First Result. The average number of hops required to find the first matching peer is nearly the same for both the networks built using the *threshold* and the $MaxMin$ algorithm (Fig. 6). Also, it is a bit smaller than the required number in a random network. Thus, only a small percentage of the network peers need to be visited to reach a matching peer. Then, it is easy to find most of the other matching peers since relevant peers are linked together.

6 Conclusions

In this paper, we have proposed building small worlds of peers based on the probability of peers matching the same set of queries. We have introduced a decentralized procedure for constructing such small worlds that is based on using routing indexes. Future work includes the definition of appropriate routing indexes that could work well to create small worlds and in addition take into account the query workload. We are also currently working on proving formally the properties of the networks constructed by our approach.

References

1. F. Banaei-Kashani and C. Shahaby. Searchable Querical Data Networks. In *International Workshop on Databases, Information Systems and Peer-to-Peer Computing*, 2003.
2. M. Bawa, G. S. Manku, and P. Raghavan. SETS: Search Enhanced by Topic Segmentation. In *SIGIR*, 2003.
3. B. Bloom. Space/Time Trade-offs in Hash Coding with Allowable Errors. *CACM*, 13(7), 1970.
4. A. Crespo and H. Garcia-Molina. Routing Indices for Peer-to-Peer Systems. In *ICDCS*, 2002.
5. A. Crespo and H. Garcia-Molina. Semantic Overlay Networks for P2P Systems. Technical report, 2002. Submitted for publication.
6. R. Morris I. Stoica, D. Karger, M. F. Kaashoek, and H. Balakrishnan. Chord: A Scalable Peer-to-Peer Lookup Service for Internet Applications. *IEEE/ACM Trans. on Networking*, 11(1):17–32, 2003.
7. A. Iamnitchi, M. Ripeanu, and I. T. Foster. Locating Data in (Small-World?) Peer-to-Peer Scientific Collaborations. In *IPTPS*, 2002.
8. G. Koloniari, Y. Petrakis, and E. Pitoura. Content-Based Overlay Networks for XML Peers Based on Multi-Level Bloom Filters. In *International Workshop on Databases, Information Systems and Peer-to-Peer Computing*, 2003.
9. A. Loser, F. Naumann, W. Siberski, W. Nejdl, and U. Thaden. Semantic Overlay Clusters within Super-Peer Networks. In *International Workshop on Databases, Information Systems and Peer-to-Peer Computing*, 2003.
10. S. Manku, M. Bawa, and P. Raghavan. Symphony: Distributed Hashing in a Small World. In *USENIX Symposium on Internet Technologies and Systems*, 2003.
11. S. Ratnasamy, P. Francis, M. Handley, R. Karp, and S. Schenker. A Scalable Content-Addressable Network. In *SIGCOMM*, 2001.
12. S. C. Rhea and J. Kubiatowicz. Probabilistic Location and Routing. In *INFOCOM*, 2002.
13. C. Schmidt and M. Parashar. Flexible Information Discovery in Decentralized Distributed Systems. In *HPDC*, 2003.
14. C. Tang, Z. Xu, and S. Dwarkadas. Peer-to-Peer Information Retrieval Using Self-Organizing Semantic Overlay Networks. In *SIGCOMM*, 2003.
15. P. Triantafillou, C. Xiruhaki, M. Koubarakis, and N. Ntarmos. Towards High Performance Peer-to-Peer Content and Resource Sharing Systems. In *CIDR*, 2003.
16. D. J. Watts and S. H. Strogatz. Collective Dynamics of Small-World Networks. *Nature*, 393:440–442, 1998.

SPROUT: P2P Routing with Social Networks[*][**]

S. Marti, P. Ganesan, and H. Garcia-Molina

Stanford University, CA, USA
{smarti,prasannag,hector}@cs.stanford.edu

Abstract. In this paper, we investigate how existing social networks can benefit P2P data networks by leveraging the inherent trust associated with social links. We present a trust model that lets us compare routing algorithms for P2P networks overlaying social networks. We propose SPROUT, a DHT routing algorithm that, by using social links, significantly increases the number of query results and reduces query delays. We discuss further optimization and design choices for both the model and the routing algorithm. Finally, we evaluate our model versus regular DHT routing and Gnutella-like flooding.

1 Introduction

Social networks are everywhere. Many people all over the world participate online in established social networks every day. AOL, Microsoft, and Yahoo! all provide instant messaging services to millions of users, alerting them when their friends log on. Many community websites, such as Friendster [4], specialize in creating and utilizing social networks. As another example, service agreements between ISPs induce a "social" network through which information is routed globally. Social networks are valuable because they capture trust relationships between entities. By building a P2P data-management system "on top of", or with knowledge of, an existing social network, we can leverage these trust relationships in order to support efficient, reliable query processing.

Several serious problems in peer-to-peer networks today are largely due to lack of trust between peers. Peer anonymity and the lack of a centralized enforcement agency make P2P systems vulnerable to a category of attacks we call misrouting attacks. We use the term *misrouting* to refer to any failure by a peer node to forward a message to the appropriate peer according to the correct routing algorithm. This includes dropping the message or forwarding the message to other colluding nodes instead of the correct peer, perhaps in an attempt to control the results of a query. For instance, in a distributed hash table (DHT) a malicious node may wish to masquerade as the index owner of the key being queried for in order to disseminate bad information and suppress content shared by other peers.

Using *a priori* relationship knowledge may be key to mitigating the effects of misrouting. To avoid routing messages through possibly malicious nodes, we would prefer forwarding our messages through nodes controlled by people we know personally,

---

[*] This research is supported in part by NSF Grant (IIS-9817799).

[**] A short position paper on this topic was presented at IPTPS 2004. This paper elaborates on the design and presents new experiments and results.

W. Lindner et al. (Eds.): EDBT 2004 Workshops, LNCS 3268, pp. 425–435, 2004.

perhaps from a real life social context. We could assume our friends would not purpose-fully misroute our messages.[1] Likewise, our friends could try and forward our message through their friends' nodes. Social network services provide us the mechanism to iden-tify who our social contacts are and locate them in the network when they are online.

Misrouting is far from the only application of social networks to peer-to-peer systems. Social networks representing explicit or implicit service agreements can also be used to optimize quality of service by, for example, minimizing latency. Peers may give queue priority to packets forwarded by friends or partners over those of strangers. Thus, the shortest path through a network is not necessarily the fastest.

In Section 2 we present a high-level model for evaluating the use of social networks for peer-to-peer routing, and apply it to the two problems we described above; yielding more query results and reducing query times.

Unstructured networks can be easily molded to conform to the social links of their participants. OpenNap, for example, allows supernodes to restrict themselves to linking only with reputable or "friendly" peer supernodes, who manage message propagation and indexing. However, structured networks, such as DHTs, are less flexible, since their connections are determined algorithmically, and thus it is more challenging to use social networks in such systems. In Section 3 we propose SPROUT, a routing algorithm which uses social link information to improve DHT routing performance with respect to both misrouting and latency. We then analyze and evaluate both our model and SPROUT in Section 4.

2   Trust Model

The basic intuition of this paper is that computers managed by friends are not likely to be selfish or malicious and deny us service or misroute our messages. Similarly, friends of friends are also unlikely to be malicious. Therefore, the likelihood of a node B pur-posefully misrouting a message from node A is proportional to (or some function of) the distance from A's owner to B's owner in the social network. Observe that in a real net-work with malicious nodes, the above intuition cannot hold simultaneously for all nodes; neighbors of malicious nodes, for example, will find malicious nodes close to them. Rather our objective is to model trust from the perspective of a random good node in the network. Likewise, we assume messages forwarded over social links would experience less latency on average because of prioritizing based on friendship or service agreements.

We now describe a flexible model for representing the behavior of peers relative to a node based on social connections. We will illustrate the model usage for two different specific issues: minimizing the risk of misrouting, and decreasing latency to improve Quality of Service.

2.1   Trust Function

We express the trust that a node A has in peer B as $T(A, B)$. Based on our assumption, this value is dependent only on the distance (in hops) d from A to B in the social network. To

---

[1] We assume a slim, but nonzero, chance that a virus or trojan has infected their machine, causing it to act maliciously.

quantify this measure of trust for the misrouting scenario, we use the expected probability that node B will correctly route a message from node A. The reason for this choice will become apparent shortly.

One simple trust function would be to assume our friends' nodes are very likely to correctly route our messages, say with probability $f = 0.95$. But their friends are less likely (0.90), and their friends even less so (0.85). Note, this is not the probability that the peer forwards each packet, but instead the probability that the peer is not misbehaving and dropping all packets. Averaged over all nodes, they are equivalent. A node's trustworthiness decreases linearly with respect to its distance from us in the social network. This would level off when we hit the probability that any random stranger node (far from us in the social network) will successfully route a message, say $r = 0.6$. For large networks with large diameters probability r represents the fraction of the network made up of good nodes willing to correctly route messages. Thus, $r = 0.6$ means that we expect that 40% of the network nodes (or more accurately network node identifiers) will purposefully misroute messages. Here we have presented a linear trust function. We consider others in the extended version of this paper [6].

When measuring QoS we would want to use a very different function. Let $T(A, B)$ be the expected additional latency incurred by a message forwarded through node B, which it received from node A. For simplicity, let us assume that $T(A, B) = \epsilon$ if a social link exists between A and B and $\Delta \cdot \epsilon$ otherwise. For example, assume $\epsilon = 1$ and $\Delta = 3$. If A has a service agreement, or is friends with, B, then B give any message it receives from A priority and forward it in about 1 (ms), otherwise it is placed in a queue and takes on average 3 (ms). We will use these same values for ϵ and Δ in our example below.

We do not claim any of these functions with any specific parameter values is an accurate trust representation of any or all social networks, but they do serve to express the relationship we believe exists between social structure and the quality of routing.

2.2   Path Rating

We wish to use our node trust model to compare peer-to-peer routing algorithms. For this we need to calculate a *path trust rating* P to use as our performance metric. The method for calculating P will be application-dependent (and we will present two specific examples below), but a few typical decisions that must be made are:

1. *Source-routing or hop-by-hop?* Will the trust value of a node on the path be a function of its social distance from the message originator, or only from whom it received the message directly?
2. *How do you combine node trust?* Is the path rating the product, sum, maximum value, or average value of the node trust values along the path? Any appropriate function could be used.

We now give as example a metric for *reliability* in the presence of misrouting. We need to compare the likelihood that a message will reach its destination given the path selected by a routing algorithm. We calculate the reliability path rating by multiplying the separate node trust ratings for each node along the path from the source to destination. For example, assume source node S wishes to route a message to destination node D. In order to do so a routing algorithm calls for the message to hop from S to A, then B, then C, and finally D. Then the reliability path rating will be $P_R = T(S, A) * T(S, B) * T(S, C) * T(S, D)$. Given that $T(X, Y)$ is interpreted as the actual probability node Y correctly routes node X's message, then P_R is the probability that the message is received and properly handled by D. Note that $T(X, Y)$ is dependent only on the shortest path in the social network between X and Y and thus independent of whether Y was the first, second, or nth node along the path.

For the Quality of Service we would want our path rating to express the expected time a message would take to go from the source to the destination. Given that $T(A, B)$ is the latency incurred by each hop we would want to use an additive function. And if each node decides whether to prioritize forwarding based on who it received the message from *directly*, and not the originator, then the function would be hop-by-hop. Calculating the latency path rating for the path used above would be $P_L = T(S, A) + T(A, B) + T(B, C) + T(C, D)$.

Though we focus on linear paths in this paper, the rating function can generalize to arbitrary routing graphs, such as multicast trees.

3   Social Path Routing Algorithm

We wish to leverage the assumed correlation between routing reliability or efficiency and social distance by creating a peer-to-peer system that utilizes social information from a service such as a community website or instant messenger service. Though there are many ways to exploit social links, for this paper, we focus on building a distributed hash table (DHT) routing algorithm. Specifically, we build on the basic Chord routing algorithm [11]. Chord was chosen because it is a well-known scheme and studies have shown it to provide great static resilience, a useful property in a system with a high probability of misrouting that is difficult to detect and repair [5]. Our technique is equally applicable to other DHT designs, such as CAN [8] or Pastry [9].

When a user first joins the Chord network, it is randomly assigned a network identifier from 0 to 1. It then establishes links to its *sequential neighbors* in idspace, forming a ring of nodes. It also makes roughly $\log_2 n$ *long links* to nodes halfway around the ring, a quarter of the way, an eighth, etc. When a node inserts or looks up an item, it hashes the item's key to a value between 0 and 1. Using greedy clockwise routing, it can locate the peer whose id is closest to the key's hash (and is thus responsible for indexing the item) in $O(\log n)$ hops. For simplicity, we will use "key" to refer to a key's hash value in this paper.

Our Social Path ROUTing (SPROUT) algorithm adds to Chord additional links to any friends that are online. All popular instant messenger services keep a user aware of when their friends enter or leave the network. Using this existing mechanism a node can determine when their friends' nodes are up and form links to them in the DHT as well. This provides them with several highly trusted links to use for routing messages. When a node needs to route to key k SPROUT works as follows:

1. Locate the friend node whose id is closest to, but not greater than, k.
2. If such a friend node exists, forward the message to it. That node repeats the procedure from step 1.

3. If no friend node is closer to the destination, then use the regular Chord algorithm to continue forwarding to the destination.

In order to improve the performance of SPROUT we apply two optimizations, which we evaluate in the extended paper [6]:

Lookahead. With the above procedure, when we choose the friend node closest to the destination we do not know if it has a friend to take us closer to the destination. Thus, we may have to resort to regular Chord routing after the first hop. To improve our chances of finding social hops to the destination we can employ a *lookahead* cache of 1 or 2 levels. Each node may share with its friends a list of its friends and, in 2-level lookahead, its friends-of-friends. A node can then consider all nodes within 2 or 3 social hops away when looking for the node closest to the destination. We still require that the message be forwarded over the established social links.

Minimum Hop Distance. Though SPROUT guarantees forward progress towards the destination with each hop, it may happen that at each hop SPROUT finds the sequential neighbor is the closest friend to the target. Thus, in the worst case, routing is $O(n)$.

To prevent this we use a *minimum hop distance (MHD)* to ensure that the following friend hop covers at least *MHD* fraction of the remaining distance (in idspace) to the destination. For example, if $MHD = 0.25$, then the next friend hop must be at least a quarter of the distance from the current node to the destination. If not then we resort to Chord routing, where each hop covers approximately half of the distance. This optimization guarantees us $O(\log n)$ hops to any destination but causes us to give up on using social links earlier in the routing process. When planning multiple hops at once, due to lookahead, we require the path to cover $\frac{MHD}{k}$ additional distance for each additional hop, for some appropriate k.

4 Results

To test our SPROUT algorithm for DHTs compare it to Chord in the following scenario. Assume the members of an existing social network wish to share files or information by creating a distributed hash table. Believing that some peers in the network are unreliable, each node would prefer to route messages through their friends' nodes if possible. We use two sources for social network data for our simulations. The first is data taken from the Club Nexus community website established at Stanford University [1]. This dataset consists of over 2200 users and their links to each other as determined by their Buddy Lists. The second source was a synthetic social network generator based on the Small World topology algorithm presented in [7]. Both the Club Nexus data and the Small World data created social networks with an average of approximately 8 links per node. We randomly inserted each social network node into the Chord id space.

For each experiment we randomly choose 500 query source nodes and, for each node, 500 random key hash values to search for (chosen uniformly from 0 to 1). We compute a path using each routing algorithm and gather statistics on path length and trust rating. Each data point presented below is the average of all 250,000 query paths.

4.1   Algorithm Evaluation

We first focus on the problem of misrouting. We use the linear trust function described in Section 2 with $f = 0.95$ and $r = 0.6$, which corresponds to 40% of the nodes misbehaving. We feel such a large fraction of bad nodes is reasonable because of the threat of Sybil attacks [3].

We compare SPROUT, using a lookahead of 1 and $MHD = 0.5$, to Chord using the Club Nexus social network data. The first and third rows of Table 1 give the measured values for both the average path length and average reliability path rating of both regular Chord routing and SPROUT. With an average path length of 5.343 and average reliability of 0.3080, Chord performed much worse in both metrics than SPROUT, which attained values of 4.569 and 0.4661, respectively. In fact, a path is over 1.5 times as likely to succeed using standard SPROUT as with regular Chord.

Table 1. SPROUT vs. Chord

	Avg. Path Length	Avg. Reliabilty
Regular Chord	5.343	0.3080
Augmented Chord	4.532	0.3649
SPROUT(1,0.5)	4.569	0.4661

But this difference in performance may be simply due to having additional links available for routing, and the fact that they are friend links may have no effect on performance. To equalize the comparison we augmented Chord by giving nodes additional links to use for routing. Each node was given as many additional random links as that node has social links (which SPROUT uses). Thus, the total number of links useable at each node is equal for both SPROUT and augmented Chord. The performance of the augmented Chord (AC) is given in the second row of Table 1. As expected, with more links to choose from AC performs significantly better than regular Chord, especially in terms of path length. But SPROUT is still 1.3 times as likely to route successfully. In the following sections we compare SPROUT only to the augmented Chord algorithm.

From our analysis of the SPROUT optimizations (see [6]) we chose to use a 1-level lookahead and an MHD of 0.5 for our standard SPROUT procedure. Though 2-level lookahead produced slightly better reliability we did not feel it warranted the longer route paths and exponentially increased node state propagation and management. Our available social network data indicates that a user has on average between 8 and 9 friends. Thus, we would expect most nodes' level-1 lookahead cache to hold less than 100 entries.

We evaluate different trust functions and parameter values in [6] and find that SPROUT outperforms AC for $r < 0.95$. When 5% or less of unknown peers are likely to misroute ($r \geq 0.95$) both algorithms perform equally well, even with f also 0.95, indicating we trust our friends no more than any stranger. While SPROUT significantly improves path reliability in a peer-to-peer network with many malicious and selfish peers, we do not suffer a reliability penalty for using it in a network with very few bad peers.

Both SPROUT and our social trust model are not limited to misrouting, but can be used towards other problems, such as Quality of Service. Using the latency trust function (with $\epsilon = 1$ and $\Delta = 3$) and latency path rater we described in Section 2, we routed messages using both SPROUT and augmented Chord to see which provides the least latency. We found that SPROUT results in roughly half (40-60%) the latency of AC. We would expect SPROUT to deliver messages twice as fast as AC by preferring to take advantage of service agreements, rather than simply minimizing hop count. For more details see our tech report [6].

4.2 Number of Friends

In a given network, a node with more friends is likely to perform better since it has more choices of social links to use. But how much better? How much improvement would a node expect to gain by establishing some trust relationship with another node? To quantify this, we generated 100 queries from each node in the Club Nexus network, calculated its path rating, and grouped and averaged the results based on the number of social links each node has.

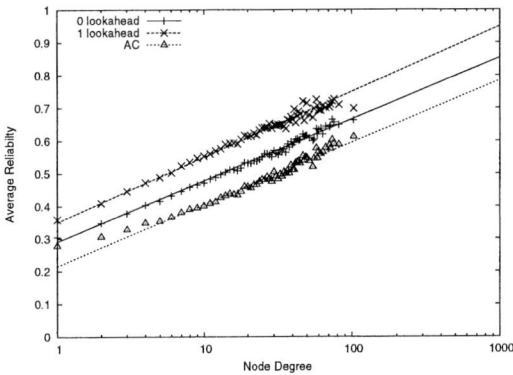

Fig. 1. Performance as a function of a node's degree. Club Nexus data

Figure 1 shows the results for SPROUT using 0- and 1-level lookahead, as well as AC for the Club Nexus data. For example, 85 nodes in the network had exactly 10 social links. The average path rating for those 85 nodes when running SPROUT with 1 lookahead was 0.553. Note that the three curves are linear with respect to the log of the node degree, indicating an exponentially decreasing benefit return for each additional social link. For instance, nodes with only 1 social peer attained a reliability rating of 0.265 with SPROUT with no lookahead, while nodes with 10 social peers scored 0.471, a difference of 0.206. A node with 10 social peers would need to grow to over 100 social peers to increase their rating that same amount (the one node with 103 social links had a rating of 0.663).

From these curves we can estimate how many links a typical node would need to have in order to attain a specified level of reliability. For instance, considering the SPROUT with 1-level lookahead curve, we see that a node would need about 100 social links to attain an average rating of 0.7, and about 600 social links to get a rating of 0.9.

Though a single node increasing its number of friends does not greatly influence its performance, what performance can nodes expect if we *a priori* set the number of friend connections each node must have? To analyze this we create a random regular social network graph of 2500 nodes where each node has an equal degree and vary this degree for each simulation run. The results are shown below in Figure 2.

The curves correspond to SPROUT with 1-level lookahead and augmented Chord. As expected, we see that both curves rise more steeply than in the previous graph. If all nodes add an extra social link the probability of successful routing will rise more than if only one node adds a link (as seen in Fig. 1). But the curves level off just below 0.9. In fact, similar simulations for larger networks showed the same results, with reliability leveling off under 0.9 at around 100 social links per node. This confirms that even at high social degree, each path is expected to take multiple hops through nodes that are, to some small amount, unreliable. Even if all nodes were exactly two social hops away from each other, this would yield a reliability of 0.95*0.9=0.855. Therefore, we would not expect a node in the Club Nexus dataset, as seen in Figure 1, reach 0.9 reliability, even with 600 links.

Though SPROUT provides greater reliability than Chord, neither algorithm performs particularly well. Our results from Table 1 showed ratings of less than 0.50, indicating less than 50% of messages would be expected to reach their destination. Perhaps DHT routing is incapable of providing acceptable performance when members of the network seek to harm it. In the next section, we evaluate the brute force method of query flooding.

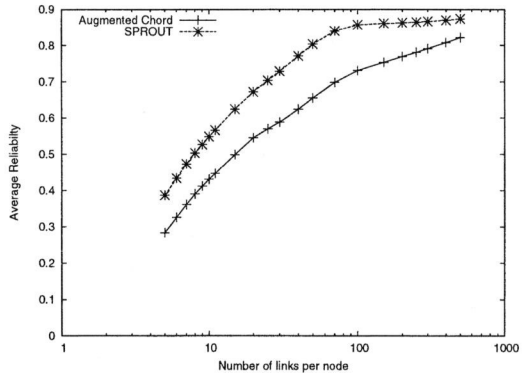

Fig. 2. Performance of SPROUT and AC for different uniform networks with varying degrees

4.3 Comparison to Gnutella-Like Networks

So far we have limited our analysis of SPROUT to Chord-like DHT routing. We were also interested in comparing the effects of misrouting on structured P2P networks to unstructured, flooding-based networks, such as Gnutella. To balance the comparison we assume the unstructured network's topology is determined by the social network, using only its social links, and apply the same linear trust function used before to calculate the probability that a node forwards a query flood message.

Because querying the network is flooding-based, we cannot use the probability of reaching a certain destination as our metric. Instead, we would like to find the expected number of good responses a querying node would receive. For a DHT we assume a node would receive all or no responses, depending on whether the query message reached the correct well-behaved index node (we do not consider the problem of inserting item keys into the DHT caused by misrouting). In an unstructured network the number of good responses located is equal to the number of responses at well-behaved nodes reached by the query flood. Because the flood is usually limited in size by a *time-to-live* (TTL), even if there are no malicious nodes in the network, not all query answers will be located.

We modelled a Gnutella-like network with a topology based on the Club Nexus data and used a TTL of 5, allowing us to reach the vast majority of the nodes in the network (over 2000 on average). We seeded the network with files based on empirically collected data from actual networks [10] and ran 10000 queries for different files from varying nodes, dropping a query message at a peer with a probability based on the trust function and the shortest path to the querying node. We averaged across 10 runs (for different file distributions) and present the results, as a function of r (the expected reliability of a node distant in the social network), in Figure 4.3.

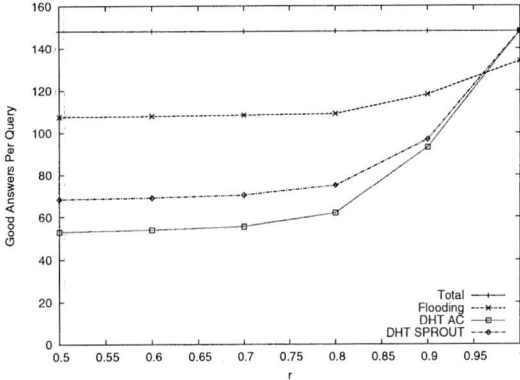

The top curve, labelled *Total*, indicates the total number of files in the entire network matching each query (on average), independent of the routing algorithm used. This value is approximately 150. The expected number of good answers received for the DHT curves was calculated as this total number times the expected probability of reaching the index node storing the queried for items. Flooding results in significantly more responses on average, a factor of almost 2 for small r. More importantly, this means we would expect to locate at least some good answers flooding when the DHT completely fails. For values of r less than 0.5 all the curves level off. If $r = 1$ then we assume no nodes in the network are malicious. Thus DHT outperforms flooding since it will always locate the index node and retrieve all the available answers.

Fig. 3. Performance of SPROUT and AC versus unstructured flooding

Note, these results are meant to be a rough comparison of these two P2P styles. The flooding model does not take into account messages dropped due to congestion. This is a much larger problem for flooding protocols than DHTs. In our simulations on the 2200 node Club Nexus network each query reached, on average, over 2000 nodes. This indicates the number of messages produced by the flood was even greater (due to duplicate messages). The DHT algorithm, on the other hand, averaged around 5 messages to reach the index node. Thus, flooding schemes will not scale to very large networks as well as DHTs.

On the other hand, in the DHT model, we are only considering the probability of a query message being misrouted. We assume all good answers are inserted at the correct index node, not taking into account that index insertions may fail just as well as index queries. If we factor in index insertion failures, the DHT curves would shift down, further increasing the relative performance difference with flooding.

Though flooding is more costly in terms of processor and network bandwidth utilization, it is clearly a more reliable method of querying in a network suffering from some amount of misrouting. A better solution may be to use a hybrid scheme where one uses DHT routing until they detect misrouting or malicious nodes, then switch to query flooding. In fact, a such a scheme is proposed in [2] and discussed in Section 5.

5   Related Work

In [2], Castro et al propose using stricter network identifier assignment and density checks to detect misrouting attacks in DHTs. They suggest using constrained routing tables and redundant routing to circumvent malicious nodes and provide more secure routing. SPROUT is complementary to their approach, simply increasing the probability that the message will be routed correctly the first time. One technique of theirs that would be especially useful in our system was their route failure test based on measuring the density of network ids around oneself and the purported destination. Not only can this technique be used to determine when a route has failed, but it can be used to evaluate the trustworthiness of a node's sequential neighbors by comparing local density to that at random locations in idspace or around friends.

6   Conclusion

We have presented a method for leveraging the trust relationships gained by marrying a peer-to-peer system with a social network, and showed how to improve the expected number of query results and the how to reduce the expected delays. We described a model for evaluating routing algorithms in such a system and proposed SPROUT, a routing algorithm designed to leverage trust relationships given by social links. Our results demonstrate how SPROUT can significantly improve the likelihood of getting query results in a timely fashion, when a large fraction of nodes are malicious. Though flooding-based search schemes are far more robust when threatened by a large number of malicious users, with the right techniques structured networks can obtain acceptable performance at far less bandwidth costs.

References

1. Orkut Buyukkokten. Club Nexus, 2001.
2. M. Castro, P. Drushel, A. Ganesh, A. Rowstron, and D. Wallach. Secure routing for structured peer-to-peer overlay networks. In *OSDI '02*, 2002.
3. John R. Douceur. The Sybil Attack. In *Proc. of the International Workshop on Peer-to-Peer Systems*, 2002.
4. Friendster Inc. Friendster Beta, 2003. http://www.friendster.com.
5. K. Gummadi, R. Gummadi, S. Gribble, S. Ratnasamy, S. Shenker, and I. Stoica. The impact of DHT routing geometry on resilience and proximity. In *Proc. ACM SIGCOMM*, 2003.
6. Sergio Marti, Prasanna Ganesan, and Hector Garcia-Molina. SPROUT: P2P Routing with Social Networks. Technical report, 2004. dbpubs.stanford.edu/pub/2004-5.
7. A. R Puniyani, R. M Lukose, and B. A Huberman. Intentional Walks on Scale Free Small Worlds. *ArXiv Condensed Matter e-prints*, July 2001. http://aps.arxiv.org/abs/cond-mat/0107212.
8. Sylvia Ratnasamy, Paul Francis, Mark Handley, Richard Karp, and Scott Shenker. A scalable content addressable network. Technical Report TR-00-010, Berkeley, CA, 2000.
9. Antony Rowstron and Peter Druschel. Pastry: Scalable, decentralized object location, and routing for large-scale peer-to-peer systems. *IFIP/ACM International Conference on Distributed Systems Platforms*, pages 329–350, 2001.

10. Stefan Saroiu, P. Krishna Gummadi, and Steven D. Gribble. A measurement study of peer-to-peer file sharing systems. In *Proceedings of Multimedia Computing and Networking 2002 (MMCN '02)*, San Jose, CA, USA, January 2002.

11. Ion Stoica, Robert Morris, David Liben-Nowell, David R. Karger, M. Frans Kaashoek, Frank Dabek, and Hari Balakrishnan. Chord: a scalable peer-to-peer lookup protocol for internet applications. *IEEE/ACM Trans. Netw.*, 11(1):17–32, 2003.

A Simulation Framework for Schema-Based Query Routing in P2P-Networks

Wolf Siberski and Uwe Thaden

Learning Lab Lower Saxony, 30539 Hannover
{siberski,thaden}@learninglab.de

Abstract. Current simulations of P2P-networks don't take any kind of schemas into account. We present a simulation-framework and first results for query routing based on extensible schema information to describe peer content, providing more value than simple categorizations like the filename as abstraction for an MP3-song. Using different parameterization, we compare the impact of introducing the HyperCuP-topology in a P2P-network for routing and possible clustering in super-peers and discuss first simulation results.

1 Introduction

Metadata and schemas are important for both peer-to-peer (P2P) networks and databases. Our open source project Edutella [15, 16] offers an infrastructure combining semantic web and peer-to-peer technologies in order to make distributed learning repositories possible and useful. It is based on the exchange of RDF metadata and allows to query different data sources. As a schema-based peer-to-peer network, Edutella extends conventional peer-to-peer networks by allowing different and extensible schemas to describe peer content, a necessary feature for information rich peer-to-peer networks. In Edutella everything is based on the Resource Description Framework (RDF) and RDF Schema, which allows to represent schemas based on classes, properties and property constraints. In our educational context schemas used in Edutella are e. g. Dublin Core (DC) or Learning Object Metadata (LOM). These are standardized categorizations one can use to store metadata going further than simply storing the filename of a music-file.

For traditional databases, schemas are nothing new, for peer-to-peer networks such approaches are just beginning to emerge. There are some aspects in that field which bring knowledge from the database community and knowledge from the P2P-community together. In their nature peers in a P2P-network are inhomogeneous regarding their technical aspects (storage-power, up- and downtime, etc.) and their usage from the topic-point of view. These facets bring the focus to the questions how to efficiently connect peers (topology) and how to extend representation and querying over P2P-networks (schemas).

Recent research has focused either concentrated on gaining knowledge using crawls of systems like Gnutella or using simulations which show message-behavior etc. on a very low (i. e. transport) level. Ideas like schema-based peer-to-peer networks cannot be simulated like that since the overlay-topology is the point of interest. On the other

W. Lindner et al. (Eds.): EDBT 2004 Workshops, LNCS 3268, pp. 436–445, 2004.

hand it is not possible to setup a large P2P-network to test how efficient a topology with different parameters is regarding search- and query-algorithms.

Using a schema-based approach, we had to find a good way how the schemas and their attributes are distributed over the network. Current research has shown that consumers in a P2P-network are interested in subsets of all available content and that they are often only interested in some content categories only [7]. E.g. for our eLearning-context we can say that students are mainly searching for resources related to their current courses. It was observed that in the domain of information retrieval the documents are distributed following Zipf's law. This means that many consumers are interested in some resources which are held by few providers. Recent (empirical) studies [9, 4] have shown that despite the randomness of the internet, it also exhibits the Zipf distribution.

The remainder of this paper is as follows: In section 2 we analyze which requirements are needed to simulate a schema-based P2P-network. Section 3 presents our simulation framework for schema-based P2P-networks. Some first results/hypotheses of our simulations are discussed in section 4.

2   Simulation Context

Ehrig et al. [8] present a theoretical model of evaluation. They discuss several aspects of a P2P-simulation and give some recommendations, but no final set of parameters. Our following list of requirements has some of their ideas and new ones combined to form a set of requirements that can be implemented and analyzed after the simulation runs.

2.1   Schema-Based Resource Description

We assume that there won't be one fixed schema to describe resources in a P2P network. Instead, peers will choose one of (more or less) standardized schemas for resource description(s). This is a trend in recent P2P systems [1, 3, 10, 14]. In Edutella we use RDFS for as schema definition language. For our simulation we only assume that a schema is identifiable and consists of arbitrary many named properties. We don't take into account any relation between properties.

2.2   Super Peer Based Topology

While the simulator framework is not tied to a specific topology, we assume a super-peer topology, where the super-peers form a backbone of the network and take care of request routing. Only a small percentage of nodes are super-peers, but these are assumed to be highly available nodes with high computing capacity. For example in our learning repository network, each university would run one such super-peer.

Super-peer routing is usually based on different kinds of indexing and routing tables, as discussed in [6] and [21]. The Edutella super-peers employ routing indexes which explicitly take schema information into account.

Super-peers in the Edutella network are arranged in the HyperCuP topology [17] which allows for $\log_2 N$ path length and $\log_2 N$ number of neighbors, where N is the total number of nodes in the network (i.e. the number of super-peers in our case). In the simulation runs described in section 4 we discuss characteristics of the hypercube topology and the influence of sorting/clustering peers and super-peers.

2.3   Existing Simulators

This section gives an overview of other P2P simulation frameworks and compares them to our work.

The **SimP2 simulator** [12] is designed to provide support and additional depth to an analysis of ad-hoc P2P-networks. The analysis is based on a non-uniform random graph model similar to Gnutella, and is limited to studying basic properties such as reachability and nodal degree. They leave out complex queries which are very important for our approach, since we want to broadcast such queries efficiently. On the other hand, SimP2 is very good for more detailed performance characteristics such as queuing delays and message loss.

3LS[19] is a discrete simulator using a central step-clock. It provides three levels: Network model, protocol model and user model. The network model uses a two dimensional matrix to define distance values between the nodes. The protocol model represents the P2P-protocol which should be investigated. Input can be simulated using the user model (which could be a interesting addition to our simulation-framework). Since 3LS is not efficient regarding memory usage, it is limited to rather small networks.

The authors of the **Packet-level Peer-to-Peer (PLP2P) Simulator** [11] state that one of the most important things in a simulation is the correct and mostly complete underlying network-structure. They assert that failure to consider low-level details can lead the simulation to inaccuracies. PLP2P provides a framework that can be used together with other simulators to achieve more accuracy in the simulations.

Narses Simulator [2] is a flow-based network simulator and thus does not concentrate on the packet-level to avoid the overhead of packet level simulators. To do this Narses offers a range of models that trade between fast runtimes and accuracy. Narses is therefore somewhere between packet level simulators and analytical models. Nevertheless the assumptions made by Narses are targeted towards reducing the complexity if simulations by approximations of physical aspects.

Evaluation Regarding our plan to simulate a schema-based peer-to-peer-network, none of the current available simulators is capable of that, since they all concentrate on the traffic or information-'flow' on a much deeper level of the OSI-model. The observations are made directly from the transport-level or by making abstraction or assumptions on the (physical) aspects which are in contrast to our needs. For our purpose we need a way to describe a specific topology in combination with schema-information, so that we can get results for search and routing in schema-based peer-to-peer networks. Furthermore most simulators cannot be used to simulate different topologies with several parameters as we need it for our task to compare different shapes of the HyperCuP-topology. To overcome these problems, we developed a simulator-framework which is described in the next section.

3   The Simulation Framework

The following sections describe our design and implementation of our simulation framework. We assume some basic knowledge on discrete event simulation.

3.1   Design

Schema based P2P-networks are a subset of P2P-networks as they are used for e. g. sharing music-files. So what we needed was a tool set for creating the "normal" requirements for a P2P-simulation like message-exchange and a simulation-stepper. For that we used a framework called SSF. Furthermore we needed to model and implement the behavior of a P2P-network that uses schemas.

Schema-Based Resource Description. The main goal of our simulation is to experiment with query routing based on schema information. To represent this information, we use schema elements which can be either complete schemas or single properties (the term property stems from semantic web terminology; in a relational database a schema property would correspond to a table column).

Query messages don't contain concrete requests, but only a list of properties used to formulate the request. Provider peers 'answer' to these requests on a probabilistic basis, depending on the schema information used by the provider and the information used in the query. For example, our model of a query which asks for *(dc:title[1] = "The Power of Metadata"' and dc:date > "1.1.2000")*, is just a list of the used properties *(dc:title, dc:date)*.

For the generation of such queries a configurable distribution is taken into account. We can set as parameters the number of available schemas and their frequency distribution, the average number of properties per schema and the average number of properties used in a query.

The same applies to peer content. When a peer is created, we do not assign content to them but only schemas and/or schema properties which this peer is presumed to use for its content. For this assignment, the same schema and property distributions are taken into account as for the query generation. Additionally, the average number of schemas and properties (and deviation) used by a peer can be configured. When a query is received by a peer and matches its assigned schema elements, an abstract response is generated with a configurable probability.

For our network it makes no difference whether the queries originate at peers or directly at super-peers. The generated queries are distributed evenly to the super-peers input queues.

This approach allows to simulate the routing behavior without needing to generate huge amounts of test data.

Super Peer Based Topology. The simulation framework assumes a super-peer topology. All simple peers have exactly one connection to a super-peer. The super-peers form their own peer-to-peer network (it would be possible to simulate a conventional P2P network by instantiating the super-peer backbone only). The super-peer network topology and protocol is pluggable. For our first experiments we used only the HyperCuP topology.

In contrast to other simulations our approach doesn't rely on a TCP/IP network simulation, but models connections between peers on a higher level. Any connection has a bandwidth (specified by messages per second) and a delay (in msec). Both properties are modeled as normal distributions with configurable deviation. As we assume that SP/SP

---

[1] dc is used here as abbreviation for the Dublin Core metadata schema.

connections typically have a higher capacity than SP/P connections, these parameters can be set separately for these connection categories.

Because super-peers are assumed to be highly available, we don't model their up- and downtime, but simulate using a static backbone. This makes it very simple to create different super-peer topologies because it isn't necessary to implement a full connection/disconnection protocol. Instead, a topology class creates all super-peers and the connections between them on simulation startup. Of course, the implementation for the real network has to consider joining and leaving super-peers. But, as super-peer joins or failures will be rare, their influence on the network performance won't be significant.

In contrast, peers will join and leave the network frequently. We model this by a giving each peer a designated lifetime, which is assigned according to a configurable distribution.

Connections (Network Characteristics). All connections are bi-directional. Each peer (including super-peers) has an incoming message queue per connection, one processing queue and an outgoing message queue per connection. We can configure the time necessary to process a message and the number of processors available at a peer. Messages between the peers are modeled as discrete events.

3.2   Implementation

Our implementation is based on the discrete simulation framework SSF (Scalable Simulation Framework [5]). The Scalable Simulation Framework is an open standard of discrete event-simulations.

The general layer is responsible for establishing the super-peer topology and the connection between peers and super-peers. Instead of using an IP network simulation as foundation, connections are specified by only two parameters, bandwidth (in number of messages per second)[2] and latency (in milliseconds). For both parameters average and deviation can be specified.

The SSF provides an interface for discrete-event simulations supporting object-oriented models to utilize and extend the framework. Extended the framework by this the potential for direct reuse of model code is maximized, while the dependencies on a particular simulator kernel implementation are minimized. The framework's primary design goal was to support high performance simulations and to make models efficient.

The SSF provides several classes that we used to map the P2P-behavior to the mode. The *Entity* is the central class in SSF. Entities can have processes for event-processing. In our simulator the peers are implemented using entities. An *Event* changes the status of the system or is used for communication between entities. Regarding our simulator when use the events as messages between the peers. *Processes* are used to handle events during the simulation. An entity can have one or more processes. *In- and out-channels* are the communication channel between the entities. An entity can have several in- and out-channels, which are always connected 1:1.

---

[2] As our network is not concerned with transport of the content, only with content description, messages don't vary much in size.

The configuration of the simulator is very simple using three XML-files which define the topology, duration of the simulation, time to live (TTL) for messages, number of peer, etc.

4   First Simulation Results

The most interesting question for us was how clustering of the peers according to their schema influences the routing efficiency in the super-peer network. Therefore, for our first experiments we focused on this issue. We had the following hypotheses:

4.1   Hypotheses

1. Clustering peers at super-peers according to their schema will reduce query distribution effort significantly.
2. Clustering super-peers according to their schema (the schema of their peers) will furthermore reduce query distribution effort.

We didn't include a hypothesis about the influence of increasing the number of peers, because in our approach this can already be predicted. If the peers are clustered, then adding new peers will not change the query distribution within the super-peer network. As we currently distribute any query to any peer which uses the corresponding schema, the number of messages between super-peers and peers will grow linearly with the number of peers. See section 5 for proposals to improve this ratio.

4.2   Experiments

We compared three different approaches:

Peers and Super-Peers Randomly Distributed. In this case peers connect to super-peers in a random fashion, independently of the schema they use (see Fig. 1a) for an example). This scenario is abbreviated with U (unclustered).

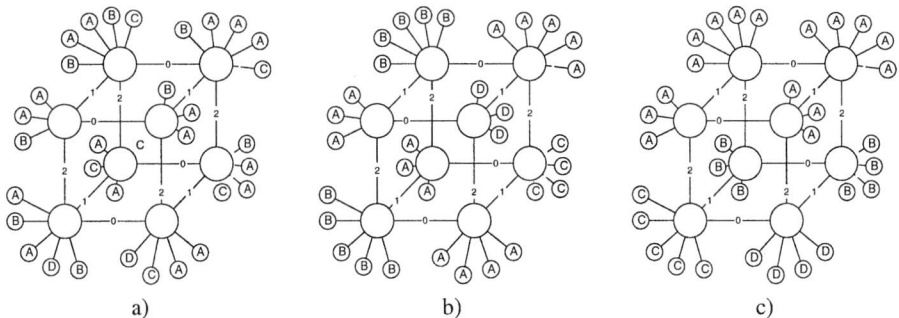

Fig. 1. Network examples with a) arbitrary peer distribution b) peers clustered by schema and c) peers and super-peers clustered

Peers Clustered, Super-Peers Randomly Distributed. Here the super-peers collect peers using the same schema. The super-peers are still placed in the hypercube at a random position, regardless of their peers schema information (Fig. 1b). We try to distribute the load evenly by assigning approximately the same number of peers to each super-peer. Therefore, for rare schemas super-peers will take the responsibility for several schemas. We use the short-hand P (peers clustered) for this scenario.

Peers and Super-Peers Clustered. In this variant we try to find optimal positions for super-peers in the hypercube as well, depending on the schema information. We have to optimize the hypercube for the most frequent schemas; a promising approach is sorting the schemas in hypercube dimensions according to their frequency. Dimension 0 is assigned to the most frequent schema, and therefore a query regarding this schema will be in the right partition of the hypercube after one hop. Queries regarding the second most frequent schema are in the right partition after two hops, etc. (see Fig. 1 c). In the following we refer to this scenario as SP/P (super-peers and peers clustered).

We simulated a network with 64 super-peers and 10000 peers. We estimate that such a network would suffice to connect a large percentage of all German university learning material providers. The number of schemas in use was set to 32 and a response probability of 5% was assumed. While our framework allows the usage of more fine grained schema elements, we chose to start with a simplified scenario, and to refine it step by step, guided by the results of the completed experiments.

For each scenario 1000 queries were distributed in the network. As the distribution algorithm doesn't depend on previously evaluated queries, the comparatively low number of queries is sufficient to avoid arbitrary results.

While our simulation framework is open to any kind of distribution of the schemas, schema properties, etc., we assume that the usage probability of the schemas follows a Zipf distribution (skew factor 0.1). Current research [9, 4] has shown that Zipf is the typical distribution in the internet context; this should apply to schema usage as well. The schema distribution is used to calculate the number of peers which use a specific schema to describe their content as well as the number of queries formulated using this schema.

4.3   Results

Figure 2 shows the sum of hops which were necessary to distribute the queries sorted by schema. For example, to distribute all queries regarding schema 0, we needed nearly 20.000 hops in scenario U, but only about 8500 in P. These results show that clustering peers at the super-peers has a substantial effect on query routing performance. The number of queries a super-peer has to handle on the average is reduced significantly. We can say that hypothesis 1 has been confirmed.

Arranging the super-peers in the hypercube according to their schemas has only a very small effect; hypothesis 2 has not been confirmed in this experiment. Assigning optimal positions to super-peers in a decentralized and efficient manner seems to be a very complex self-organizing task (especially if the hypercube has to perform a dimension increment or decrement). The first results at least indicate that clustering peers alone is a sufficient optimization.

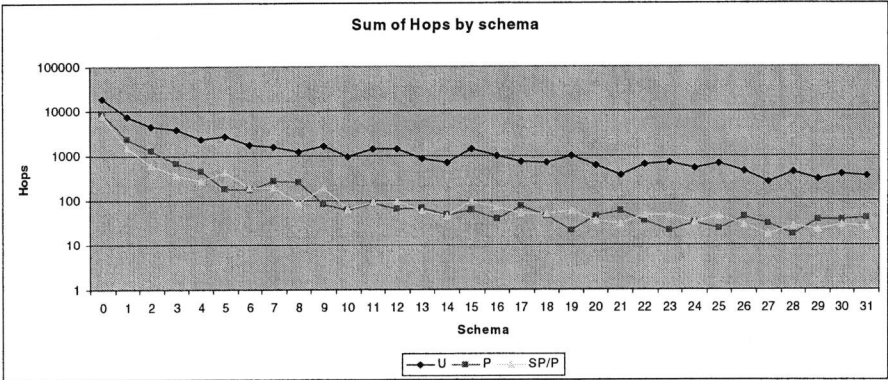

Fig. 2. Sum of super-peer hops needed to distribute queries

As we saw, clustering reduces the load of the network. However, this comes at a price regarding the load distribution, i.e. the number of queries a super peer has to handle. For scenarios P and SP this load is becomes distributed much more unevenly. The reason is that the clustered case super-peers responsible for the more frequent schemas bear a higher load, because they get more queries.

As scenario P turned out to be the most interesting, we varied the number of super-peers between 1 and 1024 to evaluate the influence of the backbone size. Fig. 3 shows the average load per super-peer for these different sizes. For example, in the case of the 4-node network, on average each super-query has to process a little more than 200 queries related to schema 0. In the (extreme) case of a 1-node 'network', the super-peer has to process all (273) queries related to schema 0. The average super-peer load is reduced when increasing the backbone size but the gain becomes insignificant for larger networks.

4.4 Consequences

Currently, a complete answer is retrieved for each query. This results in a linear increase of messages proportional to the increase of the number of peers. We are not able to compensate for this by enlarging the super-peer network.

Therefore, to reduce the amount of processing, we need to restrict the number of responding peers and/or super-peers. We see following options to achieve that goal:

- **Introduction of a Top-k Query Evaluation Approach.** The most promising technique to reduce the network load seems to restrict the number of responses. One approach would be to let each super-peer wait for responses from its own peers until it forwards the query. If sufficiently good responses can be retrieved, the query isn't further distributed. Otherwise, a result counter within the query is incremented by the number of matches found, and then the query is forwarded.
- **Result Caching.** Caching frequent matches and answering from the cache first could also result in a significant improvement. For example, [20] shows that load balancing

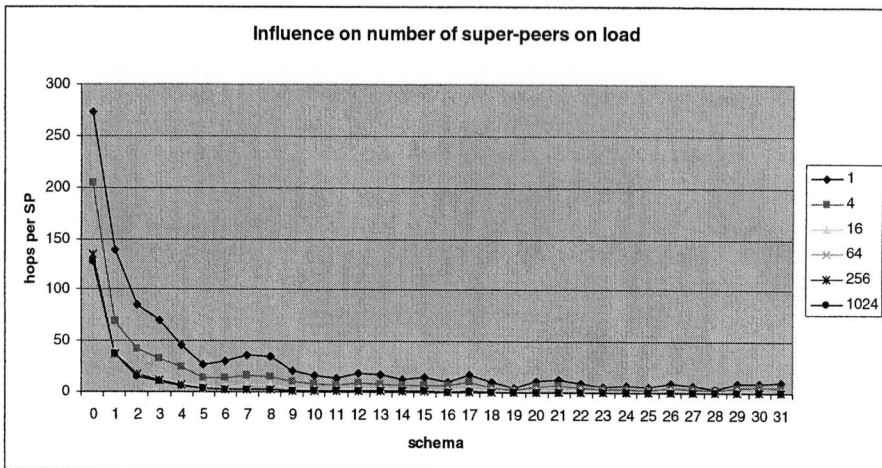

Fig. 3. Super-peer load in various network sizes

can be achieved by replicating content within a cluster of peers based on a fairness metric based on content popularity. Other approaches are described in [13] and [18].

– **Peer Preselection.** Super-peers could store statistics about the response rate for their peers and forward queries to the most promising peers first. The other peers would get the query only if the first step didn't produce sufficient results.

5   Conclusion and Further work

Current approaches don't support the simulation of schema-based P2P networks. We have collected a minimal set of requirements for the simulation of such networks and implemented a corresponding simulation framework.

We could confirm our hypothesis that schema-based clustering of peers at the super-peers improves the network performance significantly.

To get more detailed results, we will analyze the time-based measurements also, after having conducted some real-world experiments to calibrate the simulation parameters. We also plan to extend the simulator to support different response probability distributions, to model different amounts of content at peers. Our next scenarios will include peer and super-peer dynamics (up- and downtime, lifetime) as well. Additionally, we will use more fine-grained peer content and query descriptions.

This will result in an improved prediction of the behavior of our P2P networks.

References

1. Karl Aberer, Philippe Cudré-Mauroux, and Manfred Hauswirth. The chatty web: Emergent semantics through gossiping. In *Proceedings of WWW2003*, pages 197–206, New York, USA, May 2003. ACM Press.

2. M. Baker and T. Giuli. Narses: A scalable flow-based network simulator. Stanford University Technical Report, 2002.
3. P.A. Bernstein, F. Giunchiglia, A Kementsietsidis, J Mylopoulos, L. Serafini, I. Zaihrayeu. Data management for peer-to-peer computing: A vision. In *Proceedings of the Fifth International Workshop on the Web and Databases*, Madison, Wisconsin, June 2002.
4. Q. Chen. The origin of power laws in internet topologies revisited. In *21st Annual Joint Conference of the IEEE Computer and Communications Societies*, 2002.
5. James Cowie, Hongbo Liu, Jason Liu, David Nicol, and Andy Ogielski. Towards realistic million-node internet simulations. In *International Conference on Parallel and Distributed Processing Techniques and Applications*, Las Vegas, USA, Jun 1999.
6. Arturo Crespo and Hector Garcia-Molina. Routing indices for peer-to-peer systems. In *Proceedings International Conference on Distributed Computing Systems*, July 2002.
7. Arturo Crespo and Hector Garcia Molina. Semantic overlay networks for P2P systems. Technical report, Stanford University, 2003.
8. M. Ehrig, C. Schmitz, S. Staab, J. Tane, and C. Tempich. Towards evaluation of peer-to-peer-based distributed information management systems. In L. van Elst et al., editors, *Agent-mediated Knowledge Management - AMKM-2003, AAAI Spring Symposium 2003, Stanford University, March 24-26*, 2003.
9. Michalis Faloutsos, Petros Faloutsos, and Christos Faloutsos. On power-law relationships of the internet topology. *ACM SIGCOMM Computer Communication Review*, 29(4), 1999.
10. Alon Y. Halevy, Zachary G. Ives, Peter Mork, and Igor Tatarinov. Piazza: Data management infrastructure for semantic web applications. In *Proceedings of WWW2003*, Budapest, Hungary, May 2003.
11. Q. He, M. Ammar, G. Riley, H. Raj, R. Fujimoto. Mapping peer behavior to packet-level details: a framework for packet-level simulation of peer-to-peer systems. In *MASCOTS* 2003.
12. K. Kant and R. Iyer. Modeling and simulation of ad-hoc/p2p file-sharing networks. In *Tools 2003*, 2003.
13. Anirban Mondal, Kazuo Goda, and Masaru Kitsuregawa. Effective load-balancing via migration and replication in spatial grids. In *Proc. of the 14th Int. Conference on Database and Expert Systems Applications (DEXA 2003)*, Prague, Czech Republic, Sep 2003.
14. W. Nejdl, W. Siberski, and M. Sintek. Design issues and challenges for rdf- and schema-based peer-to-peer systems. *SIGMOD Records*, May 2003
15. W. Nejdl, B. Wolf, C. Qu, S. Decker, M. Sintek, A. Naeve, M. Nilsson, M. Palmér, and T. Risch. EDUTELLA: a P2P Networking Infrastructure based on RDF. In *Proceedings of WWW2002*, Hawaii, USA, May 2002.
16. Wolfgang Nejdl, Martin Wolpers, Wolf Siberski, Alexander Löser, Ingo Bruckhorst, Mario Schlosser, and Christoph Schmitz. Super-Peer-Based Routing and Clustering Strategies for RDF-Based Peer-To-Peer Networks. In *Proc. of WWW2003*, Budapest, Hungary, May 2003.
17. Mario Schlosser, Michael Sintek, Stefan Decker, and Wolfgang Nejdl. HyperCuP—Hypercubes, Ontologies and Efficient Search on P2P Networks. In *International Workshop on Agents and Peer-to-Peer Computing*, Bologna, Italy, July 2002.
18. Tyron Stading, Petros Maniatis, and Mary Baker. Peer-to-peer caching schemes to address flash crowds. In *Revised Papers from the First International Workshop on Peer-to-Peer Systems*. Springer-Verlag, 2002.
19. N. Ting and R. Deters. 3ls - a peer-to-peer network simulator. In *Third International Conference on Peer-to-Peer Computing*, 2003.
20. P. Triantafillou, C. Xiruhaki, M. Koubarakis, and N. Ntarmos. Towards high-performance peer-to-peer content and resource sharing systems. In *Proc. of the First Biennial Conference on Innovative Data Systems Research (CIDR 2003)*, Asilomar, CA, USA, Jan 2003.
21. Beverly Yang and Hector Garcia-Molina. Designing a super-peer network. In *Proceedings of ICDE2003*, March 2003.

A Distributed Algorithm for Robust Data Sharing and Updates in P2P Database Networks

Enrico Franconi[1], Gabriel Kuper[2], Andrei Lopatenko[1,3], and Ilya Zaihrayeu[2]

[1] Free University of Bozen–Bolzano, Faculty of Computer Science, Italy
franconi@inf.unibz.it, alopatenko@unibz.it
[2] University of Trento, DIT, Italy
kuper@acm.org, ilya@dit.unitn.it
[3] University of Manchester, Department of Computer Science, UK

Abstract. In this paper we thoroughly analyze a distributed procedure for the problem of local database update in a network of database peers, useful for data exchange scenarios. The algorithm supports dynamic networks: even if nodes and coordination rules appear or disappear during the computation, the proposed algorithm will eventually terminate with a sound and complete result.

1 Introduction

In the paper [5] we introduced a general logical and computational characterization of peer-to-peer (P2P) database systems. We first defined a precise model-theoretic semantics of a P2P system, which allows for local inconsistency handling. We then characterized the general computational properties for the problem of answering queries to such a P2P system. Finally, we devised tight complexity bounds and distributed procedures in few relevant special cases. The basic principles of the characterization given in [5] are: (a) the role of the coordination formulas between nodes is for data migration (as opposed to the role of logical constraints in classical data integration systems); (b) computation is delegated to single nodes (local computation); (c) the topology of the network may dynamically change; (d) local inconsistency does not propagate; (e) computational complexity can be low.

In this paper we thoroughly analyze a *distributed procedure* for the problem of local database update in a network of database peers, as defined in [5]. The problem of *local database update* is different from the problem of query answering. Given a P2P database system, the answer to a local query may involve data that is distributed in the network, thus requiring the participation of all nodes at query time to propagate in the direction of the query node the relevant data for the answer, taking into account the (possibly cyclic) coordination rules bridging the nodes. On the other hand, given a P2P database system, a "batch" update algorithm will be such that all the nodes consistently and optimally propagate all the relevant data to their neighbors, allowing for subsequent local queries to be answered locally within a node, without fetching data from other nodes at query time. The update problem has been considered important by the P2P literature; most

This work has been partially supported by the EU projects Sewasie, KnowledgeWeb, and Interop.

W. Lindner et al. (Eds.): EDBT 2004 Workshops, LNCS 3268, pp. 446–455, 2004.

notably, recent papers focused on the importance of *data exchange* and *materialization* for a P2P network [3,4].

Relevant work in semantically well founded P2P systems includes [6], which describes an algorithm for acyclic P2P systems using classical (first-order logic) semantics. The acyclic case is relatively simple – a query is propagated through the network until it reaches the leaves of the network. The work in [2] uses a notion of semantics similar to the semantics introduced in [5], but it describes only a global algorithm, that assumes a central node where all computation is performed. The paper [9] describes a local algorithm to compute query answers, but it does not allow for existential variables in the head of the coordination rules. The algorithm we present in this paper supports such variables, in a similar fashion to the global algorithm of [2].

The algorithm presented in this paper supports *dynamic* networks: even if nodes and coordination rules appear or disappear during the computation, the proposed algorithm will eventually terminate with a sound and complete result (under appropriate definitions of the latter). In addition, our algorithm is based on an asynchronous model of communications (while also supporting a synchronous alternative), which means that answering a query, and reaching the fix-point, may be faster at expense of an increase of the number of messages in the network.

2   P2P Database Systems

Our P2P framework is based on the logical model of [5].

Definition 1 (Local Database). *Let I be a nonempty finite set of indexes $\{1, 2, \ldots, n\}$, and C be a set of constants. For each pair of distinct $i, j \in I$, let L_i be a first-order logic without function symbols, with signature disjoint from L_j but for the shared constants C. A local database DB_i is a theory on the first order language L_i.*

Nodes are interconnected by means of coordination rules. A coordination rule allows a node i to fetch data from its neighbor nodes $j_1, \ldots, j_m$.

Definition 2 (Coordination Rule). *A coordination rule is an expression of the form*

$$j_1 : b_1(\mathbf{x}_1, \mathbf{y}_1) \wedge \cdots \wedge j_k : b_k(\mathbf{x}_k, \mathbf{y}_k) \Rightarrow i : h(\mathbf{x})$$

where $j_1, \ldots, j_k$, i are distinct indices, each $b_l(\mathbf{x}_l, \mathbf{y}_l)$ is a formula of L_{j_l}, and $h(\mathbf{x})$ is a formula of L_i, and $\mathbf{x} = \mathbf{x}_1 \cup \cdots \cup \mathbf{x}_k$.

Note that we are making the simplifying assumption that the equal constants mentioned in the various nodes refer to equal objects, i.e., that they play the role of URIs (Uniform Resource Identifiers). Other approaches consider *domain relations* to map objects between different nodes [10], and we plan to consider such extensions in future work.

A P2P system is just the collection of nodes interconnected by the rules.

Definition 3 (P2P System). *A peer-to-peer (P2P) system is a tuple of the form $MDB = \langle LDB, CR \rangle$, where $LDB = \{DB_1, \cdots, DB_n\}$ is the set of local databases, and CR is the set of coordination rules.*

A user accesses the information hold by a P2P system by formulating a query at a specific node.

Definition 4 (Query). *A* local query *is a first order formula in the language of one of the local databases* DB_i.

The semantics of a P2P system and of queries is defined in [5]. In this paper, we assume that all nodes are relational databases; coordination rules may contain conjunctive queries in both the head and body (without any safety assumption and possibly with built-in predicates). Under these assumptions computing of answers is reducible to data fetching [2,5].

To describe the P2P networks we introduce the notion of a *dependency edge* between nodes of a P2P network.

Definition 5. *There is a* dependency edge *from a node i to node j, if there is a coordination rule with head at node i and body at node j.*

Note that the direction of a dependency edges is the opposite to that of the rules. The direction of a rule is the direction in which data is transfered, whereas the dependency edge has the opposite orientation. In this paper we use $\mathcal{MDB}$ to denote a P2P system, using terms such as *P2P system* or *a network*; please note that we consider the general case when the network is *cyclic*. $\mathcal{I}$ is used to denote a set of all nodes in given $\mathcal{MDB}$, $\mathcal{C}$ denotes the set of all coordination rules, and $\mathcal{L}$ the set dependency edges between nodes in a network derived from $\mathcal{C}$. Subsets of $\mathcal{I}$ are denoted by $\mathcal{A}$. We assume that $\mathcal{I}$, $\mathcal{L}$, and $\mathcal{C}$ are always finite sets.

Definition 6. *A dependency path for a node i is a path* $\langle i_1, i_2, \ldots, i_n \rangle$ *of dependency edges, such that 1)* $i_1 = i$*; 2)* $\langle i_1, \ldots, i_{n-1} \rangle$ *is a simple path (no one node met twice).*

$A : a(X,Y)$

$B : b(X,Y)$

$C : c(X,Y), f(X)$

$D : d(X,Y)$

$E : e(X,Y)$

$r1 : E : e(X,Y) \rightarrow B : b(X,Y)$

$r2 : B : b(X,Y), b(Y), Z \rightarrow C : c(X,Z)$

$r3 : C : c(X,Y), c(Y,Z) \rightarrow B : b(X,Z)$

$r4 : B : b(X,Y), b(X,Z), X \neq Z \rightarrow A : a(X,Y)$

$r5 : A : a(X,Y) \rightarrow C : f(X)$

$r6 : A : a(X,Y) \rightarrow D : d(Y,X)$

$r7 : D : D(X,Y), D(Y,Z) \rightarrow C : c(X,Y)$

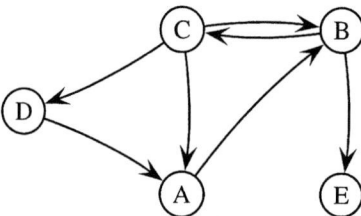

#	path	#	path	#	path	#	path
A	ABCA	B	BE	C	BE	D	ABE
A	ABE	B	BCAB	C	BC	D	ABCD
A	ABCB	B	BCB	C	DABC	D	ABCB
A	ABDA	B	BCDAB	C	ABC	D	ABCA
				C	ABE		

Fig. 1. A sample schema of a P2P system, together with its dependency edges and the maximal dependency paths

Definition 7. *A maximal dependency path for a node i is a dependency path such that if we add any node to the path, the result will not be a dependency path. In this paper, when we describe dependency paths for a node i, we omit the first node (i).*

As an example of a P2P system with its dependency paths, consider Figure 1.

3   The Distributed Update Algorithm

The problem we want to solve is to propagate to all nodes all the information which is distributed among all the databases, so that queries can be answered locally. The main idea behind the distributed update algorithm is that nodes update their local databases by importing data from their neighbors (called acquaintances) using the definitions of coordination rules w.r.t. these neighbors. The global update procedure is started by some super-node, which sends global update requests to its acquaintances, these acquaintances propagate these requests to their acquaintances, and so on. The work of the algorithm seems easy until we have loops in the dependency paths. In this case, query results from some node can go through a chain of nodes and return to the given node. In order to avoid infinite loops in propagation of already computed data in the system, node N stops propagating of some result set R iff a) N is contained in the path R has passed through, and b) there is no new data in R for N. In this case we will say that node N reaches a fix-point. This procedure can be proved to be sound and complete with respect the semantics presented in [5]. The algorithm presented here does not present possible optimization; these exploit the knowledge of specific topological structures, and allow for more fine grained queries to acquaintances and answer from acquaintances (delta optimization) in order to minimize data transfer and duplication.

It is assumed that when a node joins the P2P network it knows only its acquaintances. Therefore, the first step of the algorithm is to let each node know the network topology. Each node first looks for the set of its maximal dependency paths (Topology discovery algorithm). At the end of this first phase, all nodes are aware of the relevant part of the network topology - i.e., each node will know about all the maximal dependency paths starting from it; in the P2P literature [7] it is assumed reasonable if a node is aware of $log(n)$ 'neighbor' nodes, where n is a size of network. The topology discovery is initiated by a "super-peer", which should be selected to optimize the distribution of messages during discovery time; a super-peer do not have any other property differentiating it from other nodes. It is possible that the topology changes while the discovery process is ongoing; in Section 4 we analyze this case.

The algorithm for the actual database update is the same as the one for the topology discovery, with two main differences: (1) in the discovery phase the topology discovery algorithm stops when a node is reached twice, while the update algorithm has to continue the computation until a fix-point is reached; and (2) the discovery algorithm does not perform actual database queries and propagation. Both phases of the algorithm are executed asynchronously in parallel; we use the notation NAME_OF_FUNCTION$_i$ to mean the execution of that function at node i. In Figure 2 you can see a sample execution of the algorithm for our example P2P system.

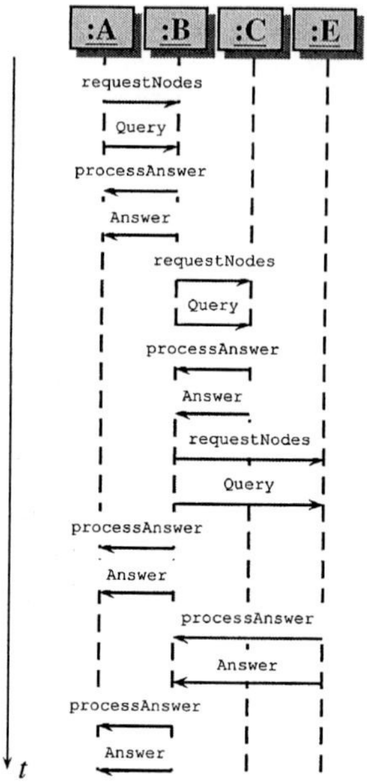

Fig. 2. A sample execution of the discovery and update algorithm

Each node is given the following data structure:

– *state_d*, a variable that describes the state of knowledge about the network. It can have the value **discovery**, that means that the discovery process is undergoing and the knowledge is incomplete, or **closed**, when the knowledge about the network is complete. Initially it is undefined.
– *state_u*, a variable that describes the status of the data at a node. It has the value **open** when the node has no complete data, or **closed** when the node has reached the fix-point.
– *finished*, a boolean variable indicating that the network discovery through the node is finished.
– *Rules(rule, node, flag)*, a relation that describes the set of coordination rules which have the node as target. The attributes of this relation are *rule*, the id of a rule, *node*, the id of the source node for that rule, and a *flag* (see the algorithm). We assume that initially each node knows all rules of which it is a target.
– *Paths(path, flag, closed)*, a relation that describes the maximal dependency paths for the node. Its attributes are: *path*, a string that represents the path, and *flag*, *closed* (see the algorithm). We assume that initially the relation is empty.
– *Edges(source, target)*, a relation that describes all dependency relations in the part of the network reachable from the node.
– *ID* is the identifier of the node, assumed to be unique in the network.
– *owner*, an array which contains pairs of node IDs, the first being a node ID on behalf of which the node is searching for data, and the second being the node ID which sent the request.

In the algorithm we use the function **id(rule)** to take the ID of a rule's ID and return the ID of the source node of the rule.

A1: Network Topology Discovery

The algorithm is executed by the 'super-peer' which starts the process of network discovery. All the other nodes will only run the QUERY and PROCESSANSWER algorithms when they are requested.

DISCOVER($Rules, ID$)
  if $|Rules| == 0$
        $state_d = closed$; $Paths = \emptyset$; **return**
    if $state_d == \perp$
      $state_d = discovery$
      foreach $r \in Rules$
          REQUESTNODES$_{id(r)}$(ID, ID)
      $owner = owner \cup \langle \emptyset, ID \rangle$

A2: Topology Discovery: Process Request

Process the request sent by another node; ID_s is an ID of the node sending request, ID_o is the ID of the node on behalf of which the request is sent.

REQUESTNODES(ID_s, ID_o)
  if $Rules == \emptyset$
        $state_d = closed$; $finished = true$
    if $ID_o \notin \pi_2(owner)$
      foreach $r \in Rules$
          REQUESTNODES$_{id(r)}$(ID, ID_o)
    else
        $finished = true$
        $owner = owner \cup \langle ID_s, ID_o \rangle$
        PROCESSANSWER$_{ID_s}$($ID_o, Edges \cup \langle ID, ID_s \rangle, state_d$, finished)

A3: Topology Discovery: Process the Answer from Another Node

ID_o is a ID of a node on behalf of which discovery is done, *set* is a set of answers (dependency edges between nodes), and *state* is the answer completeness status, *status* is an indicator that discovery in a given branch is finished, **me** is an ID of the rule to which the current answer relates.

PROCESSANSWER($ID_o, set, state, status$)
  $Edges = Edges \cup set$
  if $state ==$ **closed**
      $update\ Rules\ set\ flag = true\ where\ rule = me$
    if $status ==$ **true**
        $update\ Rules\ set\ closed = true\ where\ rule = me$
      if $\forall Rules flag == true$
        $state_d = closed$
        if $\forall Rules finished == true$
          $finished = true$
          if $ID == ID_o$

$$\textbf{if } \forall Rules\, finished == true$$
$$stated_d = closed$$
foreach (
$$\langle ID_s, ID_o \rangle \in owner)$$
$$\textsc{ProcessAnswer}_{ID_s}(ID_o, Edges, state_d, \textbf{finished})$$

A4: Database Update: Process Query Sent by Another Node

ID_s is the ID of the node which did send the request, Q is a query (the head of the coordination formula), SN is a sequence of nodes' IDs describing a path for the query evaluation.

$$\textsc{Query}(ID_s, Q, SN)$$
$$QA = \text{Compute-local-answer}(Q)$$
$$Answer_{ID_s}(ID, QA, ID + SN, state_u)$$
$$owner = owner \cup ID_s, first(SN)$$
$$\textbf{if } state_u == open \land ID \notin SN$$
$$\quad \textbf{foreach } r \in Rules$$
$$\qquad Query_{id(r)}(ID, Query(r), ID + SN)$$

A5: Database Update: Process the Answer Sent by Another Node

ID is an ID of the node which sent the answer, QA is the answer as a set of tuples, SN is a sequence of nodes' IDs, state is a flag indicating if the answer is complete.

$$\textsc{Answer}(ID, QA, SN, state)$$
$$update = \textsc{UpdateLocalData}(rule, QA)$$
$$\textbf{if } state == complete$$
$$\quad \text{update Rules set flag} = true \text{ where rule} = rule(Q)$$
$$\quad \textbf{if } update = \emptyset$$
$$\qquad \text{update Paths set flag} = true \text{ where path} = SN$$
$$\quad \textbf{if } update \neq \emptyset$$
$$\qquad \text{update Paths set flag} = false \text{ where path} = SN$$
$$\qquad \textbf{if } \forall t \in Rules \pi_{flag}(t) == true$$
$$\qquad\quad state_u = closed$$
$$\qquad\quad \textbf{if } \forall t \in Paths \pi_{flag}(t) == true$$
$$\qquad\qquad state_u = closed$$
$$\qquad\qquad \textbf{foreach } node \in \pi_1(owner_u)$$
$$\qquad\qquad\quad QA = \text{ComputeAnswer}()$$
$$\qquad\qquad\quad Answer_{node}(ID, QA, SN, state_u)$$

A6: Database Update: Local Update Algorithm

Updates the database to make it consistent with the view extensions (i.e., the rules) and the original content. Rule is the identifier of a rule, QA is a set of tuples.

$$\textsc{UpdateLocalData}(rule, QA)$$
if (
$$QA \not\equiv \emptyset)$$
$$\quad \textbf{foreach } ($$
$$\qquad tuple\ t \in QA) \textbf{ foreach } ($$
$$\qquad\quad relation\ R \in definition(View_{rule}))$$
$$\qquad\qquad \textbf{if } \pi_R(t)\neg \in R$$
$$\qquad\qquad\quad \text{insert } (\pi_R(t)) \text{ into R with new values for existential}$$

The following theorem states the correctness of the proposed update algorithm, and its complexity.

Theorem 1. *1. (Soundness and completeness) A node reaches the state closed iff the algorithm has reached the fix-point at this node;*
2. *(Termination) Every node of the network eventually reaches the state closed;*
3. *(Complexity) The complexity of the algorithm database update at each node is 2EXPTIME in the number of nodes.*

4   Dynamic Behavior of the P2P Network

One of the distinctive characteristics of P2P systems is that the network can vary dynamically. Assume that the network $\mathcal{MDB}$ consist initially of a set of nodes $\mathcal{J}$, and that $\mathcal{C}$ is an initial set of coordination rules with $\mathcal{L}$ being the initial set of dependency edges. We model network dynamicity by adding/removing coordination rules between nodes, and therefore deletion of a node is modeled by deleting all coordination rules that relate to this node. With respect to query answering adding/removing nodes with coordination rules is easily seen to be equivalent to the assumption that all nodes are present from the start, and that only coordination rules are changed.

We define an atomic network change operation as follows.

- *addLink(i,j,rule,id)*: add the coordination rule *rule* from node *j* (the body) to node *i* (the head). *id* is the name of a rule, which should be unique for a given pair of nodes.
- *deleteLink(i,j,id)*: delete the coordination rule *id* between nodes *i* and *j*

Definition 8. *1. A change U of a network $\mathcal{MDB}$ is a sequence of atomic change operations over $\mathcal{MDB}$.*
2. *A finite change of a network is a finite sequence of atomic changes.*
3. *An initial subchange U_1 of a change U is a initial prefix of U*
4. *A subchange U_A of U in respect to $A \subset \mathcal{J}$ is a set of atomic operations of U, relevant to A and ordered with the same order as in U*

We assume that in the case of atomic change the network will be notified about the change in the following cases:

1. in case of *addLink(i,j,rule,id)*, the node *i* (which will be able to fetch data by this rule) gets a notification; *addRule(i, j, rule, id)*
2. in case of *deleteLink(i,j,id)*, the node *i* (which will be unable to feth data by this rule) gets a notification. *deleteRule(i, j, id)*

Definition 9. *1. A sound answer of a query Q in a network subject to runtime changes, is an answer to the query that is included in the result that we would obtain if we executed all the addLink statements before running Q, and did not execute the deleteLink statements at all.*

2. *A* complete answer *of a query Q in a network subject to runtime changes, is an answer to the query that contains the result that we would obtain if we executed all the deleteLink statements before running Q, and did not execute the addLink statements at all.*

The basic idea behind this definition is that we cannot know in advance what the state of the database will be at termination time. Therefore, in the definition we require that a sound and/or complete answer will be classically sound and/or complete with respect to the part of the database that is *unchanged*. The result with respect to the part that is changed will depend on the order and timing of the execution of the changes. In this sense, the answer to a query in a network subject to "small" changes will be still meaningful with respect to the majority of the data that resides in the stable parts of the network. The following theorem states that our update algorithm behaves well with respect to change.

Theorem 2. *1. (Soundness and completeness) For a finite change of a network, the update algorithm will terminate, and it gives sound and complete answers to queries in the network subject to runtime changes.*
2. (Termination) In the case of an infinite change to the network, the update algorithm may not terminate.
3. (Complexity) For a finite runtime change of the network, the complexity of the update algorithm at each node is in 2EXPTIME with respect to the size of the change.

5   Implementation

We implement database peers on top of *JXTA* [8]. JXTA specifies a set of protocols which provide implementation of basic, as well as rather sophisticated P2P functionalities.

The first level logical architecture of a node, inspired by [1], is presented on Figure 3. A node consists of *P2P Layer*, *Local Database* (LDB) and *Database Schema* (DBS). DBS describes part of LDB, which is shared for other nodes. The P2P Layer consists of *User Interface* (UI), *Database Manager* (DBM), *JXTA Layer* and *Wrapper*. Nodes

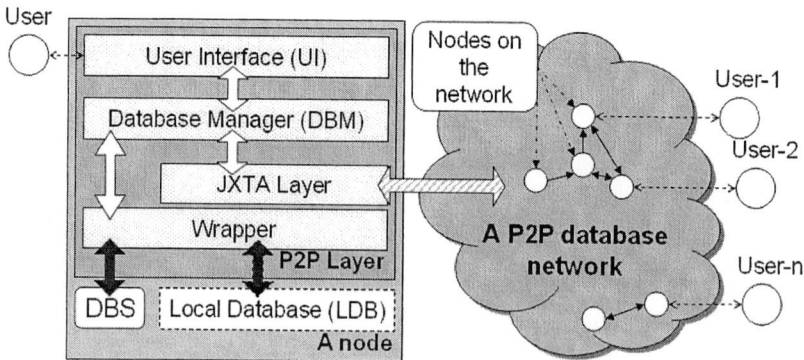

Fig. 3. First level architecture

connect to a P2P database network by means of connecting to other peer(s), as it is schematically shown on Figure 3 (see the arrow from JXTA Layer to the network and arrows between nodes in the network).

Current version of the prototype supports both global and query-dependent updates handling, distributed query answering, and implements the topology discovery algorithm. When a node starts, it creates pipes with those nodes, w.r.t. which it has coordination rules, or which have coordination rules w.r.t. the given node. Several coordination rules w.r.t. a given node can use one pipe to send requests and data. If some coordination rules are dropped and a pipe becomes unassigned a coordination rule, then this pipe is also closed.

Preliminary experiments were done to measure the scalability of our approach with respect to a size of the P2P network. We are currently organizing more precise experiments.

Up to 31 nodes participated to the preliminary experiments. The local relational databases are based on DBLP data (http://dblp.uni-trier.de/xml) and contained about 20000 records about publications (about 1000 per node), organised in 3 different relational schemas. We considered two different data distributions. In the first one there is no intersection between initial data in neighbor nodes. In the second, there is 50% probability of intersection between initial data in nodes linked by coordination rules; the intersection between data in other nodes is empty. Three types of topologies have been considered: trees, *layered* acyclic graphs, and cliques.

By looking at the execution time and the number of messages exchanged between nodes, the preliminary experiments confirmed the expectation that in the simple topological structures (like the tree and the layered acyclic graphs) the execution time is linear with respect to the depth of the structure.

References

1. P. Bernstein, F. Giunchiglia, A. Kementsietsidis, J. Mylopoulos, L. Serafini, and I. Zaihrayeu. Data management for peer-to-peer computing: A vision. *WebDB'02*, 2002.
2. D. Calvanese, E. Damaggio, G. De Giacomo, M. Lenzerini, and R. Rosati. Semantic data integration in p2p systems. In *International Workshop On Databases, Information Systems and Peer-to-Peer Computing (DBISP2P'03)*, 2003.
3. N. Daswani, H. Garcia-Molina, and B. Yang. Open problems in data-sharing peer-to-peer systems. In *ICDT'03*, 2003.
4. R. Fagin, P. G. Kolaitis, R. J. Miller, and L. Popa. Data exchange: Semantics and query answering. In *ICDT'03*, pages 207–224, 2003.
5. Enrico Franconi, Gabriel Kuper, A. Lopatenko, and L. Serafini. A robust logical and computational characterisation of peer-to-peer database systems. In *International Workshop On Databases, Information Systems and Peer-to-Peer Computing (DBISP2P'03)*, 2003.
6. A. Y. Halevy, Z. G. Ives, D. Suciu, and I. Tatarinov. Schema mediation in peer data management systems. In *ICDE'03*, 2003.
7. J. M. Hellerstein. Toward network data independence. *SIGMOD Rec.*, 32(3):34–40, 2003.
8. Project JXTA, 2004. See http://www.jxta.org.
9. L. Serafini and C. Ghidini. Using wrapper agents to answer queries in distributed information systems. In *Int. Conf. on Advances in Information Systems (ADVIS-2000)*, 2000.
10. L. Serafini, F. Giunchiglia, J. Mylopoulos, and P. A. Bernstein. Local relational model: A logical formalization of database coordination. In *CONTEXT'03*, pages 286–299, 2003.

XPeer: A Self-Organizing XML P2P Database System*

Carlo Sartiani, Paolo Manghi, Giorgio Ghelli, and Giovanni Conforti

Dipartimento di Informatica – Università di Pisa,
Via F. Buonarroti 2, 56127 Pisa, Italy
{sartiani,manghi,ghelli,confor}@di.unipi.it

Abstract. This paper describes XPeer, a *zero-administration* system for sharing and querying XML data. The system allows users to share XML data without significant human intervention, and to pose XQuery FLWR queries against them. The proposed system can be used in any application field, being a general purpose XML p2p DBMS, even though its main application is the management of resource descriptions in *GRID* environments.

1 Introduction

The last few years have seen the emerging of the *peer-to-peer* (p2p) computational paradigm. Systems conforming to this paradigm appear as *open-ended* and dynamic networks of peers willing to share computational resources, ranging from CPU cycles to local data, and even to algorithms (for instance, knowledge discovery algorithms).

The p2p paradigm was recently adopted in the database community to overcome the limitations of distributed database systems, namely the static topology and the heavy administration work, and to exploit the dissemination of data sources over the Internet.

One key factor in the success of p2p systems, mostly in the field of content sharing, is their easy administration. On the contrary, existing distributed database systems require heavy administration efforts, both in the design phase and at run-time: indeed, these systems are based on the presence of global and local schemas, together with their mappings, whose definition and maintenance are a duty of the DBA. Nevertheless, existing p2p systems for XML databases still require significant administration tasks: in Piazza [6], for instance, human intervention is still necessary for defining schema mappings between peers, which implies significant efforts for the DBA, and decreases the dynamicity of the system.

Our Contribution. This paper describes a *zero-administration* p2p system for sharing and querying XML data (XPeer). The system allows users to share XML data and to pose XQuery FLWR queries against them without any significant human intervention (the user still has to write her own queries). The system, based on a hybrid p2p architecture, *self-organizes* its superpeer network, and allows for arbitrary changes in the network topology.

---

* This work was partly funded by the FIRB GRID.IT project.

W. Lindner et al. (Eds.): EDBT 2004 Workshops, LNCS 3268, pp. 456–465, 2004.

Paper Outline The paper is organized as follows. Section 2 describes some important issues that emerge in the management of p2p XML databases. Section 3, then, presents an overview of the system, while Section 4 illustrates the system architecture in more detail. Section 5, next, outlines the techniques used in XPeer for processing queries. Section 6 discusses some related works. In Section 7, finally, we draw our conclusions and describe some future work.

2   Issues in P2P XML Data Management

The problem of managing p2p XML databases is quite complex. The source of most issues is the dynamic nature of these systems, where both data and topology may suddenly change. Hence, a closer look at these aspects is necessary.

Changing Topology. Peer-to-peer systems are usually described as *open-ended* networks of peers willing to share resources. Peers are autonomous, in the sense that they are free to choose the data to contribute to the system, to manage local data without external constraints, and to connect and disconnect at any time. As a consequence, the system is formed by a collection of nodes $S = \{p_1, \ldots, p_n\}$ that can evolve over time. Topology changes mostly affect the indexing structures used for routing queries. For instance, if a node p_i containing data (let's say a set of XML nodes s) relevant for a query q suddenly becomes unreachable, then any index entry associating p_i to s should be updated to avoid unnecessary messages, or, in the worst case, *run-time* problems.

Local Updates. Peer autonomy implies that peers have the right to update their data, even if shared, at any time. In particular, peers can perform both *value* and *schema* changing updates (unlike in relational databases, the loose structure of XML data blurs the distinction between value and schema updates).

Value and schema updates influence query mediation and query routing since sudden data changes may invalidate existing query plans or routing structures, hence imposing potentially expensive updates of distributed index structures. Moreover, most *schema-driven* data management approaches (see [6]) are severely affected by local updates, hence requiring human intervention for adapting the system to the new data.

3   XPeer Overview

XPeer is an XML p2p database system, which manages data dispersed over an *open-ended* network of autonomous peers. In XPeer no constraints are imposed over exported data, i.e., a peer may export whatever kind of data, provided that data are encoded in the XML format, and described by a schema, and it may freely update its local data; moreover, nodes can join and leave the system at any time, so the system has a dynamic topology. Exported data are integrated in a *blind* way, i.e., no *global schema* is defined: this solution allows for a significant decrease in the administration load of the system. Of course, this fundamental choice restricts the applicability of the approach to situations where schema mapping can be avoided, or can be performed out of the p2p system (i.e., by a local schema adapter). We believe the choice is perfectly reasonable in the application field we are targeting first (resource description).

XPeer adopts a hybrid p2p architecture [14], where peer nodes may also perform administrative tasks. System nodes, hence, may act both as peers and as *superpeers*.

XPeer is a general purpose XML p2p database system, so it can be used in any application field. Still, its main application is the management of resource descriptions in a *GRID-like* environment: in particular, XPeer should form the basic infrastructure for extending (and, eventually, replacing) the *LDAP-based* resource discovery layer of existing GRID systems.

3.1   Data Model and Query Language

Data in the system are represented as in most XML database systems, i.e., as unordered forests of node-labeled trees. Each tree is augmented with the indication of the hosting peer (*location* in the following) as well as with a freshness parameter fr, which indicates when the last update on the tree was performed ($\perp$ indicates that the freshness is undefined, and it is necessary to ensure that the model is closed). To support freshness parameters, the data model has a universal constant τ, which denotes the current global time in the system: since query results are assumed to be incomplete, the assumption of the existence of a global time is feasible.

The query language of choice is the FLWR subset of XQuery [3] without universally quantified predicates and sorting operations (the orderby clause). The choice of the FLWR core of XQuery distinguishes XPeer from most existing p2p systems, which are limited to simple *key-lookup* queries, or to linear path queries, and which require significant modifications to support *full* database queries [7].

4   XPeer Architecture

XPeer is a *hybrid* p2p system composed by a dynamic set $S = \{p_1, \ldots, p_n\}$ of autonomous peers, which share data and execute global queries on the database. Some nodes in S (in most cases, those with adequate computational power and/or network bandwidth) perform administration tasks too: these nodes, called *superpeers*, form a set $SP \subseteq S$. Peers become superpeers on a voluntary basis, and retain their peer role. We favor a hybrid p2p architecture wrt a hierarchical one (e.g., the GRID GRIS/GIIS system) since it offers more robustness to failures and it can adapt more easily to network changes.

4.1   Peer Network

Peers share XML data and execute queries on top of these data. Peers export a description of the data being shared in the form of a tree-shaped DataGuide [5], called *tree-guide*, which is automatically inferred from the data by means of a tree search algorithm. Leaf nodes in the schema are endowed with statistical information about value ranges, to allow the system to better identify relevant data sources during query compilation. The following Example shows a sample XML document and its tree-guide.

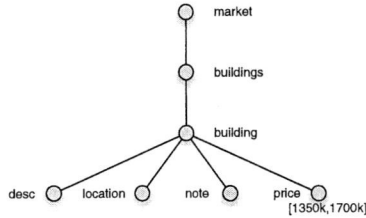

Fig. 1. A sample tree-guide

Example 1. Consider the following document, hosted by a peer p_1, describing buildings in a real-estate market database.

```
<market>
    <buildings>
        <building>
            <desc> Marvelous luxury house in the Hamptons </desc>
            <location> Hamptons </location>
            <price> 1600000 </price>
        </building>
        <building>
            <desc> Very nice flat in the Upper East Side </desc>
            <location> Upper East Side, Manhattan </location>
            <price> 1350000 </price>
            <type> comdo </type>
        </building>
        <building>
            <desc> Elegant luxury house in the countryside </desc>
            <location> Greensboro </location>
            <price> 1700000 </price>
        </building>
    </buildings>
</market>
```

The corresponding tree-guide contains each distinct path in the document, endowed with statistical information about value ranges (e.g., the range $1350000 - 1700000$ for price elements), as shown in Figure 1.

Peers are logically organized into clusters of nodes, where each cluster contains one superpeer, which is in charge with the management of the cluster: the compilation of user queries and the management of peer information. Peer clustering allows the system to decrease the efforts required for compiling queries. To this aim, clusters are formed, whenever it is possible, on a *schema-similarity* basis, i.e., peers exporting data with similar schemas are clustered together (the system still works even if nodes in the same cluster have very different schemas).

Inside any cluster, some peer may (partially or totally) replicate the content of other peers in the cluster. Replicas are built to balance the workload in the cluster and to exploit peers with huge computational resources, and are valid up to a given time. The replication process, as many other processes in XPeer, happens on a voluntary basis.

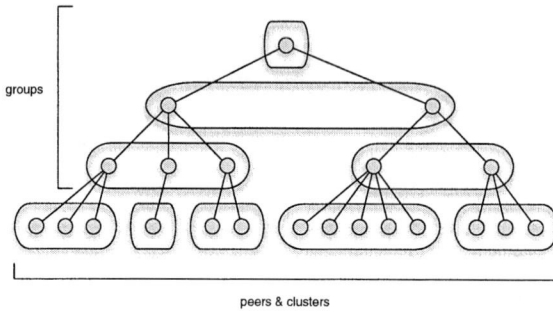

Fig. 2. Overall logical system architecture

4.2 SuperPeer Network

Superpeers have the duties of tracking topology changes, managing schema information, and compiling user queries. Superpeers are organized to form a tree, where each node hosts schema information about its children; superpeers having the same father form a *group* (which is very close to a peer cluster). The resulting logical topology is shown in Figure 2.

Superpeers host two kinds of schema information about their children: the list of the schemas of their children (the *schema list*); and the union of these schemas (the *superpeer schema*). The schema list is used during query compilation for identifying relevant data sources, or superpeers whose descendants can contain relevant data; the superpeer schema, instead, is passed to the father as schema of the superpeer, and it is built without any schema integration activity, so that no human assistance is required. Since tree-guides may have, in the worst case, the same size as the documents they are representing, the schema of the root superpeer may have, in the worst scenario, the same dimension as the whole p2p database. However, as shown in [5], this may happen only when a) each local database is formed by non-overlapping rooted paths, and b) there are no local databases having some common rooted path; this scenario is so infrequent that we can safely use tree-guides as document schemas. The following Example shows a sample superpeer schema.

Example 2. Consider the following XML document, hosted by a peer p_2, describing seller information in the real-estate market.

```
<market>
   <sellers>
      <seller>
         <name> Patrick Bateman </name>
         <address> 25, Park Avenue </address>
         <phone> ... </phone>
      </seller>
      <seller>  <name> Tim Price </name> </seller>
   </sellers>
</market>
```

This document can be represented by the tree-guide shown in Figure 3(a). Assuming that both peers p_1 (see Example 1) and p_2 have the same superpeer sp, then the superpeer schema of sp is depicted in Figure 3(b).

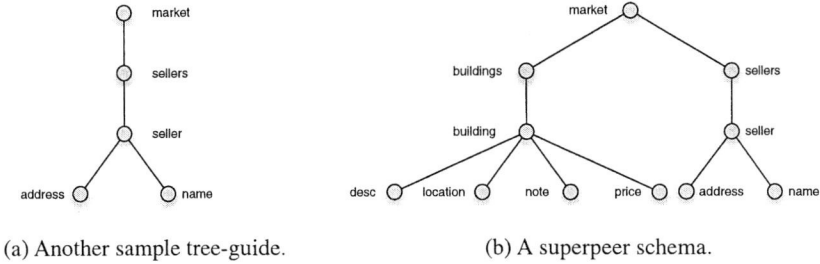

(a) Another sample tree-guide.   (b) A superpeer schema.

Fig. 3. Another tree-guide and a super-peer schema

4.3 Network Evolution

The topology of the network can evolve over time. To adapt the organization of the superpeer hierarchy to changes in the network, superpeers may split clusters and groups, and may ask for new superpeers. In particular, when the workload for a given superpeer sp becomes too hard, sp first tries to relocate some of its children in other clusters/groups (*network balancing*); if the problem persists, sp then asks the system for new superpeers, and delegates them part of its workload (*network extension*); if the workload is still too heavy, sp can finally disconnect some of its children (*peer de-gnoming*). On the other hand, when the workload for a given superpeer sp becomes too light, sp may decide to import some children from busy superpeers, or it may decide to relocate its children to another superpeer, and then to exit the superpeer network (*network contraction*).

5   XPeer Query Processing

XPeer supports the FLWR core of XQuery, the standard query language for XML data being developed by W3C [3]. Since data are usually dispersed among many peers, XPeer does not support the preservation of document order in query results.

FLWR queries are translated into algebraic expressions, and are executed on the system by relying on *data-integration-like* techniques. To speed up query execution and to decrease peer and superpeer workload, the system exploits mechanisms for replicating peer content, and for caching query plans and query results; these mechanisms can be ignored on an explicit request by the user.

5.1   XPeer Query Algebra

The query algebra of XPeer, further described in [11], is an evolution of the query algebra for centralized XML data described in [12]. The query algebra consists of three classes of operators. The first class contains operators that navigate unordered forests of node-labeled trees, binding nodes to variables, and that build new XML trees from existing variables bindings (*path* and *return*); the second class, instead, contains operators for manipulating tuples of variable bindings, as in standard OO query algebras [2] [4] (σ, π, $\bowtie$, $DJoin$, etc); the third class, finally, is formed by operators for managing *locations* (the algebraic counterpart of peers), and, in particular, for uniting their content

(*LocUnion*) and for inserting replication constraints into query plans (*Choice*). Since location choices are guarded by temporal parameters, the query algebra data model has been enriched with the universal constant τ, describing the system global time, and with time labels for locations.

The following example shows a sample algebraic expression.

Example 3. Consider the following XQuery query:

```
for $b in input()//building,
    $d in $b/desc,
    $p in $b/price
return <entry> {$d, $p} </entry>
```

This query returns the description and the price of each building in the *real-estate* market database. Assume that the database ($db1$) is formed by data dispersed over locations loc_1, loc_{11}, loc_{13}, and loc_{17}, and that $loc_{11}(db1)$ is replicated at loc_{17} till time δ; furthermore, assume that the query was submitted at time τ' so that $\tau' < \delta$. Then, the query can be expressed by the following algebraic expression:

$$return_{entry[\nu\$d,\nu\$p]}\big($$
$$path_{(//,\$b,in)building[(/,\$d,in)desc[\emptyset],(/,\$p,in)price[\emptyset]]}\big($$
$$(loc_1 \bullet (loc_{11} \mid^{\delta}_{db1} loc_{17}) \bullet loc_{13} \bullet loc_{17})^1(db1)))$$

5.2   Query Compilation

Query compilation is performed in two phases. In the first step, a query is submitted by the user to a peer p_i. p_i translates the query into a triple $Q = (q, \tau', \delta_{\tau'})$, where q is a *location-free* algebraic expression, i.e., an algebraic expression with "holes" (called *spots*) in place of locations, τ' is the query submission time, and $\delta_{\tau'}$ is a user-defined freshness parameter; in particular, $\delta_{\tau'}$ indicates that the system may use replicas and caches synced after time $\tau' - \delta_{\tau'}$, and allows the user to specify freshness and quality requirements for the result of the query (e.g., $\delta_{\tau'} = 0$ means that only up-to-date caches and replicas can be used, while $\delta_{\tau'} = \infty$ means that any existing cache or replica can be used).

In the second phase, p_i sends the query Q to the superpeer network, via the superpeer of its own cluster, for the compilation of a *location assignment* ρ, i.e., a function assigning unions ($\bullet$) and choices ($\mid$) of locations to location spots. This compilation is performed in a hierarchical way by matching the twigs of q with schema information, and by traversing the superpeer hierarchy till any interesting location has been detected. In particular, the superpeer responsible for the cluster of p_i matches the twigs of the query with the schemas of its children peers, hence finding all relevant locations in the cluster; then, the superpeer sends the query to the super-peer responsible for its group, which in turn matches the query twigs against the schemas of its children, and resends the query to clusters that may contain relevant data. The query is also propagated up in the hierarchy to find all relevant locations. The query compilation process, hence, requires the system to propagate the query till the root of the super-peer network, but still limits the exploration of the network to a fraction of the hierarchy.

Once the location assignment ρ is computed, ρ is passed to the issuing peer p_i for query execution; by making p_i responsible for the execution of its query, the system minimizes the load of the superpeer network.

5.3   Query Execution

Once the issuing peer p_i has received the location assignment ρ for a query Q, it applies common algebraic rewriting to the fully specified algebraic expression, such as selection push-down and distribution of unions, and then starts executing the query, which is split into *single-location* sub-queries that are sent to the corresponding peers; p_i waits for query results, and then executes operations, such as joins, involving data coming from multiple sources. Query subexpressions are locally optimized and executed by system peers, hence allowing each peer to choose the best execution strategy for any given algebraic expression.

Query decomposition is performed by exploiting an algorithm close to that of YAT [13]: the algorithm just browses the algebraic tree in the search of maximal single-location subexpressions, which correspond to peer sub-queries.

6   Related Works

Maier's System. In [9] authors describe a *coordinator-free* architecture for distributed XML query processing in the context of p2p systems. The architecture is based on the key idea of *mutant query plans* (MQP) [8]. An MQP is a logical query plan, where leaf nodes may consist of URN/URL references, or of materialized XML data. MQPs are themselves serialized as XML elements, and are exchanged among the nodes of the system. When a node S receives an MQP P, S can resolve URN references, materialize URL references, evaluate MQP sub-plans, re-optimize MQP sub-plans, or just route P to another server; when P is reduced to XML code only, it is sent to the *target* node, i.e., the node originating the query. As a consequence, an MQP traverses the system, carrying partial results and unevaluated sub-plans, until it is fully evaluated, i.e., it becomes a constant XML fragment.

The proposed system heavily exploits the semantic homogeneity of the data supplied by peers, hence it appears not adequate when data are semantically heterogeneous. Moreover, while MQPs allow the system to avoid centralization points, the correctness of their routing algorithms in the presence of network problems is far from being clear.

DBGlobe. In [10] authors describe DBGlobe, a p2p system for global computing. The key points of the project are the management of mobile peers, the use of services for dealing with heterogeneity and mismatching problems, as well as the use of Active XML [1] as the paradigm for service invocation/execution and data exchange.

Although very interesting, the DBGlobe system requires heavy administration activities for its build-up and its maintenance; moreover, it is not clear how the system can react to failures in its administrative layers.

Piazza. In [6] authors give an overview of Piazza, a peer data management system for XML data. The Piazza project focuses on the use of schemata, and, in particular, on the definition of schema integration and mapping techniques for p2p systems.

The architecture of Piazza is basically a hierarchical p2p architecture, where peers are fully autonomous, and may contribute data with schemas, while a central node hosts an index structure structure for query routing and performs query reformulation. Each peer has a schema, the *peer schema*, which describes how the given peer views the data offered by the system; peer visions of the world are usually different, so the need for peer schema reconciliation techniques emerges. Moreover, the peer schema is somehow independent from the schema of the data the peer may store, so a second class of mappings is required. Peers contributing data also have a second schema, the *storage schema*, which describes the structure of the data.

Each query submitted by a given peer P is posed against the peer schema of P, and it must be reformulated to work against the storage schema of the relevant peers in the system.

While very promising, the Piazza approach still requires human intervention for the definition of schema mappings.

7   Conclusions and Future Work

This paper describes the architecture of XPeer, a p2p XML data management system. The architecture of the system is *self-organizing*, in that the superpeer network can adapt its structure to changes in the system network topology and in the query workload. Furthermore, the system requires no human intervention for its administration, hence being a *zero-administration* DBMS.

XPeer is a general purpose XML p2p database system, so it can be used in any application field. Still, its main application is the management of resource descriptions in a *GRID-like* environment: in particular, XPeer should form the basic infrastructure for extending (and, eventually, replacing) the *LDAP-based* resource discovery layer of existing GRID systems.

XPeer is currently being implemented on top of an existing persistent XML query engine, so at this time no remarks about its performance and scalability properties can be done. In addition to implementing XPeer, we are currently investigating the problem of correctness of query results in the presence of incomplete query plans.

References

1. Serge Abiteboul, Omar Benjelloun, Ioana Manolescu, Tova Milo, and Roger Weber. Active XML: Peer-to-Peer Data and Web Services Integration. In *28th International Conference on Very Large Data Bases (VLDB 2002)*.
2. A. M. Alashqur, Stanley Y. W. Su, and Herman Lam. Oql: A query language for manipulating object-oriented databases. In *Proceedings of the Fifteenth International Conference on Very Large Data Bases (VLDB 1989)*.
3. Scott Boag, Don Chamberlin, Mary F. Fernandez, Daniela Florescu, Jonathan Robie, and Jérôme Siméon. XQuery 1.0: An XML Query Language. Technical report, World Wide Web Consortium, May 2003. W3C Working Draft.

4. Sophie Cluet and Guido Moerkotte. Classification and optimization of nested queries in object bases. Technical report, University of Karlsruhe, 1994.
5. Roy Goldman and Jennifer Widom. DataGuides: Enabling query formulation and optimization in semistructured databases. In *Proceedings of 23rd International Conference on Very Large Data Bases (VLDB 1997)*.
6. Alon Y. Halevy, Zachary G. Ives, Peter Mork, and Igor Tatarinov. Piazza: data management infrastructure for semantic web applications. In *Proceedings of the Twelfth International World Wide Web Conference (WWW2003)*.
7. Matthew Harren, Joseph M. Hellerstein, Ryan Huebsch, Boon Thau Loo, Scott Shenker, and Ion Stoica. Complex Queries in DHT-based Peer-to-Peer Networks. In *Peer-to-Peer Systems, First International Workshop, IPTPS 2002*.
8. Vassilis Papadimos and David Maier. Mutant query plans. *Information & Software Technology*, 44(4):197–206, 2002.
9. Vassilis Papadimos, David Maier, and Kristin Tufte. Distributed Query Processing and Catalogs for Peer-to-Peer Systems. In *CIDR 2003*.
10. Evaggelia Pitoura, Serge Abiteboul, Dieter Pfoser, George Samaras, and Michalis Vazirgiannis. DBGlobe: a service-oriented P2P system for global computing. *Sigmod Record*, 32(3):77–82, 2003.
11. Carlo Sartiani. A Query Algebra for XML P2P Databases, 2003. Manuscript draft. Available at `http://www.di.unipi.it/~sartiani/papers/eve.pdf`.
12. Carlo Sartiani and Antonio Albano. Yet Another Query Algebra For XML Data. In Mario A. Nascimento, M. Tamer Özsu, and Osmar Zaïane, editors, *Proceedings of the 6th International Database Engineering and Applications Symposium (IDEAS 2002)*.
13. Jérôme Siméon. *Intégration de sources de données hétérogènes*. PhD thesis, Université Paris XI, 1999.
14. Beverly Yang and Hector Garcia-Molina. Designing a Super-peer Network. In *Proceedings of the 19th International Conference on Data Engineering (ICDE 2003)*.

Bit Zipper Rendezvous
Optimal Data Placement for General P2P Queries*

Wesley W. Terpstra, Stefan Behnel,
Ludger Fiege, Jussi Kangasharju, and Alejandro Buchmann

Darmstadt University of Technology (TUD),
Department of Computer Science,
D-64283 Darmstadt, Germany
{terpstra,behnel,fiege}@gkec.tu-darmstadt.de,
jussi@tk.informatik.tu-darmstadt.de,
buchmann@informatik.tu-darmstadt.de

Abstract. In many distributed applications, pairs of queries and values are evaluated by participating nodes. This includes keyword search for documents, selection queries on tuples, and publish-subscribe. These applications require that all values accepted by the query be evaluated. To carry out this evaluation we will present the peer-to-peer based Bit Zipper Rendezvous which partitions query-value pairs as opposed to values only. Even for problems that allow an efficient value-based partition, the Bit Zipper complements existing solutions with its generality. Where flooding to N nodes used to be the only fall-back, the Bit Zipper is a replacement needing only $O(\sqrt{N})$. For problems requiring that all pairs be evaluated, we will show that the Bit Zipper Rendezvous is optimal.

1 Introduction

Recently, peer-to-peer (P2P) applications have emerged as an important new class of applications. They provide many attractive properties, such as self-organization and healing, robustness, load balancing, and scalability. These properties make the P2P approach appealing for large distributed applications. P2P systems have been used or proposed for a number of applications such as keyword search for documents, file storage, and publish-subscribe. Now, if we take a broader view on these applications, we can see that many of them contain the rendezvous problem.

The *rendezvous problem* is where several parameters involved in an operation need to be present at the same computer for evaluation. These parameters typically come in pairs and their evaluation takes place at some node in the P2P system. As for the above examples, keywords are searched for in documents and notifications are tested against subscriptions.

We claim that a good data placement strategy can address the rendezvous problem in the above applications. *Data placement strategies* are rules which decide where to place parameter data on the participating nodes.

---

* This work was partially funded by the German National Science Foundation (DFG) as part of the Graduate Colleges "Enabling Technologies for E-Commerce" and "System Integration for Ubiquitous Computing". A long version of this paper is provided as technical report in [19].

W. Lindner et al. (Eds.): EDBT 2004 Workshops, LNCS 3268, pp. 466–475, 2004.

Partitioning parameters by their value is a very efficient rule used for data placement. These *partitioning strategies* place each parameter in exactly one partition; this is the root of their efficiency. For evaluation to be possible, pairs must have their component parameters placed in the same partition. When all required evaluations can be performed, a partitioning strategy is correct. Unfortunately, one cannot always correctly partition by parameter value.

When an efficient, correct parameter partition cannot be found, another strategy must be used. Flooding is the traditional last resort. Naively, flooding applications place all parameters of one type on every participant. This assures a rendezvous with the locally stored parameters of the other type and allows evaluation of all pairs. However, it implies that participating nodes have linear load in the flooded parameter.

In this paper, we present a general-purpose solution with sub-linear load. It is specifically designed to address those situations where potentially all of the pairs of parameters might need to be evaluated. We also show that for rendezvous problems which require all pairs to be evaluated, our strategy is optimal.

The next section provides an overview of the rendezvous problem by presenting concrete examples of applications, and it overviews distributed hash tables (DHTs) as a rendezvous approach. Section 3 presents our general purpose approach, the Bit Zipper Rendezvous data placement strategy, followed by section 4 which shows its optimality for some important types of applications. A formal proof of the complexity this paper states for our algorithm can be found in the long version of this paper [19]. We finally discuss the implications of our research and prior art in sections 5 and 6.

2   The Rendezvous Problem

When moved onto a peer-to-peer platform, a number of important applications can benefit from the P2P characteristics mentioned above. The central rendezvous problem is described and exemplified below, and DHTs are introduced as means to implement a rendezvous strategy.

2.1   The Essential Problem

Stated generally, nodes in the rendezvous problem play three roles. In one role, nodes inject queries; in the other, they inject data. The final role is that of an intermediate router. To execute queries, the queries must either be shipped to the data, as in classic database queries, or the data must be shipped to the queries, as in filter and sensor networks. The new option offered by peer-to-peer systems is that the data and queries can *both* be shipped to nodes playing the third role—a rendezvous point where data and queries meet.

The rest of the paper interprets operations and data homogeneously; only a single application-specific operation is assumed to be executed on pairs of data from the first two roles. The two roles are distinguished according to their anticipated dynamism in the peer-to-peer network. The more dynamic parameter is designated *right* and the lesser is *left*.

The principal rendezvous problem is then to intelligently place data items at nodes; this involves choosing rendezvous nodes, and routing to them.

2.2   Examples

Publish-Subscribe. Pub-sub is an interest-oriented communication model [4]. Nodes transmit—or publish—information which is to be received—or consumed—by others. Consumers receive information that matches an expression they have specified; this expression is called a subscription. Thus, the recipient group is self-selecting by virtue of their interests.

In a distributed publish-subscribe network, subscriptions are left parameters located at some nodes. Right parameters are notifications that are forwarded to consumers in case of matching subscriptions. Clearly, the notifications must be selected by subscriptions and thus rendezvous.

Subscriptions and notifications may sometimes be successfully partitioned. For instance, subscriptions to types of information exploit a categorization of published data. However, there are many cases where such partitioning fails.

Distributed Keyword Search. Keyword search involves searching for documents by specifying words they must contain. Here it is assumed that the documents are rarely modified compared to the frequency of the queries. The left parameters are the relatively static documents and the right parameter are the keyword queries. This problem is easily solved by a centralized system using inverted-indexes, but for P2P systems it remains unsolved. After shipping queries to rendezvous nodes, one might copy the publish-subscribe idea and store these queries to get notified about new documents in the future.

2.3   Rendezvous in Distributed Hash Tables

A popular means of addressing the rendezvous problem is distributed hash tables (DHTs) [3, 9, 12, 14, 16, 21]. DHTs form an abstraction to overlay networks that provides a key-based routing scheme. The recipient of a message is determined dynamically by a distributed routing algorithm. However, as opposed to traditional networking, both the delivery path and the destination node can change over time. This easily accommodates topology changes.

By determining (hash-)keys from the parameter values, DHTs provide an obvious lookup mechanism for rendezvous nodes. However, this is partitioning by parameter value, which is not always possible. Nevertheless, DHTs do provide a number of features that make them perfectly suitable as a substrate for our data placement strategy.

DHT routing schemes are based on keys, $\mathcal{K}$. Different DHTs use between 128 to 256 bits for their fixed length keys. For concreteness, we assume that there are 160 bits: 1 to 160. If $k \in \mathcal{K}$, then k_i is defined to be the i-th bit of k.

Every participating node has one randomly chosen identifier, $n \in \mathcal{K}$. $\mathcal{N} \subseteq \mathcal{K}$ is the set of all node keys. $N = |\mathcal{N}|$ is the number of participating nodes. The lookup mechanism is a distributed algorithm implementing the responsibility function $\pi : \mathcal{K} \to \mathcal{N}$. For each key $k \in \mathcal{K}$, π returns the eventual destination node $n = \pi(k)$ of a message sent to k.

DHTs are defined with respect to some distance metric. They route a key, k, progressively closer to $\pi(k)$ by decreasing distance under their routing metric. This implies that all nodes are responsible for their own key; $\pi(n) = n$. When a *Euclidean distance metric* is used in a DHT, $\pi^{-1}(n)$ will be an interval. This property of the responsibility function is required for our data placement strategy to remain performant. Therefore, Kademlia [9] may not be used as substrate.

A message transported by a *prefix routing* protocol resolves a destination's key one bit at a time for as long as possible. Most DHTs do this either implicitly or explicitly. Our data placement strategy is easy to implement and follows normal routing paths only if a DHT has this property. Unfortunately, CAN [12] does not. Tapestry is actually based on postfix routing, but the difference is negligible for our purpose.

Summarizing, we can say that DHTs provide a way of distributing responsibility for keys uniformly at random. The majority [3, 14, 16, 21] are based on a Euclidean metric and prefix routing. These DHTs are perfect candidates for the Bit Zipper Rendezvous.

3   Bit Zipper Rendezvous

The Bit Zipper approach partitions *pairs* of parameters and distributes them randomly. It places each parameter in a large, but sub-linear number of these partitions. This strategy is applicable even when there is no correct value-based partitioning scheme for parameters separately.

The next subsection presents a method to assign every parameter to a number of pair partitions. Building on a DHT, these parameters are mapped to nodes in section 3.2 and routed in section 3.3.

3.1   Partitioning Pairs

Applications involving the rendezvous problem evaluate pairs of parameters. For some applications, nearly all of the pairs might need to be evaluated. Simply partitioning parameters separately can lead to the component parameters of a pair being placed in separate partitions; this prevents evaluation

However, partitioning *pairs* of left and right parameters does not prevent evaluation since all pairs remain intact. Each parameter is involved in many pairs and has to be placed in many pair partitions. These pair partitions are identified by DHT keys, thus mapping every parameter to a large number of DHT keys.

Parameters are assigned a randomly chosen seed key. Taking the seeds of two parameters together, one will be able to determine the DHT key where their pair is placed. Naturally, parameters must be placed at all such possible keys.

The placement follows a zipper-like bit pattern that gives the Bit Zipper its name. It is illustrated in figure 1. The b part is a configurable optimization that will be explained in section 3.4. In this pattern, every even bit in a right parameter's seed, r, is held fixed; whereas, every odd bit in a left parameter's seed, l, is fixed. The key which equals the two seeds for all fixed bits, m, is the partition where their pair is placed.

Given a seed, s, we must identify the partitions, m, of all possible pairs involving s. Formally, we define the right and left rendezvous key sets, as

$$\mathscr{R}(s) := \{m \in \mathscr{K} : \forall i \in [1, 160] : ((i \equiv 0) \bmod 2 \text{ or } i \leq b) \implies m_i = s_i\} \quad (1)$$
$$\mathscr{L}(s) := \{m \in \mathscr{K} : \forall i \in [1, 160] : ((i \equiv 1) \bmod 2 \text{ and } i > b) \implies m_i = s_i\} \quad (2)$$

$\longleftarrow b \longrightarrow$ $\square$ = fixed bit

r   1 0 0 1 0 |1| 1 |1| 0 |0| 1 |0| 1 |1| 1 |0| 1 |1| 1 |1| 1 |1| 0 |0| 0 |1|

l   0 0 1 1 1 0 |0| 1 |0| 1 |1| 0 |0| 0 |1| 1 |0| 0 |0| 1 |0| 0 |1| 0 |0| 0

m   1 0 0 1 0 1 0 1 0 0 1 0 0 1 1 0 0 1 0 1 0 1 1 0 0 1

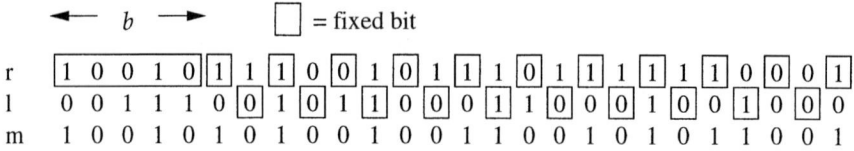

Fig. 1. Partition key m for example seeds r and l

Ignoring b, we mean here that $\mathscr{R}(s)$ is the set of all keys which share all the even bits of the seed s and $\mathscr{L}(s)$ the set of all keys which share all the odd bits.

The correctness of this strategy follows from the fact that $|\mathscr{R}(r) \cap \mathscr{L}(l)| = 1$; that is, there is exactly one partition key for every pair of left and right seeds. This is mathematically clear since the bit selecting predicates in the definitions of $\mathscr{R}$ and $\mathscr{L}$ are logical inverses.

3.2 Mapping Partitions to Nodes

$\mathscr{R}(s)$ and $\mathscr{L}(s)$ define how to select partitions or rendezvous keys. To find the actual rendezvous nodes, simply apply the DHT responsibility function, π. When $r \in \mathscr{K}$ is the seed used for a right parameter, it is placed on the set of rendezvous nodes $\pi(\mathscr{R}(r))$. Similarly, a left parameter with seed $l \in \mathscr{K}$ is placed on the set of rendezvous nodes $\pi(\mathscr{L}(l))$.

When a new parameter is placed on a rendezvous node, the node pairs the new parameter with all the parameters of the opposite type available on that node. Those pairs that the node is actually responsible for are then evaluated.

Since there is one rendezvous key in common for all pairs (r, l),

$$\emptyset \neq \mathscr{R}(r) \cap \mathscr{L}(l) \implies \emptyset \neq \pi(\mathscr{R}(r) \cap \mathscr{L}(l)) \subseteq \pi(\mathscr{R}(r)) \cap \pi(\mathscr{L}(l))$$

there is at least one rendezvous node in common. Unfortunately, there may in fact be several. Therefore, a rendezvous node, z, should check that it is responsible for the rendezvous key ($z \in \pi(\mathscr{R}(r) \cap \mathscr{L}(l))$) before operating on a pair of parameters. This way, we ensure that a given pair is evaluated at most once.

3.3 Modified DHT Routing

Although the sets $\mathscr{R}(s)$ and $\mathscr{L}(s)$ contain an extremely large number of keys, [19] argues that their mapping to rendezvous nodes is radically better than flooding. Specifically, a right parameter is placed on expected $2\sqrt{N}t^{-1}$ nodes and a left parameter is placed on expected $2\sqrt{N}t$ nodes. The t is a tunable constant related to b which trades off load in left parameters against load in left parameters.

In order to build a P2P application, this data placement strategy must be routed over a DHT. Rather than routing to each of the rendezvous keys separately, routing is carried out to all of them simultaneously.

The algorithm is a relatively simple adjustment to prefix routing. Normally, prefix routing DHTs resolve a bit at a time; this leads to a single routing path from source to destination. In our data placement strategy, some of the target key bits are fixed, but others are not. Whenever the predicate in equation 1 does not specify bit equality, the

DHT simply routes right parameters in both the direction of a zero and of one. Similarly, the predicate in equation 2 is used for routing left parameters.

This means that delivery will follow the normal routing paths used for the rendezvous keys themselves. However, the shared intermediate nodes are only contacted once. Since every second step doubles the number of reached nodes, the interior nodes grow as two geometric series. By summing these series, the total nodes involved in routing will be $6\sqrt{N}t^{-1}$ for right parameters and $6\sqrt{N}t$ for left.

3.4   Balancing Non-uniformity

In many applications, the left and right parameters will not be equal in dynamism or size. It is easy to exploit their ratio to further optimize the placement by dividing the nodes into groups. Left parameters are placed in each of these groups; however, right parameters stay within the group that originated them. This can heavily reduce the number of nodes impacted by the dynamism of the right parameters.

As explained in [19], the most heavily loaded node will have expected $\frac{2R}{\sqrt{N}}t^{-1}$ right parameters and expected $\frac{2L}{\sqrt{N}}t$ left parameters placed on it. The constant t is selected to make the trade-off as desired.

Coming back to the balance factor, b, as seen in figure 1, it is defined depending on t as $b = 2\log t$. This balance factor is a global constant for the whole system and fixes the number of groups as $2^b = t^2$. For this reason, it should be selected carefully to reflect the constraints of the application.

A node is in the group identified by the first b bits of its random node id. As right parameters stay in the originating group, the first b bits of their seed should match the origin node. Figure 1 and equations 1 and 2 use b in this way.

4   Optimality Sketch

For applications which require that all pairs of right and left parameters be operated upon, this data placement strategy is optimal. This includes linear scans and difficult variants of publish-subscribe. We present here a brief and informal sketch of our optimality.

Theorem 1. *In any routing algorithm over N nodes which evaluates RL pairs of right and left parameters, there exists a node which receives at least $\frac{R}{\sqrt{N}}t^{-1}$ right and $\frac{L}{\sqrt{N}}t$ left parameters for some t.*

Proof. There are RL pairs of right and left parameters to be operated on. Therefore, there exists a node which evaluates $P = \frac{RL}{N}$ pairs. Suppose this node has X right parameters placed on it. Choose the balance factor $t = \frac{R}{X\sqrt{N}}$. Then $X = \frac{R}{\sqrt{N}}t^{-1}$.

The node can only operate on the product of all the right and left parameters placed on it. Therefore, there must be at least

$$\frac{P}{X} = \frac{\frac{RL}{N}}{\frac{R}{\sqrt{N}}t^{-1}} = \frac{L}{\sqrt{N}}t$$

many left parameters placed on this node.

5   Related Work

Distributed Keyword Search. There have been a number of proposals for implementing distributed keyword search. The majority of them are based on inverted indexes. An inverted index stores a list of documents for every possible keyword. To execute a query, the lists for involved keywords are intersected. The problem in a distributed network is that transferring these lists means a high network overhead for potentially uninteresting provisional results.

Gnawali [5] proposes a "Keyword-Set Search System" (KSS) that uses keyword sets rather than single keywords. Their intention is to reduce the number of lists that must be retrieved. On the other hand, keeping all pairs squares the number of lists per document and thus the cost for updates. All triples cubes the cost. Reynolds and Vahdat [13] evaluated about 100,000 WWW queries during a 10-day period and found that 71.5% of them consisted of two or more keywords and about 40% contained three or more words. This puts the Gnawali [5] approach in a bad light.

Li, Loo et al. [7] like Reynolds and Vahdat [13] also aim at fast distributed list intersection. However, they start by comparing two partitioning techniques: by document and by keyword. Keyword partitioning requires transmitting the document lists, whereas document partitioning involves merely asking each partition to execute the query. According to their analysis, keyword partitioning in a DHT requires bandwidth that is about two orders of magnitude higher than in document partitioning.

Gnutella [8] is a well known decentralized system using document partitioning. However, it uses flooding to query all the partitions. The next version of Gnutella introduced ultra peers [8] to control the flooding, but this approach only reduces the number of flooded nodes. Harren et al. [6] propose to cut keywords into n-grams (fixed size substrings) and to index these. Their approach allows substring search and reduces the impact of typos. This will result in longer document lists, exacerbating the problem.

Like Gnutella, we propose to partition by document. However, instead of flooding, we propose to use the Bit Zipper to place the document meta data on $2\sqrt{N}$ nodes, and have queries pass through only $6\sqrt{N}$ nodes. On each node, a local inverted index could be used to execute the query, or one could use the technique of Harren et al. for more generality. With a network of four million users, we would require $\frac{1}{166}$-th of the bandwidth of Gnutella per node for an exhaustive search while distributing the computational load randomly over all nodes. If the work of Li, Loo et al. [7] is correct, this would place us over four orders of magnitude beyond the reach of distributed inverted indexes.

Publish-Subscribe. Subject-based publish-subscribe (SBPS) partitions notifications into hierarchically organized categories. This partitioning reduces the problem size immensely. Current SBPS systems like Scribe [15] and Bayeux [22] try to distribute their message load over large distributed systems. Coupled with the reduced problem size, they become highly scalable. Newsgroups show that SBPS scales quite well up to certain limits. However, newsgroup cross-posting shows that there are cases where the artificial hierarchy is too restrictive, or simply not relevant. On the other hand, high volume newsgroups have the problem of being too broad.

Pietzuch [11] and JMS [17] follow an approach that adds attribute filtering to the subject-based routing. This maintains the scalability attained from subject-based problem size reduction. Furthermore, it addresses the issue of high volume newsgroups by allowing filtering to be applied to reduce the noise. However, overly restrictive topics and conflicting categorizations remain a problem.

Content-based pub-sub (CBPS), on the other hand, uses filters over the content of notifications as its primary routing policy. Therefore, it reduces the load on subscribers by allowing them to specify their interests very precisely, without the problem of conflicting categorization. REBECA [10] exemplifies pure CBPS, routed over a distributed broker tree. The filters are used to determine whether or not to forward a notification. The problem with REBECA is that although clients are not heavily loaded, central brokers often carry linear load. Our previous approach [20] addresses this concern by eliminating the tree-like structure and using conceptually many trees. Unfortunately, this approach worked as attenuated broadcast. When perfect attenuation is too costly, this degenerates to flooding.

Tam et al. [18] partition based on the content of notifications. This indexing approach is commonly known from database systems. It combines high selectivity with good performance. Unfortunately, for some subscriptions, there can be no matching index. In databases, these queries would be solved by a linear scan. As mentioned in section 4, the Bit Zipper is the optimal solution for linear scans. Thus, our strategy provides an efficient fall-back mechanism which corresponds to the database table itself. In this manner, all queries can be dealt with, and the administrator can make index choices solely for performance gains.

6 Conclusion

In distributed rendezvous problems which frustrate partition by value, flooding to all N nodes was the best known technique. Our general-purpose data placement strategy can address these same problems with a cost of only $O(\sqrt{N})$ messages. Furthermore, when these rendezvous problems exhibit all-pairs evaluation, our strategy is asymptotically optimal. This includes important problems such as distributed linear scan and general content-based publish-subscribe.

The Bit Zipper Rendezvous fits naturally on most distributed hash tables. The additional routing cost in such a self-maintaining configuration is only a small multiplicative factor. Through partitioning *pairs* of left and right parameters, it achieves randomized load distribution. Hence, the load distribution will be asymptotically homogeneous.

For problem domains like publish-subscribe, where efficient parameter partitioning techniques exist, our work is complementary. When there are no matching indexes, our strategy provides a fall-back. This work paves the way for general purpose systems like databases where unanticipated queries may be posed.

The question of whether distributed keyword search requires the same message load remains open. However, since flooding (aka. partition by document [7]) was previously the fastest decentralized technique, our new result should in theory perform radically better. An implementation will show whether our predictions are correct.

References

1. *The 2001 Conference on Applications, Technologies, Architectures, and Protocols for Computer Communications (SIGCOMM)*, San Diego, California, USA, 2001.
2. *The 1st International Workshop on Peer-to-Peer Systems (IPTPS02)*, MIT Faculty Club, Cambridge, MA, USA, Mar. 2002.
3. K. Aberer. P-Grid: A Self-Organizing access structure for P2P information systems. In *Proc. of the 6th Intl. Conference on Cooperative Information Systems (CoopIS 2001), Trento, Italy*, 2001.
4. P. T. Eugster, P. A. Felber, R. Guerraoui, and A.-M. Kermarrec. The many faces of publish/subscribe. *ACM Computing Surveys*, 35(2), 2003.
5. O. D. Gnawali. A keyword set search system for Peer-to-Peer networks. Master's thesis, Massachusetts Institute of Technology, June 2002.
6. M. Harren, J. M. Hellerstein, R. Huebsch, B. T. Loo, S. Shenker, and I. Stoica. Complex queries in DHT-based Peer-to-Peer networks. In *Proc. of the 1st Intl. Workshop on Peer-to-Peer Systems (IPTPS02)* [2].
7. J. Li, B. T. Loo, J. Hellerstein, F. Kaashoek, D. R. Karger, and R. Morris. On the feasibility of Peer-to-Peer web indexing and search. In *Proc. of the 2nd Intl. Workshop on Peer-to-Peer Systems (IPTPS03)*, Berkeley, CA, USA, Feb. 2003.
8. Q. Lv, S. Ratnasamy, and S. Shenker. Can heterogeneity make gnutella scalable? In *Proc. of the 1st Intl. Workshop on Peer-to-Peer Systems (IPTPS02)* [2].
9. P. Maymounkov and D. Mazieres. Kademlia: A peer-to-peer information system based on the XOR metric. In *Proc. of the 1st Intl. Workshop on Peer-to-Peer Systems (IPTPS02)* [2].
10. G. M̈uhl. *Large-Scale Content-Based Publish/Subscribe Systems*. PhD thesis, Darmstadt University of Technology, Sept. 2002.
11. P. Pietzuch and J. Bacon. Hermes: A distributed event-based middleware architecture. In *Proc. of the 1st Intl. Workshop on Distributed Event-Based Systems (DEBS'02)*, Vienna, Austria, July 2002.
12. S. Ratnasamy, P. Francis, M. Handley, R. Karp, and S. Shenker. A scalable content addressable network. In *Proc. of the 2001 ACM SIGCOMM Conference* [1].
13. P. Reynolds and A. Vahdat. Efficient peer-to-peer keyword searching. Technical report, Duke University, Sept. 2001.
14. A. Rowstron and P. Druschel. Pastry: Scalable, decentralized object location, and routing for large-scale Peer-to-Peer systems. In *Middleware 2001*, Nov. 2001.
15. A. Rowstron, A.-M. Kermarrec, M. Castro, and P. Druschel. SCRIBE: The design of a large-scale event notification infrastructure. In *Proc. of the 3rd Intl. COST264 Workshop on Networked Group Communication (NGC 2001)*, London, UK, 2001.
16. I. Stoica, R. Morris, D. Karger, F. Kaashoek, and H. Balakrishnan. Chord: A scalable Peer-To-Peer lookup service for internet applications. In *Proc. of the 2001 ACM SIGCOMM Conference* [1].
17. Sun Microsystems Inc. Java message service specification 1.1, 2002.
18. D. Tam, R. Azimi, and H.-A. Jacobsen. Building Content-Based Publish/Subscribe systems with distributed hash tables. In *1st Intl. Workshop on Databases, Information Systems, and P2P (DBISP2P)*, Berlin, Germany, Sept. 2003.
19. W. W. Terpstra, S. Behnel, L. Fiege, J. Kangasharju, and A. Buchmann. Bit zipper rendezvous - optimal data placement for general p2p queries. Technical report, TU Darmstadt, 2004. http://www.dvs1.informatik.tu-darmstadt.de/publications/pdf/zipper.pdf.
20. W. W. Terpstra, S. Behnel, L. Fiege, A. Zeidler, and A. Buchmann. A Peer-to-Peer Approach to Content-Based Publish/Subscribe. In *Proc. of the 2nd Intl. Workshop on Distributed Event-Based Systems (DEBS'03)*, San Diego, CA, USA, June 2003.

21. B. Zhao, J. Kubiatowicz, and A. Joseph. Tapestry: An infrastructure for fault-tolerant wide-area location and routing. Technical report, Computer Science Division, U. C. Berkeley, Apr. 2001.

22. S. Zhuang, B. Zhao, A. Joseph, R. Katz, and J. Kubiatowicz. Bayeux: An architecture for scalable and fault-tolerant wide-area data dissemination. In *Intl. Workshop on Network and OS Support for Digital A/V (NOSSDAV'01)*, June 2001.

Query Answering in Peer-to-Peer Data Exchange Systems

Leopoldo Bertossi and Loreto Bravo

Carleton University, School of Computer Science, Ottawa, Canada
{bertossi,lbravo}@scs.carleton.ca

Abstract. The problem of answering queries posed to a peer who is a member of a peer-to-peer data exchange system is studied. The answers have to be consistent wrt to both the local semantic constraints and the data exchange constraints with other peers; and must also respect certain trust relationships between peers. A semantics for *peer consistent answers* under exchange constraints and trust relationships is introduced and some techniques for obtaining those answers are presented.

1 Introduction

In this paper the problem of answering queries posed to a peer who is a member of a peer-to-peer data exchange system is investigated. When a peer P receives a query and is going to answer it, it may need to consider both its own data and the data stored at other peers' sites if those other peers are related to P by data exchange constraints (DECs). Keeping the exchange constraints satisfied, may imply for peer P to get data from other peers to complement its own data, but also not to use part of its own data. In which direction P goes depends not only on the exchange constraints, but also on the *trust relationships* that P has with other peers. For example, if P trust another peer Q's data more than its own, P will accommodate its data to Q's data in order to keep the exchange constraints satisfied. Another element to take into account in this process is a possible set of local semantic constraints that each individual peer may have.

Given a network of peers, each with its own data, and a particular peer P in it, a *solution for* P is -loosely speaking- a global database instance that respects the exchange constraints and trust relationships P has with its immediate neighbors and stays as close as possible to the available data in the system. Since the answers from P have to be consistent wrt to both the local semantic constraints and the data exchange constraints with other peers, the *peer consistent answers* (PCAs) from P are defined as those answers that can be retrieved from P's portion of data in *every* possible solution for P. This definition may suggest that P may change other peers' data, specially of those he considers less reliable, but this is not the case. The notion of solution is used as an auxiliary notion to characterize the correct answers from P's point of view. Ideally, P should be able to obtain its peer consistent answers just by querying the already available local instances. This resembles the approach to *consistent query answering* (CQA) in databases [1, 4], where answers to queries that are consistent with given ICs are computed without changing the original database.

We give a precise semantics for peer consistent answers to first-order queries. First for the *direct case*, where transitive relationships between peers via ECs are not auto-

W. Lindner et al. (Eds.): EDBT 2004 Workshops, LNCS 3268, pp. 476–485, 2004.

matically considered; and at the end, the *transitive case*. We also illustrate, by means of extended and representative examples, mechanisms for obtaining PCAs. One of them is first order (FO) query rewriting, where the original query is transformed into a new query, whose standard answers are the PCAs to the original one. This methodology has intrinsic limitations. The second, more general, approach is based on a specification of the solutions for a peer as the stable models of a logic program, which captures the different ways the system stabilizes after satisfying the DECs and the trust relationships.

An instance r of a relational database can be seen a a set of ground atoms. Accordingly, an instance r' is a *repair* of instance r wrt a set of integrity constraints IC if $r' \models IC$ and r' minimally differs from r in terms of inclusion of set of tuples [1].

2   A Framework for P2P Data Exchange

In this section we will describe the framework we will use to formalize and address the problem of query answering in P2P systems.

Definition 1. A *P2P data exchange system* $\mathfrak{P}$ consists of:

(a) A finite set $\mathcal{P}$ of peers, denoted by A, B, C, ..., P, Q, ...
(b) For each peer P, a database schema $\mathcal{R}(P)$, that includes a domain $D(P)$, and relations $R(P), \ldots$ However, it may be convenient to assume that all peers share a common, fixed, possibly infinite domain, D. Each $\mathcal{R}(P)$ determines a FO language $\mathcal{L}(P)$. We assume that the schemas $\mathcal{R}(P)$ are disjoint, being the domains the only possible exception. $\mathcal{R}$ denotes the union of the $\mathcal{R}(P)$s.
(c) For each peer P, a database instance $r(P)$ corresponding to schema $\mathcal{R}(P)$.
(d) For each peer P, a set of $\mathcal{L}(P)$-sentences $IC(P)$ of ICs on $\mathcal{R}(P)$.
(e) For each peer P, a collection $\Sigma(P)$ of *data exchange constraints* $\Sigma(P, Q)$ consisting of sentences written in the FO language for the signature $\mathcal{R}(P) \cup \mathcal{R}(Q)$, and the Q's are (some of the) other peers in $\mathcal{P}$.
(f) A relation $trust \subseteq \mathcal{P} \times \{less, same\} \times \mathcal{P}$, with the intended semantics that when $(A, less, B) \in trust$, peer A trusts itself less than B; while $(A, same, B) \in trust$ indicates that A trusts itself the same as B. In this relation, the second argument functionally depends on the other two. By default a peer trusts its own data more than that of other peers.   □

Each peer P is responsible for maintaining its material instance wrt $IC(P)$, independently from other peers. In particular, we assume $r(P) \models IC(P)$. However, when local data is virtually changed to accommodate to other peers' data, the local ICs could be virtually violated. It is possible to keep the local ICs satisfied also at query time by using methodologies for consistent query answering, i.e. for consistently answering queries in databases that fail to satisfy certain ICs [4]. A peers may submit queries to other peers in accordance with the restrictions imposed its DECs and using the other peer's relations appearing in them.

Definition 2. (a) We denote with $\overline{\mathcal{R}}(P)$ the schema consisting of $\mathcal{R}(P)$ extended with the other peers' schemas that contain predicates appearing in $\Sigma(P)$. (b) For a peer P and an instance r on $\mathcal{R}(\mathrm{P})$, we denote by $\bar{r}$, the database instance on $\overline{\mathcal{R}}(\mathrm{P})$, consisting of the union of r with all the peers' instances whose schemas appear in $\overline{\mathcal{R}}(\mathrm{P})$. (c) If r is an instance over a certain schema $\mathcal{S}$ and $\mathcal{S}'$ is a subschema of $\mathcal{S}$, then $r|\mathcal{S}'$ denotes the restriction of r to $\mathcal{S}'$. In particular, if $\mathcal{R}(\mathrm{P}) \subseteq \mathcal{S}$, then $r|\mathrm{P}$ denotes the restriction of r to $\mathcal{R}(\mathrm{P})$. (d) We denote by $\mathcal{R}(\mathrm{P})^{less}$ the union of all schemas $\mathcal{R}(\mathrm{Q})$, with $(\mathrm{P}, less, \mathrm{Q}) \in trust$. Analogously is $\mathcal{R}(\mathrm{P})^{same}$ defined.   □

From the perspective of a peer P, its own database may be inconsistent wrt the data owned by another peer Q and the DECs in $\Sigma(\mathrm{P}, \mathrm{Q})$. Only when P trust Q the same as or more than itself, it has to consider Q's data. When P queries its database, these inconsistencies may have to be taken into account. Ideally, the answers to the query obtained from P should be consistent with $\Sigma(\mathrm{P}, \mathrm{Q})$ (and its own ICs $\Sigma(\mathrm{P})$). In principle, P, who is not allowed to change other peers' data, could try to repair its database in order to satisfy $\Sigma(\mathrm{P}) \cup IC(\mathrm{P})$. This is not a realistic approach. Rather P should solve its semantic conflicts or incompleteness of data at query time, when it queries its own database and those of other peers. Any answer obtained in this way should be sanctioned as correct wrt to a precise semantics.

The semantics of peer consistent query answers for a peer P is given in terms of all possible minimal, virtual, simultaneous repairs of the local databases that lead to a satisfaction of the DECs while respecting P's trust relationships to other peers. This repair process may lead to alternative global databases called the *solutions* for P. Next, the peer consistent answers from P are those that are invariant wrt to all its solutions. A peer's solution captures the idea that only some peers' databases are relevant to P, those whose relations appear in its trusted exchange constraints, and are trusted by P at least as much as it trusts its own data. In this sense, this is a "local notion", because it does not take into consideration transitive dependencies (but see Section 5).

Definition 3. (direct case) Given a peer P in a P2P data exchange system and an instance r on $\mathcal{R}$, an instance r' on $\mathcal{R}$ is a *solution for* P if r' is a repair of r wrt to $\Sigma(\mathrm{P}) \cup IC(\mathrm{P})$ that does not change the more trusted relations, more precisely: (a) $r' \models \bigcup \{\Sigma(\mathrm{P}, \mathrm{Q}) \mid (\mathrm{P}, less, \mathrm{Q}) \text{ or } (\mathrm{P}, same, \mathrm{Q}) \in trust\} \cup IC(\mathrm{P})$; (b) $r'|P = r|P$ for every predicate $P \in \mathcal{R}(\mathrm{Q})$, where Q is a peer with $(\mathrm{P}, less, \mathrm{Q}) \in trust$; (c) r' minimally differs from r in the sense that $(r' \smallsetminus r) \cup (r \smallsetminus r')$ is minimal under set inclusion among those instances that satisfy (a) and (b).   □

Intuitively, a solution for P repairs the global instance wrt the DECs with peers that P trusts more than or the same as itself, but leaving unchanged the tables that belong to more trusted peers. As a consequence of the definition, tables belonging to peers that are not related to P or are less trustable are not changed. That is, P tries to change its own tables according to what the dependencies to more or equally trusted peers prescribe.

The solutions for a peer are used as a conceptual, auxiliary tool to characterize the peer consistent answers; and we are not interested in them *per se*. Solutions are virtual and may be only partially computed if necessary, if this helps us to compute the correct answers obtained in/from a peer. The "changes" that are implicit in the definition of solution via the set differences are expected to be minimal wrt to sets of tuples which are inserted/deleted into/from the tables.

In these definitions we find clear similarities with the characterization of consistent query answers in single relational databases [4]. However, in P2P query answering, repairs may involve data associated to different peers, and also a notion of priority that is related to the trust relation.

Example 1. Consider a P2P data exchange system with peers P1, P2, P3, and schemas $\mathcal{R}_i = \{R^i, \ldots\}$. (a) Instances $r(\text{P1}) = \{R^1(a, b), R^1(s, t)\}$, $r(\text{P2}) = \{R^2(c, d), R^2(a, e)\}$, $r(\text{P3}) = \{R^3(a, f), R^3(s, u)\}$. (b) $trust = \{\ (\text{P1}, less, \text{P2}), (\text{P1}, same, \text{P3})\ \}$. (c) $\Sigma(\text{P1}, \text{P2}) = \{\ \forall xy(R^2(x, y) \rightarrow R^1(x, y))\ \}$; $\Sigma(\text{P1}, \text{P3}) = \{\ \forall xyz(R^1(x, y) \wedge R^3(x, z) \rightarrow y = z)\ \}$. Here, the global instance is $r = \{R^1(a, b), R^1(s, t), R^2(c, d), R^2(a, e), R^3(a, f), R^3(s, u)\}$. It has two repairs according to Definition 3, namely $r' = \{R^1(a, b), R^1(s, t), R^1(c, d), R^1(a, e), R^2(c, d), R^2(a, e)\}$; and $r'' = \{\ R^1(a, b), R^1(c, d), R^1(a, e), R^2(c, d), R^2(a, e), R^3(s, u)\}$.   □

Definition 4. Given a FO query $Q(\bar{x}) \in \mathcal{L}(\text{P})$ posed to P, a ground tuple $\bar{t}$ is a *peer consistent* answer to Q for P iff $r'|\text{P} \models Q(\bar{t})$ for every solution r' for P.   □

Example 2. (example 1 continued) The query $Q : R^1(x, y)$ posed to P1 has as peer consistent answers the tuples: $(a, b), (c, d), (a, e)$, because those are the tuples found in relation R^1 in the restriction to P1's schema in every solution for P.   □

Notice that this definition is relative to a fixed peer, and not only because the query is posed to one peer and in its query language, but also because this notion is based on the "direct or local" notion of solution for a single peer, which considers its "direct neighbors" only. This is a first step towards the general case of transitive dependencies, that will be explored in Section 5. However, this restricted case is the basis for the transitive case, because P does not see beyond its neighbors; and when P requests data to a neighbor, say Q, the latter may have to find local solutions of its own by considering its direct neighbors. The transitive case has to combine these local solutions.

Peer consistent answers to queries can be obtained by using techniques similar to those for CQA, e.g. query rewriting [1, 4]. However, there are important differences, because now we have some fixed predicates in the repair process.

Example 3. (example 1 continued) If P1 is posed the query $Q : R^1(x, y)$, asking for the tuples in relation R^1, its answers can be obtained through the rewritten query Q': $[R^1(x, y) \wedge \forall z_1((R^3(x, z_1) \wedge \neg \exists z_2 R^2(x, z_2)) \rightarrow z_1 = y)] \vee R^2(x, y)$, which requires from P1 to submit queries to its peers. The final answers are $(a, b), (c, d), (a, e)$, precisely the answers obtained in Example 2.   □

Notice that a query Q may have peer consistent answers for a peer which are not answers to Q when the peer is considered in isolation, which makes sense, because the peer may import data from other peers.[1]

This query rewriting approach differs from the one used for CQA. In the latter case, literals in a query are resolved (by *resolution*) against ICs in order to generate residues

---

[1] Another difference with CQA, where all consistent answers are answers to the original query; at least for conjunctive queries and *generic* ICs [4].

that are iteratively appended as extra conditions to the query. In the case of P2P data systems, the query may have to be modified in order to include new data that is located at a different peer's site. This cannot be achieved by imposing extra conditions alone, but instead, by relaxing the query in some sense. Since query answering in P2P systems includes sufficiently complex cases of CQA, a FO query rewriting approach to P2P query answering is bound to have limitations in terms of completeness [4]. Instead, we will now propose a more general methodology based on answer set programming.

3   Referential Data Exchange Constraints

An answer set programming approach to the specification of solutions for a peer can be developed. Those specifications will be similar to those of repairs of single relational databases under referential integrity constraints [2]. However, as we have seen, there are important differences with CQA.

In most applications we may expect the DECs for a peer to be inclusion dependencies or referential constraints, which will be used by this peer to either import data from or to validate its own data with another peer. We now give an example of an even more more involved referential constraint that shows the main issues around this kind of specifications.

Example 4. Consider a P2P system with peers P and Q, with schemas $\{R_1(\cdot,\cdot), R_2(\cdot,\cdot)\}$, $\{S_1(\cdot,\cdot), S_2(\cdot,\cdot)\}$, resp.; and assume that P is querying its database subject to its DEC that mixes tables of the two peers on each side of the implication:

$$\forall x \forall y \forall z \exists w (R_1(x,y) \wedge S_1(z,y) \rightarrow R_2(x,w) \wedge S_2(z,w)), \tag{1}$$

We consider the case where $(\text{P}, less, \text{Q}) \in trust$, i.e. P considers Q's data more reliable than its own. If (1) is satisfied by the combination of the data in P and Q, then the current global instance constitutes P's solution. Otherwise, alternative solutions for P have to be found, keeping Q's data fixed in the process. This is the case, when there are ground tuples $R_1(d,m) \in r(\text{P}), S_1(a,m) \in r(\text{Q})$, such that for no t it holds both $R_2(d,t) \in r(\text{P})$ and $S_2(a,t) \in r(\text{Q})$.

Obtaining peer consistent answers for peer P amounts to virtually restoring the satisfaction of (1), by virtually modifying P's data. In order to specify P's modified relations, we introduce virtual versions R_1', R_2' of R_1, R_2, containing the data in peer P's solutions. In consequence, at the solution level, we have the relations R_1', R_2', S_1, S_2. Since P is querying its database, its original queries will be expressed in terms of relations R_1', R_2' only (plus, possibly, built-ins).

The contents of the virtual relations R_1', R_2' are obtained from the material sources R_1, R_2, S_1, S_2.[2] Since S_1, S_2 are fixed, the satisfaction of (1) requires R_1' to be a subset of R_1, and R_2', a superset of R_2. The specification of these relations is done in extended disjunctive logic programs with answer set (stable model) semantics [13]. The first rules for the specification program Π are:

$$R_1'(x,y) \leftarrow R_1(x,y), \; not \; \neg R_1'(x,y). \qquad R_2'(x,y) \leftarrow R_2(x,y), \; not \; \neg R_2'(x,y), \tag{2}$$

---

[2] We can observe that the virtual relations can be seen as virtual global relations in a virtual data integration system [18, 20].

which specify that, by default, the tuples in the source relations are copied into the new virtual versions, but with the exception of those that may have to be removed in order to satisfy (1) (with R_1, R_2 replaced by R_1', R_2'). Some of the exceptions for R_1' are specified by

$$\neg R_1'(x, y) \leftarrow R_1(x, y), S_1(z, y), \; not \; aux_1(x, z), \; not \; aux_2(z). \tag{3}$$

$$aux_1(x, z) \leftarrow R_2(x, w), S_2(z, w). \qquad aux_2(z) \leftarrow S_2(z, w). \tag{4}$$

That is, $R_1(x, y)$ is deleted if it participates in a violation of (1) (what is captured by the first three literals in the body of (3) plus the first rule in (4)), and there is no way to restore consistency by inserting a tuple into R_2, because there is no possible matching tuple in S_2 for the possibly new tuple in R_2 (what is captured by the last literal in the body of (3) plus the second rule in (4)). In case there is such a tuple in S_2, we either delete a tuple from R_1 or insert a tuple into R_2:

$$\neg R_1'(x, y) \lor R_2'(x, w) \leftarrow R_1(x, y), S_1(z, y), \; not \; aux_1(x, z), S_2(z, w),$$
$$choice((x, z), w). \tag{5}$$

That is, in case of a violation of (1), when there is tuple of the form (a, t) in S_2 for the combination of values (d, a), then the *choice operator* [14] non deterministically chooses a unique value for t, so that the tuple (d, t) is inserted into R_2 as an alternative to deleting (d, m) from R_1. The *choice* predicate can be replaced by a standard predicate plus extra rules that choose a unique value for t [14]. No exceptions are specified for R_2', which makes sense since R_2' is a superset of R_2. Then, the negative literal in the body of (2) can be eliminated. However, new tuples can be inserted into R_2', what is captured by rule (5). Finally, the program must contain as facts the tuples in the original relations R_1, R_2, S_1, S_2.

If P equally trusts itself and Q, both P and Qs' relations are flexible when searching for a solution. The program becomes more involved, because now S_1, S_2 may also change; and virtual versions for them must be specified   □

This example shows the main issues in the specification of a peer's solutions under referential DECs. The program with choice operator can be translated into one with standard answer set (or stable model) semantics [14]; and the solutions are in one to one correspondence with the answer sets of the program. Actually, each answer set S corresponds to a solution $r'(S)$ for peer P which coincides with the original, material, global instance on the tables other than R_1, R_2, whereas for the latter the contents are of the form $\{\bar{t} \mid R_i'(\bar{t}) \in S\}$, $i = 1, 2$, resp. The absence of solutions for a peer is captured through the non existence of answer sets for program Π.

Since program Π represents in a compact form all the solutions for a peer, the peer consistent answers from a peer can be obtained by running a query program expressed in terms of the virtually repaired tables, in combination with the specification program Π. For this the combined program is run under the skeptical answer set semantics, for which a system like DLV [19] can be used. For example, the query $Q(x, z) : \exists y (R_1(x, y) \land R_2(z, y))$ issued to peer P, would be peer consistently answered by running the query program $Ans_Q(x, z) \leftarrow R_1'(x, y), R_2'(x, y)$ together with program Π. Although only (the new versions of) P's relations appear in the query, the program may make P import Q's data.

In the presence of referential DECs, the *choice operator* may have to choose values from the infinite underlying domain, but outside the active domains. There are several options, some of them already considered for CQA: (a) Live with an open infinite domain; (b) Assign null values without propagation through DECs [2]; (c) Consider an appropriate finite and closed proper superset of the active domains [6]; (d) Introduce fresh constants whenever needed from a separate domain [8]. We do not commit to any of these options here, but this choice and the class of referential ECs (e.g. presence cycles) may determine, e.g. decidability of peer consistent answering [7–9, 16].

If a peer P has local ICs $IC(P)$ to be satisfied, also at query time, then the program that specifies its solutions should take care of its ICs. A simple but radical way of doing this consists in using program denial constraints. If in Section 3 we had for peer P the local functional dependency (FD) $\forall x \forall y \forall z (R_1(x, y) \land R_1(x, z) \rightarrow y = z)$, then program would include the program constraint $\leftarrow R_1(x, y), R_1(x, z), y \neq z$, having the effect of pruning those solutions that do not satisfy the FD. However, a more flexible -or "robust" [11]- alternative for keeping the local ICs satisfied, consists in having the specification program split in two layers, where the first one builds the solutions, without considering the local ICs, and the second one, repairs the solutions wrt the local ICs, as done with single inconsistent relational databases [2]. A more uniform approach consists in identifying $IC(P)$ with $\Sigma(P, P)$ and considering $(P, same, P) \in trust$.

Finally, we should notice that obtaining peer consistent answers has at least the data complexity of consistent query answering, for which some results are known [7, 9, 12]. In the latter case, for common database queries and ICs, Π_2^P-completeness is easily achieved. On the other side, the problem of skeptical query evaluation from the disjunctive programs we are using for P2P systems is also Π_2^P-complete in data complexity [10]. In this sense, the logic programs are not contributing with additional complexity to our problem.

4   A LAV Approach

There are some clear connections between P2P query answering and virtual integration of data sources by means of mediator based systems [16, 21]. There are basically two approaches to the latter problem. According to *global-as-view* (GAV), each virtual table at the mediator (global) level is expressed as a view of the collection of relations in the data sources. According to *local-as-view* (LAV), relations in the (local) data sources as expressed as views of the virtual global relations. GAV is more natural and simpler for query evaluation than LAV, but LAV is simpler to deal with when sources leave and enter the integration system. GLAV is a mixture of the two approaches (see [18] for a survey).

The logic programming-based approach proposed in Section 3 can be assimilated to the GAV approach, because tables in the solutions are specified as views over peer's schemas. However, a LAV approach could also be attempted, and we also introduce virtual, global versions S_1', S_2' of S_1, S_2. The source relations R_1, R_2, S_1, S_2 are defined as views of the virtual relations in a solution, namely by $R_1(x, y) \leftarrow R_1'(x, y).$, $R_2(x, y) \leftarrow R_2'(x, y).$, $S_1(x, y) \leftarrow S_1'(x, y).$, $S_2(x, y) \leftarrow S_2'(x, y).$; and are declared closed, open, clopen and clopen, resp. [15]. These labels depend on the IC (1) and the trust relationships; actually by the fact that R_1, R_2 can change, but not S_1, S_2. More precisely, the closure of R_1 corresponds to the fact that (1) can be satisfied by deleting tuples from R_1, then the contents of the view defined in there must be contained in the original material source relation. The openness of R_2 indicates that we can insert tuples into R_2 to satisfy the constraint, and then, the extension of the solution contains the original source. Since, S_1, S_2 do not change, they are declared as both closed and open, i.e. clopen.

If a query is posed to peer P, it has to be first formulated in terms of R'_1, R'_2, and then it can be peer consistently answered by querying the integration system subject to the global IC: $\forall xyz \exists w(R'_1(x,y) \wedge S'_1(z,y) \rightarrow R'_2(x,w) \wedge S'_2(z,w))$. A methodology that is similar to the one applied for consistently querying virtual data integration systems under LAV can be used. In [5] methodologies for open sources are presented, and in [3] the mixed case with both open, closed and clopen sources is treated. However, there are differences with the P2P scenario; and the methodologies need to be adjusted as discussed below.

The methodology presented in [3] for CQA in virtual data integration is based on a three-layered answer set programming specification of the repairs of the system: a first layer specifies the contents of the global relations in the minimal legal instances (to this layer only open and clopen sources contribute), a second layer consisting of program denial constraints that prunes the models that violate the closure condition for the closed sources; and a third layer specifying the minimal repairs of the legal instances [5] left by the other layers wrt the global ICs. For CQA, repairs are allowed to violate the original labels.

In our P2P scenario, we want, first of all, to consider only the legal instances that satisfy the mapping in the table and that, in the case of closed sources, include the maximum amount of tuples from the sources (the virtual relations must be kept as close as possible to their original, material versions). For the kind of mappings that we have in the table, this can be achieved by using exactly the same kind of specifications presented in in [3] for the mixed case, *but* considering the closed sources as clopen. In doing so, they will contribute to the program with both rules that import their contents into the system (maximizing the set of tuples in the global relation) and denial program constraints. Now, the trust relation also makes a difference. In order for the virtual relations to satisfy the original labels, that in their turn capture the trust relationships, the rules that repair the chosen legal instances will consider only tuple deletions (insertions) for the virtual global relations corresponding to the closed (resp. open) sources. For clopen sources the rules can neither add nor delete tuples.[3] This methodology can handle universal and simple referential DECs (no cycles and single atom consequents, conditions that are imposed by the repair layer of the program), which covers a broad class of DECs. The DEC in (1) does not fall in this class, but the repair layer can be adjusted in order to generate the solutions for P.[4]

---

[3] This preference criterion for a subclass of the repairs is similar to the *loosely-sound semantic* for integration of open sources under GAV [17].

[4] For the specification, c.f. the appendix in http://arxiv.org/abs/cs.DB/0401015

5   The Transitive Case

It is natural to consider *transitive* DECs when a peer A, that is being queried, gets data from a peer B, who in its turn -and without A possibly knowing- gets data from a peer C to answer A's request. Most likely there is no explicit DEC from A to C; and we do not want to derive them. In order to approach peer consistent query answering in this more complex scenario, it becomes necessary to integrate the local solutions, what can be achieved by integrating the "local" specification programs. In this case, we prefer to define the global solutions directly from the the the stable models of the combined program obtained from the specification of direct interactions. This is more natural and simpler than extending to the global case the definition of solution for the direct case.[5] Of course, there might be no solutions, what is reflected in the absence of stable models for the program. A problematic case appears when there are implicit cyclic dependencies [16].

Example 5. (example 4 continued) Let us consider another peer C with a relation $U(\cdot, \cdot)$. The following exchange constraint $\Sigma(Q, C)$: $\forall x \forall y (U(x, y) \rightarrow S_1(x, y))$ exists from Q to C and $(Q, less, C) \in trust$, meaning that Q trusts C's data more than its own. When P requests data from Q, the latter will request data from C's relation U. Now, consider the peer instances: $r_1 = \{(a, b)\}, s_1 = \{\}, r_2 = \{\}, s_2 = \{(c, e), (c, f)\}$ and $u = \{(c, b)\}$. If we analyze each peer locally, the solution for Q would contain the tuple $S_1(c, b)$ added; and P would have only one solution, corresponding to the original instances, because the DEC is satisfied without making any changes. When considering them globally, the tuple that is locally added into Q requires tuples to be added and/or deleted into/from P in order to satisfy the DEC. The combined program that specifies the global solutions consists of rules (2), (4) plus both (3) and (5), but with S_1 replaced by S_1' in the body. Finally, we add $S_1'(x, y) \leftarrow S_1(x, y), \; not \; \neg S_1'(x, y)$, which is a persistence rule for S_1; and $S_1'(x, y) \leftarrow U(x, y), \; not \; S_1(x, y)$, which enforces the satisfaction of $\Sigma(Q, C)$. The solutions obtained from the stable models are: $r' = \{S_2(c, e), S_2(c, f), U(c, b), S_1'(c, b), R_2'(a, f), R_1'(a, b)\}, r'' = \{S_2(c, e), S_2(c, f), U(c, b), S_1'(c, b)\}, r''' = \{S_2(c, e), S_2(c, f), U(c, b), S_1'(c, b), R_2'(a, e), R_1'(a, b)\}$. □

Acknowledgements. Research funded by NSERC Grant 250279-02 and a grant from the CITO/IBM-CAS Student Internship Program. L. Bertossi is Faculty Fellow of the IBM Center for Advanced Studies, Toronto Lab. We appreciate conversations with Ariel Fuxman and Pablo Barcelo.

References

1. M. Arenas, L. Bertossi, and J. Chomicki. Consistent Query Answers in Inconsistent Databases. In *Proc. ACM Symposium on Principles of Database Systems (PODS 99)*, ACM Press, 1999, pp. 68–79.
2. P. Barcelo, L. Bertossi, and L. Bravo. Characterizing and Computing Semantically Correct Answers from Databases with Annotated Logic and Answer Sets. In *Semantics in Databases*, Springer LNCS 2582, 2003, pp. 1–27.

---

[5] The approaches to P2P data exchange semantics in [8, 11] also appeal to this kind of 2-step process, however in a framework based on epistemic logic.

3. L. Bertossi and L. Bravo. Consistent Query Answers in Virtual Data Integration Systems. Book chapter in 'Inconsistency Tolerance in Knowledge-bases, Databases and Software Specifications', Springer, to appear.

4. L. Bertossi and J. Chomicki. Query Answering in Inconsistent Databases. In *Logics for Emerging Applications of Databases*, J. Chomicki, G. Saake and R. van der Meyden (eds.), Springer, 2003.

5. L. Bravo and L. Bertossi. Logic Programs for Consistently Querying Data Sources In *Proc. International Joint Conference on Artificial Intelligence (IJCAI 03)*, Morgan Kaufmann, 2003, pp. 10–15.

6. L. Bravo and L. Bertossi. Disjunctive Deductive Databases for Computing Certain and Consistent Answers to Queries from Mediated Data Integration Systems To appear in *Journal of Applied Logic*.

7. A. Cali, D. Lembo, and R. Rosati. On the Decidability and Complexity of Query Answering over Inconsistent and Incomplete Databases. In *Proc. ACM Symposium on Principles of Database Systems (PODS 03)*, ACM Press, 2003, pp. 260-271.

8. D. Calvanese, E. Damaggio, G. De Giacomo, M. Lenzerini, and R. Rosati. Semantic Data Integration in P2P Systems. In *Proc. International Workshop on Databases, Information Systems and Peer-to-Peer Computing (DBISP2P 03)*, Springer LNCS 2944, 2004.

9. J. Chomicki and J. Marcinkowski. Minimal-Change Referential Integrity Maintenance Using Tuple Deletions. arXiv.org paper cs.DB/0212004. To appear in *Information and Computation*.

10. E. Dantsin, T. Eiter, G. Gottlob, and A. Voronkov. Complexity And Expressive Power Of Logic Programming. *ACM Computer Surveys*, 2001, 33(3), 374-425.

11. E. Franconi, G. Kuper, L. Lopatenko, L. Serafini. A Robust Logical and Computational Characterisation of Peer-to-Peer Database Systems. In *Proc. International Workshop on Databases, Information Systems and Peer-to-Peer Computing (DBISP2P 03)*, Springer LNCS 2944, 2004.

12. A. Fuxman and R.J. Miller. Towards Inconsistency Management in Data Integration Systems. In *Proc. IJCAI-03 Workshop on Information Integration on the Web*.

13. M. Gelfond and V. Lifschitz. Classical Negation in Logic Programs and Disjunctive Databases. *New Generation Computing*, 1991, 9:365–385.

14 F. Giannotti, D. Pedreschi, D. Sacca, C. Zaniolo. Non-Determinism in Deductive Databases. In *Proc. International Conference on Deductive and Object-Oriented Databases (DOOD 91)*, Springer LNCS 566, 1991, pp. 129–146.

15. G. Grahne and A. Mendelzon. Tableau Techniques for Querying Information Sources through Global Schemas. In *Proc. International Conference on Database Theory (ICDT 99)*, Springer LNCS 1540, 1999, pp. 332–347.

16. A.Y. Halevy, Z.G. Ives, D. Suciu, and I. Tatarinov. Schema Mediation in Peer Data Management Systems. In *Proceedings International Conference on Data Engineering (ICDE 03)*, 2003, pp. 505-518.

17. D. Lembo, M. Lenzerini, and R. Rosati. Source Inconsistency and Incompleteness in Data Integration. In Proc. Knowledge Representation meets Databases (KRDB 02), 2002.

18. M. Lenzerini. Data Integration: A Theoretical Perspective. In *Proc. ACM Symposium on Principles of Database Systems (PODS 02)*, ACM Press, 2002, pp. 233-246.

19. N. Leone *et al.* The DLV System for Konwledge Representation and Reasoning. arXiv.org paper cs.LO/0211004. To appear in *ACM Transactions on Computational Logic*.

20. A. Levy. Logic-Based Techniques in Data Integration. In *Logic Based Artificial Intelligence*, J. Minker (ed.), Kluwer, 2000, pp. 575-595.

21. I. Tatarinov *et al.* The Piazza Peer Data Management Project. *ACM SIGMOD Record*, 2003, 32(3):47-52.

Semantic Query Routing and Processing in P2P Database Systems: The ICS-FORTH SQPeer Middleware*

George Kokkinidis and Vassilis Christophides

Institute of Computer Science – FORTH,
Vassilika Vouton, PO Box 1385, GR 71110, Heraklion, Greece
and
Department of Computer Science, University of Crete,
GR 71409, Heraklion, Greece
{kokkinid,christop}@ics.forth.gr

Abstract. Peer-to-peer (P2P) computing is currently attracting enormous attention. In P2P systems a very large number of autonomous computing nodes (the peers) pool together their resources and rely on each other for data and services. More and more P2P data management systems rely nowadays on intensional (i.e. schema) information for integrating and querying peer bases. Such information can be easily captured by emerging Semantic Web languages such as RDF/S. However, a fully-fledged framework for evaluating semantic queries over peer RDF/S bases (materialized or virtual) is missing. In this paper we present the ICS-FORTH SQPeer middleware for routing and processing RQL queries and RVL views. The novelty of SQPeer lies on the use of intensional active schemas for determining relevant peer bases, as well as, constructing distributed query plans. In this context, we consider optimization opportunities for SQPeer query plans.

1 Introduction

Peer-to-peer (P2P) computing is currently attracting enormous attention, spurred by the popularity of file sharing systems such as Napster [19], Gnutella [10], Freenet [7], Morpheus [18] and Kazaa [14]. In P2P systems a very large number of autonomous computing nodes (the peers) pool together their resources and rely on each other for data and services. P2P computing introduces an interesting paradigm of decentralization going hand in hand with an increasing self-organization of highly autonomous peers. This new paradigm bears the potential to realize computing systems that scale to very large numbers of participating nodes while ensuring fault-tolerance.

However, current P2P systems offer very limited data management facilities. In most of the cases searching information relies on simple selection on a predefined set of index attributes or IR-style string matching. These limitations are acceptable for file-sharing applications, but in order to support highly dynamic, ever-changing, autonomous social organizations (e.g., scientific or educational communities) we need richer facilities

---

* This work was partially supported by the EU project SeLeNe (IST-2001-39045).

W. Lindner et al. (Eds.): EDBT 2004 Workshops, LNCS 3268, pp. 486–495, 2004.

in exchanging, querying and integrating structured and semi-structured data. To build such net-centric information systems we essentially need to adapt the P2P computing paradigm to a distributed data and knowledge management setting. In particular, we would like to support loosely coupled communities of databases where each peer base can join and leave the network at will.

The importance of intensional (i.e., schema) information for integrating and querying peer bases has been highlighted by a number of recent projects [20] [11]. In particular, the notion of Semantic Overlay Networks (SONs) [8], appears to be an intuitive way to group together peers sharing the same schema information. Thus, peers employing one or more topics (or concepts) of the same thematic hierarchy, are semantically related and belong to the same SON. This approach facilitates query routing, since a peer can easily identify relevant peers instead of broadcasting (flooding) query requests on the network. A natural candidate for representing such topic hierarchies (or more complex domain models) is the Resource Description Framework/Schema Language (RDF/S). RDF/S (a) enables a *modular design* of descriptive schemas based on the mechanism of *namespaces*; (b) allows easy *reuse* or *refinement* of existing schemas through *subsumption* of both class and property definitions; (c) supports partial descriptions since *properties* associated with a resource are by default *optional and repeated* and (d) permits *super-imposed descriptions* in the sense that a resource may be multiply classified under several classes from one or several schemas. These modelling primitives are crucial for P2P databases where monolithic RDF/S schemas and resource descriptions cannot be constructed in advance and users may have only incomplete descriptions about the available resources. In this context, several declarative languages for querying and defining views over RDF description bases have been proposed in the literature such as RQL [13] and RVL [17]. However, a fully-fledged framework for evaluating semantic queries over peer RDF/S bases (materialized or virtual) is still missing.

In this paper, we present the ongoing SQPeer middleware for routing and processing semantic queries in P2P database systems. More precisely, we make the following contributions. In Section 2.1 we illustrate how conjunctive RQL queries expressed against a SON RDF/S schema can be represented in our middleware as *semantic query patterns*. In Section 2.2 we introduce a novel technique for advertising peer RDF/S bases using intentional information. In particular, we are employing *active-schemas* for declaring the parts of a SON RDF/S schema, which are actually (or can be) populated in a peer base. Active-schemas are essentially RVL (materialized or virtual) views of peer bases. In Section 2.3 we sketch a semantic query routing algorithm, which matches a given RQL query against a set of active-schemas in order to determine relevant peers. More precisely, this algorithm relies on query/view subsumption techniques to produce *semantic query patterns annotated with routing information*. In Section 2.4 we describe how SQPeer *query plans* are generated from annotated semantic query patterns taking into account the involved data distribution (e.g., vertical, horizontal). Then, we show how a query plan is executed with the deployment of appropriate communication *channels* between the relevant peers. In Section 2.5 we discuss several *compile* or *run-time optimization opportunities* for the generated SQPeer query plans. Finally, Section 3 summarizes our contributions and presents our future work.

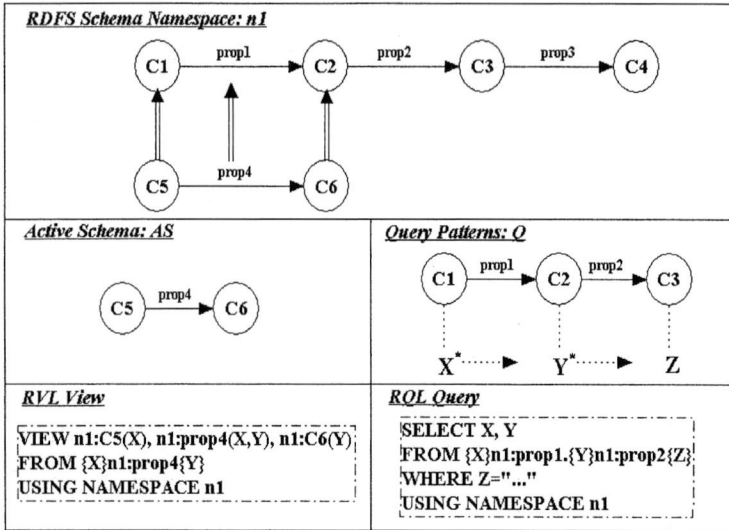

Fig. 1. RDF/S schema namespace, peer active-schema and query pattern graph

2   Semantic Query Routing and Processing in SQPeer

In order to design an effective query routing and processing middleware for peer RDF/S bases, we need to address issues, such as how peer nodes *formulate* queries and *advertise* their bases over a SON, as well as how they *route* and *process* queries and how the resulting distributed query plans are *optimized*. In the following subsections, we will present the main design choices for SQPeer in response to the above fundamental issues.

2.1   RQL Peer Queries

Each peer node in SQPeer provides RDF descriptions that conform to a number of RDF schemas. Peer nodes with the same schema can be considered to belong to the same SON[1]. In the upper part of Figure 1 we can see an example of the schema graph of a specific namespace (i.e., n1) with four classes, C1, C2, C3 and C4, that are connected with three properties, prop1, prop2 and prop3. There are also two subclasses, C5 and C6, of classes C1 and C2 respectively, which are related with the sub-property prop4 of the property prop1.

Queries in SQPeer are formulated by client-peers in RQL, according to the RDF schemas they use to create their description bases or to define virtual views over their legacy (XML or relational) databases. In this context, we need to reason about query/ view containment in order to guide query routing through the peer bases of the system. To this end, we introduce the notion of *query patterns* capturing the schema informa-

---

[1] In a more sophisticated scenario, peer nodes contributing RDF descriptions specified by an RVL view are members of the same SON

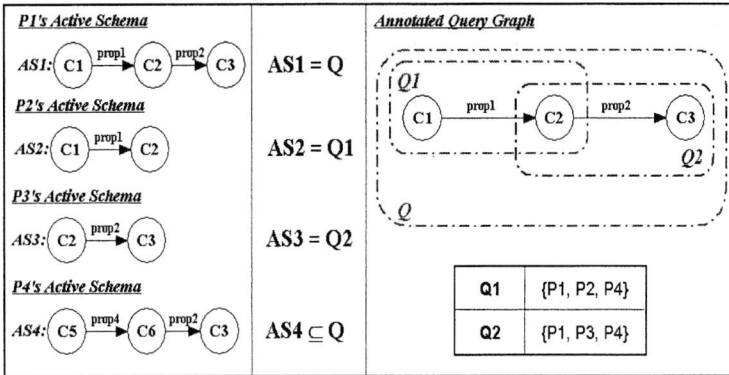

Fig. 2. An annotated RQL query graph

tion employed by an RQL query. This information is mainly extracted from the path expressions appearing in the from clause.

In the bottom right part of Figure 1 we can see an RQL query returning all the resources binded by the variables X and Y. In the from-clause, the employed path expressions imply a join on the Y resource variable between the target of the property prop1 and the origin of the property prop2. The where-clause filters the returned resources according to the value of variable Z. Filtering conditions are not taken into account by RQL query patterns. The right middle part of Figure 1 illustrates the query pattern graph of query Q, where X and Y resource variables are marked with "*" to denote projections. A graphical end-user interface[2] may be used to create and visualize such query pattern graphs. Since the query pattern graph involves only path expressions and projections, we focus only on conjunctive RQL queries.

2.2 Peer Base Advertisement

In the context of a SON, each peer node should be able to advertise its base to other peers. Peer base advertisement in SQPeer relies on virtual or materialized RDF schema(s). Since these schemas contain numerous RDF classes and properties not necessarily populated with data in a peer base, we need a fine-grained notion of schema-based advertisements. The *active-schema* of a peer node is essentially a subset of the employed RDF schema(s) for which all RDF classes and properties are (in the materialized scenario) or can be (in the virtual view scenario) populated. The active-schema may be broadcasted to (or requested by) other peer nodes, thus informing the rest of the P2P system of what is actually available inside the peer bases.

The bottom left part of Figure 1 illustrates the RVL statement of a peer active-schema. This statement "populates" the classes C5 and C6 and the property prop4 (in the view-clause) with appropriate instances from the peer's base (in the from-clause). In the middle left part of the figure we can see the corresponding active-schema graph obtained by this view. This view can be a materialized RDF/S schema with actual resource descriptions

---

[2] See for instance the RQL interactive demo at http://139.91.183.30:8999/RQLdemo/

or can be a virtual one populated with data from a relational or an XML peer base. A more complex example is illustrated in the left part of Figure 2, comprising the active-schemas of four peers. Peer P1 contains resources related through the properties `prop1` and `prop2`, while peer P4 contains resources related through the properties `prop4` and `prop2`. Peer P2 contains resources related by `prop1`, while peer P3 contains resources related by `prop2`. We can note the similarity in the representation of active-schemas and query pattern graphs.

Representing active-schemas and query pattern graphs in an intensional way makes easier to maintain a distributed knowledge of the P2P system, while yielding significant performance gains. First, by representing in the same way what is queried by a peer and what is contained in a peer database, we can reuse the RQL query/RVL view subsumption techniques, as proposed in the Semantic Web Integration Middleware (SWIM [6]). Second, compared to global schema-based advertisements [20], we expect that the load of queries processed by each peer is smaller, since a peer receives only relevant to its content queries. This also affects the amount of network bandwidth consumed by the P2P system.

2.3   Semantic Query Routing

Query routing is responsible for finding the relevant to a query peers by taking into account data distribution (vertical, horizontal and mixed) of peer bases committing to a SON RDF/S schema. The query/view subsumption techniques of [6], are employed to determine which part of a query can be answered by an active-schema and rewrite accordingly the query sent to a peer.

The query-routing algorithm takes as input a query graph and annotates each involved path pattern with the peers that can actually answer it, thus outputting an annotated query graph. A pseudocode description on how this algorithm works is given below.

Query-Routing Algorithm:

```
1. A peer P receives an RQL query Q.
2. Peer P parses the query Q and creates the corresponding query
   pattern graph by obtaining the involved paths.
3. For each pattern, the matching algorithm is performed.
   (a) Compare the path pattern with all known active-schemas.
   (b) If the active-schema graph is subsumed by the selected path
       pattern, then it is annotated with the name of the peer
       owning the active-schema.
4. Output annotated query graph.
```

An example of a query graph, which is composed of two path patterns, Q1 and Q2, is illustrated in Figure 2. In the middle part of Figure 2 we can also see how the matching is performed with the active-schemas of our example peers. P1's active-schema is equal to the path patterns Q1 and Q2, so both path patterns are annotated with P1. P2's active-schema is equal to path pattern Q1 and P3's active-schema is equal to Q2, so Q1 and Q2 are annotated with P2 and P3 respectively. Finally, P4's active-schema is subsumed by path patterns Q1 and Q2, since `prop4` is sub-property of `prop1`. Similarly to P1, Q1 and Q2 are annotated with P4. In the right part of Figure 2 we can see the annotated graph created by this matching.

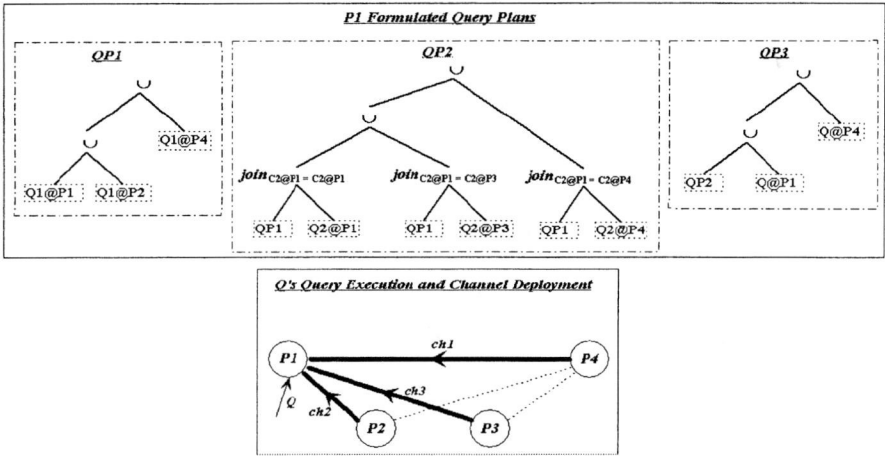

Fig. 3. A SQPeer query execution example

2.4   Semantic Query Processing

Query processing in SQPeer takes the responsibility of generating distributed query plans according to the information returned by the routing algorithm. These query plans are then executed by the relevant peers. Communication *channels* [22] enable this distributed execution and create the necessary foundation for exchanging appropriate data between the appropriate peers.

Through channels, peers are able to route query plans and exchange the corresponding results according to the queries requested by client-peers. In addition, channels permit each peer to further route and process the queries received, since it can be connected with more peers independently of the previous routing operations. Finally, channel deployment can be adapted during query execution in order to response to network failures or peer nodes processing limitations. Each channel has a root and a destination node. The root node of a channel is responsible for the management of the channel and for creating a locally unique id for it. Data packets are sent through each channel from the destination to the root node. Beside query results, these packets can also contain "changing plan" and failure information or other statistics useful for run-time query adaptability.

The query-processing algorithm receives as input an annotated query graph and outputs its corresponding query plan. A pseudocode description on how this algorithm works is also given below.

Query-Processing Algorithm:

```
1. Peer P receives an annotated query graph AQ for the RQL query Q.
2. If P doesn't answer any part of the query Q
        Send query to a neighbor peer (according to the
        architectural alternative);
   Else
        Create a new query plan QP;
3. Starting from a root of the graph, check every query path
   pattern PP in a sequential order, until AQ is fully processed;
```

```
4. If PP the root
      Execute horizontal data distribution algorithm with input
      (QP, PP, AQ);
   Else
      Execute vertical data distribution algorithm with input
      (QP, PP, AQ);
      Execute horizontal data distribution algorithm with input
```
(QP, PP, EQ $\bigcup$ AQ), where EQ the previously processed query;
```
5. Output formulated query plan QP.
```

Vertical data distribution algorithm with input (QP, PP, AQ):

1. Obtain set of peers, e.g. $P'=\{P1,\ldots,Pn\}$, from the annotated query graph that can answer PP.
2. For each peer of the set, e.g. Px, create query plan $QPx = QP\ join_{Cp@P=Cq@Px}\ AQ@Px$, where Cp and Cq are the classes on which the join of the two queries is executed.
3. Create query plan $QP = QP1 \bigcup QP2 \bigcup \ldots \bigcup QPn$

Horizontal data distribution algorithm with input (QP, PP, AQ):

1. Obtain set of peers, e.g. $P''=\{P1,\ldots,Pn\}$, from the annotated query graph that can answer PP.
2. For each peer of the set, e.g. Px, expand query plan as $QP = QP \bigcup AQ@Px$

Figure 3 illustrates an example of how the RQL query Q shown in Figure 1, can be executed over the P2P database system described in Section 2.2. The query is first sent to peer P1 which initially executes the query-routing algorithm in order to obtain the annotated query graph of Figure 2. P1 runs the query-processing algorithm and since it can answer a part of the query, creates a new query plan. The algorithm selects as a root of the annotated query graph, the path pattern Q1, for which it runs the horizontal distribution algorithm. This algorithm outputs query plan QP1, shown in Figure 3, since P1, P2 and P4 can execute query path pattern Q1. Next, path pattern Q2 is selected and the vertical data distribution algorithm executes and returns the query plan QP2. For each of the peers that can process Q2, we join the sub-queries sent with the results obtained from query plan QP1. P1 additionally follows the horizontal data distribution for obtaining more complete results. Since P1 and P4 can answer the whole query Q, P1's query plan will evolve to QP3: $QP2 \bigcup Q@P1 \bigcup Q@P4$. The final query plan and the deployment of the channels in SQPeer can also be seen in Figure 3. As seen from the example, taking into account the vertical distribution ensures correctness of query results, while considering horizontal distribution in query plans favours completeness.

Possible rewritings of the queries sent to remote peers in terms of different descriptive schemas may be necessary. This functionality can be implemented in SWIM [6], which supports powerful mappings to RDF/S of both structured relational and semistructured XML databases.

After the creation of the query plan, the peer holds the responsibility of executing this plan and deploy the necessary channels in the system. From the query plan the peer obtains the set of peers that need to be conducted for executing the query. For each of these peers, a channel is created with the root being the peer executing the algorithm and the destination being the peer examined. Although each of these peers may contribute in the execution of the plan by replying to more than one sub-queries, only one channel is of course necessary.

2.5   Query Optimization

In SQPeer we distinguish two possible optimizations of distributed query plans. First, compile-based optimization depends on statistics held by each peer and allows to choose between different execution policies, i.e. data or query shipping [16]. These statistics involve response times from previously contacted peers or result sizes from previous executions of the same query. The speed of the connection between the peers can be used to decide between different channel deployments. The processing load of the peers can be also considered, since a peer that processes fewer queries, even if its connection is slow, may offer a better execution time. This processing load can be handled by the existence of slots in each peer, which show the amount of queries that can be handled simultaneously.

On the other hand, run-time adaptability of query plans is an essential characteristic of query processing when peer bases join and leave the system at free will or more in general when system resources are exhausted. For example, the optimizer may alter a running query plan by observing the throughput of a certain channel. This throughput can be measured by the number of incoming or outgoing tuples (i.e., resources related through a property). The root node of each channel is responsible for identifying possible problems caused by environmental changes and for handling them accordingly. It should also inform all the involved nodes that are affected by the alteration of the plan. Finally, the root node should create a new query plan by re-executing the routing and processing algorithm and not taking into consideration those peers that became obsolete.

3   Summary and Future Work

In this paper, we have presented the ICS-FORTH SQPeer middleware offering sophisticated query routing and processing middleware in P2P data management systems. We presented how (conjunctive) RQL path queries expressed against a SON RDF/S schema can be represented as semantic query patterns and how peers can advertise their bases using active-schemas expressed in the same formalism. We sketched a semantic query routing algorithm, which relies on query/view subsumption techniques to annotate semantic query patterns with information concerning relevant peers. We also presented how SQPeer query plans are created and executed by taking into account the data distribution in peer bases. Finally, we have discussed several compile and run-time optimization opportunities for SQPeer query plans.

SQPeer's query processing and routing algorithms can be used independently of the particular P2P architectural setting. We consider two such architectural alternatives. The first alternative corresponds to an ad-hoc P2P architecture (like Freenet or Gnutella), where SONs are formed in a self-adaptive way. More precisely, when a peer initially joins the system, it identifies and connects to other peers committing to the same RDF/S schema of the SON. The second alternative is closer to a hybrid P2P architecture based on the notion of Super-Peer Nodes (like Morpheus or Kazaa), where SONs are created in a more static way. In particular, each super-peer node is responsible for the creation and further management of a SON. It should be stressed that while in the ad-hoc architecture, peers handle both the query routing and processing load, super-peers are only responsible for routing and their sub-peers for processing the queries. Additionally, super-peers contain a global knowledge of the active-schemas of the peers in a SON and therefore they can create a query plan offering completeness in the results. Finally, super-peers may possibly play the role of a mediator in a scenario where a query expressed in terms of a global-known schema needs to be reformulated in terms of the schemas employed by the local peer bases by using appropriate mapping rules.

Recent projects address query processing issues in P2P database systems, such as Query Flow [15], ubQL [22], Mutant Query Plans (MQPs) [21] and AmbientDB [2]. Compared to these projects, SQPeer does not require an a priori knowledge of the relevant to a query peers and exhibits more optimization opportunities for distributed query plans. Other projects address mainly query routing issues in SONs, such as the Edutella project [20] [4], RDFPeers [5] and [9]. Unlike these projects, SQPeer's query routing and processing algorithms considers both vertical and horizontal distribution, while exploiting the full power of RDF/S-based SONs and in particular the subsumption of classes or properties. Finally, although the use of indices and super-peer topologies facilitate query routing, the cost of updating (XML or RDF) distributed indices when peers join and leave is important compared to the cost of maintaining active-schemas (i.e. views), as in the case of SQPeer.

Several issues remain open with respect to the optimization of distributed and adaptive queries in SQPeer borrowing ideas from related works [1] [3] [12]. We plan to study the trade-off between result completeness and processing load using the concepts of Top N (or Bottom N) queries [16]. In the same direction, we can use constraints regarding the number of peer nodes that each query is broadcasted and further processed.

Acknowledgment

We would like to thank Val Tannen for fruitful discussions on peer channels.

References

1. R. Avnur and J.M. Hellerstein. Eddies: Continuously Adaptive Query Processing. In *ACM SIGMOD*, pages 261–272, Dallas, TX, 2000.
2. P. Boncz and C. Treijtel. AmbientDB: relational query processing in a P2P network. In *Proceedings of the International Workshop on Databases, Information Systems and Peer-to-Peer Computing (DBISP2P)*. Springer Verlag, 2003.
3. R. Braumandl, M. Keidl, A. Kemper, D. Kossmann, A. Kreutz, S. Seltzsam, and K. Stocker. ObjectGlobe:Ubiquitous Query Processing On The Internet. In *VLDB Journal*, pages 48–71, 2001.
4. I. Brunkhorst, H. Dhraief, A. Kemper, W. Nejdl, and C. Wiesner. Distributed Queries and Query Optimization in Schema-Based P2P-Systems. In *Proceedings of the International Workshop on Databases, Information Systems and Peer-to-Peer Computing (DBISP2P)*, Berlin, Germany, 2003.

5. M. Cai and M. Frank. RDFPeers: A Scalable Distributed RDF Repository based on A Structured Peer-to-Peer Network. In *Proceedings of the 13th International World Wide Web Conference (WWW)*, New York, 2004.
6. V. Christophides, G. Karvounarakis, I. Koffina, G. Kokkinidis, A. Magkanaraki, D. Plexousakis, G. Serfiotis, and V. Tannen. The ICS-FORTH SWIM: A Powerful Semantic Web Integration Middleware. In *Proceedings of the First International Workshop on Semantic Web and Databases (SWDB), Co-located with VLDB 2003*, Humboldt-Universitat, Berlin, Germany, 2003.
7. I. Clarke, O. Sandberg, B. Wiley, and T.W. Hong. Freenet: A Distributed Anonymous Information Storage and Retrieval System. In *Proceedings of the International Workshop on Design Issues in Anonymity and Unobservability*. Springer Verlag, 2001.
8. A. Crespo and H. Garcia-Molina. Semantic Overlay Networks for P2P Systems. Technical report, Stanford Technical Report, 2003.
9. L. Galanis, Y. Wang, S.R. Jeffery, and D.J. DeWitt. Processing Queries in a Large P2P System. In *Proceedings of the 15th International Conference on Advanced Information Systems Engineering (CAiSE)*, 2003.
10. The Gnutella file-sharing protocol. Available at : http://gnutella.wego.com.
11. A.Y. Halevy, Z.G. Ives, P. Mork, and I. Tatarinov. Piazza: Data Management Infrastructure for Semantic Web Applications. In *Proceedings of the 12th International World Wide Web Conference (WWW)*, 2003.
12. Z.G. Ives, A.Y. Levy, D.S. Weld, D. Florescu, and M. Friedman. Adaptive Query Processing for Internet Applications. In *IEEE Data Engineering Bulletin*, pages 19–26, 2000.
13. G. Karvounarakis, S. Alexaki, V. Christophides, D. Plexousakis, and M. Scholl. RQL: A Declarative Query Language for RDF. In *Proceedings of the 11th International World Wide Web Conference (WWW)*, Honolulu, Hawaii, 2002.
14. The Kazaa file-sharing system. Available at : http://www.kazaa.com.
15. A. Kemper and C. Wiesner. HyperQueries: Dynamic Distributed Query Processing on the Internet. In *Proceedings of the International Conference on Very Large Data Bases (VLDB)*, Rome, Italy, 2001.
16. D. Kossmann. The State of the Art in Distributed Query Processing. In *ACM Computer Surveys*, pages 422–469, 2000.
17. A. Magkanaraki, V. Tannen, V. Christophides, and D. Plexousakis. Viewing the Semantic Web Through RVL Lenses. In *Proceedings of the 2nd International Semantic Web Conference (ISWC)*, 2003.
18. The Morpheus file-sharing system. Available at : http://www.musiccity.com.
19. The Napster file-sharing system. Available at : http://www.napster.com.
20. W. Nejdl, M. Wolpers, W. Siberski, C. Schmitz, M. Schlosser, I. Brunkhorst, and A. Loser. Super-Peer-Based Routing and Clustering Strategies for RDF-Based P2P Networks. In *Proceedings of the 12th International World Wide Web Conference (WWW)*, Budapest, Hungary, 2003.
21. V. Papadimos, D. Maier, and K. Tufte. Distributed Query Processing and Catalogs for P2P Systems. In *Proceedings of the 2003 CIDR Conference*, 2003.
22. A. Sahuguet. *ubQL: A Distributed Query Language to Program Distributed Query Systems*. PhD thesis, University of Pennsylvania, 2002.

Query Processing in Super-Peer Networks
with Languages Based on Information Retrieval:
The P2P-DIET Approach*

Stratos Idreos[1], Christos Tryfonopoulos[1], Manolis Koubarakis[1], and Yannis Drougas[2]

[1] Intelligent Systems Laboratory, Dept. of Electronic and Computer Engineering,
University of Crete, Greece
{sidraios,trifon,manolis}@intelligence.tuc.gr
[2] Dept. of Computer Science and Engineering, University of California Riverside, USA
drougas@cs.ucr.edu

Abstract. This paper presents P2P-DIET, an implemented resource sharing system that unifies one-time and continuous query processing in super-peer networks. P2P-DIET offers a simple data model for the description of network resources based on attributes with values of type text and a query language based on concepts from Information Retrieval. The focus of this paper is on the main modelling concepts of P2P-DIET (metadata, advertisements and queries), the routing algorithms (inspired by the publish/subscibe system SIENA) and the scalable indexing of resource metadata and queries.

1 Introduction

We consider the problem of *selective dissemination of information (SDI)* or *publish/subscribe* in peer-to-peer (P2P) networks [2, 7, 10, 14]. In an SDI scenario, a user posts a *continuous query* or *profile* to the system to receive notifications whenever certain *resources* of interest are *published*. Our work has culminated in the implementation of P2P-DIET [9, 11], a service that unifies one-time and continuous query processing in P2P networks with super-peers.

P2P-DIET combines one-time querying as found in other super-peer networks [16] and SDI as proposed in DIAS [10]. P2P-DIET has been implemented on top of the open source DIET Agents Platform[1] and it is currently available at http://www.intelligence.tuc.gr/p2pdiet. The new concept (in the data model) is that of advertisement. Other *new* features that distinguish P2P-DIET from DIAS and other recent systems [2, 7, 14] (client migration, dynamic IP addresses, stored notifications and rendezvous, fault-tolerance mechanisms, and message authentication and encryption) are not discussed and can be found in [8]. The contributions of this paper are the following:

---

* This work was supported in part by the European Commission projects DIET (5th Framework Programme IST/FET) and Evergrow (6th Framework Programme IST/FET). Christos Tryfonopoulos is partially supported by a Ph.D. fellowship from the program Heraclitus of the Greek Ministry of Education.
[1] http://diet-agents.sourceforge.net/

W. Lindner et al. (Eds.): EDBT 2004 Workshops, LNCS 3268, pp. 496–505, 2004.

- We briefly present our super-peer architecture, the protocols for handling advertisements, publications, queries, answers and notifications and discuss how they relate to the protocols of SIENA [2] and EDUTELLA [13].
- We introduce the *new filtering algorithm* BestFitTrie used by super-peers in P2P-DIET for matching textual resource metadata with continuous queries. We compare BestFitTrie with appropriate extensions of the algorithms used by SIFT [15], and discuss their relative strengths and weaknesses.

The rest of the paper is organized as follows. Section 2 briefly presents the metadata model and query language used for describing and querying resources in the current implementation of P2P-DIET. Section 3 discusses the protocols for processing advertisements, publications, queries, answers and notifications. Section 4 presents BestFitTrie and compares it with other alternatives. Section 5 concludes the paper. There is no related work section; instead, comparison of P2P-DIET with related systems is interspersed with our presentation.

2   The Data Model $\mathcal{AWP}$

In [12] we presented the data model $\mathcal{AWP}$ for specifying queries and *textual* resource metadata. Here, we give a brief description of the main concepts of $\mathcal{AWP}$ since it is the data model used in the rest of the paper. $\mathcal{AWP}$ is based on the concept of *attributes* with values of type *text*. The query language of $\mathcal{AWP}$ offers *Boolean* and *proximity operators* on attribute values as in the work of [3] which is based on the Boolean model of IR.

Let Σ be a finite *alphabet*. A *word* is a finite non-empty sequence of letters from Σ. Let $\mathcal{A}$ be a countably infinite set of attributes called the *attribute universe*. In practice attributes will come from *namespaces* appropriate for the application at hand, e.g., from the set of Dublin Core Metadata Elements[2]. If $A \in \mathcal{A}$ then $\mathcal{V}_A$ denotes a set of words called the *vocabulary* of attribute A. A *text value* s of length n over a vocabulary $\mathcal{V}$ is a total function $s : \{1, 2, \ldots, n\} \to \mathcal{V}$.

A *publication* n is a set of attribute-value pairs (A, s) where $A \in \mathcal{A}$, s is a text value over $\mathcal{V}_A$, and all attributes are *distinct*. The following is a publication:

$\{ (AUTHOR, "John\ Smith"), (TITLE, "Information\ dissemination\ in\ P2P\ systems"),$
$(ABSTRACT, "In\ this\ paper\ we\ show\ that\ ...") \}$

A *query* is a conjunction of atomic formulas of the form $A = s$ or $A \sqsupseteq wp$, where wp is a word pattern containing conjunctions of words and proximity formulas with only words as subformulas, for example:

$AUTHOR = "John\ Smith" \wedge TITLE \sqsupseteq p2p \wedge (information \prec_{[0,0]} dissemination)$

The above query requests all resources that have *John Smith* as their author, and their title contains the word *p2p* and a word pattern where the word *information* is immediately followed by the word *dissemination*.

---

[2] http://purl.org/dc/elements/1.1/

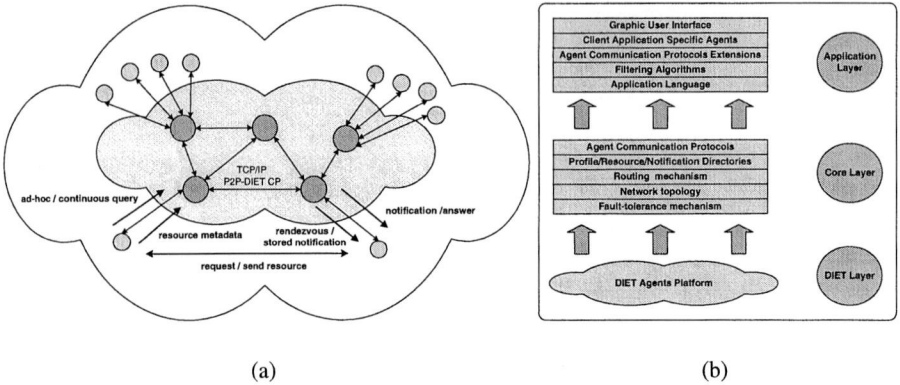

(a)   (b)

Fig. 1. The architecture and the layered view of P2P-DIET

Advertisements in P2P-DIET come in two kinds and are used to prune the paths of queries broadcasted in the super-peer network. An *attribute advertisement* is a subset of the attribute universe $\mathcal{A}$. An *attribute/value advertisement* is a set of pairs $(A, \{s_1, \ldots, s_n\})$ where every $A \in \mathcal{A}$ and every $s_1, \ldots, s_n$ are text values. Intuitively, advertisements are *intentional* descriptions of the content a peer expects to publish to the network. In this matter we follow SIENA [2] and EDUTELLA [13]. The former kind of advertisement gives only the attributes used by a peer to describe its content (e.g., a peer might use only $TITLE$ and $AUTHOR$), while the latter also lists the expected values of certain attributes (e.g., a peer might have only John Smith, John Brown and Tom Fox as authors). Attribute/value advertisements can be interpreted as disjunctions of equalities of the form $A = s_i$.

3   Architecture, Routing and Query Processing

A high-level view of the P2P-DIET architecture and its software layers is shown in Figure 1. There are two kinds of nodes: *super-peers* and *clients*. All super-peers are equal and have the same responsibilities, thus the super-peer subnetwork is a *pure* P2P network (it can be an arbitrary undirected graph). Each super-peer serves a fraction of the clients and keeps *indices* on the resources of those clients.

Resources (e.g., files in a file-sharing application) are kept at client nodes, although it is possible in special cases to store resources at super-peer nodes. Clients request resources directly from the resource owner client. A client is connected to the network through a single super-peer node, which is the *access point* of the client. It is not necessary for a client to be connected to the same access point continuously; *client migration* is supported in P2P-DIET. Clients can connect, disconnect or even leave from the system silently at any time. To enable a higher degree of decentralization and dynamicity, we also allow clients to use *dynamic IP addresses*. If clients are not on-line, notifications matching their interests are stored for them by their access points and delivered once clients reconnect. If resource owners are not on-line, requesting clients can set up a rendezvous to obtain the required resources. Additionally, P2P-DIET supports a simple fault-tolerance protocol based on *are-you-alive* messages between super-peers, and between super-peers and their clients. Finally, P2P-DIET provides message authentication and message encryption using public key cryptography.

The super-peer subnetworks in P2P-DIET are expected to be more stable than typical pure P2P networks such as Gnutella. As a result, we have chosen to use routing algorithms appropriate for such networks, *shortest path trees* and *reverse path forwarding* [5].

Advertisements. P2P-DIET clients *advertise* the resources they expect to publish in the system by sending an advertisement message to their access point. Advertisements are then forwarded in the super-peer backbone. Whenever a resource is published by a client, P2P-DIET makes sure that it satisfies the advertisements made previously by the same client or else a new advertisement message, that contains the extra information for this client must be submitted to the client's access point and forwarded in the super-peer backbone.

One-Time Queries. In the typical *one-time query scenario*, a client C can pose a query q to its access point AP through a `query` message. The message contains the identifier of C, the IP address and port of C and the query q. AP broadcasts q to all super-peers using reverse path forwarding. The advertisements present at each super-peer are used to prune broadcasting paths. An attribute advertisement a blocks further propagation of query q if a does not cover q. An attribute/value advertisement a blocks further propagation of query q if q and a are inconsistent. *Answers* are produced for all matching network resources, by the super-peers that hold the appropriate resource metadata. A super-peer that generates an answer a, forwards a directly to C using the IP address and port of C included in the query q. Each super-peer can be understood to store a relation $resource(ID, A_1, A_2, \ldots, A_n)$ where ID is a resource identifier and $A_1, A_2, \ldots, A_n$ are the attributes of A used by the super-peer. In our implementation, relation $resource$ is implemented by keeping an *inverted file index* for each attribute A_i. The index maps every word w in the vocabulary of A_i to the set of resource IDs that contain word w in their attribute A_i. Query evaluation at each super-peer is then implemented efficiently by utilizing these indices in the standard way [1].

Continuous Queries. Clients may *subscribe* to their access point with a *continuous query*. Super-peers *forward* posed queries to other super-peers. Thus, matching a query with metadata of a published resource takes place at a super-peer that is *as close as possible* to the origin of the resource. A continuous query published by a client C is identified by the identifier of C and a very large random number, *query id* assigned by C at the time that the query was generated. A notification is generated at the access point AP_1 where the resource was published, and travels to the access point AP_2 of every client that has posted a continuous query matching this notification following the *shortest path* from AP_1 to AP_2. Then, the notification is delivered to the interested clients for further processing.

Each super-peer manages an *index* over its continuous queries. Using this index, a super-peer can generate notifications when resource metadata items are published by its clients. Additionally, each super-peer manages a *continuous query poset* that keeps track of the subsumption relations among the continuous queries posted to the super-peer by its clients or forwarded by other super-peers. This poset is again inspired by SIENA [2] and it is used to minimize network traffic: in each super-peer no continuous query that is less general than one that has already been processed is actually forwarded.

4   Filtering Algorithms

In this section we present and evaluate BestFitTrie, a main memory algorithm that solves the filtering problem for *conjunctive queries* in $\mathcal{AWP}$. Because our work extends and improves previous algorithms of SIFT [15], we adopt terminology from SIFT in many cases.

BestFitTrie uses two data structures to represent each published document d: the *occurrence table* $OT(d)$ and the *distinct attribute list* $DAL(d)$. $OT(d)$ is a hash table that uses words as keys, and is used for storing all the attributes of the document in which a specific word appears, along with the positions that each word occupies in the attribute text. $DAL(d)$ is a linked list with one element for each distinct attribute of d. The element of $DAL(d)$ for attribute A points to another linked list, the *distinct word list* for A (denoted by $DWL(A)$) which contains all the distinct words that appear in $A(d)$.

To index queries BestFitTrie utilises an array, called the *attribute directory* (AD), that stores pointers to word directories. AD has one element for each distinct attribute in the query database. A *word directory* $WD(B_i)$ is a hash table that provides fast access to roots of *tries* in a *forest* that is used to organize *sets of words* – the set of words in wp_i (denoted by $words(wp_i)$) for each atomic formula $B_i \sqsupseteq wp_i$ in a query. The proximity formulas contained in each wp_i are stored in an array called the *proximity array* (PA). PA stores pointers to trie nodes (words) that are operands in proximity formulas along with the respective proximity intervals for each formula. Another hash table, called *equality table* (ET) indexes text values s_i that appear in atomic formulas of the form $A_i = s_i$.

When a new query q arrives, the index structures are populated as follows. For each attribute $A_i = s_i$, we hash text value s_i to obtain a slot in ET where we store the value A_i. For each attribute $B_j \sqsupseteq wp_j$, we compute $words(wp_j)$ and insert them in one of the tries with roots indexed by $WD(B_j)$. Finally, we visit PA and store pointers to trie nodes and proximity intervals for the proximity formulas contained in wp_j.

We now explain how each word directory $WD(B_j)$ and its forest of tries are organised. The idea is to store sets of words compactly by exploiting their *common elements*, to preserve memory space and to accelerate the filtering process.

Definition 1. *Let S be a set of sets of words and $s_1, s_2 \in S$ with $s_2 \subseteq s_1$. We say that s_2 is an* identifying subset *of s_1 with respect to S iff $s_2 = s_1$ or $\nexists r \in S$ such that $s_2 \subseteq r$.*

The sets of identifying subsets of two sets of words s_1 and s_2 with respect to a set S is the same if and only if s_1 is identical to s_2.

The sets of words $words(wp_j)$ are organised in the word directory $WD(B_j)$ as follows. Let S be the set of sets of words currently in $WD(B_j)$. When a new set of words s arrives, BestFitTrie selects an identifying subset t of s with respect to S and uses it to organise s in $WD(B_j)$. The algorithm for choosing t depends on the current organization of the word directory and will be given below.

Throughout its existence, each trie T of $WD(B_j)$ has the following properties. The nodes of T store sets of words and other data items related to these sets. Let $sets\text{-}of\text{-}words(T)$ denote the set of all sets of words stored by the nodes of T. A node of T stores more than one set of words iff these sets are identical. The root of T (at depth 0) stores sets of words with an identifying subset of cardinality one. In general, a node n of T at depth i stores sets of words with an identifying subset of cardinality $i+1$. A node n of T at depth i storing sets of words equal to s is implemented as a structure consisting of the following fields:

- $Word(n)$: the $i+1$-th word w_i of identifying subset $\{w_0, \ldots, w_{i-1}, w_i\}$ of s where $w_0, \ldots, w_{i-1}$ are the words of nodes appearing earlier on the path from the root to node n.
- $Query(n)$: a linked list containing the identifier of query q that contained word pattern wp for which $\{w_0, \ldots, w_i\}$ is the identifying subset of $sets\text{-}of\text{-}words(T)$.
- $Remainder(n)$: if node n is a leaf, this field is a linked list containing the words of s that are not included in $\{w_0, \ldots, w_i\}$. If n is not a leaf, this field is empty.
- $Children(n)$: a linked list of pairs (w_{i+1}, ptr), where w_{i+1} is a word such that $\{w_0, \ldots, w_i, w_{i+1}\}$ is an identifying subset for the sets of words stored at a child of w_i and ptr is a pointer to the node containing the word w_{i+1}.

The sets of words stored at node n of T are equal to $\{w_0, \ldots, w_n\} \cup Remainder(n)$, where $w_0, \ldots, w_n$ are the words on the path from the root of T to n. An identifying subset of these sets of words is $\{w_0, \ldots, w_n\}$. The purpose of $Remainder(n)$ is to allow for the delayed creation of nodes in trie. This delayed creation lets us choose which word from $Remainder(n)$ will become the child of current node n depending on the sets of words that will arrive later on.

The algorithm for inserting a new set of words s in a word directory is as follows. The first set of words to arrive will create a trie with the first word as the root and the rest stored as the remainder. The second set of words will consider being stored at the existing trie or create a trie of its own. In general, to insert a new set of words s, BestFitTrie iterates through the words in s and utilises the hash table implementation of the word directory to find all *candidate tries* for storing s: the tries with root a word of s. To store sets as compactly as possible, BestFitTrie then looks for a trie node n such that the set of words $(\{w_0, \ldots, w_n\} \cup Remainder(n)) \cap s$, where $\{w_0, \ldots, w_n\}$ is the set of words on the path from the root to n, has maximum cardinality. There may be more than one node that satisfies this requirements and such nodes might belong to different tries. Thus BestFitTrie performs a depth-first search down to depth $|s| - 1$ in *all* candidate tries in order to decide the optimal node n. The path from the root to n is then extended with new nodes containing the words in $\tau = (s \setminus \{w_0, \ldots, w_n\}) \cap Remainder(n)$. If $s \subseteq \{w_0, \ldots, w_n\} \cup Remainder(n)$, then the last of these nodes l becomes a new leaf in the trie with $Query(l) = Query(n) \cup \{q\}$ (q is the new query from which s was extracted) and $Remainder(l) = Remainder(n) \setminus \tau$. Otherwise, the last of these nodes l points to two child nodes l_1 and l_2. Node l_1 will have $Word(l_1) = u$, where $u \in Remainder(n) \setminus \tau$, $Query(l_1) = Query(n)$ and $Remainder(l_1) = Remainder(n) \setminus (\tau \cup \{u\})$. Similarly node l_2 will have $Word(l_2) = v$, where $v \in$

$s \setminus (\{w_0, \ldots, w_n\} \cup \tau)$, $Query(l_2) = q$ and $Remainder(l_2) = s \setminus (\{w_0, \ldots, w_n\} \cup \tau \cup \{u\})$. The complexity of inserting a set of words in a word directory is *linear* in the size of the word directory but *exponential* in the size of the inserted set. This exponential dependency is not a problem in practice because we expect *queries to be small* and the crucial parameter to be the size of the query database.

The filtering procedure utilises two arrays named $Total$ and $Count$. $Total$ has one element for each query in the database and stores the number of atomic formulas contained in that query. Array $Count$ is used for counting how many of the atomic formulas of a query match the corresponding attributes of a document. Each element of array $Count$ is set to zero at the beginning of the filtering algorithm. If at algorithm termination, a query's entry in array $Total$ equals its entry in $Count$, then the query matches the published document, since all of its atomic formulas match the corresponding document attributes.

When a document d is published, BestFitTrie hashes the text value $C(d)$ contained in each document attribute C and probes the ET to find matching atomic formulas with equality. Then for each attribute C in $DAL(d)$ and for each word w in $DWL(C)$, the trie of $WD(C)$ with root w is traversed in a breadth-first manner. Only subtrees having as root a word contained in $C(d)$ are examined, and hash table $OT(d)$ is used to identify them quickly. At each node n of the trie, the list $Query(n)$ gives implicitly all atomic formulas $C \sqsupseteq wp$ that can potentially match $C(d)$ if the proximity formulas in wp are also satisfied. This is repeated for all the words in $DWL(C)$, to identify all the qualifying atomic formulas for attribute C. Then the proximity formulas for each qualifying query are examined using the polynomial time algorithm $prox$ from [12]. For each atomic formula satisfied by $C(d)$, the corresponding query element in array $Count$ is increased by one. At the end of the filtering algorithm the equal entries in arrays $Total$ and $Count$ give us the queries satisfied by d.

To evaluate the performance of BestFitTrie we have also implemented algorithms BF, SWIN and PrefixTrie. BF (Brute Force) has no indexing strategy and scans the query database sequentially to determine matching queries. SWIN (Single Word INdex) utilises a two-level index for accessing queries in an efficient way. PrefixTrie is an extension of the algorithm Tree of [15] appropriately modified to cope with attributes and proximity information. Tree was originally proposed for storing *conjunctions of keywords* in secondary storage in the context of the SDI system SIFT. Following Tree, PrefixTrie uses *sequences* of words sorted in lexicographic order for capturing the words appearing in the word patterns of atomic formulas (instead of sets used by BestFitTrie). A trie is then used to store sequences compactly by exploiting *common prefixes* [15].

Algorithm BestFitTrie constitutes an improvement over PrefixTrie. Because PrefixTrie examines only the prefixes of sequences of words in lexicographic order to identify common parts, it misses many opportunities for clustering. BestFitTrie keeps the main idea behind PrefixTrie but searches exhaustively the current word directory to discover the best place to introduce a new set of words. This allows BestFitTrie to achieve better clustering as PrefixTrie introduces redundant nodes that are the result of using a lexicographic order to identify common parts. This node redundancy can be the cause of deceleration of the filtering process as we will show in the next section. The only way to improve beyond BestFitTrie would be to consider *re-organizing* the word directory

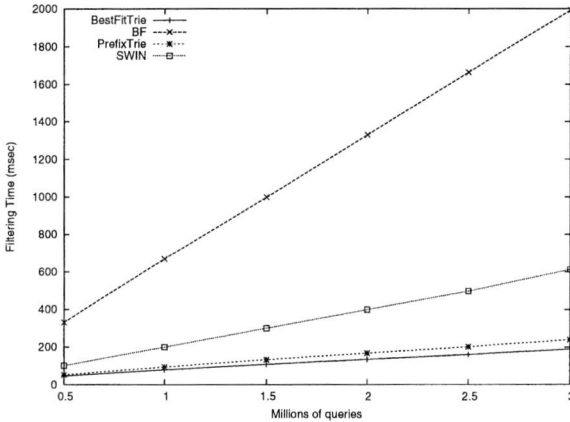

Fig. 2. Effect of the query database size in filtering time

every time a new set of words arrives, or periodically. We have not explored this approach in any depth.

4.1 Experimental Evaluation

We evaluated the algorithms presented above experimentally using a set of documents downloaded from ResearchIndex[3] and originally compiled in [6]. The documents are research papers in the area of Neural Networks and we will refer to them as the NN corpus. Because no database of queries was available to us, we developed a methodology for creating user queries using *words* and *technical terms* (phrases) extracted automatically from the ResearchIndex documents using the C-value/NC-value approach of [6].

All the algorithms were implemented in C/C++, and the experiments were run on a PC, with a Pentium III 1.7GHz processor, with 1GB RAM, running Linux. The results of each experiment are averaged over 10 runs to eliminate any fluctuations in the time measurements.

The first experiment targeted the performance of algorithms under different query database sizes. In this experiment, we randomly selected one hundred documents from the NN corpus and used them as incoming documents in query databases of different sizes. The size and the matching percentage for each document used was different but the average document size was 6869 words, whereas on average 1% of the queries stored matched the incoming documents.

As we can see in Figure 2, the time taken by each algorithm grows linearly with the size of the query database. However SWIN, PrefixTrie and BestFitTrie are less sensitive than Brute Force to changes in the query database size. The trie-based algorithms outperform SWIN mainly due to the clustering technique that allows the exclusion of more non-matching atomic queries. We can also observe that the better exploitation of the commonalities between queries improves the performance of BestFitTrie over PrefixTrie, resulting in a significant speedup in filtering time for *large query databases*.

---

[3] http://www.researchindex.com

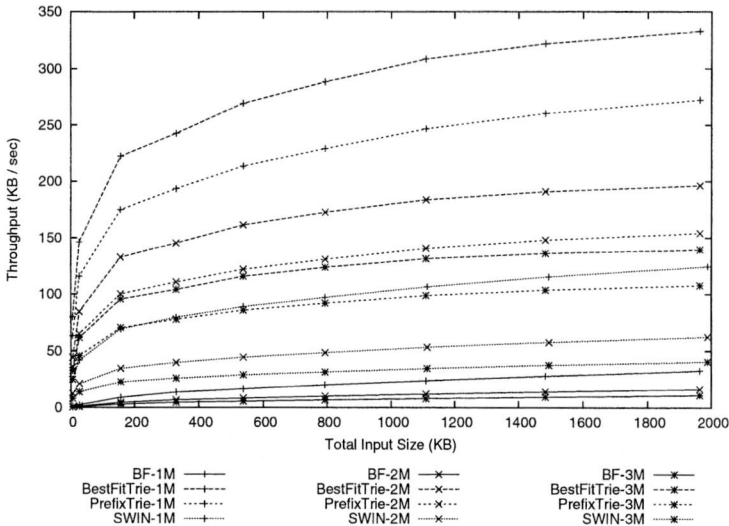

Fig. 3. Throughput for some algorithms for $\mathcal{AWP}$

Figure 3 shows that BestFitTrie gives the best filtering performance by processing a load of about 150KB (about 9 ResearchIndex papers) per second for a query database of 3 million queries.

In terms of space requirements BF needs about 15% less space than the trie-based algorithms, while the rate of increase for the two trie-based algorithms is similar to that of BF, requiring a fixed amount of extra space each time. Thus it is clear that BestFitTrie speeds up the filtering process with a small extra storage cost, and proves faster than the rest of the algorithms, managing to filter user queries about 10 times faster than the sequential scan method. Finally, the query insertion rate that the two trie-based algorithms can support is about 40 queries/second for a database containing 2.5 million queries.

We have also evaluated the performance of the algorithms under two other parameters: *document size* and *percentage of queries matching a published document*. Finally we have developed various heuristics for ordering words in the tries maintained by PrefixTrie and BestFitTrie when *word frequency* information (or *word ranking*) is available as it is common in IR research [1]. The details of these experiments are omitted due to space considerations.

5   Conclusions

We presented P2P-DIET, a service that unifies one-time and continuous query processing in P2P networks with super-peers. Currently our work concentrates on implementing the super-peer subnetwork of P2P-DIET using topologies with better properties and compare it analytically and experimentally with our current implementation. Our first steps in this direction are presented in [4].

References

1. R. Baeza-Yates and B. Ribeiro-Neto. *Modern Information Retrieval.* Addison Wesley, 1999.
2. A. Carzaniga, D.S. Rosenblum, and A.L. Wolf. Design and Evaluation of a Wide-Area Event Notification Service. *ACM TOCS,* 19(3):332–383, August 2001.
3. C.-C. K. Chang, H. Garcia-Molina, and A. Paepcke. Predicate Rewriting for Translating Boolean Queries in a Heterogeneous Information System. *ACM TOIS,* 17(1):1–39, 1999.
4. P.A. Chirita, S. Idreos, M. Koubarakis, and W. Nejdl. Publish/Subscribe for RDF-based P2P Networks. In *Proceedings of ESWS 2004,* May 2004.
5. Y.K. Dalal and R.M. Metcalfe. Reverse Path Forwarding of Broadcast Packets. *CACM,* 21(12):1040–1048, December 1978.
6. L. Dong. Automatic term extraction and similarity assessment in a domain specific document corpus. Master's thesis, Dept. of Computer Science, Dalhousie University, Halifax, Canada, 2002.
7. B. Gedik and L. Liu. PeerCQ:A Decentralized and Self-Configuring Peer-to-Peer Information Monitoring System. In *Proceedings of the 23rd ICDCS,* May 2003.
8. S. Idreos and M. Koubarakis. P2P-DIET: A Query and Notification Service Based on Mobile Agents for Rapid Implementation of P2P Applications. Technical report, TR-ISL-2003-01, Intelligent Systems Laboratory, Dept. of Electronic and Computer Engineering, Technical University of Crete, June 2003.
9. S. Idreos, M. Koubarakis, and C. Tryfonopoulos. P2P-DIET: Ad-hoc and Continuous Queries in Super-peer Networks. In *Proceedings of EDBT 2004,* volume 2992 of *LNCS,* pages 851–853, March 2004.
10. M. Koubarakis, T. Koutris, P. Raftopoulou, and C. Tryfonopoulos. Information Alert in Distributed Digital Libraries: The Models, Languages and Architecture of DIAS. In *Proceedings of ECDL 2002,* volume 2458 of *LNCS,* pages 527–542.
11. M. Koubarakis, C. Tryfonopoulos, S. Idreos, and Y. Drougas. Selective Information Dissemination in P2P Networks: Problems and Solutions. *ACM SIGMOD Record, Special issue on Peer-to-Peer Data Management, K. Aberer (editor),* 32(3), September 2003.
12. M. Koubarakis, C. Tryfonopoulos, P. Raftopoulou, and T. Koutris. Data models and languages for agent-based textual information dissemination. In *Proceedings of CIA 2002,* volume 2446 of *LNCS,* pages 179–193, September 2002.
13. W. Nejdl, M. Wolpers, W. Siberski, C. Schmitz, M. Schlosser, I. Brunkhorst, and A. Loser. Super-peer based routing and clustering strategies for RDF-based peer-to-peer networks. In *Proceedings of the 12th WWW Conference,* 2003.
14. P.R. Pietzuch and J. Bacon. Peer-to-Peer Overlay Broker Networks in an Event-Based Middleware. In *Proceedings of DEBS'03,* June 2003.
15. T.W. Yan and H. Garcia-Molina. Index Structures for Selective Dissemination of Information Under the Boolean Model. *ACM TODS,* 19(2):332–364, 1994.
16. B. Yang and H. Garcia-Molina. Designing a super-peer network. In *Proceedings of ICDE 2003,* March 5–8 2003.

A Query-Adaptive Partial Distributed Hash Table for Peer-to-Peer Systems

Fabius Klemm, Anwitaman Datta, and Karl Aberer

School of Computer and Communication Sciences,
Swiss Federal Institute of Technology (EPFL), Lausanne, Switzerland
{Fabius.Klemm,Anwitaman.Datta,Karl.Aberer}@epfl.ch

Abstract. The two main approaches to find data in *peer-to-peer* (P2P) systems are *unstructured* networks using flooding and *structured* networks using a distributed index. A distributed index is usually built over *all keys* that are stored in the network whether they are queried or not. Indexing all keys is no longer feasible when indexing *metadata*, as the key space becomes very large. Here we need a query-adaptive approach that indexes only keys worth indexing, i.e. keys that are queried at least with a certain frequency. In this paper we study the cost of indexing and propose a query-adaptive *partial distributed hash table* (PDHT) that does not keep all keys in the index. We model and analyze a scenario to show that query-adaptive partial indexing outperforms pure flooding and "index-everything" strategies. Furthermore, our scheme is able to automatically adjust the index to changing query frequencies and distributions.

Keywords: peer-to-peer (P2P), partial distributed hash table (PDHT), query-adaptive indexing, metadata.

1 Introduction

There have been several proposals to store and retrieve data in decentralized unreliable peer-to-peer networks. In most of the solutions the two alternatives so far have been to index *all or nothing*. In unstructured networks, such as Gnutella, peers use flooding or multiple random walks [2, 6] to resolve queries and do not build and maintain any index. These mechanisms can be used for arbitrary, complex search requests on *metadata* as they are not restricted to certain keys to find values in the network. On the other hand queries generate a large number of messages.

In structured peer-to-peer networks [1, 9, 12], also called distributed hash tables (DHTs), peers collaborate to construct and maintain a distributed index, which allows very efficient searches, but are, however, restricted to searches on the indexed keys [5]. Moreover, traditional DHTs do not consider the query distribution and devote equal resources to all keys.

When it comes to indexing metadata, a big difficulty lies in *selecting useful keys* for the index. Which metadata is actually used in queries depends on the application. Furthermore, the popularity of keys can change dramatically over time. Let us consider a distributed, decentralized peer-to-peer news system. Peers generate *news articles*, which are described by metadata. These metadata files consist of *element-value* pairs, such as title = "Weather Iráklion", author = "Crete Weather Service", date = "2004/03/14",

W. Lindner et al. (Eds.): EDBT 2004 Workshops, LNCS 3268, pp. 506–515, 2004.

and size = "2405". Queries may contain predicates on the different metadata attributes, such as *element1* = *value1* AND *element2* = *value2*. In case we decide to index a specific metadata attribute we generate keys by hashing single or concatenated key-value pairs, such as proposed in [4]. From this little example we can already see that indexing $key1 = hash$(title = "Weather Iráklion" AND date = "2004/03/14") makes much more sense than indexing $key2 = hash$(size = "2405") as $key1$ is much more likely to be queried.

In this paper we propose an algorithm that selects the keys that are *worth* indexing (such as $key1$). We first study the cost of maintaining a key-value pair in the index in the presence of peers going on-/off-line and frequent key updates. Routing table maintenance costs are considerable, as P2P clients are extremely transient in nature [2]. Searching a key in the index is much cheaper than searching an unstructured network. However, we claim that the cost of keeping a rarely queried key (such as $key2$) in the index can become higher than the cost saving offered by efficient index search. We therefore introduce an analytical model, to decide whether a key with a given query frequency is worth indexing. Second, we propose an extension for DHTs, which does not index all keys occurring in the network but is able to select those keys that are worth indexing.

Note that our proposal is generic enough such that it can be used for any of the DHT based systems. The main contribution of this paper is to analyze the cost of indexing, which allows to decide whether a key is worth indexing and thus to realize a hybrid peer-to-peer system. The main objective of the analysis has been to provide an intuitive understanding of such hybrid designs of P2P systems, and we make several simplifying assumptions to obtain a qualitative understanding. Given the diversity of existing DHT system designs, a generic analysis for all DHT based systems is beyond the scope of this work. Therefore, we concentrate on what can be called the traditional DHTs [1, 9, 12]. However, the analysis is generic enough such that it can be adapted to suit most other DHT proposals.

The paper is structured as follows: In Sections 2 and 3 we shall present an analytical model for partial indexing. Section 4 examines a realistic example of partial indexing. In Section 5 we propose a decentralized selection algorithm that dynamically chooses keys worth indexing and purges unnecessary keys from the index. Section 6 finishes with discussion and conclusions.

2   To Index or Not to Index?

In this section we propose an analytical model to decide whether a key is worth indexing. Keys that are not queried frequently enough are not worth indexing as they only increase the index size. The bigger the index, the more peers are necessary to store the index. On the other hand, if there are no queries, there is no need to maintain a DHT. Depending on the *query distribution*, each key is queried with a certain frequency. We are now interested in finding the lowest query frequency $fMin$ a key must have to be worthwhile indexing.

The decision to index a key depends on the following variables:

- $cIndKey$: The cost of storing one key in the index for one round.[1]
- $cSUnstr$: The cost of searching a key in an unstructured network.
- $cSIndx$: The cost of searching the index.
- $fQry_k$: The number of queries for key k per round (*query frequency*).

A key k should be indexed if it is queried often enough to amortize the indexing cost:

$$fQry_k \cdot (cSUnstr - cSIndx) - cIndKey > 0 \qquad (1)$$

If a key is not queried frequently enough, it is better not to index it. Since $cSUnstr - cSIndx > 0$ the minimum frequency a key must have to be worthwhile indexing is:

$$fQry_k > \frac{cIndKey}{cSUnstr - cSIndx} \qquad (2)$$

We set $fMin$ to the smallest value $fQry_k$ such that (2) holds. We now assume that queries for keys are *Zipf distributed* with parameter α [11] and that there are $keys$ number of unique keys. The probability of a query for the key at position $rank$ is:

$$prob_{rank} = \frac{rank^{-\alpha}}{\sum_{x=1}^{keys} x^{-\alpha}} \qquad (3)$$

With $numPeers$ peers and an average query frequency of $fQry$ per peer per round, all peers together send a total of $numPeers \cdot fQry$ queries each round. A key therefore has the following probability of being queried at least once per round:

$$probT_{rank} = 1 - (1 - prob_{rank})^{numPeers \cdot fQry} \qquad (4)$$

With (4) we now set $maxRank$ to the highest $rank$ such that $probT_{rank} \geq fMin$, i.e. $maxRank$ is the number of keys worth indexing. The probability that a random Zipf distributed query can be answered from the index is:

$$pIndxd = \frac{\sum_{x=1}^{maxRank} x^{-\alpha}}{\sum_{x=1}^{keys} x^{-\alpha}} \qquad (5)$$

3   Model

As we have seen in the preceding section, the decision to index depends on the cost of indexing a key ($cIndKey$), the cost of searching the unstructured network ($cSUnstr$), and the cost of searching the index ($cSIndx$). We are now looking for realistic models for these parameters assuming standard solutions for P2P overlay networks being used. As is a standard practice in P2P systems we consider the number of messages as the main cost (as opposed to storage and processing cost).

---

[1] One round is a fixed period of time. We shall later set one round to one second.

3.1   *cSUnstr*

We assume that the unstructured network has a Gnutella-like topology, where each peer has a few open connections to other peers. However, the Gnutella flooding-based query algorithm is not optimal even for unstructured networks. We therefore assume that a search algorithm is used that consumes less network traffic, such as multiple random walks as presented in [6]. We will explain in the next section that we replicate keys with a certain factor at random peers. We furthermore assume that the search algorithm in the unstructured network finds any key if it exists in the network. When searching an unstructured network, some peers receive several copies of the same query, depending on the network connectivity [6]. We therefore use a message duplication factor *dup*. With *numPeers* and a random replication with factor *repl* the cost of searching an unstructured network is then:

$$cSUnstr = \frac{numPeers}{repl} \cdot dup[\text{msg}] \tag{6}$$

3.2   *cSIndx*

Search in traditional DHTs is with logarithmic cost.[2] With *maxRank* keys in the index, a given replication factor, and each peer having a storage capacity of *stor* keys, we need *numActivePeers* peers to store the index. We assume that if the total number of peers is greater than the number of peers necessary to store the index (*numPeers* > *numActivePeers*), only *numActivePeers* peers participate in building and maintaining a DHT. For the remaining peers, to perform searches, it is sufficient to know at least one online peer that is participating in the DHT (i.e. the set of *numActivePeers*). The cost of searching the index in a binary key space[3] is then:

$$cSIndx = \frac{1}{2} \cdot \log_2(numActivePeers)[\text{msg}] \tag{7}$$

3.3   **cIndKey**

The cost of keeping a key in the index for one round depends on the following two factors:

Routing Table Maintenance Cost: *cRtn* Peers continuously join and leave the system. To assure a certain level of routing reliability, the peers must keep their routing tables up-to-date. One possible strategy is to *probe* routing entries with a given rate to detect offline peers [7]. The amount of probe messages depends on the routing table size, which is $O(\log(numActivePeers))$. Stale routing entries can be replaced with low overhead by piggybacking routing information on queries. Therefore, we need only messages to

---

[2] Recently, several DHTs with sub-logarithmic search costs have been proposed, such as in [8]. However, in this paper we concentrate on traditional DHTs [1, 9, 12] as both the qualitative insights and the proposed algorithm will hold even though the quantitative results will change.

[3] For simplicity we assume a binary key space. However, the analysis can also be generalized for a k-ary key space.

detect stale routing entries (by probing) but assume no additional messages to repair those routing entries. The amount of probe messages is an application dependent environment constant (such as determined in [7]), which we call *env*.

Suppose that we need *numActivePeers* peers to build a DHT big enough to index *maxRank* keys. The maintenance cost for routing tables *per key* per second is then: The cost to detect stale routing entries (*env*) multiplied by the size of the routing table $\log_2(numActivePeers)$ times the number of participating peers (*numActivePeers*) divided by the number of keys kept in the index (*maxRank*):

$$cRtn = env \cdot \log_2(numActivePeers) \cdot numActivePeers/maxRank[\text{msg/s}] \quad (8)$$

Update Cost: *cUpd* The second part of *cIndKey* is the cost of inserting, overwriting, or deleting a key in the index thereby assuring consistency among the replicas. An update works as follows: The replicas in the index maintain an *unstructured replica subnetwork* among each other. When updating a key, it is inserted at one responsible peer in the index at the cost of searching the index (*cSIndx*) and then gossiped to the other responsible peers in the subnetwork of replicas. Therefore, the update cost also depends on the replication factor (*repl*), which is given by the application. [3] studied the cost of updates between replicas based on a hybrid push/pull rumor spreading algorithm. Peers that are offline and go online again pull for missed updates. We assume a message duplication factor of *dup2* for flooding the replica subnetwork. Given that *fUpd* is the average update frequency per key per second the cost of updating a key is:

$$cUpd = (cSIndx + repl \cdot dup2) \cdot fUpd[\text{msg/s}] \quad (9)$$

Thus we obtain the cost of indexing a key per round:

$$cIndKey = cRtn + cUpd[\text{msg/s}] \quad (10)$$

The cost of searching the unstructured network (*cSUnstr*) is usually considerably higher than the cost of searching the index (*cSIndx*) and the cost of keeping a key in the index (*cIndKey*). However, we will see that searching rarely queried keys in the unstructured network is cheaper than proactively keeping them in the index. Only keys that are queried at least with a certain frequency (*fMin*) should stay in the index.

4   Evaluation of the Model

We now provide a simple scenario in order to instantiate our model with concrete parameters. In doing so, we choose values as have been observed in the context of P2P networks by various researchers [6, 7, 11]. Thus, we endeavor to provide a simple and practical decentralized solution under realistic assumptions for a longstanding drawback of DHTs, that of judiciously indexing metadata.

We imagine a news system with the following characteristics: It should be able to store 2,000 unique news articles, randomly replicated with factor 50. We assume that there exists a mechanism to determine a proper replication factor for the index and content files (news articles) to meet target levels of availability and to avoid unnecessary high update cost [13]. Such mechanisms lie beyond this work and are therefore not further discussed. Index and content are replicated with the same factor to assure the same search reliability in structured and unstructured networks.

Table 1. Parameters of the sample scenario

Description	Param.	Value
Total number of peers	$numPeers$	20,000
Number of peers building the DHT	$numActivePeers$	
Number of unique keys	$keys$	40,000
Storage capacity for indexing per peer	$stor$	100
Replication factor	$repl$	50
α of query Zipf distribution	α	1.2 [11]
Frequency of queries per peer per second	$fQry$	1/30 1/s to 1/7200 1/s
Avg. update freq. per key	$fUpd$	$1/(3600 \cdot 24)$ 1/s
Route maintenance constant	env	1/14 [7]
Message duplication factors	$dup, dup2$	1.8 [6]

As discussed in Section 1, for each article we generate 20 keys from the metadata describing the article. It is a standard approach in information retrieval to avoid indexing stop words, such as "the", "and", etc. We assume that the set of such stop words is globally known to all peers in the system and are ignored. To index 2,000 news articles we therefore get 40,000 keys. Each peer has a storage capacity of 5 articles plus a cache of 100 *key-value pairs* that can be used for indexing. With replication factor of 50 we therefore need 20,000 peers to store and index all articles.

Each article is replaced every 24 hours on average. New articles are actively replicated together with their metadata files. The average *query frequency per peer* varies from one query every 30 seconds, in very busy periods of the day, to one every 2 hours, in calmer times. Thus, with 20,000 peers and 40,000 keys, the average *key query/update ratio* varies between 1440/1 and 6/1. Furthermore, the queries are Zipf-distributed with $alpha = 1.2$ as observed in [11].

For this analysis we use the route maintenance cost that [7] studied for Pastry [10]. Using a Gnutella trace with 17,000 peers, they analyzed that around 1 message per peer per second is necessary. With (8) we therefore get a routing maintenance constant of $env = 1/\log_2(17,000) \approx 1/14$. This constant might be different in other maintenance approaches and environments. In this scenario, the maintenance cost ($cRtn$) clearly outweighs the update cost ($cUpd$).

We first assume that each peer knows which keys it can find in the index and for which it has to do a broadcast search.[4] This assumption is not realistic but at the moment we are interested in the best performance possible with partial indexing (lower bound in terms of messages in the given system model). We will discuss in the next section a more realistic environment, in which peers do *not* know whether a key is in the index. Table1 summarizes the parameters.

---

[4] We use "broadcast search" and "search in the unstructured network" interchangeably.

We can now calculate the total cost for pure indexing and broadcast searches as well as for partial indexing:

Total Cost of Indexing all Keys: Cost of the full index per second, where $maxRank = keys$, plus the cost of searching the index ($cSIndx$). The total number of queries per second is $fQry \cdot numPeers$:

$$indexAll = keys \cdot cIndKey + fQry \cdot numPeers \cdot cSIndx \, [\text{msg/s}] \qquad (11)$$

Total cost of searching all queries in the unstructured network:

$$noIndex = fQry \cdot numPeers \cdot cSUnstr \, [\text{msg/s}] \qquad (12)$$

Total Cost for Ideal Partial Indexing: We index only the $maxRank$ most popular keys, which costs $cIndKey$ per key per second. If a query can be answered from the index (with probability $pIndxd$), we have only the index search cost ($cSIndx$). Otherwise $(1 - pIndxd)$ we have to search the unstructured network ($cSUnstr$).

$$partial = maxRank \cdot cIndKey + oIndxd \cdot fQry \cdot numPeers \cdot cSIndx$$
$$+ (1 - pIndxd) \cdot fQry \cdot numPeers \cdot cSUnstr \, [\text{msg/s}] \qquad (13)$$

We used the analytical model to evaluate the behavior of the system for a changing query load ($fQry$).

Fig. 1(a) shows the cost when indexing and broadcasting all queries, and with ideal partial indexing. Ideal partial indexing is considerably cheaper for all query frequencies as the savings in Fig. 1(b) show. In Fig. 2(a) we can see that the index size decreases with lower query frequencies as the index only stores the keys worth indexing. As the queries are Zipf distributed even a small index can answer a high percentage of queries.

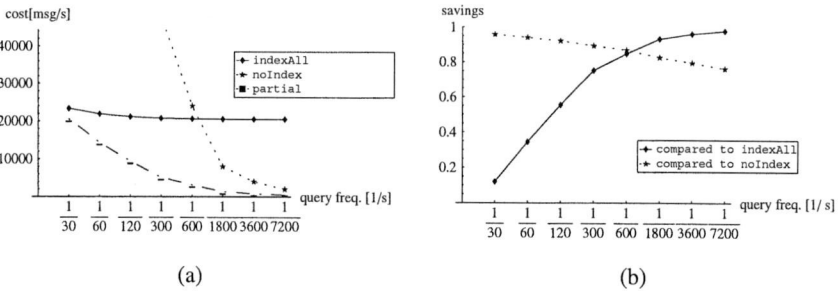

Fig. 1. (a) Query frequency per peer (x-axis) vs. total sent messages per second (y-axis) when all keys are indexed (*indexAll*, solid), when all queries are answered by broadcast (*noIndex*, dashed stars), and for ideal partial indexing (*partial*, dashed squares). (b) Savings of ideal partial indexing compared to indexing all keys (*indexAll*, solid) and compared to broadcasting all queries (*noIndex*, dashed)

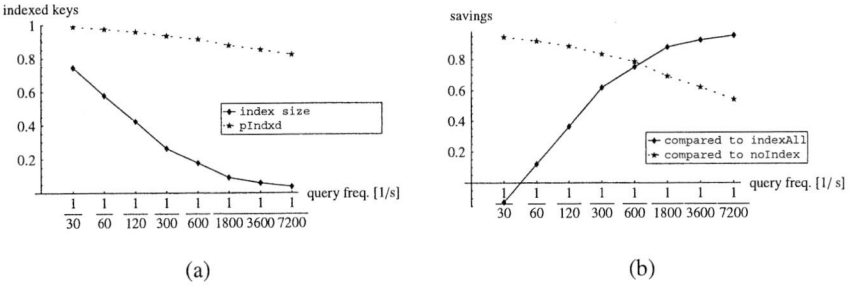

Fig. 2. (a) Percentage of indexed keys with ideal partial indexing (*index size*, solid) and percentage of queries that can be answered from the index (*pIndxd*, dashed). (b) Savings with proposed selection algorithm compared to indexing all keys (*indexAll*, solid) and compared to broadcasting all queries (*noIndex*, dashed)

5   Selection Algorithm

In the preceding section we made the idealizing assumption that every peer knows whether a key should be indexed. In this section we now present a simple decentralized algorithm to select keys worth indexing.

5.1   How to Select Worthwhile Keys?

When a peer wants to answer a query, it first searches the index. If there is no result, the peer initiates a broadcast search and inserts the resulting key-value pair into the index. Each key has an expiration time $keyTtl$, which determines how long the key stays in the index. The expiration time of a key is reset to a predefined value whenever the peer that stores the key receives a query for it. Thus, peers evict those keys from their local storage that have not been queried for $keyTtl$ rounds. The effect is that only frequently queried keys stay in the index whereas the unpopular keys, which are not worth indexing, time out. This approach does not take the relative frequency of queries into account but only whether there was any query for a particular key.

With (3) and (4), the probability that a query can be answered from the index, i.e. that the key has been queried at least once in the last $keyTtl$ rounds, is:

$$pIndxd = \sum_{rank=1}^{keys} \left((1 - (1 - probT_{rank})^{keyTtl}) \cdot prob_{rank} \right) \tag{14}$$

The number of keys in the index is:

$$keys = \sum_{rank=1}^{keys} (1 - (1 - probT_{rank})^{keyTtl}) \tag{15}$$

Purging timed-out keys leads to poor replication synchronization. Therefore, peers propagate queries in the unstructured replica subnetwork if they cannot answer them. The index search cost therefore increases by the cost of flooding the replica network:

$$cSIndx2 = cSIndx + repl \cdot dup2 \, [\text{msg}] \qquad (16)$$

A peer first searches the index ($cSIndx2$). If it does not find the key in the index, it searches the unstructured network ($cSUnstr$) and inserts the resulting key into the index ($cSIndx2$). Therefore, proactive updates ($cUpd$) are no longer necessary and the cost of keeping a key in the index consists only of the routing cost ($cRtn$). The cost of partial indexing therefore is:

$$partial = keys \cdot cRtn + pIndxd \cdot fQry \cdot numPeers \cdot cSIndx2 + (1 - pIndxd)$$
$$\cdot fQry \cdot numPeers \cdot (cSIndx2 + cSUnstr + cSIndx2) \, [\text{msg/s}] \quad (17)$$

Fig. 2(b) shows the savings with the proposed selection algorithm. The selection algorithm causes some overhead but still realizes substantial savings (except for very high query frequencies) compared to strategies that index all keys or broadcast all queries.

With the selection algorithm the cost of indexing is higher than with ideal partial indexing for four reasons: I. Not all keys that are supposed to be in the index are in the index at the time they are queried. We chose a $keyTtl$ of $1/fMin$. A key worth indexing can time out before it is queried again. II. Keys that are not worth indexing are inserted into the index for $keyTtl$ rounds. III. Index search cost ($cSIndx2$) is higher than ideal search cost ($cSIndx$). IV. A peer does not know whether a query is indexed. It always searches the index and then also broadcasts the query if necessary.

It is important that peers insert keys into the index with the right expiration time ($keyTtl$). The value of $keyTtl$ can be calculated by estimating $cSUnstr$, $cSIndx$, and $cIndKey$. A too small value results in fewer savings at high query frequencies, a too big value at lower frequencies. Analytical results show that an estimation error of $\pm 50\%$ of the ideal $keyTtl$ decreases the savings only slightly. A mechanism to self-tune $keyTtl$ based on the query distribution and frequency is part of future work.

6   Discussion and Conclusions

We have argued that in structured P2P systems the indexing cost cannot be neglected, particularly the cost of maintaining routing tables. Depending on the query frequency of a key, it can be cheaper not to index it. To outline a design for a query adaptive partial DHT, we first provided an analysis based on global knowledge. Then we proposed a very simple, nonetheless effective mechanism for selective (partial) indexing based on only locally available information at peers, without the need of global coordination. Our self-organizing and adaptive mechanism does not make the system theoretically optimal as we do not assume global coordination. However, the results show that our approach leads to performance benefits and compares well with the theoretical optimal solution. It adapts to changing query frequencies and distributions, which is especially useful when indexing metadata, as the range of the key space that is actually queried depends on the applications and can dramatically change over time. Future work includes refinements of the analytical model and improvements in the proposed selection algorithm and its implementation.

References

1. K. Aberer. P-Grid: A self-organizing access structure for P2P information systems. In *Sixth Inter-national Conference on Cooperative Information Systems (CoopIS 2001)*, 2001.
2. Y. Chawathe, S. Ratnasamy, L. Breslau, N. Lanham, and S. Shenker. Making Gnutella-like P2P systems scalable. In *Proceedings of ACM SIGCOMM 2003*.
3. A. Datta, M. Hauswirth, and K. Aberer. Updates in highly unreliable, replicated peer-to-peer systems. In *23rd International Conference on Distributed Computing Systems (ICDCS)*, 2003.
4. P. Felber, E. Biersack, L. Garces-Erce, K. W. Ross, and G. Urvoy-Keller. Data indexing and query-ing in P2P DHT networks. In *ICDCS 2004*.
5. M. Harren, J. M. Hellerstein, R. Huebsch, B. T. Loo, S. Shenker, and I. Stoica. Complex queries in dht-based peer-to-peer networks. In *Proc. of IPTPS '02*, 2002.
6. Q. Lv, P. Cao, E. Cohen, K. Li, and S. Shenker. Search and replication in unstructured peer-to-peer networks. In *16th International Conference on Supercomputing*, June 2002.
7. R. Mahajan, M. Castro, and A. Rowstron. Controlling the cost of reliability in peer-to-peer over-lays. In *IPTPS*, 2003.
8. G. S. Manku. The power of lookahead in small-world routing networks. In *STOC*, 2004.
9. S. Ratnasamy, P. Francis, M. Handley, R. Karp, and S. Shenker. A scalable content-addressable network. In *SIGCOMM*, August 2001.
10. A. Rowstron and P. Druschel. Pastry: Scalable, distributed object location and routing for large-scale peer-to-peer systems. In *IFIP/ACM International Conference on Distributed Systems Platforms (Middleware)*, November 2001.
11. K. Sripanidkulchai. The popularity of Gnutella queries and its implications on scalability. In *O'Reilly's OpenP2P.com*, 2001.
12. I. Stoica, R. Morris, D. Karger, M. F. Kaashoek, and H. Balakrishnan. Chord: A scalable peer-to-peer lookup service for internet applications. In *Proceedings of ACM SIGCOMM 2001*.
13. A. Vahdat, J. Chase, R. Braynard, D. Kostic, P. Reynolds, and A. Rodriguez. Self-organizing sub-sets: From each according to his abilities, to each according to his needs. In *First Inter-national Work-shop on P2P Systems*, March 2002.

P2PR-Tree: An R-Tree-Based Spatial Index for Peer-to-Peer Environments

Anirban Mondal, Yi Lifu, and Masaru Kitsuregawa

Institute of Industrial Science,
University of Tokyo 4-6-1 Komaba, Meguro-ku, Tokyo, Japan
{anirban,yilifu,kitsure}@tkl.iis.u-tokyo.ac.jp

Abstract. The unprecedented growth and increased importance of geographically distributed spatial data has created a strong need for efficient sharing of such data. Interestingly, the ever-increasing popularity of peer-to-peer (P2P) systems has opened exciting possibilities for such sharing. This motivates our investigation into spatial indexing in P2P systems. While much work has been done towards expediting search in file-sharing P2P systems, issues concerning spatial indexing in P2P systems are significantly more complicated due to overlaps between spatial objects and the complexity of spatial queries. Incidentally, existing R-tree-based structures for distributed environments (e.g., the MC-Rtree) are *not* adequate for addressing the sheer scale, dynamism and heterogeneity of P2P environments. Hence, we propose the P2PR-tree (Peer-to-Peer R-tree), which is a new spatial index specifically designed for P2P systems. The main features of P2PR-tree are two-fold. First, it is hierarchical and performs efficient pruning of the search space by maintaining minimal amount of information concerning peers that are far away and storing more information concerning nearby peers, thereby optimizing disk space usage. Second, it is completely decentralized, scalable and robust to peers joining/leaving the system. The results of our performance evaluation demonstrate that it is indeed practically feasible to share spatial data in a P2P system and that P2PR-tree is able to outperform MC-Rtree significantly.

Keywords: Spatial indexing, P2P systems, R-tree, scale, dynamism.

1 Introduction

Spatial data occurs in several important and diverse applications associated with geographic information systems (GIS), computer-aided design (CAD), resource management, development planning, emergency planning and scientific research. During the last decade, tremendous improvements in data gathering techniques have contributed to an unprecedented growth of available spatial data at geographically distributed locations and this coupled with the trend of increased globalization has created a strong motivation for the efficient global sharing of such data. Interestingly, the growing importance and ever-increasing popularity of peer-to-peer (P2P) systems such as Napster [10] and Kazaa [7], which have the capability of facilitating data sharing among hundreds of thousands of distributively-owned computers worldwide, has opened new and exciting possibilities for global sharing of spatial data. This motivates our investigation into spatial indexing

W. Lindner et al. (Eds.): EDBT 2004 Workshops, LNCS 3268, pp. 516–525, 2004.

in P2P systems. Interestingly, spatial data sharing in P2P systems can be of tremendous benefit to users looking for a hotel room or a museum or some landmark within a certain spatial location.

While much work has been done towards expediting search in file-sharing P2P systems [3, 11, 14], issues associated with the indexing of spatial data in P2P systems have received little attention. Understandably, several challenging issues such as overlaps between spatial objects, avoidance of data scattering and the complexity of spatial queries make the problem of spatial data indexing in P2P systems significantly more complicated than that of sharing files. Incidentally, spatial indexes have been extensively researched in centralized environments (e.g., the R-tree [6], the R*-tree [1], the R+-tree [13]) as well as in traditional distributed domains such as clusters (e.g., the dR-tree [9], the M-Rtree [8] and the MC-Rtree [12]). Existing R-tree-based techniques use centralized mechanisms in which a centralized 'master' node supervises and directs queries to all other nodes in the system. However, we believe that such centralization is *not* appropriate for P2P systems partly due to the fact that all updates and searches passing through a centralized peer may result in severe performance problems (and even more so if the centralized peer goes offline[1]) and partly due to the fact that it is practically extremely challenging to maintain updated information about other peers at a centralized peer when data can be added/deleted autonomously by any peer in the entire system or peers can join/leave the system anytime. In essence, a completely decentralized spatial indexing technique, which is scalable enough to handle hundreds of thousands of peers and also dynamic enough to deal with peers joining/leaving the system anytime, is called for.

This paper proposes the P2PR-tree (Peer-to-Peer R-tree), which is a new spatial index specifically designed for P2P systems. The main features of P2PR-tree are two-fold.

1. It is hierarchical and performs efficient pruning of the search space by maintaining minimal amount of information concerning peers that are far away and storing more information concerning nearby peers, thereby optimizing disk space usage.
2. It is completely decentralized, scalable and robust to peers joining/leaving the system, thereby making it well-suited to P2P environments.

We conducted simulation experiments to test the effectiveness of P2PR-tree for spatial select (window) queries. The results indicate that it is indeed practically feasible to share spatial data in a P2P system and that P2PR-tree is able to outperform MC-Rtree significantly. The remainder of this paper is organized as follows. Section 2 discusses related work, while Section 3 discusses the problem context as well as our proposed scheme for spatial indexing in P2P environments. Section 4 reports our performance evaluation. Finally, we conclude in Section 5 with directions for future work.

2   Related Work

The problem of spatial indexing has motivated several research efforts. In this regard, the R-tree [6] is one of the most popular spatial index structures. Each spatial data object

---

[1] Irrespective of how a centralized peer may be selected, no guarantee can be provided about the peer remaining online all the time.

in the R-tree is represented by a Minimum Bounding Rectangle (MBR). Leaf nodes in the R-tree contain entries of the form *(oid, rect)* where *oid* is a pointer to the object in the database and *rect* is the MBR of the object. Non-leaf nodes contain entries of the form *(ptr, rect)* where *ptr* is a pointer to a child node in the R-tree and *rect* is the MBR that covers *all* the MBRs in the child node. Variants of the R-tree include the R^+-tree [13] and the R*-tree [1].

R-tree-based distributed spatial indexes include the M-Rtree [8], MC-Rtree [12] and the dR-tree [9]. In case of the M-Rtree, all the internal nodes of the parallel R-tree are stored at one single dedicated machine that is regarded as the master server, while the leaf nodes are declustered across several other machines. The leaf level at the master server contains the (MBR, siteid, pageid) tuples for each global leaf node. In order to identify the page and site where the leaf page is located, the (siteid, page id) is used. An improvement to the M-Rtree is the MC-Rtree where the master node contains *only* the client ids of the data nodes (and *not* page ids), while the data rectangles are kept indexed by R-trees in the client machines. Intuitively, MC-Rtree exploits parallelism better than the M-Rtree since the client machines find the page ids in parallel. The dR-tree uses an R-tree-based two-tier indexing mechanism which facilitates efficient data migration and load-balancing in clusters. More recently, an R-tree-based indexing structure for P2P systems has been proposed in [5] in the context of sensor networks. The proposed index structure in [5] can be interpreted as a P2P version of the centralized R-tree. However, our work differs from the proposal in [5] in several ways. Here, we state only two of the major differences. First, our approach is completely decentralized without any notion of cluster leaders, while the work in [5] assumes the existence of cluster leaders. Second, the execution of nearest neighbour queries have been optimized in [5], while we focus on optimizing window queries.

3   Distributed Spatial Indexing in P2P Environments

This section first discusses the context of the problem and then proposes the *P2PR-tree* for efficiently locating objects in spatial P2P environments.

Problem Context

Given a set of hundreds of thousands of geographically distributed and distributively owned data providing peers, the problem is to search efficiently for a given spatial object such that the queried object can be retrieved within response times that would be acceptable to most users.

Every peer has a globally unique identifier *peer_id* (when a peer leaves the system and then joins the system, the ID remains preserved.) We need to adopt any existing identification scheme used for P2P systems. Every peer stores data concerning certain spatial regions. Note that spatial attributes usually remain relatively static, but non-spatial attributes may change e.g., a hotel's geographical location can be reasonably expected to remain the same over a significantly long period of time, but the number of available rooms in the hotel can change very frequently. Moreover, every incoming query is assigned a unique identifier *Query_id* by the peer P_i at which it arrives. *Query_id* consists of *peer_id* and *tm*, where *tm* is a distinct number generated by P_i using the time of arrival of the query as a seed. Observe that this ensures uniqueness of *Query_id* since more than one query cannot arrive at the same peer at *exactly* the same time. We define a peer P_i as *relevant* to a query Q if it contains at least a non-empty subset of the answers to Q, otherwise P_i is regarded as *irrelevant* w.r.t. Q. Note that it is possible for more than one peer to store information concerning the same spatial region and possibly even the same spatial objects. Moreover, it is *not* necessary that each peer indexes all the spatial objects that are within the covering MBR of the region that it indexes. This may be primarily attributed to the fact that the owner of each peer autonomously decides the spatial objects about which he wishes to store information. We shall henceforth designate the covering MBR of the region indexed by a peer as the *peerMBR* of that peer.

The P2PR-Tree

In case of P2PR-tree, the universe is first divided *statically* into a set of *blocks* (each block being a rectangular tile). The set of blocks will constitute level 0 of our proposed index as we shall see later. Each block is *statically* divided into a set of *groups* (each group is a rectangular tile) and the set of groups constitute level 1 of our index. Each group is *dynamically* divided into further rectangular tiles and these set of tiles, designated as *subgroups*, forms level 2 of our index. Depending upon the circumstances, subgroups may be *dynamically* divided further into sets of rectangular tiles, which we shall designate as subgroups of level 3. Note that we shall use the term *subgroups* generically throughout this paper to indicate sets of rectangular tiles which form level i of our index, where $i \geq 2$.

The static decomposition of space has an important advantage from the perspective of P2P systems. Whenever a new peer joins the system, it just needs to contact one peer which will inform it about the covering MBRs of the blocks and *at least one* peer in each block. Using this block structure information, the peer can decide which block(s) it belongs to. (In case the region indexed by a peer overlaps more than one block, the peer will be assigned to both blocks.) Once the peer knows its block(s), it contacts one peer inside its block for the group-related MBR information and at least one peer inside each group. Using the group structure information, the peer will know which group it belongs to. Once the peer assigns itself to that group, it finds out which subgroup it should assign itself to and so on. Note that this strategy optimizes disk space usage significantly by maintaining minimal information about peers that are far away and more detailed information concerning peers that are nearby. Interestingly, this kind of static decomposition of space is able to deal efficiently with peers joining and leaving the system. On the other hand, if we had dynamically divided the universe into blocks, information about any splits in blocks would have to be sent to an extremely large number of peers. Moreover, in case of a dynamic way of dividing the universe into blocks and groups, it would have been extremely challenging to keep the block-related and group-related information updated, given the dynamic nature of P2P systems. However, the dynamic method of splitting is an attractive option when the number of peers is low since the dynamic method can deal with highly skewed data distributions which the static technique cannot. Hence, for levels other than block and group levels, we perform dynamic decomposition of space, as we shall see shortly. Notably, the maximum number of peers in a group is pre-specified at design time and we shall denote it by G_{Max}. Moreover, the maximum number of peers in subgroups (at different levels of the distributed index) is also specified at design time and we shall refer to it as SG_{Max}.

Assume the universe is divided into 4 blocks, namely b1,b2,b3,b4. Now let us take a closer look at a specific block, say b1, to understand detailed issues concerning how P2PR-tree works. Figure 1a depicts the distribution of peerMBRs in each of the 4 groups (namely g1,g2,g3,g4) of b1, while Figure 1b presents the corresponding index structure. In Figure 1, P1,P2,P3,P4, P5,P6, P8,P9,P10 denote the peerMBRs of peers whose *peer_ids* are 1,2,3,4,5,6, 8,9,10 respectively. In Figure 1b, B1,B2,B3,B4 represent the covering MBRs of b1,b2,b3,b4 respectively, while G1,G2,G3,G4 represent the covering MBRs of g1,g2,g3,g4 respectively. For the sake of clarity, we display the index structure with special emphasis *only* on G1 and G2. Observe that the number of peerMBRs in

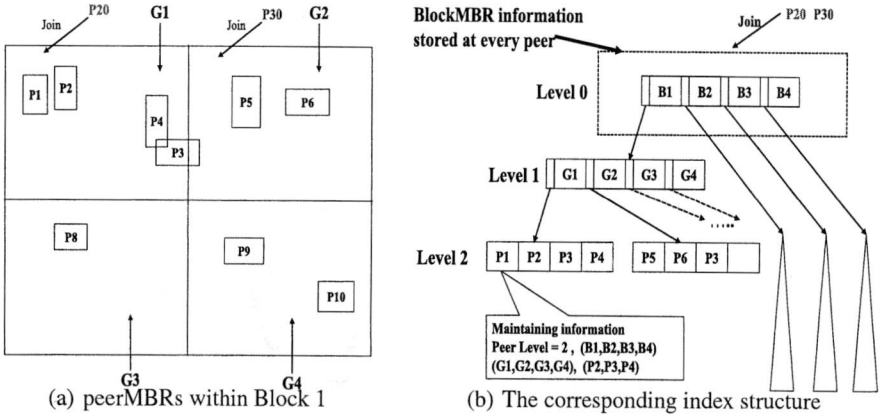

(a) peerMBRs within Block 1   (b) The corresponding index structure

Fig. 1. Illustrative example depicting our indexing scheme

each group is *not* the same e.g., while G1 has 4 peerMBRs, G3 has only 1 peerMBR. This kind of skew occurs primarily because the static decomposition of space is *not* based upon the actual data distribution during run-time. Given that peers may join/leave the system at any time, the number of peerMBRs corresponding to a given group can be reasonably expected to keep changing dynamically, the implication being that skews among groups are inevitable because it is *not* feasible to have a priori knowledge concerning the dynamically changing data distributions in each of the groups. Similarly, a moment's thought indicates that such data skews may also occur at any other level of our distributed index. Interestingly, it is also possible for a peerMBR to overlap multiple groups e.g., P3 overlaps both G1 as well as G2. In case a peerMBR overlaps more than one group, the corresponding peer will be assigned to both the groups. Hence, in the index structure shown in Figure 1b, P3 appears *twice* since P3 has been assigned to both G1 and G2. Note that we define P_L, the level of a peer, based upon its position in the distributed index e.g., P_L in case of peer 6 is 2 in Figure 1b.

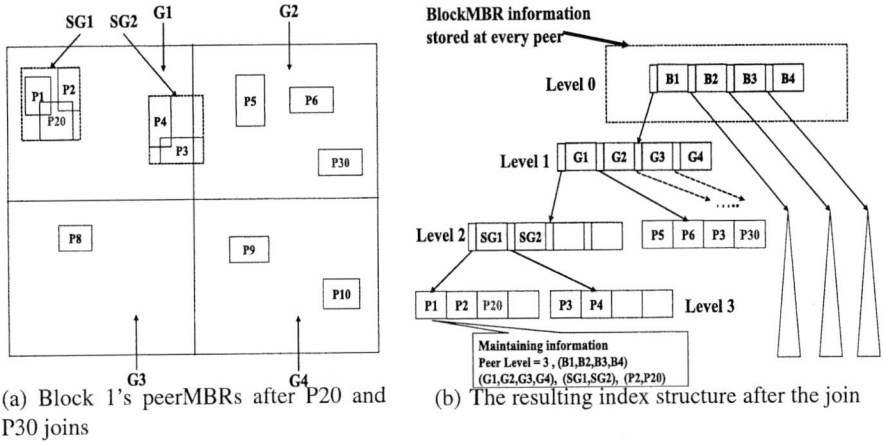

(a) Block 1's peerMBRs after P20 and P30 joins

(b) The resulting index structure after the join

Fig. 2. Example to show the effect of peers joining

Now let us understand how the index is modified in response to new peers joining the system. Figure 2a depicts what happens when two new peers join the system with their respective peerMBRS P20 and P30. For this example, let us assume the values of G_{Max} and SG_{Max} to be 4. Observe that P30's joining the system is straightforward since it does *not* result in an overflow. However, P20's joining is significantly more complicated since its joining causes an overflow in G1, thereby causing G1 to split further into subgroups SG1 and SG2. For splitting purposes, we propose to adopt an existing clustering technique [2] for performing node splitting in R-trees. The main idea behind the proposal in [2] is that the node splitting problem in R-trees is essentially a problem of finding a good set of clusters and the proposal also moves beyond the traditional two-way node splitting of R-trees to make node splitting more flexible, the prime objective being to find *real* clusters as opposed to two groupings.

Observe that the node splitting caused P1 and P2 to move from level 2 to level 3 of the index. From Figure 2b, it is clear that P2PR-tree does *not* provide global height-balance. In Figure 1b, we have shown the information that P1 maintains to facilitate search. As we see from Figure 1b, P1 maintains information concerning the entire covering MBRs of each of the blocks, namely B1,B2,B3,B4 and the covering MBRs of all the 4 groups in its own block (i.e., G1,G2,G3,G4) in addition to the peerMBRs P2,P3,P4. Observe from Figure 2b how the information maintained by P1 is changed after splitting occurs.

Search Mechanism

Now we shall discuss how efficient search can be conducted via P2PR-tree. For our search mechanism, every query is associated with a Q_L, the significance of Q_L being that it determines which level of the distributed index the query is currently traversing. When a new query is issued to any peer in the system, its Q_L is 0 and whenever a query is forwarded to peer(s) at another level of the distributed index, the value of Q_L is incremented by one. This guarantees that queries traverse down the distributed index and precludes the possibility of any query traversing up the index. Whenever a query Q arrives at any peer P_i in the system, P_i checks whether its peerMBR intersects with Q and if so, P_i searches its own R-tree, returns results (if any) and the search is terminated. Otherwise, P_i checks the value of Q_L associated with Q and depending upon the value of Q_L, P_i forwards Q to the relevant block(s) or group(s) or subgroup(s) or peer(s) as the case may be. (If Q_L is 0, Q should be forwarded to the relevant block(s); if Q_L is 1, Q should be sent to relevant group(s); if Q_L is 2, Q must be sent to relevant subgroup(s) and so on.)

P_i sending Q to a particular block B_i constitutes Q being sent to one peer in that block. Note that this implicitly assumes that every peer knows at least one peer in each block. While the system is operational and the peers issue queries to each other, it is likely that more peers will interact and come to know each other. Hence, over a period of time, it might be possible for a peer in a specific block to know N peers in each of the other blocks. Given that P_i knows N peers at block B_i to which it wishes to forward Q, P_i first sends Q randomly to any one peer P_j among the N peers that it knows. If it does *not* receive an acknowledgement message from P_j within a pre-specified maximum time limit, designated as TIME_OUT, P_i forwards the query to another peer among the N peers that it knows. In case all the N peers that P_i knows in B_i are unavailable, P_i will *not* be able to forward Q to B_i. For the sake of convenience, we shall henceforth refer to the set of N peers that a peer knows in each block (or in each group/subgroup) as the *routing peers* or simply *routers*. Note that the mechanisms for sending a query to a particular group or subgroup are essentially similar to that of sending a query to a specific block.

4   Performance Study

We conducted simulation experiments to evaluate the performance of our proposed indexing strategy. Our simulation environment comprised a machine running the Solaris 8 operating system. The machine has 4 CPUs, each of which has a processing power of 900 MHz. Main memory size of the machine is 16 Gigabytes, while the total disk space is 2 Terabytes. For all our experiments, we divided the universe into 10 blocks and we divided each block into 10 groups. Moreover, we set the value of TIME_OUT to 20 seconds. Transfer time between peers (inter-block) was randomly varied between 80 ms to 120 ms, while the transfer time between peers (inter-group) was varied between 45 ms to 55 ms. Transfer time between peers within the same group/subgroup was randomly varied between 10 ms to 15 ms. Note that an interarrival rate of n queries/second implies that n queries were issued in the entire P2P system every second. By availability of $x\%$, we mean that at any given time, a peer has an $x/100$ probability of being online (available). Furthermore, the number of *routers* being set to y means that each peer knows y peers (for routing purposes, hence we designate them as *routers*) in each block in the system and y routers in each group of its own block and y routers in each subgroup of its own group and so on.

Each of the 1000 peers that we used in all our experiments stored more than 200000 spatial objects. Each peer uses an R-tree for its own directory management. As in existing works, we assumed that one R-tree node fits in a disk page (page size = 4096 bytes).

The height of each of the R-trees at each of the 1000 data providing peers was 3 and the fan-out was 64. Our performance study was conducted using a real dataset known as *Greece Roads* [4]. We had enlarged this dataset by translating and mapping the data. The main metric that we have used for the performance study is query response time.

Incidentally, existing works on spatial indexing have *not* really addressed issues concerning P2P environments, let alone decentralized indexing techniques. In order to compare our work meaningfully against existing works, we use MC-Rtree as reference. Recall that MC-Rtree is one of the most efficient distributed R-tree-based techniques. (We do *not* compare our approach with the M-Rtree since the MC-Rtree has been shown to outperform the M-Rtree.) For the MC-Rtree approach, we select a specific peer in every block as the block leader. Each of these block leaders maintains an MC-Rtree which indexes the peerMBRs of all the peers whose spatial regions are fully contained within their blocks or intersect with their blocks. We ensured that every block leader had adequate disk space for storing the MC-Rtree. For the sake of convenience, we shall henceforth refer to this strategy as *MC-Rtree*.

Now let us study the effect of varying the zipf factor when the query interarrival rate is fixed. In order to model skewed workloads, we used the Zipf distribution over 1000 buckets to decide the number of queries to be directed to each of the 1000 peers. We modified the value of the *zipf factor* to obtain variations in workload skew. Notably, a value of 1 for the zipf factor implies a heavily skewed workload, while a value of 0 indicates a uniform workload distribution. We generated window queries by enlarging the individual data MBRs at each of the peers. Figure 3a indicates the results when the query interarrival rate was fixed at 20 queries/second, while the results for query interarrival rate of 100 queries/second is shown in Figure 3b. The number of routers was set to 5 and the availability was fixed at 65%.

From the results in Figure 3a, we find that as the skew increases, the average response time also increases for the MC-Rtree. This occurs because *every* query has to be routed through *at least one* of the centralized master peers which store the MC-Rtree for their respective blocks. As a result, there are large job queues at these centralized master peers, thereby causing significantly increased waiting times at these peers which ultimately causes severely increased query response times. The greater the workload skew, the more serious is the routing bottleneck. In contrast, the decentralized nature of P2PR-tree implies that routing is performed in a completely distributed fashion, thereby ensuring the absence of any serious routing bottlenecks. This explains why P2PR-tree exhibits far superior performance as compared to MC-Rtree. The same explanation is also applicable to the results in Figure 3b. Observe that in Figure 3b, the actual values of response times are much higher than in Figure 3a. This is because high interarrival rates make the routing bottleneck associated with the centralized master peers much more pronounced than in case of low interarrival rates. Incidentally, apart from the routing bottleneck, MC-Rtree also needs to contend with individual peers becoming bottlenecks due to a large number of queries being directed to a few 'hot' peers (because of the highly skewed workload) within a short time interval. Interestingly, the phenomenon of individual peers becoming bottlenecks due to skewed workload at high interarrival rates also occurs in case of P2PR-tree which explains why unlike the results in Figure 3a, the results in

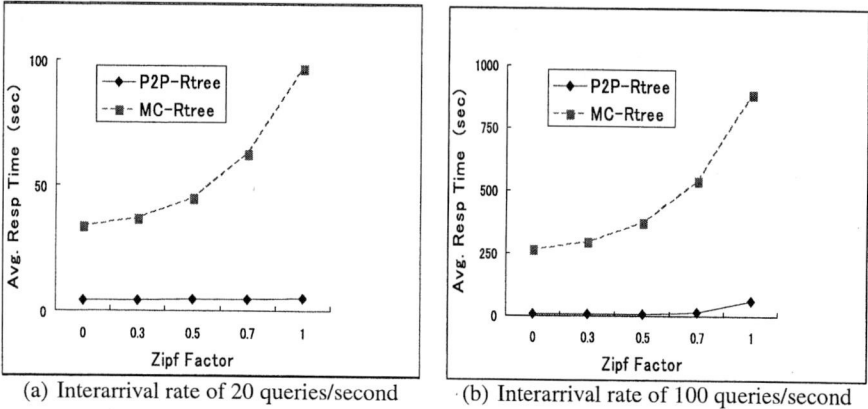

(a) Interarrival rate of 20 queries/second   (b) Interarrival rate of 100 queries/second

Fig. 3. Effect of variations in workload skew

Figure 3b indicate an increase (albeit slight) in the average response time for P2PR-tree when the interarrival rate is high (i.e., 100 queries/second).

5   Concluding Remarks

The increased importance of geographically distributed spatial data coupled with the popularity of P2P computing has motivated our research into spatial indexing in P2P systems. Since existing R-tree-based structures are *not* adequate for P2P environments, we have proposed a new R-tree-based spatial index that is well-suited to P2P environments. Our performance evaluation demonstrates that it is indeed practically feasible to share spatial data in a P2P system. However, this work has *not* addressed in detail issues concerning a single peer indexing multiple regions that are far apart in space. Moreover, this work does *not* examine performance-related issues concerning a single query intersecting more than one block/group/subgroup. We intend to investigate these issues in detail in the near future. We also wish to make detailed performance comparisons with the proposal in [5]. Furthermore, we intend to investigate issues concerning replication for performance as well as availability reasons and additionally, we plan to examine issues concerning load-balancing in this context for improving user response times.

References

1. N. Beckmann, H.P. Kriegel, R. Schneider, and B. Seeger. The R*-tree: an efficient and robust access method for points and rectangles. *Proc. ACM SIGMOD*, 1990.
2. S. Brakatsoulas, D.Pfoser, and Y. Theodoridis. Revisiting R-tree construction principles. *citeseer.nj.nec.com/586207.html*.
3. A. Crespo and H. G. Molina. Routing indices for Peer-to-Peer systems. *Proc. ICDCS*, 2002.
4. Datasets. http://dias.cti.gr/~ytheod/research/datasets/spatial.html.
5. M. Demirbas and H. Ferhatosmanoglu. Peer-to-peer spatial queries in sensor networks. *Proc. P2P*, 2003.

6. A. Guttman. R-trees: A dynamic index structure for spatial searching. *Proc. ACM SIGMOD*, 1984.

7. Kazaa. http://www.kazaa.com/.

8. N. Koudas, C. Faloutsos, and I. Kamel. Declustering spatial databases on a multi-computer architecture. *Proc. EDBT*, 1996.

9. A. Mondal, M. Kitsuregawa, B.C. Ooi, and K.L. Tan. R-tree-based data migration and self-tuning strategies in shared-nothing spatial databases. *Proc. ACM GIS*, 2001.

10. Napster. http://www.napster.com/.

11. A. Rowstron and P. Druschel. Pastry: Scalable, decentralized object location and routing for large-scale peer-to-peer systems. *Proc. IFIP/ACM*, 2001.

12. B. Schnitzer and S.T. Leutenegger. Master-client R-trees: A new parallel R-tree architecture. *Technical Report COMP-98-01, University of Denver*, 1998.

13. T. K. Sellis, N. Roussopoulos, and C. Faloutsos. The R^+-tree: A dynamic index for multi-dimensional objects. *Proc. VLDB*, 1987.

14. I. Stoica, R. Morris, D. Karger, M. F. Kaashoek, and H. Balakrishnan. Chord: A scalable peer-to-peer lookup service for internet applications. *Proc. ACM SIGCOMM*, 2001.

Web Data Protection:
Principles and Research Issues

Elena Ferrari

Università dell'Insubria, Via Valleggio, 11, 22100 Como, Italy
`elena.ferrari@uninsubria.it`

Abstract. Protection of web documents is a challenging task which requires to address several issues, ranging from the development of suitable policy languages to policy enforcement. In this paper, we discuss the main problems that need to be faced in providing a comprehensive framework for securing web documents and outline possible techniques and mechanisms that can be adopted. Additionally, we discuss research trends in the field and we show the relations that exist between web data protection and clustering information over the web.

1 Introduction

Today the Web is becoming the main means to exchange and disseminate information for private users as well as for companies and organizations. Over the web, information dissemination and exchange often takes the form of documents that are made available at web servers, or that are actively broadcasted by web servers to interested clients. In such a scenario, it is thus fundamental to develop models, techniques, and mechanisms for securing web documents. Protecting web documents means ensuring three main properties: *confidentiality*, *integrity*, and *authenticity*. Ensuring document confidentiality means ensuring that document contents are only disclosed to subjects authorized according to the specified access control policies. By document integrity we mean that document contents are modified only by authorized subjects. Finally, ensuring authenticity means that a subject receiving a document can verify that the document comes from the source to which it was required and that it was not altered during its transmission. Therefore, any solution for protecting web documents, must satisfy the confidentiality, integrity and authenticity requirements of both the requesting subject and the information owner.

We believe that three are the main ingredients for providing a comprehensive solution to web document protection. The first is the availability of an high-level language for specifying security policies. The language must be expressive enough to model the security requirements of different domains and applications. Then, there is the need of defining suitable architectures according to which documents can be released to the interested subjects, and, finally, we need to put in place a suite of security mechanisms supporting the enforcement of the specified policies according to the selected architectures.

In this paper, we consider all these three aspects, by first stating the requirements and then discussing the most promising approaches that can be used for each of the above aspects. Additionally, we discuss some research trends in the area, with particularly

W. Lindner et al. (Eds.): EDBT 2004 Workshops, LNCS 3268, pp. 526–535, 2004.
© Springer-Verlag Berlin Heidelberg 2004

emphasis on the relations between protecting web documents and clustering information over the web. More precisely, the remainder of this paper is organized as follows. Next section deals with the policy language and outlines its main requirements. Section 3 deals with architectural issues, whereas Section 4 focuses on security mechanisms. Section 5 discusses research trends. Finally, Section 6 concludes the paper.

2 Policy Language

The first step in the definition of a comprehensive framework for web data protection is the availability of a flexible language able to express the security requirements of heterogeneous application domains. In conventional information systems, security policies mainly regulate the accesses of subjects to the protected objects. Such policies are referred to as *access control policies*. Access control policies entail a set of authorizations that can be conceptually viewed as triples (s, o, p), where s is a subject id, o is the id of the protected object, and p is the privilege (e.g., read, write) that s is authorized to exercise on o. This simple paradigm, mainly based on the identity of the requesting subject, does not fit very well in the web scenario, since it requires the management of a huge number of authorizations, due to the highly dynamic subject population and the huge and heterogeneous collections of data characterizing the web. Additionally, other classes of policies, besides access control policies, could be relevant in the web environment. In the following sections, we first discuss such classes of additional policies, then we discuss the requirements that the policy language must posses.

2.1   Security Policies

It is important to note that although some proposals exist of access control policy languages specifically tailored to the characteristics of web documents (see [9] for an overview), the investigation of other classes of policies that can be useful in the web environment is still in its infancy. In what follows, we discuss some of these additional classes of policies. A first class of policies that can be devised deals with authenticity requirements. Over the web, authenticity requirements are as important as integrity and confidentiality ones. Up to now what has been developed is a variety of signature techniques [10] to sign any piece of digital information. However, we believe that the availability of techniques for digitally signing a data object is not enough to deal with authenticity issues. What is needed, on top of the signature mechanisms, is the ability of specifying who must sign a document (or a portion of it), according to the rules of the considered organization/domain. A key requirement is thus that the policy language is able to support the specification of *signature policies*. A signature policy [5] states the duty of a subject of signing a document (or document portion(s)). The main difference between an access control policy and a signature policy is thus that the first expresses the possibility of exercising a privilege on a given document, whereas the second expresses the *duty* of signing a document or a document portion.

Example 1. As an example, consider the XML document illustrated in Figure 1, which models an employee dossier, providing information on employee's activities within

```
<Employee_dossier Emp_ID="EID">
    <Resume Date="7/8/2004">
        <Personal_Data Name="John" ... >
            <Reserved>
                <Health> ... </Health>
                <Criminal> ... </Criminal>
            </Reserved>
        </Personal_Data>
        <Education>
            <Qualification> ... </Qualification>
            ...
        </Education>
        <Activity >
            <Professional_Experience> ... </Professional_Experience>
            ...
        </Activity>
    </Resume>
    <Evaluation>
        <Manag_Eval> ... </Manag_Eval>
        <Board_Dir_Eval> ... </Board_Dir_Eval>
        <HR_Eval> ... </HR_Eval>
    </Evaluation>
    <Career>
        <Position Role="Secretary" Salary="1000" Date="8/18/2003"/ >
        ...
    </Career>
</Employee_dossier>
```

Fig. 1. An example of XML document

an organization. The document contains the employee's resume, the evaluation of the employee activities, and information about his/her career. The Resume element contains some reserved data about the employee's health and criminal records. The Evaluation element contains three evaluations on the employee performance, made by the manager of the employee, the members of the board of directors, and the head of the human resources department, respectively. An example of signature policy for such document is the one which imposes that the manager must sign the employee's evaluation.

Additionally, signature policies can be further classified according to the number of subjects that are required to sign a document. For instance, policies can be used to specify both *simple* or *joint signatures*, where a simple signature is a signature made by only one subject, whereas joint signatures require that more than one subject must sign a document (or a document portion). For instance, the request for attending a conference must be signed both by the technical and the administrative manager of the requesting employee for getting approval. Furthermore, as far as joint signatures are concerned, sometimes it is useful to specify an order (total or partial) according to which the various signatures must be generated, and other requirements may be devised as well. Thus, the development of a comprehensive signature policy specification language is still an open issue.

Another class of policies that can be useful to support in the web environment deals with the distributed and cooperative updates of web documents. This is a key point since Internet has made possible a wide spectrum of distributed cooperative applications in several areas, such as collaborative e-commerce, distance learning, telemedicine, and e-government. In this scenario, it is often the case that different subjects must update different portions of the same document, following an order which is dictated by the internal rules of the organization. For instance, with reference to the XML document in Figure 1, it can be required that the `Career` element is first modified by a secretary and then verified by a manager. To be able to express such rules, what is needed is thus the support for *document flow policies* [4], that is, policies regulating the set of subjects that must receive a document for updating and/or reading it. The specification language must thus support the possibility of generating totally or partially specified lists of subjects that will have to receive a document and the possibility of specifying which subjects can modify a flow policy by adding/deleting some receivers.

2.2   Policy Language Requirements

What is needed is thus an high level language able to specify at least all the above-mentioned kinds of policies, and specifically tailored to web documents characteristics and their users. We believe that a first requirement for such a language is to be XML-based [12], in that XML is today the standard for data representation and exchange over the Internet. Apart from being XML-based, the language must posses a set of requirements, that we list in what follows:

Flexible Subjects Qualification. The traditional identity-based approach to access control is no longer appropriate to the web environment, because in such a scenario other information, besides the user identity, can be relevant to perform security checks. In this respect, several research efforts have been carried on for defining more flexible ways of qualifying the subjects to which a security policy applies. For instance, Role-based Access Control (RBAC) introduces the notion of role [6], that is, a named collection of privileges needed to perform a certain task within an organization. For the web scenario, a promising approach is that of using *subject credentials* [14]. A credential is a sort of subject profile, containing information relevant for security purposes (for example, the position of a subject within an organization, his/her age or nationality). Policies are then expressed by specifying conditions against the subject credentials. Each subject has one or more credentials issued by a Certification Authority (CA), which certifies the credential content. Policies can then be specified based on credentials and credential properties; as such they identify a set of subjects, that is, those whose credentials satisfy the constraints specified in the policies. Similar to security policies also credentials can be encoded using an XML-based language (see for instance [3]).

Additionally, information on user behavior (such as access logs) can be exploited in the specification and enforcement of policies. As an example consider a policy specifying that a subject can access a document only if he/she did not access another document before (for instance, because two documents taken together are sensitive, individually not), or a policy limiting the number of times a document can be accessed in a given period.

Protection Objects Specification. A further requirement is related to the objects to which a policy applies. Since web documents may have very different security requirements, we believe that the language must be able to support a wide range of protection granularity levels, ranging from set of documents, to single documents, to selected portions within a document. Additionally, since often a web document may have an associated extensional description of its structure, the language must be able to exploit such description in the specification of policies. For example, XML documents may conform to a DTD or an XMLSchema. This means that the policy language must be able to express both policies at the DTD/XMLschema level and policies at the instance level, where a policy specified at the schema level is automatically inherited by all the schema instances.

Additionally, also protection objects can have a profile associated with them, that can be exploited in the specification of policies. A protection object profile (similar to subject credentials) can convey additional information on the object which can be used for security checks.

Finally, the policy language must be able to express both policies based on the structure of the documents and policies based on their content. This because, it is often the case that documents with the same structure contain information of very different sensitivity degrees.

Up to now, the most relevant proposal of a standard language for specifying security policies is the XACML standard proposed by OASIS [8]. XACML is a language for specifying role-based access control policies. However, the language does not provide the support for signature and document flow policies. A first step in the definition of a comprehensive language able to satisfy all the above discussed requirements is $\mathcal{X}$-Sec, the XML-based language under development in the framework of the Author-$\mathcal{X}$ project [2]. The language provides the support for all the above-mentioned policies as well as for the notion of credential. Additionally, it supports both content-dependent and content-independent security policies and a wide spectrum of protection granularity levels. More details can be found in [2, 4, 5].

3 Architectures

The second step in developing a comprehensive solution to web documents protection is the design of architectures for a secure dissemination of information, according to the specified security policies. In this respect, a first dimension according to which architectures can be classified is the dissemination mode they adopt. Basically, information delivery can be done according either to a pull or a push mode. The push mode is the traditional user on demand way of performing access control. The other dissemination mode, referred to as push mode, is today becoming more and more attractive since it fits very well with the web characteristics. According to the push approach, a document source periodically (or whenever some relevant event arises) broadcasts data to its clients, without the need of an explicit request. Clearly, even in this case, we need mechanisms to satisfy the authenticity, confidentiality, and integrity requirements of both the receiving subjects and information owners.

Additionally, whichever dissemination mode is adopted, documents can be distributed according to either a two-party or a third-party architecture. A two-party architecture is the classical architecture in which there is a distinction between the owner of the information, which is responsible for specifying security policies, enforcing them, and answering subject requests, and one or more clients, which require information to the owner. Clearly, this architecture has the drawback that the owner could become a bottleneck for the whole system. For this reason, third-party architectures for data publishing over the web are today receiving growing attention, due to their scalability properties and to the ability of efficiently managing large number of subjects and great amount of data. In a third-party architecture, there is a distinction between the owner and the publisher of information. The owner is the producer of the information, whereas publishers are responsible for managing (a portion of) the owner information and for answering subject queries. The main problem in such a scenario is how the owner can ensure the security properties to its data, even if the data are managed by a third-party. The most intuitive solution is that of requiring the publisher to be trusted with respect to the considered security properties. However, the main drawback of this solution is that it is costly and not easy to be implemented, since it is difficult to verify that large web-based systems are trusted. For this reason, an important research direction is that of defining security mechanisms able to ensure security properties even without assuming the publisher to be trusted. Examples of such mechanisms will be given in the next section.

4   Security Mechanisms

The last component of a comprehensive solution to web data protection, is the definition of a suite of security mechanisms able to enforce the specified policies in the selected architecture. In this section, we first describe the mechanisms that can be put in place for supporting the push and pull mode. Then, we discuss security mechanisms in the context of third-party architectures.

4.1   Information Push

A trivial solution for information push support is to generate a different view for each different subject that must receive the document, on the basis of the specified access control policies, and then sign them using standard digital signature techniques [10]. However, the drawback of this solution is that, since information push has been mainly conceived for document distribution to a large community of subjects, this approach is not practically scalable. An alternative solution that avoids such drawback is that of using encryption techniques. The idea is to selectively encrypt and sign the documents according to the specified access control and signature policies. Each portion to which the same access control policies apply is encrypted with the same key, whereas a unique signature is applied to all the document portions covered by the same signature policies [5]. Then, each subject receives additional information (e.g., decryption keys) that make him/her able to correctly decrypt and verify the authenticity of the received document. Clearly, the interaction between signature and access control policies must be carefully considered, in that the portions to which the same signature must be applied can be different from the portions that must be encrypted with the same key. For instance, suppose than one of the receiver subjects has the authorization to view only a part of a signed portion. Thus, he/she is not able to validate the signature. For this reason, mechanisms must be adopted to split the signature according to the applicable access control policies. Other important open issues are how to efficiently and securely manage the encryption and signature information that must be delivered to subjects and how to efficiently support administrative operations changing the policy base.

In case of update operations performed according to an information push approach a further issue that need to be faced, if we would like to provide a distributed framework not relying on a centralized server which mediates each update operation, is how we can make a subject able to verify the correctness of the update operations performed till that point on the document, without interacting with the document server. This is still an open problem. A possible solution [4] is that of attaching some control information to the encrypted document (relying on the use of hash functions and digital signatures) that make a subject able to locally verify the correctness of the update operations wrt the specified policies.

Information Pull. The pull mode is the traditional way of enforcing access control. Thus, access control mechanisms developed for conventional DBMSs can be used and adapted to this purpose. However, the web adds further dimensions to the problem. A key issue is related to the policy language: in the web environment, a policy usually denotes a set of subjects (i.e., all the subjects whose credentials satisfy certain conditions) and a collection of documents (e.g., documents with the same structure, content and/or profile). The problem is thus how to efficiently process such policies when a request is submitted, in a way that makes easy to determine the set of policies that needs to be evaluated for deciding the result of an access request. A possible solution is that of clustering documents, according to same criteria, which must be based on the types of access requests that more frequently are submitted to the web source. For instance, documents can be clustered according to their content (e.g., all the documents on the same topics). Or, alternatively, documents can be clustered according to the credentials that a subject must posses in order to access them. In defining such clustering criteria, an important issue is to determine the impact of administrative operations changing the policy base and/or the subject credentials.

4.2   Third-Party Architectures

Third-party architectures add a further dimension when we do not assume the publishers to be trusted wrt the considered security properties. In particular, we consider authenticity and confidentiality properteis, since integrity is not so relevant in this context in that third-party architectures are mainly conceived for the management of reading operations. The problem here is which security mechanisms can be devised to enforce authenticity and confidentiality in the presence of an untrusted publisher. Consider first authenticity: it is not possible to directly apply standard digital signature techniques to ensure authenticity, since a subject may require only selected portions of a document, and thus it is not enough that the owner of the data signs each document it sends to the publisher. A possible solution [1] requires that the owner sends the publisher, in addition to the information it is entitled to manage, a summary signature, generated using a technique based on Merkle hash trees [7], which is based on a bottom-up computation. When a subject submits a request to a publisher, requiring any portion of the managed data, the publisher sends him/her, besides the query result, also the signatures of the documents on which the request is performed. In this way, the subject can locally recompute the same bottom-up hash value signed by the owner, and by comparing the two values he/she can verify whether the publisher has altered the content of the request answer and can thus verify its authenticity. The problem with this approach is that, since the subject may be returned only selected portions of a document, he/she may not be able to recompute the summary signature, which is based on the whole document. For this reason, the publisher must send the subject a set of additional hash values, referring to the missing portions that make the subject able to locally perform the computation of the summary signature. More details on this approach can be found in [1].

As far as confidentiality issues are concerned an approach can be that of sending the publisher an encrypted copy of the data it has to manage (where different portions are encrypted with different keys according to the access control policies specified by the owner). However, in that case we have to assume the existence of a trusted party which covers the task of key management. When a subject needs to perform a query, it submits an encrypted query to the publisher, that is, a query stating the search conditions in an encrypted form. In such a way, the publisher can evaluate the query on the encrypted data, without having the decryption keys, by simply comparing the encrypted values. Obviously, this approach works only for queries based on equality conditions. Developing a schema for more general classes of queries is still an open problem.

5   Research Trends

This paper has provided an overview of the main issues and developments in securing web documents. In this section, we discuss some research trends in the area. In particular, what we would like to explore in this section are the relations and the possible synergies that can be devised between web data protection and clustering information over the web, because we believe that this could lead to interesting developments and research work.

The first research direction is how to exploit clustering information in the specification of security policies. For instance, several methods have been proposed [13] for clustering web users according to their interests and for extracting knowledge from user access paths, or for discovering logical information units over the web [11]. All these information can be exploited in the specification of policies. For instance, information on user access paths can be exploited to specify policies that prevent users to infer sensitive information from accessing a set of documents, each of which contains an information that taken individually is not sensitive but taken as a whole can convey sensitive information.

Another important issue is how to combine information obtained by clustering users with information conveyed by subject credentials. The idea here is whether we can use clustering and credential information to provide a delivery of information to users which is on the one hand tailored to their interests and on the other done according to some security policies.

Further, a cluster over the web can be seen as a any other protection object. As such, it must be protected by proper security policies. It is thus necessary to investigate whether access control models developed so far for web documents must be revised to deal with clusters.

6 Concluding Remarks

Protecting web documents is a challenging task which requires to address several issues. In this paper, we have discussed some of them, by showing which are the main challenges, and which are the most promising solutions for languages, architectures, and security mechanisms. Clearly, there are several other areas for further research. A challenging research directions, which so far has not been widely explored deals with the relations between web data protection and clustering information over the web. In this paper, we have discussed some of the research activities that can be done in such area.

Acknowledgements

The author wishes to thank Dr. Athena Vakali, Aristotle University, Thessaloniki, Greece, for useful discussions on the relations between web data protection and clustering information over the web.

References

1. Bertino, E., Carminati, B., Ferrari, E. Thuraisingham, B., Gupta, A. Selective and Authentic Third-party Distribution of XML Documents. *IEEE Transactions on Knowledge and Data Engineering*, to appear.
2. E. Bertino, S. Castano, E. Ferrari. Author-$\mathcal{X}$: a Comprehensive System for Securing XML Documents, *IEEE Internet Computing*, 5(3):21–31, May/June 2001.
3. E. Bertino, S. Castano and E. Ferrari. On Specifying Security Policies for Web Documents with an XML-based Language. In *Proc. of the 1st ACM Symposium on Access Control Models and Technologies (SACMAT'01)*, Chantilly, Virginia, USA, May 2001. ACM Press.
4. E. Bertino, E. Ferrari, G. Mella. Flow Policies: Specification and Enforcement. In *Proc. of the Workshop on Information Assurance (WIA04)*, Phoenix, Arizona, USA, April 2004.
5. E. Bertino, E. Ferrari, L. Parasiliti Provenza. Signature and Access Control Policies for XML Documents. In *Proc. of ESORICS 2003, 8th European Symposium on Research in Computer Security*, Gjovik, Norway, October 2003. Lecture Notes in Computer Science 2808.
6. D. F. Ferraiolo, R. S. Sandhu, S. I. Gavrila, D. R. Kuhn, R. Chandramouli. Proposed NIST Standard for Role-based Access Control. *ACM Transactions on Information and System Security (TISSEC)*, 4(3), 2001.
7. R.C. Merkle. A Certified Digital Signature. In *Advances in Cryptology-Crypto '89*, 1989.
8. OASIS eXtensible Access Control Markup Language TC. XACML 1.0 Specification Set (18 Feb. 2003). OASIS Standard. Available at: http://www.oasis-open.org/committees/tc_home.php?wg_abbrev=xacml
9. C. Geuer Pollmann. The XML Security Page. http://www.nue.et-inf.uni-siegen.de/~geuer-pollmann/xml_security.html
10. W. Stallings. Network Security Essentials: Applications and Standards. *Prentice Hall, 2000*.
11. K. Tajima, K. Hatano, T. Matsukura, R. Sano, K. Tanaka. Discovery and Retrieval of Logical Information Units in Web. *Proc. of the Workshop on Organizing Web Space (WOWS)*, Berkeley, CA, 1999.

12. World Wide Web Consortium. Extensible Markup Language (XML) 1.0, (Second Edition) 2000. Available at `http://www.w3.org/TR/2000/REC-xml-20001006`.

13. J. Xiao, Y. Zhang, X. Jia, T. Li Measuring Similarity of Interests for Clustering Web-users. *Proc. of the 12th Australasian conference on Database Technologies*, Queensland, Australia, 2001.

14. M. Winslett, N. Ching, V. Jones, I. Slepchin. Using Digital Credentials on the World Wide Web. *Journal of Computer Security*, 7, 1997.

Clustering Structured Web Sources: A Schema-Based, Model-Differentiation Approach

Bin He, Tao Tao, and Kevin Chen-Chuan Chang

Computer Science Department,
University of Illinois at Urbana-Champaign,
Urbana IL 61801, USA
{binhe,taotao}@uiuc.edu, kcchang@cs.uiuc.edu

Abstract. The Web has been rapidly "deepened" with the prevalence of databases online. On this "deep Web," numerous sources are *structured*, providing schema-rich data. Their schemas define the *object domain* and its *query capabilities*. This paper proposes clustering sources by their *query schemas*, which is critical for enabling both *source selection* and *query mediation*, by organizing sources of with similar query capabilities. In abstraction, this problem is essentially clustering categorical data (by viewing each query schema as a transaction). Our approach hypothesizes that "homogeneous sources" are characterized by the same hidden generative models for their schemas. To find clusters governed by such statistical distributions, we propose a novel objective function, *model-differentiation*, which employs principled hypothesis testing to maximize statistical heterogeneity among clusters. Our evaluation shows that, on clustering the Web query schemas, the model-differentiation function outperforms existing ones with the hierarchical agglomerative clustering algorithm.

1 Introduction

Recently, the Web has been rapidly "deepened" with the prevalence of databases online and thus presents challenges for *large-scale* information integration. On this "deep Web" (database-backed Web sources), numerous online databases provide dynamic *query*-based data access through their *query interfaces*, instead of static URL links. Our recent survey [1] in December 2002 estimated between 127,000 to 330,000 deep Web sources. The deep Web thus presents challenges for *large-scale* information integration: While there are myriad useful databases, how can a user *find* the correct sources and *query* them in a correct way?

While tantalized by the need for effectively accessing the deep Web, such *metaquery* over large-scale structured sources has largely remained unexplored. As a first step toward metaquerying, this paper studies clustering sources by their *query schemas*, i.e., attributes in their query interfaces. For instance, for the advanced query interface of *amazon.com*, the query schema is {author, ... , publisher}. Specifically, given a set of query schemas representing structured sources, our task is thus to construct a *hierarchy* of clusters, each representing an object domain of "structurally-homogeneous" sources.

In abstraction, this problem is essentially clustering *categorical data*. We can view a schema as a *transaction* and thus a special type of categorical data. As such data is

W. Lindner et al. (Eds.): EDBT 2004 Workshops, LNCS 3268, pp. 536–546, 2004.

domain	number of sources	domain	number of sources
Airfares	53	Hotels	38
Automobiles	102	Jobs	55
Books	69	Movies	78
CarRentals	24	MusicRecords	75

Fig. 1. Our dataset of sample deep web sources: 494 sources in 8 domains

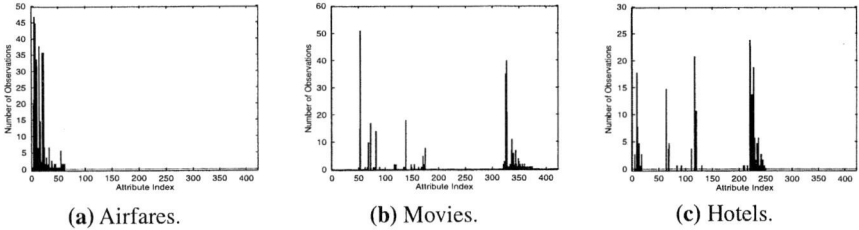

(a) Airfares.   (b) Movies.   (c) Hotels.

Fig. 2. Attribute frequencies of different domains

typically sparse in a high-dimensional space, conventional clustering based on similarity measures does not work well. Several recent efforts have thus developed new *objective functions*, e.g., context-linkages [2] and entropy [3].

In this paper, we pursue model-based clustering with a new objective function, motivated by our observations on the query schemas. In particular, we collected a dataset of deep Web sources using Web directories (e.g., InvisibleWeb.com, BrightPlanet.com) and search engines (e.g., Google.com). As Figure 1 summarizes, the dataset consists of 494 sources in 8 domains.

First, we observe that query schemas are *discriminative* representative of structured sources. Specifically, we count attribute frequencies for each domain (i.e., the aggregate occurrences of an attribute across all sources in the same domain). Figure 2 lists the attribute frequencies (y-axis) of 3 domains (Airfares, Movies and Hotels) over all the attributes (x-axis) in the 8 domains. We observe that each domain contains a dominant range of attributes, distinctive from other domains. For example, Airfares only covers the first 53 attributes and does not overlap with Movies. Hotels has its dominant range of attributes from index 200 to 250 (while overlapping with Airfares in some of the first 53 attributes).

Second, we observe that the aggregate schema vocabulary of sources in the same domain tends to converge at a relatively small size with respect to the growth of sources. As detailed in [1], for each domain, the vocabulary growth rates (i.e., the slopes of these curves) decrease rapidly with respect to the increase of sources. This observation indicates that homogeneous sources (in the same domain) share some *concerted* vocabulary of attributes.

These two observations together motivate our approach: The "discriminative" observation suggests using query schemas as "representatives" of sources in their clustering. Further, the "concerted" observation leads us to hypothesize the existence of a hidden schema model (for each domain), which probabilistically generates schemas from a finite vocabulary of attributes. This hypothesis naturally implies *model-based* clustering:

to form clusters according to their underlining models. Further, the "discriminative" observation hints a novel objective function, *model-differentiation* or MD, which seeks to maximize *statistical heterogeneity* among clusters. Rather than relying on ad-hoc cluster-similarity measures, MD takes principled statistical hypothesis testing, called *test of homogeneity* [4], to evaluate if multiple clusters are generated from homogeneous distributions.

Specifically, we develop Algorithm MD_{hac} for clustering query schemas to build a domain hierarchy. First, we develop the statistical model of a cluster as a *multinomial distribution* of attributes observed in the cluster. Second, we adopt χ^2 testing for evaluating the homogeneity among clusters. Third, for hierarchy construction, we use the general hierarchical agglomerative clustering approach [5–7].

We experimented with about 500 real sources in 8 domains (e.g., Airfares, Automobiles, Books). Our goals are two-fold: (1) to evaluate the effectiveness of schema-based clustering for organizing structured sources into domain hierarchies, and (2) to evaluate the performance of the MD objective by comparing to the existing approaches using context linkages, log-likelihood, and entropy. The results show effectiveness in both aspects.

In summary, the contributions of this paper are:

- We propose schema-based clustering for structured deep Web sources. To our knowledge, this work is the first attempt to organize structured Web sources by their query schemas.
- We propose model-differentiation as a new objective function for clustering, which allows principled statistical measure for determining cluster homogeneity. Our evaluation shows that, on clustering the Web query schemas, the model-differentiation function outperforms existing ones.

We review related work in Section 2. Section 3 discusses our statistical cluster modeling, proposes the MD objective function and develops Algorithm MD_{hac}. Section 4 reports our experiments and Section 5 concludes this paper.

2   Related Work

We relate our work to the literature in two aspects. *First*, in terms of the *problem*, this paper studies clustering structured sources on the Web. Our goal of clustering sources to facilitate large-scale integration or "metaquery" has largely been unexplored. On one hand, for structured sources, *information integration* has mainly assumed relatively small-scaled, pre-configured systems (e.g., Information Manifold [8], TSIMMIS [9]). On the other hand, research efforts on large-scale search has mostly focused on *text* sources [10–12]. Our focus mixes both of the above: We aim to enable *large-scale* metaquery over *structured* databases.

Second, in terms of the *techniques*, this paper proposes model-differentiation for clustering schema data. Clustering of categorical data has recently been more actively studied, e.g., STIRR [13], CACTUS [14], ROCK [2], and COOLCAT [3]. STIRR treats clustering as a partitioning problem of hypergraph and solves it based on non-linear dynamical systems. CACTUS considers a cluster as a set of pairwise strong connected attributes by measuring attribute occurrences. ROCK, COOLCAT and this paper are pursuing the same direction of defining a new similarity measure involving the *global context* (such as properties of a entire cluster) instead of local pairwise measure. ROCK uses context linkages between data points, and COOLCAT uses entropy of clusters. As an alternative, we develop the model-differentiation measure, which maximizes the statistical heterogeneity among clusters. Section 4 compares these related approaches.

Our statistical approach belongs to the general idea of model-based clustering [5, 6]. In general, such clustering assumes that data is generated from a mixture of distributions, each of which defines a cluster. This general approach is traditionally not specific to categorical data. More recently, reference [7] proposes a multivariate multinomial distribution (in which each feature is an independent multinomial distribution) for categorical data. In comparison, the model we propose for schema data (or transactional data) is "joint" multinomial, where all features are from one multinomial distribution (Section 3.1).

All the existing model-based works essentially use likelihood as the objective function to maximize. In contrast, we propose model differentiation (Section 3.2) by maximizing the statistical heterogeneity among clusters. In our extended report [15], we show that these two objective functions are *equivalent* in assessing the global clustering results. However, they indeed imply *different* greedy "local" similarity measures (which Section 3.3 will develop). Our experiments are also compatible with the likelihood-based HAC clustering. In practice, we apply statistical χ^2-testing to evaluate the model differences. Note that some HAC algorithms (e.g., the statistical package SPSS) use χ^2-testing for measuring the difference between two clusters of numeric data. In contrast, we exploit χ^2-testing for clustering categorical data by constructing the generative model.

3 MD-Based Clustering

As motivated in Section 1, we are pursuing a MD-based approach to cluster schema data. In the literature, model-based clustering has been widely discussed. The general idea can be stated as: The population of interest consists of G different clusters, generated by G different models. Given a set of data points (a set of schemas) $\mathbf{X} = \{\mathbf{x_1}, ..., \mathbf{x_n}\}$, where each $\mathbf{x_i}$ is independently generated from one of the G models, $\mathcal{M}_1,...,\mathcal{M}_G$, the probability of generating $\mathbf{x_i}$ in the kth model is $Pr(\mathbf{x_i}|\mathcal{M}_k)$. A clustering of $\mathbf{X}$ is a partition of $\mathbf{X}$ into G groups: denoted by $(\mathbf{X}; P) = (C_1, ..., C_G)$, where P partitions $\mathbf{X}$. The objective of model-based clustering is to identify the partition P that all the $\mathbf{x_i}$ generated from the same model $Pr(\bullet|\mathcal{M}_k)$ are partitioned into a single group.

To realize this model-based clustering for query schemas, we design a model as a multinomial distribution (Section 3.1) and develop model-differentiation as the new *objective function* of clustering based on statistical hypothesis testing. Specifically, guided by this objective function, we adopt the commonly used χ^2 testing (Section 3.2). Unlike the clustering work in statistics software, which also use χ^2 testing, we apply it for categorical data based on the generative model. Since we are pursuing a hierarchical clustering approach, we apply the widely used HAC (hierarchial agglomerative clustering) algorithm, which needs a measure to quantify the "similarity" between two clusters. In particular, we derive a new similarity measure from the MD objective function for HAC algorithm. (Section 3.3).

3.1   Hypothesis Modeling

To develop the MD-based clustering, we need to define the generative model. To begin with, we first introduce our model definition as multinomial distribution. Specifically, we assume attributes are independent each other, which is a commonly used assumption for text data [16]. Then we describe how a model generates a schema in statistical way and further how to generate a cluster of schemas.

First, to define the model for the task of schema clustering, we need to describe what is a schema. We view a query schema as a set of attributes for a query interface, as Section 1 introduced. For simplicity, in later examples, we denote attributes in letters A, B,....

Our first attempt is to consider a schema as a set of *distinct* attributes. Therefore, we view the generation of a schema as *sampling without replacement* [4] from a set of attributes, which means the result of a trial (to select an attribute) is not the same as any previous trials. (The trials are therefore "stateful".) That is, we can consider a schema with n attributes as an experiment with n trials; once one attribute is selected, it will not be selected again in the subsequent trials. However, while this model is accurate, its "stateful" trials result in complicated homogeneity testing.

Our second attempt is to approximate the generation process by *sampling with replacement* [4], where the attributes can be repeatedly selected in a schema. With this alternative strategy, to generate a schema Q in some cluster C, the model $\mathcal{M}$ behind C is a *multinomial model* with parameters $p_1,...,p_N$. More specifically, a multinomial model $\mathcal{M}$ for C consists of an exhaustive set of N mutually exclusive events (In our problem, the events are in fact the attributes.) $A_1,...,A_N$ (which covers all the attributes observed in C) with associated probabilities $p_1,...,p_N$, $\sum_{j=1}^{N} p_j = 1$. We denote $\mathcal{M}$ as $\mathcal{M} = \{A_1{:}p_1,...,A_N{:}p_N\}$. Each trial of $\mathcal{M}$ generates one of the N events. The probability of generating an attribute A from $\mathcal{M}$ in a single trial is

$$Pr(\mathsf{A}|\mathcal{M}) = \begin{cases} p_i, & \exists i : \mathsf{A} = A_i \\ 0, & otherwise \end{cases} \tag{1}$$

Under this multinomial model, a schema Q is characterized by its observed attributes frequencies. We thus view Q (of length n) as $Q = \{A_1{:}y_1,...,A_N{:}y_k\}$, $\sum_{i=1}^{N} y_i = n$, where y_i is the frequency (number of occurrences) of attribute A_i in Q. That is, Q (of length n) is generated from $\mathcal{M}$ as the result of n independent trials with the following probability, by definition of standard multinoimal distribution [4]:

$$Pr(Q|\mathcal{M}, n) = n! \prod_{i=1}^{N} \frac{Pr(A_i|\mathcal{M})^{y_i}}{y_i!}. \tag{2}$$

Consider a cluster of schemas $C = \{Q_1, Q_2, ..., Q_m\}$, where each schema Q_j (with length n_j) is generated by the same model $\mathcal{M} = \{A_1{:}p_1,...,A_N{:}p_N\}$. Since each Q_j is a multinomial experiment of n_j trials, we can view C as an experiment with $\sum_{j=1}^{m} n_j$ trials by concatenating the trials in all schemas. That is, we consider C is a series of sampling from the same mutinomial distribution $\mathcal{M}$ (i.e., the same $p_1,...,p_N$), with all these independent trials. The theoretical explanation is as follows: Let all $Q_j = \{A_1{:}\mathsf{y_{j1}},...,A_N{:}\mathsf{y_{jN}}\}$, where $\mathsf{y_{ji}}$'s are random variables denoting the frequencies of A_i, share the same multinomial distribution $\mathcal{M} = \{A_1{:}p_1,...,A_N{:}p_N\}$. For the entire C, we define new random variables $\mathsf{z_1},...,\mathsf{z_N}$ as aggregate attribute frequencies. That

	A_1	A_2	A_3	...	A_n	sum
C_1	O_{11}	O_{12}	O_{13}	...	O_{1n}	X_1
C_2	O_{21}	O_{22}	O_{23}	...	O_{2n}	X_2
...	...	...	...	...	...	...
C_m	O_{m1}	O_{m2}	O_{m3}	...	O_{mn}	X_m
sum	Y_1	Y_2	Y_3	...	Y_n	S

Fig. 3. Contingency table for testing

is, $z_i = \sum_{j=1}^{m} y_{ji}$. In [15], we show that $z_1, ..., z_N$ also form the same multinomial distribution $\mathcal{M}$ with $\sum_{j=1}^{m} n_j$ trials. Therefore, under this multinomial view, we can express C as aggregate attribute frequencies, i.e., $C = \{A_1:z_1,...,A_N:z_N\}$.

The simple multinomial modeling simplifies hypothesis homogeneity testing (by directly fitting the contingency table as shown in Section 3.2). However, the modeling is inaccurate: It may generate some schemas that are not observable in the real world. For instance, it may generate a schema {author, author, title}, where author is repeated twice. While the modeling seems crude (like other typical "independent" assumption in, say, Naive Bayes Classifier for text), our empirical study shows that the simple model performs well.

As a remark, this modeling is much simpler than what we define in our previous work MGS [17]. The MGS work addresses matching schemas across sources already given in the same domain. (Therefore, this paper is a preliminary step to provide input for MGS.) The MGS modeling assumes a two-level model structure to capture concepts and synonyms for the goal of synonym discovery. This paper assumes a much simpler model because it is sufficient to capture the attribute frequencies across different domains for the purpose of clustering.

3.2 Model-Differentiation: A New Objective Function

A clustering must be guided by some *objective function* that specifies the property of the ideal clusters. Regardless of the objective function, the basic idea of clustering is to put similar data together and dissimilar data apart. For model-based clustering, similar data might be generated from the same underlying models, while dissimilar data are from different models. Thus, we achieve better clustering result when the underlying models are more distinguishable.

Therefore, we define the objective function of clustering as some function $\mathcal{H}$ that characterizes the heterogeneity of models under a partition P, denoted by $\mathcal{H}(\mathbf{X}; P)$. The goal of clustering is to find the partition P maximizing function $\mathcal{H}$, i.e., $\arg\max_P \mathcal{H}(\mathbf{X}; P)$. In statistics, the homogeneity of distributions can be measured by *test of homogeneity* using statistical hypothesis testing. More specifically, if we have a partition function P partitioning $\mathbf{X}$ into clusters $C_k(1 \leq k \leq G)$, we can test the hypothesis "$C_k(1 \leq k \leq G)$ are generated by same distribution" with standard testing approaches. The result of testing is a probabilistic variable λ to indicate the confidence that we accept the hypothesis. Thus the heterogeneity of models is $1 - \lambda$. Formally, the MD-based clustering is to find

$$\arg\max_{P} \mathcal{H}(\mathbf{X}; P) = \arg\max_{P} \mathcal{H}(C_1, ..., C_G)$$
$$= \arg\max_{P} \{1 - \lambda(C_1, ..., C_G)\}$$
$$= \arg\min_{P} \lambda(C_1, ..., C_G), \tag{3}$$

where $\lambda(C_1, ..., C_G)$ is the hypothesis testing on a partition P with G clusters.

Specifically, given a partition P on the observed data $\mathbf{X}$, we apply χ^2 hypothesis testing to compute $\lambda(C_1, ..., C_G)$. In statistics, χ^2 testing can be used to test the homogeneity among multiple clusters with multinomial distributions by constructing a *contingency table*. Since we show that a cluster of schemas is also from a multinomial distribution, we can directly apply the test of homogeneity by fitting the attribute frequencies in the cluster into the contingency table, which reflects the fact that our modeling simplifies the testing.

Formally, assume there are m clusters $C_1, ..., C_m$, and each of them is generated from its own multinomial distribution (Section 3.1). There are n different attributes altogether, denoted by $A_1, ..., A_n$. Figure 3 is the contingency table to show this set of data. In particular, O_{ij} stands for the attribute frequency of A_j in cluster C_i. X_i is the sum of all the O_{ij} in ith row and Y_j is the sum of all the O_{ij} in jth column. That is, $X_i = \sum_{j=1}^{n} O_{ij}$ and $Y_j = \sum_{i=1}^{m} O_{ij}$. S is the sum of all O_{ij} in the table. Thus $S = \sum_{i=1}^{m} X_i = \sum_{j=1}^{n} Y_j$. We want to test the hypothesis: $\forall j, 1 \leq j \leq n$, $p_{j1} = p_{j2} = ... = p_{jm} = \frac{Y_j}{S}$, where p_{ji} is the probability of observing attribute A_j in C_i. This hypothesis is tested by considering the random variable

$$D^2(C_1, ..., C_m) = \sum_{i=1}^{m} \sum_{j=1}^{n} \left[\frac{(O_{ij} - X_i \times \frac{Y_j}{S})^2}{X_i \times \frac{Y_j}{S}} \right]. \tag{4}$$

It can be shown that D^2 has asymptotically a χ^2 distribution with $(n-1)(m-1)$ degree of freedom, denoted by df [18]. Note that we have to use both the values of D^2 and df to decide how similar the m clusters are. D^2 value itself is not a valid indicator for the similarity of clusters without being qualified the degree of freedom. Therefore we need to translate these two values into a single similarity measure. In statistics, we can compute the P-value given D^2 and df, denoted by $PV(D^2, df)$. The P-value is the probability value λ in Equation 3, indicating the confidence that we accept the hypothesis that the m clusters are generated from the same distribution. The objective function $\mathcal{H}$ is then

$$\mathcal{H}(C_1, ..., C_G) = 1 - PV(D^2, df). \tag{5}$$

The computation of P-value is expensive and requires numerical integration. Therefore, in practice, we develop an alternative measure, $\tilde{\mathcal{H}}$, by applying a normalized D^2 value. In particular, to make the D^2 values of different degrees of freedom (resulted from different clusters) comparable, we use the D^2 values with a commonly adopted significance level 0.5% as the normalization factors, denoted by $D_s^2(df)$ with different degrees of freedom. We consider $\tilde{\mathcal{H}}$ as the ratio between the computed D^2 value and the D_s^2 with the same df:

$$\tilde{\mathcal{H}}(C_1, ..., C_G) = \frac{D^2}{D_s^2(df)}. \tag{6}$$

Require: SchemaSet **X**, ObjectiveFunction $\mathcal{F}$, NumberOfClusters G
1: /* **Form a list of initial** V **clusters** */
2: $C_k = X_k, (1 \leq k \leq V)$
3: /* **Derive similarity measure** */
4: $s =$ a similarity measure derived from $\mathcal{F}$
5: /* **HAC main framework** */
6: **for** $K = V, V - 1, ..., G$ **do**
7:     /* **Compute pairwise similarities** */
8:     $k^*, l^* = \arg\min_{k,l} \mathcal{H}(C_k, C_l), (1 \leq k < l \leq K)$
9:     /* **Merge the most similar two clusters** */
10:     $C_{<k^*,l^*>} = \text{MERGE}(C_{k^*}, C_{l^*})$
11: **end for**

Fig. 4. HAC algorithm MD$_{hac}$

3.3   HAC Algorithm and MD-Based Similarity Measure

For constructing domain hierarchy, we adopt the general HAC clustering approach, which is widely used for data clustering [19]. Figure 4 illustrates the general HAC framework [7]. In HAC, we need to measure the similarity of clusters. That is, given a set of clusters, $C_1,...,C_V$, we compute all the pairwise values $s(k, l)$, where s is a similarity function derived from the objective function of clustering. The criterion of defining similarity function $s(k, l)$ is to maximize the objective function in each step. The two clusters with the smallest $s(k, l)$ are merged in each iteration. The algorithm stops when there are G clusters left.

Specifically, for the MD-based clustering, we derive $s(k, l)$ from $\mathcal{H}(\mathbf{X}; P)$ (defined in Section 3.2) as follows: In each iteration of HAC, we merge the clusters with the smallest $\mathcal{H}$ value (i.e., the most similar two models) and therefore we define $s(k, l)$ to be

$$s(k, l) = \mathcal{H}(C_k, C_l). \tag{7}$$

For the space limitation, we illustrate MD$_{hac}$ in more details in the extended report [15].

4   Experiments

To evaluate the MD$_{hac}$ algorithm, we test it with 8 domains of structured sources on the deep Web. We compare our model-differentiation based approach with likelihood [7], entropy (COOLCAT) [3] and context linkage (ROCK) [2] based approaches using HAC algorithm and analyze the results. Also, we show the domain hierarchy built by MD$_{hac}$.

4.1   Experiment Setup

We collected 494 sources over 8 domains, totally covering 422 attributes. For each source, we manually extract attributes from its query interface by extracting noun phrases, and then judge its corresponding domain. This is our ground truth of "correct" clustering. In

MD$_{hac}$	Af	Am	Bk	Cr	Ht	Jb	Mv	Mr
C_1	0	101	0	0	2	4	0	0
C_2	0	0	62	0	0	1	9	2
C_3	0	0	0	24	0	0	0	0
C_4	0	0	0	0	35	0	0	1
C_5	0	0	0	0	0	50	1	0
C_6	53	0	0	0	1	0	0	0
C_7	0	0	0	0	0	0	8	67
C_8	0	1	7	0	0	0	62	7

(a) Conditional entropy of MD$_{hac}$: 0.32.

LK$_{hac}$	Af	Am	Bk	Cr	Ht	Jb	Mv	Mr
C_1	0	100	0	0	2	8	0	0
C_2	0	0	62	0	0	1	7	2
C_3	0	0	0	0	35	6	0	1
C_4	0	0	0	0	0	0	56	5
C_5	0	2	7	0	0	0	10	2
C_6	0	0	0	0	0	0	7	67
C_7	53	0	0	0	1	0	0	0
C_8	0	0	0	24	0	40	0	0

(b) Conditional entropy of LK$_{hac}$: 0.42.

EP$_{hac}$	Af	Am	Bk	Cr	Ht	Jb	Mv	Mr
C_1	0	100	0	0	2	4	0	0
C_2	0	0	62	0	0	0	5	2
C_3	0	0	0	24	0	0	0	0
C_4	0	0	0	0	35	6	0	1
C_5	0	0	0	0	0	0	57	5
C_6	0	0	0	0	0	0	8	67
C_7	53	0	0	0	1	0	0	0
C_8	0	2	7	0	0	45	10	2

(c) Conditional entropy of EP$_{hac}$: 0.38.

CL$_{hac}$	Af	Am	Bk	Cr	Ht	Jb	Mv	Mr
C_1	34	0	0	0	1	0	0	0
C_2	19	0	0	0	0	0	0	0
C_3	0	99	7	0	2	7	1	1
C_4	0	1	62	24	0	1	4	1
C_5	0	0	0	0	35	21	0	1
C_6	0	0	0	0	0	26	1	0
C_7	0	0	0	0	0	0	70	42
C_8	0	2	0	0	0	0	4	32

(d) Conditional entropy of CL$_{hac}$: 0.61.

Fig. 5. Comparison of four similarity measures in HAC

the experiment, we compare the automatic algorithms with our ground truth, to evaluate the accuracy of clustering.

To measure the result of clustering, we adopt the *conditional entropy* introduced in [20]. For a given number of clusters G, the value of the conditional entropy is within the range from 0 to $\log G$, where 0 denotes the 100% correct clustering, $\log G$ denotes purely random clustering result, i.e. the sources from every single domain are evenly distributed into all clusters. Thus, the closer the conditional entropy value is to 0, the better the result is.

4.2   Experimental Results

We design two suites of experiments. *First*, we compare our approach MD$_{hac}$ with the three existing approaches: likelihood based approach (LK$_{hac}$), entropy based approach (EP$_{hac}$) and context linkage based approach (CL$_{hac}$) for clustering the sources of 8 domains. For fair comparison, we only replace the similarity measure of test of model difference (Equation 6) with the likelihood based measure, entropy based measure and context linkage based measure. All the rest settings stay the same.

To make the other measures clear, we briefly list each of them below. Reference [7] introduces the likelihood based similarity measure for HAC algorithm as Equation 8. The basic idea is that in each merging step in HAC, the two clusters generating the maximal likelihood after merging will be merged.

$$s(k, l) = \mathcal{L}(C_k) + \mathcal{L}(C_l) - \mathcal{L}(C_{<k,l>}). \qquad (8)$$

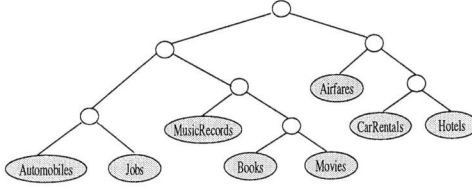

Fig. 6. Domain hierarchy built by MD_{hac}

COOLCAT [3] introduces entropy as the objective function, from where we derive the following similarity measure for HAC algorithm, with the same idea as the derivation of Equation 8 in [7].

$$s(k, l) = |C_k|E(C_k) + |C_l|E(C_l) - |C_{<k,l>}|E(C_{<k,l>}). \tag{9}$$

ROCK [2] introduces context linkage as the similarity measure:

$$s(k, l) = \frac{link[C_k, C_l]}{(n_k + n_l)^{(1+2f(\theta))} - n_k^{(1+2f(\theta))} - n_j^{(1+2f(\theta))}}. \tag{10}$$

The result in Figure 5 shows the comparison of the four measures in HAC algorithm. The numbers in the figure indicate the number of Web sources in each cluster from each domain. For example, in Figure 5 (a), 101 stands for that there are, in cluster C_1, 101 web sources from automobile domain. We use the abbreviations Af, Am, Bk, Cr, Ht, Jb, Mv and Mr to denote the 8 domains Airfares, Automobiles, CarRentals, Hotels, Jobs, Movies and MusicRecords respectively. Figure 5 illustrates two results: 1) It is feasible to address the clustering of structured sources as the clustering of query schemas. The matrix of MD_{hac}, LK_{hac} and EP_{hac} do show correct clustering for most data. The result of CL_{hac} is not good perhaps because its similarity measure may not fit the schema data well; 2) MD_{hac} achieves, on clustering web schemas, the best performance (smallest conditional entropy) among all the measures. In particular, compared with the second best measure, EP_{hac}, MD_{hac} has better clustering results for Jobs and Movies.

Second, we show the effectiveness of MD_{hac} to build the domain hierarchy (as Section 1 motivated). After clustering 8 domains, we continue to build the domain hierarchy in the same way as the HAC approach. The result in Figure 6 illustrates that Automobiles and Jobs are merged in the same subtree, MusicRecords, Books and Movies in another subtree, and Airfares, CarRentals and Hotels in a third subtree. This hierarchy is consistent with our observation in the real world (i.e.,object domains are characterized by their query schemas): Books, MusicRecords and Movies are all media and often sold together online, and so are Airfares, CarRentals and Hotel reservations. Automobiles and Jobs are together because they share many location information, such as city, state and zip code.

5   Conclusion

This paper studies the clustering of deep Web sources. Motivated by our observations, we propose to cluster sources by their query schemas and develop a new model-differentiation objective function for clustering. Guided by the MD objective, we develop a new similarity measure for the HAC algorithm. Our experiments show the effectiveness of our approach by comparison with some related existing techniques.

References

1. K.C.C. Chang, B. He, C. Li, and Z. Zhang. *Structured databases on the web: Observations and implications.* Technical Report UIUCDCS-R-2003-2321, Dept. of Computer Science, UIUC, 2003.
2. S. Guha, R. Rastogi, and K. Shim. ROCK: A robust clustering algorithm for categorical attributes. *Information Systems*, 25:345-366, 2000.
3. D. Barbara, Y. Li, and J. Couto. Coolcat: An entropy-based algorithm for categorical clustering. In *Proceedings of CIKM Conference*, 2002.
4. H.D. Brunk. *An introduction to mathematical statistics.* Blaisdell Pub. Co, 1965.
5. J.D. Banfield and A.E. Raftery. Model-based gaussian and non-gaussian clustering. *Biometrics*, 49:803-821,1993.
6. C. Fraley. Algorithms for model-based Gaussian hierarchical clustering. *SIAM Journal on Scientific Computing*, 20:270-281, 1999.
7. M. Meila and D. Heckerman. *An experimental comparison of several clustering and initialization methods.* Technical report, Microsoft Research, MSR-TR-98-06, 1998.
8. A.Y. Levy, A. Rajaraman, J.J. Ordille. Querying heterogeneous information sources using source descriptions. In *Proceedings of the VLDB Conference*, 1996.
9. Y. Papakonstantinou, H. García-Molina and J. Ullman. Medmaker: A mediation system based on declarative specifications. In *Proceedings of the ICDE Conference*, 1996.
10. J.P. Callan, M. Connell, and A. Du. Automatic discovery of language models for text databases. In *Proceedings of the SIGMOD Conference*, 1999.
11. P. G. Ipeirotis, and M.S. Luis Gravano. Probe, count, and classify: Categorizing hidden web databases. In *Proceedings of the SIGMOD Conference*, 2001.
12. W. Meng, K.L. Liu, C.T. Yu, X. Wang, Y. Chang, and N. Rishe. Determining text databases to search in the internet. In *Proceedings of the VLDB Conference*, 1998.
13. D. Gibson, J.M. Kleinberg, P. Raghavan. Clustering categorical data: An approach based on dynamical systems. *VLDB Journal*, 8:222-236, 1998.
14. V. Ganti, J. Gehrke, and R. Ramakrishnan. CACTUS – Clustering categorical data using summaries. In *Proceedings of Knowledge Discovery and Data Mining*, pages: 73-83, 1999.
15. B. He, T. Tao, and K.C.C. Chang. *Clustering structured web sources: A schema-based, model-differentiation approach.* Technical Report UIUCDCS-R-2003-2322, Dept. of Computer Science, UIUC, 2003.
16. J. Ponte and W. Croft. A language modelling approach to information retrieval. In *Proceedings of the 21st ACM SIGIR Conference on Research and Development in Information Retrieval*, 1998.
17. B. He and K.C.C. Chang. Statistical schema matching across web query interfaces. In *Proceedings of the 2003 ACM SIGMOD Conference*, 2003.
18. A. Agresti. *Categorical Data Analysis.* John Wiley & Sons, Inc. New Jersey, 2002.
19. A.K. Jain, M.N. Murty, and P.J. Flynn. Data clustering: A review. *ACM Computing Surveys*, 31:264-323, 1999.
20. P. Berkhin. Survey of clustering data mining techniques. Technical report, Accrue Software, 2002.

Clustering XML Documents
Using Structural Summaries*

Theodore Dalamagas[1], Tao Cheng[2], Klaas-Jan Winkel[3], and Timos Sellis[1]

[1] School of Electr. and Comp. Engineering,
National Technical University of Athens,
Zographou, 15773, Athens, Greece
{dalamag,timos}@dblab.ece.ntua.gr
[2] Department of Computer Science,
University of California,
Santa Barbara, CA 93106, USA
taocheng@cs.ucsb.edu
[3] Faculty of Computer Science,
University of Twente,
7500, AE Enschede, The Netherlands
winkel@cs.utwente.nl

Abstract. This work presents a methodology for grouping structurally similar XML documents using clustering algorithms. Modeling XML documents with tree-like structures, we face the 'clustering XML documents by structure' problem as a 'tree clustering' problem, exploiting distances that estimate the similarity between those trees in terms of the hierarchical relationships of their nodes. We suggest the usage of tree structural summaries to improve the performance of the distance calculation and at the same time to maintain or even improve its quality. Experimental results are provided using a prototype testbed.

1   Introduction

Grouping together structurally similar XML documents refers to the application of clustering methods using distances that estimate the similarity between tree structures in terms of the hierarchical relationships of their nodes.

Clustering by structure can be a useful task for many applications. Since the XML language can encode hierarchical data, clustering XML documents by structure can be exploited in any application domain that needs management of hierarchical structures, for example: (a) the discovery of structurally similar web navigational pathways, or tree-like patterns, (b) the discovery of structurally similar macromolecular tree patterns in bioinformatics [5, 10]. Moreover, many XML documents are constructed from data sources without DTDs. XTRACT [7] and DDbE[1] are systems that automatically extract

---

* Work supported in part by DELOS Network of Excellence on Digital Libraries, IST programme of the EC FP6, no G038-507618, and by PYTHAGORAS EPEAEK II programme, EU and Greek Ministry of Education.

[1] http://www.alphaworks.ibm.com/tech/DDbE

W. Lindner et al. (Eds.): EDBT 2004 Workshops, LNCS 3268, pp. 547–556, 2004.

DTDs from XML documents. Identifying groups of XML documents with similar structure can be useful for such systems, where a collection of XML documents should be first grouped into sets of structurally similar documents and then a DTD can be assigned to each set individually.

The main contribution of this work is a methodology for grouping structurally similar XML documents. Modeling XML documents as rooted ordered labeled trees, we face the 'clustering XML documents by structure' problem as a 'tree clustering' problem. We propose the usage of tree structural summaries that have minimal processing requirements instead of the original trees representing the XML documents. We present a new algorithm to calculate tree edit distances and define a structural distance metric to estimate the structural similarity between XML documents. Using this distance, we perform clustering of XML datasets. Experimental results indicate high quality clustering and performance. Using structural summaries instead of the original trees, improves further the performance of the distance calculation without affecting its quality.

We start discussing background information on tree editing issues. Section 3 introduces a metric of structural distance and Section 4 suggests the tree structural summaries. Section 5 presents a new algorithm to calculate tree edit distances. Section 6 discusses evaluation results, and, finally, Section 7 concludes our work.

2   Tree Editing

The *XML data model* is a graph representation of a collection of atomic and complex objects that without the IDREFS mechanism becomes a *rooted ordered labeled tree* [1]. Since we use such rooted ordered labeled trees to represent XML data, we exploit the notions of *tree edit sequence* and *tree edit distance* originating from editing problems for rooted ordered labeled trees [10]. A *tree edit sequence* is a sequence of tree edit operations (insert node, delete node, etc) to transform T_1 to T_2. Assuming a cost model to assign costs for every tree edit operation, the *tree edit distance* between T_1 and T_2 is the minimum cost among the costs of all possible tree edit sequences that transform T_1 to T_2.

All of the algorithms for calculating the tree edit distance for two ordered labeled trees (tree edit algorithms) [2, 3, 11, 12, 16] are based on dynamic programming techniques related to the string-to-string correction problem [14]. In this work, we consider Chawathe's algorithm [2] as the basic point of reference for tree edit distance algorithms, since it is the fastest available ($O(MN)$, M, N the number of nodes in trees) and permits insertion and deletion only at leaves. We believe that using insertion and deletion only at leaves fits better in the context of XML data. For example, it avoids deleting a node and moving its children up one level. The latter destroys the membership restrictions of the hierarchy and thus is not a 'natural' operation for XML data. We next discuss briefly the Chawathe's algorithm.

Chawathe in [2] suggests a recursive algorithm to calculate the tree edit distance between two rooted labeled trees, using a shortest path detection technique on an *edit graph*. The edit graph of trees T_1 and T_2 is an $(M + 1) \times (N + 1)$ grid of nodes, having a node at each (x, y) location, $x \in [0 \dots (M + 1)]$ and $y \in [0 \dots (N + 1)]$. Edit scripts on such trees can be represented using directed lines connecting the nodes in the edit graph. A horizontal line $((x-1, y), (x, y))$ denotes deletion of $T_1[x]$, where $T_1[x]$ refers to the xth node of T_1 in its preorder sequence. A vertical line $((x, y-1), (x, y))$ denotes insertion of $T_2[y]$. Finally, a diagonal line $((x-1, y-1), (x, y))$ denotes update of $T_1[x]$ by $T_2[y]$.

Figure 1 shows an example of an edit graph which represents an edit script to transform tree T_1 to tree T_2. Notice that T_1 becomes T_2 by $(Rep(T_1[2], c), Rep(T_1[3], d), Ins(T_2[4], T_1[1], 3)$. Every edit script that transforms T_1 to T_2 can be mapped to a path

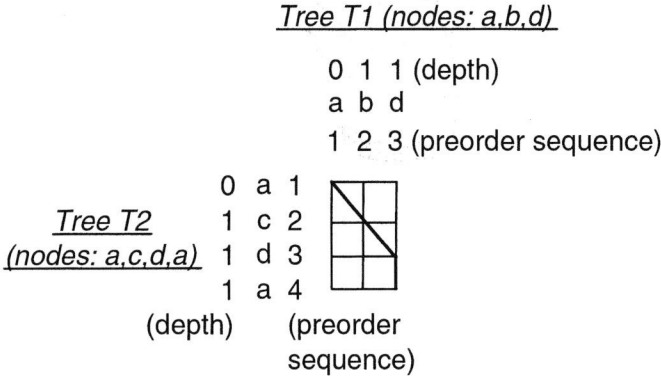

Tree T1 (nodes: a,b,d)

0 1 1 (depth)

a b d

1 2 3 (preorder sequence)

	0 a 1	
Tree T2	1 c 2	
(nodes: a,c,d,a)	1 d 3	
	1 a 4	

(depth)   (preorder
                   sequence)

Fig. 1. An example of an edit graph

in an edit graph. The tree edit distance between two rooted ordered labeled trees T_1 and T_2 is the shortest of all paths to which edit scripts are mapped in an edit graph.

3 Structural Distance

We next define a structural distance metric to estimate the structural similarity between rooted ordered labeled trees that represent XML documents. This distance can be calculated using tree edit algorithms which determine node operations to transform a tree to another one (like the ones presented in the previous section).

Definition 1. *Let T_1 and T_2 be two trees that represent two XML documents, $\mathcal{D}(T_1, T_2)$ be their tree edit distance and $\mathcal{D}'(T_1, T_2)$ be the cost to delete all nodes from T_1 and insert all nodes from T_2. The structural distance S between T_1 to T_2 is defined as $S(T_1, T_2) = \frac{\mathcal{D}(T_1, T_2)}{\mathcal{D}'(T_1, T_2)}$.*

The $S(T_1, T_2)$ is low (high) when the trees have similar (different) structure and high (low) percentage of matching nodes (0 (1) is the min (max) value). In the example illustrated in Figure 2, $\mathcal{D}'(T_1, T_2) = 12$, since 5 nodes must be deleted from T_1 and 7 nodes must be inserted from T_2, thus $S(T_1, T_2) = 0.4166$, since tree distance is 5.

We emphasize on the efficient computation of the structural distance metric (a) showing how to maintain the structural information present in XML documents using compact

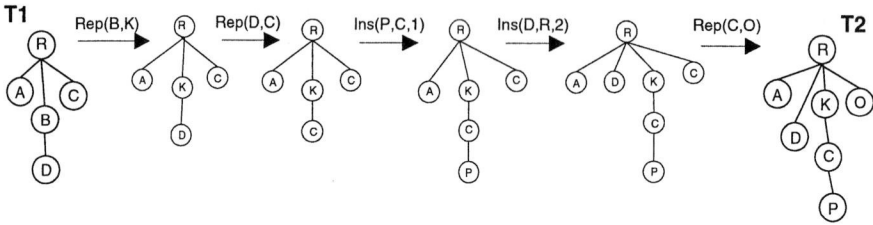

Fig. 2. The sequence of tree edit operations to transform T_1 to T_2 with minimum cost: total cost=5 (assuming unit cost for each operation)

trees, called structural summaries and (b) proposing a new algorithm to calculate tree edit distances to use it for the structural distance calculation.

4   Tree Structural Summaries

Nesting and repetition of elements is the main reason for XML documents to differ in structure although they come from a data source which uses one DTD. A *nested-repeated node* is a non-leaf node whose label is the same with the one of its ancestor. Following a pre-order tree traversal, a *repeated node* is a node whose path (starting from the root down to the node itself) has already been traversed before. Figure 5 has an example of redundancy: trees T_1 and T_3 differ because of nodes A (nested-repeated) and B (repeated).

We perform *nesting reduction* and *repetition reduction* to extract structural summaries for rooted ordered labeled trees which represent XML documents. For nesting reduction, we traverse the tree using pre-order traversal to detect nodes which have an ancestor with the same label in order to move up their subtrees. For repetition reduction, we traverse the tree using pre-order traversal, too, ignoring already existed paths and keeping new ones, using a hash table. The two algorithms are presented in Figures 3 and 4.

Figure 5 presents an example of structural summary extraction from T_1. Applying the nesting reduction phase on T_1 we get T_2, where there are no nested-repeated nodes. Applying the repetition reduction on T_2 we get T_3 which is the structural summary of T_1.

5   Calculating Tree Edit Distances

Our approach for calculating tree edit distances uses a dynamic programming algorithm which is close to Chawathe's algorithm [2] in terms of the tree edit operations that are used. However, the recurrence that we use does not need the costly edit graph calculation of the latter (see Section 2 as well as the timing analysis in Section 6.1). We next present our tree edit distance algorithm.

Permitted tree edit operations are *insertion, deletion* and *replacement* of nodes (insertion and deletion restricted to leaf nodes). Method $CalculateDistance(r_1, r_2)$ calculates the tree edit distance of T_1 and T_2, with roots r_1 and r_2, respectively:

```
void reduceNesting(TreeNode node) {
    TreeNode pos = FindAncestor(node);
    if (pos == null) {
        for (int i=0; i<node.numOfChildren(); i++)
            reduceNesting(node.getChild(i));
    }
    else {
        for (int i=0; i<node.numOfChildren(); i++)
        {
            node.getChild(i).setParentNode(pos);
            pos.addChild(node.getChild(i));
            node.getChildNodes().remove(i);
            i=i-1;
        }
    }
}
```

Fig. 3. Nesting reduction

```
void reduceRepeat(TreeNode node, String currentPath) {
    String path = currentPath + "/" + node.getNodeName();
    if (!hash.containsKey(path)) {
        hash.put(path, node);
        for (int i=0; i<node.numOfChildren(); i++)
            reduceRepeat(node.getChild(i), path);
    }
    else {
        TreeNode destination = (TreeNode)hash.get(path);
        int numOfOldChildren = destination.numOfChildren();
        for (int i=0; i<node.numOfChildren(); i++)
            destination.addChild(node.getChild(i));
        node.DeleteNode();
    }
    for (int i = numOfOldChildren;
        i<destination.numOfChildren(); i++)
            reduceRepeat(destination.getChild(i), path);
}
```

Fig. 4. Repetition reduction

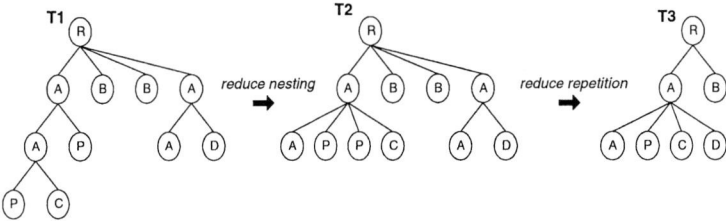

Fig. 5. Structural summary extraction

```
int CalculateDistance(TreeNode s, TreeNode t) {
    int[][] D=new int[numOfChildren(s)+1][numOfChildren(t)+1];
    D[0][0]=UpdateCost(LabelOf(s), LabelOf(t));
    for (int i=1; i≤numOfChildren(s); i++) D[i][0]= [i-1][0]+numOfNodes(sᵢ);
    for(int j=1; j≤numOfChildren(t); j++) D[0][j]=D[0][j-1]+numOfNodes(tⱼ);
    for (int i=1; i≤numOfChildren(s); i++)
        for (int j=1; j≤numOfChildren(t); j++)
            D[i][j]=Min(D[i-1][j-1]+CalculateDistance(sᵢ,tⱼ), D[i][j-1]+numOfNodes(tⱼ),
                D[i-1][j]+numOfNodes(sᵢ));
    Return D[numOfChildren(s)][numOfChildren(t)]; }
```

where: s_i (t_j) is the i_{th} (j_{th}) subtree of node s (t), $numOfChildren(s)$ returns the number of child nodes of node s, $numOfNodes(s)$ returns the number of nodes of the subtree rooted at s, $UpdateCost(LabelOf(s), LabelOf(t))$ returns the cost to make the label of node s the same as the label of node t (0 if $LabelOf(s) = LabelOf(t)$ or 1 otherwise).

In the algorithm, $D[i][j]$ keeps the tree edit distance between tree T_1 with only its first i subtrees and tree T_2 with only its first j subtrees. Assuming unit cost (1) for an insert or delete operation, we use $numOfNode(s_i)$ to represent the cost to delete the ith subtree of node s and $numOfNodes(t_j)$ to represent the cost to insert the jth subtree of node t. We next describe in detail how the algorithm computes the minimum distance between trees:

1. Having the value $D[i][j-1]$ and the number of nodes in the subtree rooted at t_j, we spend $d_1 = D[i][j-1] + numOfNodes(t_j)$ to transform the subtree rooted at s to the subtree rooted at t. Since the cost of an *insert node* operation is 1, we use $numOfNodes(t_j)$ to represent the cost to insert the j_{th} subtree of node t in the subtree rooted at s.

2. Similarly, having the value $D[i-1][j]$ and the number of nodes in the subtree rooted at s_i, we spend $d_2 = D[i-1][j] + numOfNodes(s_i)$ to transform the subtree rooted at s to the subtree rooted at t. Since the cost of a *delete node* operation is 1, we use $numOfNodes(s_i)$ to represent the cost to delete the i_{th} subtree of s.

3. Having the value $D[i-1][j-1]$, we spend
   $d_3 = D[i-1][j-1] + CalculateDistance(s_i, t_j)$
   to transform the subtree rooted at s to the subtree rooted at t. $CalculateDistance$ is recursively called for the i_{th} and j_{th} children of nodes s and t, respectively.

$D[i][j]$ keeps the minimum from d_1, d_2 and d_3 values. Figure 6 shows an example of $D[][]$ calculation. $D[2][3]$ is the distance between T_1 with only its first 2 subtrees and T_2 with only its first 3 subtrees.

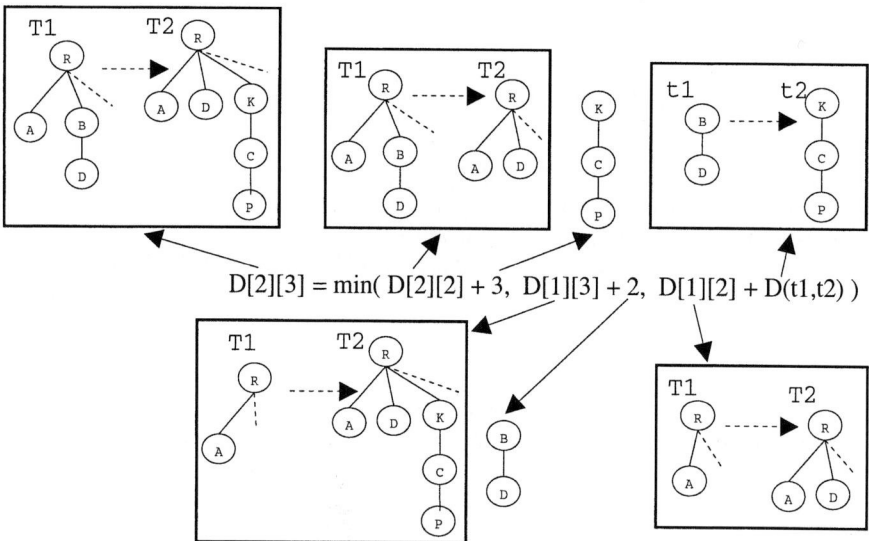

$$D[2][3] = min(\ D[2][2] + 3,\ \ D[1][3] + 2,\ \ D[1][2] + D(t1,t2)\ )$$

Fig. 6. Calculating $D[2][3]$ for T_1 and T_2

We call the function $CalculateDistance$ once for each pair of nodes at the same depth in the 2 structural summary trees, so the complexity is $O(MN)$, where M is the number of nodes in the tree rooted at s, and N is the number of nodes in the tree rooted at t.

6   Evaluation

We implemented a testbed to perform clustering on synthetic and real data, using structural distances[2]. Two sets of 1000 synthetic XML documents were generated from 10 real-case DTDs[3], varying the parameter $MaxRepeats$ to determine the number of times a node will appear as a child of its parent node. For real data set we used 150 documents from the ACM SIGMOD Record and ADC/NASA[4].

We chose single link hierarchical clustering method to be the basic clustering algorithm since it has been shown to be theoretically sound, under a certain number of reasonable conditions [13]. However, the structural distance metric can be exploited by any other clustering algorithm to discover groups of structurally similar XML documents. To determine the most appropriate clustering level for the single link hierarchies, we adopted $C-$index [8], by calculating its values, varying the clustering level in different steps.

While checking time performance is straightforward, checking clustering quality involves the calculation of metrics based on priori knowledge of which documents should be members of the appropriate cluster. Thus, the evaluation procedure raises the following issues:

1. The number of clusters discovered should ideally match the number of DTDs where the XML documents are based on. To estimate the number of clusters, we adopt the C-index in the single-link clustering method.
2. The clusters discovered should be mapped to the original DTDs where the XML documents are based on. For this reason, we performed the following tasks:
   (a) We derived DTDs $D_1^c, D_2^c, \ldots, D_k^c$ for every cluster $C_1, C_2, \ldots, C_k$, using the XML documents assigned to that cluster[5].
   (b) We parsed the derived DTDs $D_1^c, D_2^c, \ldots, D_k^c$ and the original DTDs $D_1, D_2, \ldots, D_m$, creating derived trees $t_1^c, t_2^c, \ldots, t_k^c$ trees and original trees $t_1, t_2, \ldots, t_m$, respectively[6].
   (c) For every original tree t_i, $1 \le i \le m$, we calculated the structural distances $\mathcal{S}(t_i, t_1^c), \mathcal{S}(t_i, t_2^c), \ldots, \mathcal{S}(t_i, t_k^c)$. The lowest of these values $\mathcal{S}_{min}(t_i, t_p^c)$, $1 \le p \le k$, indicates that the original DTD D_i corresponds to cluster C_p. After that, we had a mapping between the original DTDs and the clusters produced.

We note that the C-index method might give a number of clusters which is different than the number of DTDs where the XML documents are based on ($m \ne k$), that is there might be clusters not mapped to any of the original DTD. In such case, clustering quality metrics will be affected.

To evaluate the clustering results, we used two popular metrics: *precision PR* and *recall R* [13]. Let (a) a_i be the number of the XML documents in the extracted cluster

---

[2] All the experiments were performed on a Pentium III 800MHz, 192MB RAM.
[3] IBM's Alphaworks generator (DTDs: www.xmlfiles.com and www.w3schools.com)
[4] www.acm.org/sigmod/record/xml and xml.gsfc.nasa.gov
[5] using AlphaWorks Data Descriptors by Example: www.alphaworks.ibm.com/tech/DDbE
[6] DTD parser: www.wutka.com/dtdparser.html

C_i that were indeed members of that cluster (correctly clustered), (b) b_i be the number of XML documents in C_i that were not members of that cluster (misclustered) and (c) c_i be the number of XML documents not in C_i, although they should be C_i's members. Then, $PR = \sum_i a_i/(\sum_i a_i + \sum_i b_i)$ and $R = \sum_i a_i/(\sum_i a_i + \sum_i c_i)$. High precision and recall indicate excellent clustering quality.

6.1   Timing Analysis

We compared the time to derive the two structural summaries from two trees representing two XML documents, and calculate their structural distance <u>vs</u> the time to calculate the structural distance between the two original trees. We tested both Chawathe's algorithm and our algorithm using randomly generated XML documents, with their number of nodes ranging from 0 to 2000. The time decrease (%) for calculating the structural distance between 2 XML documents using their summaries instead of using the original trees lays around 80% on average for Chawathe's and around 50% on average for our algorithm. Figure 7 presents the time decrease (%) for calculating the structural distance between 2 XML documents, using our algorithm instead of Chawathe's algorithm (52% on average). Chawathe's algorithm is slower due to the pre-calculation of the edit graph (it spends more than 50% of the time needed for the overall distance calculation). To give a sense about the scaling of the calculations, Figure 8 presents the timing performance for our algorithm, with or without summaries.

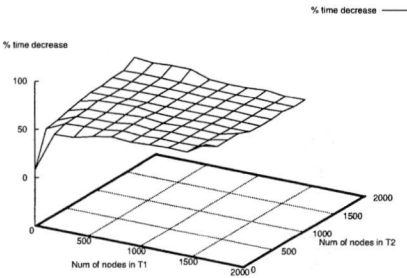

Fig. 7. Time decrease (%) for structural distance calculation using our algorithm instead of Chawathe's

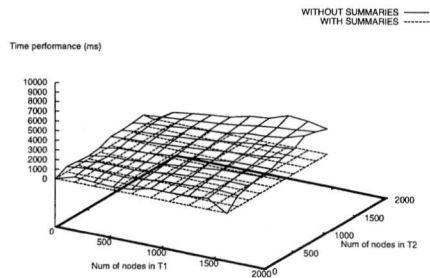

Fig. 8. Calculating the structural distance between 2 trees using our algorithm: time performance with or without summaries (ms)

6.2   Clustering Evaluation

We performed single link clustering on synthetic and real data, using structural distances returned from Chawathe's algorithm and our algorithm, with or without structural summaries, and calculated PR and R values.

Table 1 presents the PR and R values using the two algorithms on synthetic and real data. For both algorithms, we note that for small trees ($maxRepeats = 3$) with only a few repeated elements and, thus, with the structural summaries being actually the original trees, the clustering results are the same with or without summaries. On the other hand, for larger trees ($maxRepeats = 6$) with many repeated elements, clustering quality is improved in Chawathe's and maintained in high levels in our algorithm. For real data, summary usage maintains the already high quality clustering results obtained without using summaries, for both algorithms. We should note that the differences in the clusters obtained by the two algorithms in identical datasets, although both calculate the minimum cost to transform a tree to another one, are due to the cost models used for the tree edit operations. This does not affect the evaluation procedure, since our concern is to show the effect of summaries on clustering quality in both algorithms.

The evaluation results indicate that structural summaries maintain the clustering quality, that is they do not hurt clustering. Thus, using structural summaries we can clearly improve the performance of the whole clustering procedure, since summaries have lower processing requirements than the original trees. A further decrease can be achieved exploiting our algorithm since it shows improved performance compared to Chawathe's.

7   Conclusions

This work studied methods to cluster XML documents by structure, exploiting structural distances and structural summaries. We defined a structural distance metric to estimate the structural similarity between two XML documents. We proposed structural summaries that have minimal processing requirements, maintaining the structural relationships of the elements in an XML document. Also, we presented a new algorithm to calculate tree edit distances. Finally, we implemented a testbed to perform clustering on synthetic and real data, using structural distances. Our results showed that structural summaries clearly improved the performance of the clustering procedure, while maintaining the clustering quality. Moreover, our structural distance algorithm showed improved performance compared to Chawathe's.

Methods for file change detection (see for example [4]) are related to our work, but most of them do not compute the minimal tree edit sequence. Other works, like [15], concentrate on unorder trees. To the best of our knowledge, the only work directly compared with ours is [9]. Their set of tree edit operations include two new ones which refer to whole trees. They preprocess the trees to detect whether a subtree is contained in another tree. There are no results about PR and R values. In our work, we diminish the

Table 1. PR, R values for clustering synthetic and real data (**CH**: Chawathe's algorithm, **D**: our algorithm, **n** (**y**): without (with) summary, **3** (**6**): maxRepeat=3 (6))

Synthetic data	
CH-n-3: 11 clusters, $PR = 0.71$, $R = 0.90$	**CH-y-3**: 11 clusters, $PR = 0.71$, $R = 0.90$
CH-n-6: 11 clusters, $PR = 0.58$, $R = 0.89$	**CH-y-6**: 12 clusters, $PR = 0.83$, $R = 0.96$
D-n-3: 11 clusters, $PR = 1.00$, $R = 0.98$	**D-y-3**: 11 clusters, $PR = 1.00$, $R = 0.98$
D-n-6: 12 clusters, $PR = 1.00$, $R = 0.97$	**D-y-6**: 11 clusters, $PR = 1.00$, $R = 0.98$
Real data	
CH-n: 4 clusters, $PR = 1.00$, $R = 0.98$	**CH-y**: 3 clusters, $PR = 1.00$, $R = 1.00$
D-n: 4 clusters, $PR = 1.00$, $R = 0.98$	**D-y**: 3 clusters, $PR = 1.00$, $R = 1.00$

possibility of having repeated subtrees using structural summaries instead of expanding the tree edit operations. Summaries are used as an index structure to speed up the tree distance calculation. Such an approach can reduce the performance cost in every algorithm that estimates the structural distance between trees.

As a future work, certain properties of the structural distance should be explored and confirmed. Positivity, symmetry and triangular inequality are such properties. The experimental results show that these properties hold (see for example Figures 7, 8 for the symmetry) but formal study is needed to confirm it. Also, we will study how to employ vector-based representation of tree structures (like in [6]) to further explore the problem of clustering by structure.

References

1. S. Abiteboul, P. Buneman, and D. Suciu. *Data on the Web.* Morgan Kaufmann, 2000.
2. S. S. Chawathe. Comparing hierarchical data in external memory. In *Proc. of the VLDB Conference, Edinburgh, Scotland, UK*, 1999.
3. S. S. Chawathe, A. Rajaraman, H. Garcia-Molina, and J. Widom. Change Detection in Hierarchically Structured Information. In *Proc. of the ACM SIGMOD Conference*, USA, 1996.
4. G. Cobena, S. Abiteboul, and A. Marian. Detecting changes in XML documents. In *Proc. of the ICDE Conference*, San Jose, USA, 2002.
5. H. G. Direen and M. S. Jones. Knowledge management in bioinformatics. In A. B. Chaudhri, A. Rashid, and R. Zicari, editors, *XML Data Management*. 2003. Addison Wesley.
6. S. Flesca, G. Manco, E. Masciari, L. Pontieri, and A. Pugliese. Detecting similarities between XML documents. In *Proc. of WebDB'02*, 2002.
7. M. Garofalakis, A. Gionis, R. Rastogi, S. Seshadri, and K. Shim. XTRACT: A system for extracting document type descriptors from XML documents. In *Proc. of the ACM SIGMOD Conference,Texas, USA*, 2000.
8. G. W. Milligan and M. C. Cooper. An examination of procedures for determining the number of clusters in a data set. *Psychometrika*, 50, 1985.
9. A. Nierman and H. V. Jagadish. Evaluating structural similarity in xml documents. In *Proc. of the WebDB Workshop*, Madison, Wisconsin, USA, June 2002.
10. D. Sankoff and J. Kruskal. *Time Warps, String Edits and Macromolecules, The Theory and Practice of Sequence Comparison.* CSLI Publications, 1999.
11. S. M. Selkow. The tree-to-tree editing problem. *Information Processing Letters*, 6:184–186, 1977.
12. K. C. Tai. The tree-to-tree correction problem. *Journal of ACM*, 26, 1979.
13. C. J. van Rijsbergen. *Information Retrieval.* Butterworths, London, 1979.
14. R. Wagner and M. Fisher. The string-to-string correction problem. *Journal of ACM*, 21(1):168–173, 1974.
15. Y. Wang, D. DeWitt, and Jin-Yi Cai. X-Diff: An effective change detection algorithm for XML documents. In *Proc. of the ICDE Conference*, Bangalore, India, 2003.
16. K. Zhang and D. Shasha. Simple fast algorithms for the editing distance between trees and related problems. *SIAM Journal of Computing*, 18:1245–1262, 1989.

A Scalable Randomized Method to Compute Link-Based Similarity Rank on the Web Graph

Dániel Fogaras[1,2] and Balázs Rácz[1,2]

[1] Computer and Automation Research Institute of the
Hungarian Academy of Sciences*
[2] Budapest University of Technology and Economics
fd@cs.bme.hu, bracz+c31@math.bme.hu

Abstract. Several iterative hyperlink-based similarity measures were published to express the similarity of web pages. However, it usually seems hopeless to evaluate complex similarity functions over large repositories containing hundreds of millions of pages. We introduce scalable algorithms computing SimRank scores, which express the contextual similarities of pages based on the hyperlink structure. The proposed methods scale well to large repositories, fulfilling strict requirements about computational complexity. The algorithms were tested on a set of ten million pages, but parallelization techniques make it possible to compute the SimRank scores even for the entire web with over 4 billion pages. The key idea is that randomized Monte Carlo methods combined with indexing techniques yield a scalable approximation of SimRank.

1 Introduction

Calculating the similarity of two web pages is a fundamental building block of webmining algorithms. For example, clustering algorithms classify the pages based on some similarity function; related queries of web search engines enumerate the pages most similar to some source page. Both applications require fast computable similarity values that resemble the human users' similarity preferences.

Successful application areas of link analysis include ranking [13, 17] and clustering [1], as well as similarity search. The similarity scores of this paper are also evaluated solely from the hyperlink structure of web pages. Link-based methods are efficient since the link structure forms a homogenous language-independent dataset. Recent link-based similarity algorithms iterate some equations expressing basic intuitions about similarity preferences. SimRank recursively refines the cocitation measure [12]. The algorithm of [8] follows the philosophy of HITS [13] claiming that related pages form a dense bipartite subgraph within the link structure. Additional similarity metrics for the web graph are presented in [9,14], for example using network flows in local subgraphs. Several more metrics based on cocitation are evaluated in [7] that are not complex enough (e.g. can be spammed or utilize only the 1–2 neighborhood of the queried pages).

* Research was supported by grants OTKA T 42559 and T 42706 of the Hungarian National Science Fund, and from NKFP-2/0017/2002 project Data Riddle.

W. Lindner et al. (Eds.): EDBT 2004 Workshops, LNCS 3268, pp. 557–567, 2004.

Unfortunately, the available implementations of complex link-based algorithms (Sim-Rank, HITS-based and network flows) do not scale well to massive datasets. All of them require random access to the web graph (link structure), while the size of a web graph can far exceed the available main memory. Additionally, the memory and time requirements of SimRank are quadratic in the number of pages, which is irrealistic over large repositories. In contrast, PageRank requires only linear time iterations, and its external memory issues are solved in [6].

This paper introduces novel algorithms computing SimRank scores that scale well to large repositories. For example, on a collection of 10M pages the basic SimRank algorithm would require up to 10^{14} steps and main memory to compute the SimRank scores for all pairs of pages. On the other hand, our main algorithm precomputes roughly 100 sets of fingerprints with each set of size 800MB, and the SimRank of two pages can be computed with two disk seeks later in each set. We also give heuristics to reduce the total size of the database by a factor of 10 in a distributed system.

Our solution simulates random navigational pathways and stores them as *finger-prints* in the index database. The expected similarity of two fingerprints equals to the SimRank scores that can be derived from the random surfer pair model of [12]. Thus, our randomized algorithm approximates SimRank scores from several independent fingerprints. For text-based similarity search fingerprints and Monte Carlo methods were already successfully applied, see [4, 11].

This paper is organized as follows. In Section 2 and 3 we present the main algorithm and the heuristics to compact the index. In Section 4 we formally analyze the error of approximation due to randomization. In Section 5, we show that indexing and query evaluation can be very effectively parallelized to deal with extremely large repositories. Our algorithms were tested on a web crawl with 10M pages, and the method of [10] is applied to numerically compute the overall quality of our output SimRank scores, as described in Section 6.

1.1   Algorithms Scaling to the Whole Web Graph

In this section we declare the strict computational complexity, memory usage and parallelization requirements for our SimRank algorithms. An algorithm that fulfills such requirements can be scaled on a distributed system even to a graph with billions of vertices like the whole webgraph. Similar requirements appear in [18], furthermore these characterize the computational environment in which Google's PageRank scores are computed [3, 17].

The following components of similarity search need to be discussed:

- **Indexing:** Preprocess the web graph and compute a database to support fast queries later. We will refer to this as the *index* database, following the conventions of text based information retrieval [20].
- **Similarity query:** calculate $\mathrm{sim}(v, w)$ for the webpages v and w using the index database.
- **Top query:** for a given query page v enumerate the k most similar pages to v, i.e., the pages with largest $\mathrm{sim}(v, \cdot)$ scores, where $k \approx 100 - 500$.

The main contributions of this paper are the algorithms of Sections 2 and 3 fulfilling the following requirements:

- **Computational Complexity:** once the index database is ready the time needed to evaluate a similarity query is independent of the graph's size; the time needed for a top query is proportional to the size of the result list. Indexing is a linear time algorithm in both the number of vertices and the number of edges of the web graph.
- **Memory Usage:** Indexing uses no more than $\mathcal{O}(V)$ main memory, where V denotes the number of vertices. The whole hyperlink structure resides in the external memory (disk), so the edges can only be accessed sequentially as a stream. The process of reading the stream of edges will be referred to as an *edge-scan*. Our main goal will be to minimize the required number of edge-scans. This memory access scheme is usually referred to as a *semi-external memory graph algorithm* [15].
- **Database Access:** Query performs a constant number of index database accesses.
- **Parallelization:** Both indexing and querying can be implemented to utilize the computing power and storage capacity of tens to thousands of large to medium sized servers, and achieve response times suitable for (human) real-time usage.

1.2   SimRank

In this part we briefly recall the definition of SimRank and the random surfer pair model from [12]. According to the recursive intuition behind SimRank *"two web pages are similar, if they are referenced by similar pages."* This is formalized by the following *SimRank equations.* If $v = w$, then $\mathrm{sim}(v, w) = 1$; otherwise

$$\mathrm{sim}(v, w) = \frac{c}{|I(v)|\,|I(w)|} \sum_{v' \in I(v)} \sum_{w' \in I(w)} \mathrm{sim}(v', w'),$$

where $I(x)$ denotes the set of pages (vertices) linking to x, and $c \in (0, 1)$ the so called *decay factor* is a constant. If either $I(v)$ or $I(w)$ is empty, then $\mathrm{sim}(v, w)$ is 0 by definition. For a given directed graph and decay factor c the $\mathrm{sim}(\cdot, \cdot)$ *SimRank* scores are defined as the solution of the above system of equations for all v, w vertices.

Besides the recursive intuition and equations SimRank can be also interpreted by the *random surfer pair model.* This interpretation will play a crucial role throughout our paper, so we recall this approach from [12], too. The random surfer pair model assumes that *a pair of vertices (web pages) is similar, if two random walks starting from the corresponding vertices and following the links backwards (are expected to) meet within a few steps.* Based on this a rich family of similarity functions can be defined by varying the weight that is given if the random walks first meet after exactly X backward steps. The next theorem of [12] states that by choosing weights exponentially decreasing with X the obtained similarity scores are equivalent to the SimRank scores.

Theorem 1. *Let $X_{v,w}$ denote the first meeting time of two independent uniform random walks started from vertices v and w on the transposed webgraph. Then the $\mathbb{E}(c^{X_{v,w}})$ values solve the SimRank equations with decay factor c.*

2   Our Algorithm

Our novel approach calculates the SimRank values based on Theorem 1 using a Monte Carlo method: to evaluate $\mathrm{sim}(v, w)$ we will simulate N independent pair of random

---

Algorithm 1 Indexing (external memory method)

N=number of fingerprints, L=length of paths. Uses subroutine GenRndInEdges that generates a random in-edge for each vertex in the graph and stores its source in an array.

```
1: for i := 1 to N do
2:    for all j vertices of the web graph do /*start a path from each vertex*/
3:        PathEnd[j] := j
4:    end for
5:    for k:=1 to L do
6:        NextIn[] := GenRndInEdges()
7:        for all j vertices of the web graph do /*prolong the current paths with the new in-edges*/
8:            PathEnd[j]:=NextIn[PathEnd[j]]
9:        end for
10:       save PathEnd[] as Path_k[]
11:   end for
12:   merge the Path_k[j] arrays for k = 1..L into Fingerprint[i][j][k].
13: end for
```

---

walks starting from these pages on the transposed graph, and estimate SimRank by the average of the exponentially weighted meeting time. A naive implementation would just simulate random walks upon a query on $\text{sim}(v, w)$. Unfortunately this requires random access to the edge set of the graph which is prohibited by the memory requirements.

2.1   Fingerprints and Indexing

We will pre-compute N random walks for each vertex v, and store these paths in an index. For practical purposes we truncate the random walks at a finite length L.[1] Upon a query $\text{sim}(v, w)$ we load the two sets of paths from the index database and compute the average weighted meeting time. This requires two database accesses.

A random walk of length L starting from a vertex v and following the hyperlinks backwards will be referred to as a *fingerprint* of v. This captures the intuition that fingerprints depict the surroundings of vertices in the web graph. Fingerprint[i][j][k] denotes the kth node of the ith fingerprint of vertex j, where $i = 1..N$, $j = 1..V$ and $k = 1..L$.

2.2   External Memory Indexing Algorithm

Unfortunately the naive indexing approach generates fingerprints using random access to the edges of the graph, which reside in external memory. So instead of simulating random walks for each vertex separately, we simulate them together. Assume we have already computed the first k elements of all fingerprint paths. Then with one iteration we calculate the $(k + 1)^{\text{th}}$ elements of all fingerprints. To accomplish this, we generate a random in-edge for each vertex v of the graph, and prolong those partial fingerprints with this edge that have v as their last element. [2] (See Algorithm 1.)

---

[1] This is equivalent to iterating the SimRank equations L times. As observed in [12] 5–10 iterations corresponding to $L \approx 5 - 10$ is sufficient for the applications.

[2] This results in a slight distortion of the original concept, namely that the random walks of different vertices are not totally independent. Fortunately this does not cause a problem since they are independent until the first meeting point, but are *coupled* to stick together after that.

Complexity and Space Requirements. Once we have the random in-edges, the indexing algorithm is linear in V, the number of vertices of the graph, requiring V cells of memory. Furthermore, the required $N \cdot L$ sets of random in-edges can be generated either with $\frac{N \cdot L}{M/V}$ edge-scans (where M denotes the available memory) over the edges as a data stream, or by $\mathcal{O}(\log(E/M)) + 1$ edge-scans by sorting the edges with an external memory sorting algorithm and generating all sets of InEdges with one additional scan.

The preparation and evaluation of top queries employ standard methods of inverted indices and are not discussed here, see for example [20].

3 Reducing the Index Size

The algorithm described in this section uses significantly smaller sized index. In addition, the response time of top queries is also reduced by replacing frequent database accesses with more intensive main memory usage. Unfortunately, the applied heuristics compute similarity scores slightly differing from the original concept of SimRank; the effects of the distortion will be analyzed experimentally in Section 6.1.

A subgraph H with exactly one random edge linking to each vertex will be referred to as a *compacted fingerprint*, while the L sized path in H starting from v and following the links backwards[3] will be treated as a *fingerprint of vertex v*. The *compacted SimRank* score $\text{sim}(v, w)$ is calculated as the exponentially decreasing-weighted first meeting time of the fingerprints of v and w, analogously to the previous section.

Notice that the compacted fingerprint H contains the fingerprints for all vertices, and H has no more than V edges, where V denotes the number of vertices in the original graph. Storing these compacted fingerprints reduces the index size by a factor of L. In addition, the H graph with V edges still fits into the main memory according to the requirements of Section 1.1. This enables us to run more complex graph algorithms on H, for example the top query will be calculated by a (modified) breadth first search.

3.1 Indexing and Query Evaluation

The indexing method generates a compacted fingerprint H for each simulation with the same GenRndInEdges() function as in the previous section The main difference is, that the algorithm does not save the actual paths for each vertex, but it saves the generating InEdges[] array as IndexIn[i][] and the respective graph (i.e. the edges of subgraph H) transposed as IndexOut[i][].

To evaluate $\text{sim}(v, w)$ queries we simulate the random walks from v and w respectively by following the edges pointed by IndexIn[]. This requires random access to IndexIn[], which still fits into the main memory as the array has size V. The top query for vertex q will be evaluated as depicted on Algorithm 2. Basically for each independent simulation, we have to generate all the paths that intersect the path of vertex q. So first we calculate the fingerprint path of q using the IndexIn[] array. Then for each node of that path we enumerate the outgoing paths using the transposed fingerprint IndexOut[]. For the kth element of q's path we take exactly k steps forward in all possible directions

---

[3] This path is unique as each vertex is linked to by one (or zero) edge in H.

Algorithm 2 Top query (compacted SimRank)

Input: the query page q, L=length of path, N=number of fingerprints, c=decay factor.
Output: list of p pages with positive similarity to q, ordered by $\text{sim}(p, q)$.
SimilarPages is an initially empty (hashed) associative container that is indexed by the vertices of the web graph and holds the similarities to q. Non-existent entries return 0.

1: **for** $i := 1$ **to** N **do**
2:     Ancestor := q /*This variable holds the kth element of q's fingerprint ($k = 0$ currently). Wee look for other paths that lead into this point in k steps.*/
3:     **for** $k := 1$ **to** L **do**
4:         Ancestor := IndexIn[i][Ancestor]/*One step backward*/
5:         D:={Ancestor}/*The descendants of Ancestor*/
6:         **for** l:=1 **to** k **do** /*k steps forward*/
7:             D:=$\cup_{j\in D}$IndexOut[i][j]
8:         **end for**
9:         **for all** $j \in D$ **do**
10:             SimilarPages[j]:=SimilarPages[j]+$\frac{c^k}{N}$
11:         **end for**
12:     **end for**
13: **end for**
14: **return** SimilarPages sorted by value

pointed by IndexOut[]. This will generate us all the vertices with positive similarity to q, and thus has a time complexity linear in the output size.

Both similarity and top query algorithms uses random access to H for each simulation. With the parallelization techniques discussed later in Section 5, it is possible to avoid loading the compacted fingerprints one-by-one to the main memory upon a query.

4   How Many Fingerprints are Needed?

In this section we will try to estimate how well our methods approximate the actual SimRank values and how many fingerprints are sufficient for adequate results in a real-world application. It is obvious by Theorem 1, that for a sufficiently large number of fingerprints N, the results returned by our randomized methods $\widehat{\text{sim}}(u, v)$ converge to $\text{sim}(u, v)$, the actual SimRank. However, storage requirement and run time are linear in N, so we want to minimize it. In this section we will show that about 100 fingerprints are sufficient for applications.

For a given query $\text{sim}(u, v)$ the fingerprints give N independent identically distributed random variables $X_1, \ldots, X_N$, each of which has an expected value of $\text{sim}(u, v)$. By the central limit theorem—which is commonly applied from $N = 30$—the result we calculate $\widehat{\text{sim}}(u, v) = \frac{1}{N} \sum_{i=1}^{N} X_i$ is of normal distribution around the expected value $\text{sim}(u, v)$ with standard deviation $\frac{1}{\sqrt{N}} \mathbb{D}(X)$. This $\mathcal{O}(\frac{1}{\sqrt{N}})$ convergence is unfortunately not enough for our purposes.

Instead, note that in implementations we do not require the actual values to be very close to SimRank, but to have the ordering defined by $\widehat{\text{sim}}$ on a query result set follow closely the actual similarities. In this case we have much better results:

Theorem 2. *The probability of interchanging two documents in a query result list converges to 0 exponentially, i.e. if* $\text{sim}(u, v) > \text{sim}(u, w)$ *then* $\Pr\{\widehat{\text{sim}}(u, v) < \widehat{\text{sim}}(u, w)\}$ $\rightarrow 0$ *exponentially in* N.

Analyzing the proof (which unfortunaltely had to be omitted due to space limitations) suggests that $N = 100$ gives more than adequate precision for a search engine. If the result list is ordered by some other function (for example PageRank), then even less fingerprints are enough, to distinguish between unrelated pages, low similarity and top similarity pages.

5   Scaling to the Whole Web

In this section we will shortly summarize the possibilities for parallelizing the algorithms described earlier. Our aim is to apply the methods for graphs as large as the whole web graph, i.e. a few billions of vertices. The platform considered here for such applications is a very large cluster of PC category machines [2], interconnected by some form of network. We will consider requirements for minimum operation, load balancing and fault tolerance to show that our methods are applicable even in the largest publicly available search services.

The key observation is the possibility of distributing the independent fingerprints to N different machines [19]. We will call this *coarse horizontal parallelization*. In this case the index builds can run in parallel with the necessary edge-scans distributed as broadcast data over the cluster. Each computer uses its own random number generator to calculate a different and independent set of fingerprints. The resulting indices are stored only locally. The query to evaluate will also be broadcasted to all the participating machines, which return their individual result list for merging by the front-end server. The network transfer required is proportional to the length of the result list (the number of pages with positive similarity to the query page) even with the most naive approach. Alternatively, a more advanced distributed top query method can be used for merging the result sets with much less network traffic, or even to permit partial evaluation at the index servers. Distributed top queries were deeply studied recently, see for example [5].

This utilizes at most N machines, each of which has enough memory for V cells for indexing, or query with compacted SimRank. For query with the original SimRank the only resource required is database accesses (disk seeks).

Thanks to the robustness of Monte Carlo methods this method offers intrinsic load balancing and fault tolerance support. Assume we have more than N machines, and each of them has got an index. For an adequate precision result it is enough to ask *any* N machines and merge the result list. This offers nice and smooth load balancing support for an arbitrary number of index servers. As for fault tolerance, skipping one fingerprint, and merging $N - 1$ result lists instead of N does not change the result list significantly, thus *failed servers do not influence proper operation*. This enables a very effective combination of load balancing and fault tolerance: if the query load is larger than the available number of machines can serve, then the number of fingerprints used for a single query is decreased automatically, thus loosing some precision but maintaining adequate response times. Or in case of underload, precision can be increased for free to achieve better results.

6 Experiments

In our experiments the value *sibling* Γ [10] measures the quality of the similarity ranking by comparing it to a ground truth similarity ordering extracted from the Open Directory Project (ODP, [16]) data, a hierarchical collection of webpages. The category tree of ODP provides ground truth *similarity pairs* by claiming that $\text{sim}(u, v) < \text{sim}(u, w)$ should hold for certain ODP pages u, v, and w. A similarity pair will be referred to as *comparable* if both $\text{sim}(u, v)$ and $\text{sim}(u, w)$ are larger than a minimal similarity threshold, which was set to zero in our experiments. To evaluate sibling Γ for SimRank scores we need to check if the above inequality holds for the comparable similarity pairs or not. The resulting $\Gamma \in (-1, 1)$ value is 1, if all the above inequalities hold for the SimRank scores; while $\Gamma = -1$, if all pairs are ordered reversely. For our algorithms $\Gamma \approx 0.5$, implying that a pair of comparable similarity pairs chosen at random is ordered correctly by our algorithm with probability over 0.75. Notice that high Γ quality can be achieved even with very few comparable pairs. Therefore we decided to measure the number of comparable similarity pairs in addition to sibling Γ. See [10] for the further details about sibling Γ measure.

Evaluating Γ statistics requires a webgraph containing ODP pages with rich hyperlink structure for the SimRank computation. Starting from ODP pages of categories Computers and Science, our repository was collected by a crawler restricted to follow links within the sites of ODP pages in November, 2003. We obtained a webgraph with $V = 11\text{M}$ vertices, $E = 150\text{M}$ links and 161K ODP pages. Our experiments were performed on a machine with an 1.4GHz Intel Xeon processor, 5Gbyte main memory and Linux OS. The fingerprints were computed in 40 minutes, the index was truncated to the 161K ODP pages and had a total size of 1.3Gbyte (including the inverted index).

6.1   Experimental Results

Our numerical experiments address the problem of finding the optimal settings over the 3-dimensional parameter space: path length L, decay factor c and number of fingerprints N. To perform a full optimization was beyond the scope of our computing capacity, so we fixed the default values $L = 10$, $N = 100$ and $c = 0.65$; then the parameters were analyzed independently by varying only one parameter at a time, see Fig. 1.

The left hand side bars of the clustered bar charts of parts *a)* and *b)* on Fig. 1 show that both the number of comparable pairs and the quality increase with L. Recall that the SimRank scores approximated with path length L correspond to L iteration of the recursive equations. Thus, the growing quality testifies the recursive intuition of SimRank. However, more recursion slightly reduces the quality among the pages with low SimRank scores, as Γ was slightly decreasing after $L = 7$.

The right hand side bars of parts *a)* and *b)* show the quality loss for the compacted SimRank scores compared to SimRank. According to the charts, the longer the paths are the more quality loss occurs on average. However, in a real application it may be reasonable to trade the quality difference to the advantage of the reduced index database compacted to L times smaller.

The amount of comparable pairs in figure *c)* increases linearly with N. The reason is simple: more fingerprint paths cross each other, and thus make more similarity

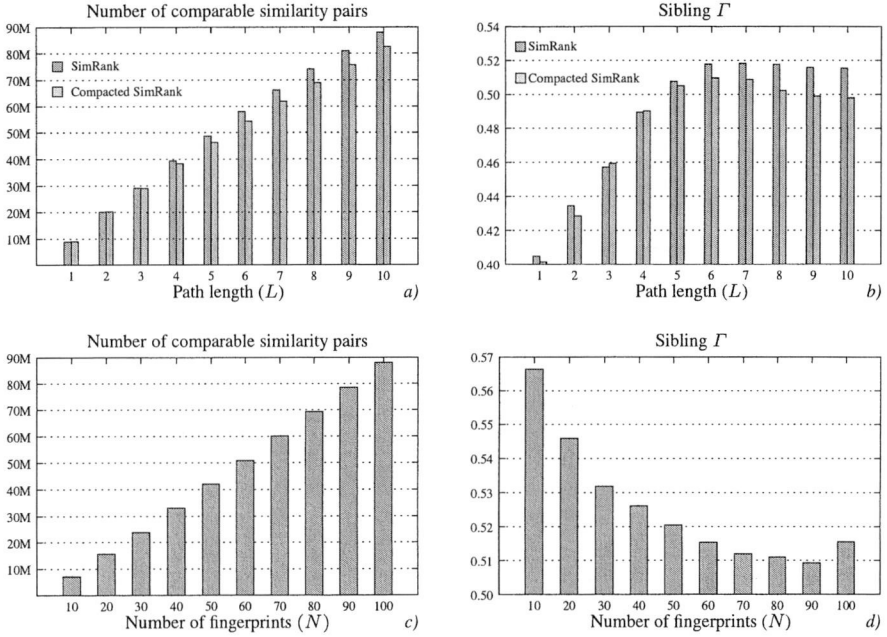

Fig. 1. Measuring the quality of SimRank scores with different parameter settings

pairs comparable. Part *d)* generally shows quality fall in sibling Γ. We argue that in case of $N = 10$ the pairs with positive approximated SimRank scores have relatively large SimRank, and such pairs approximate the ground truth similarity better than those having smaller SimRank values.

Due to space limitations the effects of decay factor is omitted from the diagrams. We experienced that the decay factor c is inversely proportional to sibling Γ, while the number of similarity pairs remains unchanged. When $c \to 0$ and N is fixed, the weight given for a shorter meeting time will largely supercede the weight given for longer meeting times. Our measurements imply that shorter paths should generally be given higher weight than the sum of arbitrary number of longer paths.

7   Conclusion and Future Work

We showed a method for computing the SimRank similarity scores for web pages. SimRank is purely based on the link structure of the web graph, just as PageRank, but has previously had algorithms with quadratic memory requirement and running time. Our method uses linear time randomized fingerprint-based calculations and can be implemented on V pages using V cells of memory, which can be further reduced to constant by using external memory sorts. When parallelized on a cluster of machines this method can cope with the whole webgraph making it suitable for the largest scale commercial web search engines, featuring load balance and fault tolerance intrinsically. Furthermore, we presented an approximation with lower precision, but drastically reduced index database sizes that can be entirely served from main memory in case of extreme workloads.

We strongly believe that fingerprint-based Monte Carlo methods can have further applications in web-mining. For example, we plan to construct scalable approximation methods for clustering web pages and tracing web communities.

Acknowledgement

We wish to thank Katalin Friedl, András Benczúr, Tamás Sarlós for valuable discussions and comments; Máté Uher for crawling the test repository of web pages.

References

1. P. Berkhin. Survey of clustering data mining techniques. Technical report, Accrue Software, San Jose, CA, 2002.
2. E. Brewer. Lessons from giant-scale services.
3. S. Brin and L. Page. The anatomy of a large-scale hypertextual Web search engine. *Computer Networks and ISDN Systems*, 30(1-7):107–117, 1998.
4. A. Broder. On the resemblance and containment of documents. In *Proceedings of the Compression and Complexity of Sequences 1997*, page 21. IEEE Computer Society, 1997.
5. N. Bruno, L. Gravano, and A. Marian. Evaluating top-k queries over web-accessible databases. In *Proceedings of the ICDE Conference*, 2002.
6. Y. Y. Chen, Q. Gan, and T. Suel. I/O-efficient techniques for computing PageRank. In *Proceedings of the eleventh international conference on Information and knowledge management*, pages 549–557. ACM Press, 2002.
7. M. Cristo, P. Calado, E.S. de Moura, N. Ziviani, and B. Ribeiro-Neto. Link information as a similarity measure in web classification. In *String Processing and Information Retrieval*, pages 43–55. Springer LNCS 2857, 2003.
8. J. Dean and M. R. Henzinger. Finding related pages in the World Wide Web. *Computer Networks (Amsterdam, Netherlands: 1999)*, 31(11–16):1467–1479, 1999.
9. G. Flake, S. Lawrence, C. L. Giles, and F. Coetzee. Self-organization of the web and identification of communities. *IEEE Computer*, 35(3):66–71, 2002.
10. T. H. Haveliwala, A. Gionis, D. Klein, and P. Indyk. Evaluating strategies for similarity search on the web. In *Proceedings of the 11th World Wide Web Conference (WWW)*, pages 432–442. ACM Press, 2002.
11. N. Heintze. Scalable document fingerprinting. In *1996 USENIX Workshop on Electronic Commerce*, November 1996.
12. G. Jeh and J. Widom. SimRank: A measure of structural-context similarity. In *Eighth ACM SIGKDD International Conference on Knowledge Discovery and Data Mining*. ACM, 2002.
13. J. Kleinberg. Authoritative sources in a hyperlinked environment. *Journal of the ACM*, 46(5):604–632, 1999.
14. W. Lu, J. Janssen, E. Milios, and N. Japkowicz. Node similarity in networked information spaces. In *Proceedings of the 2001 conference of the Centre for Advanced Studies on Collaborative research*, page 11. IBM Press, 2001.
15. U. Meyer, P. Sanders, and J. Sibeyn. *Algorithms for Memory Hierarchies, Advanced Lectures*. LNCS, Springer, 2003.
16. Open Directory Project (ODP). http://www.dmoz.org.

17. L. Page, S. Brin, R. Motwani, and T. Winograd. The PageRank citation ranking: Bringing order to the web. Technical report, Stanford Digital Library Technologies Project, 1998.
18. C. R. Palmer, P. B. Gibbons, and C. Faloutsos. ANF: a fast and scalable tool for data mining in massive graphs. In *Eighth ACM SIGKDD International Conference on Knowledge Discovery and Data Mining*, pages 81–90. ACM Press, 2002.
19. J. S. Rosenthal. Parallel computing and Monte Carlo algorithms. *Far East J. Theor. Stat.*, 4:207–236, 2000.
20. I. H. Witten, A. Moffat, and T. C. Bell. *Managing gigabytes (2nd ed.): Compressing and indexing documents and images*. Morgan Kaufmann Publishers Inc., 1999.

A Framework for Cluster Management

Barbara Catania and Anna Maddalena

Dipartimento di Informatica e Scienze dell'Informazione,
Università degli Studi di Genova (Italy)
{catania,maddalena}@disi.unige.it

Abstract. To represent and manipulate data extracted from Web-server logs or applicational logs, clustering techniques can be used. The generated clusters are often different in types, are generated by using different algorithms, and should be homogeneously manipulated together with other knowledge mined from data, for example association rules or decision trees. The problem thus arises of using an homogeneous framework in which cluster results can be represented and manipulated, possibly together with other data mining results. In this paper, we show how the pattern modeling framework presented in [5, 10] can be used to this purpose.

1 Introduction

A huge quantity of data can be collected by observing user navigation sessions on Web pages. The *clickstream analysis* is an important technique to extract additional knowledge about users behavior from those data. In particular, data mining techniques can be used to characterize user profiles to support content Web sites specialization and tailor Web sites on users preferences. To perform a clickstream analysis, clustering techniques can be applied to data extracted from Web-server logs (i.e., click sequences) or applicational logs (i.e., users profile information) to identify clusters of users sharing similar behavior. Moreover, by analyzing Web site contents, clusters of documents (e.g., HTML or XML documents) sharing similar content can be retrieved.

Once clustering has been applied, users should be able to manipulate and analyze the generated information (clusters). However, often clusters are different in types, are generated by using different algorithms, and should be homogeneously manipulated together with other knowledge, mined from source data, such as association rules or decision trees. All these requirements call for a uniform framework in which clusters can be represented and manipulated, possibly together with other data mining results.

In this paper, we suggest the usage of the framework for pattern representation proposed in [5, 10] for cluster management. Patterns are concise, but rich in semantic, representation of data. Moreover, due to the diffusion of the (Semantic) Web, the ability to manipulate different types of patterns is becoming a fundamental issue for any "intelligent" data-intensive and distributed application. The framework presented in [5, 10] is general enough to manage in an homogeneous way different kinds of patterns extracted from different real-world application domains (e.g. market-basket analysis/association rules, click-stream analysis/click sequences, etc.). In such a framework, each pattern is represented by its structure, raw data from which it has been generated, and some

W. Lindner et al. (Eds.): EDBT 2004 Workshops, LNCS 3268, pp. 568–577, 2004.

pattern measures, expressing the quality of the pattern representation with respect to raw data. Moreover, the framework provides a pattern manipulation language, by which patterns can be generated, deleted, and updated, as well as a pattern query language, by which patterns can be retrieved and combined according to various conditions. Even if several approaches have been proposed in the literature to represent and query patterns [1–3, 8, 9] they usually deal with specific types of patterns (typically association rules) and support just operations for pattern generation. As far as we know, the pattern languages defined in PANDA are the first extensive approach for pattern management and retrieval [4].

Clustering results can be considered patterns. Thus, they can be represented according to the PANDA logical model, and they can be manipulated and queried by using the Pattern Manipulation Language (PML) and the Pattern Query Language (PQL) proposed in [4]. The aim of this paper is to show how clustering results can be represented and managed under such a framework.

The remainder of this paper is organized as follows. In Section 2, the pattern management framework is presented. In Section 3 clustering results are represented as patterns by using the proposed model. Then, Section 4 shows how cluster management can be performed by using languages provided by the framework. Finally, in Section 5 we outline some conclusions.

2   The Framework

In the following, after introducing a reference architecture for pattern management, we briefly present a framework for pattern representation and manipulation, as defined in the context of the European project PANDA (PAtterns for Next-generation DAtabase systems) [5, 10]. In particular, we first present the pattern-based management system architecture, then the model to represent patterns, and, finally, languages to deal with them.

2.1   Pattern Based Management System

A pattern is a compact but rich in semantics representation of raw data. A Pattern-Base Management System (PBMS) (see Figure 1) is a system for handling patterns defined over raw data, to efficiently support pattern matching and to exploit pattern-related operations generating intensional information.

On the bottom layer of the architecture, we find raw data. Raw data can be collected or produced by a set of devices, and then organized and stored within databases or files. Knowledge discovery algorithms are applied over these data and generate patterns to be fed into the PBMS. In particular, within the PBMS, it is worth to distinguish three different layers. The *pattern layer* populated with patterns. The *type layer* holds built-in and user-defined types for patterns. The *class layer* holds definitions of pattern classes, i.e., collections of semantically related patterns.

According to the PANDA approach [10], we assume that raw data reside in the raw data layer and are managed by their native systems (e.g. a DBMS) whereas patterns are

Data Management System   Pattern Management System

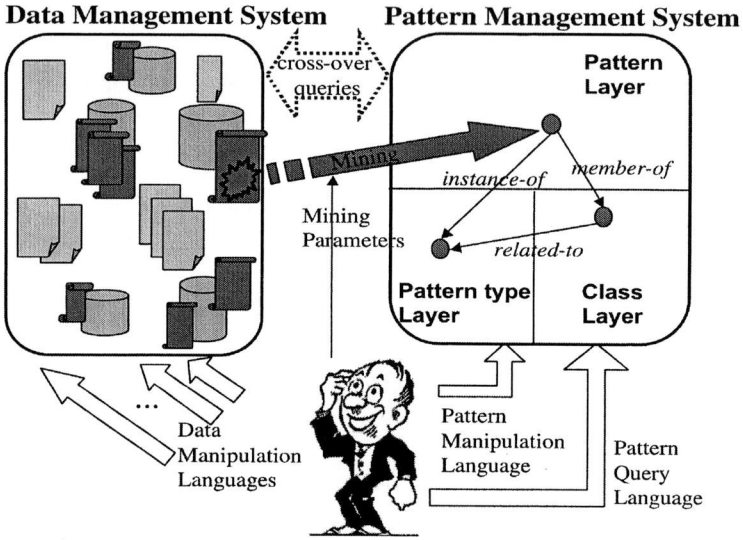

Fig. 1. The PBMS architecture

stored and managed within the PBMS, represented according to a specific pattern model and manipulated by using specific pattern languages.

2.2   The Model

The model is based on the concepts of pattern types, patterns, and pattern classes [5, 10]. A *pattern type* represents the intensional form of patterns, giving a formal description of their structure and relationship with source data. It is defined as a tuple of five elements.

- The *structure schema*, which defines the pattern space by describing the structure of the patterns, instances of the pattern type.
- The *source schema*, which defines the related source space by describing the dataset from which patterns, instances of the pattern type being defined, are constructed.
- The *measure schema*, which describes the measures which quantify the quality of the data source representation achieved by the pattern; it permits to evaluate how accurate and significant for a given application each pattern is.
- The *formula*, which describes the relationship between the source space and the pattern space, thus carrying the semantics of the pattern. Inside f, attributes are interpreted as free variables ranging over the components of either the source or the pattern space. Note that, though in some particular domains f may exactly express the inter-space relationship, in most cases it will describe it only approximatively.

Patterns are instances of a specific pattern type. Thus, they are composed of the following elements:

- a pattern *identifier*;
- a *structure* that positions the pattern within the pattern space defined by its pattern type;

- a *data source* that identifies the specific dataset the pattern is related to;
- a *measure* that estimates the quality of the raw data representation achieved by the pattern;
- a *formula* which relates the pattern to the source data. The pattern instance formula is obtained by the formula f in the pattern type by: (i) instantiating each attribute appearing in the *structure schema* with the corresponding value specified in the pattern structure; (ii) letting the attributes appearing in the *data source schema* range over the source space.

In the following, we use dot notation to identify pattern components. Thus, $p.source$ stands for the source of pattern p.

A *class* is a set of patterns with the same pattern type and constitutes the key concept in defining a pattern query language.

In order to increase the expressivity of the logical model, some interesting relationships between patterns have also been introduced (for formal details see [5]). Among them, we recall: (i) *specialization*, a sort of *IS-A* relationship (e.g. clusters of integer points can be seen as a specialization of generic clusters of points); (ii) *composition*, between a pattern and those used to define its structure; an example of composition is a clustering result, since it is a set of simple clusters, each representing a specific subset of the source data; (iii) *refinement*, between a pattern and those belonging to its source component; in this case, the pattern is generated from a source dataset which itself consists of other patterns. Clusters of association rules are an example of the usage of the refinement relationship.

As we will see in Section 4, patterns are generated by using specific algorithms. For instance, we can generate patterns of type $Cluster$ from the same dataset by applying different clustering algorithms (e.g. complete-link vs. single-link [7]). From a formal point of view, each algorithm corresponds to at least two functions: one generating the structure (*structure function*) and one computing the measures of patterns of a given type over a certain dataset (*measure function*). We assume that for each pattern type, there exist some libraries of structure and measure functions, stored in some PBMS catalog.

2.3 Pattern Languages

In the PBMS framework, a *Pattern Query Language* (PQL) and a *Pattern Manipulation Language* (PML) have been defined [5]. Queries are executed against classes. In particular, projection has been revisited in order to project out structure and measure components. Selection allows one to select patterns satisfying a certain condition, involving any possible pattern component. Operators to navigate hierarchies between patterns are also provided. Join operators are also proposed to combine patterns. Moreover, the PQL supports operations binding patterns with raw data, the so called *cross-over queries* since for their execution two different systems - the PBMS and the system where raw data are stored - have to be used.

Besides query operators, traditional manipulation operators (insertion, deletion, and update) have been re-interpreted to be able to cope with patterns. In particular, pattern insertion is represented by an extraction operator, which extracts a pattern from a raw dataset by applying a specific mining algorithm. Patterns can also be generated by recomputing pattern measures against a new dataset. Among update operators, we recall synchronization, which performs the re-computation of pattern measures to reflect data source modifications.

3   Cluster Representation

In the following, we show how different types of information extracted by cluster algorithms can be represented inside the pattern framework. For the sake of simplicity, we assume that the data sources correspond to N-dimensional point sets and we provide examples in a 2-dimensional space. In particular, we show how the framework can be used for representing: (i) *simple clusters*, i.e. collections of raw data items; in this paper, we are interested in circular shaped clusters of points; (ii) *clustering results*, i.e. sets of simple clusters, usually obtained as result of a clustering algorithm [6]; (iii) *complex clusters*, i.e. clusters of existing clusters or other mined information.

3.1   Simple Clusters

A simple cluster is a collection of raw data items. In a Web context, it may for example correspond to all the users mostly navigating Web sites concerning sport events. To represent simple clusters inside the framework, we must decide how to represent their structure, which measures associate with each cluster, and how to represent the relationship between the cluster itself and raw data it represents.

Structure. Since we are interested in circular shaped clusters of points, a cluster can be represented as a N-dimensional circle with a *center* and a *radius*. The center represents the cluster representative[1] and the radius the maximum distance between the representative and other cluster points. The center is a N-dimensional point and the radius is a real number.

Data source. The data source of the pattern is a set of N-dimensional points, i.e. a set of real coordinates $(X_1, X_2, \ldots, X_N)$. It defines the source space of the pattern, i.e. the set of points from which the cluster has been generated.

Measures. The measure schema models the quality measures associated with each cluster, for example their average intra-cluster distance [7]. This measure expresses the quality of the representation of raw data achieved by the pattern. By evaluating the distribution of elements into a cluster; in some sense, we express the "cohesiveness" and "compactness" of the cluster.

Formula. The formula provides precise or approximated information concerning the subset of the source dataset represented by the pattern. In this case, the precise representation would coincide with the exact set of points represented by the cluster. However, such a representation could be quite expensive, due to the high set of points probably

---

[1] A representative is an element, not necessary belonging to the data set from which the cluster has been generated, that characterizes all other elements in the cluster.

represented by each single cluster. A different approach thus consists in providing an approximated representation of such set. For example, it may correspond to the set of points belonging to the circle represented in the cluster structure.

In the following, the pattern type $Cluster$ modeling 2-dimensional simple clusters is provided. Then, an example of a pattern for such pattern type is presented:

Name:	Cluster
StructureSchema:	disk: TUPLE(center: TUPLE(CX: real,CY: real), rad: real)
DatasourceSchema:	SET(X: real, Y: real)
MeasureSchema:	AvgIntraClusterDistance: real
Formula:	$(X - disk.center.CX)^2 + (Y - disk.center.CY)^2 \le disk.rad^2$

Pid:	337
Structure:	disk: TUPLE(center:TUPLE(CX:2,CY:3), rad:4.2)
DataSource:	users(X,Y)
Measure:	AvgIntraClusterDistance: 0.9
Formula:	$(users.X - 2)^2 + (users.Y - 3)^2 \le (4.2)^2$

In the pattern instance, *users* is a relational view concerning observations about users behavior during their navigation in a certain Web site. It may contain, for example, for each user, his/her age and the total number of his/her navigation sessions during a day. On the other hand, the pattern measure component contains the effective average intra-cluster distance. Finally, the pattern formula is obtained by instantiating the pattern type formula with structure component values and data source component variable names of the pattern instance. It thus provides the exact equation used to identify the approximated set of points represented by the cluster.

3.2   Clustering Results

We define a clustering to be the result of the application of a clustering algorithm. The *structure* of a clustering corresponds to a set of simple clusters. The *data source* is still a set of N-dimensional points. The quality *measure* associated with this pattern is a clustering validity measure, expressing the "goodness" of the whole clustering result obtained by applying the chosen clustering technique. Examples of such measures are the *Overall Similarity* measure, the *Entropy*, and the *F-measure* [7]. The overall similarity measures cluster cohesiveness, evaluating the similarity of each element pair belonging to the same cluster. A point of the source space is represented by a clustering result if it is represented by at least one simple cluster belonging to the clustering. Based on this consideration, the *formula* of a clustering can be defined as the disjunction of all formulas associated with each cluster involved in the clustering.

For instance, a pattern type Clustering for the whole clustering result in a 2-dimensional space and an example of pattern instance are the following:

Name:	Clustering
StructureSchema:	cl: SET(disk: TUPLE(center: TUPLE(CX:real, CY:real),rad: real))
DataSourceSchema:	SET(X: real, Y: real)
MeasureSchema:	OverallSimilarity:real
Formula:	$\bigvee_{k \in cl}((X - k.disk.center.CX)^2 + (Y - k.disk.center.CY)^2 \le k.disk.rad^2)$

Pid:	38
Structure:	cl: { disk: TUPLE(center(CX:2, CY:3), rad:4),
	disk: TUPLE(center:(CX: 2, CY: 4), rad:3.5),
	disk: TUPLE(center:(CX: 2.2, CY: 3), rad:6) }
DataSource:	users(X,Y)
Measure:	OverallSimilarity:0.85
Formula:	$((X - 2)^2 + (Y - 3)^2 \le 4^2) \lor ((X - 2)^2 + (Y - 4)^2 \le 3.5^2) \lor$
	$((X - 2.2)^2 + (Y - 3)^2 \le 6^2)$

In the pattern instance, the structure is a set of tuples, each representing a simple cluster. The data source is the view *users* (see Section 3.1). The measure contains the overall similarity real value. Finally, the formula is obtained by instantiating free variables in the pattern type formula with the corresponding pattern variables.

3.3 Complex Clusters

By exploiting the power of composition and refinement relationships between patterns, we can model complex clusters, i.e., clusters or clustering results defined over other clusters or data mining results. By using the composition relationship, we can model clustering by using the Cluster pattern type in the clustering structure definition. By using the refinement relationship, we can define clusters of other clusters or even of other data mining results; in this last case, the source data corresponds to sets of patterns, instances of other pattern types.

As an example, we consider multilevel clustering, which is actually an example of both composition and refinement. At the first level of a multilevel clustering, clusters are generated from data points. Thus, the pattern types Cluster and Clustering can be used to represent them. Clusters at the upper levels of the clustering hierarchy are generated by further applying the clustering algorithm to the collection of clusters obtained as result of the previous step. In that case, the source data corresponds to a set of clusters (pattern type Clustering can be used to represent such data), thus a refinement relationship has to be used to model this information, but, at the same time, the representative of each cluster is a cluster itself, thus requiring a composition relationship to correctly model the structure. The following is an example of a pattern type for the second level of the hierarchy (dist is a distance function between clusters):

Name:	Clustering_refined
StructureSchema:	disk: TUPLE(center: Cluster,rad: real)
DatasourceSchema:	cc:Clustering
MeasureSchema:	OverallSimilarity:real
Formula:	$x \in cc.cl \land dist(disk.center,x.disk.center) \le disk.rad^2$

4 Cluster Management

In the following, we show how patterns modeling clustering results can be manipulated and queried by using some of the operators provided by the pattern languages [4].

Extraction. The application of a clustering algorithm produces a clustering. In the pattern framework, it becomes a generation operation which creates new patterns from a raw dataset, and inserts them in the PBMS. Thus, the *extraction* manipulation operation

$\mathcal{E}$ must be used by specifying: a mining function representing the clustering algorithm the user wants to apply; the pattern type of the result (for example **Cluster**); the dataset of raw data, used as input for the extraction operation, corresponding to the data source over which clusters have to be generated.

Suppose to apply a complete-link algorithm [6] (by means of a mining function μ_{c_link}) to a set QS of 2-dimensional points representing user age and average navigation session time, collected from the Web server, and to insert the output of the clustering into class C_{2D}. These operations can be specified in PML as follows:

- $SP = \mathcal{E}(Cluster, QS, true, \mu_{complete\_link})$
- $\mathcal{I}_C(SP, C_{2D})$

The first operation extracts a set of patterns SP of type Cluster from the dataset QS by applying the complete-link algorithm. No special insertion conditions are specified, thus all output patterns are inserted in the PBMS. The second operation inserts generated patterns into class C_{2D}.

Synchronize. Observations concerning user Web navigation result in a huge quantity of data characterized by a high level of dinamicity. Since modifications in raw datasets are very frequent, the need arises of verifying whether an existing pattern still holds for the source data and, possibly, changing the corresponding measures.

Suppose, for instance, that new data have been collected by the Web server. Clusters SP previously extracted from Web server log information have to be updated to reflect modifications occurred in the data source. This behavior can be achieved by applying a PML synchronization operation, as follows ($\mu_{Cl\_Measure}$ is a measure function for clusters):

- $\mathcal{S}(SP, \mu_{Cluster\_Measure})$

Retrieval of Cluster Representatives. In many cases, it is important to be able to retrieve representative elements of clusters. Suppose we want to retrieve all points that are representatives of clusters in class Cl_1. A projection operation π can be applied to project out the radius component from the pattern structure and the pattern measures. This query can be expressed in PQL as $\pi_{(<center>,<>)}(Cl_1)$ and it returns a set of patterns with the following type:

StructureSchema: center: TUPLE(CX: real, CY: real)
DataSourceSchema: SET(X: real, Y: real)
MeasureSchema: –
Formula: true

Note that the resulting pattern type has no name, since it is generated at run time and it is not made persistent in the PBMS. Moreover, the formula becomes just $true$ since by projecting out rad from the original formula, any values for CX and CY satisfy it.

Retrieval of Clusters with Certain Properties. Selection of clusters satisfying specific conditions is an important operation in clickstream analysis. In our framework, it is supported by the PQL selection operator, which also supports advanced selection criteria, such as pattern similarity ($=^s$). Examples of PQL selection queries are:

- Find clusters in class Cl_1 having radius greater than 1 and average intra-cluster distance lower than 0.75: $\sigma_{(disk.rad>1)AND(AvgIntraClusterDistance<0.75)}(Cl_1)$.
- Find all clusters in class Cl_1 similar to cluster my_C: $\sigma_{=^s my_C}(Cl_1)$.
- Find clusters in Cl_1 mined from a data source d containing the set V: $\sigma_{V \subseteq d}(Cl_1)$.

Retrieval of Cluster Information Within a Clustering. When composition or refinement relationships are used in defining a pattern type, specific operations can be used to navigate such hierarchies. For example, using pattern type Clustering_refined (see Section 3.3), we may want to move the focus from the whole clustering result to its member clusters. The PQL decomposition operation, $\mathcal{C}_a$, makes it possible.

Let C_{ing} be a class over pattern type Clustering_refined, $\mathcal{C}_{Cluster}(C_{ing})$ returns a set of patterns of pattern type Cluster representing the cluster representatives. Selection can then be used to restrict the resulting set. For example, if we are interested only in clusters with radius 1, we can use the following query: $\sigma_{disk.rad=1}(\mathcal{C}_{Cluster}(C_{ing}))$.

Join Two Clusters Together. In some cases, it can be useful to join two different clusters having the same representative to obtain a new ones. From an applicational point of view, this corresponds to merging clusters sharing the same representative and could be useful when various clustering results over similar datasets have been generated and we want to generate a more compact representation. Given a pair of clusters, we assume that the resulting cluster is generated only if their datasets have the same schema (thus, patterns correspond to semantically equivalent data). The resulting cluster is characterized by the following components (see Figure 2).

Structure. The resulting cluster is a circular cluster too, characterized by the same center than the input clusters and with radius equal to the maximum of the radius of the input clusters (since the new cluster must cover points belonging to both clusters).

DataSource. The data source of the new pattern is the union (defined, since their schemes are compatible) of the data sources of the two input clusters.

Measures. All the measures of the input clusters are retained but no value is assigned to them, since, as the source has changed, they have to be recomputed.

Formula. The resulting cluster represents each point satisfying at least one formula of the input patterns. Thus, the disjunction of the input formulas is taken.

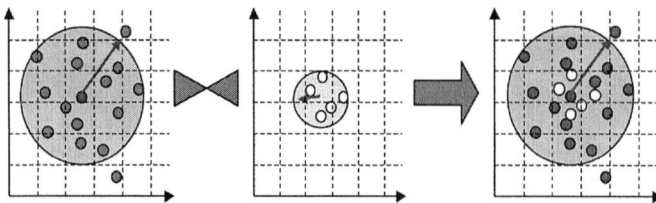

Fig. 2. The join operation

To get this result, we can use the $\bowtie$ operator over two classes Cl_1 and Cl_2 of type **Cluster**. To perform the join, we have to specify a *join predicate*, specifying when a pair of clusters have to be joined, and a *composition function*, specifying how the resulting cluster has to be created. In our example, the join predicate F has to check data source compatibility, whereas the composition function c has to be defined according to what we specified above. The PQL expression for the join operation is then: $Cl_1 \bowtie_{F,c} Cl_2$.

5   Concluding Remarks

Cluster management requires an uniform representation of cluster results and sufficiently expressive operations for cluster manipulation. In this paper, we presented how typical clustering results can be represented and managed in the context of a framework for pattern representation first presented in [10]. The proposed examples show that the pattern framework is a good environment for performing cluster management. An important issue, when dealing with clusters, concerns how their semantics can be represented and managed. To this purpose, the framework could be extended with ontologies characterizing the semantics of raw data attributes and measures. As a future work, we plan to investigate this issue, in order to provide a richer semantic representation and manipulation for clusters. Additionally, in order to experimentally assess the validity of the proposed approach, we plan to use the pattern framework prototype we are developing as a testbed for cluster management.

References

1. Common Warehouse Metamodel (CWM). http://www.omg.org/cwm, 2001.
2. Java Data Mining API. http://www.jcp.org/jsr/detail/73.prt, 2003.
3. Predictive Model Markup Language (PMML). http://www.dmg.org/pmmlspecs_v2/pmml_v2_0.html, 2003.
4. E. Bertino, B. Catania, and A. Maddalena. Towards a Language for Pattern Manipulation and Querying. In *Proceedings of the 1st Int. Workshop on Pattern Representation and Management*, Heraklion, Greece, March 18, 2004.
5. E. Bertino, B. Catania, M. Golfarelli, M. Halkidi, A. Maddalena, S. Skiadopoulos, S. Rizzi, M. Terrovitis, P. Vassiliadis, M. Vazirgiannis, and E. Vrachnos. The Logical Model for Patterns. Technical Report TR-2003-02, PANDA, 2003.
6. J. Han and M. Kamber. *Data Mining: Concepts and Techniques*. Academic Press, 2001.
7. A.K. Jain, M.N. Murty, and P.J. Flynn. *Data Clustering: a Review. ACM Computing Surveys*, 31(3):264–323, 1999.
8. T. Imielinski and A. Virmani. MSQL: A Query Language for Database Mining. *Data Mining and Knowledge Discovery*, 2(4):373–408, 1999.
9. R. Meo, G. Psaila, and S. Ceri. An Extension to SQL for Mining Association Rules. *Data Mining and Knowledge Discovery*, 2(2):195–224, 1999.
10. S. Rizzi, E. Bertino, B. Catania, M. Golfarelli, M. Halkidi, M. Terrovitis, P. Vassiliadis, M. Vazirgiannis, and E. Vrachnos. Towards a Logical Model for Patterns. In *Proceedings of the 22nd International Conference on Conceptual Modeling (ER 2003)*, Chicago, 2003.

DiXeminator: A Profile-Based Selective Dissemination System for XML Documents

Elisa Bertino[1], Giovanna Guerrini[2], and Marco Mesiti[3]

[1] Computer Sciences Department,
Purdue University, USA
bertino@cs.purdue.edu
[2] Dipartimento di Informatica,
Università di Pisa, Italy
guerrini@disi.unige.it
[3] Dipartimento di Informatica e Comunicazione,
Università degli Studi di Milano, Italy
mesiti@dico.unimi.it

Abstract. Current approaches for the selective dissemination of XML documents are not suitable for an automatic adaptation of user profiles to her current preferences because either they rely on user preferences specified by filling up forms or they require to process a high number of documents. In this paper we present the architecture of DiXeminator, a selective dissemination system for XML documents based on profiles. Profiles, represented through XML Schema, concisely represent the kind of documents a user subscribing the service is interested in. Profiles are used for filtering out irrelevant documents relying on user preferences. Moreover, profiles are kept up to date taking into account the documents the user effectively accesses or refuses.

1 Introduction

As the amount of XML data available on the Web and the number of pervasive applications making use of these data increase, systems that support *selective dissemination of information* (*SDI systems*) are more and more popular [1, 4, 8, 10, 12]. A selective dissemination system manages user profiles as well as streams of incoming documents. For each incoming document, the system searches for the set of user profiles that match it in order to identify the users to whom the document should be broadcasted. Users can set their preferences when they connect the first time to the system (by filling up a form) or the preferences can be dynamically discovered by monitoring the documents users frequently access. A key capability of an SDI system is the effective filtering of a continuous stream of XML documents according to user preferences. Another key capability is the adaptability of user profiles to new preferences. It is not reasonable, indeed, to assume that user preferences do not change.

In this paper we present the architecture of DiXeminator, a selective dissemination system for XML documents based on *user profiles*. Our system receives a continuous stream of XML documents and, by matching them against the user profiles, filters out the users that are not interested in the documents. Then, documents are broadcasted only

W. Lindner et al. (Eds.): EDBT 2004 Workshops, LNCS 3268, pp. 578–587, 2004.
© Springer-Verlag Berlin Heidelberg 2004

to interested users. Moreover, the system collects user feedbacks to keep the profiles up to date.

A key characteristic of DiℵXeminator is that user profiles are modeled as XML Schemas [11]. By means of an XML Schema it is possible to concisely represent the set of documents relevant for a user. A document, which is *valid* with respect to the XML Schema, perfectly adheres to the conditions the user specifies to select the documents she is interested in. Moreover, a user profile can specify constraints on the values of data content elements. Since users can be interested in documents of different types, a user profile is often specified as a set of subschemas, each one of them representing a type of documents. Figure 1 reports an example of profile. The profile contains two subschema. The first one represents documents dealing with books, whereas the second one represents documents containing Sigmod record publications.

The user profile can initially be specified by the user or automatically inferred from documents the user previously deemed valuable, by means of document clustering and schema extraction techniques [7, 10]. Actually, the two approaches can be combined in order to obtain more coincise representations. Schema extraction techniques can be adopted to identify patterns/templates of documents and clustering techniques can be employed to group together similar patterns/templates. Finally, from each group an XML Schema can be determined that concisely represents the documents from which it has been extracted.

Incoming streams of documents are matched against the user profiles in order to establish the users to whom the documents should be broadcasted. Whenever a user accepts the document, because she locally stores the received document or sends a positive feedback to DiℵXeminator, or rejects it, because she discards the received document or sends a negative feedback, structural and content information are extracted from the document and exploited for enhancing the user profile. Moreover, DiℵXeminator monitors the Web navigation of its users in order to determine the new kinds of documents they are interested in. This information, gathered by the user feedbacks and the monitors, is used for updating the user profiles accordingly.

The presence of a huge amount of users, together with a high number of kinds of documents they could be interested in, introduces however scalability issues. Therefore, a mechanism for grouping together users interested in the same kind of documents is required along with query capabilities for efficiently selecting only the user profiles that can effectively match the document to be broadcasted. DiℵXeminator addresses these issues by introducing the concept of *profile types* and their hierarchical organization that allows us to easily identify the users that are interested in the same sets of documents.

DiℵXeminator takes advantage of previous work we have carried out for estimating the structural similarity between an XML document and a DTD [2]. The measure is employed for computing the *degree of relevance* of the document with respect to the DTD. Moreover, it takes also advantage of our work on the evolution of DTD structure relying on documents classified against it [3, 5]. DiℵXeminator takes finally advantage of other approaches developed for the selective dissemination of text documents [1, 4, 8, 10, 12]. The most similar approach is the one proposed by Stanoi et al. [10]. Such an approach integrates profile inference with data dissemination and exploits the structured content of XML documents. Profiles are inferred by clustering documents previously

```
<?xml version="1.0"?>
<xsd:schema xmlns:xsd="http://www.w3.org/2001/XMLSchema">
 <xsd:element name="BookStore">
  <xsd:complexType>
  <xsd:sequence>
    <xsd:element name="Book" maxOccurs="unbounded">
    <xsd:complexType>
    <xsd:sequence>
      <xsd:element name="Title" type="xsd:string"/>
      <xsd:element name="Author" type="myAuthor" maxOccurs="5"/>
      <xsd:element name="Date" type="xsd:string"/>
      <xsd:element name="ISBN" type="xsd:string"/>
      <xsd:element name="Publisher" type="xsd:string" minOccurs="0"/>
    </xsd:sequence>
    </xsd:complexType>
    </xsd:element>
  </xsd:sequence>
  </xsd:complexType>
 </xsd:element>
 <xsd:element name="SigmodRecord">
  <xsd:complexType>
  <xsd:sequence>
    <xsd:element name="issue" minOccurs="0" maxOccurs="unbounded">
    <xsd:complexType> <xsd:sequence>
      <xsd:element name="volume" type="xsd:string"/>
      <xsd:element name="number" type="xsd:string"/>
      <xsd:element name="article" maxOccurs="unbounded">
      <xsd:complexType> <xsd:sequence>
        <xsd:element name="title" type="xsd:string"/>
        <xsd:element name="initPage" type="xsd:string"/>
        <xsd:element name="lastPage" type="xsd:string"/>
      </xsd:sequence> </xsd:complexType>
      </xsd:element>
    </xsd:sequence> </xsd:complexType>
    </xsd:element>
  </xsd:sequence>
  </xsd:complexType>
 </xsd:element>
 <xsd:simpleType name="myAthor">
  <xsd:restriction base="xsd:string">
   <xsd:enumeration value="Serge Abiteboul"/>
   <xsd:enumeration value="Stefano Ceri"/>
  </xsd:restriction>
 </xsd:simpleType>
</xsd:schema>
```

Fig. 1. An example of profile

deemed valuable by the user according to a similarity measure that takes into account document structure. However, the similarity is accepted and measured at nodes, and then weights combined taking the structure into account. The document structures are required to coincide exactly, and no partial structural matches are allowed. By contrast, our approach uses an intensional representation of the documents the user is interested in. Moreover, it supports both approximate structural and content matches, and uses a hierarchy of profile types in order to minimize the number of matches to be executed.

The remainder of this paper is organized as follows. Next section introduces the representation of documents, profiles and profile types. Section 3 deals with the main components of the architecture of DiXeminator. Section 4 concludes the paper and outlines future research directions.

2   Documents, Profiles and Profile Types

In this section we briefly discuss our tree representation for documents and profiles. Then, we introduce profile types and their hierarchical organization. This hierarchical organization is really relevant in order to face the scalability issues of Di𝒳eminator.

2.1   Documents and Profiles

Documents and profiles are represented as labeled trees. The tree representation is exploited when matching a document against a profile and for the evolution of profile structures. Formal definitions and properties of this representation can be found in [2,5]. In the tree representation of a document, internal nodes represent elements, whereas leaves represent data content elements.

Figure 1 shows an example of profile. Note that, the profile contains the specification of two kinds of documents: `bookStore` and `SigmodRecord` documents. In the tree representation of a profile, internal nodes represent either element types, operators used for binding together elements (sequence, all, choice, ecc..) or operators specifying whether elements or groups of elements are optional or repeatable. Specifically, the operators that can be used for labeling internal nodes of a profile are {AND, ALL, OR, [n,m] }. The AND operator represents a sequence of elements, the ALL operator represents a set of elements for which the order is not relevant, the OR operator represents an alternative of elements (exactly one of the alternatives must be selected). The notation [n,m] is used for representing the number of repetitions or the optionality of elements. In particular, [0,1] denotes optional elements, [0,n] denotes repeatable optional elements, [1,n] denotes repeatable mandatory elements (that is, at least an occurrence should be present). Leaves of a profile, by contrast, represent basic types (integer, string, boolean,...) or specific constraints on the content of data content elements. The possibility XML Schema offers for restricting the set of valid values for data content elements by means of *facets* [11] is exploited in Di𝒳eminator for specifying simple constraints on the profile about the documents the user is interested in.

Example 1. Consider the profile in Figure 1. The profile specifies that the user is interested in any sigmod record publication and only in the books which author is either Serge Abiteboul or Stefano Ceri. These constraints are reported in the tree representation of the profile as shown in Figure 2. As future work, we plan to introduce new kinds of constraints for specifying typical information retrieval operators.   △

2.2   Hierarchy of Profile Types

Consider the following situation. Two XML Schemas can be used for representing the same kind of information but they do not have the same structure. Therefore, when we have to broadcast a document of such a kind we need to match it against the two schemas. Consider also the situation in which two users present a profile with the same structure. The same degree of relevance is computed for the two users.

In order to deal with the previous situations (that is, group together XML Schemas representing the same kind of information and apply the filtering algorithm only once on the same profile) we introduce *profile types*. A profile type is a triple $(id, profiles, users)$. The *id* component is a meta level description of the profile type. In the current

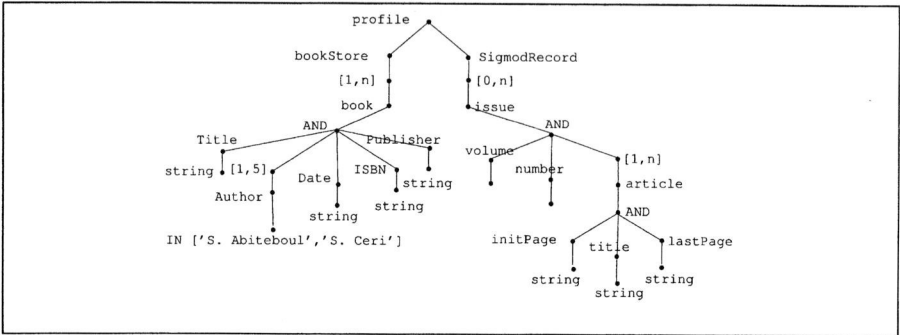

Fig. 2. Tree representation of the profile in Figure 1

stage of development it corresponds to the name of the outermost element of an XML Schema (e.g. BookStore, cdStore considering the profile in Figure 1). The *profiles* component is a set of profiles that belong to the same description. For example, if we wish to model the profile type cdStore, the *profile* component contains the XML Schemas that model CDs. Finally, the *users* component is a set of DiXeminator users.

Profile types are organized in a hierarchy. Given two profile types, $T_1 = (id_1, P_1, U_1)$ and $T_2 = (id_2, P_2, U_2)$, T_2 is a subtype of T_1, if and only if id_2 is considered as a more specific meta level description of a profile type than id_1, and $U_2 \subseteq U_1$. A dummy root node, called top, is present. The set of users associated with top is the entire set of users subscribing DiXeminator.

Example 2. Figure 3 shows an example of hierarchy. Suppose the profile in Figure 1 is associated with user Bob. Since Bob is interested in bookStore and SigmodRecord profile types, his identifier is contained in the corresponding nodes of the hierarchy and in all the ancestor nodes (till the root top).   △

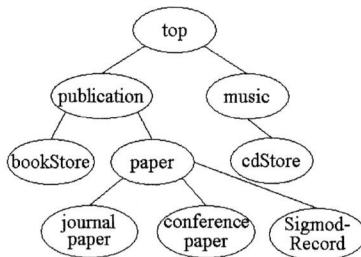

Fig. 3. Hierarchy of profile types

3   DiXeminator Architecture

Figure 4 reports the main components of the architecture of DiXeminator. Rectangles denote the main functional components of the system, cylinders denote data stores, thick arrows denote the profile flow. Document flow is represented by means of the big arrow that pass through the filtering component. We remark that documents are considered only once by the filtering component. This component is in charge of determining the users interested in a document and of extracting structural and content information that will be exploited in the following phases of profile evolution. The information that is exchanged among components is thus a summary of the document structure and content. This is very important because it makes the system more efficient. In the remainder of the section we provide details of the main components of the architecture.

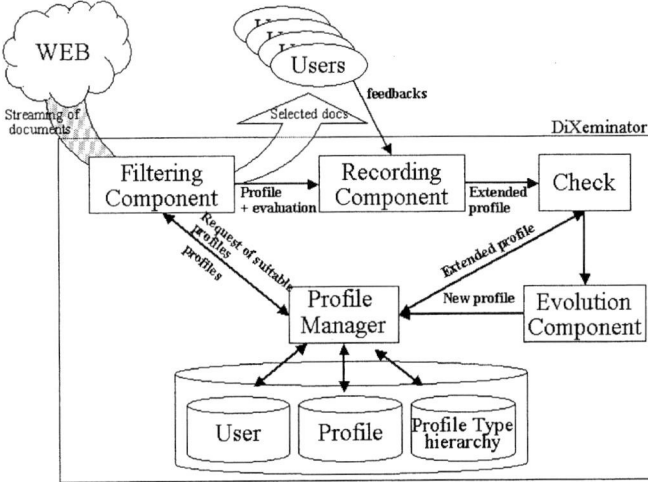

Fig. 4. Architecture of DiℋEminator

3.1 Filtering Component

The *filtering* component is the most important component of the system because it is in charge of processing the incoming stream of documents and of broadcasting them to the interested users. This is the only component that works on line, thus it should perform its tasks efficiently.

Figure 5 reports the $Filter$ procedure, which is the main procedure of this component. Given a document d this procedure selects the profiles and broadcasts them to the interested users. Such a procedure exploits different functions. The *ProfileFor* function, which belongs to the ProfileManager component, selects profiles that, once matched against d, could return a positive degree of relevance. The function compares the tag t of the root of d with the profile types contained in the hierarchy. The comparison is not a simple syntactic match, but we consider the possibility that t is syntactically (relying on an edit distance function [9]) or semantically (relying on a Thesaurus [6]) similar to the description of the profile type. For all the identified matches the corresponding profiles are grouped together and returned.

The $Match$ function evaluates the relevance degree of document d with respect to a profile p_i (one of those profiles returned by function $ProfileFor$). This function

```
Procedure Filter(d : XMLdocument)
begin
    {p₁, . . . , pₙ} = ProfileManager.ProfileFor(d);
    for i = 1 to n do
    begin
        let (S_D, p̄ᵢ) = Match(d, pᵢ); /*degree of relevance of d against pᵢ */
        if (S_D > σ) begin
            {u₁, . . . , uₘ} = ProfileManager.UserFor(pᵢ);
            broadcast(d, {u₁, . . . , uₘ});
            RecordingComponent.FeedBackWaitingQueue(p̄ᵢ);
        end
    end
end
```

Fig. 5. The $Filter$ procedure

evaluates the degree of relevance of the document with respect to the profile by evaluating the similarity between the two structures. The value S_D that function $Match$ returns is the ratio between the common features and the common and divergent features identified between the two structures. This evaluation takes into account both the level in which the common and divergent features are detected and the possibility that tags are syntactically or semantically similar. Details of function $Match$ can be found in [2, 5].

Moreover, function $Match$ returns the profile $\bar{p}_i$ which is the profile p_i with some structural and content information extracted from d. If the degree of relevance is above the fixed threshold, it means that there are users interested in this document, otherwise the document is discarded because it is irrelevant for the user. This threshold, which is a number between 0 and 1, is specified by the user and indicates the strength of desired similarity between her profile and the document to be delivered.

By means of the $UserFor$ function, the users presenting the profile p_i are detected and the document is distributed to them. The $feedbackWaitingQueue$ function is then invoked on profile $\bar{p}_i$. This function inserts $\bar{p}_i$ in a queue waiting for a user feedback. The feedback along with the extracted information are used for subsequent evolutions.

3.2   Recording Component

The *recording* component is in charge of receiving a profile with the extracted data from a document d and making it persistent when the user sends a positive feedback. The profile is, thus, extended with auxiliary data structures recording the information made persistent that will be exploited for the evolution phase. Such data structures are associated with each node of the profile. The profile with the auxiliary data structures is called *extended profile*.

In each element of the profile we store information about the elements with the same tag found in that position in the hierarchical structure of the document. In particular, for elements that do not perfectly match the constraints imposed by the profile specification we store the frequency of each subelement, the frequency in which group of subelements appears together, the subelements that are not required in the profile, and the subelement of the profile that are missing. These kinds of information will be considered in the evolution phase to determine the new structure of the profile.

Two approaches can be followed for handling profiles and extracted data when we are waiting for user feedbacks. First, the extracted data are made persistent immediately

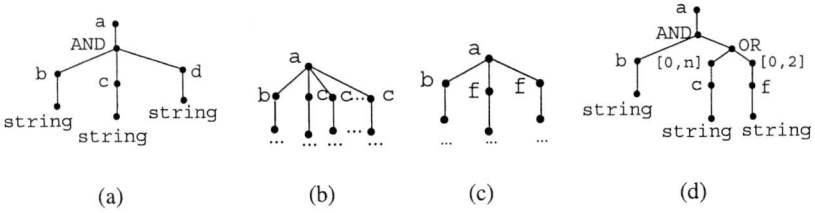

Fig. 6. (a) Profile, (b,c) documents matched against (a), (d) Profile after evolution

and, in case of negative feedback, removed from the extended profile. Second, the profile is left unchanged and when the positive feedback arrives it is made persistent. In both cases, a queue of profiles waiting for feedbacks should be maintained. We follow the second approach because it does not require to analyze again the document from which we extracted the information. However, we plan to experimentally validate our choice because if negative feedbacks are rare, the first approach could be more efficient.

3.3 Check Component

The *check* component is responsible for determining whether the evolution phase should be activated. Specifically, we decided to trigger the evolution phase for a profile when, among the documents matched against that profile, the percentage of non relevant documents, and the percentage of non relevant elements in the documents, are above a fixed threshold (which is initially set by the system and then tuned by user feedbacks). Thus, we compute the sum of the percentage of non relevant elements for each document, normalized by the number of examined documents. Let Doc_P be the set of all documents matched against P and τ be a fixed activation threshold, the evolution phase for a profile P is triggered when:

$$\frac{\sum_{D \in Doc_P} \frac{\#\{e | e \ element \ in \ D \ non \ relevant \ for \ P\}}{\#\{e | e \ element \ in \ D\}}}{\#Doc_P} > \tau$$

3.4 Evolution Component

The *evolve* function of the *evolution* component is responsible for generating a new set of profiles and works at different granularities, ranging from a very coarse granularity, regenerating the whole profile, to a very fine granularity, regenerating the structure of a single element in the profile. By making use of the information collected in the recording phase, some association rules are extracted that represent relationships between presence/absence of subelements of an element. Based on such rules and on some heuristics we have identified, the new profile is generated. Details of the approach are reported in [3, 5]. The following example presents the intuition of our approach.

Example 3. Suppose the profile P in Figure 6(a) has been specified for a user and documents similar to those reported in Figure 6(b,c) have been matched against it. From such documents the following considerations can be pointed out:

- element c in P is specified as mandatory with only one occurrence whereas in the matched documents it can be optional (see Figure 6(c)) or can appear more than once (see Figure 6(b));
- element f is not specified in P and when it is present it always appears twice;
- the presence of element c implies the presence of element b, the presence of element f implies the presence of element b, the presence of c implies the absence of element f, the presence of element f implies the absence of element c;
- element d required in P is not present in any documents matched against it.

By means of the policies developed in [3, 5] we can conclude that: element d can be eliminated from the specification of P; element c can be repeated an arbitrary number of times and it is an alternative of element f which in turn can be repeated twice. Therefore, the new profile in Figure 6(d) is generated.   △

3.5   Profile Manager

The *profile manager* plays a central role in our architecture. This component is in charge of handling user information, profiles, the profile types and their hierarchical organization. This manager directly interacts with the database management system in which such data are stored. The profile manager should minimize the interaction with the database management system in order to improve the performance of Di$\mathcal{X}$eminator.

Whenever the filtering component requires profiles to match against an incoming document, the profile manager has to identify the profiles that could return a positive degree of relevance by consulting the hierarchy of profile types. Specifically, the profile manager retrieves the profile types whose identifier match against the document root (by means of function $ProfileFor$ introduced in Section 3.1). This approach allows us to filter out profile types (and thus profiles) that should not match the document with a high degree of relevance. Moreover, by considering the hierarchical organization of the profile types, the profile manager easily identifies only once the users to whom the document should be broadcasted.

Another activity of the profile manager is to handle profile updates. Whenever a profile is updated from the evolution component, the profile manager modifies the corresponding profile stored in the database and also maintains up to date the hierarchy of profile types. Moreover, if a user is not interested anymore in a profile type, the profile manager eliminates her identifier from the profile type and from all the descendant profile types.

4   Concluding Remarks

In this paper we presented the architecture of Di$\mathcal{X}$eminator, a new selective dissemination system for XML documents based on user profiles. We wish to remark that users of a Di$\mathcal{X}$eminator system can be other Di$\mathcal{X}$eminators. That is, Di$\mathcal{X}$eminators can be composed in order to redirect documents from a Di$\mathcal{X}$eminator with high level filters to other Di$\mathcal{X}$eminators with more specific filters.

The proposed system can lead to further research directions. Currently, profiles are XML Schemas representing the document types the user is interested in. We plan to extend the system in order to handle profiles that contain only relevant portions of documents the users are interested in. In this way the presence of certain elements in a document can be exploited as a characteristic of the kind of document, thus improving the performance of the system. Another research direction concerns the development of an index structure for improving the retrieval of user profiles that should be used for filtering. A further research direction concerns the extension of XML Schema formalism in order to represent information retrieval operators for expressing some sophisticated constraints on data content elements. A final research direction concerns the integration of an access control mechanism into the Di𝒳eminator system. In this way, the filtering process takes into account the privileges the users have on the documents.

References

1. R. A. Baeza-Yates and G. Navarro. Integrating contents and structure in text retrieval. *SIGMOD Record*, 25(1):67–79, 1996.
2. E. Bertino, G. Guerrini, and M. Mesiti. A Matching Algorithm for Measuring the Structural Similarity between an XML Document and a DTD and its Applications. *Information Systems*, 29(1):23–46, 2004.
3. E. Bertino, G. Guerrini, M. Mesiti, and L. Tosetto. Evolving a Set of DTDs According to a Dynamic Set of XML Documents. In *EDBT 2002 Workshop Revised Papers*, LNCS(2490), pages 45–66, 2002.
4. M. Franklin and S. Zdonik. "Data in Your Face": Push Technology in Perspective. In *Proc. of Int'l Conf. on Management of Data*, pages 516–519, 1998.
5. M. Mesiti. *A Structural Similarity Measure for XML Documents: Theory and Applications*. PhD thesis, University of Genova, Italy, 2002.
6. A. Miller. WordNet: A Lexical Database for English. *Communications of the ACM*, 38(11):39–41, November 1995.
7. A. Nierman and H. Jagadish. Evaluating Structural Similarity in XML Documents. In *Proc. of the 5th Int'l Workshop on the Web and Databases*, 2002.
8. J. Pereira, F. Fabret, F. Llirbat, and D. Shasha. Efficient Matching for Web-based Publish/Subscribe Systems. In Proc. of *Int'l Conf. Cooperative Information Systems*, LNCS(1901), pages 162–173, 2000.
9. S. V. Rice, H. Bunke, and T. A. Nartker. Classes of Cost Functions for String Edit Distance. *Algorithmica*, 18(2):271–280, 1997.
10. I. Stanoi, G. Mihaila, and S. Padmanabhan. A Framework for the Selective Dissemination of XML Documents based on Inferred User Profiles. In *Proc. of 19th IEEE Int'l Conf. on Data Engineering*, 2003.
11. W3C. XML Schema, 2001.
12. T. Yan and H. Garcia-Molina. The Sift Information Dissemination System. *TODS*, 24(4):529–565, 1999.

Query Recommendation Using Query Logs in Search Engines

Ricardo Baeza-Yates[1], Carlos Hurtado[1], and Marcelo Mendoza[2]

[1] Center for Web Research,
Department of Computer Science,
Universidad de Chile
{rbaeza,churtado}@dcc.uchile.cl
[2] Department of Computer Science,
Universidad de Valparaiso
marcelo.mendoza@uv.cl

Abstract. In this paper we propose a method that, given a query submitted to a search engine, suggests a list of related queries. The related queries are based in previously issued queries, and can be issued by the user to the search engine to tune or redirect the search process. The method proposed is based on a query clustering process in which groups of semantically similar queries are identified. The clustering process uses the content of historical preferences of users registered in the query log of the search engine. The method not only discovers the related queries, but also ranks them according to a relevance criterion. Finally, we show with experiments over the query log of a search engine the effectiveness of the method.

1 Introduction

A key factor for the popularity of today's Web search engines is the friendly user interfaces they provide. Indeed, search engines allow users to specify queries simply as lists of keywords, following the approach of traditional information retrieval systems [2]. Keywords may refer to broad topics, to technical terminology, or even to proper nouns that can be used to guide the search process to the relevant collection of documents.

Despite that this simple interaction mechanism has proved to be successful for searching the Web, a list of keywords is not always a good descriptor of the information needs of users. It is not always easy for users to formulate effective queries to search engines. One reason for this is the ambiguity that arise in many terms of a language. Queries having ambiguous terms may retrieve documents which are not what users are searching for. On the other hand, users typically submit very short queries to the search engine, and short queries are more likely to be ambiguous. From a study of the log of a popular search engine, Jansen *et al* [5], conclude that most queries are short (around 2 terms per query) and imprecise.

Users searching for the same information may phrase their queries differently. Often, users try different queries until they are satisfied with the results. In order to formulate effective queries, users may need to be familiar with specific terminology in a knowledge domain. This is not always the case: users may have little knowledge about the

W. Lindner et al. (Eds.): EDBT 2004 Workshops, LNCS 3268, pp. 588–596, 2004.

information they are searching, and worst, they could not even be certain about what to search for. As an example, a tourist seeking for *summer rentals* ads in Chile may not know that the vast majority of such ads in the Web are for apartments in *Viña del Mar*, a popular beach in the central part of Chile. In contrast, local users may have the expertise to submit queries with the term *Viña del Mar*, when they are looking for a location to spend their vacations. The idea is to use these expert queries to help non-expert users.

In order to overcome these problems, some search engines have implemented methods to suggest alternative queries to users[1]. Their aim is to help the users to specify alternative related queries in their search process. Typically, the list of suggested queries is computed by processing the query log of the search engine, which stores the history of previously submitted queries and the URLs selected in their answers. A central problem that arises in this context is how to model the information needs associated to a query. Some models proposed in previous work (e.g., [3]) represent a query as the set of URLs clicked by users for the query. This approach have limitations when it comes to identifying similar queries, because two related queries may output different URLs in the first places of their answers, thus inducing clicks in different URLs. In addition, as an empirical study shows [1], the average number of pages clicked per answer is very low (around 2 clicks per query). Our data shows the same.

As in traditional document retrieval, in query recommendation one may expect that the ordering in which the queries are returned to the user plays a central role in the quality of the service, even more important than the set of recommendations itself. As far as we know, a problem not yet addressed is the definition of a notion of *interest* for the suggested queries.

1.1   Contributions

In this paper we present an algorithm to recommend related queries to a query submitted to a search engine. Groups of related queries are found by running a clustering process over the queries and their associated information in the logs.

The clustering process is based on a term-weight vector representation of queries, obtained from the aggregation of the term-weight vectors of the clicked URLs for the query. Semantically similar queries may not share query-terms but they do share terms in the documents selected by users. Thus our framework avoids the problems of comparing and clustering sparse collection of vectors, in which semantically similar queries are difficult to find, a problem that appears in previous work on query clustering. Further, our query vectors can be clustered and manipulated similarly to traditional document vectors.

We provide a relevance criterion to rank the suggested queries. We rank the queries according to two criteria: (a) the similarity of the queries to the input query (query submitted to the search engine); and (b) the support, which measures how much the answers of the query have attracted the attention of users. It is important to have a measure of *support* for the recommended queries, because queries that are useful to many users (searching for related information) are worth to be recommended in our

---

[1] Some search engines (e.g., Lycos, Altavista, AskJeeves) provide query recommendations to users, however there is not much public information on the methods they use to do so.

context. The combination of measures (a) and (b) defines the *interest* of a recommended query.

Finally, we present an experimental evaluation of the algorithm, using logs from a popular search engine for the Chilean Web (TodoCl.cl).

1.2   Related Work

Baeza-Yates [1] presents a survey on the use of Web logs to improve different aspects of search engines.

Wen et al. [6] propose to cluster similar queries to recommend URLs to frequently asked queries of a search engine. They use four notions of query distance: (1) based on keywords or phrases of the query; (2) based on string matching of keywords; (3) based on common clicked URLs; and (4) based on the distance of the clicked documents in some pre-defined hierarchy. Befferman and Berger [3] also propose a query clustering technique based on distance notion (3). Notions (1)-(3) are difficult to deal with in practice, because distance matrices between queries generated by them from real query logs are very sparse, and many queries with semantic connections appear as orthogonal objects in such matrices. Ad-hoc clustering algorithms are needed to deal with this problem. Notion (4) needs a concept taxonomy and requires the clicked documents to be classified into the taxonomy as well.

Fonseca *et al* [4] present a method to discover related queries based on association rules. Here queries represent items in traditional association rules. The query log is viewed as a set of transactions, where each transaction represent a *session* in which a single user submits a sequence of related queries in a time interval. Their notion of query session is different than the notion we use in this paper. The method shows good results, however two problems arise. First, it is difficult to determine sessions of successive queries that belong to the same search process; on the other hand, the most interesting related queries, those submitted by different users, cannot be discovered. This is because the support of a rule increases only if its queries appear in the same query session, and thus they must be submitted by the same user.

Zaiane and Strilets [8] present a method to recommend queries based on seven different notions of query similarity. Three of them are mild variations of notion (1) and (3). The remainder notions consider the content and title of the URLs in the result of a query. Their approach is intended for a meta-search engine and thus none of their similarity measures consider user preferences in form of clicks stored in query logs.

Another approach adopted by search engines to suggest related queries is *query expansion* [2, 7]. The idea here is to reformulate the query such that it gets closer to the term-weight vector space of the documents the user is looking for. Our approach is different since we study the problem of suggesting related queries issued by other users and query expansion methods construct artificial queries. In addition, our method may recommend queries that are related to the input query but may search for different issues, thus redirecting the search process to related information of interest to previous users.

Outline. The remainder of this paper is organized as follows. In Section 2 we present the method proposed for computing and ranking related queries. Section 3 describes and shows the results of the query clustering process. In Section 4 we present the experimental evaluation of the method. Finally, in Section 5 we conclude and outline some prospects for future work.

2   Discovering Related Queries

Our algorithm considers only queries that appear in the query-log. A single query (list of terms) may be submitted to the search engine several times, and each submission of the query induces a different *query session*. In this paper, we use a simple notion of query session similar to the notion introduced by Wen *et al.* [6] which consists of a query, along with the URLs clicked in its answer.

$$\texttt{QuerySession} := (\texttt{query}, (\texttt{clickedURL})^*)$$

A more detailed notion of query session may consider the rank of each clicked URL and the answer page in which the URL appears, among other data that can be considered for improved versions of the algorithm we present in this paper.

The query recommender algorithm operates in the following steps:

1. Queries along with the text of their clicked URLs extracted from the Web log are clustered. This is a preprocessing phase of the algorithm that can be conducted at periodical and regular intervals.
2. Given an *input query* (i.e., a query submitted to the search engine) we first find the cluster to which the input query belongs. Then we compute a rank score for each query in the cluster. The method for computing the rank score is presented next in this section.
3. Finally, the related queries are returned ordered according to their rank score.

The rank score of a related query measures its interest and is obtained by combining the following notions:

1. **Similarity of the Query.** The similarity of the query to the input query. It is measured using the notion of similarity introduced in Section 3.1.
2. **Support of the Query.** This is a measure of how relevant is the query in the cluster. We measure the support of the query as the fraction of the documents returned by the query that captured the attention of users (clicked documents). It is estimated from the query log as well.

One may consider the number of times the query has been submitted as the support of a query. However, by analyzing the logs in our experiments we found popular queries whose answers are of little interest to users. In order to avoid this problem we define the support of a query as the fraction of clicks in answers of the query. As an example, the query *rental offices* has a low popularity (2.52%) in its cluster, but users in the cluster found this query very effective, as its support in Figure 3 shows.

The similarity and support of a query can be normalized, and then linearly combined, yielding the rank score of the query. Another approach may consider to output a list of suggestions showing the two measures to users, and to let them tune the weight of each measure for the final rank.

3   Query Clustering

3.1   Query Similarity

In order to compute the similarity of two queries, we first build a term-weight vector for each query. Our vocabulary is the set of all different words in the clicked URLs. *Stopwords* (frequent words) are eliminated from the vocabulary considered. Each term is weighted according to the number of occurrences and the number of clicks of the documents in which the term appears.

Given a query q, and a URL u, let $\text{Pop}(q, u)$ be the popularity of u (fraction of clicks) in the answers of q. Let $\text{Tf}(t, u)$ be the number of occurrences of term t in URL u. We define a vector representation for q, $\boldsymbol{q}$, where $q[i]$ is the i-th component of the vector associated to the i-th term of the vocabulary (all different words), as follows:

$$q[i] = \sum_{URL u} \frac{\text{Pop}(q, u) \times \text{Tf}(t_i, u)}{\max_t \text{Tf}(t, u)} \tag{1}$$

where the sum ranges over all clicked URLs. Note that our representation changes the inverse document frequency by click popularity in the classical tf-idf weighting scheme.

Different notions of vector similarity (e.g., cosine function or Pearson correlation) can be applied over the proposed vectorial representation of queries. In this paper we use the cosine function, which considers two documents similar if they have similar proportions of occurrences of words (but could have different length or word occurrence ordering).

3.2   Computing the Clusters

We considered queries extracted from a 15-day query-log of the Todocl search engine. The log contains 6042 queries having clicks in their answers. There are 22190 clicks registered in the log, and these clicks are over 18527 different URLs. Thus in average users clicked 3.67 URLs per query.

We compute the clusters by successive calls to a k-means algorithm, using the CLUTO software package[2]. We chose an implementation of a k-means algorithm for the simplicity and low computational cost of this approach, compared with other clustering algorithms. In addition, the k-means implementation chosen has shown good quality performance for document clustering. We refer the reader to [9] for details.

The quality of the resulting clusters is measured using a criterion function, adopted by common implementations of a k-means algorithm [10]. The function measures the total sum of the similarities between the vectors and the centroids of the cluster that are assigned to. Since in a single run of a k-means algorithm the number of clusters k is fixed, we determine the final number of clusters by performing successive runs of the algorithm. Figure 1 shows the quality of the clusters found for different values of k (function criterion FC). The curve below (DIFF) shows the incremental gain of the

---

[2] CLUTO is a software package developed at the University of Minnesota that provides algorithms for clustering collections of documents in high-dimensional vectorial representations. For further information see http://www-users.cs.umn.edu/ karypis/cluto/.

overall quality of the clusters. We selected $k = 600$, for which we obtain a 0.6 average distance of each point to its cluster centroid. We ran the clustering algorithm on a Pentium IV computer, with CPU clock rate of 2.4 GHz, 512MB RAM, and running Windows XP. The algorithm took 64 minutes to compute the 600 clusters.

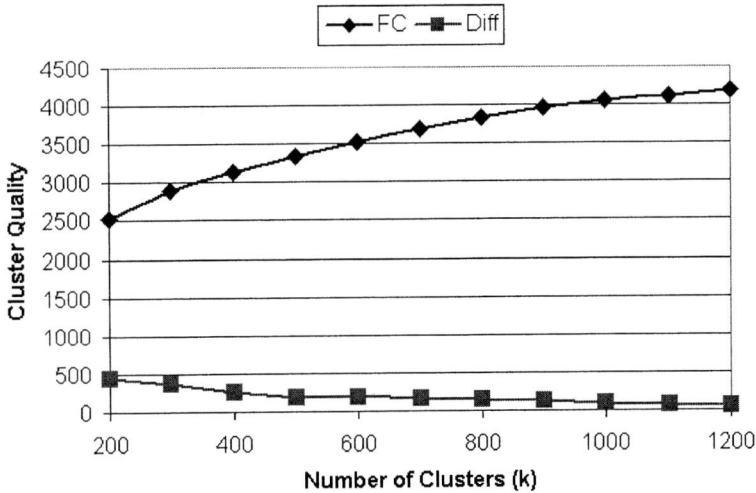

Fig. 1. Cluster quality vs. number of clusters

4 Experimental Evaluation of the Algorithm

In our experiments we consider ten queries: (1) *theater* (*teatro*); (2) *rental apartments viña del mar* (*arriendo de departamentos en viña del mar*); (3) *chile rentals* (*arriendos chile*); (4) *recipes* (*recetas*); (5) *roads of chile* (*rutas de chile*); (6) *fiat*; (7) *maps of chile* (*mapas de chile*); (8) *resorts of chile* (*resorts de chile*); (9) *newspapers* (*diarios*) and (10) *tourism tenth region* (*turismo décima región*).

The ten queries were selected following the probability distribution of the 6042 queries of the log. The original queries along with the results shown in this section are translated from Spanish to English. Figure 2 shows the clusters to which the queries belong. In addition, we show the cluster rank, the quality of each cluster (average internal similarity), the cluster size (number of queries that belongs to each cluster) and the set of feature terms that best describe each cluster. Right next to each feature term, there is a number that is the percentage of the within cluster similarity that this particular feature term can explain.

Figure 3 shows the ranking suggested to Query 3 (*chile rentals*). The second column shows the popularity of the queries in the cluster. The third column shows the support, and the last column depicts the similarity of the queries. The queries are ordered according to their similarity to the input query. The figure shows that algorithm discovered

Q	Cluster Rank	ISim	Size	Query Selected	Descriptive Keywords
q_1	15	0,98	8	theater	productions (18, 4%) *Campbell* productions (7, 7%) dance (4, 5%)
q_2	81	0,709	15	rental apartments *Viña del Mar*	real estate (21, 7%) property (17, 0%) used (11, 1%)
q_3	124	0,618	9	*Chile* rentals	storehouse (5, 3%) warehouses (4, 6%) office (3, 0%)
q_4	136	0,588	7	recipes	food (28, 4%) soft drinks (9, 4%) eggs (2, 2%)
q_5	147	0,581	14	roads of *Chile*	maps (10, 8%) springs (4, 2%) ski (4, 0%)
q_6	182	0,519	8	*Fiat*	spare parts (28, 2%) shock absorber (3, 9%) mechanic (3, 1%)
q_7	220	0,481	7	maps of *Chile*	maps (50, 3%) geological (1, 1%) *Mapcity* (1, 0%)
q_8	306	0,420	11	resorts of *Chile*	hotels (69, 2%) region (1, 4%) bay (0, 5%)
q_9	421	0,347	7	newspapers	journal (25, 6%) *el mercurio* (18, 1%) *estrategia* (1, 9%)
q_{10}	597	0,264	7	tourism tenth region	*Montt* (17, 9%) *Osorno* (5, 5%) *Chaitén* (3, 7%)

Fig. 2. Clusters for the experiment

semantically connected queries that are build upon different keyword. As an example, for a non-expert user the keyword *lehmann* may be unfamiliar for searching rental adds. However, this term refers to a rental agency having a significant presence in Web directories and ads of rentals in Chile. Notice that our algorithm found queries with related terms, some of which would be difficult to use for users .

In order to asses the quality of the results, we follow a similar approach to Fonseca *et al* [4]. The relevance of each query to the input query were judged by members of our department. They analyzed the answers of the queries and determined the URLs in the answers that are of interest to the input query. Our results are given in graphs showing precision vs. number of recommended queries. Figure 4 shows the average precision for the queries considered in the experiments.

The figure shows the precision of a ranking obtained using the similarity, support, and popularity of the queries. The graphs show that using the support measure, in average, we obtain a precision of 80% for the first 3 recommended queries. For both popularity and similarity, the precision decreases. Our results show that the similarity criterion for ranking queries could be improved by considering how effective are queries in returning pages that are preferred by users, which is measured using our notion of support.

Query	Pop. (%)	Support (%)	Similarity
rentals	23,74	0,24	0,998
real estate	1,44	0,1	0,9852
lehmann properties	0,72	0,1	0,963
properties	56,83	0,19	0,7203
parcel purchase	3,6	0,1	0,7089
rental offices	2,52	0,19	0,655
free advertisement	5,76	0,29	0,602
rental apartments	3,6	0,24	0,396

Fig. 3. Ranking of queries recommended to the query *Chile rentals*

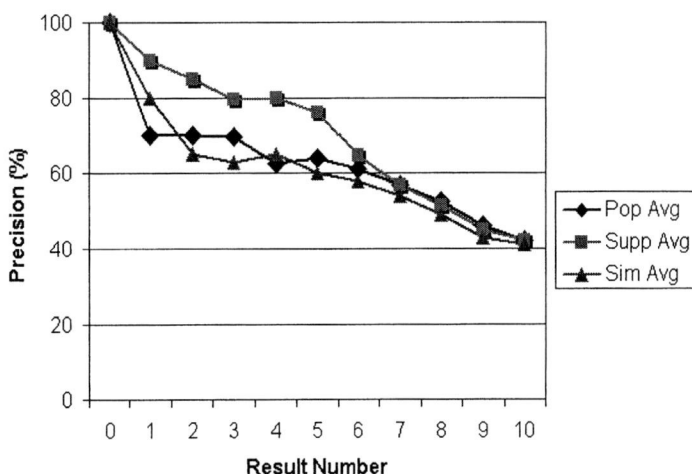

Fig. 4. Average retrieval precision for the queries considered in the experiments

5   Conclusion

We have presented a method for suggesting related queries based on a clustering process over data extracted from the query log. We are currently preforming experiments with larger logs and considering more queries, to improve the empirical evaluation of our approach. In addition, we are trying to do query expansion (which can be seen as automatic query recommendation) using the keywords associated to clusters. We also consider to improve the notion of support of a query. One direction for doing so is to only consider clicks in the query answer to documents that are similar to the term-weight representation of the input query.

As future work we consider to improve the notion of interest of the suggested queries and to develop other notions of interest for the query recommender system. For example, finding queries that share words but not clicked URLs. This might imply that the common words have different meanings if the text of the URLs also are not shared. Hence we can detect polysemic words. On the other hand, if words are not shared and the many terms in the URLs are shared, that may imply a semantic relation among words that can be stored in an ontology.

Acknowledgments. This research was supported by Millennium Nucleus, Center for Web Research (P01-029-F), Mideplan, Chile. M.Mendoza was partially supported by the Universidad de Valparaíso DIPUV-03 project.

References

1. R. Baeza-Yates. Query usage mining in search engines. *Web Mining: Applications and Techniques, Anthony Scime, editor. Idea Group*, 2004.
2. R. Baeza-Yates and B. Ribeiro-Neto. *Modern Information Retrieval*, chapter 3, pages 75–79. Addison-Wesley, 1999.
3. D. Beeferman and A. Berger. Agglomerative clustering of a search engine query log. In *KDD*, pages 407–416, Boston, MA USA, 2000.
4. B. M. Fonseca, P. B Golgher, E. S. De Moura, and N. Ziviani. Using association rules to discovery search engines related queries. In *First Latin American Web Congress (LA-WEB'03)*, November, 2003. Santiago, Chile.
5. M. Jansen, A. Spink, J. Bateman, and T. Saracevic. Real life information retrieval: a study of user queries on the web. *ACM SIGIR Forum, 32(1):5-17*, 1998.
6. J. Wen, J. Nie, and H. Zhang. Clustering user queries of a search engine. In *Proceedings at 10th International World Wide Web Conference*, pages 162–168. W3C, 2001.
7. J. Xu and W. B. Croft. Improving the effectiveness of information retrieval with the local context analysis. *ACM Transaction of Information Systems*, 1(18):79–112, 2000.
8. O. R. Zaiane and A. Strilets. Finding similar queries to satisfy searches based on query traces. In *Proceedings of the International Workshop on Efficient Web-Based Information Systems (EWIS)*, Montpellier, France, September, 2002.
9. Y. Zhao and G. Karypis. Comparison of agglomerative and partitional document clustering algorithms. In *SIAM Workshop on Clustering High-dimensional Data and its Applications*, 2002.
10. Y. Zhao and G. Karypis. Criterion functions for document clustering. Technical report, University of Minnesota, MInneapolis, MN, 2002.

An Overview of Web Data Clustering Practices

Athena Vakali[1], Jaroslav Pokorný[2], and Theodore Dalamagas[3]

[1] Department of Informatics,
Aristotle University of Thessaloniki,
Thessaloniki, 54124, Greece
avakali@csd.auth.gr
[2] Faculty of Mathematics and Physics,
Charles University,
118 00 Praha 1, Czech Republic
pokorny@ksi.mff.cuni.cz
[3] School of Electr. and Comp. Engineering,
National Technical University of Athens,
Zographou, 15773, Athens, Greece
dalamag@dblab.ece.ntua.gr

Abstract. Clustering is a challenging topic in the area of Web data management. Various forms of clustering are required in a wide range of applications, including finding mirrored Web pages, detecting copyright violations, and reporting search results in a structured way. Clustering can either be performed once offline, (independently to search queries), or online (on the results of search queries). Important efforts have focused on mining Web access logs and to cluster search engine results on the fly. Online methods based on link structure and text have been applied successfully to finding pages on related topics. This paper presents an overview of the most popular methodologies and implementations in terms of clustering either Web users or Web sources and presents a survey about current status and future trends in clustering employed over the Web.

1   Introduction

Nowadays, more and more people rely on the World Wide Web to acquire knowledge and information by navigating Websites. However, the exponentially growing of the Web implies difficulties in the way people interact, search, do business etc. Therefore, issues related with organizing the Web content and the structure of a Website become quite popular in recent research efforts.

A lot of previous work has focused on Web data clustering (e.g. [2, 5]). Web data clustering is the process of grouping Web data into "clusters" so that similar objects are in the same class and dissimilar objects are in different classes. Its goal is to organize data circulated over the Web into groups / collections in order to facilitate data availability and accessing, and at the same time meet user preferences. Therefore, the main benefits include: increasing Web information accessibility, understanding users' navigation behaviour, improving information retrieval and content delivery on the Web.

W. Lindner et al. (Eds.): EDBT 2004 Workshops, LNCS 3268, pp. 597–606, 2004.

We can broadly categorize Web data clustering into (I) *users' sessions-based* and (II) *link-based*. The former uses the Web log data and tries to group together a set of users' navigation sessions having similar characteristics. In this framework, Web-log data provide information about activities performed by a user from the moment the user enters a Web site to the moment the same user leaves it [6]. The records of users' actions within a Web site are stored in a log file. Each record in the log file contains the client's IP address, the date and time the request is received, the requested object and some additional information -such as protocol of request, size of the object etc. Figure 1 presents a sample of a Web access log file from an educational Web server (the

```
216.239.46.60 - - [04/Jan/2003:14:56:50 +0200] "GET
/~lpis/curriculum/C+Unix/Ergastiria/Week-7/filetype.c.txt HTTP/1.0"
304 -
216.239.46.100 - - [04/Jan/2003:14:57:33 +0200] "GET
/~oswinds/top.html HTTP/1.0" 200 869
64.68.82.70 - - [04/Jan/2003:14:58:25 +0200] "GET /~lpis/systems/r-
device/r_device_examples.html HTTP/1.0" 200 16792
216.239.46.133 - - [04/Jan/2003:14:58:27 +0200] "GET
/~lpis/publications/crc-chapter1.html HTTP/1.0" 304 -
209.237.238.161 - - [04/Jan/2003:14:59:11 +0200] "GET /robots.txt
HTTP/1.0" 404 276
209.237.238.161 - - [04/Jan/2003:14:59:12 +0200] "GET
/teachers/pitas1.html HTTP/1.0" 404 286
216.239.46.43 - - [04/Jan/2003:14:59:45 +0200] "GET
/~oswinds/publications.html HTTP/1.0" 200 48966
```

Fig. 1. A sample of Web Server Log File

Department of Computer Science in Aristotle University of Thessaloniki). Usually, we need to do some data processing, such as invalid data cleaning and session identification [8]. Data cleaning removes log entries (e.g. images, javascripts etc) that are not needed for the mining process. In order to identify unique users' sessions, heuristic methods are (mainly) used [6], based on IP, and session time-outs. In this context, it is considered that a new session is created when a new IP address is encountered or if the visiting page time exceeds a time threshold (e.g. 30 minutes) for the same IP-address. Then, the original Web logs are transferred into user access session datasets for analysis. The above process is illustrated in Figure 2. Clustering users' sessions are useful for discovering both groups of users exhibiting similar browsing patterns and groups of pages having related content based on how often URL references occur together across them. Therefore, clustering users' sessions is more important in some Web applications, such as on-line monitoring user behaviour, on-line performance analysis, and detecting traffic problems.

Clustering of Web documents helps to discover groups of pages having related content. In general, a Web document can be considered as a collection of Web Pages (a set of related Web resources, such as HTML files, XML files, images, applets, multimedia resources etc.). The main contributions of clustering the Web documents are to improve both the Web information retrieval (e.g. search engines) and content delivery on the Web. In this framework, the Web topology can be regarded as a directed graph, where the nodes represent the Web pages with URL addresses and the edges among nodes represent the hyperlinks among Web pages. Therefore, new techniques are used in order to recognize

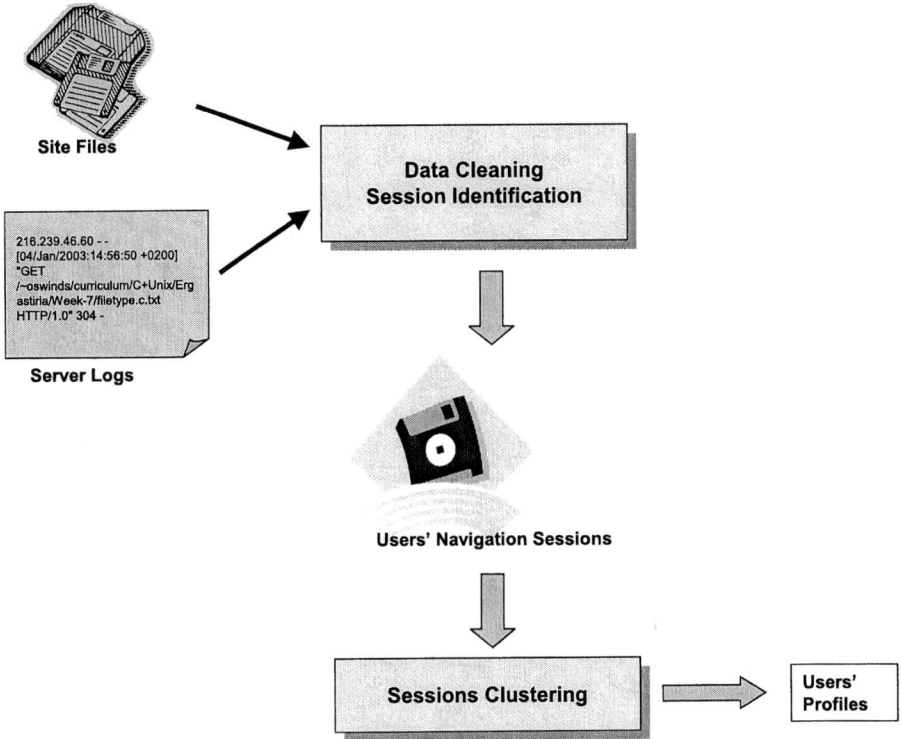

Fig. 2. Clustering users navigation sessions: An overview

and group hypertext nodes into cohesive documents. In this context, the idea of compound documents [11] and logical information units [29] has been evolving recently. A compound document is a set of Web pages that contains at least a tree embedded within the document. A necessary condition for a set of Web pages to form a compound document is that their link graph should contain a vertex that has a path to every other part of the document. Moreover, the notion of Web page communities [18] has gain ground lately in order to organize Web sources and meet Web user requirements. More specifically, a Web community is defined as a set of Web pages that link to more Web pages in the community than to pages outside of the community. A Web community enables Web crawlers to effectively focus on narrow but topically related subsets of the Web.

Much of previous work has focused on understanding the Web user needs and on organizing Web data sources (e.g. pages, documents) [3, 4, 5, 28]. Clustering methodologies have been proven beneficial in terms of grouping Web users in clusters such that the various information circulation activities can be facilitated. In this framework, the XML language is nowadays the standard Web data exchange format. Using XML, one can annotate pages or data exchanged in the Web using tags, providing interoperability and enabling automatic processing of Web resources. Clustering of XML documents brings new challenges, since an XML document encodes not only data but also structure, in one entity [1].

The rest of the paper is organized as follows. Sections 2 and 3 survey the most popular methodologies for Web data clustering. Section 4 presents the XML data clustering perspectives and future trends. Finally, Section 5 concludes the paper and gives some future remarks.

2   Users' Sessions-Based Clustering

The algorithms for users' sessions clustering may be classified into two approaches: similarity-based and model-based (or probabilistic).

2.1   Similarity-Based Clustering Approach

Similarity measures have been proposed towards capturing Web users' common practices whereas effective Web users' logs processing has resulted in the definition of users' session patterns. The first step is to determine the attributes that should be used to estimate similarity between users' sessions (in other words, we determine the users' session representation). Then, it is determined the "strength" of the relationships between the attributes (similarity measures/correlation distance). Finally, clustering algorithms (hierarchical or partitional) are applied in order to determine the classes/clusters to which each user session will be assigned. The hierarchical algorithms define a hierarchy of clustering, merging always the most similar clusters. On the other hand, the partitional approaches (e.g. k-means) define a "flat" clustering into a pre-determined number of clusters (with minimal costs).

Originally, sessions clustering efforts considered sessions as unordered sets of "clicks", where the number of common pages visited was a similarity indication between sessions. The most popular measures that are used are euclidean distance, cosine measure, and Jaccard coefficient. Later on, it was recognized that the order of visiting pages is important, since for example visiting a page A after a page B is not the same information as knowing that both A and B belong to the same session. In this context, the most indicative similarity-based clustering approaches, which have been proposed in the past, can be summarized as follows:

- **Sequence Alignment Method** (SAM) [20], where sessions are chronologically ordered sequences of page accesses. SAM measures similarities between sessions, taking into account the sequential order of elements in a session. SAM distance measure between two sessions is defined as the number of operations that are required in order to equalize the sessions (dynamic programming method to match related sessions).
- **Generalization-Based Clustering** [16] uses page URLs to construct a hierarchy, for categorizing the pages (partial ordering of Web pages, leaf is the Web page file, non-leaf nodes are the general pages). Then, the pages in each user session are replaced by the corresponding general pages and clustered using the BIRCH algorithm [34].
- **Clickstream (Sessions) Analysis** [25] evaluates the similarities between two clickstreams. More specifically, the similarity between two clickstreams requires finding similarity / distance between two page views. Since semantic analysis is not possi-

ble, the degree of similarity between two page views is proportional to their relative frequency of co-occurrence. In this context, authors in [3] cluster two clickstreams using as criterion the length of the largest subsequence common (LCS) between two clickstreams.

2.2 Model-Based (or Probabilistic) Clustering Approach

Model-based clustering techniques have been widely used and have shown promising results in many applications involving Web data [2,4]. More specifically, in the model-based approach the users' sessions clusters are generated as follows:

1. A user arrives at the Web site in a particular time and is assigned to one of a predetermined number of clusters with some probability. The number of clusters is determined by using several probabilistic methods, such as BIC (Bayesian Information Criterion), bayesian approximations, or bootstrap methods [14].
2. The behaviour of each cluster is governed by a statistical model and the user's behavior is generated from this model to that cluster.

Each cluster has a data-generating model with different parameters for each cluster. Therefore, this model can be well defined, if only we learn the parameters of each model component, which are the probability distribution used to assign users to the various clusters and the number of components. The model structure can be determined by model selection techniques and parameters estimated using maximum likelihood algorithms, e.g., the EM (Expectation-Maximization) algorithm [10]. Markov models (e.g. first order Markov models, or Hidden Markov models) [2,4] are the most indicative models that are used for users' sessions. Once the model is learned, we can use it to assign each user to a cluster or fractionally to the set of clusters. Compared to similarity-based methods, model-based methods offer better interpretability since the resulting model for each cluster directly characterizes that cluster. Model-based clustering algorithms often have a computational complexity that is "linear" in the number of data objects under certain practical assumptions.

3 Link-Based Clustering

Due to the high heterogeneity of Web documents, the information seeking on the Web has many difficulties. Recently, researchers suggested to apply clustering to Web documents in order to improve the Web searching process [5]. In this approach the Web is treated as a directed graph. Previous researches have shown that the Web presents strong connectivity, which means that the Web pages with similar topical content have "dense" links between them. Therefore the goal is to cluster in the same group the Web pages with similar content and this can be achieved by eliminating arcs between dissimilar pages. The advantage of this approach than the previous one (users' sessions-based clustering) is that the similarity/dissimilarity of pages is determined by the structure of Website. Another interesting feature of this approach is that it does not need to specify the number of clusters as a separate parameter. On the other hand, the users' sessions-based algorithms have several tuneable parameters (such as the number of clusters) that may affect significantly the clustering method.

In this context, various approaches for clustering of Web documents using the Website topology have been proposed in the literature. The most indicative of them are the following:

– **Web Communities** were proposed [18] on the basis of the evolution of an initial set of hubs (pages that points to many relevant ones) and authorities (relevant pages that pointed to by many hubs), such that the behavior of users is captured with respect to the popularity of existing pages for the topic of interest [21]. More specifically, a Web graph consists of several hundred thousand of sub-graphs, the majority of which correspond to communities with a definite topic of interest. In this framework, several approaches have been proposed (e.g. Maximum Flow and Minimal cuts, graph cuts and partitions, PageRank algorithm etc.) in order to identify them [12].
– **Compound Documents** are represented as Web graphs, which are either strongly connected or nearly so. In graph theory, a directed graph is strongly connected if there is a path from every vertex to every other vertex. Authors in [11] present new techniques for identifying and working with such compound documents. In this work, the compound documents are identified if they contain at least one of the following graph structures within their hyperlink graph:

  - Linear paths: There is a single ordered path through the document, and navigation to other parts of the document are usually secondary (e.g. news sites with next link at the bottom)
  - Fully connected: These types of documents have on each page, links to all other pages of the document (e.g. short technical documents and presentations)
  - Wheel documents: They contain a table of contents (toc) and have links from this single toc to the individual sections of the document (toc is a kind of hub for the document)
  - Multi-level documents: Complex documents that may contain irregular link structures such as multilevel table of contents

4   XML Data Clustering Perspectives and Future Trends

The XML language is becoming the standard web data exchange format, providing interoperability and enabling automatic processing of web resources. Using XML, one can annotate pages or data exchanged in the Web using tags. Tags can be exploited by web scripts or programs to identify data easier, since they give meaning and structure to data. To this extend, an XML document encodes data and structure in one entity, perfectly suited for describing semistructured data [1], that is schema-less and self-describing pieces of information.

Processing and management of XML documents have already become popular research issues [1]. Clustering XML documents refers to the application of clustering algorithms to detect groups of XML documents that share similar characteristics. The estimation of *similarity* is closely related to the *distance metric* exploited by the clustering algorithm. We consider the clustering of XML documents as a problem with two dimensions: *content* and *structure*. The content dimension needs distances that estimate similarity in terms of the textual content inside elements in XML documents, while the structure dimension needs distances that estimate similarity in terms of the structural relationships of the elements in XML documents. We next discuss each one of these two dimensions.

4.1 Clustering XML Documents: The Content Dimension

Clustering XML documents by content is mainly based on the application of traditional IR techniques [31] to define distance metrics that capture the content similarity for pieces of text. A new requirement for such a task arises from the need to support *granularity of indexes* in XML documents. Applications may restrict the context of interest for the clustering procedure to certain XML elements instead of the whole document. Flexible models to manipulate structured documents, taking into consideration their granularity, have been examined in older works for SGML document management [23] and structured text databases retrieval [32]. The main issues to consider in the case of content dimension in the clustering procedure are:

1. the generation of *dynamic statistics*: these statistics include statistical information (for example frequencies) for the terms inside tags, for various parts of the XML documents,
2. the design of *hierarchical indexes*: these indexes should calculate efficiently the distance metrics required by the clustering procedure for various parts of the XML documents, and should be easily maintained to reflect changes in statistics.

Current work examples where such issues are explored include XML retrieval systems like JuruXML [22], XXL [30], XIRQL [15], and hierarchical indexing methodologies, like the flexible indexes [9], and the dynamic generation of vector spaces [17].

Another interesting issue arises from viewing XML documents under a data-centric approach. Treating elements as *categorical attributes* (e.g. values "red", "green","blue" for the element color as categorical attribute) or the values of elements as *market basket data* (e.g. values of the element price) brings a data mining perspective in the task of grouping XML documents by content. The challenge is the application of data mining techniques (like for example the ROCK algorithm for clustering categorical attributes [19]) in the context of XML documents, under the requirement of granularity.

4.2 Clustering XML Documents: The Structure Dimension

Modeling XML documents with tree models [1], we can face the 'clustering XML documents by structure' problem as a 'tree clustering' problem, and exploit *tree edit distances* to define metrics that capture structural similarity [26]. Assuming a set of tree operations (e.g. insert, delete, replace node) and a cost model to assign costs for each one, the tree edit distance between two trees T_1 and T_2 is the minimum cost among the costs of all possible tree edit sequences that transform T_1 to T_2. The tree edit distance can estimate the structural similarity between trees that represent XML documents, and can be included in clustering procedures to identify clusters of structurally similar XML documents.

However, since tree edit distance calculations are quite intensive, vector-based approaches that capture the hierarchical relationships of tree structures should be also explored as a basis to design appropriate efficient indexes.

The main issues to consider in the case of structure dimension in the clustering procedure are:

1. the need or not for ordering in the elements of XML documents,
2. the difference in the importance of elements as structural primitives in the hierarchy imposed by the XML document: the deletion of a top element, e.g. vehicles, might be more important than the deletion of a bottom element, e.g. three-wheel-bicycles, in an XML document.
3. semantic dissimilarities: different tags might refer to semantically similar elements, e.g. elements price and cost.

Current work examples where such issues are explored include change detection methodologies [7], clustering methodologies like [24], indexes that used for time series management, and bitmaps to model tree-like structures [13, 33].

5   Conclusions

It seems that both Web modelling and Web searching need to be improved. An emphasis is put on increasing expressiveness of modelling tools and Web content capturing. New research directions include:

– developing techniques to efficiently cluster the entire web based e.g. on similarity searches in high dimensional spaces,
– developing scalable robust fuzzy techniques to model noisy data sets containing an unknown number of overlapping categories,
– developing techniques like e.g. locality sensitive hashing, in which web pages are hashed in such a way that similar pages have a much higher probability of collision than dissimilar pages,
– exploring new techniques to handle linguistic and textual features.

Another sources of new research directions appear in considering so called deep Web. Many of its sources are structured (stored in relational DBMSs) according to a specified schema. Such schemas define the object domain of a source (e.g., goods, movies) and its query capabilities (e.g., by price, actor). Clustering sources by their query schemas (i.e., attributes in query interfaces) is possible. This approach is essentially clustering categorical data. Clusters are often governed by statistical distributions.

The last but not least is a dynamics of the Web. The methods mentioned usually work on a Web samples that are static, i.e. they represent only a snapshot of the real Web. It is a challenge to model a dynamic Web and to develop methods for an efficient implementation of its structure and content.

References

1. S. Abiteboul, P. Buneman, and D. Suciu. *Data on the Web*. Morgan Kaufmann, 2000.
2. P. Baldi, P. Frasconi, and P. Smyth. *Modeling the Internet and the Web* Wiley, 2003.

3. A. Banerjee and J. Ghosh. Clickstream clustering using weighted longest common Subsequences. In *Proceedings of Workshop on Web Mining, SIAM Conference on Data Mining*, pages 33-40, Chicago, USA, April 2001.

4. I. V. Cadez, D. Heckerman, C. Meek, P. Smyth, and S. White. *Model-based clustering and visualization of navigation patterns on a Web site*. Data Mining and Knowledge Discovery, 7(4):399-424, 2003.

5. S. Chakrabarti. *Mining the Web*. Morgan Kaufmann, 2003.

6. Z. Chen, A. Wai-Chee Fu, and F. Chi-Hung Tong. Optimal algorithms for finding user access sessions from very large Web logs. *World Wide Web: Internet and Information Systems*, 6:259-279, 2003.

7. G. Cobena, T. Abdessalem and Y. Hinnach. *A comparative study for XML change detection*. Technical Report, INRIA, France, 2000.

8. R. Cooley, B. Mobasher, and J. Srivastava. Data preparation for mining World Wide Web browsing patterns *Knowledge Information Systems*, 1:5-32, 1999.

9. H. Cui and J.-R. Wen. Hierarchical indexing and flexible element retrieval for structured document. In *Proceedings of ECIR*, 2003.

10. A. P. Dempster, N. M. Laird, and D. B. Rubin. *Maximum likelihood from incomplete data via the EM algorithm*. Statistics Society B, 39:1-22, 1997.

11. N. Eiron and K. S. McCurley. Untangling compound documents on the Web. In *Proceedings of ACM Hypertext,*, pages 85-94, 2003.

12. G. W. Flake, S. Lawrence, C. Lee Giles, and Frans Coetzee. *Self-organization and identification of Web Communities* IEEE Computer,35(3), 2002.

13. S. Flesca, G. Manco, E. Masciari, L. Pontieri and A. Pugliese. Detecting similarities between XML documents. In *Proceedings of WebDB Workshop*, 2002.

14. C. Fraley and A. Raftery. *How many clusters? Which clustering method? Answers via model-based cluster analysis*. Computer Journal, 41, 1998.

15. N. Fuhr and K. Großjohann. XIRQL: a query language for information retrieval in XML documents. In *Proceedings of ACM SIGIR*, 2001.

16. Y. Fu, K. Sandhu, and M-Y Shih. Clustering of Web users based on access patterns. In *Proceedings of WEBKDD*, 1999.

17. T. Grabs and H.-J.Org Schek. Generating vector spaces on-the-fly for flexible XML retrieval. In *Proceedings of XML and IR Workshop*, 2002.

18. G. Greco, S. Greco, and E. Zumpano. *Web communities:models and algorithms*. World Wide Web, 7(1):58-82, 2004.

19. S. Guha, R. Rastogi and K. Shim *ROCK: A robust clustering algorithm for categorical attributes*. ACM SIGMOD Record, 25(5), 2000.

20. B. Hay, K Vanhoof, and G. Wetsr Clustering navigation patterns on a Website using a sequence alignment method. In *Proceedings of 17th International Joint Conference on Artificial Intelligence*,Seattle, Washington, USA, August, 2001.

21. J. M. Kleinberg. Authoritative sources in a hyper-linked environment. In *Proceedings of the 9th ACM-SIAM Symposium on Discrete Algorithm*, 1998.

22. Y. Mass, Matan Mandelbrod, E. Amitay, Yoelle Maarek, and Aya Soffer Juru XML - an XML retrieval system at INEX'02 In *Proceedings of INEX*,Dagstuhl, Germany, December 2002.

23. S. H. Myaeng and D-H Jang. A flexible model for retrieval of SGML documents. In *Proceedings of ACM SIGIR*, 1998.

24. A. Nierman and H. V. Jagadish Evaluating structural similarity in XML documents. In *Proceedings of the WebDB Workshop*, Madison, Wisconsin, USA, June, 2002.

25. R. Kothari, P. A. Mittal, V. Jain, and M. K. Mohania. On using page cooccurrences for computing clickstream similarity. In *Proceedings of the 3rd SIAM International Conference on Data Mining.*, San Francisco, USA, May 2003.

26. D. Sankoff and J. Kruskal. *Time warps, string edits and macromolecules, the theory and practice of sequence comparison*. CSLI Publications, 1999.
27. R. R. Sarukkai. *Link prediction and path analysis using Markov chains*. Computer Networks, 33:377-386, 2000.
28. Z. Su, Q. Yang, H. H. Zhang, X. Xu, and Y. Hu Correlation-based document clustering using Web logs. In *Proceedings of the 34th Annual Hawaii International Conference on System Sciences (HICSS-34)*, Maui, Hawaii, January, 2001.
29. K. Tajima, K. Hatano, T. Matsukura, R. Sano, and K. Tanaka. Discovery and retrieval of logical information units in Web. In *Proceedings of the Workshop on Organizing Web Space (WOWS 99)*, pages 13-23, Berkeley, USA, August 1999.
30. A. Theobald and G. Weikum. The Index-Based XXL Search engine for querying XML data with relevance ranking. In *Proceedings of the EBDT Conference*, 2002.
31. R. Baeza-Yates and B. Ribiero-Neto *Modern information retrieval*. Addison-Wesley, 1999.
32. R. Baeza-Yates and G. Navarro. *Integrating contents and structure in text retrieval*. ACM SIGMOD Record, 25(1), 1996.
33. J. Yoon and V. Raghavan and V. Chakilam and L. Kerschberg. *BitCube: A three-dimensional bitmap indexing for XML documents*. Journal of Intelligent Information Systems, 17, 2001.
34. T. Zhang, R. Ramakrishnan, and M. Livny. BIRCH: An efficient data clustering method for very large databases. In *Proceedings of the International Conference Management of Data (ACM-SIGMOD)*, pages 103-114, Montreal, Canada, June, 1996.

Author Index

Lecture Notes in Computer Science

For information about Vols. 1–3225

please contact your bookseller or Springer

Lecture Notes in Computer Science 3268

Commenced Publication in 1973
Founding and Former Series Editors:
Gerhard Goos, Juris Hartmanis, and Jan van Leeuwen

Editorial Board